Going Alone

Going Alone

The Case for Relaxed
Reciprocity in Freeing
Trade

Edited by Jagdish Bhagwati

The MIT Press
Cambridge, Massachusetts
London, England

This book was set in Palatino on 3B2 by Asco Typesetters, Hong Kong, and was printed and bound in the United States of America.

Library of Congress Cataloging-in-Publication Data

Going alone : the case for relaxed reciprocity in freeing trade / edited by Jagdish Bhagwati.
    p.   cm.
 Includes bibliographical references and index.
  ISBN 0-262-02521-3 (hc. : alk. paper)
  1. Commercial policy. 2. International economic relations. 3. International trade. I. Bhagwati, Jagdish N., 1934–
HF1411 .O497   2002
382′.71′09—dc21   2002016513

For Robert Baldwin and John Chipman
Generous friends and great international economists

Contents

Foreword

The great cause of removing tariffs, quotas, and other impediments to free trade among nations has proceeded, since the end of World War II, largely through reciprocal agreements: One nation agrees to reduce certain of its import restrictions in return for one or more other nations agreeing to do the same. These are odd sorts of contracts, because each nation's commitments would serve its own interests even if undertaken independently of commitments by other nations. But there is an economic logic and a political logic to reciprocal trade agreements and, logic aside, the agreements have been an evident success. The economic logic is that, although reducing my trade barriers will itself be good for my economy, my gains will be even greater if I can induce you to reduce your barriers. The political logic is an application of the theory of interest groups: Government policymaking tends to be dominated by producer interests, and reciprocal trade negotiations can harness the expansionist interests of a nation's producer-exporters to overcoming the protectionist interests of its producer-importers. And the practical evidence is that the postwar progress of reciprocal agreements, including the General Agreement on Tariffs and Trade (GATT) and trade liberalization under its auspices, has been accompanied by large gains in trade and economic welfare among the participating nations.

Both the logic and the evidence are, however, incomplete. Reciprocal reductions in trade restrictions may be just as beneficial if pursued sequentially as simultaneously, especially if the simultaneous ones require each nation to postpone its reductions until its diplomats get home from Geneva. The trade agenda generated by interest-group competition may be less than ideal and will certainly introduce economic distortions of its own, especially when pursued at the regional level. And it is easy to find beneficial trade reforms that were undertaken unilaterally and had nothing whatsoever to do with reciprocal agreements. There is a danger that the great intellectual prestige that reciprocal trade agreements now enjoy, and the great institutional momentum they have acquired through increasingly elaborate regional and global political structures, will blind us to the deficiencies of the reciprocal approach and even inhibit continued progress.

We—economists and other academics, and practicing politicians devoted to the cause of free trade—are therefore enormously indebted to Jagdish Bhagwati and his colleagues for producing this volume of studies of the logical and practical claims of unilateral trade liberalization. "Going alone," they demonstrate, is much more than a libertarian debating point. As a practical instrument for promoting mutual free trade, unilateral action possesses economic logic and political logic as compelling as the arguments for reciprocal agreements. For example, importers are politically well-organized and influential in many international markets for intermediate goods and services; when they secure a reduction in import restrictions, one effect will be to strengthen the relative political position of exporters in other nations; the result may be a benign sequence of liberalizing moves more prompt and beneficial than tit-for-tat negotiations. And many of the most important and productive steps toward freer trade in recent times have in fact been unilateral; the studies collected here are particularly impressive in documenting this phenomenon, and they will astonish many readers who have grown accustomed to thinking of trade liberalization as something that nations do only reluctantly and by dint of diplomatic pressure.

The arguments and evidence of this volume amount to the most sophisticated analysis and defense of unilateral trade liberalization that has appeared to date. The volume is also a notable intellectual milestone: The authors—first and foremost Professor Bhagwati himself—are not only the leading trade economists of our time, but also longstanding political advocates of reciprocal, multilateral trade agreements. The American Enterprise Institute is delighted to have sponsored this work, which is certain to provoke lively controversy and deserves to achieve lasting influence.

Christopher DeMuth
President
American Enterprise Institute for Public Policy Research

Preface

The project that has led to this volume was supported by a generous grant from the Ford Foundation, with supplementary funds provided by the American Enterprise Institute (AEI).

Bernard Wasow of the Ford Foundation provided not merely conventional oversight, but a substantial amount of intellectual interest and insights. Having handled several grants for different projects in the past, from several financing sources, I must say that Wasow stands apart. I am truly grateful to him.

While several of the staff at the AEI helped most efficiently and with great dedication through the years by running the project and the conferences where the project's agenda and then emerging findings were discussed, I must also thank Mark Groombridge and Claude Barfield Jr. for their continuous interest and advice, and AEI President Chris DeMuth for his support of the project and for providing a foreword.

I must add that directing this project has been immensely rewarding. I was lucky to get several of today's distinguished economists (and one splendid political scientist, John A. C. Conybeare) to participate in the project. Unfortunately, a couple of participants dropped out halfway through the project, one a specialist on Japanese telecommunications policy response to the U.S. success and the other on Hong Kong's remarkable policy of unilateral free trade. On the other hand, I was able to draft Ross Garnaut, the brilliant Australian economist, to write an important paper on Australia's unilateral conversion to trade liberalization.

Many other economists, some of whom attended the conferences under the project's auspices, in Washington, DC, have helped generously with their comments and suggestions. I would like to thank, in particular, Kyle Bagwell, Robert Baldwin, Richard Brecher, Alan

Deardorff, Vivek Dehejia, Gene Grossman, Arnold Harberger, Pravin Krishna, Rodney Ludema, Robert Staiger, Robert Stern, T. N. Srinivasan, and Ravi Yatawara.

I am thankful also for the assistance of Bikas Joshi, Maria Coppola, and Olivia Carballo. The volume was finalized for publication when I was on leave at the Council on Foreign Relations this academic year; I would like to acknowledge the council's splendid facilities and ambience.

Jagdish Bhagwati
New York, May 2001

1

Introduction: The Unilateral Freeing of Trade versus Reciprocity

Jagdish Bhagwati

We came to the conclusion that the less we attempted to persuade foreigners to adopt our trade principles, the better; for we discovered so much suspicion of the motives of England, that it was lending an argument to the protectionists abroad to incite the popular feeling against free-traders, by enabling them to say, "See what these men are wanting to do; they are partisans of England and they are seeking to prostitute our industries at the feet of that perfidious nation ..." To take away this pretense, we avowed our total indifference whether other nations became free-traders or not; but we should abolish Protection for our own selves, and leave other countries to take whatever course they like best.

—Richard Cobden[1]

God I have loved, but should I ask return
Of God or women the time were come to die.

—W. B. Yeats, "Tara's Hills"[2]

If, on hearing your call, no one comes,
Then, go thou alone.

—Rabindranath Tagore, "Untitled Song"[3]

1.1 Introduction

The analysis of free trade divides into two distinct areas:

• whether the freeing of trade is good; and, if so,

• which are the ways, and among them the better ways, to get to freer trade.

The research under the project that has led to this volume belongs to the latter class of questions. The major ways to free trade can be set out as

• the unilateral liberalization of trade (or what I call here "going alone" or simply "unilateralism");

• the reciprocal liberalization of trade (or what might simply be called "reciprocity") in a multilateral framework such as Multilateral Trade Negotiations under General Agreement on Trade and Tariffs (GATT) or World Trade Organization (WTO) auspices;

• the reciprocal liberalization of trade under plurilateral or bilateral auspices such as Preferential Trade Agreements typically in the form of Free Trade Areas and Customs Unions;

• the unilateral reduction of *others'* (not one's own, as under conventional "unilateralism") trade barriers under the threats of sanctions, as in the use of Section 301 provisions of U.S. trade legislation (a method that I have called[4] and others now call "aggressive unilateralism").

Aggressive unilateralism was used only by the United States (though there was discussion in the European Union (EU) about deploying such an instrument, imitating the United States even as the European Commission was agitating against its use by the United States). It is really an instrument that can be deployed only by the very powerful nations and then again only against the weak nations. In U.S. experience, little was won by the United States from the EU or from Japan: even the threatened use of the Section 301 instrument against Japan in the celebrated and high-profile U.S.-Japan auto dispute led to an ill-disguised loss for the US.[5] Besides, it has now faded from the scene, with the use of Section 301 to extract unilaterally demanded trade concessions from others virtually declared by the World Trade Organization (WTO) Dispute Settlement Mechanism as WTO-illegal if undertaken.[6]

The real contest, in both theory and policy, is therefore between unilateralism and reciprocity when it comes to choosing between these methods of freeing trade. The "conventional wisdom" on the question is that economists, the free traders, favor unilateralism whereas policymakers and politicians, the "mercantilists," favor reciprocity. As always, such stereotypical contrasts have something going for them but are, in reality, too simplistic.

Thus, it is simply not true that economists have viewed reciprocity in freeing trade as necessarily mercantilist, in the sense that if you lower your trade barriers only in exchange for others lowering theirs, you behave as if freeing your own trade is making a "concession." As it happens, and this is what I argue systematically below, there is a very good case to be made for reciprocity; and I myself set it forth as long ago as 1990 when I argued the following:[7]

While this (reciprocity) approach is considered "mercantilist" by those who prefer unilateral trade liberalization by oneself, the pairing of mutual concessions has a fourfold advantage:

i. if I can get you to also liberalize while I liberalize myself, I gain twice over;

ii. if there are second-best macroeconomic considerations such as short-run balance of payments difficulties from trade liberalization, the mutuality of liberalization should generally diminish them;

iii. mutuality of concessions suggests fairness and makes adjustment to trade liberalization politically more acceptable by the domestic losers from the change; and

iv. foreign concessions to one's exporters create new interests that can counterbalance the interests that oppose one's own trade liberalization.

Equally, whereas reciprocity has become endemic in Washington today, and this is not surprising in a country which since the 1930s has been populated in varying degrees by what I and Douglas Irwin have called "reciprocitarians,"[8] and whereas prominence in the media often goes to reciprocal reduction of trade barriers through Multilateral Trade Negotiations[9] or via Preferential Trade Agreements such as NAFTA, a great deal of often unflagged unilateral trade liberalization has also occurred in recent decades (as documented in this volume). Indeed, the first dramatic case of trade liberalization, one that can justly be argued to have freed trade hugely for the first time, was the repeal of the Corn Laws in 1846 by the British prime minister, Sir Robert Peel, who admitted to having been converted to free trade by the economists of his time—and that was an act of unilateral repeal, totally outside of any reciprocal treaty framework. As I state later, Peel actually and articulately drew away from reciprocity as the way of liberalizing British foreign trade.

So, to any serious student of the issues raised by the choice between unilateral and reciprocal freeing of trade, it is obvious that the subject awaits systematic and intensive analysis, both theoretical and empirical. This, in fact, was the agenda of the project whose output is collected in this volume.

This agenda is evidently analytically challenging and relevant to policy. But its immediate motivation was the increasing and obsessive emphasis in Washington on reciprocity in trade negotiations that I just noted. Indeed, Prime Minister Peel and President Clinton seemed to me to be two statesmen standing in contrast: one abandoning reciprocity boldly for unilateralism, the other embracing reciprocity with some passion instead.[10] And, on the face of it, Peel, who towered intellectually above Clinton (who was no slouch himself, but was indeed regarded widely as a policy afficionado), seemed to have the better of the argument. Hence the project was set up to see what could be said analytically in favor of unilateralism, a task that would inevitably draw into it virtually as its flip side the question of the merits and demerits of reciprocity as well, while documenting (in different ways, recalled in section 1.3 below) the enormous extent of unilateral trade liberalization in practice (and, where possible, examining its causes).

To anticipate, the central conclusions of the analysis below then are that

• there *is* an economic case for reciprocity in freeing trade;
• but where others will not go along with oneself, it makes sense to go with unilateral freeing of trade;
• but this conventional case for unilateralism is incomplete: such unilateral freeing of trade can, and occasionally will, trigger a reciprocal response, implying what I call "sequential reciprocity."

1.2   Three Basic Propositions on Unilateralism and Reciprocity

Let me now begin by stating the basic economics of unilateralism and of reciprocity in terms of three propositions, developing the underlying arguments with necessary nuances.

PROPOSITION 1   Go alone if others do not go with you.

The classic statement of the case for going alone if others will not go with you is, of course, by my Cambridge teacher, Joan Robinson. Gifted with a talent for saying things both plainly and wittily—she is the celebrated author of the phrase "beggar my neighbor" policies that describe Nash-equilibrium behavior when countries competitively devalue and seek to switch aggregate demand away from each other—she famously remarked once that if others have rocks in their harbor, that is no reason to throw rocks into your own.

This is worth remembering, as it is a lesson that often gets lost in public debates: and the reason is, of course, an obsession with "fairness." Many wrongly think that it is unfair if one's market is open and one's trading rival's is not. This is also a mistake that many make today as they contemplate rich-country protectionism and then claim therefore that it is unfair to ask poor countries to reduce theirs.[11]

In short, we need to remember that if we refuse to reduce our trade barriers just because others do not reduce theirs, we lose from our trading partners' failure to reduce their trade barriers (as they do too) and then we lose twice over from our failure to reduce our own.[12] In many ways, when Prime Minister Robert Peel repealed the Corn Laws unilaterally in 1846 to usher in free trade in Britain, he was following this route, having been exasperated with the refusal of continental powers to pursue trade liberalization in the reciprocal framework implied by the then fashionable bilateral trade treaties.[13]

PROPOSITION 2   If others go with you, so that there is (simultaneous) reciprocity, that is still better.

For the same reason, we can argue that if others do liberalize in return for one's trade liberalization, then we gain twice over. This is, of course, broadly true. The formal argumentation for it can be tricky but is readily doable as I demonstrate very briefly below and in greater analytical depth in the appendix that draws, as is necessary in theoretical analyses, on a very precise definition of reciprocity (in contrast to the several different ways in which reciprocity is practiced in reality, as I argue from the project findings in section 1.4 below).

Thus, imagine that we have what, following Kyle Bagwell and Robert Staiger, I call a reciprocal trade liberalization that preserves the external terms of trade where it was in the previous higher-tariff equilibrium. This will necessarily increase the welfare of both countries. Why? Because, with terms of trade unchanged, and with tariffs having declined in both countries, each country will have only production and consumption gains from the reduced tariff. It is then possible to show that, compared to unilateral trade liberalization, such terms-of-trade-preserving reciprocal trade liberalization will be productive of greater gains for each country. This is a neat theorem; it also puts a formal structure on the intuition that reciprocal trade liberalization will lead necessarily to greater gain.

What can we say about bargaining so as to achieve this reciprocity (which may, however, not materialize as Peel believed had happened with earlier efforts to get European countries to go to free trade alongside Britain through bilateral treaties)? Evidently, it makes sense and is not "mercantilist," though there *is* a danger that excessive use of the language of "concessions" in trade bargaining can lead, and has indeed led, to a widespread bureaucratic and political acceptance of the wrong-headed view that import liberalization is expensive rather than gainful and must be offset by concessions for one's exports. This, in turn, has fed the popular protectionist misconception that "trade is good but imports are bad"! Evidently, such a viewpoint does create difficulties for trade liberalization: As George Orwell would have reminded us, language matters. And as we scholars believe, sloppy arguments have a tendency to come back at us: We may win battles that way but may lose the war.

Let me then suggest at least one other way in which reciprocity may be helpful. In a pluralistic system, it may help a government mobilize export-oriented lobbies who would profit from expanding foreign markets to countervail the import-competing lobbies that profit instead from reducing trade. True, as trade economists well understand, one's reduced protection itself creates incentives for exporters: Protectionism implies a bias against exports. But one may be forgiven for assuming, quite correctly, that this benefit is not easily perceived by the exporters who would benefit (indirectly) from such a change. What reciprocal trade liberalization does is to add to, in a perfectly direct and hence salient fashion, the incentives of exporters and hence to facilitate, through use of countervailing power, the reduction of one's own trade barriers.[14]

In fact, Irwin's beautifully argued account in chapter 3 of why reciprocity helped the United States liberalize trade after the Smoot-Hawley disaster, compared to the earlier decades when the Congress unilaterally decided on tariffs, assigns part of the explanation to precisely this argument.

PROPOSITION 3   If you go alone, others may liberalize later: Unilateralism then begets sequential reciprocity.

Then, we get to the interesting proposition, that if others do not see the light and wish to go on with their protectionism, we might be able to get them to follow us with a lag. So we get in effect "sequential" reciprocity. This thought is not entirely new: it had occurred to Prime Minister Peel for sure. Indeed, he argued that Britain's example, her success with the unilateral introduction of free trade, would get the recalcitrant nations to follow suit.[15] But the matter is best seen more generally, as always, in terms of supply and demand: in this instance, of protection.

The *supply* of protection can shrink if, as Peel believed, the success of unilateral free trade by a country seduces foreign nations into imitating the reasons for this success. I should add to the usual argument about diffusion through imitation of success the fact that, in the case of sectoral unilateral deregulation and liberalization of trade, there is also the slightly different argument that governments that lag behind also lose out to governments that go ahead in worldwide competition. Thus, Japan may hold on to its protected Japanese market in telecommunications but, in competing with the American firms who have grown to strength in a unilaterally liberalized home market, they cannot hack it in, say, Brazil, India, and China for sales. That then drives home to MITI in Japan the necessity to liberalize too: There is some reason to think that this has been the case in Japan and the EU, that this "ahead-of-the-curve" model of unilateral liberalization drives the laggards into their own market opening, namely, to sequential reciprocity.

But the *demand* for protection may also shrink: a possibility that Peel did not allow for but which I have argued for and some of my students (Dan Coates and Rodney Ludema, and Debashish Mitra and Pravin Krishna) have now modeled ably.[16] This happens essentially through the fact that the expansion of trade (thanks to the unilateral trade liberalization elsewhere) can strengthen the export lobbies relative to the import-competing lobbies: in jargon, the foreign political-economy equilibrium is shifted in favor of those who seek reduced rather than increased protection.

Let me add briefly here that the empirical reality, as captured in several essays in this volume (especially chapters 6–11), shows extensive resort to unilateral trade liberalization in the last two decades in Eastern Europe, in Latin America (especially Chile), in Asia (especially in Australia, New Zealand, and Indonesia, and since 1991 in India as well), and even earlier in Singapore and Hong Kong. In addition, there is evidence of unilateral liberalization in the highly innovative financial and telecommunications sectors in the United States (see chapters 12 and 14 for U.S. financial services and for U.S. telecommunications, respectively), with some evidence of sequential reciprocity by the EU and Japan (both moving to respond with their own liberalization in light of American example and success at competition when earlier they refused to do so under reciprocity and even Section 301 threats).

1.3   The Findings on These Questions

These three propositions, admittedly in more intuitive form, were precisely what I had in mind as requiring systematic and intensive scrutiny, both analytical and empirical, when the project was set up and I invited several prominent scholars to address the pertinent issues. As reflected in the three parts into which this volume is divided, the project was divided into three segments:

• Part I deals with historical experience on unilateral trade liberalization and reciprocity. A natural starting point was precisely Prime Minister Peel's pioneering shift to unilateral free trade with the repeal of the Corn Laws in 1846. Astonishingly, you will recall, he had expressed hope for what I have called here sequential reciprocity, based on his faith that Britain's success with free trade would induce others to follow the British example. The interesting question historically is: Did Peel turn out to be right? John Conybeare, a leading political scientist and historian of such questions, probes this matter in some depth in chapter 2 and tells us the following: true, there was indeed trade liberalization in Europe subsequent to the repeal of the Corn Laws, but it is not easy to establish strong Peel-like sequential reciprocity links. Clearly, more research is needed; the Conybeare essay is a tantalizing first step.

• Part II considers the experience with unilateral trade liberalization worldwide in recent decades. Of particular note are the external trade liberalizations carried out by Singapore, as demonstrated convincingly by Arvind Panagariya in chapter 8, and by Australia and New Zealand, the former studied in depth by Ross Garnaut in chapter 6 and the latter with cogency by Lewis Evans and Martin Richardson in chapter 7. These are "genuinely" unilateral liberalizations: They were not part of reciprocal negotiations, whether bilateral[17] or multilateral, nor were they a result of conditionality imposed bilaterally or multilaterally, as by the World Bank or the International Monetary Fund (IMF) (for, in that case, as I argue below, the quid pro quo exists but lies outside trade benefits and arises in the form of aid inflows). Patrick A. Messerlin's essay in chapter 9 on Central Europe's unilateral trade liberalization also makes for interesting reading since it shows how countries recoiling from communism, central planning and autarky embraced democracy, markets and openness. The interesting and important case of extensive unilateral trade liberalization by Chile is addressed in chapter 10 by Sebastian Edwards and Daniel Lederman, and the experience of Latin America more comprehensively is reviewed by Rachel McCulloch in chapter 11.[18]

These country experiences had much to do with unilateral trade liberalization but little to do with sequential reciprocity in the sense that the unilaterally liberalizing country hoped that its action would prompt its trading partners to respond subsequently with their own liberalization. But that is not to say that the example of success with trade liberalization did not play a part in the decision of other countries to reduce their own barriers unilaterally instead of persisting in protectionism.[19]

• Part III shows how unilateral trade liberalization has occurred in certain sectors, such as finance and telecommunications, and has prompted sequential reciprocity in rival countries as well. This has typically happened in the United States where, while the ethos of reciprocity is exceptionally strong, these sectors have been characterized by the reality of "going alone." And others, such as the EU and Japan, which were reluctant laggards and unwilling to indulge in simultaneous reciprocity, have followed suit sequentially, more or less. The U.S. experience has been reviewed for the finance sector by Lawrence J. White in chapter 12 and in telecommunications by Cynthia Beltz Soltys in chapter 14. Koichi Hamada in chapter 13 has examined the Japanese Big Bang in its financial sector from the unilateralist perspective.[20]

This set of contributions takes us significantly closer to understanding the way in which unilateral trade liberalization has worked historically and in modern times, both at the country and the sectoral level. But we need more work, especially at the sectoral level, examining the U.S. experience more fully and also extending the analysis to Japan, the EU, and other nations.

But the project illuminated not just the three major propositions that I have highlighted as its major findings. It has also been of great value in taking further our understanding of trade reciprocity itself and of the underlying factors that led to the unilateral trade liberalizations in practice. I will now consider each in turn.

1.4   Reciprocity: Conceptual Clarifications

Like most concepts in economics, such as the budget deficit or the unemployment rate, reciprocity in trade liberalization seems simple enough but in fact can mean a multitude of things, each with its uses. This became manifest early in the project. What emerged were insights that led me to think of several typologies.

The basic typology used in a central way in this volume is of course what I have already been dealing with. Reciprocity here divides into "simultaneous" and "sequential." The former is when a nation exchanges a trade barrier reduction for another, as part of its trade bargain. Now, such a "contractual" reciprocity may involve the return concession accruing down the road so that the simultaneous reciprocity is over time. The essence of simultaneous reciprocity therefore is that it occurs within the bargain, not that it is instantaneous or that the actual exchange of concessions accrues at the same time.

By contrast, what I call "sequential" reciprocity and one that underlies Proposition 3 earlier, is one that occurs, not because it is agreed to by the negotiators, but because it is induced by a unilateral, nonreciprocal act of unilateral trade liberalization.

Then again, one must keep in mind, as I noted in *Protectionism* based on the first Bertil Ohlin Lectures in Stockholm, that reciprocity can be either "full" reciprocity, namely, where equality of market access (e.g., matching of tariff rates) is sought, or "first-difference" reciprocity where matching of concessions at the margin is all that is sought.[21] Clearly, most Multilateral Trade Negotiations (MTN) negotiations have amounted, where rough balancing of concessions is sought, to first-difference reciprocity. But, in Free Trade Areas (FTAs) and Customs Unions (CUs), as under Article 24 of the GATT or the Enabling Clause, the intention has to be to reach full reciprocity since that is what the acceptance of full dismantling of intra-FTA or intra-CU trade barriers amounts to.

But then there are two other typologies, which must also be kept in view for clarity of analysis of the question of unilateralism in trade liberalization. Thus reciprocity can occur within trade and outside of trade: Namely, the quid pro quo may be the securing of trade concessions for grant of trade concessions or the quid pro quo may be concessions on nontrade dimensions.

The "within trade" reciprocity can be subdivided into three different types that the project participants variously encountered: (1) where tariff cuts are balanced, the most recent practice of agreeing on zero-tariff sectors being the most extreme example; (2) where (estimated) trade volumes from trade concessions are balanced, a practice that Alice Enders discusses in chapter 4 as the one that the U.S. negotiators seemed to favor when the GATT architects were discussing reciprocity and a practice whose remnants are to be found in the compensation provisions of the GATT when tariff concessions are withdrawn;[22] and (3) where reciprocity is sought only very broadly and includes offering concessions that cut across sectors and without quantitative balancing of either cuts in trade barriers or volumes of trade that result therefrom: a practice that J. Michael Finger, Ulrich Reincke, and Adriana Castro testify to in chapter 5 in describing what happened by way of reciprocity in the Uruguay Round.

The project threw up several instances where countries were apparently freeing trade unilaterally but the quid pro quo was absent only in the form of reverse trade concessions. It obtained instead on nontrade dimensions, so that what looked like genuinely unilateral trade liberalization was actually not. Such "outside of trade" reciprocity divides in turn into quid pro quos that arise in the form of aid, as when the IMF or the World Bank, or other multilateral or bilateral funding agencies, provide funds only if trade liberalization is undertaken, and those that arise, as the case of Taiwan studied by Arvind Panagariya in chapter 8 illustrates well, in the form of bargains that are tantamount to avoiding punishment (on security, aid, trade, and other dimensions) rather than securing rewards. Evidently, therefore, one must not deduce that all cases where one sees trade liberalization undertaken outside of a trade reciprocity framework, as in an MTN Round, are automatically genuine cases of unilateral trade liberalization where no quid pro quo is simultaneously extracted or given.

But a second typology relates to the complexity introduced for reciprocitarians by the fact that any attempt at balancing first-difference reciprocity has to face up to the fact that there are more than two countries. This is the so-called third-country problem. Bilaterally, one can always try to balance concessions whichever way one seeks to do so (whether on trade volumes or tariff cuts or broadly across sectors). But what does one do when one has trade, and possibly trade agreements or treaties, with third countries? The reciprocitarians have always had to choose a strategy on how to accommodate bilateral trade reciprocity in the multilateral context. Essentially, this third-country problem has been resolved in both treaty-making and trade-institution-devising arenas in two ways:

- unconditional MFN, and
- conditional MFN,

though I should include absence of any MFN (i.e., most favored nation clause) also as a remote possibility.

Unconditional MFN

Under unconditional MFN, any trade concession made bilaterally must be extended to third countries that then enjoy the right to market access on the most favored terms extended to any other country. This principle is embodied conventionally in treaties signed with specific third countries that then typically extend such MFN rights reciprocally.

The GATT was built on such a reciprocated agreement to extend MFN to all members, with some built-in exceptions such as Article 24 permitting preferential trade agreements under well-defined restrictions and, later, with exceptions provided to developing countries in various ways.

Conditional MFN

Under conditional MFN, there is no automatic extension of bilateral reduction of tariffs and other trade barriers to third nations. Rather, there is a presumption, and in treaties an obligation, that the concessions will be extended to third nations (signatory to such a treaty) *provided* they make acceptable reciprocal trade concessions. The General Agreement on Trade in Services (GATS) favors this approach, so that the WTO, unlike GATT which was based on unconditional MFN, is now a blend of both unconditional and conditional MFN since it includes both GATT and GATS.[23]

Now, conditional MFN is clearly a way of ensuring reciprocity between any pair of nations, in whatever way it is defined, since no "unrequited" concessions are made to third nations. No third country gets a "free lunch." A third nation receives only the right to get to the dining table, not the right to sit down and sup. To receive, it must give.

But unconditional MFN leaves open the possibility of "free riders" if one is a reciprocitarian. So, does it not handicap trade liberalization, even though MFN has well-known advantages such as nondiscrimination that the great international economists of earlier generations, including Frank Taussig and Gottfried Haberler of Harvard and Jacob Viner of Princeton, recognized? We now appreciate their concerns better as we see the proliferation of discrimination worldwide through multiplying Free Trade Agreements.[24]

Or, to raise a related question that affects the issues in this volume more directly, how can one work with unconditional MFN and still manage to be a reciprocitarian in trade negotiations? As it happens, there are several ways in which the free-rider problem has been minimized or tolerated in practice, some seen in this volume and others in other research and reflection:

• ways have been devised that have reduced unconditional MFN in reality to conditional MFN; or

• free riding has been accepted as legitimate; or

• free riding has been dismissed as unimportant and not worth bothering about; or

• sequential reciprocity has been regarded as likely and hence the free rides are assumed to be unlikely to endure; or

• the likelihood of actually getting the potential free riders to pay has been enhanced by suitable institutional innovation (as James Meade, who devised the so-called multilateral-bilateral way of conducting the GATT-based Multilateral Trade Negotiations using unconditional MFN, is supposed to have done, as documented by Alice Enders in chapter 4).

I will address each of these ways now.

1. If reciprocity with third nations is really desired, unconditional MFN may be reconciled with it by ensuring that the bilateral deals, characterized by attempted pairwise reciprocity, are restricted by

and large to products of export interest only to the bilaterally liberalizing countries. That way, through product-selection bias, third
countries could not get a free ride or at least one that is worth much.

This is what has led the GATT negotiations (see Enders in chapter
4) to be on a "principal suppliers" basis with the initial liberalizing
moves in the MTN confined to those who have a substantial position
in a product. Michael Finger has also remarked that the reason why
developing countries did not make much progress on textiles and
agriculture is partly a reflection of the fact that they were free riders
who were exempted form reciprocity and hence products of interest
to them were bypassed by the rich countries playing actively in successive MTNs. The one time that these subjects moved was in the
Uruguay Round; but by then, the developing countries had begun to
play with their own concessions.[25]

ii. But if unconditional MFN was reduced to acting pretty much as
conditional MFN did, it would surely be disappointing. In reality,
however, that is only part of the story. Other factors have been at
play in preserving the true character of unconditional MFN.

Among these is the fact that free riding may be considered legitimate when the free rider cannot pay. Here, I may recall the benign
view that economists such as Alfred Marshall of Cambridge University held on the question. They argued, at the turn of the last century, that British free trade should be unilateral, without demanding
reciprocity from the developing countries. To quote Marshall: "it
would have been foolish for nations with immature industries to
adopt England's [free trade] system pure and simple."[26] Though
Marshall, Edgeworth and other leading English economists were
indeed skeptical of the advisability and utility of protection, they
shared with John Stuart Mill an indulgence toward infant-industry
protection, Mill having been the father of this argument.

Indeed, this type of reasoning was behind also the legitimation of
exemption from reciprocity for the poor countries at the GATT, with
successive changes provided for the purpose as the postwar period
unfolded. In fact, developing countries long enjoyed an easy exemption from reciprocity in bargaining, and indeed in the disciplines that
GATT members were otherwise subjected to, all amounting to what
came to be called Special & Differential (S&D) Treatment. It is only
with the Uruguay Round that S&D has come increasingly under the
axe.

iii. But the fact that free riding by the developing countries was ignored also reflected their insignificance in trade at the time. It was simply not worth making a fuss: The free rider was dwarfish and could get into the bus inconspicuously, taking up little space.

iv. But one can take a more complex view, one that I have developed myself,[27] that sees an enlightened self-interest strategy in this benign approach to not demanding reciprocal concessions from the insignificant multitude of developing nations. If the developing countries, bent on protectionism, were asked to join in reciprocal reductions of trade barriers, they would have likely abstained from the GATT system (as indeed was the danger as they lined up behind the United Nations Conference on Trade and Development or UNCTAD). By indulging them at only a negligible cost in terms of markets foregone, and committing them and the GATT to the view that this free ride would last till they developed and then had to "graduate," the postwar hegemonic power, the United States, could lead trade liberalization efforts and simultaneously build up commitment to the Liberal International Economic Order and to the GATT. This would then serve to help open the developing-country markets under GATT's auspices, through new MTN Rounds, when these markets had become truly important (as they now have).

Unlike in Charles Kindleberger's view of the hegemon being altruistic and setting rules and making institutions as a "public good," much like providing a public service from "leadership" and altruistic motives, the view here is then of what I have called by contrast a "selfish" hegemon. Its short-run policy of apparently selfless altruism leads to bigger long-run gain.

v. But unconditional MFN liberalization may be considered acceptable to the advocates of conditional MFN if only one could think of institutional ways of minimizing the free-rider problem. Here, the institution of the GATT and its MTN Rounds, as envisaged by James Meade (in his preference for the "multilateral-bilateral" approach) from the British side in the negotiations over postwar trade arrangements, became the preferred option. As Alice Enders observes in chapter 4, "The multilateral character of the negotiations would be secured by the simultaneous engagement of countries in the process of bilateral tariff negotiations [conducted on the principal-supplier and a "selective, product-by-product" approach] in one location."

It is certainly plausible that this "single location and negotiation" approach, underlying the successive MTN Rounds under GATT auspices, has served to reduce the free-rider problem while not eliminating it, making unconditional MFN more palatable to the reciprocitarians.

1.5   Explaining Unilateral Trade Liberalization: Ideas, Interests, and Institutions

So, one can conclude that reciprocity, despite the foregoing analysis of its many meanings and conceptual complexities and the difficulty of working with it in the real world of trade negotiations among multiple countries, has indeed played a role in reducing trade barriers in a nondiscriminatory way, both historically (as evident from Irwin's analysis of the U.S. experience in chapter 3) and in the modern period (as evident from the experience with the GATT's success with its MTN Rounds).

But the project's main findings relate, as already indicated, to the success of unilateral trade liberalization as well. So, the final question I must address is: What have we learned about the reasons why unilateral trade liberalization has occurred? In my 1988 book, *Protectionism*, I introduced the tripartite division of the causes of trade liberalization: ideas, interests, and institutions. This has proven to be influential; it can be used here to analyze the causes of unilateral trade liberalization specifically. Indeed, both the Asian analysis by Panagariya (chapter 8), and the New Zealand analysis by Evans and Richardson (chapter 7), use it to advantage in this volume; and Garnaut's discussion of Australia (chapter 6) clearly reflects this type of analysis as well.

Ideas

This divides in turn into the role of ideas per se and the role of individuals who brought these ideas to bear on the shift to unilateral trade liberalization.

The idea of unilateral trade liberalization (in the form of Proposition 1 in section 1.2) is of course quite old. But it was reinforced by policy *experience*: that is, by "example" as Prime Minister Peel believed when he repealed England's Corn Laws. Conybeare's investigation does not demonstrate unequivocally that Europe followed England's example, as Peel had assumed it would. But the role of example has certainly worked in modern contexts. This is borne out for countries such as India, studied by Panagariya in chapter 8, and for Central Europe as it turned from central planning and autarky, studied by Messerlin in chapter 9.

Equally, the example of one's own failure, not necessarily of others' success but possibly in conjunction with it, surely helped as well. India, Latin America, and Central Europe had all tried autarky or its less fearsome variants and had failed. In reforms, nothing succeeds like (past) failure! The reformers rooting for unilateral trade liberalization in these countries and regions had the advantage that there was a wide perception, I would say recognition, that opting out of trade and even direct foreign investment had failed. As Galbraith once remarked about Friedman, and I endorse the wit but not the economics, "Milton's misfortune is that his theory has been tried"!

But many chapters in this volume highlight the role of *individuals*, both in strategic governmental and quasi-governmental positions and also among intellectuals and economists who worked long to change public opinion through ceaseless public policy writings, who were critical to the unilateral shift to freer trade. In this context, the chapters by Panagariya, Garnaut, and Evans and Richardson are the most direct and fascinating while some examples of interest can be obtained also from many of the other chapters in part II in particular. In fact, remember that Prime Minister Peel in the 1840s was himself one of these key individuals, in the right place at the right time; and the developments in political economy, underlining evidently the convincing arguments for free trade, evidently played a major and self-acknowledged role in Peel's conversion to free trade and then to its unilateral version.[28]

Interests

As for interests, I must also note the role played by Richard Cobden and John Bright, the leaders in the Anti-Corn Law League, and the lobbying interests of the manufacturing classes that wanted cheap corn, in providing the necessary political support for Peel's intellectual-conversion-based decision to repeal the Corn Laws and usher in free trade unilaterally.

The role of exporting interests in pushing for greater freeing of trade, and as countervailing power to the import-competing interests that wish to close markets instead, is of course well understood and has been written about for almost two decades. The rise of globalized multinationals in keeping up the momentum for trade liberalization has been studied in this context.[29] But this volume produces several vignettes as when the role played by users of foreign inputs, made hugely expensive by protectionist policies, is also argued by Panagariya as a major factor in the eventual business push for more openness in trade in South Asia.

In addition, Panagariya reminds us that the exporting interests in powerful countries abroad can act as levers of openness in countries in politically dependent status. He argues this for Taiwan, which had to respond to U.S. lobbying pressures. This was also true of successful U.S. threats under Section 301 against South Korea (with exceptions only where the politics was immensely difficult, as with rice and cars). Such unilateral trade liberalization, however, falls into the category distinguished above as really a form of reciprocity going outside of trade: One's trade liberalization has its quid pro quo in removal of punitive threats or promise of benefits like security.

The role of *innovation* is also emphasized in the creation of genuinely unilateral, new sectoral liberalization. Lawrence J. White's analysis in chapter 12 of the U.S. financial liberalization, virtually all unilateral, and Cynthia Beltz Soltys's story in chapter 14 of how the U.S. telecommunication market was liberalized illustrate very well how rapid technical change was the effective driver.

Institutions

Perhaps the most dramatic argument for the role of institutions in driving unilateral trade liberalization comes from the Central European experience in Messerlin's chapter 9. The restoration of democracy after decades of Soviet-imposed communism changed the economic game as well. The shift to democracy was accompanied by a shift to economic policies such as freer trade that were associated with noncommunist systems.

The shift worked because there was no real politics to contend with at the outset. Borrowing from Mancur Olson's way of looking at this, I might say that there were no pressure groups to oppose or to propose change: More or less, ideas alone mattered.[30] It was not that the end of the Cold War had destroyed old economic lobbies that would oppose change; the Cold War had destroyed a system that had virtually no such lobbies in the political space to begin with!

The other chapter in this volume that is of interest from the viewpoint of the role of institutions is Irwin's chapter 3. It shows, however, how the Reciprocal Trade Agreements Act (RTAA) that followed the Smoot-Hawley tariff was an institutional change that replaced the earlier unilateralism of tariff setting by the Congress with reciprocity in trade bargaining by the Executive (i.e., the administration) and thereby overcame the bias toward protectionism that the Congress exhibited. So Irwin applauds the shift to reciprocity and deplores the earlier unilateralism, because the latter paradoxically served institutionally to undermine, not promote, trade liberalization! A paradox indeed.

1.6   Concluding Remarks

But there is much else that the curious and careful reader will find in these thoroughly researched papers. All I have done is to highlight the major issues, and findings, as I see them.

I recommend the smorgasbord. But what the reader will find on the sumptuous table is by no means confined to what I see and like. I urge that she explore. If she does, she ought to be rewarded.

Appendix: Formalizing the Argument for (Simultaneous) Reciprocity

Consider the theoretical argument, free from any political-economy argumentation, for unilateral free trade (UFT) and then, in light thereof, the case for reciprocity.[31]

Model 1: All Countries Are "Small": Unilateral Free Trade (UFT)

Assume that all trading nations are atomistic, so that they cannot influence the prices in world trade. This is the familiar "small country" assumption. Consider also that for unexplained reasons, each nation starts from an initial tariff-ridden equilibrium and then asks whether unilateral freeing of trade or a reciprocal one is desirable.[32]

It is immediately evident that unilateral free trade will be the choice of every country. No one country can do anything effective, such as closing its markets, to get others to change their tariffs by way of reciprocity; a policy of reciprocity is simply not feasible given the country's atomistic position. Every country therefore has the incentive to choose UFT in the absence of any leverage on world prices.

Of course, in the worldwide free trade (WFT) equilibrium that must emerge in this model, world efficiency is achieved and the equilibrium is Pareto-efficient. But this does not mean that, compared to its welfare in the initial tariff-ridden equilibrium, every country will become better off (ruling out lump-sum redistribution between nations, as I do throughout this appendix). The reason obviously is that the world prices facing a country in the WFT equilibrium may be worse than those faced by it in the initial tariff equilibrium, so that the loss from protection is eliminated but the terms of trade are worse. But this prospect will not mean that this country will not opt for UFT; it remains its best choice (since what it does or does not do cannot affect what others do, and these others will choose UFT and hence worsen the terms of trade for this country *anyway*). Evidently, there is no argument here for reciprocity of tariff cuts.

Model 2: Countries Are "Large": Argument for Reciprocity

But this is no longer so once the trading countries are assumed to be large, namely, with the power to influence their terms of trade by varying the volume of trade. In this case, a unilateral move toward free trade is not necessarily a welfare-improving policy for a country since its optimal tariff now is positive and a reduction in the tariff barrier below that could be welfare-worsening. Thus, UFT proponents would have to assume that the ability to influence the terms of trade is "negligible" in reality and that it is therefore best to proceed under the assumption that the trading countries are "small."

But that is a theoretically unsatisfactory position. If we allow for the "large" country assumption, then we must necessarily admit the possibility that UFT is welfare-worsening and hence is not a policy that will be embraced by the country.[33]

However, once we admit reciprocity, it is also obvious that the optimal-tariff-generated welfare level for a large country can be improved upon if this county's loss from its own liberalization was more than compensated by increased gains from a suitably large reciprocal liberalization by its trading partners. Recall from the text that this is, in fact, the case that I made in 1990 when I proposed four different reasons leading to reciprocity in preference to UFT, the first being the one that I have just stated and will now argue more rigorously.

But this justification for reciprocity is not really complete since the welfare of the partner countries is not examined. Of course, one may assume that a similar argument in favor of reciprocity can be assumed for them. But we still need to show rigorously that, through suitable reciprocal tariff cuts, *every* trading country (in a world of "large" countries) can improve its welfare with certainty and hence countries have an incentive to choose reciprocal tariff cuts instead of continuing at the initial tariff-ridden equilibrium.[34] This can be done, as I proceed to do now, demonstrating first the propositions stated earlier regarding the large-country case.

The Model and Initial Situation
Consider a two-country model throughout (except for a brief analysis of MFN at the end of this section). Then, in figure 1A.1, with

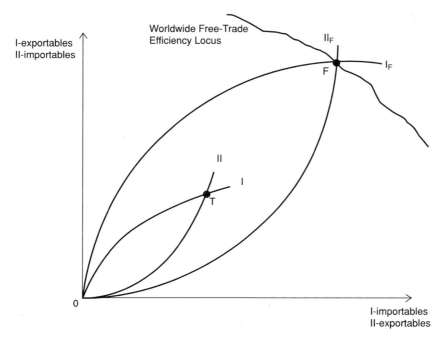

Figure 1A.1

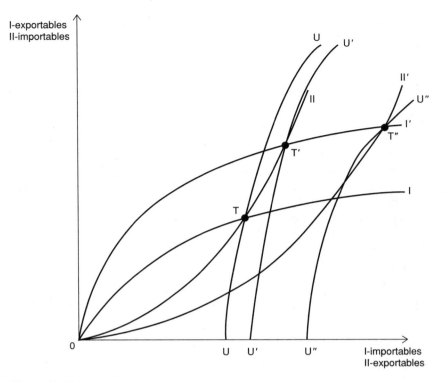

Figure 1A.2(a)

countries I and II trading with each other, their initial tariff-ridden offer curves I and II intersect at T. Their free trade offer curves I_F and II_F intersect at F, which lies on the worldwide free trade efficiency locus. T clearly is Pareto-inefficient.

Bhagwati's 1990 Argument

Suppose now that country I undertakes unilateral trade liberalization. Then in figures 1A.2(a) and 1A.2(b), its offer curves shifts to I′ and the equilibrium shifts to T′. Consider then a reciprocal trade liberalization by country II which shifts its offer curve to II′ and the trade equilibrium to T″. In figure 1A.2(a), the unilateral tariff reduction by I leads to increased welfare U′ since, at T, the country is above its optimal tariff in the initial (and new) equilibrium. Then, the reciprocal trade liberalization by II, leading to a shift in II's offer curve to II′, leads to a *further increase* in I's welfare to U″, exactly as argued earlier.[35]

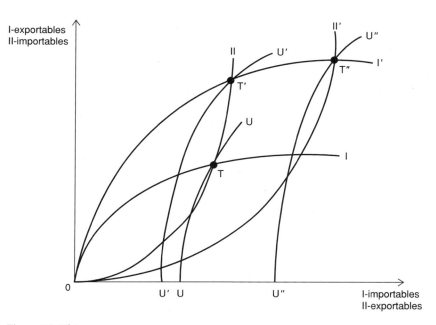

Figure 1A.2(b)

In figure 1A.2(b), the alternative case is illustrated where the unilateral liberalization by country I leads instead to reduced welfare at U′, because the initial tariff at T is below the optimal tariff and a further move away from the optimal tariff is welfare-reducing.[36] If country II then liberalizes sufficiently (as in the case illustrated), it will more than compensate for the loss of welfare for country I from U to U′ from its own liberalization, and hence lead to an overall welfare increase for country I to U″ from the initial level U.

The Zone of Reciprocal Trade Liberalization Making Each Country Better Off

But, on the one hand, this is a somewhat unsatisfactory way to deal with the advantage of benefits from reciprocity since the attention is exclusively on the welfare gain of one country. It is possible to strengthen the case for reciprocal trade liberalization, on the other hand, by showing that it can be suitably designed in such a way that each nation benefits from it, without invoking lump-sum transfers. To demonstrate this, and to establish the zone within which such trade liberalization will lie, consider figure 1A.3.

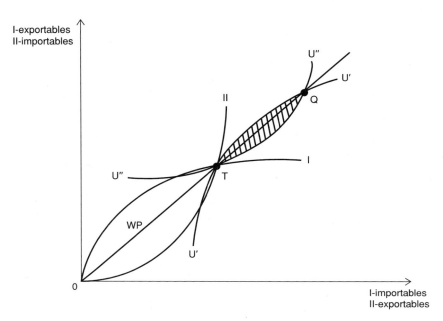

Figure 1A.3

With OI and OII still the tariff-inclusive offer curves of the two countries I and II, the initial tariff-ridden equilibrium is at their intersection at T. Now, however, draw the trade indifference curves U′ and U″ through T. As known from Johnson,[37] each country's domestic price-ratio line will be tangent to its trade indifference curve through T. Because of the tariff, that price line must be steeper than the world terms of trade or price line WP for country I and flatter than it for country II. Hence, we must necessarily have the trade indifference curves through T define a zone such as the striped area TQ in figure 1A.3.

If country I were to liberalize its trade so that its new offer curve moves through zone TQ, and if country II reciprocally liberalizes so that its new, shifted offer curve intersects country I's shifted offer curve within zone TQ, then each country will necessarily have become better off. And, mind you, we have not invoked lump-sum transfers.

The Terms-of-Trade-Preserving Reciprocal Trade Liberalization within this Zone of Mutual Gain: A Special Case

Consider now the case where we move into zone TQ but along the path set by the initial terms of trade, WP. For any trade liberalization by I, the shifted offer curve of I will go through TS. Choose then the tariff liberalization that makes the shifted II curve go through the same point, yielding the intersection of the two shifted curves.

It is easy to see why this pattern of reciprocal tariff cuts by I and II is beneficial to both nations. For, with terms of trade constant, the only effect of a tariff cut is to yield production and consumption gains to each country.[38] In a two-country world, therefore, we have an algorithm that tells us how we could ensure a mutually gainful reciprocal trade liberalization. Let I cut its tariff: this will worsen its terms of trade. Let II then liberalize its trade until the original terms of trade are restored. Both I and II will have then improved their welfare.

Of course, at each successive reduced-tariff-equilibrium, assuming that the countries proceed to seek yet higher welfare levels, we must redraw the zone TQ with respect to it rather than the original T and repeat the argument with reference to it. Note that, as is evident from figure 1A.4 and the depiction there of the free trade equilibrium at F on the worldwide free trade efficiency locus, the terms of trade WP at free trade will generally be different from the WP under the initial tariff-ridden trade equilibrium.[39] So, the end game of our terms-of-trade-preserving reciprocal trade liberalization algorithm will not be (fully) free trade, except in the case where the two countries are fully symmetric (or the terms of trade at T are fortuitously the same as in free trade). Free trade (at F) will generally be achievable through reciprocal elimination of all tariffs, with gain for each (compared to T), only with lump-sum redistribution among the trading countries.

Extension to MFN
The preceding argument applies to more than two countries, with MFN. Just consider the country II's offer curve to be the net offer curve of n different countries. As long as there is no discrimination among them, as MFN would ensure, the argument that everyone would benefit from a reciprocal tariff reduction that preserves the world terms of trade would follow immediately. Of course, with n countries in the game, there will generally be multiple solutions: A number of alternative combinations of tariff cuts among them could be compatible with equilibrium at any point along TS in figure 1A.4, for instance.

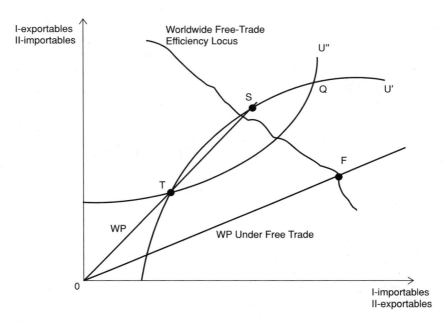

Figure 1A.4

Notes

I have profited from the comments and suggestions of Douglas Irwin, Arvind Pana-
gariya, T. N. Srinivasan, Kyle Bagwell, Pravin Krishna, Debashish Mitra, Don Davis,
Alan Deardorff, Robert Feenstra, and Gene Grossman. The comments of Richard
Brecher and Rodney Ludema have been particularly important.

1. Quoted in J. A. Hobson, *Richard Cobden—The International Man* (New York: Holt,
1919), 41. Cobden was, of course, the great crusader for the repeal of the Corn Laws.
His portrait, along with that of John Bright, hangs in London's celebrated Reform
Club—though Prime Minister Robert Peel's does not since he was, beyond the repeal
of the Corn Laws, not a "reformer." As Martin Wolf of the *Financial Times*, a brilliant
and indefatigable proponent of freer trade, and I were recently having coffee with
these two men looking down from the walls at us, I mischievously remarked to Wolf
about the delightful coincidence of two of the greatest free traders of the twentieth
century sitting under the portraits of two of the greatest free traders of the nineteenth!

2. From "Tara's Hills."

3. From this Indian Nobel Laureate's untitled celebrated song.

4. Cf. Jagdish Bhagwati and Hugh Patrick (eds.), *Aggressive Unilateralism*, (Ann Arbor:
Michigan University Press, 1990); and Jagdish Bhagwati, *The World Trading System at
Risk*, (Princeton: Princeton University Press, 1991).

5. See my exposé of the reality of U.S. loss in contrast to the propaganda by the USTR of a U.S. victory, in Jagdish Bhagwati, "The U.S.-Japan Car Dispute: A Monumental Mistake," *International Affairs* 72, no. 2 (1996): 261–279, reprinted as chapter 21 in my collected public policy essays, *A Stream of Windows: Unsettling Reflections on Trade, Immigration, and Democracy* (Cambridge: MIT Press, 1998).

6. This case involved the EU as the plaintiff and the United States, of course, as the defendant. Technically, the United States won the ruling because 301 was not declared intrinsically WTO-illegal but only if used. For all practical purposes, it was therefore the EU that had won the decision and therefore decided not to appeal it. The panel reported on December 22, 1999; see WTO/DS152/R, especially paragraph 8.1.

7. See chapter 1 in Bhagwati and Patrick, *Aggressive Unilateralism*, 15. The first of these four arguments was then developed formally in Jagdish Bhagwati, "The Choice between Reciprocity and Unilateral Freeing of Trade," mimeo., Columbia University, April 1997; it forms the basis for the appendix.

8. Cf. Bhagwati and Douglas Irwin, "The Return of the Reciprocitarians: U.S. Trade Policy Today," *The World Economy* 10: 109–130.

9. Because MTNs are marked by reciprocal reductions of trade barriers (though, with important reservations discussed in later sections of this chapter), my good friends Kyle Bagwell and Robert Staiger, who have done important work of their own recently on reciprocity, call it "GATT-think," drawing on Paul Krugman. But this is surely inapt. Reciprocity enters the scene with *negotiations*, whether at the GATT or the WTO or in bilateral or plurilateral trade treaties, and is what Prime Minister Peel was renouncing in unilaterally repealing England's Corn Laws. So, one should say "negotiations-think" not "GATT-think."

10. Cf. my op-ed, "President Clinton versus Prime Minister Peel: The Obsession with Reciprocity," *The Financial Times*, August 24, 1995, and a more expansive version of the essay in my 1998 book, *A Stream of Windows*. I should perhaps attribute the passionate embrace of reciprocity to the U.S. Congress and to the U.S. Trade Representative, Ambassador Mickey Kantor. But President Clinton's own embrace of aggressive unilateralism against Japan, even if less inflammatory, was evident in the early years of his first term, and as a consequence it affected his choice of staff and infected many others in his administration.

11. Cf. Jagdish Bhagwati and Arvind Panagariya, "Wanted: Jubilee 2010 Against Protectionism," mimeo., Council on Foreign Relations, February 2001. It has also appeared as an op-ed in *The Financial Times*, March 30, 2001. UN Secretary General Kofi Annan has also picked up this idea and brought it to the attention of the assembled NGOs in Brussels recently at the UNCTAD-World Bank meeting on the least developed countries' problems in the summer of 2001.

12. We must, of course, add the usual riders when there is national monopoly power in trade. Thus, unilateral trade liberalization is beneficial only if the optimal tariff is zero (i.e., there is no national monopoly power in trade) or when the reduction in barriers is from a level above the optimal tariff and does not go so far below the optimal tariff as to actually bring a welfare loss. Similar qualifications are necessary when firm-level imperfect competition exists.

13. As I note later, however, Peel also believed that sequential reciprocity would likely follow.

14. The distinction between direct (hence visible and salient) and indirect effects of reforms is extremely important in discussing the political economy of reform. I am afraid this point is not as well appreciated by political scientists such as Robert Bates, whose work on reforms in African agriculture aggregates the two types of reforms to arrive at "net" incentives. Get me a peasant who will passively accept the withdrawal of a subsidy on his fertilizers because a change in the exchange rate will make agriculture more profitable sufficiently to outweigh the loss of subsidy (and that too, based on Bates's or the World Bank's model)!

15. His views have been extensively documented in my 1988 book *Protectionism*. Also see the article by Douglas Irwin, "Political Economy and Peel's Repeal of the Corn Laws," *Economics & Politics* 1 (1989): 41–59.

16. See Rodney Ludema and Daniel E. Coates, "A Theory of unilateralism and Reciprocity in Trade Policy," Georgetown University Working paper. March 1989, and published in the *Journal of Development Economics*, 2001. See also Pravin Krishna and Debashish Mitra, "A Theory of Unilateralism and Reciprocity in Trade Policy," Brown University Department of Economics Working Paper, April 1999. The models used by these authors are quite different but both demonstrate how the foreign demand for protection can get affected by one's own tariff liberalization.

17. Australia and New Zealand did form a Free Trade Area, the first NAFTA, and of course participated in tariff cutting in the GATT Rounds, in addition to the significant unilateral trade liberalization.

18. I had originally included Hong Kong in the project since it is a case of a country that has remained a unilateral free trader for a long time. Unfortunately, the commissioned paper, by a team headed by Kar-yiu Wong, could not be completed in time.

19. The reasons why countries in the project have unilaterally liberalized are considered in section 1.5.

20. Unfortunately, Motoshige Itoh of Tokyo University could not complete a paper on Japanese experience with telecommunications.

21. See Jagdish Bhagwati, *Protectionism* (Cambridge: The MIT Press), 35–36.

22. Reciprocity is defined unambiguously in terms of trade volumes only in the context of compensation and retaliation. Thus, Enders states that "a specific example of retaliation based on this rule of thumb was the EEC's request to the GATT Council in March and April 1988 to authorize the retaliatory withdrawal of equivalent concessions granted to the United States in respect of specific products, following the adoption in 1987 of the panel report on United States—Taxes on Petroleum and Certain Imported Substances" (chap. 4, 109n57). Besides, typically the trade retaliation practiced under Section 301 of the United States, whether GATT-consistent or not, proceeds by calculating the trade-volume effect of whatever is objected to abroad and attempting to inflict a similar damage to the offending country's exports (while choosing products for retaliation on different economic and political considerations, of course).

23. WTO is in fact a tripod, with the third leg being intellectual property protection, alongside GATT and GATS.

24. On the drawbacks of these preferential trade agreements, which violate intrinsically the MFN principle vis-à-vis nonmembers, see the many writings of Arvind Panagariya and myself. For many of the most important contributions, see Jagdish

Bhagwati, Pravin Krishna, and Arvind Panagariya (eds.), *Trade Blocs* (Cambridge: MIT Press, 1998).

25. This argument is well known to several trade economists but is lost sight of by some well-meaning but misguided non-governmental organizations (NGOs) and, with far less excuse, by some World Bank bureaucrats who keep talking about how "unfair" the world trading system is, in having rich-country protectionism, as if it was a result simply of wickedness by the rich countries! Moreover, the governments of the poor countries who repeat this claim of "unfairness" are unaware that "fairness" in trade is a code word for "justifiable" protectionism in the rich countries, and they do themselves harm by appropriating this terminology as an acceptable way of looking at the world trading system.

26. Quoted in J. M. Keynes, ed., *Official Papers of Alfred Marshall* (Macmillan: London, 1926), 392.

27. Cf. chapter 30 in my collection of public policy essays, *A Stream of Windows*.

28. I might recall with amusement the time I was on the platform at an APEC Seminar in Auckland, New Zealand, with the country's dynamic trade minister, Dr. Lockwood. He spoke passionately in favor of unilateral trade liberalization, decrying reciprocity. He argued that asking for reciprocity was like telling your girl friend "I won't drop my pants unless you take off yours." I did not wish to contradict a free trader on the stage. But over coffee later, I told him that unfortunately, since sex normally requires two parties, and it is not much use dropping your pants if your girlfriend does not, any sexual analogy can only work for reciprocity, not for unilateral trade liberalization!

29. I developed this theme in *Protectionism*, and the political scientists John Odell and Helen Milner have also written on this theme.

30. Namely, that events such as wars can destroy old lobbies and facilitate change. See Mancur Olson.

31. This appendix is based on my widely circulated but unpublished manuscript from five years ago, "The Choice between Reciprocity and Unilateral Freeing of Trade," Columbia University, April 1997. Comments from Richard Brecher, Rodney Ludema, Arvind Panagariya, and T. N. Srinivasan at the time were most helpful.

32. A fully satisfactory analysis should derive the initial tariff equilibrium as well. But I stay here with the conventional assumption that somehow tariffs have been inherited, perhaps imposed by an earlier government, and the current government is free to decide whether free trade is good for it and, if so, is free to choose the way of getting to it.

33. I am not even admitting the further complication of trade retaliation by countries when they are not "small."

34. Of course, remember again that with any particular tariff-retaliation mechanism specified, such as in the celebrated Johnson-Cournot analysis, a large country could well emerge better off under a tariff-*increasing* policy than under the reciprocity that I analyze. Cf. Harry G. Johnson, "Optimum Tariffs and Retaliation," *Review of Economic Studies* 21 (1953–54): 142–153. But I discount this possibility as a likely outcome in the real world.

35. See chapter 1 in Bhagwati and Patrick, *Aggressive Unilateralism*.

36. Successive moves away from the optimal tariff, in either direction, are monotonically welfare-worsening, except for a multiple-equilibrium possibility in the presence of inferior goods, as noted by me and by Murray Kemp in the late 1960s.

37. Cf. Johnson, "Optimum Tariffs and Retaliation."

38. This idea was suggested to me by listening to Kyle Bagwell on reciprocity. See Kyle Bagwell and Robert Staiger, "An Economic Theory of GATT," *American Economic Review* 89, no. 1 (March 1999): 215–248.

39. The efficiency locus consists of all points of tangency between the trade indifference curves of both countries. Within any zone TQ, there must be such tangency points. Therefore, as pointed out to me independently by Richard Brecher and Rodney Ludema, a segment of the efficiency locus must lie within TQ. S may, however, lie below the efficiency locus rather than above it as illustrated.

I   Historical Experience

2

Leadership by Example?: Britain and the Free Trade Movement of the Nineteenth Century

John A. C. Conybeare

Supported by the principles of political economy, Great Britain was determined to set an example of free trade—unilaterally if necessary—for all the world to follow, hoping that through such a system, England might maintain her leading position as the metropolis in an Empire of Free Trade, such as Torrens described as early as 1815.

—Bernard Semmel, *The Rise of Free Trade Imperialism*

2.1 Introduction

The passage quoted previously summarizes one of the pieces of conventional wisdom about Great Britain's unilateral move to free trade in the middle of the nineteenth century. Whatever the motives driving the goal of free trade (and maintaining industrial dominance is only one of the many possible factors), it is also useful to pursue a less-examined question: Was unilateralism successful? Did it inspire other countries to emulate Britain, yielding the free trade movement that flourished internationally from the late 1840s into the 1870s?

Questions of motivation are difficult to answer when it comes to issues of contemporary public policy, and much more problematic when attempted with regard to decisions taken over a hundred years ago. Hence I will take a somewhat indirect path toward the question of whether British trade policy induced other countries to follow the same course, during the brief mid-century period when the commercial policies of most European countries reduced the magnitude of trade restrictions.

The first issue is the almost universal assumption that Britain did move to a policy of unilateral free trade. Questions have arisen about both the degree of free trade in Britain, relative to other countries, and the extent to which changes in trade policy were really unilateral. A second issue is to isolate the reasons for Britain's policy change toward freer trade. The extent to which other countries emulated Britain might have been influenced by whether they felt that Britain's motives were selfishly redistributive, and that Britain might gain far more from free trade than its trade partners, due to Britain's more advanced industrial structure. The next step is to examine how much trade liberalization actually occurred in the decades following 1840s. Finally, I return to the main question of setting out the possible reasons for other countries engaging in trade liberalization, and the extent to which their actions or motives may be attributed to Britain's example.

2.2   Who Was the Freest Trader of Them All?

Perfectly free trade, the absence of governmentally implemented barriers to trade, is obviously rare. Yet there is little disagreement that the middle decades of the nineteenth century saw a considerable weakening of formal trade barriers between states. Such changes could have been manifested in a number of ways, exhaustively catalogued in Gregory (1968 [1921]). All of these are essentially variations on a few possible outcomes of trade negotiations between states A and B that may also affect a third party (state C).

Negotiations between A and B may be of three types: unilateral concessions by one party, a bilateral most-favored-nation (MFN) agreement between the two, or a bilateral agreement stating the contingencies under which tariffs may be raised. The implications for third parties (state C) fall into the following categories:

1. C receives the same benefits by way of unconditional MFN treatment by A and/or B. This was likely in the nineteenth century if state C was a major trading nation.

2. C receives these benefits by way of unconditional MFN treatment to which it is entitled as a signatory to a trade agreement that also binds A and B; examples would be the early nineteenth-century Zollverein, a customs union that in 1834 linked eighteen German states, or the present-day General Agreement on Trade and Tariffs (GATT) and its successor, the World Trade Organization (WTO).

3. C receives the benefits of tariff reductions by A or B conditional upon offering its own concessions acceptable to A and/or B. The

prevalence of two-tier tariff rates in the late nineteenth century, under which A and B chose whether to extend to C a high or a low tariff rate, made conditionality easy to effect.

4. C is excluded from receiving the benefits of concessions exchanged between A and B. Military motives frequently generated such outcomes. After Germany refused to renew its military alliance with Russia in 1892, the former consistently attempted to exclude Russia from receiving any gains from Germany's trade negotiations with other states.

Given these many forms of trade liberalization and associated qualifications, it is worth considering the question of how free trading Britain actually was in reality. The implicit premise of the leadership-by-example argument is that Britain was free trading, or at least the most free trading country after the 1840s. Britain's turn to free trade was largely unilateral, symbolized by the abolition of the Corn Laws (agricultural import duties) in 1847. Export duties had been removed in 1842, and between 1842 and 1845, the number of items subject to import duties was reduced from 750 to 520. By 1860, there were only 48 dutiable items (Kenwood and Lougheed 1983). However, it has also been pointed out that British protectionism prior to the 1840s was never as consistently severe as in the popular impression. The chronological peak in import duties was reached in 1822 (when customs duties were 64 percent of the value of imports), but the rapid rise to this level had begun only with the revenue needs of the Napoleonic wars (Imlah 1958).

The question of how free-trading Britain actually was has been the subject of some debate, resolving principally into measurement issues. Nye (1991b) writes of the "myth of free trade Britain and fortress France" and claims that until the 1890s Britain was less free trading than France. During the middle years of the nineteenth century, he notes that French customs revenues (as a proportion of net import values) were consistently about 30 percent below that of Britain. Irwin (1993) suggests that this interpretation is misleading because it is based on inferences drawn from data on revenue rather than actual rates of duty, and much of British tariff revenue came from a few highly taxed luxury imports.

The argument is not entirely new; others have pointed out that Britain never moved completely to free trade and kept some tariffs (e.g., wine, silk) high after the 1840s for revenue or bargaining purposes. Iliasu (1971) notes that even after the unilateral tariff reductions of the 1840s, Britain left some duties high for bargaining with Spain, France, Portugal, and Brazil, but the tactic apparently had the desired effect in few instances. In 1865, for example, Britain signed a treaty with Austria whereby Britain lowered tariffs on timber in exchange for lower tariffs on manufactures (Lazer 1999).

Also relevant here is that MFN with Britain did not automatically extend to the empire; this had to be negotiated. Access to empire markets became increasingly problematic after the colonies attained tariff autonomy in 1846 (Foreman-Peck 1983). India, not being a colony, was never granted such autonomy, and Britain could continue to bargain for access to Indian markets, a major outlet for British textiles. Chronic conflicts ensued over India's need for revenues and the opposition of British manufacturers to duties (Davis and Huttenback 1986).

Since British tariffs on industrial products were low or nonexistent, free trade primarily affected imports of raw materials, so that the effective rate of protection (the nominal rate of duty on a final product, adjusted for the duty paid on inputs) for British manufactures might actually have been rising as free trade was introduced. Assuming that most tariffs on manufactured outputs were zero (or close to zero), reductions of tariffs on inputs would raise the effective rate of protection from a negative value toward zero. The fact that the cotton textile manufacturers (importers of raw cotton) were the primary lobbyists for free trade (see Anderson and Tollison 1985) is consistent with this inference.

Despite all of these qualifications, protection was effectively a dead political issue by the 1850s. There were few strong economic interests in favor of returning to protection. Agriculture adjusted to free trade more easily than expected, and manufacturing industry maintained a global competitive advantage well into the 1880s (see Irwin 1994). Free trade, and free markets generally, also acquired religious approval, noticed some time later and outlined in its historical evolution by Max Weber in his famous essay on the role of the "Protestant ethic" in the rise of market capitalism.

Unilateral free trade was not seriously debated again until the last two decades of the century (see Bhagwati and Irwin 1987). By the 1890s, "fair" trade, with its emphasis on strict reciprocity was becoming a popular slogan. This was also a time of severe trade rivalry with Germany (see Hoffman 1964 [1933]), especially over manufactured exports, and the increasing entanglement of trade politics with the rigidifying system of military alliances of the period before World War I. Yet the themes of the tariff debates in Britain at this time were still similar to those of the early decades of the century (Coats 1968).

All things considered, the British political commitment to free trade was a mostly unilateral and remarkably robust phenomenon, despite the qualifications cited above. Protectionist politicians ignored this at their peril. The free trade debate of the 1840s split the Tories, the free traders under Peel joining the Liberals (formerly Whigs), and the rest of the Tories reforming as the Conservative Party under Disraeli, who never again seriously opposed free trade. The Conservatives remained out of office until 1874, except for brief minority governments in 1852, 1858–1859, and 1866–1868.

When the Liberals split in 1886 over Home Rule for Ireland, the Liberal Unionists allied with the Conservatives, and the Unionists' commitment to free trade helped constrain protectionist sentiment in the Conservative ranks. In 1903 Colonial Secretary Joseph Chamberlain committed the Conservatives (including a reluctant Prime Minister Balfour) to Imperial Preference (an intra-Empire free trade area) and the party again split, the free traders (including Winston Churchill) joining the Liberals. The protectionist Conservative Party was severely defeated in the elections of 1906. As Friedberg (1988, 22) poignantly observes, Chamberlain's actions "broke his health, ended his active career, split his adopted party, and restored the Liberals to office after ten years of opposition and frustration." The critical political factor was that Liberals effectively wielded an argument that had also been used in the 1840s: Protection is a tax on food. Since near universal manhood suffrage had been in place since the Franchise Act of 1884, the electoral implications of a higher cost of living were doubtless even more politically harmful to protectionists than they had been in elections during the 1840s.

It was not until the World War I that Britain began to turn away from free trade. The McKenna duties of 1915 (named after the chancellor of the exchequer) imposed a 33.3 percent tariff on certain items (e.g., motor vehicles), ostensibly for revenue and to save shipping space, but were continued until 1938, when they were incorporated into the general tariff. Various other tariff measures were introduced in the 1920s, culminating in the Import Duties Act of 1932, imposing a 10 percent ad valorem tariff across the board (see Capie 1983). As before the war, the Conservatives favored protection. The Labour

Party adopted the free trade stand of the dying Liberal Party (which had last formed a government in 1916) and replaced the latter as the official opposition to the Conservatives. This pattern mirrored that observed in the United States at the time: Democrats preferred free trade, and Republicans protection.

2.3   Why Did Britain Move to Free Trade?

To what extent was the free trade movement driven by the expectation of imitation by other states? Unfortunately, there is a plethora of plausible, overlapping explanations for Britain's move to free trade, grouped in the following discussion into six categories. The first five pertain primarily to the question of why public policy became committed to lower trade barriers, and the sixth more to the issue of why the implementation of that commitment was unilateral, rather than relying on bilateral or multilateral bargaining. It should also be noted that a commitment to unilateral free trade does not necessarily imply that Britain believed others would follow; the policy would be equally consistent with the conjecture that Britain felt it would gain irrespective of foreign reactions, at least as long as foreign reactions would not be perversely negative (i.e., raising tariffs in response to British openness, a point that came up in tariff debates later in the century, and to which I return later).

Interest Group Lobbying

As they are still wont to do in the present day, those speaking for sectional interests went to some pains to phrase their demands in terms of a "national interest" (Grampp 1982). Prying beneath these superficial arguments, Anderson and Tollison (1985) argue that the Anti Corn Law League had tremendous financial power in elections during the 1840s and was backed by Midland textile producers who wanted lower duties on raw cotton and cheaper food for workers. The radical social reformer and parliamentary organizer of the vote on the Corn Laws, Richard Cobden, received cash payments of £75,000 from the Executive Council of the League after the end of the campaign, and another £40,000 from a "private subscription" (Prentice 1853; Anderson and Tollison 1985).

The textile industry may also have believed that free trade would inspire foreign reciprocity, stimulating British textile exports. Cobden certainly encouraged them in this hope (Barnes [1930] 1965). Yet this was not an argument pushed hard by the league, most likely because it would expose them to assertions that unilateral free trade might lead to Britain being exploited by others, one of the constant refrains of those opposed to unilateral free trade and revived again in the last decades of the century.

More general studies of industrial structure and lobbying for protection, such as McKeown (1989) and Schonhardt (1991), correlate the vote on repealing the Corn Laws with variables representing constituency interests. The results are generally as one would expect: MPs voted according to what they perceived to be the effect on the major economic interests in their constituencies.

Strong bureaucratic interests, notably the Treasury and the Board of Trade, consistently endorsed free trade. Throughout the nineteenth century most appointees to the Board of Trade remained members of "the Cobden Club," and career bureaucrats generally favored laissez-faire policies (Platt 1968). Whether these bureaucrats' sense of their organizational mission was generated by ideological commitment (as Platt implies) or material interest is unclear, but their policy stands were unambiguous. Their influence may well have been particularly strong during the debate and resolution of the Corn Law issue in the 1830s and 1840s, when party discipline was extremely weak, and the centralization of legislative initiative in the cabinet had not yet occurred (Cox 1987).

During the three decades prior to World War I, the bureaucracy again played a major role in providing wavering politicians with counterarguments to the new protectionists, or "fair" traders. Sir Robert Giffen, the Board of Trade's chief statistician from 1876 to 1897 (and former editor of *The Economist* from 1868 to 1876), produced numerous reports critical of the evidence presented by the fair traders. During the debate over Imperial Preference in 1903, the president of the Board of Trade, Charles Ritchie, was able to delay Chamberlain's efforts to commit the Conservatives to protection by threatening to resign.

The Treasury did not hesitate to join the fray on the side of the Board of Trade. In 1903, shortly after Chamberlain broke Cabinet discipline and publicly called for a debate on trade policy (despite Balfour's desperate attempts to delay such a debate), the Treasury produced a memorandum suggesting the following:

The Preferential system ... seems fraught with danger to the Empire: It may imperil its trade, hamper its finances, lead to strained relations with foreign countries, drag Colonial questions into Party politics, and increase the difficulty of the struggle for life [in] the poorest classes. (qtd. in Friedberg 1988, 61)

Domestic Political Goals

The period of Britain's turn to free trade was also a time of major social and political unrest (including a revolution in France in 1830, and another in 1848 that finally brought down the monarchy), culminating in a spate of mostly unsuccessful revolutions throughout Europe in 1848. Britain was spared the overt revolutionary violence that occurred on the continent, partly because it moved to enact social welfare reforms (e.g., Poor Law of 1834), legislated work conditions (e.g., the Factory Acts of the 1830s), expanded the franchise with a series of voting reforms (beginning with the Reform Act of 1832), and did not actively repress the nascent trade union movement begun by the Chartists (the laws prohibiting trade union activity, the Combination Laws, were repealed in 1825).

Conservatives still feared that revolutionary activity would spread to Britain, compounded in Ireland by famine conditions. Hence one of the most accepted conventional views of the abolition of the Corn Laws is that the goal was to defuse revolutionary pressure with cheaper food. This consideration has been alleged to be the primary incentive for Tory Prime Minister Robert Peel, who believed that the trade reforms of the early 1840s had demonstrated that the final repeal of the Corn Laws would raise wages, maintain social stability, and revive commerce in general (Irwin 1989).

Reduced Reliance on Tariff Revenues

The reintroduction of the income tax in 1841 reduced the need for tariffs, and the tariff reduction measures taken in the same years (e.g., alterations in the sliding scale of corn duties and the abolition of taxes on imports and exports of wool) were explicitly linked to the lower need for duties. Though the regressive implications of high import duties may well have contributed to the motivation to move to free trade, reintroducing the income tax was rather more a condition of moving to free trade rather than a reason for seeking it. Yet by 1860 tariff revenue was still 33 percent of total government revenue, falling to 23 percent in 1880, and 16 percent in 1910 (Mitchell 1975). In any case, it is not implausible to regard the abolition of the Corn Laws as part of the fiscal reforms that had been taking place since the early 1840s.

Ideas, Ideology, and Morality

Arguments about the role of ideas and ideology are notoriously hard to demonstrate, but may nevertheless be relevant, especially in situations where a state maintains a strong commitment to a policy over a long period of time, across generations of leaders and long-term structural changes in the nation's economy. It is an important consideration here because the commitment to free trade was so long-term and so robust. The strength of new ideas may well derive partly from economic interests, as Stigler clearly suggests in his pithy opinion that "if Cobden had spoken only Yiddish and, and with a stammer, and Peel had been a narrow, stupid man, England would have moved toward free trade in grain as its agricultural classes declined and its manufacturing and commercial classes grew" (1982, 63–64). Yet as I will note in what follows, ideas that drive long-term social change may well have bases distinct from economic interests.

A belief in the economic and moral virtues of unfettered markets is often seen as a key to understanding the politics of economic policy in the nineteenth century (see Irwin 1996). Free trade is like eating your spinach—it is good for you. The message of classical laissez-faire economics is often attributed great importance in the move to freer trade. Kindleberger (1975) favors this motive, suggesting that the leaders of British government and industry were persuaded by the rhetoric of Adam Smith's arguments in favor of the welfare-enhancing effects of unrestricted (for the most part) markets, though the individuals who propounded the free trade principles were often those who also stood to gain materially from free trade. Grampp's assessment of the move to free trade goes further than Kindleberger's and suggests that the driving force was a few key political figures—in particular, Lord Liverpool (sometime Tory Prime Minister between 1812 and 1822): "These men believed a freer trade would raise the country's real income, that the country must set itself on that course, but that it must do so with due regard to the

revenue needed by the government and to the legitimate claims of
people who would be adversely affected" (Grampp 1987, 86).

Semmel (1970, 159) suggests that for people like Cobden, free
trade was a "scriptural principle" rather than an economic efficiency
argument. Hilton (1988) goes further, elaborating on the theme that
free trade and free markets generally were seen by evangelicals as
one part of the trials with which God tests mankind, and offers the
opportunity for redemption (the manifestation of which, in this case,
would presumably be successful adjustment to the adversity created
by market forces without appealing to government intervention). The
more extreme evangelicals believed that God causes disasters to
punish humankind and saw the hardships of market forces to be not
only a test of humankind's ability to survive without resort to government regulation of the economy but also a form of divine retri-
bution for sin.

In addition to the evangelical aspects of arguments for free trade
many, including Cobden and Quaker John Bright, also believed that
it would promote world peace. This argument had been made earlier, more on logical and philosophical than moral grounds, by Im-
manuel Kant in his famous 1794 essay "On Perpetual Peace": The
ties of commerce will lead human reason to see a strong self interest
in peace, an idea that can be traced at least as far back as Aristotle.
The following excerpt from one of Cobden's speeches conveys the
argument well:

Free trade! What is it? Why, breaking down the barriers that separate nations; those barriers, behind which nestle the feelings of pride, revenge, ha-
tred and jealousy, which every now and then burst their bounds and deluge
whole countries with blood; those feelings which nourish the poison of war
and conquest, which assert that without conquest we can have no trade,
which foster that lust for conquest and dominion which sends forth your
warrior chiefs to scatter devastation through other lands, and then calls
them back that they may be securely enthroned in your passions, but only to
harass and oppress you at home. (qtd. in Barnes [1930] 1965, 268)

Yet material interest was never far from even the loftiest rationales
for free trade. Cobden frequently reiterated that he hoped for reciprocity from foreign powers (Semmel 1970).

The free trade debate became entangled in discussions of the goals
of and rationales for imperialism. Paradoxically, some of the proponents of peace through free trade also appear to have approved the
use of military force to keep markets open (e.g., the Opium Wars

with China between 1839 and 1842), and it is probably not a coincidence that the era of unilateral free trade also heralded a period known to some as the "imperialism of free trade" (Robinson and Gallagher 1953), during which underdeveloped countries could expect force to be used to encourage them to keep markets open to British exports and to repay debts to British banks.

The debate over "the imperialism of free trade" originated as a historical reflection upon the publicly stated beliefs of the Manchester School (of which Cobden was an adherent) that free trade was in truth "anti-imperialist." Robinson and Gallagher's primary concern was to correct this flattering self-depiction of the free traders and to argue that there was little difference between early and late Victorian imperialism. The former was merely "informal" empire, the use of force to keep trade open. The association of the free traders with informal imperialism has not gone unchallenged. Platt (1968) disputed the historical accuracy of Robinson and Gallagher's thesis and argued that Britain rarely used force to open markets. Opening up underdeveloped areas, by whatever means, helped cause severe friction with other European powers over mutual access to colonial markets (especially in Africa, where Britain and France nearly came to blows in 1898 over the Fashoda Crisis).

National Power and Wealth

Grampp (1987) and Semmel (1970) suggest that domestic sectional interests were weak and uninfluential in the free trade debates, and they attribute primary importance to politicians concerned with economic power and wealth: Free trade would maintain British power as the "workshop of the world." The Anti-Corn Law League (ACLL) was also prone to add the assertion that free trade would be a preemptive strike to maintain British industrial dominance (Semmel 1970).

Benjamin Disraeli (leader of the protectionist Tories in the Commons, from the 1840s until becoming prime minister in 1868) ridiculed this argument, and pointed out that Holland had once had a similar fantasy (Semmel 1970). Dutch pretensions to commercial hegemony were destroyed in a series of naval wars with Britain in the seventeenth century. Tories generally took the line that other states' tariff policies would not be influenced by Britain. Unfortunately, the "workshop of the world" argument was taken seriously by other countries. Suspicion of British motives in Germany and the United

States was so great that in 1856 Cobden remarked that "the less we attempted to persuade foreigners to adopt our trade principles, the better" (Semmel 1970, 177).

Failure of Previous Bilateral Negotiations

This portion of the chapter pertains primarily to the question of why, once free trade was accepted as desirable, it was pursued unilaterally, irrespective of whether one sees unilateralism as a deliberate tactic or merely as a second-best fallback position with no consciously articulated calculations other than the belief that free trade would be in Britain's interests regardless of foreign reactions.

During the eighteenth century, British trade negotiations were conducted on the basis of strict reciprocity (e.g., the Methuen Treaty with Portugal in 1703 exchanged preferential tariffs on items of mutual interest). By 1823 it was perceived that the policy of playing off one trade partner against another, with offers of preferential access, had failed. It had simply led to increased foreign tariffs (as bargaining chips) and retaliation by others when Britain gave a concession to one country. The Reciprocity of Duties Act (1823) offered MFN status to all willing to negotiate, and between 1824 and 1827, treaties were negotiated with France, Prussia, Austria, Sweden, the Hanse, Denmark, the United States, and most of the new states of Latin America (Iliasu 1971).

What Britain failed to get were actual tariff reductions. Negotiations to do so were long, unsuccessful, and marred by intense suspicion of British intentions—Britain would not, foreign countries uncharitably surmised, offer reciprocity unless it would be the primary beneficiary (Iliasu 1971). If true, this might imply that other states viewed the goal of trade negotiations for each participant as that of maximizing relative rather than absolute gains. This atavistic remnant of mercantilist thinking could not have been helpful to the goal of mutual tariff reduction.

Great efforts were made to negotiate tariff reductions with France in the 1830s. Both threats (increases in the duty on French silks) and promises (diplomatic alliance) were made (Ratcliffe 1978). The perception that they had been cheated in an earlier trade treaty with Britain (the Eden Treaty of 1786, that allowed Britain to continue to ban the import of French silk, while reducing French textile tariffs) made it harder to respond positively to British moves (Rose 1908).

Similarly frustrating negotiations went on with Prussia and Austria in the early 1840s. Prussia backed away from proposed duty increases on iron after explicit threats of retaliation from Britain, but not without a parting shot from Foreign Minister von Bulow: "We prize good relations with England but we won't let her impose on us. It's England who needs us, who needs markets for its manufactures, while what she takes from Germany is subjected to heavy taxes" (Gordon 1969, 84). In 1842 Metternich expressed Austria's position to a British trade representative in more pithy prose: "Take our corn and we will take your manufactures" (Semmel 1970, 149). Both of these exercises in reciprocity produced few substantive results.

These experiences convinced the British government that "tariff reductions would have to be based exclusively on domestic benefit rather than the hope of foreign counter concessions" (Gordon 1969, 87). Irwin (1989) agrees, suggesting that the failure of proponents of reciprocity (such as the economist Torrens) was less because arguments about the adverse terms-of-trade effects of unilateral free trade were unappreciated, but because of a general belief by the early 1840s that Britain could not influence the trade policies of most other countries by explicit bargaining or by implicit reciprocity.

There is little question that the turn to unilateralism in the 1840s was partly a response to the failure of bilateralism to achieve tariff reductions, as distinct from mere MFN status. Several caveats should be noted. Britain did not totally abandon bilateralism, and easily reverted to that bargaining tactic when useful:

1. The Cobden-Chevalier Treaty of 1860 with France (a bilateral exchange of trade concessions) has been cited as representing the abandonment of the policy of seeking free trade "by example." Free traders opposed the treaty because it was not unilateral. Oddly though, Iliasu (1971) says that the reason was not trade related, but due to a mutual desire for diplomatic rapprochement in the expectation of conflict with Austria over northern Italy. Whether politically or economically motivated, this treaty was a salient exception to the strategy of unilateralism.

2. Britain continued to negotiate bilateral MFN treaties, which protected her from the worst excesses of foreign tariffs (Saul 1960). Such treaties did this by keeping Britain on the lower rates of the two-tier tariff schedules that became common during the nineteenth century.

There were two types of multiple-tier tariff systems that hampered British exports. The minimum-maximum tariff (an example of which was the French Méline tariff of 1892) gave the minimum to countries that were considered cooperative. More widespread prior to the World War I was the general-conventional system (used by, e.g., Germany), which put all countries initially on the high general tariff and invited them to bargain for trade conventions that would entitle them to a lower rate. MFN status with a country having the general-conventional system would have always guaranteed to Britain that country's lowest rates. A parliamentary command paper (Great Britain 1903) lists sixty-seven MFN treaties in force at that time. Treaties with Denmark and Sweden dated back to the 1660s, but most were concluded between the 1850s and the 1870s. Yet what incentive would states have to agree to an MFN treaty with a unilateral free trader? One such incentive has already been cited: Britain kept some tariffs high for future bargaining.

3. Also noted above is that Britain still bargained over access to colonies. In 1870, 20 percent of exports and imports were with the Empire (Capie 1983), which both gave Britain a bargaining chip and muted the effect of foreign tariffs. As most of the empire gained tariff autonomy, Britain herself faced increasing tariff barriers in colonial markets. As Davis and Huttenback (1986, 230) wryly note, "Much to Britain's chagrin, faith in the wonders of free trade was limited to Britain herself." This development partly accounts for the increasing interest in Imperial Preference, or what Torrens had in the early part of the century called a "colonial Zollverein" (Semmel 1970, 195).

Involvement in conflicts over empire tariffs occasionally dragged Britain into unwelcome disputes. In 1897, when Canada gave a special tariff concessions to British manufactures, Germany protested that this was a violation of an earlier MFN treaty giving Germany equal access to British dominions. Britain canceled the treaty, and Germany and Canada engaged in a tariff war (Ashley 1910). Britain and Germany continued, as major trade partners, to give each other MFN on an annual basis (Hoffman [1933] 1964).

4. Even if we accept British liberalization as unilateral, we cannot preclude an expectation of emulation, if not reciprocity. The distinction between unilateralism and reciprocity is rarely unambiguously clear. This is particularly true of the trade measures taken by Britain

in the period immediately prior to the abolition of the Corn Laws, so that one should perhaps say that Britain's trade liberalization was not "truly" unilateral until after 1847 (Gordon 1969). Even after that time, it was in Britain's strategic interest for countries to remain in some degree of uncertainty about the strength of its commitment to free trade, in the absence of emulation.

2.3 Did Others Liberalize after Britain?

The repeal of the Corn Laws had little immediate effect on foreign tariffs. Williams's history of British commercial policy up to 1850 notes that British attempts to encourage emulation from Austria, Russia and Belgium elicited no positive response (Williams 1972). Yet most countries were busy lowering tariffs after the 1840s (see Kindleberger 1975), with the exception of Russia and the United States.

Cross-nationally comparable tariff data for this period are difficult to obtain, though the imperfect proxy of import duties as a proportion of import values (table 2.1) does suggest a general decline in protection during the period after the 1840s.

Table 2.1
Customs duties as a percentage (%) of import value, selected countries, 1820–1900

	1820	1830	1840	1850	1860	1870	1880	1890	1900
Austria	na	na	na	3	3	2	1	3	7
Belgium	na	na	na	5	3	2	1	1	2
Denmark	na	na	na	na	na	10	12	11	8
France	38	22	16	16	7	3	5	8	9
Germany	na	na	na	13*	12*	na	6	9	8
Italy	na	na	na	na	na	8	10	18	12
Neth.	na	na	na	3	2	1	1	1	1
Russia	21	33	33	32	21	13	15	35	33
Spain	na	na	na	25	16	10	16	16	18
Sweden	na	na	na	19	16	12	10	11	11
Switzerland	na	na	na	na	na	na	na	3	4
UK	22	34	25	21	11	7	5	5	5

Sources: Mitchell (1975), Flora (1983).
Note: na indicates data not available in sources cited.
*Prussia only.

The Cobden-Chevalier Treaty between Britain and France in 1860 produced a flurry of MFN treaties in Europe, but mostly between France and other European powers (Belgium, Prussia, Italy, Switzerland, Sweden, Norway, Netherlands, Austria). The concessions Britain granted to France were unilaterally extended to the rest of the world; France extended its concessions to Britain to other parties only through MFN treaties. The French Assembly of the new Third Republic denounced the Cobden Chevalier Treaty in 1873, but unilaterally continued to give Britain the same rates until the Méline tariff of 1892 (Smith 1980; Verdier 1994). Nye (1991a) interprets the Cobden-Chevalier Treaty as an indication of Britain's recognition of the failure of unilateralism, and he suggests that the subsequent flurry of MFN treaty making around Europe led to more trade liberalization than did the unilateralism of the period immediately after the abolition of the Corn Laws in 1847.

Whatever imitation effect did occur was short-lived. From the late 1870s, most European states raised import barriers and became entangled in tariff wars (Conybeare 1987). The conventional explanation for this return to protection is the sustained European depressions (especially in agriculture) of the latter decades of the century (Gourevitch 1986). Infant industry arguments in "late industrializing" countries may have also contributed, as may have domestic lobbying for tariffs. In Germany the marriage of "iron and rye" and in France the "bourgeois-peasant alliance" were manifested in the higher rates of the German tariff of 1879 and the Méline Tariff of 1892 (Smith 1980; Henderson 1975; Kindleberger 1951). In both France and Germany the results of these coalitions were higher tariffs on both agriculture and industrial products, to please both sectors. In the context of this discussion of British unilateralism, the return to protection might also reflect confidence on the part of other powers that Britain's free trade policies were truly unilateral and unlikely to be removed in retaliation.

The "return" to protectionism in the last decades of the century (see, e.g., Gourevitch 1986) is seen by many as the end of Britain's success at inducing other states to open their markets. On a contrary note, it is worth observing that if revenue data is a reasonable proxy for unavailable tariff data, the return to protectionism—and hence the extent to which British unilateralism should be considered a failure in the longer term—has been exaggerated. The data in table 2.1 show that French duties did rise after 1870 but never came close to approaching the magnitude attained in the 1820s. Similarly, the "high" German protectionism of the later decades of the century appears to have been far below the Prussian tariff rates (around 20%) that were considered very liberal in the earlier decades of the century. Russia appears to have been the only European state that returned to the tariff levels of the 1820s and 1830s. Tariffs were lower at the end of the century than at the beginning (as were transport costs, due to the steamship), and to the extent that one is willing to attribute the beginnings of free trade to British unilateralism, the lack of a genuine return to protection at the end of the century is further evidence of the robustness of British policy and its impact on other states.

In the 1890s, another brief round of treaty making was centered on Germany—the Caprivi round, during which Germany signed treaties with Italy, Switzerland, Belgium, Serbia, Spain, Romania, and Russia. The motive was most likely diplomatic—France allied with Germany's erstwhile ally, Russia, and Britain had rejected Germany's overtures for a military alliance. This was a time of close coordination of trade and military alliance policies among the continental European powers.

The prevalence of bilateral MFN treaty making during the second half of the nineteenth century—inspired by British unilateralism or Cobden-Chevalier—was not without dysfunctional aspects.

First, it should be noted that nineteenth-century MFN treaties were unlike MFN negotiations that have occurred under the auspices of the GATT/WTO during the past fifty years. Under contemporary institutions, concessions exchanged between GATT/WTO members are automatically extended to all members of the club. MFN treaties during the nineteenth century, whether conditional or unconditional, did not automatically extend to third parties unless that party also had an MFN treaty with the contracting states. However, by the end of the century, bilateral MFN treaties linked together most of the major trading states of Europe, and so came to resemble a GATT-like system.

A memorandum written for the League of Nations claimed that the nineteenth-century MFN system incurred large transaction costs,

compelling states to join in the game of haggling: first, to revise their tariffs at certain fixed intervals...; second, to incorporate in their tariffs new rates carrying a considerable trading margin; and third, to go through a period in which negotiations were carried on simultaneously in quick succession with a considerable number of states. (Page 1927, 8)

The U.S. Tariff Commission (1934) particularly objected to the "padding" of tariffs prior to negotiations, though the reluctance of the United States to engage in negotiations prior to World War I is more likely related to the disinclination of Congress to allow the executive to preempt congressional power over foreign trade. Germany in particular is cited for such actions prior to entering the round of Caprivi treaties in the 1890s.

Page (1927) also notes that the system quickly broke down after World War I, because of the large number of new states in the tariff negotiating game. International negotiations also became more problematic because countries that had hitherto played little active role in the system became more active, if not belligerent (e.g., the U.S. and Japan), and some states raised (already high) tariffs to protect war-created industries (e.g., Australia). British unilateralism in the previous century had faced a much easier task: It had to confront only a few "tough" bargainers (namely, France and Prussia/Germany), its other trade partners being either malleable empire countries, states with whom no negotiations were possible (the U.S.), or small European countries more vulnerable to subtle hints (e.g., Netherlands).

The gains from MFN agreements could also be undermined by making new categories in a country's tariff schedule. An egregious example is the German cattle tariff of 1902: wanting to lower the cattle tariff for Switzerland, but bound to an MFN treaty with Russia, the government created a new low tariff rate for cattle grazed at a high altitude.

By the end of the nineteenth century many countries had moved to a formal two-tier tariff system. This increased the pressure on countries to be constantly in negotiation to maintain their MFN status in these markets. A state without MFN status in the markets of its trade partner risked being punished in every category of the partner's tariff schedule, rather than merely for certain items where third countries might have secured a more advantageous rate.

2.4   Why Did Other Countries Liberalize?

Did the trade liberalization movement of the middle of the nineteenth century occur because other countries were following Britain's example? McKeown (1983) claims that the liberalization that occurred after the 1840s was without any British pressure, supported by evidence that Britain got no better terms from small weak countries than from larger ones. The problem here is one of judging motives and intent. The outcome is consistent with a number of explanations.

Interest Groups and Ideology

Recall the familiar arguments about the difficult-to-separate variables of interest-group pressure and ideology. Kindleberger (1975) has provided a number of such explanations with respect to the states of Western Europe. Unfortunately, these often appear rather ad hoc, since the data necessary to test such hypotheses (e.g., the industrial structure of a country) is usually unavailable for most countries in the nineteenth century, with the exceptions of the United States and Britain. The relatively high economic growth rates of the midcentury doubtless also reduced sectional demands for protection. Annual rates of growth for total and per capita GNP increased up to 1870 (to 2.4% and 1.5%, respectively) and declined thereafter until 1900 (Bairoch 1976).

Political Sidepayments

British diplomatic or military support was a valued prize. This appears to have been a prime motivation behind Napoleon III's enthusiasm for the Cobden-Chevalier commercial treaty with Britain in 1860. For nonmajor, non-European powers, the threat of British military intervention was always present. It was common to use military force against defaulting sovereign debtors (e.g., Egypt in 1870 and Turkey in the 1890s). What distinguished late-nineteenth-century imperialism from the earlier so-called imperialism of free trade (the alleged use of force only to keep trade open) was that when military power was used, it was for physically annexing by force, rather than merely keeping markets open.

Some scholars claim to observe a "contagion" effect, closely related to the argument that other countries followed Britain's example. A recent paper by Lazer (1999) makes this argument about the round of MFN treaties following Cobden-Chevalier. The model itself is a version of the familiar dynamic Prisoners' Dilemma game. The implication for judging British influence is, I think, that once Britain negotiated the treaty with France, and unilaterally extended the concessions to everyone, third parties then had an incentive to negotiate with France to get the same rates as Britain. But this was not so much following Britain as safeguarding their interests in the French market.

Following the British Example

Britain's position in world trade meant that it could hardly not have had an effect on lesser trading powers, even ones with economic (or overall national) power close to that of Britain. Nye (1991), for example, estimates that British openness significantly increased the elasticity of demand for French exports and so encouraged lower French duties. Despite McCloskey's (1980) argument that free trade actually hurt Britain by causing a deterioration in the terms of trade (a counterargument to which may be found in Irwin 1988), ample evidence exists that foreigners believed Britain did well by free trade.

Unfortunately, believing that Britain benefited from free trade did not necessarily encourage others to follow, for at least two reasons. One is that insofar as other states accepted the "workshop of the world" argument made by some within Britain, it caused them to speculate about the possible predatory intent (based on economies of scale?) behind British free trade, and hence fueled the "late industrialization" or infant industry protection arguments popular in continental Europe. Second, belief that Britain may have itself gained from free trade did not necessarily exclude the temptation to also believe that other states might gain relatively or absolutely by trying to "take advantage" of British free trade. Some influential British policymakers attributed such thoughts to other states by the 1890s.

Hence the possibility exists that the unilateral free trade tactic made other countries even less motivated to lower their tariffs. Lazer (1999) suggests that once it became clear that the British commitment to free trade was relatively permanent and really unilateral, they became less inclined to make concessions that would benefit Britain (e.g., Austria canceled its trade treaty with Britain in 1875) (Lazer 1999). Ironically, when the question came up again in the 1890s of whether Britain should "bargain" rather than maintain unilateral free trade, the Treasury argued that such a move would lead to foreign retaliation (Friedberg 1988). Threats to abandon free trade had little credibility, except in a few cases, such as the sugar agreement of 1903 (Saul 1960).

One can sympathize with "the Weary Titan [that] staggers under the too vast orb of its fate" (Joseph Chamberlain, qtd. in Friedberg 1988, vii). Many of those who purported to speak for the Weary Titan appear to have concluded, by the 1890s, that Britain would be disadvantaged no matter what its trade policy: Unilateralism would cause Britain to suffer free riding or worse; reciprocal bargaining would not be credible and might lead to retaliation. The mood of the times was not unlike that frequently expressed in the United States today. Alfred Marshall was expressing a widely held view when he wrote:

England is not in a strong position for reprisals against hostile tariffs, because there are no important exports of hers, which other countries need so urgently as to be willing to take them from her at a considerably increased cost; and because none of her rivals would permanently suffer serious injury through the partial exclusion of any products of theirs with which England can afford to dispense. (Marshall's Official Papers, qtd. in Saul 1960, 135)

One might also raise the question of who was emulating whom. The Prussian Maasen tariff of the 1820s reduced duties on manufactured imports to 20 percent and inspired Huskisson to tell the House of Commons that "I trust that the time will come when we shall be able to say as much for the tariff in this country" (Henderson 1975, 33). The Zollverein predated the repeal of the Corn Laws by some twenty years and was strongly opposed by Britain and France, both of which actively worked to reduce the number of states induced to join the Zollverein (Luard 1984; Henderson 1975).

A common belief in Britain from the early decades of the century, no doubt stemming partly from the chronic failure of bilateral negotiations, was that foreign tariffs would not be influenced by Britain except in a negative way. Imlah (1958, 149) cites a House of Commons select committee report of 1840, which argued that high tariffs would and were leading to retaliation by foreign governments, suggesting that Britain could only hope to influence foreign governments by setting an example. Hence Cobden's fervently hopeful proclamation that "if you abolish the Corn Laws honestly, and adopt free trade in its simplicity, there will not be a tariff in Europe that will not be changed in less than five years to follow your example" (qtd. in Barnes [1930] 1965, 268). Irwin (1998) found four distinct perspectives on this issue: a group around Ricardo who thought British tariffs should be independent of conjectures about foreign reactions (either because irrelevant or beyond British influence), unilateralists who believed foreign countries would emulate Britain, bilateralists who believed that unilateralism should be invoked if negotiations failed, and adherents to strict reciprocity who followed Torrens in the belief that unilateral free trade would harm the British terms of trade.

Yet the notion that foreign countries would copy Britain was largely rejected by many Tories, and Peel was careful to justify free trade as good for its own sake, irrespective of foreign action. Most observers note that post-1840s liberalization occurred without any British pressure, though such influence by example was a clear hope of many. The select committee report of 1840 expressed this aspiration in the unselfconsciously patronizing manner that is so quintessentially English, suggesting that free trade would

give an example to the world at large, which, emanating from a community distinguished above all others for its capital, it enterprise and its intelligence, and the extent of its trading relations, could not but exercise the happiest effects and consolidate the great interests of peace and commerce by associating them intimately and permanently with the prosperity of the whole family of nations. (qtd. in Imlah 1958, 149–150)

Some more contemporary observers (e.g., the German economist Carl Fuchs 1905) felt that until it became clear that Britain's commitment to freer trade really was unilateral, other states perceived it to be short-term and conditional and moved to lock in the benefits with MFN treaties with Britain. Hence one of the problems of inference here is that the underlying motive of the foreign powers that did follow Britain's example could have been reciprocity rather than following an example that might lead to greater national income.

Yet because this is an argument about a policy "climate," empirical evidence is very hard to present. The hypothesis that Britain was followed, consciously or otherwise, is almost untestable, at least beyond a simple observation of chronological sequence of measures. A more persuasive test would be to look for specific instances in which there is some more clearly documented evidence of linkage, where foreign leaders clearly articulated a connection between Britain's trade policy and their own.

The example of the U.S. Walker Tariff of 1846 illustrates the difficulties of distinguishing between emulation and reciprocity. The United States is perhaps the least felicitous example of the inspirational impact of British unilateralism, since the United States remained (with Russia) one of the highest tariff states during the nineteenth century, though it did enter a brief period of lower tariffs from the 1840s to the Civil War. As one of the countries least likely to imitate British free trade, the United States also had by 1860 the largest shares of British trade, providing 21 percent of British imports and taking 16 percent of its exports (Mitchell 1975).

Primary documents indicate that commentators on both sides of the Atlantic believed that the abolition of the Corn Laws was instrumental in helping the Walker Tariff pass. Apparently no threats were made, so one might see this as one example of spontaneous emulation of Britain. At least one parliamentary speaker in the Commons debates in 1846 spoke of how the abolition of the Corn Laws would lead to reciprocity by the United States (James and Lake 1989). Since it is unlikely that the abolition of the Corn Laws could have been conditional upon U.S. reactions, this may be one of the few examples where British unilateralism could plausibly be asserted to have stimulated unilateral emulation, or at least reward. Yet even here it is not entirely clear that some spirit of reciprocity could not be imputed to either or both sides. Lord Lyndhurst suggested to the Commons in 1838 that he feared the United States would shift its imports of manufactured goods to Germany if Britain did not lower its barriers on U.S. agricultural products (Semmel 1970).

Thus, though publicly stated as unilateral trade liberalization measure, British policy during the middle decades of the nineteenth century may well have been interpreted by foreign countries to contain an implicit threat and an expectation of reciprocity.

2.5 Conclusion

Barnes's ([1930] 1965, 268) history of the Corn Laws gloomily opined that "this hope, that other countries would follow Great Britain in free trade, ... has proved a great disappointment." This judgment on British unilateralism was implicitly invoked in rationales for Britain's return to across-the-board tariffs in the interwar period. Lord Londonderry, presenting the Import Duties Act of 1932 to the House of Lords, said: "Foreign nations have been able to disregard us in any negotiations which we were capable of putting forward ... Now we find ourselves in a totally different position. Instead of approaching the nations of the world as a supplicant, we come before them as a powerful negotiator" (qtd. in Jones [1934] 1983, 234). Nevertheless, given Britain's large share of world trade, it is hard to imagine the free trade movement having much force without British cooperation.

Consider, for example, the impact of the Smoot Hawley tariff, at a time when the United States had replaced Britain as the largest world trading power. The chronology of the internationalization of the free trade movement from the 1840s to the 1870s is certainly consistent with this interpretation. But once the basic move was made, there is little indication that other states were explicitly copying Britain. Whether this is truly lack of emulation or simply lack of evidence pertaining to the motivations of national leaders, it is difficult to judge. The Cobden-Chevalier Treaty of 1860 may not be indicative of much about British trade strategy (for or against unilateralism), since it appears to have been concluded largely for military reasons.

Insofar as British unilateralism may be given credit for the free trading policies of the middle of the nineteenth century, should we extrapolate this experience to the current trade policies of the United States? Lake (1991) has perceptively suggested a few reasons for caution.

One reason Britain could afford to be magnanimous in its unilateralism was that it could (or so the British hoped) rely on Empire markets to mitigate the effects of other countries failing to cooperate. In 1870 the Empire took 21 percent of British exports and provided 23 percent of its imports; and these shares continued to rise up to World War I (the respective market shares being 27% and 35% in 1914) (Capie 1983).

In addition to having an Empire market as insurance, another difference is that, at the peak of its commercial hegemony, Britain accounted for a much larger share of world trade than the United States (about 24% in 1870), whereas in 1960 the United States provided 15 percent of world trade. World trade yielded half Britain's national product for most of the last century. U.S. global economic power, argues Lake, has been based on its share of world production and its domestic market size (traded goods accounting for much less than 20% of national income by the 1960s). This characteristic might tempt U.S. policymakers to focus more on reciprocity tactics rather than unilateralism.

Oscar Wilde reminds us, in *The Importance of Being Earnest*, that "the truth is rarely pure, and never simple." Perhaps the best one can say is that British commitment to free trade—whether truly unilateral or otherwise—was a necessary but not sufficient condition for the emergence, however brief, of more open international markets in the nineteenth century. This is an appropriate lesson for U.S. policymakers today.

Acknowledgments

I would especially like to thank Jagdish Bhagwati and Douglas Irwin for comments on earlier drafts.

References

Anderson, Gary, and Robert Tollison. 1985. "Ideology, Interest Groups and the Repeal of the Corn Laws." *Journal of Institutional and Theoretical Economics* 141, no. 2 (June): 197–212.

Ashley, Percy. 1910. *Modern Tariff History*. 2nd ed. London: John Murray.

Bairoch, Paul. 1976. "Europe's Gross National Product: 1800–1975." *Journal of European Economic History* 5, no. 2 (Fall): 273–340.

Barnes, Donald. [1930] 1965. *A History of the English Corn Laws*. New York: Kelly.

Bhagwati, Jagdish N., and Douglas A. Irwin. 1987. "The Return of the Reciprocitarians—U.S. Trade Policy Today." *The World Economy* 10, no. 2 (June): 109–130.

Capie, Forrest. 1983. *Depression and Protectionism: Britain between the Wars*. London: Allen and Unwin.

Coats, A. W. 1968. "Political Economy and the Tariff Reform Campaign of 1903." *Journal of Law and Economics* 11 (April): 181–229.

Conybeare, John. 1987. *Trade Wars*. New York: Columbia University Press.

Cox, Gary W. 1987. *The Efficient Secret: The Cabinet and the Development of Political Parties in Victorian England*. New York: Cambridge University Press.

Davis, Lance, and Robert Huttenback. 1986. *Mammon and the Pursuit of Empire: The Political Economy of British Imperialism, 1860–1912*. New York: Cambridge University Press.

Flora, Peter. 1983. *State, Economy and Society in Western Europe, 1815–1975: A Data Handbook*, Vol. 1. Chicago: St. James Press.

Foreman-Peck, James. 1983. *A History of the World Economy since 1850*. Totowa, NJ: Barnes & Noble.

Friedberg, Aaron. 1988. *The Weary Titan: Britain and the Experience of Relative Decline, 1895–1905*. Princeton: Princeton University Press.

Fuchs, Carl. 1905. *The Trade Policy of Great Britain and Her Colonies since 1860*. London: Macmillan.

Gordon, Nancy. 1969. "Britain and the Zollverein Iron Duties, 1842–1845. *Economic History Review* 22, no. 1 (April), 2nd series: 75–87.

Gourevitch, Peter. 1986. *Politics in Hard Times: Comparative Responses to International Economic Crises*. Ithaca: Cornell University Press.

Grampp, William. 1982. "Economic Opinion When Britain Turned to Free Trade." *History of Political Economy* 14 (Winter): 496–520.

Grampp, William. 1987. "How Britain Turned to Free Trade." *Business History Review* 61, no. 1 (Spring): 86–112.

Great Britain. 1903. Commercial No. 9 (October). "Return of Most Favoured Nation Clauses in Existing Treaties of Commerce and Navigation between Great Britain and Foreign Powers." London: HMSO.

Gregory, T. E. G. 1968 [1921]. *Tariffs: A Study in Method*. New York: Kelly.

Henderson, W. O. 1975. *The Rise of German Industrial Power, 1834–1914*. Berkeley: University of California Press.

Hilton, B. 1988. *The Age of Atonement*. Oxford: Clarendon Press.

Hoffman, Ross. [1933] 1964. *Great Britain and the German Trade Rivalry. 1875–1914*. New York: Russell.

Iliasu, A. A. 1971. "The Cobden-Chevalier Commercial Treaty of 1860." *Historical Journal* 14, no. 1: 67–98.

Imlah, Albert. 1958. *Economic Elements of Pax Britannica*. Cambridge: Harvard University Press.

Irwin, Douglas. 1988. "The Welfare Effects of British Free Trade: Debate and Evidence from the 1840s." *Journal of Political Economy* 96, no. 6 (December): 1142–1164.

Irwin, Douglas. 1989. "Political Economy and Peel's Repeal of the Corn Laws." *Economics and Politics* 1 (Spring): 41–59.

Irwin, Douglas. 1993. "Free Trade and Protection in Nineteenth Century Britain and France revisited: A Comment on Nye." *Journal of Economic History* 53, no. 1 (March): 146–152.

Irwin, Douglas. 1994. "The Political Economy of Free Trade: Voting in the British General Election of 1906." *Journal of Law and Economics* 37 (April): 75–108.

Irwin, Douglas. 1996. *Against the Tide: An Intellectual History of Free Trade*. Princeton: Princeton University Press.

Irwin, Douglas. 1998. "The Reciprocity Debate in Parliament, 1842–1846." In *Free Trade and Its Reception*, ed. Andrew Marrison. London: Routledge.

James, Scott, and David Lake. 1989. "The Second Face of Hegemony: Britain's Repeal of the Corn Laws and the American Walker Tariff of 1846." *International Organization* 43, no. 1 (Winter): 1–29.

Jones, Joseph. [1934] 1983. *Tariff Retaliation: Repercussions of the Hawley-Smoot Bill*. New York: Garland.

Kenwood A. G., and A. L. Lougheed. 1983. *The Growth of the International Economy, 1820–1980.* London: Allen & Unwin.

Kindleberger, C. P. 1975. "The Rise of Free Trade in Western Europe, 1820–1875." *Journal of Economic History* 35 (March): 20–55.

Kindleberger, C. P. 1951. "Group Behaviour and International Trade." *Journal of Political Economy* 59, no. 1 (February): 29–46.

Lake, David. 1991. "British and American Hegemony Compared." In *History, the White House and the Kremlin,* ed. Michael Fry, 106–122 London: Pinter.

Lazer, David. 1999. "The Free Trade Epidemic of the 1860s." *World Politics* 51, no. 4 (July): 447–483.

Luard, Evan. 1984. *Economic Relations among States.* New York: St. Martin's.

McCloskey, D. 1980. "Magnanimous Albion: Free Trade and the British Income." *Explorations in Economic History* 17 (July): 303–320.

McKeown, Timothy. 1983. "Hegemonic Stability Theory and Nineteenth Century Tariff Levels in Europe." *International Organisation* 37 (Winter): 73–92.

McKeown, Timothy. 1989. "The Politics of Corn Law Repeal and Theories of Commercial Policy." *British Journal of Political Science* 19: 353–380.

Mitchell, Brian. 1975. *European Historical Statistics, 1750–1970.* New York: Columbia University Press.

Nye, John. 1991a. "Changing French Trade Conditions, National Welfare and the 1860 Anglo-French Treaty of Commerce." *Explorations in Economic History* 28: 460–477.

Nye, John. 1991b. "The Myth of Free Trade Britain and Fortress France." *Journal of Economic History* 51, no. 1 (March): 23–46.

Page, W. T. 1927. "Memorandum on European Bargaining Tariffs." Submitted to the Preparatory Committee of the League of Nations, Economic and Financial Section, CECP 97, Geneva.

Platt, D. C. M. 1968. *Finance, Trade and Politics in British Foreign Policy, 1815–1914.* London: Oxford University Press.

Prentice, A. 1853. *History of the Anti-Corn Law League.* London: W. & F. G. Cash.

Ratcliffe, Barrie. 1978. "The Tariff Reform Campaign in France, 1831–1836." *Journal of European Economic History* 7, no. 1 (Spring): 61–138.

Robinson, Ronald, and John Gallagher. 1953. "The Imperialism of Free Trade." *Economic History Review* 6, no. 1 (August), 2nd series: 1–15.

Rose, J. Holland. 1908. "The Franco-British Commercial Treaty of 1786." *English Historical Review* 23, no. 92 (October): 709–724.

Saul, S. B. 1960. *Studies in British Overseas Trade.* Liverpool: Liverpool University Press.

Schonhardt, C. 1991. "Specific Factors, Capital Markets, Portfolio Diversification, and Free Trade: Domestic Determinants of the Repeal of the Corn Laws." *World Politics* 43, no. 4 (July): 545–569.

Semmel, Bernard. 1970. *The Rise of Free Trade Imperialism*. Cambridge: Cambridge University Press.

Smith, Michael. 1980. *Tariff Reform in France, 1860–1900*. Ithaca: Cornell University Press.

Stigler, George. 1982. *The Economist and Preacher and Other Essays*. Chicago: University of Chicago Press.

U.S. Tariff Commission. 1934. *Tariff Bargaining under Most Favoured Nation Treaties*. Washington, DC: GPO.

Verdier, Daniel. 1994. *Democracy and International Trade: Britain, France and the United States, 1860–1990*. Princeton: Princeton University Press.

Williams, Judith B. 1972. *British Commercial Policy and Trade Expansion*. Oxford: Clarendon Press.

3

Reciprocity and the Origins of U.S. Trade Liberalization

Douglas A. Irwin

3.1 Introduction

The liberalization of British trade policy in the nineteenth century illustrates a failure of reciprocity followed by the triumph of unilateralism, starting with the repeal of the Corn Laws in 1846 and continuing for decades thereafter. The liberalization of U.S. trade policy in the twentieth century, by contrast, illustrates a failure of unilateralism followed by the success of reciprocity, starting with the passage of the Reciprocal Trade Agreements Act (RTAA) in 1934 and continuing for decades thereafter.

The broad goal of this chapter is to analyze why the political structure of U.S. trade policymaking was not conducive to unilateral efforts to liberalize trade policy and how the 1934 innovation in that structure ultimately contributed to the success of reciprocal methods of tariff reduction. This chapter focuses on the pivotal period of the 1930s and 1940s, when the United States shifted from a tariff code determined solely by Congress, usually acting at the behest of domestic import-competing producers, to one in which tariffs were subject to executive negotiations with foreign countries. This shift in tariff-making authority, originally the subject of sharp partisan dispute, soon received bipartisan support. As a result, the United States embarked on a sustained path of trade liberalization that helped reduce the average U.S. tariff from about 50 percent in the early 1930s to about 10 percent by the early 1950s, as shown in figure 3.1.[1]

3.2 Congressional Unilateralism

Just as Congress is the "keystone to the Washington establishment," to borrow the phrase of the political scientist Morris Fiorina (1977),

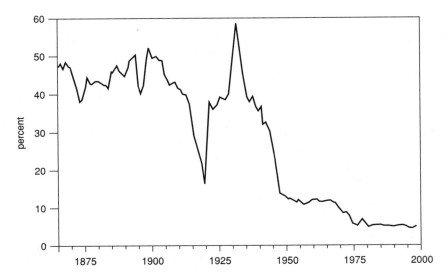

Figure 3.1
Average U.S. tariff, 1865–1999 (tariff revenue divided by dutiable imports)

Congress is the keystone to U.S. trade policy. Article 1, section 8, of the Constitution invests Congress with the power to impose and collect import duties and to "regulate Commerce with foreign Nations." Such duties also raise fiscal revenue, and all revenue measures (and hence most trade legislation) must originate in the House Ways and Means Committee.

From the Civil War until the early 1930s, Congress would set about revising the tariff code about every seven years. The rates in that code, consisting of a single column list of import duties, were determined completely unilaterally. Congress derived considerable electoral benefits from setting the tariff, and therefore it treated the determination of import duties on hundreds of individual products as an exclusively domestic concern of its own province. Congress set tariff rates independent of (and generally without regard for) the tariff policies of other countries and jealously guarded its prerogative over the tariff vis-à-vis the president, who typically played a minor role in tariff revisions.

How are we to assess Congress as the institutional forum in which tariff rates were determined? During this period, the fiscal role of tariffs was important because import duties raised about half of federal government revenues. Many tariffs, however, were imposed not for their revenue-raising potential but to serve the economic interests of domestic producers. Members of Congress, whose sole objective is frequently taken to be reelection, voted for such tariffs at the behest of producer and labor interest groups in their state or district, who sought to obtain protection from the competition of foreign producers. A standard collective action reason is usually given to explain why those seeking tariffs dominate the process by which Congress set import duties, while those harmed by such duties— exporters, downstream users, and other consumers, for example— are less well represented politically. The benefits of a tariff are concentrated on a few, identifiable domestic producers who are willing to make the necessary investments in seeking political influence to obtain tariff protection, whereas the costs of any given tariff are dispersed across many consumers who do not find it worthwhile to oppose the policy.[2]

Not all domestic interests opposed to import competition succeed in obtaining tariff protection, however, because of organizational costs and the free-rider problem. A tariff, to some extent, operates as a public good: The imposition of an import duty protects not only firms that made political investments to obtain that protection, but all firms producing goods that fall under a certain tariff category regardless of the degree to which they contributed to the political action. A free-rider problem arises in that some domestic interests desire tariff protection but wish to avoid incurring the costs of political action. Economic and geographic concentration mitigates these problems for certain industries. Economic concentration reduces the transactions costs of political organization and improves the ability of the organization to monitor which firms are contributing to the political cause. Such concentration also can be effectively increased by expanding the number of tariff categories in the legislation.[3] In its deliberation on the Smoot-Hawley tariff in 1929–1930, for example, the Senate conducted roll call votes on tariff rates for such specific commodities as wooden clothespins, zinc, boric acid, and so on.

Geographic concentration also helps mitigate the free-rider problem by ensuring that representatives from a certain state or region takes a strong interest in the economic fortunes of a particular industry. Congressmen from Louisiana, for example, assiduously supported a high tariff on sugar to protect cane growers, and those from Pennsylvania vigorously pressed for high tariffs on steel products. On the other hand, geographic concentration also means that only a few members of Congress will have a direct political interest in high tariffs for those goods. (The number of senators who would reap direct electoral benefits of higher clothespin or zinc tariffs, for example, is extremely small.) This gives rise to vote trading, or logrolling, in which a coalition is formed among several different, narrow interests. Congressmen representing either clothespin or zinc producers could not by themselves win a vote for a higher clothespin or zinc tariff, for example, but they might be able to form a winning coalition if they agreed to vote in favor of each others' tariff.

The Smoot-Hawley tariff of 1930 has long been thought to provide the classic example of logrolling in action.[4] After clearing the Senate Finance Committee, the bill was considered by the Senate acting first as a "committee of the whole," a procedure that permitted open-ended debate during which time any senator could offer amendments and request votes on tariff rates for specific goods. A coalition of Democrats and progressive Republicans voted to reduce many tariffs on manufactured goods in the "committee as a whole" period of January–March 1930.

The Senate proper then considered the resulting bill in March 1930, and senators could again offer amendments and request new votes on specific tariff rates, even if it had been voted on during the committee of the whole period. At this point, opponents of the reductions in the industrial tariffs had time to regroup and propose new amendments. A different coalition emerged, one not based on broad agriculture versus industry interests but on vote-trading among unrelated goods, and succeeded in raising tariffs.[5] The reversals of the previous tariff reductions gave rise to claims of vote trading and backroom deals, special interest lobbying, and buy-offs. Sen. Robert LaFollette (R-Wis.) characterized the Senate bill as follows:

the product of a series of deals, conceived in secret, but executed in public with a brazen effrontery that is without parallel in the annals of the Senate.... it seems to me that a vote for this bill condones the vote-trading deals by which some of the most unjustifiable rates in the bill were obtained.... this Congress has demonstrated how tariff legislation should not be made. (*Congressional Record*, March 24, 1930, 5976–5977)

This instability (indeterminacy) in congressional voting suggests that Congress will create mechanisms to enforce logrolling agreements and thereby provide for policy stability. Political scientists have studied how specific institutional and organizational features of Congress, such as strong committee structures or strong political parties, are suited to sustain cooperative redistributive bargains (see Weingast and Marshall 1988; Shepsle and Weingast 1994). A strong committee structure and powerful party leadership in the House ensured that there would be no floor votes on the bill, insuring that redistributive bargains struck in unobserved deals in committee would stick. In the Senate, these arrangements and rules were less strong, hence the floor voting on individual tariffs, but the majority party was eventually able to end the debate by invoking a cloture rule.

Congressional tariff-making was not always a smoothly functioning process because the tariff was such a complex and controversial political issue. An ever expanding list of imported goods complicated the task of gathering and processing information on trade matters. Tariff legislation became lengthier and increasingly time-consuming.[6] Aggrieved interests complained that Congress was not getting or acting upon the right information. Business groups such as the Chamber of Commerce and the National Association of Manufacturers did not want to end protection, but wanted to "take the tariff out of politics" and put the tariff on a more impartial, rational footing, less subject to the whims of special-interest politics. Export interests complained that the system failed to allow for lower tariffs on intermediate goods or for reciprocal bargaining to reduce foreign barriers against U.S. exports.

Despite the complaints, the process of congressional tariff-making was relatively immune to pressures for change. The protectionist bent of Congress was seemingly entrenched, more so than ever (so it appeared) after the Smoot-Hawley tariff. Schattschneider (1935) ended his study of congressional politics of the Smoot-Hawley tariff despondently, noting that "a survey of the pressure politics of the revision of 1929–30 shows no significant concentration of forces able to reverse the policy and bring about a return to a system of low tariffs or free trade." Yet Schattschneider's judgment was premature and, ultimately, too pessimistic.

3.3 Forces in Congress for Trade Liberalization

That the structure and organization of Congress and economic interests would conspire to keep tariffs high did not imply a complete absence of forces in Congress favoring lower tariffs. A sharp

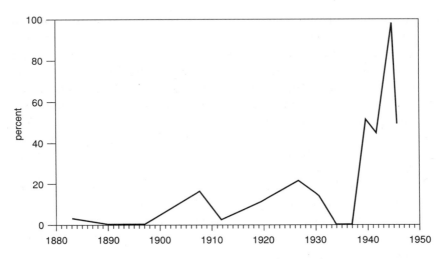

Figure 3.2
Percent of Republican senators voting for lower tariffs, 1880–1950

partisan division over tariff policy from the end of the Civil War until World War II had the Republicans supporting high tariffs and the Democrats supporting low tariffs. Figure 3.2 illustrates just how predictable this pattern of congressional voting on the tariff was by depicting the degree of party cohesion in voting on major tariff legislation by the Senate, where party leadership is typically less strong (and hence strict party-line voting less frequent) than in the House. In most instances, over 90 percent of Republicans voted in favor of high tariffs and against lower tariffs. The Republicans drew much of their political support from manufacturers in the Northeast and Midwest, and hence they enacted high protective tariffs. They argued that such tariffs preserved the home market for domestic producers and secured high domestic wages for labor by making foreign producers pay for their access to the U.S. market.

By contrast, over 90 percent of Democrats voted in favor of lower tariffs or against higher tariffs. The Democrats, drawing their support largely from farmers in the South, believed that the tariff should be designed mainly for revenue purposes with only moderate protection given to import-competing interests. They worried that high tariffs would foster monopolies ("the tariff is the mother of the trust") and excessively burden consumers and small businesses. Progressive Republicans, often in a coalition with the Democrats, agreed that the tariff should be protective, but also wanted to reform the tariff system of its inequities and limit its costs to consumers.

Trade policy would have been more liberal during this period if there had been a period of sustained control of government by the Democrats. But the political dominance of the Republicans helped ensure that average U.S. tariffs stood at roughly 40–50 percent in the decades prior to the RTAA. In the brief periods when they were in control of government, the Democrats would undertake tariff reductions, but there was no way for the Democrats to ensure that those low tariffs would be sustained once they were voted out of office.

In fact, Democratic tariff legislation was consistently reversed when the Republicans regained power. In the decades after the Civil War, the Democrats controlled both houses of Congress and the presidency for just one brief period (1893–1895), during which time they passed the Dingley Tariff of 1894 that marginally reduced tariff rates. Less than three years later, the Republicans regained power and pushed tariffs back up again. In 1913 the Democrats regained control of Congress and the presidency and promptly passed the Underwood Tariff, the first thoroughgoing downward revision in import duties since the Civil War. Yet this effort was cut short by the outbreak of World War I, when special emergency controls on trade were imposed, and then reversed by the Republicans after the war. Thus, in the brief periods in which they controlled both Congress and the presidency, the Democrats reduced import tariffs (1894, 1913). When the Republicans regained control of government, they promptly raised import tariffs (1897, 1922), and revised or raised them at other times as well (1883, 1890, 1909, 1930).

Consequently, while a unilateral policy of protection was sustainable because of the repeated reelection of the Republicans, Democratic congresses could not commit that body to a policy of low tariffs.

3.4   Early Failures of Reciprocity

Congress so jealously guarded its powers over the tariff, refusing to relinquish control or delegate authority to other agencies, that it doomed to failure any use of the tariff as a bargaining tool in reciprocity negotiations. Although it did express concern about foreign tariffs and discriminatory policies that hindered U.S. exports, Congress was not the best forum in which the foreign ramifications of trade policy were given due consideration because it was more concerned about serving the protectionist inclinations of its constituents.

Under his foreign policy powers, the president could always negotiate a tariff reduction treaty with another country. As a practical matter, however, U.S. tariffs proved to be nonnegotiable. Such a treaty would require not just the approval of two-thirds of the Senate, but implicitly require House approval as well because it would involve a revenue matter. Foreign countries were reluctant to negotiate tariff agreements with the United States because they knew that, owing to the necessity of Congressional approval, the executive could not commit to the implementation of any signed agreement. Just three significant trade agreements—with Canada (1855–1866), Hawaii (1876–1900), and Cuba (1903–1934)—were enacted during this period.

At times Congress would include special provisions to encourage the executive to undertake trade negotiations, but the provisions were always halfhearted. The Tariff Act of 1897 was the first to authorize the president (within 2 years) to reduce certain import duties (by no more than 20 percent, in agreements lasting no more than 5 years) in conjunction with countries giving equivalent tariff concessions. Any agreement would still require the approval of both the House and Senate, but by explicitly inviting such agreements Congress implied that it would approve them, even promising not to amend any agreement. As the qualifications suggest, however, the invitation for the president to undertake negotiations was rather tepid and carefully circumscribed. Congress's endorsement of reciprocity ultimately proved empty because treaty opponents ensured that not one of the eleven agreements that resulted from this legislation even came up for a vote. Furthermore, the tariff act in which this provision appeared was apparently set up as a classic bargaining duty: Tariff rates were set 20 percent higher than otherwise to take into account their later reduction under presidential agreements, according to the U.S. Tariff Commission (1919, 202–203). In the end, the United States enacted a high bargaining tariff without having approved any of the bargains. The Tariff Act of 1913 also had a provision authorizing the president to undertake tariff negotiations, but none were held.

Congress more frequently embraced a different kind of reciprocity, one to eliminate foreign discrimination against U.S. goods by imposing penalties rather than offering concessions. The McKinley

Tariff of 1890, for example, authorized the President to impose penalty duties on the importation of sugar, molasses, coffee, tea, and hides from foreign countries that maintained "unequal and unreasonable" tariffs on U.S. goods. Reciprocity here was not the mutual reduction of tariffs but the elimination of foreign discrimination. It was to be achieved not through the carrot of bargaining but the stick of retaliation.

In 1909, Congress shifted gears and passed a two-column, "maximum-minimum" tariff schedule. The maximum schedule was designated as the general tariff, but if the president determined that another country's policies did not "unduly discriminate" against U.S. products, he could apply the minimum schedule to that country's goods. In this instance, President Roosevelt rendered the maximum schedule moot by determining that no foreign country "unduly" discriminated against the United States.

All of these measures, however, amounted to halfhearted tinkering and proved to be short-lived. The penalty duties in the McKinley tariff of 1890 were abolished by the Democratic tariff of 1894, reinstituted by the Republicans in 1897, abolished by the Democrats once again in 1913, and not reintroduced by the Republicans in 1922. The 1897 invitation for the president to bargain was absent in the 1909 law, reappeared again in 1913, but was left out of both the 1922 and 1930 tariff acts. Before 1922 "the United States tariff, although negotiable in principle, had not been very negotiable in fact," writes Kelley (1963, 27). "After 1922, even the principle of negotiability was discarded." In that year, the Republicans promulgated a "scientific" tariff, based upon the equalization of domestic and foreign costs of production, and a tariff so astutely constructed could not be reconciled with one that could be arbitrarily bargained away.

Congress's tight reigns on tariff-making also constrained the president from exercising greater international economic leadership in the interwar period. Although encouraging more liberal, nondiscriminatory trade policies was one of President Wilson's Fourteen Points promulgated after World War I, he was unable to follow through with any substantive proposals in this direction. At international economic gatherings through the 1920s, particularly the 1927 World Economic Conference, the State Department could offer platitudes but not concrete proposals, owing in part to the firm Republican control of Congress. The president, whose national constituency and foreign policy responsibilities might be expected to moderate any tariff produced by Congress, continued to be relegated to a minor position without much of a say in trade policy.

Two unheralded but key changes took place during this period, however, that would have important implications for the future course of U.S. trade policy. First, the introduction of the income tax, which the Democrats had consistently linked to tariff reform, dramatically reduced the dependence of the federal government on revenues from import duties after 1916. Tariffs raised over 90 percent of federal revenue prior to the Civil War, about 50 percent from 1870–1910, and, due to the income tax, only about 10 percent in the 1920s. The tariff was now more an instrument of trade policy than fiscal policy, and therefore could be set with objectives other than revenue in mind.

Second, the United States switched from a conditional to an unconditional interpretation of the most-favored-nation (MFN) clause in 1923. Under the conditional policy, U.S. tariff concessions to one country would not be extended to others unless "equivalent" reductions were offered. A report by the U.S. Tariff Commission (1919, 10), headed by Frank Taussig, pointed out the "troublesome complications" of employing unconditional MFN. An "equivalent" concession required definition, and numerous bilateral negotiations—which often failed—were then required to obtain such concessions from other countries. Thus, while conditional MFN aimed to achieve reciprocity, it would "inevitably result in discrimination, whether intentional or not" (Kelley 1963, 31).

The USTC report argued that "a great gain would be secured ... if a clear and simple policy could be adopted and followed," namely, that of equality of treatment, meaning unconditional MFN in which any U.S. tariff reduction would be automatically applied to all countries that had signed an MFN treaty with the United States. The 1923 decision formalized the longstanding U.S. commitment to nondiscrimination as a ruling principle in international commerce. In defending the policy in 1923, Secretary of State Charles Hughes stated: "... As we seek pledges from other foreign countries that they will refrain from practicing discrimination, we must be ready to give such pledges, and history has shown that these pledges can be made adequate only in terms of unconditional most-favored-nation treatment" (qtd. in Kelley 1963, 47).

At the time, the adoption of unconditional MFN was simply an administrative change in trade policy. The single-column tariff code meant that the United States did not actually practice conditional MFN or discriminate against others to a significant degree. "Because the United States conditional MFN policy resulted in relatively little discrimination," Kelley (1963, 35) notes, "the adoption of an unconditional MFN policy in 1923 would not be of such major significance had the United States tariff continued to be virtually non-negotiable." But after 1934 U.S. tariffs became negotiable and the use of unconditional MFN precluded the United States from discriminating against other countries with which it had MFN agreements.

Congress did not directly mandate the adoption of unconditional MFN, but the Senate approved an agreement with Germany in 1925 that contained the unconditional MFN clause.[7] The wisdom of the unconditional MFN clause was questioned by the Republican opposition in the debate over the RTAA, but the policy was not changed. It did, however, determine "the selective nature of the negotiating procedure [i.e., tariff reductions by a product-by-product, principal supplier rule rather than across-the-board] for both the bilateral and multilateral phases of the trade-agreements program," according to Kelley (1963, 35).

3.5 The RTAA of 1934: A New Approach to Reciprocity

The election of 1930 handed the Democrats control of the House and, with the aid of progressive Republicans, a working majority in the Senate on trade issues. This provided the Democrats with their first chance since the Wilson administration to change the course of U.S. trade policy. In early 1932, Democrats and progressive Republicans joined forces behind a bill that authorized the president to undertake negotiations with other countries to reduce tariffs. (While this constitutes some evidence of congressional sentiment in favor of tariff bargaining, any agreement would still require Senate approval.) President Hoover promptly vetoed it, stating that there has "never been a time in the history of the United States when tariff protection was more essential to the welfare of the American people than at present" (1977, 205–207). The tariff was "solely a domestic question" and economic conditions made its maintenance "imperative." An international conference was inappropriate because it might lead to the "abandonment of essential American policies."

Democrats got a better opportunity to put their mark on tariff policy when they were swept into power in the election of 1932. The

Democratic platform and candidate Franklin Roosevelt had criticized the Smoot-Hawley tariff during the election campaign and
proposed reciprocal trade agreements with other countries. In view
of the high unemployment rate, however, Roosevelt also promised
not to strip away protection for American industry. Despite Roosevelt's equivocations over tariff policy, his secretary of state, Cordell
Hull, was staunchly in favor of lower tariffs through international
negotiations and was the main force behind the RTAA. Hull was to
American trade policy what Cobden had been to British trade policy:
someone who fought the tough political battle for trade liberalization. Like Cobden, Hull believed in liberalization more for its role in
promoting peace among nations than for its direct economic benefits.
As early as 1916, Hull (1948, I: 81) came to believe that "unhampered
trade dovetailed with peace; high tariffs, trade barriers, and unfair
economic competition, with war," and that free trade helped promote "a reasonable chance for lasting peace."

Had they came to power in ordinary circumstances, the Democrats
might simply have enacted a unilateral tariff reduction as they had
done in 1913. Some Democrats proposed just this. In August 1931,
for example, Sen. Kenneth McKellar (D-Ten.) suggested repealing the
Smoot-Hawley tariff and enacting an immediate, across-the-board
tariff cut of 25 percent. A draft campaign speech for Roosevelt prepared by Cordell Hull in 1932 contemplated reducing tariffs unilaterally by 10 percent and then negotiating further reductions.[8]

But the economic situation in 1933 differed from that in 1913 on
two dimensions and prevented this course of action. First, the U.S.
economy was in the depths of the Depression. Most Democrats
wanted lower tariffs, but in the midst of high unemployment and
low output they could not muster the political support to consider
seriously a unilateral tariff cut.[9] Second, foreign tariffs escalated
sharply during 1930–1932 and had been supplemented with quantitative restrictions and exchange controls. While retaliatory measures
against Smoot-Hawley might have spawned some of those barriers,
a repeal of Smoot-Hawley was unlikely to eliminate them.

Thus, the domestic and foreign economic situation together undercut the case for unilateral action. Many feared that a repeal of
Smoot-Hawley would be contractionary unless opportunities were
created for increasing U.S. exports. Entrenched foreign trade barriers, it was believed, could be reduced only through negotiation.
Some business groups also began to coalesce behind the principle of

reciprocal tariff reductions. As a result, there was virtually no sentiment in Congress for unilateral tariff reductions and much greater
support for reciprocity.

In April 1933, President Roosevelt announced his intention to
request negotiating authority from Congress to undertake tariff reduction agreements with other countries, but the formal request was
delayed for a year in order to concentrate on the passage of the
National Industrial Recovery Act (NIRA) and the Agricultural Adjustment Act (AAA) through Congress. At any rate, Hull soon discovered that there was no international support for a multilateral
tariff reduction conference.[10]

The administration finally put forth its proposal in early March
1934, requesting negotiating authority to reduce U.S. tariffs in trade
agreements that would not require congressional approval. President Roosevelt stated "that a full and permanent domestic recovery
depends in part upon a revived and strengthened international trade
and that American exports cannot be permanently increased without
a corresponding increase in imports."[11]

Cordell Hull (1948, I: 357) later recalled that "in both House and
Senate we were aided by the severe reaction of public opinion
against the Smoot-Hawley Act." The notion that the passage of the
RTAA constituted a repudiation of Smoot-Hawley by Congress per-
sists to this day. But the passage of the RTAA did not reflect a
change in the underlying tariff preferences of individual politicians,
just a change in the partisan composition of Congress, namely, the
Democratic majority. By examining the votes of all members of
Congress who voted on both Smoot-Hawley and the RTAA, Schnietz
(2000) clearly demonstrates that Congress did not "learn" that the
Smoot-Hawley tariff was bad. The learning hypothesis implies that
members who voted for Smoot-Hawley later regretted its harmful
consequences and voted for the RTAA. But only 6 of the 178 House
members who voted on both measures demonstrate this type of
learning, and all were Democrats. No House Republican who voted
for Smoot-Hawley also voted in favor of the RTAA.[12] Whether the
electorate "learned" to prefer the tariff views of the Democrats is
doubtful because Smoot-Hawley probably played an insignificant
role in the Democrats's electoral success in 1930 and 1932.

The RTAA, which was technically an amendment to Smoot-
Hawley, had the following provisions:

- the president was authorized to enter into tariff agreements with foreign countries;
- the president could proclaim an increase or a decrease in import duties by no more than 50 percent, but could not transfer any article between the dutiable and free lists;
- the proclaimed duties would apply to imports from all countries on an unconditional MFN basis;
- the president's authority to enter into foreign trade agreements would expire in three years;
- any agreement could be terminated after three years with six months notice, otherwise it would survive indefinitely.[13]

The most important change from previous legislation was that Congress waived its approval of the agreements. Congress also explicitly endorsed the unconditional MFN clause, under which tariff reductions negotiated with one country would be automatically extended to others.

On the House floor a key amendment was offered to the president's proposal that served to ensure ongoing congressional influence over trade policy. While the president had proposed (with the concurrence of the Ways and Means Committee) no time limit to the negotiating authority, the House instead chose to limit the authority to three years, after which it would automatically terminate unless Congress renewed it. This feature of the RTAA strengthened Congress's hand because the threat of nonrenewal of negotiating authority would keep the executive branch politically sensitive to the legislature's concerns. Had this provision not been added, a two-thirds majority of both houses of Congress would have been required to override a presidential veto of a bill striping away his negotiating authority.

Unlike Smoot-Hawley, Congress's consideration of the RTAA attracted virtually no participation by interest groups. Haggard (1988, 112) reasons that "in contrast to 1930 ... when interest groups were the main protagonists and specific tariff rates the issue, the most important issues at stake in 1934 were institutional, centering on the transfer of authority from Congress to the executive." The RTAA was simply enabling legislation, and no one knew how the authority would be used, how successful the negotiations would be, or how extensive the agreements might be. When the RTAA was passed, Congress could not anticipate how important the legislation would become or even whether it would be sustained by future congresses. In view of the many short-lived trade policy experiments of the past three decades, it was not obvious that the RTAA would necessarily bring a lasting, durable change in U.S. trade policymaking. Perhaps this accounts for the apparently minimal participation of interest groups, even among export associations, in the RTAA's passage.

3.6   Tilting the Political Balance toward Liberalization

In its first decade of operation, the RTAA was much less important for what it accomplished in terms of agreements and tariff reductions than for what it implied in terms of changing the system of formulating U.S. trade policy.

By 1938, the United States had concluded trade agreements with eighteen countries, only three of which (Canada, France, and the Netherlands) were among the top ten U.S. export markets. (An insubstantial agreement with the United Kingdom in 1939 was operational for less than a year, cut short by World War II.) The agreements resulted in a modest reduction in the average U.S. tariff. As reported in Tasca (1938, 188ff), the U.S. Tariff Commission calculated the duties that would have been collected in 1934 had the tariff resulting from the first thirteen country agreements implemented by 1936 been in effect. This fixed weight measure indicates a decline in the average ad valorem tariff from 46.7 percent to 40.7 percent, a 13 percent drop, not much more than half of the Smoot-Hawley increase.[14] What remains unclear is the degree to which U.S. negotiators succeeded in reducing foreign tariffs on U.S. exports.

The RTAA was much more important for its impact on the structure of trade policymaking than for its immediate economic effects. As Gilligan (1997) has described, several key elements of the RTAA helped tip the political balance in favor of lower tariffs. First, the RTAA reduced access to legislative mechanisms that supported redistributive bargains and logrolling coalitions that had led to high tariffs (Shepsle and Weingast 1994; Irwin and Kroszner 1996). Congress effectively gave up the ability to legislate duties on specific goods when it delegated tariff-negotiating power to the executive. Congressional votes on trade policy were now framed simply in terms of whether or not (and under what circumstances) the RTAA should be continued, so vote trading among particular import-competing interests was no longer feasible.

Second, the RTAA delegated authority and agenda-setting power to the executive who, with a broad-based constituency, was more likely to favor tariff moderation compared with Congress. The national electoral base of the president is often thought to make the executive more likely to favor policies that could benefit the nation as a whole (such as free trade), whereas the narrower geographic representative structure of Congress would lead its members to have more parochial interests (Weingast, Shepsle, and Johnson 1981). Furthermore, the president may be more likely than Congress to take into account the broader foreign policy ramifications of trade policy that affect the country as a whole (Haggard 1988).

Third, the RTAA reduced the threshold of political support needed for members of Congress to enact tariff-reduction agreements negotiated by the executive. The renewal of the RTAA required a simple majority in Congress, whereas prior to the RTAA any foreign trade treaty negotiated by the president had to be approved by two-thirds of the Senate. Executive trade agreements thus needed only the support of the median legislator, not that in the sixty-seventh percentile (Bailey, Goldstein, and Weingast 1997). This meant that protectionist forces would have to muster greater support to block tariff-reduction agreements under the RTAA, by refusing to renew the legislation, than under a treaty, when a minority could veto it.

Finally, the RTAA helped to bolster the bargaining and lobbying position of exporters in the political process (Hillman and Moser 1996; Gilligan 1997). Previously, import-competing domestic producers were the main trade-related lobby groups on Capitol Hill because the benefits to these producers of high tariffs was relatively concentrated. Since an import duty is effectively equivalent to a tax on exports, exporters were harmed—but only indirectly—by high tariffs. The cost to exporters of any particular duty was relatively diffuse, and therefore exporters failed to organize an effective political opposition. The RTAA explicitly linked foreign tariff reductions that were beneficial to exporters to lower tariff protection for import-competing producers. By directly tying lower foreign tariffs to lower domestic tariffs (and upsetting the ability of import-competing producers to form logrolls), the RTAA may have fostered the development of exporters as an organized group opposing high tariffs and supporting international trade agreements. In addition, the reduced tariffs negotiated under the RTAA authority would tend to increase the size of the export sector and thereby enhance subsequent support for renewal.

Bailey, Goldstein, and Weingast (1997) and Schnietz (2000) interprete the RTAA as being an institutional mechanism cleverly designed by the Democrats to lock in their preferred tariff level. By making reciprocal tariff reductions via the RTAA rather than a treaty, only half of Congress (rather than two-thirds) was needed to enact lower tariffs. If the RTAA succeeded in reducing tariffs, it also would constrain future (Republican) politicians from easily reversing the policy since it was made in the context of a foreign trade agreement. With hindsight this interpretation rings true, but the RTAA's success was not guaranteed. The RTAA could easily have been reversed by the Republicans had they been returned to power, and until the early 1940s they explicitly vowed in their party platform to halt and perhaps reverse any tariff changes brought about by the RTAA.

3.7 Sustaining the RTAA: Toward the Postwar Trading System

These aspects of the RTAA may have reduced the costs (or increased the benefits) for free trade interests to organize and lobby relative to protectionist interests. The RTAA did not make free trade inevitable, however, because at any point Congress could have taken back the negotiating authority it granted. Sustaining the RTAA as an institutional change required the ongoing support of a majority in Congress. The RTAA was easily passed in 1934 because the Democrats had large majorities in both chambers of Congress at the time. As long as those majorities were maintained, the RTAA could be sustained.

Republicans, however, bitterly opposed the RTAA. Just 2 of 101 House Republicans (2 percent) and just 6 of 36 Senate Republicans (17 percent) favored passing the measure in 1934. Republicans argued that the legislation was an unconstitutional delegation of taxation powers to the president and claimed that lower tariffs would add to the severity of the Great Depression. The Republican platform of 1936 vowed to "repeal the present reciprocal trade agreement law," deeming it "destructive" for "flooding our markets with foreign commodities" and "dangerous" for entailing secret executive negotiations without legislative approval (Isaacs 1948, 258). In 1937 the Democratic majority in Congress renewed the legislation for another three years. Just 3 of 84 (4 percent) House Republicans supported the extension, while not a single Senate Republican endorsed the measure.

In their election platform of 1940, the Republicans softened their rhetoric on the RTAA, still condemning it but no longer explicitly calling for repeal.[15] Nonetheless, they still voted overwhelmingly against the 1940 renewal, with 96 percent of House Republicans and every Senate Republican voting against it. Because the trade agreements program was effectively on hold until after the war, the proposed two-year extension of the RTAA in 1943 was not controversial, and in a show of wartime unity the renewal passed with even Republican support.[16]

The Republican platform of 1944 revealed a further shift toward accepting the RTAA and the tariff reductions negotiated by the president. The Republicans would support the "removal of unnecessary and destructive barriers to international trade," but qualified this position by saying that they also wanted to "maintain [a] fair protective tariff ... so that the standard of living of our people shall not be impaired." Furthermore, the tariff should be modified "only by reciprocal bilateral trade agreements approved by Congress," apparently indicating an acceptance of the idea of reciprocity, but not of unconstrained delegation of authority to the president (Isaacs 1948, 274–275).

The biggest challenge facing the RTAA was its postwar survival. The president's negotiating authority, necessary to complete the ambitious postwar plans for the multilateral liberalization of commercial policies, expired in mid-1945. In addition, the Roosevelt Administration sought the authority to reduce tariffs up to another 50 percent from their 1945 levels over the next three years because the 50 percent maximum reduction in tariffs specified in the original 1934 act already had been made on most dutiable imports. At this critical juncture, 15 of 35 (43 percent) of the Republicans in the Senate broke with their protectionist past and voted in favor of renewal in 1945 (see figure 3.2). After the Republicans took control of Congress following the 1946 election, they continued to support the RTAA, thereby ensuring bipartisan support for trade liberalization and U.S. participation in the GATT negotiations.

This bipartisan support for the reciprocal trade agreements approach was vital to its long-run viability. The era in which changes in political control by the two parties also brought about large upward or downward revisions in the tariff (as evident in figure 3.1) had passed. What accounts for the shift in the Republican position that made the success of reciprocity possible?

One explanation for the eroding Republican opposition to the RTAA focuses on changes in the relative strength of export-related economic interests. The economic devastation in Europe as a result of World War II meant domestic firms had to contend with less foreign competition. Immediately after the war, Baldwin (1984, 8–9) notes, the United States ran "an export surplus in every major industrial group (e.g., machinery, vehicles, chemicals, textiles, and miscellaneous manufactures) except metals" and "favorable export opportunities ... helped to build support for liberal trade policies on the part of those sectors whose international competitive position was strong." U.S. exports increased sharply after the war from its prewar level: During 1937–1939, exports were on average 3.6 percent of GNP and imports 2.7 percent, but during 1945–1947 exports were on average 5.4 percent of GNP and imports 2.2 percent. The growth of export interests, both in terms of economic size and lobbying effectiveness (due to the RTAA), and the diminished threat to import-competing producers, may therefore have put sufficient pressure on the Republicans to change their long-standing support for protectionism. Irwin and Kroszner (1999) find evidence to support the notion that economic interests were pivotal to the change in the Republican position. Examining Senate voting for the RTAA in 1934 and its renewal in 1945, they find that Republican senators were sensitive to importing competing constituent interests in 1934, but were sensitive to both import-competing and export-oriented interests in 1945. The Republicans who swung behind the RTAA's renewal came from precise those states—located mainly in the Northeast—whose producers experienced the largest increase in export orientation.

A more general ideological change toward a more liberal view of trade is also thought to have occurred. As Pastor (1983, 161) put it, "the Smoot-Hawley Tariff Act of 1930 is to commerce what the Munich agreement of 1938 is to peace.... they remain indelibly imprinted on the consciousness of the world as historical errors of such magnitude that every generation of leaders has pledged to avoid repeating them." This buttressed Cordell Hull's message about trade and peace. The link between foreign policy and trade policy also may have encouraged Republicans to support the RTAA after World War II, as trade liberalization was seen as a mechanism for aiding the economies of Europe in an effort to contain Communism. Bailey (1997) finds evidence that security preferences influenced congressional trade votes in the early 1950s, lending support to this view.

Irwin and Kroszner (1999) argue that changes in the sizes of competing economic interests and changes in the effectiveness of those interests due to the RTAA provide keys to understanding both the transformation of the Republican position and the persistence of trade liberalization in the postwar era. While both of these changes may have been necessary to sustain liberalization, neither one appears to be sufficient to achieve this end. Growth in the size of the export interests that occurred during and after World War II clearly increased the relative influence of export interests. Yet a similar growth of exports, both absolutely and relative to imports, also occurred during and after World War I, but this did not generate bipartisan support for lower tariffs. Instead, it was followed by the Republican enactment of the protectionist Fordney-McCumber tariff of 1922. Without an institutional mechanism such as the RTAA for activating export interests, the simple growth in the size of export interests did not change the essential policy outcome.

Similarly, the institutional structure of the RTAA alone was not sufficient to cause the Republicans to alter their position and thereby provide durable support for trade liberalization. The RTAA was passed in 1934 over the objections of the Republicans, but by the 1940 renewal they were no closer to supporting it than they had been six years earlier. Having a mechanism in place to facilitate the organization and lobbying of exporters in favor of trade liberalization was itself apparently insufficient to institutionalize the RTAA until export interests grew larger. The expansion of exports coincides with World War II, at which point Republicans began to cross the aisle in support of the RTAA and trade liberalization.

Thus, it appears that both an institutional change (in the form of the RTAA) and a change in economic interests (as a result of World War II) were necessary, and neither sufficient, to bring about a lasting change in U.S. trade policy.

3.8 Conclusion

Under the Constitution, Congress is the focal point of U.S. trade policy. With the political parties differing in their view of the proper height of import duties, neither party could commit future legislators to a particular type of tariff policy. As a result, whenever there was a change in the partisan control of government, U.S. tariffs were adjusted up or down. In general, however, Congress proved to be an institution that gave relatively greater weight to import-competing interests seeking high tariffs than to export or consumer interests seeking more modest tariffs.

In 1934, the low-tariff Democrats enacted an institutional innovation that broke up this congressional system. Tariff-setting powers were delegated to the president in the context of reciprocal tariff-reduction agreements with other countries. This change upset the existing balance of forces that had determined tariff policy and gave a greater voice to export-oriented economic interests.

The reciprocity adopted was a form of "relaxed" reciprocity. Congress did not stipulate the degree to which reductions in the U.S. tariff should be matched by foreign tariff reductions. This issue was left to the executive, and indeed greater access to the U.S. market via lower tariffs was not initially matched by equal access to European markets, which remained more restricted due to quotas and exchange controls. What mattered more to Congress, at least in this formative period, was that the trade policy process be reciprocal in nature, not that a certain outcome (parity of concessions) be achieved.

The institutional change proved in part to be self-sustaining as export-oriented interest groups grew to have a stake in the new system. After World War II, Republican opposition to the reciprocal trade agreements approach waned and the multilateral tariff negotiations of the GATT were able to proceed.

Notes

1. While most of this reduction was due to erosion of specific duties by import price inflation rather than reductions in tariff rates (see Irwin 1998b), the important point is that politicians supported this change in the tariff.

2. Schattschneider (1935), in his famous book on the Smoot-Hawley tariff of 1930, noted how congressional committees were biased strongly in favor of accommodating the demands for higher tariffs through the principle of "reciprocal non-interference," in which producers did not oppose the efforts of others to obtain higher tariffs. See Gilligan (1997).

3. Schattschneider (1935, 23) shows that pre–Civil War tariff legislation ran fewer than 20 pages, reached about 100 pages by the turn of the century, and amounted to 200

pages with Smoot-Hawley. The tariff code grew longer because increasingly refined distinctions were made among imported products.

4. Irwin and Kroszner (1996) present anecdotal and statistical evidence of logrolling in their examination of the numerous Senate votes on individual tariff items in the Smoot-Hawley bill.

5. On January 16, 1930, for example, the Senate voted to retain the 1922 rate on sugar (instead of raising it) by a vote of 48 (18 Republicans, 29 Democrats, 1 Farmer Labor) to 38 (34 Republicans, 4 Democrats). Sen. Reed Smoot (R-Utah), the chairman of the Finance Committee, came from a state with extensive cultivation of beet sugar and refused to accept this. On March 5, the day after the Senate took the bill from the committee of the whole and was again able to consider the sugar issue, the Senate voted 47 (38 Republicans, 9 Democrats) to 39 (13 Republicans, 26 Democrats) to increase the tariff on sugar.

6. Tariff bills typically took six to twelve months to get through Congress around the turn of the century, but took over eighteen months in the case of Fordney-McCumber in 1921–1922 and Smoot-Hawley in 1929–1930.

7. In 1927 the World Economic Conference unanimously endorsed the use of the unconditional MFN clause.

8. See Tasca (1938), 14, and Haggard (1988), 106.

9. Hull (1948, I: 358) later wrote that "it would have been folly to go to Congress and ask that the Smoot-Hawley [Tariff] Act be repealed or its rates reduced by Congress."

10. As Hull (1948, I: 356) put it:

In earlier years I had been in favor of any action or agreement that would lower tariff barriers, whether the agreement was multilateral ... regional ... [or] bilateral.... But during and after the London Conference it was manifest that public support in no country, especially our own, would at that time support a worth-while multilateral undertaking. My associates and I therefore agreed that we should try to secure the enactment of the next best method of reducing trade barriers, that is, by bilateral trade agreements which embraced the most-favored-nation policy in its unconditional form—meaning a policy of nondiscrimination and equality of treatment.

11. Quoted in Tasca (1938), 300, which reproduces the text of the president's message.

12. Of the 47 senators who voted on both bills, only 2 Democrats and 1 Republican "learned."

13. The complete text of the RTAA is in Tasca (1938), 306–308.

14. The extent of the tariff reductions varied substantially across commodities, with large cuts in the "spirits, wines, and other beverages" category of the tariff schedule and virtually none in textiles.

15. The 1940 platform read: "We condemn the manner in which the so-called reciprocal trade agreements of the New Deal have been put into effect without adequate hearings, with undue haste, without proper consideration of our domestic producers, and without Congressional approval" (Isaacs 1948, 267).

16. As Isaacs (1948, 273) put it, "Its passage was not seriously opposed by the Republicans. Their leaders felt that no change in the tariff during the war would be helpful and that no attack on it would get very far."

References

Bailey, Michael, Judith Goldstein, and Barry Weingast. 1997. "The Institutional Roots of American Trade Policy: Politics, Coalitions, and International Trade." *World Politics* 49 (April): 309–338.

Baldwin, Robert E. 1984. "The Changing Nature of U.S. Trade Policy Since World War II." In *The Structure and Evolution of Recent U.S. Trade Policy*, edited by Robert E. Baldwin and Anne O. Krueger. Chicago: University of Chicago Press.

Bailey, Michael. 1997. "Iron Imperatives: Voters, Congress and the Politics of Trade-Security Linkages in the Cold War." Working Paper, Georgetown University, Government Department.

Fiorina, Morris. 1977. *Congress: Keystone to the Washington Establishment.* New Haven: Yale University Press.

Gilligan, Michael J. 1997. *Empowering Exporters: Reciprocity Delegation and Collective Action in American Trade Policy.* Ann Arbor: University of Michigan Press.

Haggard, Stephan. 1988. "The Institutional Foundations of Hegemony: Explaining the Reciprocal Trade Agreements Act of 1934." *International Organization* 42 (Winter): 91–119.

Hillman, Arye, and Peter Moser. 1996. "Trade Liberalization as Politically Optimal Exchange of Market Access." In *The New Transatlantic Economy*, edited by Matthew Canzoneri, Wilfred Ethier, and Vittorio Grilli. New York: Cambridge University Press.

Hoover, Herbert. 1977. *The Public Papers of the President of the United States: Herbert Hoover, 1932–1933.* Washington, DC: GPO.

Hull, Cordell. 1948. *Memoirs.* 2 vols. New York: Macmillan.

Irwin, Douglas A. 1998a. "From Smoot-Hawley to Reciprocal Trade Agreements: Changing the Course of U.S. Trade Policy in the 1930s." In *The Defining Moment: The Great Depression and the American Economy in the Twentieth Century*, edited by Michael Bordo, Claudia Goldin, and Eugene White. Chicago: University of Chicago Press.

Irwin, Douglas A. 1998b. "Changes in U.S. Tariffs: The Role of Import Prices and Commercial Policies." *American Economic Review* 88 (September): 1015–1026.

Irwin, Douglas A., and Randall S. Kroszner. 1996. "Logrolling and Economic Interests in the Passage of the Smoot-Hawley Tariff." *Carnegie-Rochester Conference Series on Public Policy* 45 (December): 173–200.

Irwin, Douglas A., and Randall S. Kroszner. 1999. "Interests, Institutions, and Ideology in the Republican Conversion to Trade Liberalization, 1934–1945." *Journal of Law and Economics* 42 (October): 643–673.

Isaacs, Asher. 1948. *International Trade: Tariffs and Commercial Policies.* Chicago: Irwin.

Kelley, William B. Jr. 1963. "Antecedents of Present Commercial Policy, 1922–1934." In *Studies in United States Commercial Policy*, ed. William B. Kelley Jr. Chapel Hill: University of North Carolina Press.

Pastor, Robert. 1983. "The Cry-and-Sigh Syndrome: Congress and Trade Policy." In *Making Economic Policy in Congress,* ed. Allen Shick. Washington, DC: American Enterprise Institute.

Schattschneider, E. E. 1935. *Politics, Pressures, and the Tariff.* New York: Prentice Hall.

Schnietz, Karen. 2000. "The Institutional Foundations of U.S. Trade Policy: Revisiting Explanations for the 1934 Reciprocal Trade Agreement Act." *Journal of Policy History* 12 (Nov.): 417–444.

Shepsle, Kenneth, and Barry Weingast. 1994. "Positive Theories of Congressional Institutions." *Legislative Studies Quarterly* 19 (May): 149–179.

Tasca, Henry J. 1938. *The Reciprocal Trade Policy of the United States.* Philadelphia: University of Pennsylvania Press.

U.S. Tariff Commission. 1919. *Reciprocity and Commercial Treaties.* Washington, DC: GPO.

Weingast, Barry, and William Marshall. 1988. "The Industrial Organization of Congress." *Journal of Political Economy* 96 (June): 132–163.

Weingast, Barry R., Kenneth A. Shepsle, and Christopher Johnsen. 1981. "The Political Economy of Benefits and Costs: A Neoclassical Approach to Distributive Politics." *Journal of Political Economy* 89 (August): 642–664.

4   Reciprocity in GATT 1947: From 1942 to the Kennedy Round

Alice Enders

4.1   Introduction

Reciprocity is always present in international relations based on treaties: By signing a treaty, each party assumes obligations in exchange for rights in relation to the other party or parties.[1] To this general form of reciprocity in treaties, the notion of an equivalence in the commitments assumed by the parties to an agreement is generally added.[2] Such equivalence can take many forms. For instance, members of a free trade area each assume the commitment to eliminate the tariffs on trade between them, independent of the extent of the economic benefits they anticipate to realize. In contrast to the equivalence of the formal commitment to bilateral free trade, Jagdish Bhagwati has coined the term "first-difference reciprocity" to describe the negotiated exchange of trade barrier reduction commitments on a balanced basis originally institutionalized in GATT 1947, and "full" reciprocity to refer to balanced openness on average.[3]

Since trade agreements are concluded in a world composed of many countries, a key aspect of reciprocity is the unconditional most-favored-nation (MFN) clause. When the clause is present in an agreement, each party extends to other parties the highest standard of treatment granted to any particular country, both in the present and in the future. Such a clause therefore has the effect of providing parties with the benefits of trade barrier reduction commitments they have not participated in negotiating. Robert Keohane has termed reciprocity in trade agreements with the MFN clause "diffuse" because, in his view, parties go beyond their immediate economic self-interest in granting third parties the benefits of agreements negotiated bilaterally, in contrast to the "specific reciprocity" of agreements without the clause.[4]

This chapter is concerned with the origin of first-difference reciprocity in GATT 1947 and its evolution toward full reciprocity in the first two decades of the postwar period.[5] Section 4.2 examines the proposals made to liberalize tariffs by the United Kingdom and the United States in the wartime discussions held under Article VII of the Lend-Lease Agreement. The section concludes that the multilateral-bilateral" approach to tariff liberalization of GATT 1947 reflected a compromise between the United States' bilateral approach of the Reciprocal Trade Agreements Act (RTAA) of 1934 and the insistence of the United Kingdom on a multilateral setting for tariff liberalization.

Section 4.3 describes the multilateral-bilateral approach. The term "bilateral" referred to the tariff negotiations between pairs of principal suppliers, and the term "multilateral" referred to the multicountry nature of the tariff liberalization exercise, the implementation of tariff commitments on an MFN basis, and the multilateral convention on nontariff barriers. Under the bilateral approach, tariff reduction or binding commitments were conceived as bargaining chips to be exchanged for equivalent commitments in terms of market access. Although the tariff concessions were implemented on a multilateral basis under the MFN clause, the principal supplier rule was designed to limit the effective reach of their benefits.

Section 4.4 analyzes the factors behind the evolution of GATT 1947 toward the formula approach of the Kennedy round. Although the bilateral approach rapidly exhausted its liberalization potential and therefore became an issue for the continued viability of GATT 1947, domestic political constraints in the United States prevented a shift to another approach until the establishment of the European Economic Community (EEC). This event revitalized the GATT process of tariff liberalization because the United States was forced to adopt the formula approach to achieve its trade policy objectives in the newly bipolar world economy. The final section provides concluding remarks on the role of the formula approach—and the broader conception of reciprocity underlying this approach to tariffs—in fostering trade liberalization.

4.2   Wartime Discussions

James Meade devised his proposal for an International Commercial Union in 1942 as a companion to the proposal for a multilateral clearing system for payments made by Keynes, which eventually took the form of the International Monetary Fund (IMF) in 1944. In Keynes's proposal, commercial policy was one of the instruments at the disposal of member states for the adjustment of disequilibria; for instance, countries with a persistent balance-of-payments surplus would be required to undertake expansionary policies, including a unilateral reduction of tariffs.[6] In Meade's proposal, the purpose of the Commercial Union was to reduce barriers to trade and commercial policy was therefore the subject of standalone commitments.

Meade expected that the United Kingdom would face a postwar "commercial problem" in the form of a substantial and unsustainable balance-of-payments deficit.[7] The problem, according to Meade, was to maintain the imports of food and raw materials essential to the population's living standard while eliminating the balance-of-payments deficit. In accordance with conventional Keynesian thinking, Meade believed that this objective could be achieved by a large expansion of exports through the removal of restrictive trade policies in countries outside the Commonwealth area, in particular, the United States, continental European and Latin American states, with a continued use of quantitative restrictions by the United Kingdom to block inessential imports.[8]

To this end, Meade proposed the "multilateral" approach to tariff-cutting, as the alternative to rigidly bilateral bargains that remove the opportunities for multilateral trading."[9] Each member of the commercial union "would undertake to remove altogether certain protective devices against the commerce of other members of the Union and to reduce to a defined maximum the degree of protection which they would afford to their own home producers."[10] In short, the members of the commercial union would negotiate on a tariff-cutting formula, and not on a bilateral basis for tariff reductions on particular items, and a bilateral balancing of market access concessions would therefore not be the guiding principle of the proposed commercial union.

Although the members of Meade's commercial union would be required to observe the MFN principle in their relations with each other, they would be permitted to discriminate against nonmembers and in favor of a recognized political or geographical grouping of states (e.g., imperial preference). Another feature of the proposal was the permission for countries with balance-of-payments deficits to use quantitative restrictions on imports, subject to oversight by the proposed clearing union. As Meade subsequently stated: "The ideal solution is one which permits the use of quantitative import restrictions to us if our balance of payments is unfavorable, but simultaneously prohibits the use of quantitative import restrictions by our customers if their balances of payments are not unfavorable ... A similar principle applies to exchange rates."[11]

Meade's proposal was developed at a time when the United States intended to conclude a new bilateral trade agreement with the United Kingdom under the RTAA, while pursuing the informal and exploratory discussions on postwar economic arrangements foreseen under Article VII of the Lend-Lease Agreement. The United Kingdom presented Meade's proposal as its position in the discussions in the Anglo-American Committee on Commercial Policy that took place in September 1943 in Washington.[12] The discussions went well since the committee agreed to a joint report on tariffs and preferences, according to which:

Consideration was given to the relative effectiveness and feasibility of the multilateral as compared to the bilateral method for bringing about a reduction of tariffs. In this connection a number of formulas were examined and compared without, however, at this stage attempting a selection. Consideration was also given to the substantial abolition of preferences and discriminations and the question of the relation of action in this field to the reduction of tariff barriers.[13]

What practical effect would the Anglo-American statement have had on the broad outlines of the commercial policies of the United Kingdom and the United States? The United Kingdom was already a low-tariff country. Its tariff policy consisted mainly of a 10 percent floor ad valorem rate for all products except for a small duty-free list, with the flexibility of upward and downward revision based on the recommendations of the Import Duties Advisory Committee.[14] Furthermore, the United Kingdom, as a deficit country, could have continued to impose quantitative restrictions on imports. A major change however was the proposed elimination of the "imperial" preferences granted on products imported from the Dominions under the Ottawa Agreements Act of 1932.[15] In this regard, Meade notes in his diary the difficult task that lay ahead: "When we get back to London we shall have to sell this compromise to the British powers that be, but if they have a grain of sense they will not repudiate a scheme which really contains everything which is of vital interest to us but without which all our economic (and probably many of our political?) projects for the post-war world will be impossible".[16]

More substantial changes would have been required in the United States. It had been a "high-tariff" country since the Smoot-Hawley Tariff Act of 1930, although imports from all origins were treated equally with several important exceptions (e.g., preferences to Cuba). The twenty-nine agreements negotiated under the RTAA had reduced tariffs on certain items by up to 50 percent, leading to "peaks and valleys" in the Smoot-Hawley tariff. The multilateral approach would therefore have engaged the United States in a relatively substantial across-the-board tariff reduction exercise, and would also have reduced the disparities in the United States tariff. This outcome was a key objective of the United Kingdom in the Article VII discussions: "In some British government circles and outside circles here there is a feeling that the enhanced creditor position of the United States makes it essential that there be some general lowering of the American tariff, and not merely further agreements under the Trade Agreements Act [RTAA], if a stable basis is to be found for post-war international economic relationships".[17]

More significantly, a formula approach would have fundamentally changed the conduct of trade policy making in the United States in relation to the RTAA. The purpose of the RTAA was to expand market access abroad for exporting interests in exchange for "concessions" on imported items, the latter carefully chosen to minimize adjustment of domestic industries according to the "no-injury" test proclaimed by President Roosevelt.[18] The RTAA represented a fundamental shift in United States commercial policy, according to Harry Hawkins and Janet Norwood, because the tariff "had come to be regarded as untouchable (except to raise it) by anyone who valued his political life."[19] Congressional support for the RTAA and its extensions therefore depended on concessions being offered on products that were not produced to any significant extent in the United States or on which political opposition was low.

In this context, the executive used its temporarily delegated tariff-cutting authority with circumspection. Although the RTAA did not require it, the executive assured Congress that a selective, item-by-item approach would be used to identify candidate products for tariff concessions.[20] The "principal supplier" rule was used to elaborate the list of candidate concessions, according to which the negotiating partner for a concession on an item was required to be the supplier with the largest share of imports. Grace Beckett, a historian of the period, noted that "even though other nations receive the duty reduction through the most-favored-nation treatment, the reduction is often of no particular benefit to them because they do not send large quantities of the concession product to the United States," and the principal supplier rule therefore maintained bargaining power for future agreements.[21]

An interagency Committee for Reciprocity Information held hearings and reported back to the executive. This procedure was designed to give potentially affected enterprises advance notice and a right to comment on the proposed list of concessions. Finally, the State Department issued advance public notice of the intention to negotiate together with a list of items on which concessions would be considered, but not necessarily granted. Since the United States entered the negotiations with its maximum offer on the table, the executive established the final list of concessions by invoking the principle of reciprocity for the concessions offered by the negotiating partner. The substance of the agreement was then amply documented by the Tariff Commission.[22]

In sum, a shift to the multilateral approach to tariff liberalization by the United States would have undermined the congressional agenda of selective liberalization by both enlarging the potential scope of tariff concessions to products produced in the United States and reducing the role of import-competing enterprises in the trade policymaking process. Since negotiations would have taken place on the modalities of the formula to be applied by all parties, rather than a bilateral balancing of market access commitments, a broader conception of reciprocity would have obtained. In this context, Meade reported in his diary that "Hull is still extremely unconvinced of the multilateral approach" due to the continued affection of the Tariff Commission and Congress for the bilateral approach.[23]

The Anglo-American discussions continued informally in 1944, with the American side proposing a 15 percent tariff floor with a 50 percent reduction of the tariffs above the floor, a proposal that met with Meade's approval.[24] But the United Kingdom proved unable to resume Article VII discussions at the official level mainly because the Cabinet was not prepared to endorse an elimination of imperial preference.[25] By mid-1944, the Anglo-American commercial policy plan was effectively at a deadlock within ministerial circles, which Prime

Minister Churchill was unwilling to break at the price of a schism in conservative ranks.[26]

Informal talks were held again in late 1944 and early 1945 in London. The British side continued to insist on the merit of the multilateral approach to tariff reduction:

The UK officials compared the multilateral approach with the bilateral and multilateral-bilateral approaches. While appreciating the complexities of the first approach, they believe that the last two approaches have such serious disadvantages that they should only be considered as a last resort in the event of the breakdown of attempts at the multilateral approach.

They point out that in the bilateral approach concessions are narrowed because of the obligation to generalize them under the MFN principle. Second, the principle of "equivalence of concessions" raises difficulties. Efforts had been made after 1860 and to some extent in the 1920s to get around these difficulties by trying to negotiate a string of bilateral agreements. But the results were largely destroyed by subsequent depressions ... In addition, since an early US–UK agreement would be necessary under the bilateral or multilateral-bilateral approach, and preferences would be a major issue in such an agreement, the UK at an early stage would have to make concessions on preferences which would at once be made general. Consequently, when UK negotiated later with other countries it would not be able to get concessions in return for this.[27]

The multilateral approach to tariff liberalization was adopted in March 1945 by the State Department.[28] This position was, however, immediately discarded when discussions with congressional leaders revealed that legislative support for extending the president's tariff-cutting authority under the RTAA could not be secured without a continuation of the existing approach to tariff reduction. When informed of the definitive position of the United States on this issue, the British officials lamented that it would be the end of "all we hope to achieve," "the end of everything worth having," and "the UK would go into it with no heart and no expectation of anything worthwhile coming out of it."[29] The British side made clear that without the multilateral approach to tariff reduction, no comprehensive approach to eliminating imperial preference was possible.[30]

Although the State Department was itself convinced of the superiority of the formula approach,[31] and that the multilateral approach "would be a much more drastic approach to the trade barrier problem...,"[32] the issue could not be reopened with Congress given the narrow margin of passage of the renewal statute.[33] Attention therefore was directed to developing commercial policy arrangements that permitted selective tariff reduction but that were also acceptable to the United Kingdom and Dominion governments. One proposal discussed by the United States with Canada was the simultaneous launching of trade agreements programs by a core group of countries for the purpose of negotiating with principal suppliers.[34] Canada proposed instead the "nuclear" approach, whereby a small group of countries would engage in bilateral tariff negotiations, the tariff reductions effected by such agreements would be generalized to the other participants, agreement would be reached on provisions for dealing with nontariff trade barriers, and an international conference would be convened to invite other countries to join the nucleus by appropriate tariff reduction commitments.[35]

This plan was eventually agreed upon—under duress—by the United Kingdom. At the close of World War II, the immediate end of lend-lease forced the United Kingdom to request a low-interest loan to finance purchases of food and essential raw materials in the United States. One condition for the loan set by the United States was the elimination of preferences by the United Kingdom, and the negotiations on the loan were therefore linked with a renewal of discussions on commercial policy. The final compromise on the issue of import tariffs and preferences provided that margins of preference would be capped at existing levels, automatically reduced by concessions on MFN tariffs, the latter undertaken in multilateral negotiations.[36] The multilateral character of the negotiations would be secured by the simultaneous engagement of countries in the process of bilateral tariff negotiations in one location. It was agreed that the United States should issue the report of the United States–United Kingdom Committee on Commercial Policy to bring into force multilateral trading arrangements in the form of the "Proposals for Expansion of World Trade" on December 6, 1945.[37]

The next section describes the form in which reciprocity eventually emerged in GATT 1947.

4.3   The Nature of Reciprocity in GATT 1947[38]

The GATT was negotiated as part of the draft Charter for the International Trade Organization (ITO) of the United Nations. In addition to trade barriers, this organization had the ambitious program to regulate restrictive business practices, intergovernmental commodity arrangements, and the international aspects of domestic employment policies.[39] While the discussions on the draft Charter for the ITO proceeded, the United States invited the nineteen members of the Preparatory Committee to meet in Geneva in April 1947 to negotiate tariff commitments and reductions in preference margins and to decide on the provisions of the chapter on commercial policy considered essential to safeguard the value of the tariff commitments, to be known as the General Agreement on Tariffs and Trade (GATT).[40]

The results of these negotiations entered into effect provisionally on January 1, 1948, pending the entry into force of the ITO. Since the United States did not have the authority to enter into an agreement establishing an international organization, the GATT agreement did not contain an institutional framework for the contracting parties to carry out the functions set out therein. Such a framework was contained in the draft Charter for the ITO.

Tariff Bargains

To guide the tariff negotiations, the Prepcom issued a document at the conclusion of its first meeting in London in 1946 on the procedures to be followed for the Geneva Round. These negotiations were to be conducted on a "reciprocal" and "mutually advantageous" basis, which was explicitly stated to mean that "no country would be expected to grant concessions unilaterally, without action by others, or to grant concessions to others which are not adequately counterbalanced by concessions in return."[41] The negotiations would concern both tariffs and margins of preference, the latter being capped and subject to reduction through negotiations on the level of MFN tariffs. Furthermore, these negotiations were to be conducted on a selective, product-by-product basis to afford "ample flexibility ... for taking into account the needs of individual countries and individual industries."[42] Another rule was that participants "should not seek to improve their bargaining position by tariff or other restrictive measures in preparation of the negotiations,"[43] which has become known as the "standstill commitment" and has formed part of all the negotiating rounds subsequently conducted under the auspices of GATT 1947.

According to the guidelines, participants first made requests for tariff concessions on particular items to other participants, followed by "a schedule of proposed concessions which it would be prepared to grant to all other members in the light of the concessions it would have requested from each of them."[44] This approach was known as "request-and-offer." In compiling its offer list, a participant would be guided by the principal supplier rule, according to which an item would be considered for inclusion if a negotiating partner was the supplier with the largest share of imports. All the participants would then study the request and offer lists of all the others, and classify them according to whether they were satisfactory or in need of further discussion. In the latter event, the participant in question would initiate negotiations, normally conducted on a bilateral basis given the principal supplier rule. The results of the tariff negotiations were to be contained in schedules of tariff concessions, which identified each of the principal suppliers holding the "initial negotiating right" (INR-holder).

Commitments to Safeguard the Value of Tariff Concessions

Another central aspect of GATT 1947 was the multilateral convention on the MFN principle and on the rules of conduct for nontariff measures. Regarding MFN, preferences were permitted, but capped however at existing levels; a new but more qualified vehicle for preferences was the permission to enter into free trade areas or customs unions. Regarding quantitative restrictions, there was a new commitment prohibiting their use subject to certain exceptions, and in particular for countries in balance-of-payments difficulties. (The linkage with the IMF originally proposed by Meade took form in Articles XII and XVIII of GATT 1947 that require a determination made by the IMF). Should such restrictions be used, the importing country was required to apply them on a nondiscriminatory basis.

Regarding the tariff concessions, Article II:1 of GATT 1947 provided that "each contracting party shall accord to the commerce of the other contracting parties treatment no less favorable than that provided for in the appropriate part of the appropriate Schedule annexed to this agreement." A degree of flexibility was however provided in Article XXVIII on the modification of schedules, according to which concessions would remain in place for three years—from January 1, 1948 to January 1, 1951—at which point modifications could be made in accordance with the rules set down therein.[45] The rules of Article XXVIII were designed to re-create, to the extent possible, the original context in which the tariff concessions had been negotiated. The contracting party intending to modify its tariff schedule was required to enter into negotiations with the INR-holder with the aim of reaching agreement in accordance with the following general principle: "In such negotiations and agreement, which may include provision for compensatory adjustment with respect to other products, the contracting parties concerned shall endeavour to maintain a general level of reciprocal and mutually advantageous concessions not less favourable to trade than that provided for in the present Agreement."[46]

The contracting party was also required to "consult" (as opposed to negotiate) with contracting parties, having been determined by the contracting parties acting as a collective body to have a "substantial interest."[47]

Although the aim of such negotiations and consultation was agreement, it was not required and the modification of the tariff schedule could still proceed. However, the INR-holder and contracting parties with a substantial interest would then be free to withdraw substantially equivalent concessions initially negotiated with the contracting party having modified its tariff schedule on an MFN basis. Thus, while the modifying country was free to withdraw the concession made on an item to its principal supplier in the absence of an agreement, that supplier was free in turn to withdraw the concession that had been granted as a counterpart.

4.4   The Shift to the Formula Approach

In relation to the bilateral approach to trade agreements of the interwar period, the objective of liberalizing trade was widely seen as being advanced by the GATT 1947 due to the multilateral nature of the new agreement. Although the negotiations on tariff concessions were bilateral in nature, the tariff commitments thereby assumed applied to the trade of all contracting parties to the GATT 1947. Thus, important secondary suppliers of products were able to indirectly obtain tariff concessions on products of export interest, which in turn promoted the granting of tariff concessions on imports.[48] Furthermore, the simultaneity of these negotiations implied, according to Gerard Curzon, that "the old argument of free concessions to third countries has also died."[49] As the Prepcom summed up:

The multilateral form of tariff schedules is designed to provide more stability than has existed in the past under bilateral tariff agreements, to assure certainty of broad action for the reduction of tariffs and to give to countries a right for tariff concessions on particular products which such countries might wish to obtain, but could not obtain under bilateral agreements, because of their relatively less important position as a supplier of the product concerned. The multilateral form also gives expression to the fact that each country stands to gain when another country grants tariff reductions on any product, even though primarily supplied by a third country. This point can be finally settled when the negotiations have proceeded sufficiently to enable all the varying factors to be taken into account.[50]

Another central aspect of GATT 1947 was the multilateral convention on the MFN principle and on the rules of conduct for nontariff measures. Although such a code of conduct had been a feature of bilateral trade agreements in the interwar period,[51] the GATT 1947 contained a code of conduct that was, for the first time in the history of trade agreements, simultaneously applied by all parties, irrespective of their particular situations. This code applied to all products and not only those on which tariff concessions had been made. Given the interest of the participants in preserving the privileges already negotiated in the preexisting network of bilateral trade agreements, the GATT 1947 probably represented a relatively high standard of conduct for MFN and nontariff barriers.

However, the techniques for tariff negotiations rapidly came to undermine the viability of the new trading arrangements, particularly after the United States failed to ratify the ITO. One difficulty was their lengthy and laborious nature. For instance, in the Geneva round of 1947, the 16 participants conducted a total of 108 bilateral negotiations, each with multiple meetings.[52] Although no definitive figure on the total number of meetings held by the negotiators is available, the document on the state of the negotiations issued by the Tariff Steering Committee on September 10, 1947 (the original target date for completion) indicated that 1,395 meetings had been held since the start of negotiations in May, but only 23 bilateral negotiations had successfully been concluded![53] The committee noted that completion of a number of bilateral negotiations was undermined by disagreement on the evaluation of concessions or by the limited amount of trade covered by the concessions offered.[54]

Given the need to make the negotiations manageable by selecting a core group of countries, a second difficulty was the limitation the principal supplier rule imposed on the potential scope of the negotiations in terms of products. This scope was limited to those products on which pairwise combinations of negotiating partners were possible. As a result, the developing countries that joined the GATT in the early 1950s did not generally participate in the request-and-offer exercises because they did not have principal supplier status, and could therefore not negotiate for tariff concessions on items of particular export interest. To respond to their concerns, a modification was made at the fourth round of tariff negotiations to permit coalitions of countries to request a concession on products of which they were collectively a principal supplier.[55] This modification, however, required the coalition to agree on the concessions to be offered in exchange, a condition which, given the difficulty of achieving agreement on this question, continued to undermine the effective participation of developing countries in tariff negotiations.

A third difficulty with the tariff-negotiating techniques concerned the domestic political implications of the request-and-offer approach. As was noted in section 4.2 above, the United States executive used an item-by-item approach in the RTAA to carry out the congressional agenda of selective liberalization on products not produced in the United States or on which political opposition was low. Once the GATT tariff negotiations had moved into the more difficult terrain of domestically produced products, Congress limited the tariff-cutting authority of the United States executive by the "peril point" provision. The president was required to obtain the advice of the Tariff Commission on the products on which negotiations were intended, and the commission reported on (1) the maximum decreases in duty that could be made on any such item without causing or threatening to cause serious injury to the domestic industry; and (2) the minimum increase that might be necessary to avoid serious injury or the threat thereof. If the president ignored the advice of the commission, he was required to report his reasons for doing so to Congress.[56]

Another difficulty concerned the limited extent of liberalization that such techniques could achieve between negotiating partners. Although no specific rules have ever been decided in the GATT on the value of tariff concessions, and therefore on the concept of substantial equivalence, the available evidence indicates that a concession's value is the anticipated expansion in exports—the difference between the old and new tariff rates, weighted by the price elasticity of the product, and multiplied by the average value of trade in the previous three years, taking into account the trend in the development of trade.[57] Thus, the negotiating leverage of an importing country depended on such factors as the height of the initial tariff, the value of imports, the extent to which demand is price-elastic, and so forth.

The 1951 Torquay round—the first real test of the bilateral approach—was considered to be a disappointment. The low-tariff countries of continental Europe complained that the principle of reciprocal concessions prevented satisfactory negotiations with their high-tariff neighbors designed to lead to a single market among European countries, and they proposed that the GATT concern itself not only with reducing tariffs but also tariff disparities.[58] The low-tariff countries pursued the matter in a GATT working party, which eventually led to the "GATT plan" to lower the incidence of tariffs—the percentage of duties collected in relation to the value of imports—by 30 percent in each of four categories of imports, subject to ceiling rates.[59]

The United Kingdom opposed the plan,[60] and the United States could not support the plan because, in the 1955 renewal of the tariff-cutting authority of the president, the executive branch had again assured Congress that the selective, item-by-item approach would be used in GATT tariff negotiations. The GATT plan was dropped and the fourth round of tariff negotiations was held in Geneva in 1956 on the basis of the traditional techniques of tariff negotiation. Gerard Curzon sums up the mood at the end of the Geneva round:

Apart from the United States … no one was really satisfied. Several countries had withdrawn from the negotiations because of inadequate negotiating leeway, others had only little to offer and therefore received little in exchange. Protectionist strongholds had been left untouched and it was felt that if GATT stuck to the system of commodity-by-commodity nibbling at tariffs, there would be no further progress. While the underdeveloped countries remained mute, the U.S. a prisoner of its domestic legislation and the U.K. true to the belief that Commonwealth trade was more important than trade with the continent of Europe, the delegates from continental countries went home with a feeling of frustration. If there was to be another tariff conference, they would insist on the use of new rules.

A week after the conclusion of the 1956 tariff round, the Foreign Ministers of Holland, Belgium, Luxembourg, Germany, France and Italy met in Venice to discuss the plan worked out by the Spaak Committee for eliminating tariff barriers among themselves.[61]

The establishment of the European Economic Community (EEC) in 1958 revived the GATT process of tariff liberalization in two ways.

First, the GATT rules left open only the option of a customs union or a free trade area for European economic integration because the United States and the United Kingdom refused to grant a waiver for the creation of a new preferential trade area. To eliminate tariffs on infra-EEC trade, the members undertook a staged formula cut subject to exceptions for certain products, demonstrating the merits of such an approach among countries with widely different tariffs. Second, the staged tariff reductions among EEC members placed American products at a competitive disadvantage in those markets, and the United States became intent upon reducing the external tariff of the EEC in step with these tariff reductions.

In the reciprocal negotiations of the 1960–1961 Dillon round, the United Kingdom (which intended to join the EEC) and the EEC proposed a formula cut of 20 percent to minimize internal haggling among the members on the substance of the EEC's offer. The United States was unable to respond to the offer because of "peril point" and "escape clause" provisions even though the president had obtained the authority from Congress to cut tariffs by 20 percent in the 1958 extension of the RTAA. As Secretary of State Rusk explained to President Kennedy:

Unfortunately, in the bureaucratic process of developing bargaining offers for these negotiations, the Eisenhower Administration threw away most of its chips. First, it made the decision to restrict the commodities for possible negotiation to a very limited list ... only 26.3% of our imports from the countries with which we plan to negotiate. Second, the Tariff Commission further limited the Administration's bargaining authority by setting highly debatable peril points for a large number of commodities.[62]

Although the United Kingdom and the EEC were prepared to proceed with their offer without requiring full reciprocity from the United States,[63] withstanding their domestic political pressures required at least a show of reciprocity, to which end the executive expanded the product coverage of its offer by breaching the peril points on a number of items "at a minimum political risk."[64]

This experience led President Kennedy to conclude that his tariff-cutting authority could not be used effectively in negotiations with the EEC unless fundamental changes were made in its conception. The resolution of this issue was perceived as urgent given the effects of a persistent balance-of-payments deficit on the reserve position of the dollar, linked in turn to the broader issue of the leadership position of the United States in NATO.[65] In a message to Congress on the RTAA sent on January 25, 1962, President Kennedy stated that "trade policy adequate to negotiate item-by-item tariff reductions with a large number of small independent states will no longer be adequate to assure ready access ... to a market nearly as large as our own, whose negotiators can speak with one voice but whose internal differences make it impossible for them to negotiate item by item."[66] To meet the objective of minimizing discrimination against American products as the customs union was established, President Kennedy stated:

But the traditional technique of trading one brick at a time off our respective walls will not suffice to assure American farm and factory exports the kind of access to the European market which they must have if trade between the two Atlantic markets is to expand. We must talk instead in terms of trading whole layers at a time in exchange for other layers, as the Europeans have been doing in reducing their internal tariffs, permitting the forces of competition to set new trade patterns. Trading in such an enlarged basis is not possible, the EEC has found, if traditional item-by-item economic histories are to dominate. But let me emphasize that we mean to see to it that all reductions and concessions are reciprocal, and that the access we gain is not limited by the use of quotas or other restrictive devices.[67]

The 1962 Trade Expansion Act gave the administration a five-year grant of authority to reduce tariffs by up to 50 percent (as in 1934 and 1945), to reduce tariffs by 80 percent on items for which the United States and the EEC (enlarged to include the United Kingdom) accounted for 80 percent of world trade, and to reduce tariffs on certain tropical products of export interest to developing countries without requiring reciprocity provided the EEC did the same.[68] Items exempted from this authority were those subject to escape clause action and petroleum on the grounds of national security. In relation to previous grants of tariff-cutting authority, major changes included the fact that negotiations could be conducted either on an article-by-article basis or across the board. In addition, although the act maintained the requirement of peril point findings by the Tariff Commission, the criterion for injury was made more stringent and the requirement to identify precise peril points was lifted. Finally, a new program of trade adjustment assistance was made available to firms and workers that might be injured in consequence of increased imports as a result of lowered tariffs.

The United States was determined to use its new tariff-cutting authority to the maximum to contain the discriminatory effects of the establishment of the EEC. At the same time, reciprocity considerations required the United States to persuade other GATT contracting parties to agree in advance to a 50 percent across-the-board tariff cut on industrial products and bound agricultural items, with strictly limited exceptions. However, the EEC opposed the plan on the grounds that a linear cut would be biased in favor of the United States, whose tariff peaks would remain in place and would therefore provide the United States with negotiating leverage in future tariff negotiations.[69] As a matter of fact, the EEC and the United States both had average tariffs in the 10 percent range, but 60 percent of the tariff rates of the United States were below 20 percent compared to 85 percent for the EEC.[70]

The EEC proposed instead to reduce tariff disparities by "ecretement" (removing peaks). This proposal combined a floor rate of 10–15 percent for finished industrial products, with a 50 percent cut in the difference between the existing rate and the target rate. In turn, the United States opposed ecretement on the grounds that a greater expansion of trade would occur under the linear cut, that ecretement negated the "basic philosophy of linear approach to reciprocity," and that the United States would therefore undertake more substantial tariff liberalization than the EEC, thereby violating a cardinal principle of American commercial policy.[71] The low-tariff European countries also opposed ecretement on the grounds that it would result in relatively small cuts by the EEC on many products for which they were the principal suppliers, and they insisted on the use of the principal supplier rule for negotiations on removing items from the lists of exemptions.[72] The final compromise at the GATT Ministerial Meeting in May 1963 launching the Kennedy Round was agreement that the tariff negotiations would be "based upon a plan of substantial linear tariff reductions with a bare minimum of exceptions," linked to the solution of tariff disparities, agricultural products, exceptions and nontariff problems (the effect of the American selling price method on market access for chemicals).

In November 1964, the United States tabled its preliminary list of exceptions to the 50 percent cut on nonagricultural products, strictly limited to statutorily exempted items. The EEC, vexed by the unresolved issue of tariff disparities, took instead a more expansive approach to the exceptions list. From that point on, the negotiations in the Kennedy Round were mainly concerned with bilateral negotiations between the EEC and the principal suppliers of items on its

exemptions list to remove them to the liberalization column by reciprocal additions/exclusions from their own lists of exceptions. In
the end, the United States had shifted a significant number of items
into the exceptions list, citing the need to attain an overall level of
reciprocity with its trading partners, as well as a bilateral balance
with certain partners, in particular, the EEC.[73] Still, the United States
was able to claim that "in terms of the number of participating
countries, the amount of trade involved, and the scope and depth of
trade liberalization, it was by far the greatest achievement in the
series of negotiations in the 20-year history of the GATT."[74]

4.5 Reciprocity and Trade Liberalization

The different forms of reciprocity are of interest to the trade community mainly in terms of their contribution (or absence thereof) to
the liberalization of world trade. Keohane has argued that the specific reciprocity of bilaterally balanced agreements undermines cooperation in a multilateral environment characterized by sequentially
negotiated trade agreements since the benefits of the earlier treaties
are undermined by subsequent treaties, leading to an unstable treaty
system. In his view, the widespread adoption of the unconditional
MFN clause in the interwar period led to a diffuse form of reciprocity, which was institutionalized in GATT 1947, and reflected a norm
of cooperative or unselfish behavior, whereby states overlook their
short-run economic interests.

The opposite view of the unconditional MFN clause prevailed,
however, in the 1930s as George Auld explains:

the generalized concessions unconditionally granted to third-party countries
are by no means given away. They are in fact granted for compensation. The
compensation received from third party countries consists of the reciprocal
extension to us of the treatment which they accord or may in the future accord to the most favored nation ... [so that] the destructive force of discrimination and retaliation are not set in motion, and the spirit and practice of
commercial warfare are avoided.[55]

In other words, the fact that A would benefit at the time of gen-
eralizing the concessions granted to C from forcing additional concessions from B, does not imply that such a policy would at all other
times be in its own best interest.

In determining whether the unconditional MFN clause promotes
or inhibits tariff liberalization, Keohane notes that, on the one hand,

the objective of a stable treaty system in a world of many trading nations sequentially negotiating trade agreements is achieved and, on the other hand, free riding is promoted. According to Keohane, GATT 1947 solved the problem of free riding by combining the diffuse reciprocity of the obligations of each party on nontariff barriers with the specific reciprocity of tariff negotiations based on the principal supplier rule, and simultaneous negotiations so that all the elements of the final package would be in place before agreement was required. He claims that the switch to the formula approach preserved the balance between specific reciprocity and diffuse reciprocity by the supplementary negotiations that took place between importers and their principal suppliers on a product-by-product basis.

The historical record examined in this chapter is broadly consistent with Keohane's analysis of the original form of reciprocity in GATT 1947. Indeed, the drafters of the agreement identified the problem of trade barrier reduction commitments through bilateral trade agreements with the MFN clause in a world composed of more than two countries and the advantages of multilateralism in substantially the same terms. Although the specific reciprocity of GATT in 1947 resolved in principle the issues raised by the commercial policy arrangements of the interwar period, the experience of trade liberalization in the first two decades of the existence of GATT 1947 revealed new problems.

Although the requirement of reciprocity may have spurred trade barrier reduction commitments by recalcitrant nations, it also confined the scope of liberalization due to its peculiar characteristics. In particular, reciprocity prevented the realization of broader agendas of trade integration, such as the construction of a single European market between high-tariff and low-tariff countries or the development of North-South trade by the effective participation of developing countries in the tariff negotiations. At the domestic level, the item-by-item approach was designed to permit the domestic forces most opposed to liberalization to mobilize to block tariff reduction in their sectors of economic activity. Thus, the United States experienced a growing imbalance between the requests of its trading partners and the concessions it could make, gradually undermining the process of reciprocal trade liberalization. This constraint was broken by the establishment of the EEC, which revitalized the GATT process of tariff liberalization because the United States could no longer achieve its trade policy objectives in the newly bipolar world economy using the traditional techniques of the RTAA.

The adoption of the formula approach by the United States for the Kennedy round was a significant shift in the multilateral techniques for trade liberalization, and not just a slightly modified version of the previous approach as Keohane claims. Although it is true that the second phase of the Kennedy Round consisted mainly of bilateral negotiations between the EEC and the principal suppliers of items on its exemptions list, such negotiations were fundamentally different from those conducted previously in GATT 1947. (As a passing note, such negotiations would not have been necessary had the EEC and, in particular, France agreed to a linear cut, as they had previously offered in the Dillon Round).[76] One difference was the commitment by a large number of countries to make tariff reductions across the board, and since no items were in principle to be excluded from liberalization, the domestic blocking strategies of certain interest groups were effectively undermined. Another difference was the new manner in which reciprocity was understood. The United States, for instance, emphasized an overall balance in the value of trade covered by concessions made and received, with the exception of the handful of countries effectively engaged in the negotiations, for which bilateral balancing was required on a trade basis.[77] In addition, the negotiation between the United States and the EEC was settled by a package of tariff and nontariff concessions on agricultural and nonagricultural products. The result of the shift to the formula approach was a broader notion of reciprocity than had originally been incorporated in GATT 1947.

In sum, this chapter has argued that the shift in the GATT from the specific reciprocity of 1947 to the adoption of a truly multilateral approach to tariff reduction in the Kennedy Round—as had originally been proposed by Meade two decades before—produced trade liberalization on a much broader and more significant scale than had previously been possible in GATT.

Notes

This chapter was written while the author was on leave from the Secretariat of the World Trade Organization, Geneva, Switzerland. The views in this chapter are those of the author alone, and should not be attributed to the WTO secretariat or to the WTO members, either individually or collectively. Thanks are due to Jagdish Bhagwati for comments on the draft versions of this chapter.

1. J. Lawrence Laughlin and H. Parker Willis, *Reciprocity* (New York: The Baker & Taylor Co., 1903), 1.

2. Elisabeth Zoller, *Peacetime Unilateral Remedies: An Analysis of Countermeasures* (Dobbs-Ferry, NY: Transnational Publishers, Inc.), 14.

3. Jagdish Bhagwati, *The World Trading System at Risk* (Princeton, NJ: Princeton University Press, 1991), 4.

4. Robert Keohane, "Reciprocity in International Relations," *International Organization* 40 (Winter 1986): 1.

5. GATT 1947 is distinguished from GATT 1994, which is a component of the WTO.

6. "The Counselor of the British Embassy (Opie) to the Assistant Secretary of State (Berle)," *Foreign Relations of the United States* 1 (1942): 203–221.

7. James Meade, "A Proposal for an International Commercial Union (1942)," in *The Collected Papers of James Meade*, Vol. III, International Economics, ed. Susan Howson (London: Unwin Hyman, 1988), 27.

8. Meade, "A Proposal," 29.

9. Meade, "A Proposal," 28.

10. Meade, "A Proposal," 29–30.

11. James Meade, "The Post-War International Settlement and the United Kingdom Balance of Payments (1943)," in Susan Howson, editor, *The Collected Papers of James Meade*, Vol. III: International Economics, ed. Susan Howson (London: Unwin Hyman, 1988), 37.

12. The "Law Mission" was in Washington in September–October 1943. In addition to commercial policy, the mission discussed Keynes's plan for a clearing union and the plan for a stabilization fund developed by Harry White of the U.S. Treasury. These discussions led to the Bretton Woods Agreements of 1944 establishing the IMF and World Bank.

13. The report is not available. A summary was provided to the Allies at the Moscow Conference of 1943 in the "Memorandum Concerning the Washington Meeting Between British and American Economic Experts with Reference to Article VII of the Mutual-Aid Agreement," *Foreign Relations of the United States* 1 (1943): 766. The report led to an agenda outline for discussions with other countries. See the "Telegram from Secretary of State Hull to Ambassador Harriman in the Soviet Union," *Foreign Relations of the United States* 1 (1943): 1119–1125.

14. Carl Kreider, *The Anglo-American Trade Agreement* (Princeton, NJ: Princeton University Press), 19–25.

15. Article VII apparently commits the parties to eliminate discrimination and therefore implicitly imperial preference. However, President Roosevelt wrote to Prime Minister Churchill that "it is the furthest thing from my mind that we are attempting in any way to ask you to trade the principle of imperial preference as a consideration for lend-lease" ("Personal for the Former Naval Person from the President," *Foreign Relations of the United States* 1 (1942): 535).

16. Susan Howson and Donald Moggridge, eds., *The Wartime Diaries of Lionel Robbins and James Meade, 1943–1945* (New York: St. Martin's Press, 1991), 130.

17. "The Charge in the United Kingdom (Mathews) to the Secretary of State," *Foreign Relations of the United States* 1 (1942): 164.

18. President Roosevelt transmitting the Reciprocal Trade Agreements Act to Congress, quoted by Alfred E. Eckes Jr., *Opening America's market: U.S. foreign trade policy since 1776* (Chapel Hill: The University of North Carolina Press, 1995), 142.

19. Harry C. Hawkins and Janet L. Norwood, "The Legislative Basis of United States Commercial Policy," in *Studies in United States Commercial Policy*, ed. William B. Kelly Jr. (Chapel Hill: University of North Carolina Press, 1963), 73.

20. The president was advised in his choice of items by an interdepartmental Trade Agreements Committee, chaired by the representative of the State Department, assisted in turn by the United States Tariff Commission on the import side and the Department of Commerce for the export side. See William Adams Brown Jr., *The United States and the Restoration of World Trade* (Washington, DC: The Brookings Institution, 1950), 18.

21. Grace Beckett, *The Reciprocal Trade Agreements Program* (New York: Columbia University Press, 1941), 21. In a review of tariff policies in the interwar period, the League of Nations also noted that the generalization of the unconditional MFN clause did not "in fact go far towards meeting the problem of discrimination, which was effectively practiced by means of tariff specifications so detailed that only the Parties to a bilateral negotiation were likely to benefit from the tariff reductions agreed upon" (League of Nations, *Commercial Policy in the Interwar Period: International Proposals and National Policies*, Part I: An Historical Survey, 112).

22. See, for instance, United States Tariff Commission, *Concessions Granted by the United States in the Trade Agreement with Switzerland* (Washington, DC: 1936).

23. Howson and Moggridge, *The Wartime Diaries*, 135, 137.

24. "The Ambassador in the United Kingdom (Winant) to the Secretary of State," *Foreign Relations of the United States* 2 (1944): 3.

25. "The Ambassador in the United Kingdom (Winant) to the Secretary of State," *Foreign Relations of the United States* 2 (1944): 28.

26. "The Ambassador in the United Kingdom (Winant) to the Secretary of State," *Foreign Relations of the United States* 2 (1944): 56. According to Keynes, "the substance of the commercial policy plan could be entirely preserved in a redrafted document . . . the Board of Trade drafters of statements on commercial policy [e.g., Meade] had acted too much like civil servants and not enough like politicians" ("The Charge in the United Kingdom (Bucknell) to the Secretary of State," *Foreign Relations of the United States* 2 (1944), 42).

27. "The Ambassador in the United Kingdom (Winant) to the Secretary of State," *Foreign Relations of the United States* 6 (1945): 15–16.

28. "Memorandum by the Secretary of State's Staff Committee," *Foreign Relations of the United States* 6 (1945): 26.

29. "The Ambassador in the United Kingdom (Winant) to the Secretary of State," *Foreign Relations of the United States* 6 (1945): 58.

30. "The Ambassador in the United Kingdom (Winant) to the Secretary of State," *Foreign Relations of the United States* 6 (1945): 90.

31. "Memorandum by the Executive Committee on Economic Foreign Policy," *Foreign Relations of the United States* 6 (1945): 74.

32. "Memorandum by the Assistant Secretary of State (Clayton) to Mr. Harry C. Hawkins, Minister-Counselor of Embassy for Economic Affairs at London," *Foreign Relations of the United States* 6 (1945): 45.

33. "Memorandum of Conversation, by the Chief of the Division of Commercial Policy (Brown)," *Foreign Relations of the United States* 6 (1945): 78.

34. "Memorandum of Conversation," by Mr. John Leddy, Assistant Advisor in the Division of Commercial Policy," *Foreign Relations of the United States* 6 (1945): 61.

35. "Memorandum of Conversation, by Mr. John Leddy, Assistant Advisor in the Division of Commercial Policy," *Foreign Relations of the United States* 6 (1945): 66.

36. "Minutes of a Meeting of the United States Top Committee," *Foreign Relations of the United States* 6 (1945): 157.

37. "Draft Combined Minutes of the Meeting of the United States-United Kingdom Committee on Commercial Policy," *Foreign Relations of the United States* 6 (1945): 178.

38. This section is based on the record of the discussions of the Preparatory Committee of nineteen countries established in February 1946 by the Economic and Social Council of the United Nations to prepare for the international conference on trade and employment and to prepare a draft Charter of the International Trade Organization. A first meeting was held in London in October–November 1946, and a drafting committee met in Lake Success, New York, in January–February 1947. The second meeting was held in Geneva in April–October 1947, and ended with the signature of the Final Act containing GATT 1947 and the schedules of tariff concessions.

39. "United States Draft Charter," Annexure 11, Report of the First Session of the Preparatory Committee of the United Nations Conference on Trade and Employment, EPCT/33.

40. "Multilateral Trade-Agreement Negotiations," Annexure 10, Report of the First Session of the Preparatory Committee of the United Nations Conference on Trade and Employment, EPCT/33.

41. Section C-General Nature of Negotiations, "Multilateral Trade-Agreement Negotiations," Annexure 10, Report of the First Session of the Preparatory Committee of the United Nations Conference on Trade and Employment, EPCT/33.

42. Section C-General Nature of Negotiations, "Multilateral Trade-Agreement Negotiations," Annexure 10, Report of the First Session of the Preparatory Committee of the United Nations Conference on Trade and Employment, EPCT/33.

43. Section E-Miscellaneous Rules for Guidance, "Multilateral Trade-Agreement Negotiations," Annexure 10, Report of the First Session of the Preparatory Committee of the United Nations Conference on Trade and Employment, EPCT/33.

44. EPCT/S/1, 7.

45. The original text of Article XXVIII is contained in the Final Act of the Second Meeting of the Prepcom (EPCT/214/Add.1 Rev. 1, 61). The original rule was never invoked by the contracting parties due to a decision to maintain the schedules until January 1, 1951. The renegotiation of a small number of items was carried out at the

Torquay Conference in 1951, and the life of the schedules was prolonged until the end of 1954, which date was extended to July 1, 1955. Article XXVIII was amended in 1955 to provide for greater flexibility in the timing of modifications.

46. EPCT/214/Add.1 Rev. 1, 61.

47. The Interpretative Note to Paragraph 1 of Art. XXVIII states the following:

a contracting party has principal supplying interest if that contracting party has had, over a reasonable period of time prior to the negotiations, a larger share in the market of the applicant contracting party with which the concession was initially negotiated or would, in the judgment of the CONTRACTING PARTIES, have had such a share in the absence of discriminatory quantitative restrictions maintained by the applicant contracting party. It would therefore not be appropriate for the CONTRACTING PARTIES to determine more than one contracting party, or in those exceptional cases where there is a near equality more than two contracting parties, had a principal supplying interest.

48. GATT, *An Analysis and Appraisal of the General Agreement on Tariffs and Trade*, prepared by the William L. Clayton Center for International Economic Affairs of the Fletcher School of Law and Diplomacy, Medford, MA, February 1955, for the United States Council of the International Chamber of Commerce. This report states on page 24 that the United States directly negotiated concessions on products amounting to 43 percent of exports and indirectly obtained concessions on products amounting to 8 percent of exports in 1953.

49. Gerard Curzon, *Multilateral Commercial Diplomacy* (New York: Frederick A. Praeger, 1966), 62.

50. Section E-Miscellaneous Rules for Guidance, "Multilateral Trade-Agreement Negotiations," Annexure 10, Report of the First Session of the Preparatory Committee of the United Nations Conference on Trade and Employment, EPCT/33.

51. For instance, the 1938 Anglo-American Trade Agreement provided for the parties to grant each other unconditional MFN treatment, subject to exceptions for preferences with respect to certain third countries, and in particular, imperial preference, and also required inter alia that imported products receive national treatment with respect to internal measures, the nondiscriminatory application of quantitative restrictions on imports or exports, and a competitive practice for state trading enterprises.

52. The theoretical total of 156 bilateral negotiations was reduced by the negotiations that could not take place between the members of preferential unions (e.g., Canada, Australia, New Zealand, United Kingdom) and those that were not initiated at all.

53. EPCT/S/9.

54. EPCT/S/8. The decision of the United Kingdom on the reductions in the margin of preference for the key markets of Australia and Canada held up the negotiations of those countries with their principal suppliers as well as the "key" bilateral negotiation with the United States.

55. Karin Kock, *International Trade Policy and the GATT, 1947–1967* (Stockholm: Almqvist & Wiksell, 1969), 103.

56. The "peril point" was added by Congress in the 1948 renewal of the RTAA. The 1951 peril point provision provided that the president should submit to the Tariff

Commission a complete list of products on which negotiations were intended. The commission was required to report to the president (1) the maximum decreases in duty that could be made on any such item without causing or threatening to cause serious injury to the domestic industry; and (2) the minimum increase that might be necessary to avoid serious injury or the threat thereof. If the president ignored the advice of the commission, he was required to report his reasons for doing so to Congress.

57. Statement of the Legal Advisor to the Director-General (GATT document C/M/ 220) quoted in the section on paragraph 3 of Article XXVIII in GATT, *Guide to GATT Law and Practice*, 6th ed. (Geneva: GATT Secretariat, 1994). A specific example of re-taliation based on this rule of thumb was the EEC's request to the GATT Council in March and April 1988 to authorize the retaliatory withdrawal of equivalent con-cessions granted to the United States in respect of specific products, following the adoption in 1987 of the panel report on United States—Taxes on Petroleum and Cer-tain Imported Substances.

58. Curzon, *Multilateral Commercial Diplomacy*, 87. The same view is expressed in Kock, *International Trade Policy*, 95.

59. Kock, *International Trade Policy*, 97.

60. This position was due, according to Curzon, to the peculiar circumstances in which the United Kingdom inadvertently found itself as a result of the commitment to cap preference margins under Article I of GATT 1947. This commitment prevented the United Kingdom from raising unbound items, which therefore claimed that it was deprived of benefits enjoyed by other contracting parties. The contracting parties to GATT "carefully and suspiciously studied" (66) the issue and granted a waiver under strict conditions. The United Kingdom remained unsatisfied and consequently blocked tariff liberalization proposals based on a formula approach.

61. Curzon, *Multilateral Commercial Diplomacy*, 94–95.

62. "Memorandum from Secretary of State Rusk to President Kennedy," Washington, September 11, 1961, *Foreign Relations of the United States* 9 (1960–1961), 475.

63. Three reasons were given: the fact that the United States had been adversely af-fected by the quantitative restrictions imposed by European countries in the immedi-ate postwar period, the balance-of-payment deficit of the United States, and the fact that the European countries wished to minimize discrimination against the United States resulting from the establishment of the EEC. See note 62 for reference.

64. "Memorandum from Secretary of State Rusk to President Kennedy," Washington, September 11, 1961, *Foreign Relations of the United States* 9 (1960–1961), 475.

65. The policy options that were considered by the president are found in *Foreign Relations of the United States* 9 (1960–1961), 484–495.

66. Committee on Ways and Means, House of Representatives, 87th Congress, 2nd Session, "Trade Expansion Act of 1962, President's Message," March 13, 1962 (Wash-ington, DC: U.S. Government Printing Office, 1962), 2.

67. Committee on Ways and Means, House of Representatives, 87th Congress, 2nd Session, "Trade Expansion Act of 1962, President's Message," March 13, 1962 (Wash-ington, DC: U.S. Government Printing Office, 1962), 9–10.

68. Committee on Ways and Means, House of Representatives, 87th Congress, 2nd Session, "Trade Expansion Act of 1962, President's Message," March 13, 1962 (Washington, DC: U.S. Government Printing Office, 1962).

69. "Telegram from the Department of State to the Mission to the European Communities," Washington, May 17, 1963, *Foreign Relations of the United States* 9 (1960–1961), 606.

70. "Circular Telegram from the Department of State to Certain Diplomatic Missions," Washington, May 4, 1963, *Foreign Relations of the United States* 9 (1960–1961), 599.

71. "Circular telegram from the Department of State to Certain Diplomatic Missions," *Foreign Relations of the United States* 9 (1960–1961), 599.

72. Kock, *International Trade Policy*, 104.

73. Thomas B. Curtis and John Robert Vastine Jr., *The Kennedy Round and the Future of American Trade* (New York: Praeger, 1971), 9.

74. Office of the Special Representative for Trade Negotiations, *General Agreement on Tariffs and Trade, 1964–1967 Trade Conference, Geneva, Switzerland, Report on United States Negotiations*, Vol. I, i.

75. George P. Auld, *Rebuilding Trade by Tariff Bargaining* (New York: National Foreign Trade Council, 1936), 10.

76. "Memorandum from the Under Secretary of State (Ball) to President Kennedy," Washington, March 8, 1963, *Foreign Relations of the United States* 9 (1961–1963), 582.

77. Canada, Australia, South Africa, and New Zealand did not participate in the formula cut by virtue of their trade structure, namely, that imports were concentrated in industrial products while exports were concentrated in primary products. Except for bound items, agricultural products were excluded from the formula cut. Most developing countries were also excused from participation in the formula cut on the basis of the principle of nonreciprocity.

5

Market Access Bargaining in the Uruguay Round: How Tightly Does Reciprocity Constrain?

J. Michael Finger, Ulrich Reincke, and Adriana Castro

How tightly are trade negotiators constrained to win a dollar of concession for each dollar they give? Our examination of the outcome of the Uruguay Round tariff negotiations indicates that such a constraint is not tight. None of the delegations we interviewed had attempted to calculate for themselves the extent of concessions *received*. In addition, we found that the surplus or deficit of concessions received over concessions given varied widely among countries. Measured by percentage point dollar of concessions given and received (a percentage point dollar is a reduction of the tariff by one percentage point on $1 of imports, or by trading partners on exports), the outcome of the negotiations varied enormously from one country to another. For thirteen of twenty-seven countries, *net concessions* (positive or negative) were at least 75 percent as large as concessions received.

Our interviews with delegations revealed a widespread perception of the negotiations as "equal sacrifice for the common good," under which all countries were expected to cut tariffs on the same percentage of imports. An element of ability to pay was also present, a smaller fraction of imports for developing countries. Particularly when we include *unilateral liberalization* by developing countries—including the part of it that was not bound at the Uruguay Round—we find a tendency toward equality (of percentage of imports affected) across the participating country's concessions.

Another point that delegations brought out was the importance to a delegation to look after the interests of politically important sectors—for example, rice for Japan and Korea, and textiles for the United States and the European Union (EU).

Economists widely agree that unilateral free trade augments the national economic interest. Economists perhaps even more widely accept that bargaining at the General Agreement on Tariffs and Trade (GATT) rounds has been motivated and controlled by reciprocity—each government treats its trade restrictions as assets and will reduce them only in exchange for equivalent reductions by trading partners. This presumption, that trade liberalization through the GATT is built on reciprocity, seems to be an even more solid part of economists' folklore than is a preference for free trade.

This study will explore market access bargaining—particularly tariff bargaining—at the Uruguay Round. There are two general objectives:

1. *To measure the extent of country participation in market access bargaining*—the degree to which countries agreed to reciprocal liberalization or to bind under GATT or previous World Trade Organization (WTO) rules unilateral liberalization.

2. *To analyze the basis of the success in market access bargaining that was achieved at the round.* Was the successful outcome attributable to a rigid adherence to reciprocity in bargaining—a dollar of concessions received by each party for each dollar of concession given? Or is this success the result of a more relaxed view of reciprocity, one that recognizes other reasons to agree to reduce tariffs, such as the contribution of individual liberalizations to constructing an international system within which all may prosper—or even the domestic gains that liberalization brings?

The following section explores several hypotheses or models that might explain the motives and disciplines that propel and control tariff bargaining at GATT negotiations. The following sections explain how we have measured tariff concessions given and received at the Uruguay Round, then used these findings to evaluate the relevance of the various models that we have advanced to explain tariff negotiations. Section 5.8 provides our conclusions.

5.1 Hypotheses about the Nature of Bargaining

What do trade negotiators do, what motivates them (i.e., what are they out to achieve), and how do they score their successes and failures?

Analytically speaking, one can identify two basic models that explain the motivation and the structure of a country's participation in multilateral market access negotiations. The two models, which we label the "mercantilist bargaining model" and the "common good" model, are described below. The models need not be mutually exclusive—reality may involve aspects of both of them. In this spirit, the models will be used to interpret the measured results of the Uruguay Round tariff bargaining.

The Mercantilist Bargaining Model

What You Get Is What You Pay for

The mercantilist bargaining model, to economists, is the obvious model. Trade negotiators (at least those who conduct the market access negotiations, the subject of this chapter) bargain over market access—to gain a reduction of other countries' tariffs at the cost of a reduction of one's own. Ernest Preeg (1995, 27–28), explaining why a multisector negotiated approach to liberalization is more effective than unilateral liberal or sector-specific negotiations, writes:

Governments [in the latter case] confront sharply focused political opposition that can best be neutralized by counterbalancing gains for particular export industries in other sectors. The overall "gains from trade" for consumers unfortunately lack political force. A balance of specific "benefits" and "concessions" thus constitutes the political basis for the comprehensive approach for trade negotiations.

Paul Krugman (1997, 114) is even more direct:

Anyone who has tried to make sense of international trade negotiations eventually realizes that they can only be understood by realizing that they are a game scored according to mercantilist rules, in which an increase in exports ... is a victory, and an increase in imports ... is a defeat. The implicit mercantilist theory that underlies trade negotiations does not make sense on any level ... but it nonetheless governs actual policy.

Likewise, Gilbert Winham (1986, 62) in his analysis of the Kennedy Round, notes that "the principle of reciprocity is a determinant of bargaining behavior." This principle "leads negotiators to develop certain procedures and measures for evaluating the progress of a negotiation ... [f]or example, 'duty reduction' and 'volume of imports,' ... [that] no doubt make trade bargaining easier, but do not make much sense in economic terms."

Though the Kennedy Round was a multilateral negotiation that (formally) applied an across-the-board tariff-cutting formula rather than item-by-item bargaining, Winham observes (1986, 64–65) that "participants quickly found that meaningful concessions usually could be given only between the principal supplier of individual goods and the major importers."

Within this model, what you get is what you pay for. It treats market access bargaining as an application of the straightforward mercantilist calculus that measures gaining access to foreign markets as a benefit, and giving up access to the domestic market as a cost.

Complications to the Mercantilist Bargaining Model

There are two basic sources of complications: (1) the possibility of noneconomic objectives, and (2) the frictions that might occur in balancing the interests of industries that will gain (export industries) versus those that will lose (import-competing industries) in the reciprocal bargaining of market access.

Noneconomic Objectives

War, according to Clausewitz, is the pursuit of diplomacy through other means. Often, so is trade policy. While the mercantilist bargaining model accurately describes the commercial interests that pressure government policy, the government may itself have other—noneconomic—objectives. After World War I, a number of leaders saw freedom of commerce as an important instrument for maintaining world peace. Freedom of international commerce was the third of U.S. President Wilson's Fourteen Points. To Cordell Hull, secretary of state for President Franklin D. Roosevelt, the link was straightforward: "[U]nhampered trade dovetailed with peace; high tariffs, trade barriers and unfair economic competition with war" (Hull 1948, 81).

Likewise, after World War II leadership in Europe and in the United States saw economic union in Europe and the construction of an open global trading system perhaps more as strategic objectives than as economic ones. Their view of the good of such arrangements paid more attention to the prevention of future wars than to the dollars-and-cents calculations of efficiency or welfare gains that economists are conditioned to interpret as gains.

However, the presence of such noneconomic objectives need not discredit the mercantilist bargaining model of the negotiating process. To leaders motivated by such objectives, reciprocal bargaining is a tactic by which they can move toward their objective. The reduction of trade barriers—by whatever process and without regard to the motives of the interests that support the process—moves them toward their objective. Indeed, a government that can mobilize non-economic motives into significant support for trade liberalization will be in a position to play a hegemonic role (as the United States did) and give up larger concessions than it receives in exchange.

Frictions, Transferring National Gains to National Losers

For a government motivated toward trade liberalization, the deciding trade-offs are not between it and foreign governments, but between domestic winners and losers—between exporting and import-competing domestic industries. The bargaining process ties access to foreign markets to the granting of access to the domestic market, and thereby mobilizes export interests to favor import liberalization. In the U.S. political process, an important application of the leverage export interests provide is in the passage of legislation that grants the president the authority to negotiate—that grants him the legal authority to reduce U.S. tariffs.

Overcoming resistance from import-competing industries has been, in practice, part power—using export industries to win more congressional votes than the opposition could rally—and part compensation. Adjustment assistance, which in 1980 dispensed $1.6 billion to import-competing industries and workers is the best example of compensation, though public works and other programs that would be more literally described as bribery than as compensation have also been used.[1]

Another way in which governments attempt to minimize the problem of compensating losers is by taking advantage of the large volume of intra-industry trade that characterizes the modern trading system. To the extent that concessions given by an industry can be offset by concessions received on the products exported by the same industry, the government need not develop inter-industry mechanisms for balancing losers against winners. Gilbert Winham reports (1986, 65) that during the Kennedy Round there evolved a tendency to look for such "self-balancing sectors." From a political standpoint this informal negotiating practice would be practical as it would reduce the need for cross-industry compensation mechanisms.

Taking into account that the politics of negotiations across industries will require cross-industry compensation mechanisms—and that these mechanisms will not be frictionless—does not change the basic mercantilist metric of the reciprocal bargaining model. It does, however, suggest that—other factors given—a country's concessions given and concessions received will tend toward industries where intra-industry trade is large.

A variant of the reciprocal bargaining model, relevant to developing countries that have unilaterally liberalized, focuses on binding such liberalization internationally as defense against later backsliding. Against pressures for new import restrictions the government can respond that to do so would violate an international commitment. If further pressed, the government can mobilize export interests by pointing out that under the international agreement, unauthorized import restrictions can lead to authorized retaliation by trading partners.

The Common Good Model

Individual Sacrifice for the Common Good

Many of the participants in the initial International Trade Organization (ITO) and GATT negotiations viewed their task as the construction of a *system*, from which all countries would derive significant noneconomic benefits—perhaps economic benefits also, but the emphasis was usually on noneconomic benefits. The model differs from the mercantilist bargaining model in that the benefits a participant gets are not unequivocally identified with the particular market access concessions that the country receives—the link between contribution and benefit is amorphous, resulting from the collective nature of the system rather than from any particular element of it.

Within the mercantilist bargaining model, the appropriate yardstick for an individual country's success in the negotiations would be the excess of its concessions received over its concessions given. The common good model focuses not on the successes of individual countries but on the success of the group. Within this model, *success* would be gauged in a collective way, for example, by overall reduction of trade restrictions, and *fairness* by comparing the contributions of countries to the system, for example, concessions given by one country compared with concessions given by other countries.

This model, in which negotiators see their activity as reaching agreement to accept individual sacrifice for the common good, describes well the situation in which the shared objective is noneconomic, such as creating a web of economic activity, interests, and enterprises that span international borders so as to minimize the likelihood of armed conflict. It underlies several insightful analyses of previous rounds, such as Robert Hudec's analysis (1987) of the position of developing countries in the GATT system. Hudec's focus is to explain how GATT members came to accept "special and differential treatment" as the appropriate attitude toward developing countries. In constructing any system out of the contributions of its members, it is difficult to ask poorer members to contribute proportionally with the richer.

5.2 Lessons from Experimental Economics

Experimental economics has paid considerable attention to bargaining experiments; thus, this literature can offer insights into a better understanding of both the negotiating process and the likely outcomes of international trade negotiations. In the experimental bargaining context, bargaining structures (institutions) and bargaining or market interactions turn out to be key elements in determining possible outcomes.

In simple bilateral bargaining games, researchers have found 50/50 splits to be more the rule than the exception (Davis and Holt 1993). This is true even when the bargaining is structured so that one of the subjects has the opportunity to capture all of the prize that is at stake. In situations[2] in which one party (called the "controller") enjoys the power to decide how the outcome will be allocated, these controllers recurrently fail to exploit their full bargaining position and accept an equal split. It is interesting to notice, however, that this "benevolent" behavior tends to occur more often in cases where the property rights are randomly assigned (as with the toss of a coin). If the party in control (the one making the offer) feels that he has "earned the right" to be the controller, then the incidence of an equal split offer tends to be reduced.

The important lesson from those bargaining experiments is that there is something more than individual payoff maximization in explaining behavior (and the realized outcomes). The idea of fairness plays an important role in the outcomes. Players often will not exploit their advantage and claim the entire reward unless the bargaining situation is structured so as to provide a sense that they have earned this reward, that is, a reason to think that it is reasonable and fair to do so. Benevolent controllers may be motivated by the fear of rejection of "unreasonable" proposals, or they may be concerned with the opinion of outsiders. But even in cases in which the controller is given dictatorial power—the other party cannot refuse the outcome that the controller specifies—experimenters have observed that controllers do not necessarily claim all of the prize for themselves. (Other things equal, controllers in a dictatorial position do tend to take a larger share than in cases in which the other party can refuse to accept, or block the game.)

Why, however, would a dictator be reluctant to maximize his own payoff? An attempt to answer this question looked at the case where every action and decision were absolutely anonymous so that no one would know who made which decision—not even the person who designed and ran the experiment. In this experiment, dictators dramatically increased their share of the prize, taking all of it in more than 60 percent of the trials. From these results, the experimenters conclude that opinions of outsiders do influence bargaining behavior, more so than the payoffs available to other players (Hoffman et al. 1994).

In conclusion, the findings of experimental economics suggest that the idea of fairness will be important to outcomes in a bargaining situation such as bilateral or multilateral trade negotiations. Public exposure matters, perhaps more than an abstract sense of fairness. A party in a strong bargaining position is less inclined to exploit that power when it will be evident to all participants that the stronger party has more or less dictated the outcome—that is, when he senses that a relevant peer group might not approve. However, when the process provides the party in the stronger position a sense of having earned that position, there is a notably increased tendency to exploit it.

5.3   Conversations with Negotiators

Examining quantitatively the balance of concessions given and received is one way to evaluate hypotheses about delegations' objectives and standards. It is also possible to evaluate such hypotheses by asking delegations how they negotiated and how they evaluated and presented the outcome they achieved. Such conversations were held in September 1994 after the Uruguay Round Agreements had been signed in Marrakech on April 15, 1994. These conversations brought out several related points:

- Powerful constituencies had to be accommodated.
- Selling the agreement at home—that is, gaining approval—was an important consideration, particularly in the last months when the negotiations were being mopped up.
- A sense of fairness, of appropriate contribution, was an important concept.

Accommodating Constituencies and Selling the Agreement at Home

The first two points are perhaps obvious, but their weight on how delegations evaluated the outcome of the negotiations needs a word of explanation. From our conversations we developed the impression that satisfying powerful constituencies was much more important than any evaluation of the overall balance of concessions received versus concessions given. Because of the obvious need to gain governmental approval (implementation) for any agreement reached, delegations sought to avoid calling attention to concessions given. Evaluation tended to be across general issue areas (TRIPs, antidumping, dispute settlement), and in areas in which a delegation accepted losses (i.e., areas in which the outcome was opposed at home) the delegation's presentations tended to emphasize what was gained on other items within the issue area and how the final agreement on the losing issue was better than other alternatives that had been on the table. The tendency was to present everything as a victory, nothing as a concession given.

No delegation of the ten with whom we spoke mentioned having tallied concessions received versus concessions made, either within the tariff access negotiations or across the span of the Uruguay Round agreements. One delegation did comment that SELA had provided useful tabulations of concessions tabled by trading partners of the South American and Caribbean countries.

Several delegations explained that their governments, internally, did recognize the irrelevance of a mercantilist toting up and saw the round as an instrument of their domestic reforms. But even they, in selling the round domestically, found it useful to make certain mercantilist points. For them, the mercantilism of the process was somewhat more for appearance' sake than for substance—the domestic politics of the situation rather than the international politics. The more, however, that client-oriented domestic politics was the determining characteristic of a delegation's behavior, the more mercantilist was that delegation's evaluation in substance. But even delegations whose evaluations were substantially mercantilist in concept made no attempt at a formal tallying up of *overall* domestic benefits versus domestic costs. (As already noted, there was considerable reluctance to present anything as a cost.) No delegation was aware of any calculation of concessions received such as we have presented here.

As to how powerful constituencies were assuaged, there seem to have been many ways. The U.S. delegation, for example, under pressure from the U.S. textile industry, negotiated hard-to-extract concessions on fibers and fabrics from major exporters of apparel. In other cases, a powerful domestic constituency was honored by the delegation holding out until the deadline before accepting an agreement that gave less than what the constituency wanted. The Korean delegation, for example, to emphasize that what was given was the minimum that could be given, did not concede on a commitment to increase its imports of rice until the final moments before the deadline for completing the round.

Achieving Appropriate Contributions from All

Particularly in their last month (the mopping up), the tariff negotiations devoted significant attention to ensuring that each participating country had made an appropriate contribution to the tariff reduction exercise. Delegations widely but informally accepted that the target for industrial countries was an average reduction of one-third, and for developing countries an average reduction of one-fourth.[3] Achieving these targets intertwined with how countries would receive "credit" for unilateral tariff reductions and for extensions of bindings that did not imply tariff cuts. It was also influenced by the fact that founding the World Trade Organization (WTO) was one of the Uruguay Round agreements.

No specification for measuring "officially" how much a county had reduced its tariffs was ever agreed on or, for that matter, even debated. The Punta del Este Declaration[4] (Part I.G) mandated that the Group of Negotiations on Goods "conduct an evaluation of the results obtained ... in terms of the Objectives and the General Principles Governing Negotiations," but the relevant objectives and general principles (Part I.D.—Tariffs) established only broad targets for the tariff negotiations: "to reduce or, as appropriate, eliminate tariffs including the reduction or elimination of high tariffs and tariff escalation. Emphasis shall be given to the expansion of the scope of tariff concessions among all participants."

According to delegations, the informal practice was more or less to count from applied rates in 1986 to the bound rate agreed at the Uruguay Round.[5] By this practice, countries that had, after 1986, unilaterally reduced their tariffs would be given "credit" at the round to the extent that they bound these cuts at the round. No delegation that we interviewed had actually performed such calculations.

For how to take into account bindings that did not imply tariff cuts, for example, ceiling bindings, not even an unofficial approach evolved. Toward the end of 1990, the Mexican delegation circulated a nonpaper[6] that argued that credit be given for expansions of the scope of bindings, but did not offer a method for measuring its "tariff cut equivalent." Later, the chairman of the Market Access Group provided guidelines for such measurement, including a matrix of suggested equivalents between depth of tariff cut and scope of expansion of bindings. The view of the negotiators with whom we spoke is that these guidelines were not followed—there never emerged even notional agreement on how to convert extension of bindings into a tariff cut equivalent.

Though Canada's proposal in April 1990 to create a WTO was slow to win support (Preeg 1995, 114) by the time the negotiations were coming to a close, the general sense of agreement that the WTO proposal would be approved did influence the outcome of the tariff negotiations. In the informal tallying up, negotiators informed us, delegations were reluctant not to accept a country's tariff offer that seemed a few percentage points short of the unofficial targets of one-third reduction by the industrial or one-fourth reduction by the developing countries. To do so would prevent the country from being a charter member of the WTO—leave the country out of the new institution that was being created. In such cases, notice was taken of extension of ceiling bindings, that is, the extension of ceiling bindings provided a pretext to accept an offer that countries were, for other reasons, inclined to accept.

The exercise in achieving appropriate contributions from all parties allows several generalizations about the negotiating process. First, obvious trade-offs existed from one part of the negotiations to another and the all-or-nothing character of the WTO proposal required that a country accept the disciplines of *all* the agreements if it became a WTO member. In contrast, a country could choose not to accept any or all of the Tokyo Round codes and still remain a full member of the GATT. Accepting all of these disciplines could reasonably be interpreted by trading partners as worth as much as another percentage point coverage of tariff reduction.[7]

5.4 Data and Measurements

Our basic data source was the Integrated Data Base (IDB)[8] that is maintained by the secretariat of the WTO. The IDB covers all industrial and transition economies that participated in the Uruguay Round, plus 26 of 94 developing economy participants. Complete data for the calculations described below were available for 33 countries and the European Union.[9]

There is no "official" measure of the tariff reductions exchanged at the round. Strictly speaking, each country agreed to bind its tariff rates at the levels notified—the levels reported in series MFN09F of the IDB. Legally speaking, the exchange that was consummated was this exchange of bindings.[10] We have developed three different measures of the tariff cuts that were implicitly agreed: the reciprocal reduction, the bound reduction, and the total reduction. Each of these is explained below.

The tariff reductions we report below are averages of changes, not changes of averages. The various changes were calculated tariff line by tariff line, then aggregated by country into averages, weighted by their own imports that enter at MFN rates.[11] The changes cover only reductions of MFN tariffs; they do not include the tariff equivalent of the agreed elimination of the MFA, nor do they include the agreed tariffication of NTBs on agricultural products and the agreed reduction of these tariff equivalents. Average applied rates cover all tariff lines but average bound rates cover only those tariff lines that are bound, post Uruguay Round.

Reciprocal Reduction

The calculations labeled "reciprocal reduction" were intended to measure reductions agreed at the Uruguay Round and to exclude the unilateral reductions that were, by accident of timing, introduced during the round,[12] that is, to cover reductions specifically conditioned on reciprocal reductions by trading partners.

A number of countries introduced substantial unilateral reductions of their tariff rates during the years of the Uruguay Round. Where these unilateral changes were reflected in the IDB most-favored-nation (MFN) applied rate (MFN03), we used these rates as the "before"[13] rates to calculate the reciprocal reductions. Where the MFN03 rates did not reflect the unilateral reductions, we used 1992 applied rates from the TRAINS database. The "after" rate for this calculation we took to be the minimum of the Uruguay Round final offer rate[14] (MFN09F) and the "before" rate. Thus we counted as reciprocal reductions only those instances in which the binding was a commitment to reduce the post-unilateral-liberalization applied rate.

Total Reduction

The "total reduction" measures the overall tariff reduction from "before" the Uruguay Round, chronologically speaking, to the "after" Uruguay Round rate, again chronologically speaking. The "after" rate for this calculation is the same as that used to calculate reciprocal reductions—the lower of the post–Uruguay Round bound rate and the rate that resulted from unilateral liberalization. The "before" rate is the Uruguay Round applied rate for 1986, as provided by the IDB.

Bound Reduction

The "before" rates for the calculations labeled "bound reduction" are the same as the "before" rates for the "total reduction." The "after" rates are the post–Uruguay Round bound rates.

Comparing the Three Concepts

Simplistically speaking, we have for each tariff line for each country, three tariff rates:

- A: the 1986 MFN applied rate,
- B: the 1992 MFN applied rate,
- C: the post–Uruguay Round bound rate.

The changes then are defined as follows:

- Total Reduction: from A to the smaller of B or C,
- Bound Reduction: from A to C,
- Reciprocal Reduction: from B to the smaller of B or C.

Note that the bound reduction and the reciprocal reduction do not add up to the total reduction.

Concessions Received

The second and perhaps the motivating side of the negotiations coin is concessions received. In addition to tabulating concessions given by each participant, we will also tabulate concessions received. Just as concessions given are measured by the depth of cut and the value of imports on which a country agrees to reduce its tariffs, concessions received are measured by the depth of cut of trading partners' cuts on products that a country exports, and the value of exports to those countries.

5.5   Measurement of Participation in the Tariff Negotiations

One of the objectives of the study is to document the countries' participation in the Uruguay Round. From tariff line information recorded by the GATT/WTO secretariat, we will tabulate the extent to which countries agreed at the round to reduce and to bind their import restrictions. Reductions and bindings by countries will be compared, as will be resulting levels of import restrictions and of bindings.

Arithmetically, once concessions given are calculated, by tariff line, for each country as an importer, concessions received can be tabulated for any country by aggregating over the imports of all other countries from the subject country.[15]

5.6   Tariff Concessions Given: The Common Good Hypothesis

The common good hypothesis has a straightforward empirical implication: that countries will reduce tariffs by more or less the same amount. GATT's history of special and differential treatment for developing countries suggests that this proposition will be modified by a mercantilist "ability-to-pay" equity consideration, so that developing countries will be expected to make smaller reductions than industrial countries.

Reciprocal Concessions

The size of reciprocal concessions given by selected countries are given in table 5.1. The first column follows normal GATT usage and measures the change as a percentage of the initial ad valorem or ad valorem equivalent tariff level. The second column measures the tariff reduction as the change divided by unity plus the ad valorem tariff rate. For many purposes this is a more economically meaningful measure of the impact of the tariff cut than the percentage change of the ad valorem rate. For a small country, one whose imports do not affect world prices, $dT/(1 + T)$ measures the percentage by which the domestic price of the imported product will decline as a result of the tariff cut. If the concern is market access, it would be inappropriate, for example, to treat the halving of a 2 percent tariff as equivalent to the halving of a 50 percent tariff. The latter change would allow a 20 percent improvement of the (after tariff) price the importer receives, the former a less than 1 percent improvement—as $dT/(1 + T)$ measures.

The common good model implies that countries will be expected to make equal contributions or sacrifices, perhaps modified by some accepted ability-to-pay criterion. At the Uruguay Round, ability to pay was reflected in the informal criterion that industrial countries reduce their tariffs overall by one-third, developing countries by one-fourth. To incorporate this criterion, we scaled each country's tariff reduction by the targets—33.3 percent reduction for industrial countries, 25 percent for developing countries. (Thus an industrial country that reduced its tariff by an average of 33.3 percent or a developing country that reduced its tariff by 25 percent would have an index value of 100.)

The data do not support the hypothesis that countries would be induced to make uniform reductions. As a test of the common contribution hypothesis, the most striking property of the results reported in table 5.1 is the *lack* of uniformity in contributions. As a percentage of the target contributions of a one-third reduction by the industrial countries and a one-fourth reduction for the developing countries, the actual figures for reciprocal reductions range from 0

Table 5.1
Depth of reciprocal tariff reductions agreed at the Uruguay Round by selected countries and groups

Country or group	dT/Tb (as %) (a)	$dT/(1 + Tb)$ (as %) (b)	Index,[a] dT/T (c)	Index,[b] $dT/(1 + T)$ (d)
Australia	18.2	3.18	54	158
Austria	32.2	3.60	97	178
Canada	9.6	0.87	29	43
European Union	35.5	2.13	107	105
Finland	23.1	2.43	69	120
Japan	22.6	1.02	68	50
New Zealand	5.3	0.78	16	39
Norway	17.3	2.11	52	105
Sweden	29.3	1.48	88	73
Switzerland	27.8	0.89	84	44
United States	23.2	1.03	70	51
Target, industrial	*33.3*	*2.03*	*100*	*100*
Argentina	0.0	0.00	0	0
Brazil	0.0	0.00	0	0
Chile	0.0	0.00	0	0
Colombia	0.0	0.02	0	0
Czech & Slovak U.	19.8	0.98	79	20
Hong Kong	0.0	0.00	0	0
Hungary	16.7	1.69	67	34
Iceland	0.8	0.18	3	4
India	13.8	5.52	55	110
Indonesia	0.7	0.23	3	5
Korea Rep.	42.6	5.64	170	113
Malaysia	21.5	1.84	86	37
Mexico	0.0	0.00	0	0
Peru	0.0	0.02	0	0
Philippines	5.0	1.22	20	24
Poland	10.9	1.26	44	25
Singapore	3.8	0.78	15	16
Sri Lanka	0.0	0.01	0	0
Thailand	17.1	5.29	68	106
Tunisia	0.0	0.02	0	0
Turkey	13.2	2.85	53	57
Uruguay	0.0	0.00	0	0
Venezuela	0.4	0.12	2	2
Target, developing	*25*	*5.00*	*100*	*100*

Table 5.1 (continued)

---

[a] Each country's tariff reduction as a percentage of the Uruguay Round informal targets of one-third reduction by industrial countries and one-fourth reduction by other countries.
[b] Each country's tariff reduction as a percentage of the target calculated as follows: (i) The pre–Uruguay Round average tariff for industrial countries and for developing countries were 6.5 percent and 25 percent, respectively. A one-third reduction of the 6.5 percent rate comes to 2.03, when measured by $dT/(1 + T)$; likewise a one-fourth reduction of the 25 percent rate comes to 5 percent when measured by $dT/(1 + T)$. Consequently in this column, 2.03 is the base for the index values for the industrial countries, 5 percent for the index values for the developing countries.

percent to 170 percent (column c). In the following section, we look into the possibility that the target criteria applied to the bound or the total reductions rather than to the reciprocal reductions.

Total and Bound Concessions

Table 5.2 compares the uniformity of reciprocal, bound, and total tariff reductions given at the Uruguay Round. As there was informal agreement at the round to grant credit for tariff reductions that had been made unilaterally but were now bound under the GATT/WTO, we would expect that countries would measure their contributions to the common good by the metric of bound concessions rather than concessions whose reduction was narrowly conditioned on the Uruguay Round negotiations.

Results reported in table 5.2 show that this was indeed the case. The coefficient of variation of tariff reductions[16] across all countries falls by one-half when we move from reciprocal cuts to bound cuts—for developing countries, it falls by two-thirds. It seems evident then that the binding of unilateral tariff reductions was treated at the round as an action of substantial value.

Table 5.3 shows that the same result applies when we measure the tariff reductions by the formula $dT/(1 + T)$. Again the coefficient of variation is much lower for bound reductions than for reciprocal reductions. Again, the reduced variation is mostly among the developing countries.

What then can we conclude from our examination of the "equal contributions to the common good" hypothesis?

The most dramatic finding is the lack of uniformity across countries in the depth of concessions given.

Table 5.2
Indices of reciprocal, bound and total tariff reductions given at the Uruguay Round, by selected countries

	Reciprocal[a]	Bound[b]	Total[b]
Industrial countries[c]			
Australia	54	125	195
Austria	97	105	98
Canada	29	152	152
European Union	107	132	132
Finland	69	69	na
Hong Kong	0	0	0
Iceland	2	77	77
Japan	68	203	209
New Zealand	16	174	225
Norway	52	132	132
Singapore	11	193	288
Sweden	88	114	na
Switzerland	84	98	98
United States	70	130	130
Czech & Slovak U	59	71	72
Hungary	50	77	84
Poland	33	122	152
Developing countries[d]			
Argentina	0	78	176
Brazil	0	114	282
Chile	0	113	273
Colombia	0	70	278
India	55	153	190
Indonesia	3	14	150
Korea Rep.	170	204	275
Malaysia	86	125	156
Mexico	0	93	298
Peru	0	76	184
Philippines	20	38	148
Sri Lanka	0	16	75
Thailand	68	77	240
Tunisia	0	14	55
Turkey	53	56	245
Uruguay	0	34	67
Venezuela	2	30	254
*Stdev/Mean * 100*[e]			
All countries	111	57	47
Industrial countries	66	42	51
Developing countries	168	67	39

Table 5.2 (continued)

[a] Calculated from average tariff reductions by the formula dT/T_0, where T_0 is the tariff rate before the change.
[b] Calculated from average tariff reductions by the formula dT/T_{avg}, where T_{avg} is the average of the tariff rates before and after the change.
[c] For industrial countries, the index is based on the informally presumed one-third overall reduction.
[d] For developing countries, the index is based on the informally presumed one-fourth overall reduction.
[e] Calculation of these summary statistics did not include Finland and Sweden.

Table 5.3
Variation among countries of tariff reductions given at the Uruguay Round (reduction measured as $dT/[1 + (T_0 + T_1)/2]$)

	Reciprocal reduction	Bound reduction	Total reduction
All countries[a]			
Standard deviation	1.79	4.61	8.24
Mean	1.44	5.68	11.50
Stdev/Mean * 100	125	81	72
Industrial C's[a]			
Standard deviation	1.02	3.33	4.89
Mean	1.42	4.63	5.90
Stdev/Mean * 100	72	72	83
Developing C's[a]			
Standard deviation	2.27	5.34	7.39
Mean	1.46	6.59	16.45
Stdev/Mean * 100	155	81	45

[a] The country coverage is the same as for table 5.2.

In evaluating this lack of uniformity, we should of course remember that the tariff were only a part of the negotiations. There were fourteen other negotiating groups, hence what a country gave or did not give in the tariff negotiations may reflect what the country received or did not receive in the other negotiations. The other negotiations were however mainly about rules (antidumping, dispute settlement, etc.) in which the outcome for one country was the same as for another. While there might be reason for different countries to evaluate differently the value of such an outcome, that evaluation should have been more or less the same among similar groups of countries, for example, among the industrial countries or among the developing countries.

We do not find uniformity even among groups. Excluding Hong Kong, whose free trade policies leave her no tariffs reductions to contribute, bound cuts among the industrial countries still range from about two-thirds of the 33.3 percent target to over 200 percent. Likewise, among developing countries, bound cuts for a number of countries were less than half of the target 25 percent cut; for other developing countries, bound cuts were well over 100 percent of the target—for Korea, over twice the target.

While many delegations informed us that there was a shared concern that all negotiating countries contribute equally (or equitably), loyalty to this concern seems to have been more notional than rigorous. There was minimal policing of the standard, no official tabulation of depth of cut by country, and from what we learned from delegations, minimal informal tabulation.

Binding unilateral concessions did seem to count in the round. When we take these liberalizations into account along with cuts tied to reciprocal cuts agreed at the round, the contributions across countries are considerably more uniform.

5.7 Concessions Received versus Concessions Given: The Mercantilist Bargaining Hypothesis

The view of tariff bargaining most familiar to economists focuses not on the amount of concessions that a country gives but on the net of concessions received over concessions given. According to this model, the objective of each negotiator is to gain a net advantage, or "profit," but the negotiating or competitive process pushes the level of profits toward zero. We should expect therefore that for each country the net of concessions received over concessions given will be close to zero.[17]

To evaluate this hypothesis, we tabulated the value of concessions received by each of the countries in our sample, then the net of concessions given over concessions received.[18] In the first three columns of table 5.4, we compare the depth of tariff cut received and the depth of tariff cut given for each country in our sample. (The cuts are calculated according to the more economically sensible measure $dT/\{1 + T\}$.) It is obvious that the net cuts are not uniform over countries. India agreed (reciprocal cut) to reduce its tariff by about 6 percent, in exchange for a slightly larger than 1 percent cut by trading partners on India's exports. Hong Kong, on the other hand, had no tariffs to cut, but received an average cut of almost $2^1/_2$ percent on its exports. Because the economically sensible formula $dT/(1+T)$ assigns higher values to cuts in higher tariffs than does the formula dT/T, those higher tariff countries that made substantial cuts generally tended to have negative balances.

The second, fourth, fifth and sixth columns of table 5.4 take into account not only the depth of tariff cuts but also the value of exports or imports on which the cut applies—measures concessions received and concessions given in "percentage-point dollars." We see again a very large variation in the "mercantilist balance" of concessions received over concessions given. Of thirty-three countries for which we have figures, twenty-three had an imbalance—positive or negative—at least half as large as their concessions given.

At the bottom of the table we provide two summary measures of this variation: the sum of the absolute difference divided by the sum of concessions received, and the overlap index.[19] The overlap index measures the percentage of the total number of two different things that have "mates," when both items are distributed among the same categories. For example, if one box contains one knife and nine forks, the other box contains zero knives and nine forks, then of the total of nineteen forks and knives, only two (one fork and one knife) have mates within their category, or box.[20] According to the overlap index, only 29 percent of percentage point dollars of concessions given were matched by concessions received by the same country.

5.8 Final Remarks

Though it seems obvious that mercantilism (aversion to imports, attraction to exports) provides the thrust for the GATT/WTO trade negotiations, we found little evidence that governments evaluate their own performance by a mercantilist standard of export concessions received less import access concessions given. None of the delegations we interviewed were aware of such calculations, either by their own governments or by others. Likewise, we found that when measured by net concessions received, the outcome of the negotiations varied enormously from one country to another.

While the process may be driven by the mercantilist instinct, there did seem to be imposed on it a mercantilist sense of community, or

Table 5.4
Reciprocal tariff concessions received and given at the Uruguay Round

	Percent tariff reduction[a]			Mercantilist balance, in percentage point dollars[b]		
	Received	Given	Received minus given	Concessions received	Concessions given	Received minus given, as percent of received
Australia	0.76	3.35	−2.59	21,032	88,162	−319
Austria	2.64	3.74	−1.11	74,602	108,820	−46
Canada	0.22	0.89	−0.67	5,291	26,205	−395
European Union	1.94	2.19	−0.26	578,816	627,939	−8
Finland	3.47	2.52	0.95	63,924	44,021	31
Hong Kong	2.36	0.00	2.36	60,258	0	100
Iceland	1.59	0.20	1.39	2,151	299	86
Japan	2.06	1.06	1.00	481,006	143,142	70
New Zealand	0.84	0.83	0.01	5,126	4,155	19
Norway	1.15	2.17	−1.03	24,250	44,263	−83
Singapore	1.96	0.85	1.11	50,294	32,741	35
Switzerland	2.15	0.89	1.25	100,659	46,829	53
United States	1.21	1.07	0.14	214,791	283,580	−32
Czech & Slovak U	2.06	1.05	1.01	9,773	7,312	25
Hungary	1.82	1.69	0.13	7,755	13,727	−77
Poland	1.36	1.26	0.09	8,609	7,112	17
Argentina[c]	0.98	0.00	0.98	6,331	0	100
Brazil	1.37	0.00	1.36	38,037	98	100
Chile[c]	0.50	0.00	0.50	3,291	0	100
Colombia	1.25	0.02	1.23	6,323	81	99
India	1.22	6.16	−4.94	14,380	67,172	−367
Indonesia	0.87	0.25	0.63	16,222	3,355	79
Korea Rep.	1.87	5.99	−4.12	100,809	262,918	−161
Malaysia	1.46	1.97	−0.51	36,108	28,966	20
Mexico	0.16	0.00	0.16	960	3	100
Peru	0.57	0.03	0.54	1,586	58	96
Philippines	2.43	1.29	1.14	19,748	12,847	35
Sri Lanka	1.36	0.01	1.35	1,595	33	98
Thailand	1.33	5.93	−4.60	20,564	95,953	−367
Tunisia	1.42	0.02	1.40	2,506	72	97
Turkey	1.72	3.00	−1.27	12,557	32,661	−160
Uruguay[c]	0.52	0.00	0.51	772	6	99
Venezuela	0.21	0.13	0.08	2,051	806	61
	Sum abs diff/Sum of rec'vd, as % = 137			Sum abs diff/Sum of rec'vd, as % = 58		
	Overlap index = 42			Overlap index = 29		

Table 5.4 (continued)

[a] Weighted average of change measured as $dT/(1 + T_{avg}) * 100$, where T_{avg} is the average of the before and after change rates, calculated across all tariff lines, including those on which there was no reduction.

[b] Tariff cut as measured in the first or second column multiplied by the value (in millions of dollars) of the imports or exports to which the importing country applies MFN tariff rates.

equal sacrifice (import concessions) for the common good. Delegations emphasized that as the round was coming to an end, the standard of one-third cut by the developed countries, one-fourth cut by the developing economies, became an important yardstick. This system of control is, however, anything but precise. Conceptually, the conversations and nonpapers that demonstrate a concern for equal sacrifice (tempered by ability of the developing countries to pay) did not go into how to measure tariff cuts—for example, dT/T or $dt/(1 + T)$—how to balance off depth versus scope of cut, or how to take into account that some countries started from different levels of protection—for example, it would be difficult for Hong Kong, China, or Singapore to contribute to the tariff cuts. Empirically, the data shows a lot of variation from country to country in the depth and in the scope of cuts.

We do, however, observe in the results indications that the developing countries were given credit for binding under the WTO tariff cuts that had been made unilaterally, and even for tariff cuts that were applied but not bound. Bound cuts were more uniform than the cuts the developing countries added at the Uruguay Round, total cuts—that included unbound cuts of applied rates—even more uniform than bound cuts.

Two other findings are also important, though we cannot fit them into any particular analytical model—except perhaps the obvious one of agents' self-interest:

· delegations attended to their country's powerful constituencies,

· delegations avoided calculations that would allow a comparison of one delegation's "score" with another's.

Notes

1. Zeller (1992) provides examples of the deals President John F. Kennedy made to win congressional approval of the Trade Expansion Act of 1962, which gave him the authority to negotiate in what came to be called the Kennedy Round.

2. Well-defined property rights are another property of these games.

3. At the July 7–9, 1993, G-7 summit in Tokyo, the Quadrilateral Trade Ministers announced a substantial market access agreement plus overall goals they hoped to achieve:

• selected products; reductions to zero or harmonization at low levels,
• tariffs 15 percent and above; 50 percent reduction, subject to certain exceptions and similar reductions by other exporting counties,
• other tariffs; negotiated reduction by an average of at least one-third.

The one-third reduction for industrial countries may thus have come from this agreement, but we have not identified the origin of the one-fourth target cut for developing countries.

4. The Punta del Este Declaration, formally titled, "Ministerial Declaration on the Uruguay Round," was published in GATT (1986).

5. The tariffication of NTBs on agricultural products used the 1986–1988 average of their tariff equivalent as the target, but the target was not binding.

6. In GATT/WTO usage, a "nonpaper" is a way to circulate an idea for discussion without proposing that the idea be adopted—a way to advance preliminary discussion. The nonpaper was cosponsored by nineteen other developing countries.

7. The experience shows that there are always fudge factors available. In this case, the treatment of bindings, which could be used as cover for a decision made for other reasons.

8. The IDB includes countries that account for 100 percent of non-petroleum imports of North America, Western Europe, and WTO members (at the time of the Uruguay Round) in Central and Eastern Europe. The IDB covers 90 percent of Asia's non-petroleum imports, 80 percent of Latin America's nonpetroleum imports, but only two sub-Saharan African countries (Senegal and Zimbabwe) who together account for 30 percent of sub-Saharan Africa's nonpetroleum imports.

9. Finger, Ingco, and Reincke (1996) explain in more detail the IDB and the data it contains.

10. Some of these bindings—where the MFN09F rate was below the applied rate—implied tariff reductions. Some did not. For many developing country tariff lines, the MFN09F rates were above applied rates.

11. Imports from free trade area or customs union partners were not included in the weights.

12. By the same token, we did not include tariff changes resulting from regional integration that took place during the round: for example, the formation of NAFTA; Austria, Finland, and Sweden joining the European Union.

13. "Before," of course, relates here to cause, not to chronology.

14. The Uruguay Round agreement allows for a year-by-year staged introduction of tariff reductions. Generally, the MFN final offer rates will be effective no later than January 1, 1999, but some countries have, for some commodities, negotiated later deadlines. The MFN09F rates are the final rates—after all stages are completed.

15. Concessions given are tabulated only over imports from other countries included in the sample. Thus our measures cover concessions given only to other countries in the sample, concessions received only from other countries in the sample.

16. The standard deviation divided by the mean.

17. Again, we found no evidence that any country had ever attempted to tabulate at any GATT round the amount of concessions that it had received. This fact certainly argues against the hypothesis as a description of what negotiators actually do.

18. We took into account only concessions given to the countries in our sample—concessions tabulated over imports from these countries alone.

19. We did not calculate coefficients of variation because the expected value over all countries of percentage point dollars of concessions received minus concessions given is 0.

20. The overlap index is by definition equal to

$$100^* \left[2^* \sum Min(Ri, Gi) \right] \Big/ \sum (Ri + Gi).$$

Since the total of percentage point dollars of concessions received and given are equal the overlap index for those columns must be equal to one-half the sum of the absolute differences divided by the total of concessions received.

References

Clausewitz, Carl von. 1968. *On War*. London: Penguin.

Davis, Douglas, and Charles Holt. 1993. *Experimental Economics*. Princeton: Princeton University Press.

Finger, J. Michael, Merlinda D. Ingco, and Ulrich Reincke 1996. *The Uruguay Round: Statistics on Tariff Concessions Given and Received*. Washington, DC: The World Bank.

GATT (General Agreement on Tariffs and Trade). 1986. *GATT Focus*, no. 41 (October). Geneva: GATT.

Hoffman, Elizabeth, Kevin McCabe, Keith Shachat, and Vernon Smith. 1994. "Preferences, Property Rights, and Anonymity in Bargaining Games." *Games and Economic Behavior* 7, no. 3 (November): 346–380.

Hudec, Robert E. 1987. *Developing Countries in the GATT Legal System*. London: Trade Policy Research Centre.

Hull, Cordell. 1948. *The Memoirs of Cordell Hull*, Vol. 1. New York: Macmillan.

Krugman, Paul. 1997. "What Should Trade Negotiators Negotiate About?" *Journal of Economic Literature* 35 (March): 113–120.

Preeg, Ernest H. 1995. *Traders in a Brave New World: The Uruguay Round and the Future of the International Trading System*. Chicago: University of Chicago Press.

Winham, Gilbert R. 1986. *International Trade and the Tokyo Round Negotiation*. Princeton: Princeton University Press.

Zeller, Thomas W. 1992. *American Trade and Power in the 1960s*. New York: Columbia University Press.

II

Country Experience

6   Australia: A Case Study of Unilateral Trade Liberalization

Ross Garnaut

6.1   Introduction

For two decades until the mid-1980s, Australia, with New Zealand, had the most protected manufacturing sector among the members of the OECD. This was a central element in a highly regulated and inward-looking economy. At the turn of the century, Australia, with New Zealand, has one of the more open manufacturing sectors in the OECD, perhaps the most open for goods when agriculture and minerals are included, and a relatively and increasingly internationally oriented overall economy.

This chapter analyzes the remarkable reorientation of Australian trade policy in the decade from the mid-1980s.

Australian protection and then trade liberalization are both explained mainly by reference to the domestic debate and political contests. As protection was progressively raised through the first two-thirds of the twentieth century, it was supported by the dominance of ideas that suggested that protection raised Australian economic welfare. Private vested interests interacted with a favorable climate of opinion to determine the inter-industry pattern of protection and, once protection had been provided to an industry, to lock it in place. Particular political events and sometimes crises, along with notable acts of political leadership, influenced the timing, the pace, and the extent of protectionism's triumphant march.

Trade liberalization from 1983 was preceded by the transformation of elite, although not popular, opinion toward the view that protection had negative effects on Australian economic welfare. In a new intellectual environment, vested interests in trade liberalization became more effective in the political process. Other vested interests were able to slow, but not stop, liberalization in the most highly protected industries: cars, textiles, clothing, and footwear. Discretionary acts of political leadership were important in converting the changed climate of elite opinion into policy reform.

Australia's interaction with the international economy played a role in both the rise and the fall of protectionism, but not through agreements to reduce protection in direct reciprocation of trading partners' liberalization. Indeed, in the Australian debate, "specific reciprocity" was an instrument of protectionism (Arndt 1994). More diffuse conceptions of reciprocity were, however, brought to account by forces favoring liberalization.

Section 6.2 describes changes in Australian protection policy in the twentieth century, focusing especially on the recent period of liberalization. Section 6.3 defines the broader context of policy reform in which trade liberalization was a central part. Section 6.4 discusses the political economy of trade liberalization in Australia, analyzing the interaction of ideas, vested interests, and political opportunity. Sections 6.5 and 6.6 examine the part played by Australian participation in global (GATT and WTO) and regional (APEC) discussions, negotiations, and agreements on trade liberalization. Finally, section 6.7 sums up the evidence on unilateralism and reciprocity in Australian trade liberalization.

6.2 Internationalizing a Protectionist Economy

The Australian Federation was established as a customs union of previously separate states on the first day of the twentieth century. The federation had two major constituent states: New South Wales with a generation-long commitment to rigorous free trade, and Victoria with a generation-long commitment to protection as a central element in development strategy. The polities of both New South Wales and Victoria were convinced that free trade and protection respectively were the causes of their own state's considerable economic success and prosperity.

The political parties of the new federation were organized around the contest over commercial policy. A Free Trade Party, a Protection Party, and a Labor Party had similar representation in the first Federal Parliament.

There was no clear national consensus or policy on protection in Australia's first decade. But by the end of the decade, the national polity had opted decisively for protection. Within two more decades, the Australian economic profession had supplied a "national welfare" justification for the national preference. The "Australian Case for Protection" was a precursor of the Stolper-Samuelson theorem. It demonstrated to the satisfaction of a majority of the Australian economics profession that for Australia, with its unusually rich per capita natural resource endowments, protection increased the number of people who could be employed at the relatively high wages that had been established in Australia (Anderson and Garnaut 1987).

In the victory of protection in the national policy contest, the influence of vested interests established before the federation was decisive. The combination of widespread belief, even among economists, that protection was in the national interest and the pressures of vested interests ensured that the average level of protection for manufacturing industry increased rapidly to reach unusual heights in the 1930s, then resisted the postwar tendency for liberalization in advanced economies. Australia shifted from being one of the more open of the advanced economies, to having (with New Zealand) the most highly protected manufacturing sector (table 6.1). Australian protection was so high that it greatly reduced imports of the most highly protected products, so that import-weighted averages of the kind presented in table 6.1 underestimated Australia's relative protection levels later in the period.

Not only was the average tariff rate for manufacturing as a whole well above that for other industrial countries but the rates were higher in almost every two-digit group of manufactured commodities (table 6.2).

Manufacturing protection became the keystone of a highly regulated national economy, extending through the externally oriented agricultural sector in which Australia had strong comparative advantage. It encompassed a unique system of detailed central regulation of wages and other conditions of employment, controls on the terms of domestic and international financial transactions, and extensive state ownership and sponsorship of monopolies in the services industries.

The tariff had generally been the principal instrument of Australian protection. The main exception was World War II and postwar exchange controls, extended in the late 1940s and 1950s into quantitative restrictions on imports, explained on balance-of-payments

Table 6.1
Average manufacturing tariff rates, selected industrial countries, 1902, 1913, 1925, and 1970 (%)

	1902	1913	1925	1970[a]
Australia	6	16	27	23
Belgium	13	9	15	na
Canada	17	26	23	14
Denmark	18	14	10	NA
EEC-6[b]	na	na	na	8
France	34	20	21	na
Germany	25	13	20	na
Italy	27	18	22	na
Japan	10	20	13	12
Netherlands	3	4	6	na
New Zealand	9	na	na	23
Norway	12	na	na	11
Sweden	23	20	16	7
Switzerland	7	9	14	3
United States	73	44	37	9

Sources: League of Nations, *Tariff Level Indices*, Geneva, 1927, as quoted in Little, Scitovsky, and Scott (1970, 162–163), and General Agreement on Tariffs and Trade, *Basic Documentation for the Tariff Study*, Geneva, 1972.
Reproduced from K. Anderson and R. Garnaut, *Australian Protectionism: Extent, Causes and Effects.* (Sydney: Allyn and Unwin, 1987).
Note: na indicates data not available.
[a] The 1970 estimates are not comparable with earlier estimates because the earlier estimates used f.o.b. export prices of other countries as indicators of boarder prices, instead of c.i.f. import prices for the country concerned. Thus the earlier rates are somewhat overestimated. This has little effect on the intercountry comparison for each year, however.
[b] Belgium, France, West Germany, Italy, Luxembourg, and the Netherlands.

grounds. The quantitative restrictions were dismantled by 1959 and mostly replaced by increased tariffs with similar protective effects (Corden 1996).

The structure of Australian manufacturing protection underwent great change in the 1970s, with modest effect on the average level. First, the Whitlam Labor Government cut all tariffs by 25 percent in 1973. Second, protection levels were further reduced for most manufactured products. Third, protection levels were greatly increased for the most highly protected industries—most important, textiles, clothing, footwear, and motor vehicles—mainly through the reintro-

Table 6.2
Tariff rates by manufacturing subsector, selected industrial countries, 1975[a] (%)

ISIC Group	Australia	Canada	EEC-9[c]	Japan	Sweden	United States
Food, beverages, and tobacco	10	6	8	22	5	5
Textiles	24	19	8	4	10	13
Wearing apparel	44	25	16	18	13	27
Footwear and leather[b]	28	13	6	12	7	12
Wood, wood products, and furniture	16	11	4	3	3	5
Paper, paper products, printing and publishing	5	8	6	5	2	1
Chemicals, petroleum, coal, rubber and plastic products	7	11	8	8	4	3
Nonmetallic mineral products	15	12	8	6	6	12
Base metals	5	7	5	4	4	5
Fabricated metal products	20	14	8	12	5	8
Machinery	12	8	8	12	6	6
Transport equipment	23	3	8	11	7	4
Other manufacturing	9	9	5	11	4	8
Total	13	8	8	11	5	6

Sources: Compiled by information supplied by the GATT, as reported in Industries Assistance Commission (1978, Table 1.3.3). Reproduced from K. Anderson and R. Garnaut, *Australian Protectionism: Extent, Causes and Effects* (Sydney: Allyn and Unwin, 1987).
[a] Weighted average of MFN tariff rates for all items in each industry, using weights based on the value of imports of the country concerned.
[b] Rubber footwear is included with other rubber products.
[c] EEC-9 comprises the 6 member countries listed in footnote a of table 6.1 plus Denmark, Ireland, and the United Kingdom.

duction and the successive tightening of quantitative import restrictions between 1974 and 1982.

Table 6.3 sets out changes in effective protection for manufacturing by subsectors and for agriculture up to the eve of the reform period in 1983. Note that from the 25 percent across-the-board tariff cut in 1973 until 1983 virtually no change occurred in average effective protection levels for manufacturing. The small apparent reduction, from an average of 27 percent to 25 percent, is entirely the result of a shift in the relative production weights of different sectors over the period.

The decisive dismantling of Australian protection began soon after the election of the Hawke Labor Government in 1983, with the successive removal of quantitative import restrictions on steel, household consumer durables, and some items of heavy machinery, and with reduction of tariff rates on a number of items for which protection levels had arisen as matters for policy decision. Liberalization was given momentum by far-reaching financial deregulation including the removal of exchange controls in December 1983 and the subsequent depreciation of the real effective exchange rate in the mid-1980s, which reduced the protection provided by the quantitative restrictions on imports of textiles, clothing, footwear, and cars. A revision of quantitative import restrictions on cars was announced in 1984, gradually to reduce their protective effect. A similar announcement on textiles, clothing, and footwear in 1987 was intended to have a similar effect, but technical miscalculation meant that its actual liberalizing content was small.

In May 1988, the government announced that all tariffs above 15 percent would be reduced in annual steps to 15 percent in 1992. Tariffs between 10 and 15 percent would be reduced to 10 percent. Exceptions were made for textiles, clothing, footwear, and cars. By this time, quantitative import restrictions had been removed on all items other than textiles, clothing, footwear, and cars. For textiles, clothing, and footwear, quantitative restrictions would continue to be eased slightly under the 1987 program. For cars, quantitative import restrictions were abolished with immediate effect, and tariffs reduced by 2.5 percentage points per annum, from 45 percent in 1988 to 35 percent in 1992.

A second, more radical and comprehensive across-the-board reduction of protection was announced in 1991, moving Australia into the ranks of low-protection developed countries. The tariff for cars was to continue to fall by 2.5 percentage points per annum, to 15 percent in the year 2000. For the first time, radical reduction in textiles, clothing, and footwear protection was included in the liberalization program: Quantitative import restrictions were abolished, and a schedule of tariff reductions was announced to maximum rates of 15 percent (for most textiles and footwear) and 25 percent (for clothing) by 2000. For all other manufactured goods, the maximum tariff rate was to be reduced to 5 percent by 1996.

Figure 6.1 charts the reductions in protection announced during the period of radical reform, 1983–1991. The 1991 program was implemented as announced through to its completion in 2000. A new Conservative government elected in 1996 confirmed its commitment to announced policy.

While the period of radical reform ended in 1991, the Conservative government in 1997 announced further reductions in protection for the highly protected industries after the completion of the current liberalization program in 2000. The tariff is to fall in 2005 to 10 percent for cars, textiles, and footwear, and to 15 percent for clothing.

The Labor government's reductions in tariffs for cars, textiles, clothing, and footwear were accompanied by the introduction of "export facilitation" schemes, which allowed imports free of duty for an amount of the protected goods equal to exports of those same products. The export facilitation arrangements had an economic effect similar to that of an ad valorem export subsidy at the tariff rate for the product.

The export facilitation arrangements were probably inconsistent with the WTO subsidies code introduced following the Uruguay Round. Following threats that the United States would take action within the WTO's disputes settlement mechanism, the Australian government announced in 1996 that it would end the export facilitation arrangements in 2000, replacing them with arrangements that were consistent with the new WTO rules.

6.3 Manufacturing Trade Liberalization and General Policy Reform

The Australian Federation, in the early decades of its first century, had been built on the policy pillars of protection, a racially discriminatory immigration policy ("White Australia"), a highly regulated and centralized system for settling labor disputes and determining

Table 6.3
Average effective rates of assistance to Australia's manufacturing subsectors and to agriculture, 1968–1969 to 1982–1983[a] (%)

	1968–1969	69–70	70–71	71–72	72–73	73–74	74–75	75–76	76–77	77–78	77–78	78–79	79–80	80–81	81–82	82–83
		1971–1972 production weights					1974–1975 production weights				1977–1978 production weights					
Food, beverages, & tobacco	16	17	18	19	19	18	21	20	16	13	10	14	13	10	9	9
Textiles[b]	43	42	42	45	45	35	39	50	51	57	47	47	51	55	54	54
Clothing & footwear	97	94	91	86	88	64	87	99	141	149	141	143	135	140	204	220
Wood, wood products, and furniture	26	27	26	23	23	16	18	19	18	18	18	17	15	15	14	13
Paper & paper products, printing	52	50	50	52	51	38	31	30	30	29	24	26	25	25	25	24
Chemicals, petroleum, & coal products	31	31	31	32	32	25	23	23	21	18	19	19	17	15	124	14
Nonmetallic mineral products	15	15	15	14	14	11	11	10	7	5	5	5	5	4	4	4
Basic metal products	31	30	28	29	29	22	16	16	15	14	10	10	9	10	11	11
Fabricated metal products	61	60	60	58	56	44	39	38	34	32	30	31	30	31	27	27
Transport equipment (motor vehicles and parts)[b]	50	50	51	50	51	39	45	59	54	61	48	53	59	63	71	72
	(50			49		38	54	73	67	79	73	81	89	96	108	110)
Other machinery & equipment	43	43	43	44	39	29	24	25	22	21	20	20	21	20	21	18
Miscellaneous manufacturing	34	35	35	32	31	24	27	26	25	27	30	30	29	28	27	25
Total manufacturing	36	36	36	35	35	27	27	28	27	26	23	24	23	23	25	25
Total manufacturing less textiles, clothing, footwear, and motor vehicles & parts	32	32	32	32	32	23	23	22	20	17	17	17	16	16	16	15
Total agriculture		28	28	21	14	13	8	9	9	13	13	10	7	8	9	16

Source: Industries Assistance Commission (1976a, 1980a, 1983a, 1985a). Reproduced from K. Anderson and R. Garnaut, *Australian Protectionism: Extent, Causes and Effects* (Sydney: Allyn and Unwin, 1987).

[a] The forms of assistance covered by this table include tariffs, quantitative restrictions on imports, production and export subsidies, and special pricing schemes for sugar and petroleum products. The assistance provided by the motor vehicle local content scheme is included only in the estimates based on 1977–1978 production weights. Forms of assistance not taken into account include government purchasing practices and assistance from state governments, for which some descriptive details are provided by the Industries Assistance Commission (1981e, chapter 2 and appendices 2.2 and 2.3).

[b] Estimates of assistance afforded by import quotas from 1979–1980 are based on a survey of quota transfer prices and on official tender sale prices, unlike those for previous years which are based on price comparisons.

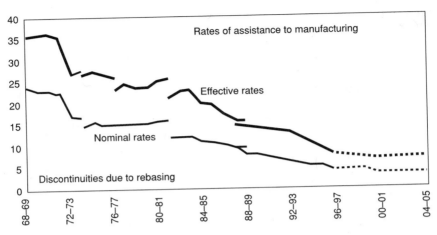

Figure 6.1
Reductions in protection announced during the period of radical reform, 1983–1991

labor conditions, and extensive government ownership and regulation of the transport, communications, and large parts of the services industries (Kelly 1992).

These certainties of historical policy were challenged late in the century. Discriminatory immigration policy was modified from 1966 on and abolished beginning in the early 1970s. But the other pillars of early Australian policy remained into the 1980s, when they came under pressures to reform in parallel with manufacturing protection.

Radical reform began in December 1983 with the floating of the Australian dollar and the abolition of all exchange controls—with the deregulation of the financial sector ahead of the real economy, and the external ahead of the domestic economy (Garnaut 1994). However unconventional the sequencing of reform, the international financial measures spurred a major increase in the external orientation of Australian business, among other things with a sharp and large increase in direct investment abroad. The depreciation of the real effective exchange rate that followed in 1985 and 1986 supported increased export orientation of Australian production and the diversification of exports into manufactured goods and services, alongside the traditional primary commodities. An expectation developed that international financial integration would be followed inevitably by increased external orientation more generally, including through trade liberalization.

The Labor government's internationally oriented economic reform was accompanied and supported by increased awareness and official promotion of integration with the rapidly growing economies in Australia's East Asian neighborhood. Such reorientation of international outlook and foreign policy was in one sense an inevitable accompaniment to an historic shift in global economic and political weight toward the Western Pacific. It was not inevitable, however, that the growth of East Asia should be embraced as an opportunity to raise Australian incomes through increased trade and specialization in line with Australia's comparative advantage. That it was so embraced provided major support for internationally oriented reform.

The Australian protection debate had always focused mainly on the manufacturing sector. Over time, however, and most comprehensively after the World War II, the general policy preference for protection interacted with the usual processes of political economy to generate "all-round protection," in which the agricultural sector was compensated for manufacturing protection through special assistance. The reform of manufacturing protection in the 1980s was accompanied by removal of most agricultural assistance. The Australian and New Zealand agricultural sectors are the most open to international market conditions of any in the developed countries.

Trade liberalization, and the expectation that this would continue to near free trade, introduced powerful pressure for reform of the other pillars of early Australian policy. Internationally oriented businesses came to realize and eventually accept that no industry or firm could expect its Australian production of tradable goods and services to survive in the new circumstances unless it was internationally competitive. The increased international orientation made businesses much more aware of the gap between world's best practice in the general economic and regulatory environment and in supply of inputs, and the conditions under which they were required to operate in Australia. Business people who had once been tolerant of inefficient regulatory arrangements and supply of inputs within the context of "all-round protection," from which they drew a share of benefits, came to see these inefficiencies as threats to their own survival. Business awareness of the costs of an inefficient policy environment spread to associated trade unions and the general community, creating conditions for widespread deregulation and privatization in transport, communications, energy, banking; for

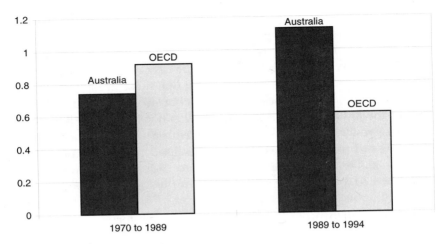

Figure 6.2
Australia's comparative productivity growth rates, 1970–1994 (percent)
Source: Industry Commission, *Assessing Australia's Productivity Performance* (AGPS: Canberra, 1997), fig. 3.

efficiency-raising taxation and general regulatory reform; and for the beginnings of reform of labor-market arrangements.

The greater international orientation of the Australian economy heightened awareness of the value of stable macroeconomic conditions, including low inflation and nominal long-term interest rates.

The whole reform program was associated with a marked shift in Australia's economic performance relative to other developed countries. Australia's total factor productivity growth in the 1990s was well above the average of the OECD members, after having lagged behind through the two preceding decades (figure 6.2).

6.4   The Political Economy of Trade Liberalization

What was the cause of the historic transformation of Australian trade policy in the 1980s and 1990s?

The background to the trade liberalization of the 1980s extends back to the 1960s, which witnessed the beginnings of change in elite (but not popular) opinion about whether protection was in the national interest.

The change in the climate of elite opinion on protection can be traced to work by academic economists through the 1960s. Economists began to examine closely and to publish studies on the costs of the highly differentiated Australian tariff. At first, the main reform advocated was movement toward a uniform tariff. By the late 1960s, the economic profession was advocating import liberalization with near unanimity and with increasing technical sophistication (Corden 1967, 1968, 1996; Lloyd 1988; Anderson and Garnaut 1987; Garnaut 1994).

The new views of the Australian economic profession gradually influenced opinion in the bureaucracy, commencing with the Tariff Board. The Tariff Board was an advisory body established in the 1920s to place a buffer between protection policymaking and vested interest groups, in recognition of the corruption of the political process associated with unconstrained pressure by private interests. The Tariff Board was established to implement the established national policy of protection, and its views in its first four decades differed little from the general community's. The first breach in the protectionist line occurred when an economist chairman, Sir Leslie Melville, resigned in quiet opposition to government policy in 1962. The importance of individual views and the character of statutory officeholders for the direction of policy was underlined following the appointment of G. A. Rattigan as chairman in 1963. Rattigan was converted by the evidence to a freer trade position and made the public hearings and reports of the board important vehicles of public education. By the end of the 1960s, the financial press, led by the *Australian Financial Review*, was giving extensive coverage to the Tariff Board's heresy and was itself playing a major role in publicizing the case against protection. The Tariff Board perspective gradually became more influential in other areas of government.

The near consensus of elite opinion in support of reduced protection in the early 1970s was not reflected in general public opinion. The polls showed (and continue to show) substantial majorities in favor of protection. Interestingly, despite persistent support for protection in the polls, the Whitlam Labor government's decision to reduce all tariffs by 25 percent in 1973 received large majority support at the time, most strongly among Labor Party voters, who otherwise tended to be somewhat stronger supporters of protection. This illustrates the autonomy of political leadership on protection policy issues, at least at times of broad agreement across the leadership of the major parties and of buoyant economic conditions.

Through the late 1960s and 1970s, lobbying by groups with vested interests in protection had become more overt and strident. Protectionist interests had not needed to be strident in earlier times, when the climate of opinion had been strongly supportive. Their more open participation in the debate was partly a reaction to the emergence in public trade policy discussion of groups with an interest in trade liberalization. The changes in parliamentary leaders' attitudes, the information made available to the public by the Industries Assistance Commission (successor to the Tariff Board from 1974), and the improved understanding within the economics profession on the effects of manufacturing protection on farm incomes encouraged farm industry groups to join the public debate, especially the National Farmers' Federation, founded in 1977. The mining sector, perhaps mindful of its political weakness and vulnerability, and comprising large corporations with deep interests in government mineral leasing and taxation policies, was late to enter the public political fray. In 1982, five mining companies without large manufacturing assets argued for movement toward a low, uniform tariff.

The established protection for the textiles, clothing, footwear, and automobile industries was so great that enterprises in them were able to invest heavily in political activity to preserve it. The establishment of strong industry organization in defense of protection lowered the costs of new political mobilization. Developments in the wider economy were introducing pressures for these manufacturing industries to decline more rapidly than others in the recession of the mid-1970s and early 1980s, and these pressures increased incentives and established a congenial "fairness" environment for the defense of established protection.

In addition, fortuitous political circumstances helped the cause of high protection for textiles, clothing, and footwear (Anderson and Garnaut 1987, chap. 6).

International practice in the most highly protected industries (especially textiles, clothing, and footwear, but also automobiles) was less liberal than in other areas of manufacturing, reflecting the rise of new centers of competitiveness in East Asia, outside the North Atlantic economies that were most influential in setting the international rules. International practice supported the introduction of quantitative restrictions on imports of these commodities, the protective effect of which could then rise with changes in economic conditions without new government decisions. Through all these influences, it was the powerful incentive of highly protected industries to invest heavily in political influence that was decisive in raising protection for textiles, clothing, footwear, and automobiles against the general trend in the years preceding radical trade policy reform.

Writing before the election of the Labor government in early 1983, Kym Anderson and I drew five main lessons from Australia's experience with protection policy. First, both the public and private interest theories of protection policymaking are relevant: Neither on its own can explain Australian policy. Second, political leadership can exercise decisive influence over policy outcomes at certain moments in history. Third, protection is extremely difficult to remove once it has been granted. Fourth, sudden increases in import penetration tend to trigger protectionist responses, even in a climate of opinion generally unfavorable to protection. Fifth, while export interest groups have not been major actors in protection policymaking for most of Australia's history, they have been influential when they have been active (Anderson and Garnaut 1987). We thought in 1983 that there would be little change in the average level of manufacturing protection "in the immediate future." Working for lower protection were the change in political and intellectual leadership opinion in favor of a more open economy, the rise in countervailing power from export interests, and the desire to build closer and more cooperative relations with Australia's East Asian neighbors. The increasing understanding of the effects of protection on export performance had brought farm and mining industry groups into the policy debate, and the increasing understanding of the effects of protection on the interstate distribution of income had brought in the principal exporting states.

Two factors were working against freer trade at that time. Long-term industry plans introduced by the Fraser conservative government in the early 1980s had greatly increased the political costs of reducing protection before 1988 (for textiles, clothing, and footwear) or 1992 (automobiles). And the deep recession of the early 1980s was unfavorable to early import liberalization.

We concluded that the prospects of future trade liberalization would be enhanced by further dissemination of information about the economic effects of protection; by compensating the states that benefited from protection for the effects of liberalization through Commonwealth-state financial arrangements; by public funding for political parties; and by Australian participation in discussions of trade liberalization within the Asia Pacific region.

The Australian move toward free trade in the 1980s and 1990s is comprehensible in the context of the lessons that we drew in 1983 from earlier Australian experience. Bob Hawke as Labor prime minister held the personal belief that closer integration into the international economy, through trade liberalization and other means, was a necessary element of economic reform to build a modern economy in Australia. This was a personal view shared by other members of his cabinet, including his treasurer and eventual challenger and successor, Paul Keating. Trade liberalization did not feature in the program upon which the government was elected, but Hawke's consistent public position from the early days of his government was that sustained economic growth in Australia required reductions in protection, and that these reductions would be implemented as employment strengthened during the economic recovery from the 1982 recession. Hawke's perspective on trade policy was reflected in decisions on each of a series of industry policy issues that arose in the early years of the government, prior to the general trade liberalization decisions of 1988 and 1991.

Hawke's political style involved consultation among a wide array of interest groups, extended public discussion, and dissemination of information well in advance of decisions for change. The National Economic Summit Conference, discussion in the new Economic Planning Advisory Council and the Australian Manufacturing Council, speeches and exhortations by the prime minister himself, and the publication of reports to the government explaining the need for change (including the author's *Australia and the Northeast Asian Ascendancy*; see Garnaut 1989) were all instruments of public education, helping to prepare a climate of public opinion that expected and favored trade liberalization.

During the Hawke years, there was considerable discussion of and some movement toward reduction of the earlier bias in the allocation of Commonwealth revenues toward the less densely populated "export states." The governments of these states, especially Western Australia, moved more strongly than in earlier years to argue the case for compensatory reductions in protection.

Public funding of political parties was introduced at the Commonwealth level, although its effect on interest group pressures was diminished considerably by escalation in the costs of election campaigns.

It was a theme of the Hawke government that close relations with East Asia and integration into Australia's Asia Pacific environment were important elements of the reform program. It was part of the case for reducing protection that significant opportunities for expanding exports were emerging from economic growth in East Asia, including export of nontraditional services and manufactured goods. Reductions in protection would make Australia's most productive industries more competitive and better able to take advantage of the East Asian opportunity. This was the position argued in *Australia and the Northeast Asian Ascendancy* (Garnaut 1989), the first contribution to mainstream public debate in Australia to argue the case for free trade rather than simply for lower protection.

The most important change in interest group behavior, toward the emergence of economy-wide trade union and business groups, was encouraged by the Hawke leadership style. The Australian Council of Trade Unions became more influential, relative to the individual unions that were its constituents, in public policy discussion and in consultation with government. The economy-wide Australian Business Council, which included representatives of mining and service industries, became the most influential of the business groups. Economy-wide perspectives gave greater weight to the national interest in liberal trade, significantly constraining the political effectiveness of the advocacy by union and business groups of continued or increased protection for textiles, clothing, footwear, and automobiles. In the new climate of opinion, more favorable to liberal trade, the National Farmers' Federation and the Australian Mining Industry Council became more active in advocacy of trade liberalization.

How important were general economic conditions to the transformation of Australian trade policy?

Australian economic reform responded to the long-term deterioration of relative economic performance that had first become apparent to close observers in the 1960s. There was a sense in which the government was responding to a crisis, which became more severe with the collapse of the world system of agricultural trade in the 1980s. The crisis, however, was slow-burning and spread over time, and there was no inevitability that the problems would be addressed when they were, in the mid-1980s, rather than, say, the 1970s or the 1990s.

The economic problems that were felt politically as crisis were short-term macroeconomic problems—the recessions of 1982–1983 and 1990–1991 and the current account deficit that followed the collapse in primary export prices in 1985–1986. The instinctive Australian response to macroeconomic crisis, based on historical precedents since the 1930s, was not to pursue internationally oriented or market-oriented reform, but rather to stimulate domestic demand (for recession) and to increase protection and exchange controls (for balance-of-payments weakness). Government used the crisis atmosphere of 1983 and 1986 to advance the reform effort, but there is no sense in which the shape of the reform program itself was determined by crisis.

The rapid growth in employment from 1983 to 1990 validated the reform program in the eyes of the electorate, and especially within the government's own (social democratic) constituency. The growth in employment was not mainly a benefit of reform—the main benefits would come later. There were, however, some links between employment growth and reform. Wage restraint through the 1983–1985 recovery contributed to employment growth, and the depreciation that occurred under floating exchange rates in the terms-of-trade crisis in 1985–1986 eased adjustment. Financial deregulation contributed in an unfortunate way to employment growth by helping monetary expansion get out of hand in 1987 and 1988, fueling unsustainable boom conditions and setting the scene for the 1990–1991 recession. Recession, when it came, was moderated somewhat in its effects on employment by the growing importance of the manufactured and service exports that were emerging from economic reform: Domestic demand contracted proportionately more in 1990–1991 than 1982–1983, but manufacturing employment rather less.

Recession from mid-1990 on reinforced the community mood against radical reform, but not before the government had announced the largest trade-liberalizing step of all at the cyclical low point in March 1991. More important for policy, recession politics introduced powerful political incentives to split the elite consensus on trade liberalization.

The Labor government's trade policy reforms had been facilitated greatly from the mid-1980s on by the support of the leadership of the conservative opposition parties. The transformation of the Opposition from conservative (status quo) to liberal trade policies, under the influence of the more general change in elite opinion, is in itself a large and important phenomenon (Kelly 1992). The transformation of Opposition policy went so far that in the early 1990s, it was a new Labor prime minister, Paul Keating, who broke the rhetorical consensus in support of trade liberalization, leaving the Opposition closer to the Labor government's earlier positions.

The Keating government's change in stance in 1992 was opportunistic, responding to the Opposition's strong endorsement of and commitment to completion of the government's liberalization program, and to moving beyond announced policy by supporting my recommendation in *Australia and the Northeast Asian Ascendancy* (Garnaut 1989) to move to complete free trade by 2000. A majority of popular opinion had always opposed trade liberalization, and Prime Minister Keating, under strong electoral competitive pressure, sought to mine a political lode that the leadership of both parties had denied themselves in the national interest since the mid-1980s. Much was made by Keating of the damage that would be done to manufacturing industry if the residual protection, after completion of the Labor program, were removed.

The government's policy retreat was tactical and rhetorical and not substantial: The only retreat on real policy was the removal of developing country preferences for newly industrialized economies in 1992. Previously, advocates of open trade had expected the preferences to be removed only by the completion of the liberalization process after 2000 (Garnaut 1989).

The Keating Labor government unexpectedly won the 1993 election. This defeat ended the conservative Opposition's dalliance with radical liberal policies on economic policy, including on trade liberalization. When the Howard Conservative government won office in the 1996 election, it was on a program of completing the Labor government's trade liberalization to 2000, but otherwise of silence on this issue.

The new conservative consensus on trade policy across the political leadership ensured that there was no revival of radical trade liberalization. But the survival of elite comprehension that open trade was in Australia's national interest, and the Labor government's commitment to the APEC goal of free trade by 2010, now endorsed by the new government, together ensured that there was some forward movement. Hence the modest further reductions in 2005 for tariffs in the most highly protected industries.

6.5 Diffuse Reciprocity: Australia and the WTO

Australia's slide into deep protectionism, and then reform to near free trade, was little influenced by failure and success in bargaining with trade partners for reciprocal liberalization. To the extent that official relations and negotiation with other countries influenced Australian policy, it was indirect. To the extent that "reciprocity" played any role, either negatively or positively, it was diffuse rather than specific.

Australia was an active member of the GATT at its formation and in its first years, seeking access to international markets for its agricultural products and policy autonomy to retain its manufacturing protectionism. The failure of the General Agreement on Tariffs and Trade (GATT) to bring agriculture adequately within its rules, and its tolerance of the proliferation of European and North American distortions of agricultural trade in the 1960s, provided a convenient pretext for Australian governments to stand aside from effective participation in the early rounds of multilateral trade negotiations. Australia, with New Zealand, was alone among developed countries in remaining outside the manufacturing trade liberalization and expansion of the early postwar decades. Australian governments held back on criticism of GATT's tolerance of increasing agricultural protectionism, lest it draw attention to Australian manufacturing trade policy.

The more differentiated Australian climate of opinion on protection in the 1970s, and realization of the high and increasing cost of other countries' agricultural protectionism, drew Australia into the Tokyo Round of multilateral trade negotiations. Australia offered to lower its bindings on many items that were bound at well above current tariff rates. Australia lowered tariffs on a range of items identified as having "water in the tariff"—in Australian parlance, items where protection kept the domestic price much (and for the supporters of protection, unnecessarily) above the cost of import-competing production.

The government explained its Tokyo Round offer to the Australian Parliament as having no effect on Australian production. The explanation was correct at the time. But there were virtues in these moves that were hidden to business, the community, and probably the government at the time: The removal of "water in the tariff," and tighter bindings, had some real liberalizing effects in later years when changed macroeconomic circumstances generated appreciation of the real effective exchange rate.

Australia did not always take its GATT tariff bindings seriously. When senior Australian GATT trade negotiators asked the government to hold back on unilateral liberalization in 1984, so that they would have "coin" for negotiation in particular with the European Community, they were advised that the government would be announcing easing of automobile quantitative import restrictions a few months later. If the negotiators could buy any market access within these months, that would be to the good. At the time, the Australian automobile tariff of 57 percent was not binding at the margin, because quantitative restrictions had a tariff equivalent closer to 100 percent. The negotiators subsequently reported the European response to Canberra: What did Australia have to "sell," until the tariff had returned to the 35 percent at which it had been bound in the early 1960s?

The Hawke Labor government's intention to reduce protection changed Australia's approach to multilateral trade negotiations. In December 1983, the prime minister during a speech in Bangkok called for a new round of multilateral trade negotiations, which would address exceptions to the multilateral trade rules that had had high costs for Australia, Thailand, and some of their Western Pacific trading partners: agriculture and textiles. This became a theme of active Australian multilateral trade diplomacy in the lead-up to and through the Uruguay Round. Following the Bangkok speech, senior trade officials from Western Pacific members of GATT met a number of times to discuss regional interest in a new multilateral round. One practical consequence was Japanese acceptance, at least within the Foreign Ministry, that agriculture would need to be brought within GATT rules. Another was realization within the ASEAN countries, that there were potential gains from active participation within multilateral trade negotiations for the first time.

A variation on this theme was the Australian initiative in the formation of the Cairns Group of agricultural exporting countries. The Cairns Group was influential in securing a place for and a substantial outcome on agriculture in the Uruguay Round.

Australian policy had been liberated by commitment to reduce protection as a matter of domestic policy. Australia made Uruguay Round offers substantially in excess of what turned out to be necessary in settlement of the round. But the offers comprised lower bindings on tariffs, reductions in which had already been announced entirely in the domestic policy context. The only important steps in Australian trade liberalization over the period of reform that were part of a reciprocal agreement occurred in the context of the Closer Economic Relations Agreement with New Zealand. A trade-diverting free trade agreement between Australia and New Zealand in the 1970s, NAFTA, had made exceptions of all important areas of potential trade creation. NAFTA was replaced by the Closer Economic Relations (CER) agreement in 1983, which soon provided for clean free trade in goods, without exceptions. For some agricultural goods, notably dairy products, New Zealand was the lowest cost potential supplier to Australia. The CER was therefore genuinely trade-creating in this and some other areas.

While specific reciprocity was of minor importance in Australian liberalization, the Hawke Government's political strategy allocated a substantial place to participation in the WTO and, after its formation under Australian leadership, in APEC. Support for trade liberalization required confidence that exports from Australia's internationally competitive industries could expand. Participation in global and regional trade policy discussion was seen as being helpful in underlining and extending the reality of substantial international market opportunity. There was enough expansion of Australian trade opportunity for this political purpose to be served in the Uruguay Round outcome.

6.6 Diffuse Reciprocity: Asia Pacific Economic Cooperation

Australia was a leading participant in discussion of Asia Pacific economic cooperation from the earliest days. It hosted the founding meeting of the Pacific Economic Co-operation Council (PECC) at the Australian National University in 1980, and PECC became the focus of discussion of the role and modus operandi of more formal regional cooperation. The first APEC meeting was suggested by Australian Prime Minister Hawke in 1989 and convened in Canberra later in that same year. Australian Prime Minister Keating was the first advocate of raising APEC meetings to heads of government level, a suggestion taken up by President Clinton in 1993 in Seattle. Keating was a strong advocate of establishing free and open trade in the Asia Pacific region, in the process leading to the Bogor Declaration in 1994.

APEC developed within a conceptual framework different from the regional economic arrangements in Europe and North America. Unilateral liberalization had been the principal path of trade reform in the Western Pacific economies that became members of APEC: Australia, New Zealand, the (then) six ASEAN states, Hong Kong, China and (although in these cases with more cross-currents) Japan, Taiwan, and Korea.

There was little interest and no inclination in the Western Pacific to turn APEC into a conventional free trade area, ultimately meeting the requirements of Article 24 of GATT, with binding agreements on a schedule of trade liberalization, toward substantially free trade in a relatively short timetable. The first objective of APEC had been to build awareness of the implications of the deep integration that had already occurred within the region through market forces taking advantage of opportunities created by unilateral bilateralization. This would introduce constraints on unilateral policy action in individual economies that would reduce the gains from trade and investment. A related objective was to expand knowledge of the extent of the opportunities that were emerging from trade liberalization and expansion within the region. Such knowledge, brought to account in the political economy of trade policy in each member, would support the efforts of individual governments to continue liberalization at home.

The guiding idea of APEC was *open regionalism* that, to the extent that it encompassed trade liberalization, was based on reduction of official barriers to intraregional trade without discrimination against outsiders (Elek 1992; Garnaut 1996; Drysdale 1998).

When in 1994, under the leadership of Indonesia's President Soeharto, the ambitions of APEC were raised with the Bogor Declaration, a novel approach to "free and open trade in the region" had to be developed. Free trade was to be achieved by 2010 for developed countries and by 2020 for developing countries by the unilateral actions of member states. The modus operandi of APEC trade liberalization was developed in subsequent leaders' meetings in Osaka in 1995 and Manila in 1996. Each economy would present an individual action plan for its own liberalization a number of years ahead. Because there were no binding agreements to meet the requirements of Article 24 of the WTO, liberalization was to be on a nondiscriminatory basis, under Article I of the WTO. This process came to be known as "concerted unilateral liberalization." From the Manila meeting, nonbinding agreements to liberalize trade in individual sectors—legal under the WTO only because they were to be implemented on a most-favored-nation (MFN) basis—became an important means of moving forward and provided impetus to new global sectoral liberalization agreements within the WTO.

There were no binding agreements backed by judicial processes for resolving disputes. The sanctions were peer pressure and realization that a process that would yield large benefits if pursued to a successful conclusion would break down if too many economies appeared not to be making progress toward the agreed end points.

In a number of Western Pacific economies, the informal, nonbinding agreements within APEC provided important support for domestic trade policy reform. President Soeharto's leadership of the meeting that formulated the declaration of open trade and investment was important background to major, forward-looking Indonesian liberalization packages in 1995 and 1996.

President Ramos of the Philippines used the hosting of the APEC Summit late in 1996 to secure congressional support for a radical trade liberalization program, lesser variants of which had been promoted by his predecessors from time to time over the previous quarter century but defeated by vested interests through the domestic political process. The Philippines, a high-protection economy as late as the early 1990s, is now committed legally to a maximum manufacturing tariff of 5 percent by 2004. This is a clear example of the power of informal processes: President Ramos's closest economic adviser on these matters has testified that progress along these lines would have been defeated by nationalist reaction in Congress if it had been put forward as a binding commitment within the WTO (Estanislao 1997).

Australia's APEC commitment to free trade by 2010 turned out to be crucial in maintaining momentum in domestic liberalization in the less congenial environment of the 1990s. The Keating government's protectionist rhetoric from 1992 never led to serious backsliding from the 1991 liberalization program, significantly because of the prime minister's personal association with the Bogor Declaration. Australia's "individual action plan" presented to the Manila APEC meeting in 1996 included the completion of the 1991 liberalization program, which was to continue to reduce tariffs on the announced timetable until 2000. Industry interests applied great pressure to the new Conservative government on its election in 1996 to modify the announced liberalization program, but were told crisply that this was impossible because commitments had been made within APEC. The need to remain credible on the general APEC commitment to free trade by 2010 was a major and probably a crucial element in the government's decision to announce in 1997 that there would be further reductions in tariffs on textiles, clothing, footwear, and motor vehicles in 2005.

Interestingly, the role of APEC in constraining backsliding from trade liberalization induced reaction from protectionist interests that assumed elements of reciprocity in the APEC program. "We are the only virgins in the brothel" became a catch cry of resistance to continued liberalization. Textiles and automobile producer interests argued for delaying further liberalization until it could be demonstrated that other APEC members were making similar progress toward free trade. Paradoxically, a program of trade liberalization that had been entirely unilateral in its origin came under attack when elements of "diffuse reciprocity" were introduced into it through APEC. The attack was unsuccessful.

Future progress toward the APEC goal of free trade in the Asia Pacific on a MFN basis eventually will need to reconcile Western Pacific commitment to unilateral liberalization, informal and non-binding agreements, and now "concerted unilateralism," with North American traditions of reciprocity. Initially, the reconciliation can come through Western Pacific acceptance that the United States and Canada are more open economies than most (but not all) others in APEC, and that conscientious implementation of their Uruguay Round commitments represents major liberalization of importance to other APEC members.

Eventually, the APEC goals will only be reached by Western Pacific members continuing to make large progress through unilateral processes; through the United States political leadership responding to realization of this progress through recognition that relatively free trade in the Asia Pacific is a sufficiently realistic objective for it to join with a serious free trade commitment of its own; and for the APEC commitment of free trade by 2020 then to be taken into the WTO in search of an agreement on global free trade (at least in goods and major services) by 2020 (Garnaut 1998).

6.7   Unilateralism, Reciprocity, and Australian Liberalization

The dismantling of Australia's high protection is overwhelmingly a case of unilateral liberalization. It was undertaken because the leading figures in Australian policy discussion and decision had come to the view that open trade was in Australia's interest, whatever policies were adopted by other countries.

Specific reciprocity was important only at the margins, in particular in relation to a few items of agricultural trade within the Agreement on Closer Economic Relations with New Zealand.

A more diffuse conception of reciprocity played some role in support of trade liberalization. Participation in the Uruguay Round of multilateral trade negotiations and APEC helped focus the Australian polity's attention on opportunities for expansion of industries in which Australia had comparative advantage, alongside the inevitable contraction of some high-cost industries in the process of import liberalization. The progress in the Uruguay Round and in unilateral liberalization in the Western Pacific sustained the credibility of this approach.

When the concept of reciprocity was important in the Australian discussion of trade policy, it was always as an argument against reduction in protection. The absence of reciprocity in the agricultural trade was one of the reasons advanced for Australia not participating in multilateral trade negotiations in the GATT in the early postwar decades. It was advanced unsuccessfully as a reason to delay liberalization in the 1980s and the 1990s. The call for specific reciprocity is being heard again in the debate about removal of the remnants of protection in manufacturing at the end of the twentieth century. Now, as in the radical trade liberalization decisions from 1983 to 1991, the prospects of progress in reducing protection are better the softer the resonance of calls for international reciprocity in the domestic policy debate.

References

Anderson, K., and R. Garnaut. 1987. *Australian Protectionism: Extent, Causes and Effects.* Sydney: Allen and Unwin.

Arndt, H. 1994. "Reciprocity." *Quarterly Review of the Nazionale de Laboro* (September): 259–269.

Corden, W. M. 1967. "Australian Tariff Policy." *Australian Economic Papers* 6, no. 9 (December): 131–154.

Corden, W. M. 1968. "Australian Policy Discussion in the Post-War Period: A Survey." *American Economic Review* 58, no. 3 (June, suppl.): 88–138.

Corden, W. M. 1996. "Protection and Liberalisation in Australia and Abroad." *The Australian Economic Review* (2d quarter).

Drysdale, P. 1998. *A Shared Global Agenda, East Asia, APEC and the ASEM Process*, ed. P. Drysdale and D. Vines. Cambridge: Cambridge University Press.

Elek, A. 1992. "Trade Policy Options for the Asia-Pacific Region in the 1990s: The Potential for Open Regionalism." *American Economic Review* 82, no. 2.

Estanislao, J. 1997. Comments at conference. *Europe, East Asia, APEC and the Asia-Europe Meeting (ASEM) Process*, London, May.

Garnaut, R. 1989. *Australia and the Northeast Asian Ascendancy*. Canberra: Australian Government Publishing Service.

Garnaut, R. 1994. "Trade Liberalization and the Washington Consensus in Australia." In *The Political Economy of Policy Reform*, ed. J. Williamson, 51–72. Washington, DC: Institute for International Economics.

Garnaut, R. 1996. *Open Regionalism and Trade Liberalisation: An Asia Pacific Contribution to the World Trade System*. Singapore: Institute of Southeast Asian Studies, and Sydney: Allen and Unwin.

Garnaut, R. 1998. "Europe and Asia Pacific Economic Cooperation." Chap. 12 in *A Shared Global Agenda? Europe, East Asia, APEC and the ASEM Process*, ed. P. Drysdale and D. Vines. Cambridge: Cambridge University Press.

Kelly, P. 1992. *The End of Certainty: The Story of the 1980s*. Sydney: Allen and Unwin.

Lloyd, P. 1988. "Protection Policy." Chap. 5 in *Survey of Australian Economics*, vol. 1, ed. F. H. Gruen. Sydney: Allen and Unwin.

7 Trade Reform in New Zealand: Unilateralism at Work

Lewis Evans and Martin Richardson

7.1 Introduction

In the last two decades, the New Zealand economy has been subject to an extremely extensive and far-reaching episode of liberalization. Reforms have included institutional changes to the central bank; the way in which government departments organize and report their affairs; reforms of labor, capital, and goods markets; and even electoral reform. Among these reforms have been extensive liberalizations of New Zealand's international trading regime.

A central distinguishing characteristic of these reforms is that they have been largely unilateral. The aim of this chapter is to consider the political forces behind these trade reforms with an eye toward explaining the political success of the unilateral approach. We seek to provide some answers to the following sorts of questions. Who were the vested interests behind New Zealand's starting point of very high protection, and how did they succeed in getting it implemented? Why were reforms mooted—what happened such that the early status quo was no longer politically feasible? Why did the trade reforms succeed (in the sense of being put in place), and how did that implementation occur so as to overcome these special interests? Why unilateralism? Why has liberalization not been complete (especially since it has been so dramatic, one might think that the final steps would be easier in some sense)? How important were multilateral and bilateral deals in affecting New Zealand's unilateral reforms? How, if at all, has New Zealand's multilateral position been affected by these reforms?

In considering these questions, we not only look at the evolution of trade policy in New Zealand in recent decades but also focus on two important sectoral groups: manufacturing and agriculture. We discuss the involvement of these groups in the reform process and the ex post consequences for them of the reforms. Our approach to the political economy of unilateralism is organized around Bhagwati's (1988) framework of Ideology, Institutions, and Interests. Finally, in order to get some idea of the political strength of various groups in New Zealand as reflected in trade policy, we use the methodology of Anderson (1998) to estimate effective rates of protection from a twenty-two-sector CGE model of the New Zealand economy.

While our focus is on trying to understand direct trade reforms, many aspects of the entire reform process have had consequences for New Zealand's trading position. Accordingly, we shall start by outlining the major economic reforms that have occurred since the early 1980s.

7.2   The Facts of the New Zealand Experience

A Timeline of Economic Reforms

New Zealand (hereafter NZ) is a country about the size of Great Britain but with a population of only 3.5 million or so. In 1995, GDP was a little under US\$60b[1] (so per capita GDP was a little under US\$17,000) and around 12 percent of this was generated in primary production, 20 percent in manufacturing, and 60 percent in services. Exports amounted to 31 percent of GDP, and raw and processed pastoral and wood products accounted for 70 percent of total merchandise exports (machinery, motor vehicles, and mineral fuels accounted for almost 45% of total merchandise imports.) In sum, NZ is a small, open economy exporting mainly primary and processed primary products.

For a large part of its history since British settlement, NZ had relied on Great Britain as a destination for its agricultural exports. This was the source of NZ's high standard of living: in the early 1950s NZ had one of the 5 highest per capita incomes in the world. The relative decline of the NZ economy in the last thirty years has frequently been pinned on external factors such as the severity with which the oil shocks of the 1970s hit the country and the accession of the United Kingdom to the EEC in 1973. However, Evans, Grimes, and Wilkinson (1996) note that NZ developed a comprehensive (and expensive) system of social legislation and became an increasingly regulated and publicly owned economy.[2] They suggest that the focus on external factors as the source of NZ's woes caused policy-makers to overlook the need for greater internal flexibility so that by the late 1970s/early 1980s NZ had extensive import controls; state ownership of assets, price, and wage controls (including exchange rate and foreign ownership controls); and high debt.

In 1984 an election was called, triggering massive flight out of the NZ dollar,[3] so much so that the Reserve Bank ceased to convert NZ$ to foreign currency the day after the election, leading to a constitutional crisis, "until the outgoing prime minister agreed to implement the instructions of the incoming government" (Evans, Grimes, and Wilkinson 1996, 5). It was with the FX and constitutional crises as background that NZ's new Labour government launched its reform program. Table 7.1 (adapted from Evans, Grimes, and Wilkinson 1996, fig. 2) presents the major components of the reforms.

Economic Performance since the Reforms

The performance of the NZ economy since the reforms were initiated has been well documented[4] so we will just summarize things very briefly here. After very high growth in 1984, NZ experienced real GDP growth of less than 2 percent in every year from 1985 to 1992 (including a fall of over 1% in 1991). However, growth picked up substantially to exceed 3.5 percent per annum from 1993 through 1997. Inflation has fallen dramatically from over 17 percent in 1986 to around 2 percent p.a. from 1991 to the present. Unemployment, historically very low in NZ, hit a high of nearly 11 percent in 1991 and now hovers at around 6 percent of the workforce while employment has risen about 19 percent since 1993. The government has operated a fiscal surplus since 1993 and used it, in large part, to retire public foreign debt. Gross government debt in 1991 was 60.5 percent of GDP, while in 1995 it was only 50.9 percent.[5] Government *overseas* debt in 1993 was 35 percent of GDP, while in 1996 it was 25 percent.

Based on casual observation, it seems that New Zealanders are still quite divided on the effectiveness and desirability of reforms since 1980. Interestingly, however, the governments responsible for the major reforms (the Labour government of 1984 and the National government of 1990) were both subsequently reelected (in 1987 and 1993, respectively), the former with an increased majority. One of

Table 7.1
A simplified chronology of reforms, 1983–1996

	1983	1984	1985	1986	1987	1988	1989	1990	1991	1992	1993	1994	1995	1996
Trade	CER	SMPs abolished		5% across-the-board tariff cut	Tariff Working Party Export subsidies			Full CER FTA						
			Import licensing removed											
		Tariff reductions												
Other goods market		Price freeze lifted		Commerce Act										
		Agricultural subsidies removed												
Financial markets	20% devaluation	NZ$ floated												
Monetary policy							Reserve Bank Act							

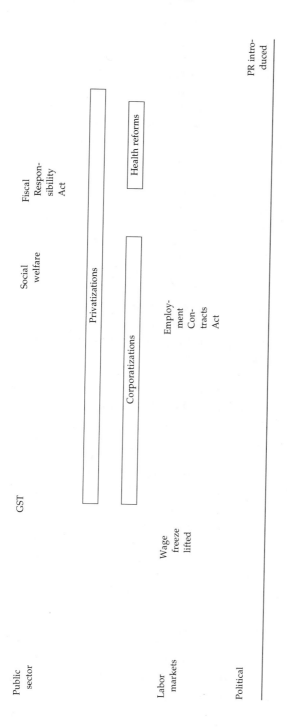

the primary architects of the Labour government's reforms, Roger Douglas, fell out with the prime minister in 1987 and was sacked in 1988. (In an interesting parallel, the finance minister in charge during many of the subsequent reforms under the 1990 National government, Ruth Richardson, was also sacked the year after the National government was reelected in 1993.) It is frequently suggested that voter anger at the reforms was stimulated by the perception that the Labour government was hijacked by a small cabal of reformers who had kept their intentions hidden until they were in power.[6] Not only does the reelection of the Labour government in 1987 cast considerable doubt on this version of events,[7] but Roger Douglas himself had "advocated the case for radical reform some years earlier in a book ..." (Evans, Grimes, and Wilkinson 1996, 7). Furthermore, academic opinion for many years had contended that the NZ economy was overregulated, particularly in the area of trade policy and many public officials, notably in Treasury, were well versed in recent developments in microeconomic theory and had been drawing on this knowledge to develop alternative policy proposals.

The Evolution of Trade Policy in New Zealand

An Overview[8]

Any attempt to quantify the evolution of New Zealand's trade policy over the last forty or fifty years is complicated by the extensive use of quantitative restrictions and (largely as a consequence of this) the wide disparity in levels of protection across sectors. What studies there have been of restrictions through the 1970s tend to be of selected industries only. So one study suggests that in the late 1950s the effective rate of protection of auto assembly was in excess of 2,400 percent and that for clothing was over 120 percent.[9] A more recent and frequently cited study of effective rates in 1982 found rates of 90 percent in textiles and over 50 percent in a number of other manufacturing industries.[10] The wide disparity in rates across sectors makes many indicators of "openness" quite misleading for New Zealand. So even in 1994, for example, while tariff revenues as a percentage of the total value of imports were only 3.4 percent in NZ, about the same as the OECD wide average, the average duty paid on dutiable lines was around 27 percent.[11]

Nevertheless, the general consensus on NZ trade policy through to the early 1980s can be summed up as follows: "[u]p to 1984, New

Zealand had probably the highest tariffs on manufactured goods of any OECD country, and was the only developed country to maintain a comprehensive system of quantitative controls."[12]

This contrasts with the following comment from the Office of the U.S. Trade Representative in 1997: "New Zealand's open trade and investment policy continues to be a bellwether for regional and global trade and investment liberalization" (USTR 1997, 267). Likewise, the WTO comments, "New Zealand has transformed its economy from among the most heavily protected and regulated into one of the most market-oriented and open in the world."[13] In 1996 the average applied tariff on all dutiable lines in NZ was only 10.3 percent (down from 27% only two years earlier and projected to fall to less than 6% by 2000), and the trade-weighted average applied tariff rate across all goods was 5.2 percent.[14]

The origins of protection in NZ have been traced back to the 1880s when a depression led to a switch in motivation for tariffs (and a general increase in the tariff level) from revenue to sectoral protection (arguably as a response to declining natural protection induced by falling ocean freight rates).[15] For our purposes, however, we note only that in 1938 a foreign exchange crisis, which dramatically reduced NZ's exchange reserves, led to blanket import licensing in NZ. Coverage fell over the next two decades but was restored to 100 percent in 1958. It gradually declined again until by the start of the 1970s about 30 percent of all imports were covered by license requirements.

At the same time, a rather haphazard pattern of tariffs emerged, motivated largely by import-substitution goals. Accordingly, most raw materials were imported duty-free and tariffs were modest on intermediates and generally high on finished goods: a pattern of cascading tariffs with correspondingly high effective rates of protection. Final goods were only protected, however, if a domestic industry existed[16] so that nominal and effective rates of protection were widely dispersed across industries.

The importance of external trade to NZ was certainly understood in this period, and the harmful consequences for exporting industries of high import restrictions was also recognized. However, the only responses to these observations were the introduction of additional distortions aimed to "compensate" exporters for the harm done to them by import restrictions and the pursuit (to a small degree) of bilateral liberalization with Australia in the form of the original

NAFTA of 1966. This focus on exporters was also heightened in the 1950s and 1960s by the perceived possibility of British entry into the European Common Market, which stimulated a desire to promote greater diversification in NZ's export base. Accordingly, explicit export subsidies were introduced in the 1960s and by the late 1970s there were many forms of explicit assistance to exporters, primarily those of nontraditional export products: export development expenditures were given tax write-offs; exporters were given greater access to import licenses; and an incremental export subsidy scheme was introduced. It has been estimated that in 1982–1983 the pretax subsidy equivalent of these incentives was over $400 million[17] or nearly 17 percent of the total value of NZ exports.

New Zealand's trade policies had been perceived for some time to have negative effects on resource allocation, and these perceptions found a strong voice in a 1968 report on the NZ economy prepared by the World Bank. The first cautious steps to serious reform were taken in 1969 at the National Development Conference, which recommended, essentially, that protection of manufactures should be "tariffied." The government of the day announced its intention to do this over a period of five years, but this triggered such a strong response from manufacturers that the proposal went to a committee that recommended more cautious implementation. In 1972 the government announced that it had decided to postpone the tariffication measures and, instead, announced significant increases in export incentives. Furthermore, in 1978 a new (and what was to become very generous) system of price supports for agricultural producers was introduced: supplementary minimum prices (SMPs).

From 1975–1977 a Tariff Review Committee undertook a substantial review of NZ's tariff structure with a view to determining the "level of tariff necessary to afford domestic producers a reasonable degree of protection." In their 1978 report they identified eleven industries where the appropriate level was considered "excessive" and special Industry Plans were developed for the restructuring of these industries by the Industries Development Commission (IDC).[18]

The first serious liberalization of trade policy came in 1979 when the government announced a number of major changes to import licensing.[19] Consequently, import licensing for non-IDC industries rapidly disappeared: In 1986 it was announced that import licensing on all non-IDC industries would end in 1988. Finally, import licensing ended for all industries in 1992.

In 1983 NAFTA was replaced by the far more comprehensive Closer Economic Relations (CER) free trade area (FTA) agreement with Australia. The original intention was to develop a full FTA by 1995 with export incentives for trans-Tasman trade removed by 1987, tariffs by 1988, and quotas by 1995. In fact this was all achieved some five years ahead of schedule, by the middle of 1990. The FTA has gone beyond many other bilateral agreements in also coordinating competition policies across the partners and removing anti-dumping measures—see Vautier and Lloyd (1997) for more details.

In 1985 the new Labour government announced its intentions of liberalizing foreign trade more rapidly than the previous government had envisaged, through reductions of high tariffs on non-IDC industries.[20] In 1986 the government also announced its intention to convert all specific tariffs to ad valorem equivalents, and in 1987 a Tariff Working Party was set up, preempting a planned major review of 1988.

This group recommended that tariffs be reduced further and more uniformity be introduced into the tariff system and, in December of that year, the government announced a plan for more radical tariff reform than initially envisaged in 1984. The "Swiss formula" of the GATT Tokyo Round was adopted to improve tariff uniformity, and tariffs (including those less than 20%) were cut in half by 1992 with IDC industries included as their plans finished.

In 1990 a schedule for further reductions beyond 1992 was announced but, with a new government, this was suspended and a more modest proposal slated.[21] Tariffs for the post-1996 era were reviewed again in 1994, and the consequences of this review are noted in table 7.2. Furthermore, any tariff that was 5 percent or less on July 1 1996 was removed by 1998. These tariff reductions were

Table 7.2
Tariff reform schedule, 1996–2000

Tariff in 1996	Tariff in 2000
Under 15%	5%*
15% to 20%	10%
Over 20%	15%**

Source: Ministry of Commerce (1994).
*Except for motor vehicle components, which will only fall to 10%.
**Auto tariffs, scheduled to be 15% in July 2000 but cut to 0% in December 2000, were in fact cut to 0 in July 1998.

scheduled to occur in four annual approximately equal steps. Finally, the few remaining specific tariffs (most notably in some apparel lines) were reduced in accordance with the schedule for their
ad valorem equivalents except for the specific tariff on used autos,
abolished along with all other auto tariffs in July 1998.

So by the year 2000 only four tariff rates were scheduled to be applied in NZ: 0 percent, 5 percent, 10 percent, and 15 percent. However, a new Labour government elected in late 1999 suspended the
tariff reductions scheduled for 2000, freezing all tariffs at their 1999
levels. New Zealand's APEC commitment to full free trade by the
year 2010 still holds; however, the previous schedule to attain this by
2006 is now in some doubt.

What have been the consequences for NZ's trade performance of
these liberalizations? New Zealand's export mix has altered substantially over the last few decades, both in terms of product lines
and in terms of markets. There is much less reliance on both "traditional" export products (wool and meat) and "traditional" markets
(particularly the U.K.) with increased diversification, both in terms
of actual destinations and in terms of the number of trading partners.[22] Of course, these trends have been occurring for some time
and cannot be attributed solely to the reforms. But NZ enjoyed an
export boom from 1991 to 1995 and, interestingly enough, it was
characterized by an increasing volume and diversity of manufactured exports, in particular: from 1991 to 1995 nonfood manufacturing export volumes grew by 11 percent per annum, on average.[23] A
great deal of this growth comes from exports to Australia: Almost
one quarter of NZ's total manufactured exports (including primary
food processing) go to Australia and the value of that trade nearly
doubled from 1988 to 1994.[24]

Some empirical work suggests that there is a structural break in
both the NZ merchandise export and import time-series around
1988–1990 with real exports growing significantly faster in the 1991–
1995 period (6.4%) than in the 1967–1989 period (4%).[25] Another
study looking at the performance of NZ exporters by markets and
by product categories measured against the performance of other
exporters[26] found that, over the period 1970–1985, the value of NZ's
exports grew substantially less than the value of world trade overall.
This was largely because of NZ's export commodity composition,
which was concentrated on primary goods with slow-growing mar-

kets. Over the period 1985–1993, NZ's overall export growth was still slower than world trade growth (and the main reason was again the product mix), but the gap had narrowed dramatically.

Focus on Manufacturing

The evolution of trade reform in NZ outlined earlier makes it clear that manufacturing has long been the focus of—and driving force behind—protective efforts. In this section we look more closely at the evolution of manufacturing protection in NZ and the position of manufacturers regarding the reforms. We then examine, in a little more detail than above, the consequences for manufacturers of the trade reforms.

As noted earlier, protection in NZ has long had a cascading pattern with high restrictions on imports of finished goods that competed with domestic products and very low or zero restrictions on raw materials and inputs or goods not produced domestically. This was a conscious import-substitution strategy predicated upon a belief that manufacturing was intrinsically valuable, a belief buttressed in later years by a desire to diversify NZ's export base. At the National Development Conference (NDC) of 1969, for example, the Manufacturing Committee was "directed to outline a national strategy for attaining the optimum growth of the manufacturing sector ... with particular reference to the development of manufacturing activity that can contribute to a major breakthrough in exports."[27] The committee stresses the belief that positive externalities are likely with manufacturing and goes on to recommend a number of measures the government should take in order to support manufacturing.

This report may be the source of the subsequent understanding of manufacturers that their protection was "needs-based." Paragraph 101 of the report reads, "[t]he essential point is that where industry requires protection this is because it has higher unit costs and cannot market an equivalent product at the same price as a competing import."[28] Nevertheless, the committee recommended that the *form* of protection should change from quantitative restrictions to tariffs for a number of reasons: (1) administrative simplicity (particularly in avoiding the decision of who gets licenses), (2) revenue, (3) international acceptability, (4) greater responsiveness to foreign supply changes, and (5) greater ease of measurement of the costs of protection.

In discussion of this committee's recommendations at the NDC plenary sessions, a number of the stronger recommendations concerning industrial policy and protection were referred to a select committee. These included the following:

212. That Government should proceed *with all practicable haste* to implement its announced policy of dismantling the import licensing system and replacing it with a policy of appropriate tariffs.

213. That Government be urged to continue the dismantling of the import licensing scheme *with all practicable speed* (our italics).

The select committee, which included the president of the Manufacturers' Federation, replaced these and other clauses with recommendation 209A that, while less enthusiastic about the speed with which tariffication should occur, was nevertheless clear in endorsing it. The final recommendation passed by the conference was the following:

209A: The manufacturing sector should be accorded a level of protection sufficient to promote steady industrial development [and] increasing manufactured exports ... This level of protection, however, should be such as to encourage competition efficiency and reasonable prices to other sectors and to consumers ... It is accordingly recommended that the system of protection should be flexible, that import licensing should be replaced by tariffs ... and that this transition should be carried out ... within a reasonable time. It is recognized, however, that there are cases where other protective measures including import licensing may be more appropriate than a tariff.

By the time of the second NDC in March 1972, however, manufacturers had cold feet: "in the light of changed conditions they no longer see recommendation 209A as appropriate to maintain a level of confidence in the manufacturing sector."[29] The review committee redrafted the recommendation (and expanded it from its original 127 words to a much-hedged and caveated 494 words in four parts with sections and subsections). The thrust of the amended 209A is that tariffication is no longer the central point of the recommendation but simply an option to be considered in consultation with industry and so forth. As noted earlier, this led to the shelving of plans for reforms of the licensing scheme. Interestingly, Federated Farmers of NZ, the Associated Chambers of Commerce of NZ, the NZ Retailers' Federation, and the NZ Bureau of Importers and Exporters all made submissions to this new committee supporting the current version of 209A (NDC 1972, 21). The changed stance of the manufacturers suggests that the committee's findings, which essentially acceded to the wishes of the Manufacturers' Federation, did not stem from a national belief in the infant industry and externality arguments floated in favor of continued high assistance to manufacturing but rather from the political power of manufacturers as a group.

When the 1979 budget announced the first tendering of licenses, it was with the intent of not only introducing some foreign competition into consumer goods industries but also getting some sense, via the size of tender premia, of the magnitude of protection that was being afforded through the licensing system. Manufacturers continued to resist tariffication even as license tendering increased, until acquiescing to a gradual program in 1984. The Treasury, in its background papers for the 1984 Economic Summit, notes that

[i]n order to pursue the goals of assistance reform in activities outside those subject to industry plans, discussions were initiated last year [1983] with the NZ Manufacturers' Federation, aimed at developing arrangements for the gradual switch from import licensing to tariffs as the prime means of protection ... The motivation for [a rule suggesting that increases in license allocations for tender would depend positively on tender premia] is to ensure that a somewhat faster rate of adjustment to import competition is faced by the most highly assisted ("tall poppy") industries *as revealed by the size of tender premia*.[30] (our italics)

Despite this, it appears that manufacturers had a sense that the premia were to determine the "scientific tariff" needed by each industry, along the lines of the Manufacturing Committee Report at the NDC some ten years earlier! So the Manufacturers' Federation could write in its newsletter of May 1984 of its understanding that the "tariff would be based on the needs of the particular industry provided those needs were not 'very high' (150–200 percent duty)."[31] The acquiescence of manufacturers in 1983 to the principle of tariffication and reform (the latter perhaps unknowingly!) was the beginning of the end as far as protection of manufacturing was concerned. The new Labour government of 1984 devalued the currency by 20 percent and explicitly argued that this "devaluation has created conditions conducive to an acceleration of this assistance reform program. In particular, the devaluation will produce an increase in the cost of imported goods (and thereby an increase in the level of protection) and an increase in export returns."[32]

The general lesson that emerges from this discussion is that the favored position of manufacturers in NZ can be attributed in part to a general belief on the part of planners and policymakers in the desirability of manufacturing per se and in part to the strength of manufacturers as a political group. One feature of protection in New Zealand that has survived all the reforms is a favoring of certain industries within the manufacturing sector. So in the 1994 tariff review for 1996–2000 the Minister of Commerce and Industry noted, "[a]s in the past special consideration has been given to the textiles, apparel, footwear and automotive industries."[33] Before turning to political economy explanations of protection of manufacturing in NZ, however, it is instructive to look more closely at the consequences for the manufacturing sector of the general reforms to date. In light of the wide scope of NZ's reforms, however, the following caveat is instructive: "When contemplating likely results from past and present liberalizations, it is important to keep in mind that trade often plays a distant second fiddle to bigger macroeconomic issues."[34]

It is clear that the initial impact of the reforms on the manufacturing sector was strongly negative but, in recent years, perhaps as a consequence of other reforms (particularly to the transport industry and to labor markets in NZ), output and exports in particular have picked up.[35] Furthermore, exporting has become more significant in most product lines for all size firms as shown in table 7.3.

It would be of some interest to know the role played by both existing firms and new entrants into manufacturing in the recent export boom. Roberts, Sullivan, and Tybout (1996) report that only about a half of export growth in their microstudy of several export booms is attributable to incumbent exporters: the rest comes from nonexporters choosing to export. In the NZ case, one study of firm behavior from 1987 to 1991 found that approximately half (1,123 out

Table 7.3
Exports as % of total sales by value

	Year	Primary food processing	Textiles	Wood products	Paper products	Chemical	Basic metals
Large firms	1982	88.2	41.5	12.2	17	16.4	39.9
	1994	65.2	53.2	26.6	16.8	18.1	75
Small and medium firms	1982	19	16.2	5.5	7.3	30.2	11.5
	1994	25.4	31.3	5.4	16.7	34.7	22.4

Source: Colgate (1995), 4–5.

of 2,551) of the manufacturing firms surveyed who were exporters in 1987 (and still existed in 1991) were no longer exporters. Over the same period, only a small fraction (about 9%) of firms that sold only to the domestic market in 1987 had become exporters by 1991.[36]

By 1998 the most significant sectors that continued to attract high protection were motor vehicles (assembly and component production) and textiles, clothing, and footwear (TCF). Nevertheless, as protection of motor vehicles has declined, imports have increased and the sector has shrunk dramatically already. New Zealand has also experienced a large increase in imported used cars from Japan in recent years, which has also contributed to domestic production falling—by almost 50 percent in the last ten years. Employment in the assembly industry at the beginning of 1997 was only 2,200 people with a little more than that employed in production of components.[37] In late 1997 the government announced that all tariffs on new and used auto imports would be abolished in the year 2000, falling from 15 percent in July of that year to 0 percent in December. Finally, it was announced in the 1998 budget that "the government has received representations from the industry that market uncertainty should be brought to an end. Therefore ... [t]ariffs on motor vehicles ... will be removed with effect from midnight tonight." Table 7.4 shows the consequences of tariff reforms for the nominal tariff on imported, completely assembled autos in NZ, and table 7.5 provides some basic statistics for passenger cars in NZ.

Table 7.4
Nominal tariff on new autos

1/1/89	1/1/90	1/7/93	1/7/94	1/7/95	1/7/96	1/7/97	1/7/98
45%	35%	32.5%	30%	27.5%	25%	22.5%	0%

Source: Border, Industry and Environmental Policy Group, Ministry of Commerce, Wellington, N2. Private correspondence.

Table 7.5
Some auto industry data

	Nominal tariff on new imports	Used imports	New imports	NZ sales of new cars	NZ production of cars
1988	50%	21,325	11,875	71,372	49,473
1996	25%	117,025	42,860	65,065	29,727

In the TCF industries, employment is somewhat larger but has also declined following liberalization. Around 31,000 people were employed in the apparel and textiles industries in 1985 and only about 20,000 in 1994.

The recent export boom in manufactures, discussed earlier, has surprised a number of commentators: NZ's comparative advantage clearly lies in primary products, and one would anticipate that if trade liberalization improves resource allocation then any export boom should come from the primary sector. That this has not been the case is probably due in part to the patchwork pattern of tariff compensation to agriculture in NZ, which attempted to lessen the export tax component of import restrictions. Furthermore, NZ's actual experience fits quite well with the thesis advanced by Olson (1987). He suggests that high protection of manufactures "facilitate[s] collective action to collude and cartelize" (256), which in turn distorts resource allocation further and leads to greater inefficiencies. Accordingly, one would anticipate very low export ratios in such sectors. Liberalization then induces an increase in exports of the protected sector. Our discussion of the evolution of the manufacturers' position in NZ certainly suggests that protection facilitated collusion on a political front and enabled manufacturers to wield surprising political power.

This discussion brings us to the political economy of protection of manufactures in NZ. Some efforts have been made to try to explain the pattern of assistance to manufacturing industries in terms of industry features. One study regressing industry *assistance* (trade protection as well as assorted subsidies and tax concessions) on industry characteristics in 1981–1982 found that assistance was higher, ceteris paribus,

• the lower the skill level of workers (measured by educational achievement),
• the lower the industry's growth rate,
• the lower were transport costs (i.e., natural protection),
• the less important were exports, and
• the higher the number of firms in the industry.[38]

Employment and labor-intensity were not found to be significant. This study omitted the motor vehicle assembly industry, for reasons of data problems, and is therefore likely to be influenced largely by the extremely high protection accorded to other industries such as textiles, apparel, and footwear. Interestingly, however, they found that geographical concentration tended to *reduce* protection although it was concentration in nonurban areas that had this effect. This fits with a suggestion by John Yeabsley that high assistance to TCF industries might be attributable, in part, to the fact that they are relatively high employers of rural women and find a political voice through that.[39]

The finding that protection increased with the number of firms in an industry runs counter to common arguments that pressure group formation and thus political effectiveness will be hampered by free-rider problems as the number of firms increases. Of course, these numbers are small anyway in the NZ case (the authors report an average of 60 versus 164 in Australia) and may reflect the incentives for entry to protected industries. These incentives will be limited, however, by quotas as opposed to tariff protection.

Another more recent study looks at the pattern of plant exit in NZ manufacturing from 1986 to 1989.[40] Over this period, the effective rate of assistance for manufacturing declined from 39 percent to 19 percent and nearly 20 percent of their initial sample of around 4,000 medium to large plants had exited by late 1989. The study attempts to explain exit with a range of plant, firm, and industry characteristics, finding that exit was more likely

• by high-cost, larger and younger plants,

• if the plant was owned by a firm that owned more than one plant,

• if it was not foreign-owned,

• the greater was the fall in the effective rate of assistance to the industry, and

• the more significant was import licensing as an element of that assistance.

While interpretation of these results as consequences of trade liberalization is a little doubtful,[41] they do suggest the unsurprising result that highly protected industries were also highly inefficient.

The Gibson and Harris (1996) study also notes that the exporters in the sample tend to have larger plants, have fewer plants per firm, use more specialized capital, and be younger than the overall sample average: "With the exception of plant age, the characteristics of successful exporters are also the major characteristics of surviving plants." A recent paper by Clerides, Lach, and Tybout (1998) examines the same episodes of export booms as Roberts, Sullivan, and Tybout (1996) and suggests that there is a self-selection of efficient firms into exporting. This in turn suggests that, ceteris paribus, exit of nonexporters as in the NZ case will tend to be efficiency-improving. Finally, a recent study by Ratnayake (1999) suggests that concentration in NZ manufacturing has declined since the reforms were initiated.

All in all, these studies suggest that the pattern of protection of manufacturing in NZ had been motivated as much by "social policy" concerns as by anything else. This fits well with the persistence of protection for certain sectors through the reforms and might explain why NZ's unilateral reforms did not jump immediately to full free trade. Indeed, from the initial major reforms in the early 1980s, the current schedule is such that NZ will have taken over two decades to reach full free trade.

Another explanation that has been put forward for the persistence of sectoral protection is that when the Labour government of 1984 introduced sweeping reforms, it essentially "outflanked" the National party, its main Opposition. In subsequent elections, and as a backlash against the reforms mounted, National chose to "differentiate their product" by pledging their support for freer trade as a *practical* matter rather than an *ideological* one.[42] Accordingly, they had few qualms about continued protection for certain sectors and, indeed, could use the commitment to more gradual trade reform as evidence of their practicality.[43]

Agriculture
The negative consequences of import protection for exporters have long been recognized in New Zealand (this is evidenced in statements by agricultural representatives at the NDC in 1969 and also explains, in part, the cascading pattern of protection that evolved up until the 1970s). The political response to this, however, has typically been to offer additional interventions designed to offset these consequences rather than to question the initial protection itself.

This interpretation of assistance to primary producers as "tariff compensation" is widespread. Lattimore and Wooding (1996, 319) note that the introduction of producer marketing boards with monopoly export rights in the 1930s was an explicit quid pro quo for increased protection of imports. Others have argued that attempts at trade "liberalization," beginning around 1962, "can be characterized as an attempt to move closer to neutrality in trade intervention by the provision of compensation to exporters for the effects of import protection"[44] and that "a stated justification of the supplementary minimum price (SMP) scheme [a price support scheme for certain agricultural products introduced in 1978] was to compensate farmers for cost excesses due to protection to the manufacturing industries."[45] Tariff compensation finds its most explicit official voice, however, in the minister of finance, the Rt. Hon. Robert Muldoon, in the 1982 Budget: "[t]he chief purpose of the export incentives is to compensate exporters for the high costs they face because of import protection."

Thus, quite ironically given its comparative advantage, New Zealand developed a system of high assistance to agriculture. Evans, Grimes, and Wilkinson (1996, 39) report that the effective rate of assistance to pastoral agriculture, looking at all forms of transfers, was in excess of 30 percent during the early part of the 1980s (largely due to SMP payments), reaching a peak of 120 percent in 1983. However, it has been argued that, apart from in 1983 (when the true effective rate of assistance was 25%) these payments did not fully compensate farmers for the losses incurred through import protection.[46]

The consequences of the reforms for agriculture have been dramatic. Evans, Grimes, and Wilkinson (1996) report that effective transfers to the sector were negative by 1990 and rationalization has been extensive: Farmland prices fell sharply with deregulation and the pattern of farming has changed—sheep numbers fell by 30 percent in the decade from 1985 to 1995, for example.

Interestingly, however, farmers as a group were big supporters (indeed leaders of the dominant farmer organization were initiators) of the reform of the early to mid-1980s. To trace the origins of this, it is helpful to expand our analysis of the state of agriculture in the period leading up to the reforms.

From the middle of the 1970s to the onset of the reforms agricultural subsidies were, as we have mentioned, designed to compensate agriculture for the high levels of protection afforded manufacturing.[47] In part this stemmed from the deteriorating balance of payments and growing public debt.[48] Evidence for concern about export performance is revealed by the establishment of an export subsidy scheme for manufactures.[49] At the same time the subsidy schemes were designed to generate extra output (i.e., exports) from *agriculture* as well.[50] These incremental subsidies sought to produce extra output at a lower government budgetary cost than if the same intended output expansion was engendered by broad-based subsidies. Evans and Morgan (1983) report many of the subsidy schemes of the late 1970s and early 1980s resulted in user costs of capital inputs that, at the time of investment, were virtually zero, and in some cases negative. This subsidization meant that the marginal rate of return to investment on farms was much higher than the average rate of return farmers were experiencing in their businesses as a whole. While it may have encouraged extra production, it did not raise the profitability of farming vis à vis that of other industries. So farmers as a group came to perceive that their share of economic rents resulting from government management of the economy was less than that they would achieve in a much less centrally controlled economy.

Farmers anticipated higher (average) rewards from comparative advantage in a deregulated economy. Just prior to the reforms, subsidies and regulation had reached the point where they were widely perceived as not sustainable. This, and the belief that in a fully deregulated economy farming would achieve a higher income share, predisposed farmer support for the reforms and farmer special interest groups have broadly supported the reforms since their inception.

In 1985, the reform of agriculture started abruptly with the removal of subsidies. It was accompanied by plans for reform of other sectors, but was almost contemporaneous with deregulation of the financial sector and the foreign exchange market. Significant state sector reform did not start until 1988 and labor market reform did not take place until 1991. With the exception of changes to the regulatory framework for natural resource use, the statutory monopoly of a number of producer boards remains the key unresolved source of statutory constraints on agriculture.[51] These boards' statutory powers include the right to levy producers, compulsory product purchase, the sole right of export, and the responsibility for the administration of quotas imposed by foreign countries. The effect of these boards on competitive supply, price signals, and efficient provision of supply, marketing, contracting, and transport services is under wide scrutiny and debate.

The general reform program also included reconsideration of legislation controlling town and country development. The Resource

Management Act of 1992 replaced all previous legislation and its goal was a framework for sustainable use of resources. The focus of the act is to promote sustainable land use while placing greater weight on effects of actions, rather than actions themselves, and on property owners' rights to make decisions. Because the Resource Management Act replaces, rather than builds on, previous case law, its introduction has injected uncertainty into planning and development procedures for agriculture. Local government authorities have the responsibility of administering the act, and they have adopted various positions on the trade-off between regulatory restriction and unfettered decision making by owners, although they are constrained by the requirement that restrictions be justified by economic analysis. There is uncertainty about the enforceability of some local government positions and promulgated regulations. In many regions, the new act has provided more freedom to subdivide properties for various purposes, and it is sustaining a trend to smaller farms that really started in the mid-1980s as farmers sought to restructure their debt.

In the context of the other planned reforms, the rapid deregulation of the financial (including foreign exchange) sectors and full funding of the government budget deficit resulted in a period of high interest rates and real exchange rate in 1985. In conjunction with the simultaneous removal of agricultural subsidies, the profitability of farming was vastly reduced and agriculture retrenched. The decline in farmland prices in the 1985–1988 period was as much as 50 percent in real terms. Restructuring was not smoothed by government-sponsored transitional arrangements, and a number of farmers were bankrupted. Others retained ownership by selling portions of their farms.

Agriculture has changed and diversified. Its commodities now account for less than 50 percent of total exports, and there has been much change in operation and the product mix. Meat and wool farms have borne the brunt of change. The decline in sheep numbers and expansion of forestry reflect the low terms of trade for sheep products and reversion from the high levels of capital stock resulting from the prereform policy of encouraging extra production with scant regard for international product price signals.[52] It also reflects the relative profitability of sheep and forestry, in part engendered by world prices and in part by the exceptional tax treatment of forestry.

Although diversification into deer farming and horticulture as well as wine production started in the 1970s and early 1980s, agriculture has been consolidated since that time. Indeed, horticultural export growth has accounted for much of the growth in agricultural value added and exports broadly defined. The strong growth of tourism in the 1990s has made it a major foreign exchange earner, and it has been associated with changes to farms to meet tourism demands.

The changed operation of farms reflects the need for individual farmers to manage their own risk rather than rely on government programs, and benefits associated with contracting directly with customers for specific products. Their larger size, permitting specialization of intensity and better access to capital markets, may entail corporate farms having advantages over the family farm in both these areas. Although they are few in number, more public corporations exist in farming than in 1984.

Industries supplying inputs to agriculture have followed agriculture's cycle. In particular, the meatpacking industry, which was once heavily regulated, has had to undergo major restructuring since entry became open in the early 1980s, as sheep numbers have declined, and in response to demands for value-added meat products rather than meat as a commodity. The restructuring has carried with it a number of bankruptcies resulting in significant losses to shareholders and farmers. The industry still has excess capacity, particularly under the current, more flexible terms of employment, and is likely to remain volatile for some time to come.

Rural NZ is continuing to change rapidly in the directions already indicated. It is affected by factors that include ancillary industries' adjustments, the major change to the regulation of resource use, and the continuing expansion of tourism. It is more diversified and has a continuing decline in the importance of traditional farming operations and products. Agriculture's contribution to GDP and exports have grown since the onset of the reforms. But between 1991 and 1996 pastoral farming's share of exports fell from 46 percent to 43 percent, and between 1994 and 1997 the contribution of farming to GDP fell from 6.2 percent to 4.9 percent.[53] Philpott (1994) estimates that during the ten years since 1984 agricultural and horticultural GDP grew by 6.4 percent per annum, and total factor productivity by 7.7 percent, much of it attributable to horticulture. He suggests that the average labor productivity of agriculture has increased more rapidly than in manufacturing over the reform period. Finally, between 1979–1981 and 1996, producer subsidy equivalents— expressed as a percentage of the value of agricultural output averaged across all OECD countries—increased from 29 percent to 36 percent.[54] For NZ the percentage decreased from 18 percent to 3 percent in the mid-1980s, and it has remained at this low level.

With this background we return again to the political economy of NZ's agricultural reform. The abrupt reduction in profitability of farming in the mid-1980s did not change the pro-deregulation stance of leaders of NZ's farming interest groups. Their response was not to change their commitment to deregulation, consequent to the plight of farmers, but rather it was to regard the costs as transitional and to speed up the process of reform by promoting further deregulation of other sectors of the economy. In particular, they have been firm advocates of reducing border protection and government expenditure. They have held this position throughout the 1986–1997 period despite some reverses in interest group membership, but without the formation of competing farmer-representative organizations.[55] It may be that the current distribution of rents is regarded as being as much to farmers' advantage as could be expected under further regulation and subsidies, especially given the increased international pressure, under the GATT agreement of the Uruguay Round, for other countries to deregulate their agriculture. Indeed, NZ's unilateral stance toward agricultural subsidies offers this country's agriculture a prominent exemplary leadership role that may aid in gaining access to markets.

7.3 The Political Economy of New Zealand's Unilateral Trade Reforms

There has been in the NZ experience a remarkable change in the direction and coalition of interest group pressures. In addition to agricultural interest groups, manufacturers have also advocated government expenditure reductions during the 1990s. Their position reflects these groups' perception that the lower this expenditure, the less pressure that monetary policy will place on interest rates and concomitantly on the exchange rate: ergo, lower government expenditure leads to a lower exchange rate. It is not the argument about this linkage that is remarkable; rather, it is that farmers and manufacturers have joined forces in their advocacy of a point of view. It reflects the long-held view of farming leaders about border protection and consequent domestic costs and the fact that exporting is now so important to manufacturing that the goals of its representative group have become aligned with many of those of farming. Prior to the 1990s, with manufacturing under a protective umbrella, the interests of the two groups were quite different. It may be that the coalition of interests will be strong enough to preserve NZ's low and declining border protection, thus making this aspect of the reforms more sustainable.

Political interest group influence has changed in other ways. In the mid-1980s the New Zealand Business Roundtable (NZBR) established a secretariat that has continued to finance and conduct studies across a wide spectrum of economic and social policy areas. The reports have not had a sectoral point of view but have typically argued for policies that entail an open and competitive economy with reduced government.[56] They have been influential, partly as a consequence of their frequently employing academics (often U.S. academics) to author their studies. Such a grouping did not exist prior to 1984, and the concordance of its views with many of the common policies of farmer and manufacturer organizations yields a consensus about the direction of the economy from the business sector that will continue to advocate low levels of border protection in NZ.

Before turning to specific issues in the political economy of NZ's unilateral trade reforms, we should stress again that no aspect of NZ's economic reforms can be analyzed in isolation. We argue below, for example, that an important (perhaps the *most* important) motivation for unilateral trade reforms was in providing credibility to the reform process itself.

Ideas

Perceptions of NZ's Performance and the Need for Change
As NZ's trade liberalization was, in many respects, just another facet of general economic liberalization, so the causes of and motivations for the latter apply equally to the former. Thus general dissatisfaction with the hands-on economic management style of the outgoing National government, for instance, may have been as important a motivator in trade liberalization as any other factor. However, we have noted already that criticism of NZ's trade policy regime, both

from within and from external commentators, had been around for some decades and had been growing. So the 1968 World Bank report on the NZ economy was quite explicit in its criticism of NZ's reliance on high protection in general and quantitative restrictions in particular: "[t]he most important single measure which can help make NZ manufacturing internationally competitive is its gradual exposure to competition from imports. This requires a removal of quantitative import restrictions and a reliance on [temporary] tariff protection [which] ... should be gradually reduced."[57] This criticism was also echoed in International Monetary Fund (IMF) and Organisation for Economic Cooperation and Development (OECD) reports through the years.

Alternatives

An important question that needs to be answered is *why* NZ chose to reform its economy in such an extensive fashion and in such a short time period. That some drastic change should occur was almost inevitable (but see Kelsey 1995, chap. 14, for a dissenting view), but it is not obvious why such a *broad* program of reforms should have been initiated. When the Labour Party took over the government in 1957, for instance, they also faced deteriorating FX reserves but responded by imposing 100 percent import licensing.

The difference probably lies in the coincidence of economic and constitutional crises and in the fact that the incoming government had (at least, some of its key members had) a coherent and already articulated philosophy of economic management. Furthermore, the outgoing government had been characterized by a general policy of extreme interventionism in the economy, and there were no clear signs that it had been at all effective. Accordingly there was a strong sense of dissatisfaction with the idea that activist government policy could be a panacea for all—or any—ills. Indeed, it's been suggested that the overwhelming support for the Labour government of 1984 was less an endorsement of their reform package (which was largely unannounced in their campaigning) than a rejection of what went before.[58]

As far as trade policy is concerned, the timing of these crises was such that real alternatives to unilateral liberalization were few. We have argued that it had been clear since the late 1960s that trade reform was needed in NZ, but neither multilateralism nor bilateralism were immediate enough to be attractive to the reformers. Speed of reform was highly emphasized by the Labour reformers.[59] The General Agreement on Tariffs and Trade (GATT) was between rounds with the Tokyo Round having left many unsettled issues, and the direction of the United States was uncertain—while encouraging a further round of GATT talks, it also passed the Trade and Tariff Act of 1984 granting presidential authority to negotiate bilateral deals. Multilateralism through GATT could not be initiated by NZ, and the delay involved in negotiating reciprocity for domestic reforms, if it could be done at all, would have been too great. Indeed, there was explicit recognition in the Treasury that NZ was too small a player to have any effects on the policies of other countries, be they trade policies or any other form of industry assistance.

The main bilateral option available was in trade with Australia and, indeed, the pace of this was accelerated, as we have noted, but in tandem with unilateral liberalization.

The Role of Individuals

Antagonists and protagonists alike attribute the reforms to a "conjunction of personalities, economics, politics and the prevailing ideology" (Kelsey 1995, 353), and it is inevitable that personalities must be involved to some extent in a country with a population the size of Toronto. Roger Douglas's role in initiating and leading the institution of the reforms, along with key advisers and other members of parliament, is clearly significant and is well documented elsewhere.[60] Nevertheless, Evans, Grimes, and Wilkinson (1996) suggest that this aspect of the reforms has been overstressed. It is certainly the case that the initial enthusiasm for reform was coincident with Labour party principles (as witnessed by subsequent comments of the then-prime minister, David Lange, who remarked in 1989, "I apologize ... for nothing of what we did to begin with ... in the course of about three years we changed from being a country run like a Polish shipyard into one that could be internationally competitive"[61]). Both those in favor of and those against the reforms also acknowledge a growing consensus among academics—and awareness among key public servants—that the NZ economy was overregulated and that liberalization to some degree was inevitable. As already suggested, this consensus did not just spring up overnight but had been foreshadowed many years earlier. The notion, then, that the reforms were somehow an aberration or purely a product of personalities seems difficult to maintain.

Surprisingly, particularly in contrast to the experience in Australia where it was a strong factor in promoting reform, explicit academic criticism of NZ's trade policy continued to be muted.[62] The infant-industry argument was generally accepted as a valid theoretical rationale for protection and, as we have seen, there was a strong belief in the external benefits of manufacturing. Even at the Economic Summit of 1984 when manufacturers themselves were facing up to the reality of life with import competition, the submission of a leading academic economist, while decrying the particularly high levels of protection in certain sectors, wrote:

[t]here are strong arguments for a continuing level of uniform protection— arguments which in our view stem largely from:

(i) Pessimism about the future growth in overseas demand for traditional agricultural export products.

(ii) The high NZ propensity to import such that faster export led growth tends to be frustrated by the spill over into imports.

... There is in fact an optimal level of protection justified by the need to ensure an industrial structure which produces the highest GDP or standard of living possible.[63]

More significant were the opinions of key policy advisers, particularly in the Treasury, which we discuss next.

Institutions

Domestic Political Institutions

The structure of NZ's political system is such that opportunities for far-reaching reforms are more easily taken than in many other systems. New Zealand operates a Westminster-style parliament but with a single House. Accordingly, there is no upper body to overrule decisions made by the elected Parliament. There is no single written constitutional document, and there are no provincial or state legislatures. Further, until 1996 the electoral system was a FPP or first-past-the-post system in which every member of Parliament was a local representative of some geographical constituency. Parliament was (and still is, though to a lesser extent with the introduction of proportional representation in 1996) dominated by two parties, Labour and National. Party loyalty has traditionally been very strong with the effect that government has effectively been by Cabinet. Accordingly, a small group of like-minded individuals can effect rapid and far-reaching change with less opposition than might be encountered in a more pluralistic system.

One very significant counter to this, however, is that the government is elected for only three years at a time. As such it has severe restraints on its ability to enact unpopular policies if they are not broadly supported. This time constraint provided an incentive for rapid reform and, as a consequence, an inducement for *packages* of reforms: In the context of significant reforms, there was simply not time to rely only on bilateralism.

The Role of Domestic Policy Advisors

The main institutions in terms of the role of domestic policy advisors are the NZ Treasury and, to a lesser extent, the Reserve Bank of New Zealand. There were other institutions engaged in public debate but with far less influence—the NZ Planning Council, for instance, issued occasional papers and reports until its demise in 1991—but the Treasury has been the main source of economic policy advice to the NZ government for some decades. The Treasury in New Zealand serves a role that in many other countries is found in a finance department as well as a treasury: it is the main source of economic analysis, briefing, and advice to government. As an advisory body it tends to stay out of open public debate, a feature that has led many critics to view it as pushing a "secret agenda" and as somehow bypassing the democratic process. So critics have perceived its "strategy" as seeking "to impart information and bring important interests on board, not to consult them about the nature and direction of change."[64]

It has been well-documented (see Evans, Grimes, and Wilkinson, for example) that a number of Treasury officials had received postgraduate training in the United States and were well versed in developments in microeconomic theory, particularly concerning public choice, contracting issues, the economics of information, and so forth. In fact, the Treasury was one of the most important conduits of such developments to New Zealand given the relative noninvolvement of academics in the policy debate at the time and the positions taken by those that *were* prepared to debate the reforms.

The Treasury put together an influential briefing document for the incoming Labour government entitled *Economic Management* and the coincidence of its views on reform with those of Roger Douglas gave added impetus to the Labour Party's commitment to reform. The

Treasury position had evolved over a number of decades as its views increasingly came into conflict with those of the National government of the 1970s and early 1980s.[65]

International Institutions

We have already noted the impact of reports on the NZ economy by institutions such as the World Bank, the IMF, and the OECD. It should also be noted that NZ's trade policy had been affected frequently by relations with major trading partners. Tariffs on autos were maintained for many years, for instance, and one reason was British pressure to maintain a tariff preference on U.K. cars. Another example was the U.S. response to NZ export subsidies in the late 1970s/early 1980s when NZ was persuaded to sign the GATT code on countervailing duties. The proximate cause of this was a threat by the United States to remove an injury test in evaluating U.S. firms' complaints about subsidized exports from NZ.[66]

The role of Closer Economic Relations with Australia (CER), particularly as far as trade reform was concerned, is an interesting but difficult one. Clearly CER was important in that it provided the first breath of competition to NZ's domestic industries. Furthermore, Lloyd (1997) has suggested that CER provided a valuable "demonstration effect" on both sides of the Tasman, showing that trade liberalization did not lead to the end of the world as we know it and thus reassuring policymakers and voters alike that further liberalization was also unlikely to be catastrophic. It is interesting to note that overall CER progress has slowed since 1990 or so and that the main reason seems to be Australian reluctance to go much further. Lloyd writes, "[i]n the 1992 negotiations the New Zealand government was anxious to see the Agreement extended [principally to capital flows and services.] ... Australia saw the agreements as a free trade agreement which had almost been completed."[67]

At a theoretical level, it has also been suggested (Richardson 1993) that FTAs might lead, endogenously, to declining external tariffs in a political economy setting. However, NZ officials have suggested that CER was more an epiphenomenon of general liberalization rather than a cause. (As already suggested, it is certainly true that progress under CER was rapidly overtaken by other developments.)

Disentangling the effects of CER from those of unilateral liberalization is an impossible task. Australia has become NZ's largest trading partner and is particularly important as a destination for manufacturing exports, but how much of this would have occurred in the absence of CER is hard to know. While lower Australian trade barriers are a factor in NZ's manufacturing export boom, so are resource reallocation effects of NZ's unilateral reforms. Further, suppose the extent of the liberalization under CER would have occurred even in the absence of each country's unilateral reforms. Then clearly it reduced the cost of unilateralism to New Zealand by eliminating tariffs on the only country that New Zealand might have had any bargaining power over at all.

A question of some interest from the trade policy perspective is what consequences, if any, NZ's liberalizations have had for its role in multilateral negotiation forums—both GATT and regional bodies such as APEC (of which NZ is a vociferous supporter although Lloyd 1997 suggests that this may be from fears of trade diversion should world trade become dominated by aggressive blocs).[68] A priori one would anticipate that it has had very little effect given that NZ is a small player in these settings. Furthermore, NZ threw its insubstantial weight in the GATT negotiations in with the Cairns group of primary exporters, which may have diluted its voice even further. As noted earlier, it is possible that NZ trade negotiators have been assisted by the reforms in that they can take a position of "leadership" as a consequence.

To the extent that NZ has some market power in certain product lines (wool, butter, some horticultural exports), NZ's increased efficiency might reduce world prices and thus increase the costs of protection in other countries. As in Richardson (1993) and Coates and Ludema (1997), a unilateral tariff reduction by one country harms import-competing producers in another and, if their political efforts are the source of protection, this may reduce protection in other countries as well.

However, even where NZ is a big exporter, it is unimaginable that these effects could occur. In the dairy industry, for example,[69] NZ exports 90 percent of its production but this still amounts to less than 2 percent of international output.[70] The NZ Dairy Board was, until 2001, a statutory export monopoly; even so, it was only the ninth largest dairy company in the world. NZ exported 151 tons of butter to the United States in 1994 when U.S. consumption was around half a million tons, and NZ butter exports to the EC are less than 4 percent of European consumption.

A much more credible mechanism by which NZ reforms could influence the policies of trading partners is via Lloyd's "demonstration effect," mentioned earlier. So the reforms have given increased weight to the NZ experience internationally: Unilateral liberalization has led to an *increase* in exports, and removal of assistance to agriculture has led to increased diversification, rationalization, and productivity in the agrarian sector. Furthermore, the NZ experience has been highly publicized internationally.[71]

New Zealand is also active in seeking bilateral deals. "In fact, New Zealand is willing to explore fresh bilateral and subregional free trade options with any of its significant trading partners."[72] Of course, given the extent of its unilateral liberalization any such deals would impose little further obligation on NZ.

One further institution we have not yet discussed in any depth is GATT and its current incarnation, the WTO.[73] As noted, NZ's reforms have been pursued unilaterally. Nevertheless, it is a signatory of GATT and an active participant in GATT negotiations (and has recently taken a successful case to the WTO regarding a dispute over a U.S. "escape clause" tariff on lamb imports). But its unilateral liberalizations have (generally) gone well beyond its obligations under the Uruguay Round agreements. With the exception of transport equipment (93%) and textiles (99.9%), 100 percent of tariff lines are bound and half of these are duty-free.[74] The import-weighted average bound tariff rate in 1996 was 10.8 percent while the average applied tariff rate was only 5.2 percent. Moreover, these figures are somewhat skewed by the existence of high tariffs on a few product lines, as noted earlier.

Interests

ERP Study

We have noted the interests that drove trade protection in NZ but what are the interests that have been best *served* by NZ's protection pattern? To answer this question, we have estimated effective rates of protection across broad sectors of the NZ economy. It has long been known that the standard definition of the effective rate of protection—the percentage change in domestic value added induced by the protective structure—is not meaningful in general equilibrium (Ethier 1977): It tells us nothing about the pattern of production, resource flows, or sectoral returns except under very stringent conditions. Accordingly, we employ an alternative definition advocated by Anderson (1998), which proposes that effective protection for industry j is measured by the level of a uniform tariff on all imports that yields the same return to a specific factor in sector j as does the existing protective structure. Its intended interpretation is that it indicates the power of the specific sector to elicit rents at the expense of society at large, and thus the political power of that sector. We accept Anderson's argument that the term "distributional effective protection" (DERP) may be substituted for "effective protection" (ERP) to best describe his concept. These measures are given by the following:

$$DERP^j \equiv (1/d) - 1$$

and

$$ERP^j \equiv \frac{t_j - \sum \alpha_{ij} t_i}{1 - \sum \alpha_{ij}},$$

where

$$d \equiv \{d : \pi^j((p^1/d), w^0) = \pi^j(p^0, w^0)\},$$

t_i is the ad valorem tariff applied to imports of j,

p^k is the distorted $(k = 0)$ or free trade $(k = 1)$ output and intermediate input price vector,

w^0 is the primary input price vector,

$\pi^j(.,.)$ is the jth industry's profit function, and

α_{ij} is the cost share of intermediate i in industry j.

Under very special conditions DERP and ERP yield the same outcomes.[75] We report both measures for the NZ economy in 1990–1991.

To calculate the uniform tariffs that are equivalent to the tariffs that were in place in NZ in 1990 (DERP), we use a computable general equilibrium model, JOANNA, that is a member of the stable of models that have been constructed by the Research Project in Economic Planning at Victoria University (see Wells and Easton 1986, 182–237). JOANNA is a twenty-two-sector model of the Johansen type (Dixon et al. 1982). Its variables are expressed and solved for as percentage changes in which form the model is linear. The version of JOANNA we have used is based upon Statistics New Zealand's inter-industry study of 1991.

The model has profit- (utility-) maximizing producers (consumers) that admit substitution between labor, capital, and intermediate inputs (8 consumption goods), and the allocation or division of aggregate intermediate goods across industries is determined by fixed coefficient input-output relationships. It incorporates downward-sloping export demand curves and imperfect substitution between domestically produced goods and their imported equivalents. We employ the static short-run version of JOANNA, and in it government consumption and total and government investment are exogenously specified. The short run is taken to be sufficiently long for investment to occur, but without additions to useable capital stock. Total investment is allocated across sectors in the manner that equates expected rates of returns (determined by the current rates of return and the ratio of desired to current capital stocks in each sector). The endogenous contemporaneous rates of return are calculated as the rent to immobile capital—the gross revenue of sector j less the cost of material inputs and labor.

JOANNA determines prices relative to a numeraire that is world prices in NZ dollars. The closure of the model requires exogenously specifying certain variables, and we choose the closure that most closely corresponds to microeconomic trade models: Trade balance and employment are fixed, and the nominal wage is endogenous.

The term "equivalent tariffs" encompasses two tariff measures. Two are required to recognize that whereas for those industries that face border protection in the form of tariffs the statutory tariff rate is the appropriate measure, this is not the case for imports subject to quotas. For these, equivalent tariffs were constructed as the difference between the landed cost of an import and its production cost in NZ. Quotas were of negligible importance in the period of our analysis.

The model was used to calculate the DERP figures of table 7.6, and the data of the model were used to produce that table's ERP data.

The industry-specific uniform tariffs (DERPs) in table 7.6 are obtained from running the model for each sector. In running the model for sector j ($j = 1, \ldots, 22$), the (otherwise endogenous) rent of sector j is held constant in the move from the existing tariff structure to one with a uniform tariff. The exogenous variables are as follows:

Table 7.6
1990 Input-output base data: DERP and ERP

Industry	Rent (return to capital) $m	% of total	Capital stock $m	% of total	Gross output $m	% of total	GDP $m	% of total	Employment 000 FTEs	% of total	DERP %	ERP %
Agriculture	1,479	4.52	32,625	9.55	9,081	5.96	4,142	5.65	123.5	9.58	0.62	-0.47
Fishing	83	0.25	536	0.16	586	0.38	214	0.29	4.3	0.33	4.68	-3.88
Forestry/logging	1,538	4.70	1,308	0.38	2,380	1.56	1,652	2.25	6.4	0.50	5.51	-0.57
Mining	555	1.69	4,737	1.39	1,392	0.91	844	1.15	5.5	0.43	-7.16	-0.63
Food/bev./tobacco	1,085	3.31	10,918	3.20	12,856	8.43	3,694	5.04	58.3	4.52	0.76	19.51
Textiles	133	0.41	2,363	0.69	2,799	1.84	773	1.05	31.6	2.45	36.58	47.15
Wood & products	349	1.07	2,266	0.66	2,087	1.37	821	1.12	17.7	1.38	2.47	9.76
Paper	720	2.20	5,914	1.73	4,635	3.04	1,814	2.47	32.5	2.52	3.09	7.46
Chemicals	761	2.33	7,516	2.20	4,231	2.78	1,492	2.04	19.4	1.50	8.02	13.19
Nonmetallics	104	0.32	1,454	0.43	1,180	0.77	356	0.49	7.0	0.54	-2.53	13.78
Basic metals	167	0.51	4,039	1.18	1,903	1.25	457	0.62	7.5	0.58	6.81	5.27
Fab. metals	680	2.08	6,055	1.77	7,876	5.17	2,410	3.29	65.3	5.06	12.18	21.65
Other manuf.	32	0.10	329	0.10	291	0.19	94	0.13	3.6	0.28	-2.53	35.56
Electricity/water/gas	1,471	4.49	29,996	8.78	4,276	2.81	2,027	2.76	12.0	0.93	2.93	-0.50
Buildings	946	2.89	4,186	1.23	11,976	7.86	3,136	4.28	91.5	7.10	3.39	-8.75
Trade & hotels	3,750	11.45	21,538	6.31	25,796	16.92	10,835	14.78	241.9	18.75	2.44	-3.22

Transport	1,076	3.29	18,597	5.45	7,226	4.74	3,440	4.69	59.0	4.57	6.95	−2.08
Communications	1,009	3.08	6,941	2.03	3,014	1.98	2,233	3.05	33.5	2.60	—	−0.67
Finance	5,180	15.82	28,410	8.32	16,910	11.09	10,146	13.84	131.7	10.20	0.27	−0.65
Own dwellings	4,312	13.17	90,288	26.44	6,783	4.45	5,048	6.89	0.0	0.00	5.03	−0.63
Private services	868	2.65	4,509	1.32	5,706	3.74	2,851	3.89	98.1	7.60	5.61	−2.72
Public services	6,447	19.69	56,951	16.68	19,454	12.76	14,820	20.22	239.8	18.59	5.73	−0.60

- industry capital-use
- aggregate real investment spending
- real investment in industries *min, egw, own, pub*
- real government consumption spending
- nominal exchange rate (numeraire)
- trade balance and aggregate intensity employed (wages endogenous)

The unreported element in table 7.6 (communications) occurs because, starting with a zero tariff, as the tariff increases the change in the rental price of this sector never falls to zero over any relevant range of tariff settings. In consequence, there is no uniform tariff that preserves the status quo in their rental price: That is, there is no solution to the model that maintains the same rental price of capital of these industries for this closure.[76]

The data of table 7.6 pertain to a period that preceded the further reductions in border protection that we have noted. Nevertheless, they indicate the broad picture that one would expect from our preceding discussion. The CGE model can be closed in various ways. Closures that substituted for fixing the trade balance and aggregate employment that we experimented with included (1) holding constant nominal wages and the trade balance and (2) fixing real household consumption and aggregate employment. These two also gave the same key picture of table 7.6 and, indeed, levels of effective protection (DERP) for textiles and fabricated metals that were close to those reported in that table.

The measures DERP and ERP are quite different. Apart from identifying the same two sectors (textiles and fabricated metals) that stood out in the level of protection that they enjoyed, the DERP and ERP outcomes are not highly correlated measures.[77] Anderson (1998) foretold this outcome and provides an example of it. The lack of correlation is indicative of the departures of the model from the requirements for an exact correspondence. In particular, the fixed coefficient requirement may be particularly stringent given that the tariff tableau is not from exactly the same year as the data of the model.

Of the two measures, we feel comfortable giving only DERP an explicit interpretation. It is the uniform tariff that would give the industry the same rent as it enjoys under the existing structure: it has no immediate welfare connotations.[78] The extraordinarily high DERP for textiles (both relative to other sectors and in absolute terms) fits with our earlier discussion of the industry and supports the conclusion that it is a sector with disproportionately great political clout. The size of this sector is very small, however it is measured, and hence the aggregate excess rent of textiles is small. One possibility is that the sector carries political power because it is labor-intensive. In fact, the data of table 7.6 indicate that, on the basis of the labor-capital ratio, it ranks the third-most labor-intensive industry. When this is combined with the likelihood that the labor in this sector is probably less skilled than that of the Private Services industry, and that it is likely to have a much larger proportion of females than the Building industry (these being the two industries that are more labor-intensive than textiles), this result buttresses strongly our earlier conjecture that protection in that sector flows from political responses to areas of less skilled labor. The other noticeably high DERP is fabricated metals. This reflects the protection of the vehicle assembly industry, but it is interesting that transport equipment itself comes in only fourth on this list with a rent-maintaining uniform tariff not much greater than that of four or five other sectors.

Other Factors

Timing: The Foreign Exchange and Constitutional Crisis of 1984

We have already noted that NZ's reforms of recent years were initiated by the Labour government of 1984 that took power with a backdrop of a foreign exchange crisis and a consequent constitutional showdown with the outgoing government. The importance of this, which has been discussed at length elsewhere,[79] lies in the opportunity for change that it presented. That this opportunity was taken so enthusiastically is perhaps surprising, but one of the key elements explaining the success of NZ's liberalization emphasized by the reformers was its comprehensiveness, as we discuss next.

Trade Reform as a Subset of General Reforms

We have stressed throughout this chapter that NZ's trade reforms cannot be considered in isolation from the other reforms that were occurring in the economy at the same time. One reason that opponents were overruled is that the reforms were extensive and affected every sector. This was quite deliberate on the part of the reformers and was justified as a means of not only making reforms *feasible* (in "buying off" groups who suffered from one set of reforms but gained from others[80]) but also gaining *credibility* for the reforms (by bringing all New Zealanders into the reform process and thus making reversals more difficult and by selling each piece of the reform as an essential part of the overall package[81]).

To what extent is there any evidence of this quid pro quo in the reform package and was it perceived differently by the reformers and sectoral interests?[82] We have seen in our discussion of agriculture that farmers very explicitly requested the dismantling of industrial protection as their price for the removal of assistance to agriculture. One could argue that farmers *did* take a broad view of the reforms, an argument buttressed by their continuing support even after the initially dire consequences for agriculture in the early to mid-1980s.

The business sector, however, was rather more divided over the reforms. While the Business Roundtable was supportive of general reform (and, again, took the broader view that deregulation was in its overall interests despite the effects of reduced assistance on particular sectors), the Manufacturers Federation only came to support the reforms grudgingly when they were already pretty much a fact of economic life. Nevertheless, the quid pro quo was again explicit here as evidenced in our earlier quotation from the minister of trade and industry's statement to the 1984 Economic Summit that the 20 percent devaluation was protection enough. It has also been suggested[83] that the reform of monetary policy to provide the greater certainty of a low-inflation environment was part of the benefits put to business interests by the reformers.

As noted earlier, there is also some suggestion that manufacturers did not understand the ultimate goals of the initial trade liberalizations, thinking that the auctioning of import licenses was intended to find premia to be used to determine the appropriate tariff to apply to each industry. This may also explain their conversion, albeit limited, to the reforms.

It is reasonable to surmise that, along with those of many commentators, farmers' and manufacturers' expectations of the adjustment period and the costs of adjustment were awry. It was largely unforeseen that a major place for manufacturing existed in the new environment, and it meant that the longer adjustment than many anticipated reinforced manufacturers' expectations that they would lose from the reforms. The persistent high real exchange rate was also not anticipated by farmer lobby groups. By the realization of this, however, key reforms were in place and reforms in the rest of the economy were being implemented. Thus there was always the expectation of a fall in interest rates and the real exchange rate, and this expectation affected farmer groups' positions. The expansion of manufacturing exports meant that manufacturers' initial expectations about the long-term impact of the reform on them had, in hindsight, been overly pessimistic. The reverse was the case for farmers. We note that there is now a concordance of interest between farmers and manufacturers, resulting from the dependence of both on exporting, that has not been present before in NZ's history. This adds credibility to the existing low barriers to entry.

One group that appears to have been "left out" by reformers was organized labor. Recalling that a Labour government began the reforms, it was always the case that the interests of labor would be considered heavily but it was argued that the real wage of workers would be increased through price reductions and price stability stemming from economic liberalization. It was out of consideration for their traditional support base in organized unions that the Labour government did not move quickly on labor market reform (something the reformers subsequently regretted) and substantial deregulation did not occur until the National government of 1990 brought in the Employment Contracts Act of 1991. Moreover, early in the restructuring of the public service, redundancy packages were significantly more generous than are generally the case under current arrangements, and this affected the position of the influential public service unions.

Returning to trade reform, we argue that unilateralism can only be completely understood as a piece of the patchwork that made the reforms a coherent whole, as the reforms were explicitly intertwined, both politically and economically. One important aspect of unilateral trade liberalization for NZ was that it facilitated the light-handed regulation regime that has characterized NZ competition law since 1986 (Evans, Grimes, and Wilkinson 1996, 31–38). Unilateral reduction of border protection was essential because it was an important part of the broader program to allow open entry into NZ markets and therefore make possible a regime of only light regulation. The argument here is that open entry and contestability render heavy-handed competition law regulation unnecessary. If such access (to the NZ market) was negotiated on a bilateral basis and so depended on intercountry negotiations, then openness would be rather more limited[84] as the provision of preferential access in a bilateral deal implies that protection against nonmembers remains. This would make a policy of light regulation unsatisfactory as a means of en-suring competitive outcomes. Thus, unilateral trade reforms can be viewed as being necessary to provide *credibility* for the competition policy reforms: If the former had been negotiated on a bilateral basis, then their necessarily more limited nature—and the possibility of their reversal—would have rendered the light regulation regime less effective and so less believable. Farmers would have been less san-guine about the removal of their subsidies had they thought that lower border protection was to be negotiated rather than simply implemented.

7.3   Conclusions

At least two possible political economy perspectives on the reforms might be drawn from the literature on political support functions and that on competing lobby groups.

First, one might argue that the incoming Labour government of 1984, as a consequence of its personalities, perhaps, placed differ-ent weights on various aspects of social welfare than did its prede-cessors; in particular, it stressed the welfare of consumers more highly than earlier producer-captured governments.

Second, one might also argue that the NZ economy had become sufficiently ossified through the creation of rent-seeking opportunities that such rents were declining through general economic decline. Ac-cordingly, pressure groups might have recognized the desirability of "starting again" rather than simply nullifying each other's directly unproductive political lobbying activity with consequent deadweight losses.

Our interpretation of the evidence is that there is some truth in both of these positions. However, the distinguishing feature of the incoming government in 1984 was less its difference in goals and more its different perception (however constructed) of the means to achieve those goals. The history of trade policy in New Zealand shows a long and abiding belief in the use of trade policy both as a tool of social policy and as a means of fostering industrial development, and the Labour government of 1984 dissented from both of these views. It perceived instead that these goals could be more effectively pursued in a growing economy and focused on achieving them indirectly through economic liberalization.

In this it was aided by sectoral interests that perceived the futility of their mutual efforts. As we have noted, farmers' representatives, in particular, were active in promoting reform even when the immediate impacts of the reforms were sharply negative for them. Manufacturers were far more reluctant initially but, ex post, have recognized that their best interests are served by continued support for economic liberalism.

We conclude by summarizing our answers to the questions with which we began.

• *What were the vested interests behind NZ's starting point of very high protection, and how did they succeed in getting it implemented?* Crudely, manufacturers. They succeeded because of a general sympathy toward economic arguments that stressed the importance of industrialization—infant industry arguments and claims of a declining terms of trade—and because industrial policy was also used as a tool of social policy, in particular, to protect employment in the politically sensitive industries of textiles and auto assembly.

• *Why were reforms mooted—what happened such that the early status quo was no longer politically feasible?* General reforms in 1984, of which trade policy was a subset, were triggered by twin crises—economic and constitutional—and by a government with a new policy agenda. There was also recognition that the existing pattern of protection and protection-compensation was largely self-defeating but resulted in substantial resource misallocation and poor marginal incentives.

• *Why did the trade reforms succeed (in the sense of being put in place), and how did that implementation occur so as to overcome these special interests?* They succeeded in that they were part of a much larger package that, in turn, succeeded for a number of reasons: political institutions, speed, scope, even-handedness. This last feature was critical in overcoming special interests in that the reforms affected all parties and could be sold by noting that losses from one reform would be offset by gains from others. Exempting certain special interests would have been politically difficult given this commitment to breadth of coverage.

• *Why unilateralism in trade reform?* Partly it was because border policy was just another interventionist instrument to be liberalized in keeping with the general reformist philosophy. Partly it was in the interests of speed. Partly, however, it was because of an explicit recognition by policy advisers (i.e., Treasury officials) that NZ is too small in international markets and policy forums to rely on multilateral bargaining as an effective means of liberalization. Also, we have argued that unilateralism was important—even essential—in giving credibility to competition policy reforms by the very fact that the trade reforms were both extensive and not dependent on international negotiations.

• *Why has liberalization not been complete (especially since it has been so dramatic, one might think that the final steps would be easier in some sense)?* Because of the social policy aspect of trade policy in textiles and, until recently, autos and because of efforts by recent governments to "distinguish" their reforms from those of previous policymakers as driven by practicality, not ideology.

• *How important were multilateral and bilateral deals in affecting New Zealand's unilateral reforms?* They were of limited importance, in the sense that NZ was committed to unilateral reforms anyway and CER was incidental to these. However, the market access consequences of CER may have affected the sustainability of the reforms in contributing to an increase in manufactured exports and thereby to the commitment of manufacturers to the reforms. Further, the existence and extent of CER reduced the costs of unilateralism by "removing" the only significant trading partner country against which NZ had any bargaining power.

• *How, if at all, has NZ's multilateral position been affected by these reforms?* It is our perception that it has been almost totally unaffected. The country is still committed to multilateral forums, particularly APEC, and the loss of "bargaining chips" through unilateral reforms is insignificant, given NZ's size. Furthermore, the reforms have enabled NZ negotiators to take the "moral high ground" in bilateral and multilateral negotiations.

Notes

We are grateful to Paul Wooding, Jagdish Bhagwati, and Pravin Krishna for helpful comments on earlier drafts of this chapter. We thank both Paul Wooding and John Yeabsley for useful discussions of issues arising in the chapter. We also thank Ganesh Nana for his ERP calculations in the JOANNA CGE model of the New Zealand economy.

1. The following data are taken from Evans, Grimes, and Wilkinson (1996), henceforth EGWT in notes.

2. Public largesse was a feature of all governments, regardless of political persuasion. After the 1972 election in which Labour ousted the previous National government, the outgoing National finance minister announced that Labour would be unable to keep its spending promises as "I've spent the lot." As it turns out, this did not constrain Labour's behavior.

3. Indeed, the government lost such quantities of reserves that it resorted to raiding the FX holdings of its overseas embassies.

4. See, for example, EGWT (1996), Bollard (1994), and OECD (1996).

5. OECD (1996).

6. Jane Kelsey, an outspoken critic of the reforms, in describing the process of the reforms, titles the second chapter of her 1995 book "Capturing the Political Machine." Wallis (1997) also makes plain this interpretation even in his paper title: "Policy Conspiracies and Economic Reform Programs in Advanced Industrial Democracies: The Case of New Zealand."

7. Another common argument is that electoral reforms—the introduction of a system of proportional representation for the 1996 election—were also triggered by this sense of capture of the policymaking process by unrepresentative interests.

8. The material in this section draws heavily on Lattimore and Wooding (1996). See also Richardson (1998).

9. See Rayner and Lattimore (1991), 66.

10. Syntec, cited in Lattimore and Wooding (1996), 335.

11. Ministry of Commerce (1994), 134.

12. OECD (1989), 39.

13. WTO (1996). While the starting point for NZ in 1984 was a highly regulated economy, it has been pointed out that this was also the case for many other OECD countries. Similarly, many other countries have pursued liberalizing policies in the last two decades but, nevertheless, NZ's reforms stand out in both their breadth and depth. See Henderson (1996).

14. APEC Individual Action Plan: Tariff Summary for 1996, from Ministry of Commerce.

15. Lattimore and Wooding (1996), 317.

16. The existence of domestic industry was not exogenous, however! Roger Douglas cites the following from a TV manufacturer in NZ:

We would go to Japan and explain ... that our government wanted us to assemble their TV sets in NZ ... They said no one [else] assembles Japanese TV sets. 'Do you have cheaper labor?' they asked. 'Make your own tubes? Transistors? Anything?' 'No,' we said. 'We just have to make them in NZ; and because there are only a few of us permitted to do this, we make good money doing it.' ... [T]he Japanese finally agreed to sell us the bits to assemble their sets in NZ. However, they explained this was very costly. They were making tens of thousands of sets a day and we only wanted parts for a few thousand a year. At great cost they contracted outside people to come in, take assembled sets apart, sort out all the pieces we needed and put them in boxes. They got engineers to write out all the instructions in English for reassembly, and shipped them on their way ... on average they charged us for the parts 110% of the price of the finished goods ... We then opened a factory, imported much machinery, paid the highest wages in the neighborhood ... and finally produced a TV set ... at twice the imported price. (Alan Gibbs, qtd. in Douglas 1993, 27–28)

17. Syntec Economic Services (1984), 30.

18. The IDC formulated plans for fifteen industries in all: textiles, motor vehicles, carpets, tires, general rubber, shipbuilding, plastics, electronics, packing, wine, tobacco, writing instruments, fruit growing, eggs, and milk.

19. That there was some reluctance is evidenced by the minister of finance's comment, rejecting the idea that forty years of import licensing should be scrapped: "I have no intention of letting efficient industries go to the wall for the sake of a theory" (qtd. in Lattimore and Wooding 1996, 326).

First, manufacturers could be granted licenses to import components where the domestically produced good had a "manifestly excessive price, or quality problems compared with imports" or where use of the domestic product would harm exports of finished goods. Second, import license tendering began. While initially small (being confined to only about 5% of the domestic market for certain consumer goods) many commentators have identified this as an important step in the ultimate dismantling of the whole licensing scheme, not least because it made visible the extraordinary premia that consumers were paying for many imports. Pickford (1987b) reports, for instance, that over 17 percent of the successful bids in the first twelve rounds of the scheme involved premia of over 50 percent of the underlying value of the license. Interestingly, by 1984 this figure had fallen to less than 3 percent: This is indicative of the way in which the tender scheme was used to liberalize licensing. Increasing values of licenses were put out to tender in successive rounds: 10 percent of the domestic market in 1984 increasing to 15 percent in 1985. If the premia paid remained low for a couple of rounds, or if total tenders were less than the amount of licenses available, this was used as an indication that licensing could be abolished on that product line.

20. Initially, all such tariffs (on goods that were also produced in NZ) above 25 percent were to be reduced by 5 percent in 1986 and by a further 10 percent in 1987 prior to a major review in 1988. Furthermore, tariff reductions on five hundred product lines not made in NZ and not subject to import licensing were also introduced. Pickford (1987a) notes that for most of these goods tariffs (some as high as 40%) were eliminated but for some the tariff was reduced to 5 percent "because of obligations to give major trading partners a preferred trading position in those areas" (75).

21. From 1992 on, general tariffs were cut by a third by 1996 with a maximum tariff of 14 percent (so any tariff no less than 21% in 1992 was cut to 14% by 1996). This one-

third reduction did not apply to certain of the "special" sectors (notably carpets, apparel, some textiles, footwear, and motor vehicles), and no tariff in excess of 5 percent in 1992 was to be reduced to less than 5 percent by 1996.

22. In 1950 over 40 percent of the value of NZ's exports came from wool, nearly 16 percent from meat, 30 percent from dairy products and less than 14 percent from other goods (Rayner and Lattimore (1991, 35). In 1995 wool accounted for less than 7 percent of the total value of exports, meat for around 13 percent, and dairy products for less than 14 percent with other goods constituting 66 percent of total exports (New Zealand Treasury (1996, 35). Similarly, while the United Kingdom took 66 percent of NZ's exports in 1950, the United States 10 percent, and Australia only 3 percent, by 1995 Australia was the largest purchaser of NZ exports, taking over 20 percent, while Japan was second at nearly 17 percent (with the U.S. third at 10% still). In 1995 only a little over 6 percent of NZ's exports (by value) went to the U.K. (New Zealand Treasury 1996, 37).

23. New Zealand Treasury (1996), 22.

24. Colgate (1995), 15.

25. Lattimore and Wooding (1996).

26. Lattimore and McKeown (1995).

27. NDC (1969b), 5.

28. NDC (1969b), 21.

29. Qtd. in NDC (1972), 9.

30. New Zealand Treasury (1984), 307–308.

31. Qtd. in Lattimore and Wooding (1996), 329.

32. From the statement of the minister of trade and industry to the Economic Summit in 1984 (Economic Summit Conference 1984, 88).

33. Minister of Industry and Commerce, December 16, 1994.

34. Levinsohn (1996).

35. Hazledine and Murphy (1996) report that while the real output of resource-based manufacturing industries grew by some 22 percent in total from 1984 to 1992 (and employment there declined some 24%), overall manufacturing grew by less than 6 percent over that period (and employment declined by almost 21%). This is somewhat misleading in that 1992 was a recession year: By 1995 unemployment had fallen from the 10.3 percent of 1992 to 6.3 percent, and manufacturing increased from 16.7 percent of total employment to 18.2 percent (OECD 1996). Nevertheless, manufacturing real GDP was over 15 percent lower in 1991 than in 1984 (Colgate 1996, 7). But exports of noncommodity manufactures grew by 3.5 percent, 9.4 percent, 19.4 percent, 12.7 percent, and 20.7 percent in each of the years 1990 through 1994 (Colgate 1995, 8).

36. Malcolm (1993), 56. This survey is likely to underestimate the move into exporting for a number of reasons: It does not include new entrants; it is not clear if the export category refers to firms that *only* export as opposed to those with domestic sales as well; and it looks at 1991, a recession year.

37. It should be noted that over 40 percent of the output of the components industry is exported, so this employment is not totally dependent on the domestic assembly industry.

38. Gibson and Lattimore (1991).

39. In 1994 there were still some eight hundred plants in the apparel industry, for example, scattered throughout the country, and employing an average of twenty employees each (Ministry of Commerce 1994). Accordingly, the results of Gibson and Lattimore may well be driven by the high protection accorded to this single very scattered sector.

40. Gibson and Harris (1996).

41. All other things equal, one would anticipate, for example, that high-cost, young plants are more likely to exit in any sample and the interesting question is then how *trade* reform changes the nature of the exit decision. If trade liberalization is adequately controlled for through the fall in ERAs, then presumably one would like to know how this interacts with the other independent variables. If trade liberalization is *not* captured by the fall in ERAs, then to interpret these numbers as consequences of reforms solely because of the time period chosen one would also need to consider an earlier post–reform period as a control. Also, macroeconomic effects may have been present and these are not controlled for: in particular, real interest rates were very high and the economy was flat over this period.

42. This also fits with the comments of NZ negotiators following the conclusion of the Uruguay Round of GATT, discussed below.

43. This argument has been suggested to us by Paul Wooding.

44. Rayner and Lattimore (1991), 10.

45. Chiao and Scobie (1990), 1.

46. Chiao and Scobie (1990).

47. The extent of agricultural subsidies for the period 1979–1997 is described by SONZA (1997), 123–124. The subsidies took a wide variety of forms. Some were the outcome of mechanisms designed to smooth farmers' fluctuating incomes. These often took the form of low-interest guaranteed loan facilities to finance producer boards' cost of carry in their activity of trading in markets (e.g., the wool market) in attempts to ameliorate the fluctuations in prices that farmers faced. Others were direct input (e.g., fertilizer) subsidies and output subsidies.

48. Statistics New Zealand (1996), 359, 564.

49. The history of export incentives is described by Wooding (1987), 96–98.

50. The widespread subsidization of the 1970s and early 1980s separated economy-wide incentives guiding production and investment decisions from the country's terms of trade, which for meat and wool, have been declining since their relatively high level of 1972–1973 (see SONZA 1997, 92–96).

51. There have been some changes. The deregulation of egg production and distribution and the Wool Board withdrawing from its buffer stock scheme are examples, but there had been little change in function or structure of the board encompassing the largest business—the New Zealand Dairy Board—until 2001.

52. Sheep numbers fell by 30 percent between 1985 and 1995. Between 1960 and 1990, the peak level of new production forest plantings was in 1985. Following the changed tax treatment of forestry (in 1991) and the lower relative profitability of sheep farming, forestry planting jumped to almost twice this peak by 1995 (Statistics New Zealand 1996, 396).

53. SONZA (1997), 120–122.

54. See SONZA (1997), 123. Producer subsidy equivalents indicate the value of transfers from domestic consumers and taxpayers to farmers, as measured by the difference between domestic and world prices.

55. It must be noted that New Zealand farmer organizations are also very active in reacting to land-use regulations brought down under the Resource Management Act 1992, and in managing issues arising under the Occupational Health and Safety in Employment Act 1992. The former act, in particular, has most significant implications for farming.

56. Membership in the NZBR is for CEOs by invitation. The NZBR represents most of the large NZ business interests drawn from all parts of the business sector. Its focus is "the general economy rather than particular sectors or industries" (NZBR Statement of Purpose.)

57. World Bank (1968), 14.

58. In fact, deregulation was proposed and did find political favor in that election. The New Zealand Party, formed only months before the election, gained a remarkable 12.6 percent of the vote on a deregulatory platform.

59. Roger Douglas elevates speed to the status of a principle of successful reform in *Unfinished Business*: "Speed is essential. It is almost impossible to go too fast" (1993), 222.

60. See, for example, Bollard (1994).

61. Kelsey (1995), 38.

62. An exception had been Wilfred Candler (professor of agricultural economics at Massey University) who many years earlier in 1963 had published an unsigned article in *The Economist* entitled "How to Progress Backward."

63. Economic Summit Conference (1984), 535.

64. Kelsey (1995), 34.

65. Bollard (1994), 90.

66. See Lattimore and Wooding (1996), 329.

67. Lloyd (1995), 274.

68. Lloyd (1997), 18.

69. The following figures are taken from WTO (1996).

70. As a percentage of total *trade* in dairy products, however, NZ is a more significant participant in world markets, accounting for approximately 25 percent of world trade. The largest exporter is the EU at about 45 percent.

71. *The Economist* magazine, in an editorial on October 19, 1996, explicitly recognized that the attention paid in the magazine to NZ, "a tiny country of only 3.5m people [roughly the same size as] Albania or Uruguay" was disproportionate to its size: "The answer, quite simply, is that the country merits it. Over the past decade or so, New Zealand has embraced more of the free market reforms that this newspaper espouses than any other industrial country."

72. Minister for International Trade, April 29, 1997.

73. Given the explicit commitment of recent NZ governments to freer trade, remarks of the NZ minister for trade negotiations on the completion of the Uruguay Round, which suggested that New Zealand had "gotten away with something" in not having to make "concessions" beyond those already undertaken unilaterally, were surprising. While his remarks reflect more his own personal position than that of his government, his perception that this was needed to sell the agreement politically does suggest a remaining mercantilism in the electorate.

74. NZ APEC individual action plan, 1997. We are grateful to officials at the BIEP group of the Ministry of Commerce for providing this information.

75. These are (a) nonjoint outputs, (b) distortion of all intermediate goods prices, and (c) fixed coefficients (Anderson 1998).

76. Anderson (1998) notes that when protection is negative, a solution may not exist.

77. So comparing the ranking of sectors by ERP and DERP, for instance, yields a Spearman's rho statistic of -0.015, which is insignificantly different from zero— namely, no correlation between the two sets of rankings.

78. Anderson suggests a rationale for the use of DERP by referring to the seminal work of Grossman and Helpman (1994) in which the rents accruing to a specific factor represent the amount a lobby group is willing to pay to the tariff-setting authority to obtain protection. Accordingly, if welfare is monotonically decreasing in the uniform tariff on all imports, then the DERP can be thought of as representing the welfare loss a policymaker is willing to incur in order to protect a particular sector. This story is not watertight, however, since there is no monotonic mapping from the *actual* welfare loss of a particular sectoral tariff to the welfare loss of the DERP.

79. See, for example, Bollard (1994).

80. "Large packages [of reforms] provide the flexibility to ensure that losses suffered by any one group are offset by gains for the same group in another area" (Roger Douglas, qtd. in EGWT 1996, 8).

81. We do not have space here to discuss the broad package of reforms in full detail beyond that we have already mentioned and what is listed in table 7.1. The interested reader is referred to EGWT (1996) for a much more comprehensive discussion of aspects of NZ's economic reforms other than in trade.

82. Jagdish Bhagwati raised this question and suggests that while a reforming government might see the "big picture" in which the immediate consequences for a particular sector are offset by other reforms, sectoral interests might take a more narrow view, focusing on the direct "impact effect" of changes specific to their sector.

83. We are grateful to Paul Wooding for raising this argument.

84. One can also argue that because bilateral deals make liberalization contingent on the actions of partner countries, by implication they involve the necessity of reversal if a partner reneges. So to the extent that such deals are sustained by the threat of punishment (as in many theoretical analyses of such agreements in supergame settings), the possibility of reversal of liberalization occurs. For NZ, countervailing threats would not have been credible in any setting. In any event, retaliation is not an issue in unilateral reforms, obviously.

References

Anderson, James E. 1998. Effective protection redux. *Journal Of International Economics* 44, no. 1, 21–44.

Bhagwati, Jagdish. 1988. *Protectionism*. Cambridge, MA: The MIT Press.

Bollard, Alan. 1994. New Zealand. In *The political economy of policy reform*, ed. John Williamson, 73–110. Institute for International Economics, Washington, DC.

Chiao, Y.-S., and G. Scobie. 1990. The cost to agriculture of import protection in NZ. Working Paper No. 90/2, Department of Economics, University of Waikato, Hamilton, New Zealand.

Clerides, S., S. Lach, and J. Tybout. 1998. Is learning by exporting important? Micro-dynamic evidence from Colombia, Mexico and Morocco. *Quarterly Journal of Economics* 113, no. 3: 903–947.

Coates, D., and R. Ludema. 1997. Unilateral tariff reduction as leadership in trade negotiations. Economics Department Working Paper 97–23, Georgetown University, Washington, DC.

Colgate, P. 1995. Trade in manufactured goods. NZIER Working Paper 95/12, NZ Institute of Economic Research, Wellington, New Zealand.

Dixon, P., B. R. Parmenter, J. Sutton, and D. P. Vincent. 1982. *ORANI; A Multisectoral Model of the Australian Economy*. Amsterdam: North-Holland.

Douglas, Roger. 1993. *Unfinished business*. Auckland: Random House Ltd.

Duncan, I., R. Lattimore, and A. Bollard. 1992. *Dismantling the barriers: Tariff policy in New Zealand*. NZIER Research Monograph #57, NZIER, Wellington, New Zealand.

Economic Summit Conference. 1984. *Proceedings and conference papers*. Wellington: Government Printer.

The Economist. 1996. October 19. London.

Ethier, W. J. 1977. The theory of effective protection in general equilibrium, effective-rate analogues of nominal rates. *Canadian Journal of Economics* 10, no. 2: 233–245.

Evans, L., and Morgan, G. 1983. "The user cost of capital and its application to New Zealand agriculture." *New Zealand Economic Papers* 17: 17–24.

Evans, L., A. Grimes, and B. Wilkinson, with D. Teece. 1996. New Zealand's economic reforms: 1984–1995. *Victoria Economic Commentaries* 1: 1996. Victoria University of Wellington, Wellington.

Gibson, J., and R. Harris. 1996. Trade liberalization and plant exit in NZ manufacturing. *Review of Economics and Statistics* 78, no. 3: 521–529.

Gibson, J., and R. Lattimore. 1991. Causes of the pattern of manufacturing industry assistance in NZ, 1981/82. *New Zealand Economic Papers* 25, no. 1: 100–122.

Grossman, G., and E. Helpman. 1994. Protection for sale. *American Economic Review* 84: 833–850.

Hazledine, T., and A. Murphy. 1996. Manufacturing industries. In *A study of economic reform: The case of New Zealand*, ed. B. Silverstone, A. Bollard, and R. Lattimore, 355–388. Amsterdam: North-Holland.

Henderson, David. 1996. *Economic reform: New Zealand in an international perspective.* Wellington: NZ Business Roundtable.

Kelsey, J. 1995. *The New Zealand experiment: A world model for structural adjustment?* Auckland: Auckland University Press and Bridget Williams Books.

Lattimore, R., and P. McKeown. 1995. NZ's international trade performance pre and post deregulation: 1970–1985 and 1985–1993. AERU Research Report No. 231, Lincoln University, Canterbury, New Zealand.

Lattimore, R., and P. Wooding. 1996. International trade. In *A study of economic reform: The case of New Zealand*, ed. B. Silverstone, A. Bollard, and R. Lattimore, 315–356. Amsterdam: North-Holland.

Levinsohn, James. 1996. Firm heterogeneity, jobs, and international trade: Evidence from Chile. Mimeo, Department of Economics, University of Michigan, Ann Arbor, MI.

Lloyd, P. J. 1995. The future of trans-Tasman Closer Economic Relations. *Agenda* 2, no. 3: 267–280.

Lloyd, P. 1997. Unilateral and regional trade policies of the CER countries. In *International trade policy and the Pacific Rim*, ed. John Piggott and Alan Woodland, 59–83. Houndsmill: Macmillan.

Malcolm, G. 1993. Business dynamics in NZ 1987–1991: Entry, growth and decline in the business sector. *NZIER Research Monograph* 61. Wellington, New Zealand: New Zealand Institute for Economic Research.

Ministry of Commerce. 1994. *Review of post-1996 tariff policy.* Wellington: Government Printer.

National Development Conference (NDC). 1969b. *Report of the Working Party on Industrial Policy, Manufacturing Committee*, NDC 4/1 Manufacturing. Wellington: Government Printer.

National Development Council (NDC). 1972. *Report of the Committee on Industrial Policy: Review of Recommendation 209A.* Wellington: Government Printer.

New Zealand Treasury. 1984. *Economic Management.* Wellington: New Zealand Treasury.

New Zealand Treasury. 1996. *New Zealand: Economic and Financial Overview*, NZ Treasury, Wellington.

Organization for Economic Cooperation and Development (OECD). 1989. *OECD economic surveys: New Zealand 1988/89.* Paris: OECD.

Organization for Economic Cooperation and Development (OECD). 1996. *OECD economic surveys: New Zealand 1996.* Paris: OECD.

Olson, Mancur. 1987. Economic nationalism and economic progress. *The World Economy* 10, no. 3: 241–264.

Philpott, B. 1994. Productivity growth by type of farming: 1972–93. Research Project on Economic Planning Paper 259. Wellington: Victoria University of Wellington.

Pickford, Michael. 1987a. Measuring the welfare effects of the tariff cuts of 19th December 1985. *New Zealand Economic Papers* 21: 75–82.

Pickford, Michael. 1987b. Industry inefficiency, monopoly and import liberalization in New Zealand—an assessment of the static welfare effects. *Economic Record* 63: 162–174.

Ratnayake, R. 1999. Industry concentration and competition: New Zealand experience. *International Journal of Industrial Organization* 17, no. 7: 1041–1057.

Rayner, A., and R. Lattimore. 1991. New Zealand. In *Liberalizing foreign trade*, Vol. 6, ed. D. Papageorgiu, M. Michaely, and A. Choksi, 8–135. Oxford: Blackwell.

Richardson, M. 1993. Endogenous protection and trade diversion. *Journal of International Economics* 34: 309–324.

Richardson, M. 1998. New Zealand Trade Policy and the 1996 WTO Review. In *The world economy: Global trade policy 1998*, ed. P. Lloyd and C. Milner, 529–547. Oxford: Blackwell.

Roberts, Mark, Theresa Sullivan, and Jim Tybout. 1996. Micro-foundations of export booms. Mimeo, World Bank, Washington, DC.

SONZA. 1997. *Situation and outlook for New Zealand agriculture.* Wellington: New Zealand Ministry of Agriculture.

Statistics New Zealand. 1991. *The New Zealand official yearbook.* Wellington: NZ Government Printer.

Syntec Economic Services. 1984. *The structure of industry assistance in New Zealand: An exploratory analysis.* (Study commissioned by NZ Government.)

United States Trade Representative (USTR). 1997. *1997 National Trade Estimate Report on Foreign Trade Barriers*, United States Trade Representative, Washington, D.C.

Vautier, Kerrin M., and Peter J. Lloyd. 1997. *International trade and competition policy: CER, APEC and the WTO.* Wellington: Institute of Policy Studies.

Wallis, Joseph L. 1997. Policy conspiracies and economic reform programs in advanced industrial democracies: The case of New Zealand. UNE Working Papers in Economics No. 38, University of New England, Armidale.

Wells, Graeme, and Brian Easton. 1986. *Economy Wide Models of New Zealand.* Wellington: New Zealand Institute of Economic Research.

Wooding, Paul. 1987. Liberalising the international trade regime. In *Economic liberalisation in New Zealand*, ed. Alan Bollard and Robert Buckle. Wellington: Allen and Unwin.

World Trade Organization (WTO). 1996. Trade Policy Review report on New Zealand, WTO, Geneva.

8   Trade Liberalization in Asia

Arvind Panagariya

Experience with trade policies has been richer in Asia than in any other part of the world. At one extreme is Hong Kong with a history of complete free trade for more than a century, and at the other is Myanmar with virtual autarky in recent decades. The spectrum in between is filled by Indonesia, Malaysia, the Philippines, Republic of Korea, Singapore, and Taiwan on the liberal side, Bangladesh, China, India, and Pakistan on the protectionist side, and Sri Lanka and Thailand in the middle.

Equally interesting, all of these countries, except Hong Kong and Myanmar, which define the two extremes, have experienced substantial trade policy changes during the second half of the twentieth century. All of them started with protectionist policies to promote industrialization but eventually turned to more liberal trade regimes. On the political front, India and Sri Lanka have been democratic, and China, Indonesia, and Singapore authoritarian throughout the period. Bangladesh, Korea, Pakistan, the Philippines, and Thailand, on the other hand, have been authoritarian during the initial decades but democratic subsequently. The movement toward democracy in the latter countries has coincided with movement toward liberal trade regimes.

In this chapter, I analyze the trade liberalization experience in Asia. A thorough analysis of this rich experience spanning over four decades and more than a dozen countries will require many volumes. Not having that luxury, I ruthlessly limit the scope of my investigation to three areas: a conceptual discussion of the benefits of unilateral and preferential liberalization, an explanation of why protection proliferated in the earlier decades, and an evaluation of the extent of and reasons behind trade liberalization to date. A key issue I address is whether liberalization in a given country was unilateral and voluntary, a result of threats by a major trading partner, a response to aid from a multilateral agency, or a part of a multilateral negotiation under the auspices of the General Agreement on Tariffs and Trade (GATT). The analysis is carried out initially at the regional level and then at the country level with Singapore, Taiwan, and India serving as examples.

8.1 The Welfare Economics of Trade Liberalization

The decision by countries to introduce new trade barriers or to remove existing ones depends on many factors. In this section, I focus on the decision by a government guided solely by the objective of social welfare maximization. Even though social welfare maximization is not the only factor guiding trade policy, it is an important one and, as we will see, has played a central role in some of the countries in Asia. Though I keep the analysis deliberately simple by restricting myself to a partial-equilibrium framework, I do not sacrifice rigor. All results can be shown to hold in a general-equilibrium framework. There are three cases to be distinguished depending on the size of the country undertaking liberalization and whether liberalization is discriminatory or nondiscriminatory.

Small Countries: The Case for Unilateral Free Trade

The case against trade barriers and for unilateral liberalization is most compelling for a small economy defined as the one that has no market power whatsoever in the world market. This case is sufficiently well known that it may seem worthless to offer an elaboration of it. But because it serves as the benchmark for my discussion of more subtle points, the elaboration is justified. Though the analysis can be carried out within a formal general-equilibrium model, in the interest of simplicity, I rely on a partial-equilibrium model.

Consider a small country—call it country A—whose domestic demand for and supply of an importable are given by $D_A D_A$ and $S_A S_A$, respectively, in figure 8.1. Make the standard assumption that there are no production or consumption taxes. Suppose that the world supply of the product is given by $P^* P^*$ with P^* as the world price. The country levies a per unit tariff $t = P - P^*$ so that the tariff inclusive price of the product in A is P. The standard story is that a removal of the tariff leads to an increase in the consumers' surplus by

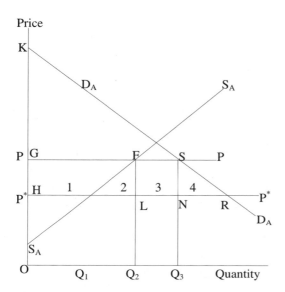

Figure 8.1

areas $1 + 2 + 3 + 4$, a reduction in the producers' surplus by area 1, a loss of tariff revenue represented by area 3, and a net gain to the country as a whole equal to area $2 + 4$. Several points can now be noted.

First, the gain of area $2 + 4$ arises solely from unilateral liberalization. Country A will reap this gain irrespective of whether the rest of the world liberalizes or not. If the rest of the world does liberalize, however, the gain to A will be larger. This is an illustration of Bhagwati's (1991) proposition: "if I can get you to also liberalize while I liberalize myself, I gain twice over."

Second, for equal tariff reductions, the gain to a small country from liberalization by partner countries is far larger than that from its own liberalization. Thus, if the rest of the world were to lower its tariff by the same amount as just considered for country A, $t = P - P^*$, the gain to A would not be limited to the small triangles 2 and 4 but would include a large rectangle (plus a triangle) whose base equals the *entire* initial quantity of imports and whose height equals the tariff reduction.[1] This can be verified by shifting P^*P^* and PP lines together down by t and measuring the net change in tariff revenue, consumers' surplus, and producers' surplus. Trade liberalization by the rest of the world improves country A's terms of trade by full amount of the reduction in the tariff. The improvement in the terms of trade, in turn, generates a large redistributive rectangle in favor of A. This fact explains partially why even small-country governments often focus on increased "market access"—a trade negotiator's jargon for partner country's liberalization—rather than unilateral liberalization.

Third, though the immediate gain to a small country from its own liberalization may be small as illustrated by the area represented by triangles 2 and 4, the eventual gain from such liberalization can be much larger. For the gain to A from the rest of the world's liberalization depends critically on the extent of its own openness. Recall the major part of the gain to A from partners' liberalization is a rectangle whose base equals the quantity of imports from the rest of the world. And the quantity of A's imports itself depends on how liberal is the country's own trade regime. To take an extreme example, if the country imposes prohibitive trade restrictions, it will reap no benefits at all from liberalization by its partner countries. A less extreme but still telling real-world example is that of India, whose trade from the 1960s to the 1980s was well below half of its potential level under a free-trade regime. Correspondingly, she failed to reap more than half of the potential benefits from liberalization of trade by its partner countries during the three decades. The country effectively failed to take advantage of the "free ride" offered by developed countries.

Fourth, a small country's unrealized gains from its own as well as partners' liberalization can be very substantial if it uses fixed import quotas or flexible quotas whose growth is outpaced by growth in import demand. As the country grows, efficiency triangles associated with unilateral liberalization and redistributive rectangles resulting from partner countries' liberalization grow as well. Once again, India's experience is illustrative of the point. Even the modest growth experienced during 1960–1990 led to a progressive rise in the implicit quota rents. In many cases, these rents had grown anywhere from 200 to 300 percent!

Fifth, the gains from unilateral liberalization need not be limited to the efficiency and redistributive effects. Even within the static framework, as discussed by Bhagwati (1982), trade restrictions may be accompanied by directly unproductive profit-seeking (DUP) activities. For instance, a higher domestic price can lead to smuggling. As demonstrated originally by Bhagwati and Hansen (1973) and developed further by Pitt (1981) and Martin and Panagariya (1984), use of real resources in smuggling can lead to further losses that cut into the tariff-revenue rectangle 3 in figure 8.1. Additionally, rent seeking in the presence of import quotas as discussed by Krueger (1974) and revenue seeking in the presence of tariffs as analyzed by Bhagwati and Srinivasan (1980) can also contribute to losses, which cut into the tariff-revenue rectangle 3 and the producers' surplus trapezium 1 in figure 8.1.

Finally, trade barriers can hamper growth while outward orientation can help it. Although econometric evidence remains inconclusive so far, a persuasive argument can be made in favor of this hypothesis (Bhagwati and Srinivasan 1999). To the extent that technology is embodied in capital goods, trade is a means of gaining access to the most efficient technology. Moreover, because entrepreneurs must compete against the most efficient producers in the world market and, due to GATT rules and fiscal considerations, the room for intervention on their behalf is limited, an outward-oriented strategy places a much tighter discipline on them than does an inward-looking strategy. Keesing (1967) made this argument as far back as three decades ago:

Reliance only on the domestic market permits a high degree of government intervention, whether in Soviet or Latin American fashion. By contrast, an outward-looking strategy compels moderation. If governments are serious about exporting manufactures, their freedom to intervene is restricted by the exigencies of keeping manufactures internationally competitive, and by trade conventions and sanctions that limit permissible methods of trade promotion. (p. 303)

Large Countries: The Role of Reciprocity

The case for unilateral liberalization on static efficiency grounds alone is weaker for a large country than for a small country. It is well known that the optimum tariff for a large country is positive. In terms of figure 8.1, for a large country, a tariff is accompanied by an improvement in the terms of trade. Therefore, in addition to the negative efficiency effects represented by triangles 2 and 4, the tariff generates a positive tariff-revenue effect (not shown in figure 8.1) through an improvement in the terms of trade. This effect is, of course, a pure redistribution from the partner country, which loses from deterioration in its terms of trade. The optimum tariff is the one that maximizes the excess of this tariff-revenue effect over negative efficiency effects.

If the initial tariff of a country is higher than the optimum tariff, unilateral liberalization is still beneficial since the gains in efficiency are larger than the losses due to deterioration in the terms of trade.[2] Once the tariff reaches the optimum, further unilateral tariff reductions produce a net loss and reciprocity from trading partners is called for. Tariff reductions by trading partners must neutralize intercountry income redistributions at least to the extent that they do not entirely offset the efficiency gains. As Bhagwati (1997) shows in a general-equilibrium model, one simple rule that accomplishes this goal is to require that tariff reductions by various countries be such that the terms of trade do not change.[3] This rule essentially mimics the small-country unilateral liberalization scenario for large countries: There are no net intercountry income redistribution effects so that each country is able to internalize the benefits of its own liberalization. As Bhagwati (1997) notes, in general this process will not lead to complete free trade unless free trade terms of trade happen to coincide with the initial terms of trade.

It is important to note, however, that the case for unilateral liberalization on conventional welfare criteria may have some force even for large countries with low levels of protection if the instruments of protection are antidumping or voluntary export restraints (VERs). Frequently, antidumping measures take the form of the exporting firm, raising its price to eliminate the "dumping margin." This amounts to *deterioration* in the importing country's terms of trade. Similarly, voluntary export restraints that transfer quota rents to exporting countries worsen the terms of trade of countries seeking those restrictions. Elimination of both of these restrictions improves the country's terms of trade and, hence, is likely to improve its welfare.

To make a case for unilateral liberalization in the absence of these considerations, we must rely on the sources of gains other than the conventional ones just discussed. Two such sources were noted above in the context of small countries: minimizing the losses from DUP activities and promoting faster growth. Advocates of unilateral liberalization by large countries must rely, explicitly or implicitly, on these sources of gain.

Preferential Trade Liberalization between Small Countries: The Return of Reciprocity

Because preferential trade liberalization has become an issue even in Asia in recent years, it is important to consider briefly its welfare economics. There are two main points to make here. First, if we adopt the small-union assumption as is appropriate for developing Asian countries, the union as a whole stands to lose from preferential liberalization. Second, because preferential liberalization leads to a shift in intra-union terms of trade, in this context, reciprocity becomes relevant for even small countries. The more a country liberalizes and the larger its intra-union imports relative to the partner, the more it loses from the arrangement (Panagariya 1996, 2000).

These points can be explained with the help of a hypothetical free trade area (FTA) between Indonesia and Singapore. In figure 8.2, I distinguish Indonesia, Singapore, and the rest of the world by subscript I, S, and W, respectively. Curve $M_I M_I$ represents Indonesia's import demand for the product on which tariff preference is given, say, videocassette recorders (VCRs). Curve $E_S E_S$ represents Singapore's supply of exports of VCRs, while $P_W E_W$ gives the supply of VCRs from the world market. It is assumed that Indonesia and

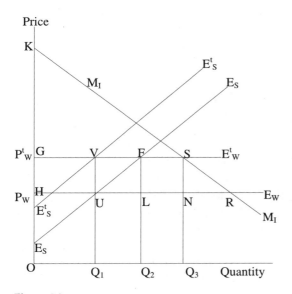

Figure 8.2

Singapore are small in relation to the world and take the world VCR price as given.

Initially, Indonesia levies a nondiscriminatory tariff on imports equal to $P_WP^t_W$ per VCR so that export supply curves of Singapore and the rest of the world, as viewed by Indonesian consumers and producers, are given by $E^t_SE^t_S$ and $P^t_WE^t_W$, respectively. The price of VCRs in Indonesia is P^t_W. The country imports OQ_1 from Indonesia and Q_1Q_3 from the rest of the world, collecting GSNH in tariff revenue. The consumers' surplus is given by triangle KSG.

Suppose now that, as a result of an FTA agreement, Indonesia eliminates the tariff on Singapore but keeps it on the rest of the world. This change shifts the export supply curve of Singapore down to E_SE_S. As long as any VCRs continue to come from the rest of the world, the price in Indonesia remains unchanged at P^t_W. Imports from Singapore rise to OQ_2, and those from the rest of the world fall to Q_2Q_3.

It is now easy to see that Indonesia and the union as a whole experience a net loss and Singapore a net gain as a result of this liberalization. Indonesia loses the rectangle GFLH of which trapezium GFUH is captured by exporting firms in Singapore. Triangle FLU is a deadweight loss due to trade diversion: Production costs along the FU segment of Singapore's export supply curve are higher than the world supply price. This triangle also represents the net loss to the union as a whole. Due to the large redistribution effect, which is a rectangle, the loss to Indonesia in this example is much larger than the deadweight loss from trade diversion, which is a triangle. And the larger the quantity of trade with Singapore, the larger the redistribution and the greater the loss. As we have already seen, if Indonesia chooses to remove the tariff on a unilateral basis, no such loss occurs. With unilateral liberalization, the lost tariff revenue benefits Indonesia's own consumers through a reduction in price. In addition, the country makes a net gain of triangle SNR from improved efficiency.

Indonesia's losses from preferential liberalization could be limited to the deadweight loss due to trade diversion, provided it could get a corresponding trade preference from Singapore on equal value of exports to the latter. The problem, however, is that if Singapore's initial tariffs are themselves low as is the case in reality, obtaining such a preference is not possible. Under such circumstances, unless Indonesia expects "noneconomic" gains from an FTA with Singapore, it is better off liberalizing trade on a unilateral basis.

8.2   Explaining the Spread of Protection in the Post-Colonial Era

Given that most developing countries have little bargaining power to get reciprocal liberalization from developed countries, the analysis in the previous section suggests a strong case for unilateral free trade by them. Yet, as the 1980s approached, with the exception of Hong Kong and Singapore, there was not a single country in Asia (or the world), which could justifiably claim to be a free trader. The decades preceding the 1980s were characterized by active promotion of protectionist policies by most developing countries. How do we explain this discrepancy between theory and policy? Following Bhagwati's (1988) taxonomy, the answer can be divided into three categories: ideas, interests, and institutions.

Ideas

The prevailing ideas and their influence on institutions that evolved played a critical role in the adoption of protectionist policies. During the 1950s and 1960s, import substitution was an ideology shared by economists and international institutions alike. Fearing that, due to a low *income* elasticity of demand, growth in developed countries will lead to a secular decline in the terms of trade of primary products, the Argentine economist Raul Prebisch argued forcefully in favor of promoting manufacturing industries in the developing countries (e.g., see United Nations 1950). Ragner Nurkse (1959), on the other hand, took the view that the *price* elasticity of demand for primary products was low so that any attempts by developing countries to expand exports will simply result in a deterioration of their terms of trade. This line of reasoning led Nurkse to a pessimistic view of exports as the engine of growth and to import substitution as the natural strategy of development.[4] Nurkse's message was, in turn, accepted and echoed by economists in Latin America and elsewhere in the world. Working as advisors to various developing-country governments, they aided the spread of protectionist policies throughout the developing world.[5]

The success of planning in the Soviet Union in its early years also helped the spread of protectionist ideas. In 1950s when developing countries were choosing among different paths to development, the Soviet planning experience and growth strategy happened to be an unequivocal success. Consequently, some countries readily embraced planning and what was clearly an inward-looking strategy of development.

The influence of the Soviet experience was most pronounced in the case of India. Indeed, some economists (Little 1982 and Srinivasan 1996) have argued that the Indian fascination with import substitution and emphasis on heavy industry had little to do with Prebisch and Nurkse and much to do with the perceived success of the Soviet industrialization. Srinivasan (1996) traces the ideas behind the Indian policy framework back to the 1930s and early 1940s when several individuals and groups, including a National Planning Committee under the chairmanship of Nehru, drew up plans of India's development once independence was achieved.

Interests

The lobbying interests created by initial import substitution reinforced the policies of governments that were already favorably disposed toward protection. Over time, with the growth in domestic productivity lagging behind that in the outside world, there were ever increasing demands for protection by established producers. Moreover, as these producers entered new activities, the net of protection grew wider and tighter.

This growth in domestic protectionist interests coincided with an essential lack of interest on the part of developed countries in developing-country markets. Unlike today, in the immediate post-colonial era the latter were willing to accommodate protection in the developing countries. While developed countries cannot be blamed for protectionist policies that developing countries adopted at their own initiative, the complacency of the former did contribute to a greater proliferation of trade restrictions and, subsequently, a slower dismantling of them. Thus, recall that during the 1960s and 1970s, imbalances in payments had plagued many developed countries as well. Yet, throughout the period, under the auspices of the General Agreement on Tariffs and Trade (GATT), they kept the process of trade liberalization among themselves moving ahead. But they did not bring sufficient pressure to bear upon developing countries to liberalize their trade regimes. Instead, yielding to the pressure from developing countries, they gave the latter modest one-way tariff preferences. Later in the 1980s and 1990s, having exhausted the scope for tariff liberalization in industrial products among themselves and recognizing that the developing-country markets had now become too big to ignore, developed countries did switch strategies—rather aggressively—with definite results in favor of liberalization.

A key question, which this discussion fails to answer, is why Hong Kong and Singapore more or less escaped entirely the wave of protectionism that swept the rest of the developing world during the decades following World War II. The fact that these countries were "small" is clearly insufficient to explain this observation, since there were many other even smaller countries that fell prey to the protectionist wave. The answer, therefore, would seem to lay in the initial conditions. Both Singapore and Hong Kong had virtually no agricultural or mineral resources and, in the 1950s, were already dependent heavily on external markets for imports as well as exports. This was in contrast to countries such as India, which had a large population and land area, exported large volumes of primary product, and derived a much greater proportion of their income from agriculture than from industry. The domestic interests in these latter countries saw a large *potential* market for manufactures at home. Given their limited experience in manufactures exports, the option of securing this market for domestic producers was an attractive one.

Institutions

The institutional arrangement with respect to the exchange-rate regime contributed to the spread of protectionism.[6] Under fixed exchange rates, which characterized the international monetary system during the 1950s and 1960s, balance-of-payments crises played a key role in the proliferation of trade restrictions. Countries such as Singapore, Hong Kong, and Malaysia, which had a comfortable foreign-exchange reserves position and did not face balance-of-payments crises, were less likely to invoke protectionist measures. At the other extreme, countries such as India, which felt continuously threatened by balance-of-payments crises, sought refuge in trade restrictions. Once trade restrictions had been adopted, political power was reconfigured with import-competing interests seizing control and ensuring that restrictions remained in place even after the crisis had passed.

Yet another institutional factor, itself influenced heavily by the prevailing ideology, was the tolerance of quantitative restrictions in the developing countries by GATT. Article XVIII of GATT permitted developing countries to adopt across-the-board, permanent quantitative restrictions under the slightest threat of balance-of-payments crises. Simultaneously, the International Monetary Fund (IMF) readily sanctioned the use of exchange-control measures to deal with imbalances in payments.

8.3   Problems in Defining Openness and Trade Liberalization

Before we turn to a description of trade liberalization experience, it is useful to note some basic difficulties in measuring openness and the change in it. Since these difficulties have been discussed at length in the literature, I do not intend to go over them in detail.[7] But three conceptual issues are important to narrow down the scope of the evidence on which I focus.

First, in defining openness, there is a great deal of preoccupation in the literature with the real exchange rate. While the real exchange rate does have an influence on how a country's exports and imports respond to the changes in trade restrictions, being itself an endogenous variable, it cannot serve as a policy variable. Nor is it especially helpful in evaluating the *welfare* effects of trade liberalization. Furthermore, whether the real exchange rate is overvalued or undervalued and by how much at any point in time itself depends on how the "equilibrium" real exchange rate is defined. And there is little agreement on the definition of the equilibrium real exchange rate. The question, at what level should the real exchange rate be in order for a country to be defined as a free trader, is rarely attempted. This is in contrast to trade barriers: Their absence implies the country is a free trader. In view of this difficulty with respect to the real exchange rate, in this chapter, I will look at openness in terms of traditional trade barriers only.

Second, in evaluating openness and the extent of liberalization in East Asia, an analyst faces a serious conceptual problem on account of a simultaneous existence of or change in import restrictions and export incentives. According to the Lerner Symmetry Theorem, the outcome under a uniform import duty and a uniform export subsidy at the same rate is identical to that under free trade. Because almost all East Asian countries used import restrictions simultaneously with export incentives and subsequently also removed them simultaneously or in quick succession, it becomes difficult to judge both the degree of initial protection and eventual liberalization. For example, if a country with 15 percent tariff and 10 percent export subsidy lowers the tariff to 5 percent and removes the export subsidy, it is likely to be judged as having liberalized even though the net effect of the changes is nil. Alternatively, if the country just eliminates the export subsidy, few practitioners will judge it to have increased protection though that is precisely the effect of the change. This is not a purely academic point. For example, Westphal and Kim (1982) and Westphal (1990) have judged the net effect of trade interventions in Korea and Taiwan during the late 1960s and 1970s as either a neutral regime or one biased in favor of exports. If one accepts that view, by definition, there could not have been any liberalization in these countries subsequently. Alternatively, to the extent that policies supporting exports were dismantled first, protection in these countries increased before it was reduced.

Finally, and closely related to the previous point, if one wants to judge the degree of protection in terms of the outcome with respect to trade, the task becomes even more complicated. The point is made most conveniently with the help of an example. Most observers agree that Korea's aggregate exports during the 1970s were no less than what they would have been in the absence of all interventions. The observed aggregate import flows are, nevertheless, judged to be less than what they would have been under a free trade regime. But these two observations can be true simultaneously only if Korea's current account was in surplus. In reality, the current account was consistently in deficit until 1977. Thus, one must either argue that actual exports were less than what they would have been under free trade or that the net impact of trade interventions taken as a whole was minimal. Neither position is easy to defend.

In the following, I will sidestep these and other complications and follow the more common practice of identifying a removal of restrictions on imports with liberalization and paying limited or no attention to changes in export subsidies. Indeed, given the large number of countries I am dealing with, unless absolutely necessary, I will simplify my task by ignoring interventions in exports altogether, whether they be taxes or subsidies. Even then, we face serious problems with summary measures, which must inevitably be employed.

Thus, in the case of nontariff barriers, the available summary measures calculate the proportion of imports or output covered by various restrictions. These measures do not distinguish among restrictions on the basis of their severity. For example, a ban on imports gets the same weight in the measure as licensing even if licenses are issued freely.

Similarly, in evaluating the extent of tariff liberalization, we can use measures of nominal or effective protection. The former are more appropriate for evaluating consumption distortions and the latter for production distortions. In each category, we have the option to choose among simple, import-weighted, production-weighted, and consumption-weighted averages and collection rates. On the whole, a production-weighted effective protection rate is more appropriate to measure distortions in production, and a consumption-weighted nominal tariff for consumption distortion. But the former is calculated only occasionally and the latter almost never. The most frequently calculated measure is a simple average followed by an import-weighted average. A simple average is likely to overestimate the ideal average since many high rates are likely to have water in them. An import-weighted average, on the other hand, is likely to underestimate the ideal measure since it is likely to give the least weight to products with highest tariffs. Given these difficulties, the measures considered below should be viewed as suggestive of the direction of change without placing too much faith in their magnitudes. And simple averages should not be compared to weighted averages.

8.4   Trade Liberalization in Asia: An Overview

In describing trade liberalization in Asia, I follow the traditional division of the continent into East Asia and South Asia. The major countries in East Asia are China, Hong Kong, Indonesia, Korea, the Philippines, Singapore, Taiwan, and Thailand, and those in South Asia include Bangladesh, India, Pakistan, and Sri Lanka.[8] Broadly speaking, the countries in East Asia have been export hawks and those in South Asia export pessimists. In terms of trade policies, East Asia has been more liberal than South Asia though vast differences exist among countries within each region, especially East Asia.

Before we turn to measures of trade liberalization, it is useful to take a brief look at some basic characteristics of the countries. This can be done with the help of tables 8.1 and 8.2.[9] Table 8.1 reports annual growth rates over 1960–1990 by decades and for 1991–1995. Table 8.2 gives selected economic indicators for 1980, 1990, and 1995. From these tables, a link between growth and openness can be established at least for countries lying on extremes. The highly open

Table 8.1
Real average annual rates of growth (% GDP)

Year	1960–1970	1970–1980	1980–1990	1990–1995
Hong Kong	10.0	9.2	6.9	5.6
Singapore	8.8	8.3	6.4	8.7
Indonesia	3.9	7.2	6.1	7.6
Korea	8.6	9.6	9.6	7.2
Malaysia	6.5	7.9	5.2	8.7
Philippines	5.1	6.0	1.0	2.3
Thailand	8.4	7.1	7.6	8.4
China	5.2	5.2	10.2	12.8
Bangladesh	3.7	2.3	4.3	4.1
India	3.4	3.4	5.8	4.6
Pakistan	6.7	4.9	6.3	4.6
Sri Lanka	4.6	4.1	4.2	4.8
Industrial market East	5.2	3.2	3.2	2.0
USA	4.3	2.8	3.0	2.6
Japan	10.9	4.3	4.0	1.0
Germany	4.4	2.6	2.2	N.A.
Brazil	5.4	8.1	2.7	2.7
Mexico	7.2	6.3	1.0	1.1

Source: From World Development Reports (WDR): Various issues [WDR's data source: U.N. System of National Accounts].

economies of Hong Kong and Singapore have grown consistently rapidly while the least open economy, India, has performed consistently poorly except arguably during the 1980s when some liberalization and foreign debt helped prop up the growth rate to 5.8 percent. In the middle of these two extremes, we have countries such as Korea and Taiwan, which have grown consistently rapidly and, at least in terms of exports-to-GDP and imports-to-GDP ratios, appear highly open. Countries in South Asia that have generally done poorly, except possibly Sri Lanka, have been relatively closed when measured by these ratios as well as trade polices.

Reductions in Tariffs and Nontariff Barriers

The information on trade policies in this section is drawn mainly on the United Nations Conference on Trade and Development (UNCTAD) (1994), which provides an excellent documentation of

Table 8.2
Broad performance indicators

	Year	GNP per capita	Share in world population (million)	Share in world exports (%)	Export to GDP ratio (%)	Import to GDP ratio (%)
Hong Kong	1980	4,240	5.10	0.95	71.86	81.67
	1990	11,490	5.8	2.29	115.14	115.58
	1995	22,990	6.2	3.38	120.94	134.18
Singapore	1980	4,430	2.40	0.93	165.35	204.87
	1990	11,160	2.8	1.47	150.16	173.35
	1995	26,730	3.0	2.30	141.31	148.76
Indonesia	1980	430	146.60	1.06	28.08	13.89
	1990	570	181.3	0.72	23.96	20.38
	1995	980	193.3	0.88	22.93	20.66
Malaysia	1980	1,620	13.90	0.63	52.92	44.19
	1990	2,320	18.2	0.82	69.42	69.05
	1995	3,890	20.1	1.44	86.78	91.14
Philippines	1980	690	49.00	0.28	17.69	25.56
	1990	730	62.9	0.22	18.26	29.51
	1995	1,050	68.6	0.34	23.59	38.20
Thailand	1980	670	47.00	0.31	20.23	28.65
	1990	1,420	57.2	0.64	28.28	40.92
	1995	2,740	58.2	1.10	33.80	42.37
Korea	1980	1,520	38.20	0.84	27.95	35.60
	1990	5,400	43.3	1.81	26.64	28.62
	1995	9,700		2.43	27.46	29.67
Taiwan	1980	2,348	N.A.	N.A.	N.A.	N.A.
	1990	7,729	N.A.	N.A.	N.A.	N.A.
China	1980	290	976.70	0.87	6	7
	1990	370	1,149.5	1.71	17	14
	1995	620	1,200.2	2.89	21.33	18.51
Bangladesh	1980	130	88.50	0.04	6.83	21.89
	1991	220	110.60	0.05	7.34	14.83
	1995	240	119.80	0.06	10.90	22.32
India	1980	240	673.20	0.34	4.71	9.05
	1991	330	866.50	0.53	7.96	9.20
	1995	340	929.40	0.60	9.49	10.65
Pakistan	1980	300	82.20	0.13	12.06	24.93
	1991	400	115.80	0.20	16.22	20.97
	1995	460	129.90	0.16	13.18	18.90

Table 8.2 (continued)

	Year	GNP per capita	Share in world population (million)	Share in world exports (%)	Export to GDP ratio (%)	Import to GDP ratio (%)
Sri Lanka	1980	270	14.70	0.05	24.57	53.96
	1991	500	17.20	0.09	32.08	47.11
	1995	700	18.10	0.07	29.41	40.15

Source: World Development Report, U.N. System of National Accounts, and IFS Trade Statistics.
Note: N.A. indicates data not available.

tariff and nontariff barriers. For countries not covered by UNCTAD (1994), I have used alternative sources. A second comprehensive source of information, used in sections 8.4 and 8.5, is GATT's Trade Policy Review Mechanism that, starting from 1989, publishes comprehensive reviews of trade barriers every two years for the four largest trading entities (counting the European Communities as one), every four years for the next largest sixteen entities, and every six years for other contracting parties with possible exceptions made for the least developed member countries. Trade Policy Reviews (TPRs) offer very detailed information relating to virtually all policies influencing trade flows. Their main limitation is that they often provide a snapshot only and do not trace changes in trade barriers over time. Sometimes even when two or more TPRs are available for a country, it is difficult to relate the information across them. For example, they may report the simple average tariff in one but the weighted average tariff in the other.

For East Asia, an additional source of information is the publication by the Pacific Economic Cooperation Council (PECC) (1995) of the Asia Pacific Economic Cooperation (APEC). PECC (1995) draws on UNCTAD (1994), APEC economy notifications, and other sources. A limitation of the publication, however, is that the information in it often fails to provide explanations of what appear to be contradictory pieces of information coming from different sources.[10] For South Asia and some countries in East Asia, I also draw on the Asian Development Bank's (ADB's) recent country studies, which I codirected with Narhari Rao.[11]

To the extent that countries chose tariff bindings under the Uruguay Round Agreement that were well above their applied tariff rates, I have refrained from describing them in this chapter. I discuss the bindings in individual country profiles as a part of multilateral liberalization only in the cases in which they lead to an actual lowering of tariffs. In my judgment, bindings with water pave the way for future liberalization but by themselves amount to little liberalization. Countries such as Hong Kong and Korea have chosen bindings that are well above their applied tariffs, arguing that the former give them bargaining power in future negotiations. But it is difficult to imagine that other countries will take these bindings seriously in the face of applied tariffs that are much lower.

Table 8.3 provides summary indicators of nontariff barriers. Except for the Philippines, Taiwan, and Bangladesh, these indicators have been taken from UNCTAD (1994) and, thus, use a consistent methodology. Broadly speaking, the unweighted average is a measure of the proportion of products subject to nonautomatic licensing. The weighted average, on the other hand, can be interpreted as an indicator of the proportion of imports affected by nonautomatic licensing. The UNCTAD (1994) figures are available for three different years, which are not uniform across countries but do fall into three time periods that are uniform, 1984–1987, 1988–1990, and 1991–1993.

From table 8.3, it is evident that Hong Kong and Singapore have had minimal nontariff barriers (NTBs). The few that existed in the 1984–1987 period were dismantled by 1989. Malaysia compares favorably in terms of the level of NTBs but had achieved less success in the removal of the small proportion of the barriers that remained in 1987. Taiwan is yet another country that was virtually free of NTBs by 1985.

Among the remaining countries in East Asia, Indonesia began with the most extensive system of nontariff barriers in 1987 with almost 95 percent of products covered by some form of nontariff barrier. And remarkably, by 1992, it had virtually abolished all NTBs. Based on the unweighted average for all products during 1984–1987, the Philippines, Thailand, and Korea follow Indonesia in that order. But by 1991–1993, they had all achieved comparable levels of liberalization of NTBs with Thailand remaining slightly more protected. China remains an anomaly where NTBs seem to have risen and then declined with a net increase in protection over the period covered. But given the direct state intervention in trade, the indicator used in table 8.3 is less meaningful in China's case.

Leaving aside Sri Lanka, which had undertaken a major liberalization of its nontariff barriers in 1977, South Asia began with very substantial NTBs during 1984–1987. Based on the information in table 8.3, Bangladesh and Sri Lanka have gone a long way toward dismantling NTBs, and Pakistan has also made some progress. Though India also liberalized to some degree, in 1992 it was still suffering from very substantial NTBs. Recalling, however, that India's liberalization program began in earnest only in June 1991, table 8.3 does not capture a major part of the changes in NTBs that have taken place. These changes will be discussed later in the chapter.

Table 8.4 offers summary measures of tariffs. All information in this table, except that relating to the Philippines and Taiwan, comes from UNCTAD (1994). The years for the UNCTAD countries fall into the periods 1980–1983, 1984–1987, 1988–1990, and 1991–1993. The overall picture in table 8.4 is broadly consistent with that emerging from NTBs in table 8.3. Consistent with its free trade status, Hong Kong has had no tariffs during the period covered. Singapore has had an average tariff of less than 1 percent on an unweighted basis and less than 2 percent on a weighted basis. Malaysia's average tariff has also been low but, despite room for liberalization, there appears to have been limited liberalization. Indeed, if we take 1981 as the starting year, average tariff in 1992 was slightly higher.

If we go by the import-weighted average tariff, leaving aside China, which is complicated, and Taiwan, for which we do not have comparable information, the remaining countries in East Asia had comparable levels of tariffs during 1980–1983. But in terms of the simple average, the Philippines, Thailand, and Indonesia had much higher tariffs than Korea. With the exception of Thailand, all three countries have achieved significant liberalization. As we see later, this liberalization has continued beyond the years included in table 8.4. Because of revenue reasons, Thailand has regressed over the period covered in table 8.4.

Finally, though tariff levels in South Asia, with the possible exception of Sri Lanka, remain extremely high for the latest year shown in table 8.4, there too a substantial *reduction* in tariffs has taken place. As we see later in this chapter, in the case of Bangladesh, India, and Sri Lanka, substantial further reductions in tariff barriers have taken place in recent years not shown in table 8.4. Thus, on balance, the evidence for liberalization is across the board.

Table 8.3
Nontariff barriers in Asia

Country and year	Primary products		Manufactured products		All products	
	Unweighted average	Weighted average	Unweighted average	Weighted average	Unweighted average	Weighted average
Hong Kong						
1985	6.9	38.7	2.1	3.3	3.4	14.3
1989	0.8	1.9	0.3	0.3	0.5	0.9
1993	0.8	1.9	0.3	0.3	0.5	0.9
Singapore						
1987	15.3	12.6	14.1	12.8	14.7	12.9
1989	3.0	3.3	0.2	0.2	1.0	1.3
1993	1.2	2.1	0.00	0.0	0.3	0.7
Indonesia						
1987	98.9	98.4	93.1	89.8	94.7	92.5
1990	15.7	14.9	7.0	10.8	9.4	12.1
1992	4.6	11.2	2.0	5.3	2.7	7.3
Korea						
1987	17.6	13.6	5.5	14.6	8.8	14.2
1990	12.4	38.6	0.8	0.5	4.0	13.3
1992	9.0	8.6	0.2	0.2	2.6	3.0
Malaysia						
1987	4.5	6.3	3.2	9.1	3.7	8.2
1988	1.6	1.6	3.0	8.0	2.8	6.0
1992	1.2	1.6	2.4	7.0	2.1	5.1

Philippines						
1980					51.8	
1985					35.1	
1990					8.0	
1992					2.5	
Taiwan						
July 1970					42.9	
July 1972					17.9	
June 1985					2.5	
June 1987					1.6	
Thailand						
1985	24.4	28.6	7.8	16.3	12.4	20.2
1989	7.9	12.1	8.8	3.7	8.5	6.5
1991	8.8	12.0	4.2	6.2	5.5	8.2
China						
1987	17.8	19.7	7.9	16.1	10.6	17.2
1990	27.2	58.9	21.9	34.4	23.2	42.6
1993	11.5	40.7	11.3	19.2	11.3	26.4
Bangladesh						
1985–1986					56.7	
1989–1990					25.4	
1991–1992					15.6	
1993–1994					8.8	

Table 8.3 (continued)

Country and year	Primary products		Manufactured products		All products	
	Unweighted average	Weighted average	Unweighted average	Weighted average	Unweighted average	Weighted average
India						
1987	91.6	96.9	76.5	83.1	80.7	87.4
1990	74.4	88.8	61.7	53.1	65.4	65.2
1992	71.7	87.8	58.9	47.8	62.6	61.3
Pakistan						
1984	85.4	93.8	82.0	81.6	83.1	85.4
1988	17.4	19.6	28.0	25.7	25.4	23.8
1992	6.8	40.7	17.3	16.5	14.5	24.7
Sri Lanka						
1987	11.7	48.0	14.1	17.3	13.9	27.1
1990	10.6	56.3	9.5	12.1	10.1	27.1
1993	2.8	11.1	4.0	11.1	3.8	11.2

Sources: UNCTAD (1994), except for Philippines, Taiwan, and Bangladesh. Philippines: Intal et al. (1996). Taiwan: Baldwin, Chen, and Nelson (1995). Bangladesh: World Bank (1996). The basis of calculation for Philippines, Taiwan, and Bangladesh may differ.

Explaining the Post-1980 Wave of Trade Liberalization

How do we explain the massive liberalization that has taken place in the past ten to fifteen years? The answer is multifaceted and can again be organized around Bhagwati's (1988) taxonomy of ideas, institutions, and interests.

Ideas

First, the phenomenal success of Hong Kong, the Republic of Korea, Singapore, and Taiwan—which came to be known variously as the newly industrialized economies (NIEs), East-Asian tigers, four dragons, and the gang of four—administered a major blow to the proponents of export pessimism. These countries demonstrated that it was possible for developing countries to become highly successful exporters of manufactures, which did not suffer from low import-demand elasticities. The experience helped quash the myth that changes in the exchange rate could not be trusted to correct deficits in external payments and thus opened the way for trade liberalization without the fear of a balance-of-payments crisis.

Second, the success of the outward-oriented NIEs in promoting growth had a more direct, contagion effect. The NIEs were emulated by neighboring Indonesia, Malaysia, Thailand, and the Philippines who were, in turn, emulated by their neighbors, Vietnam and China. The success of China helped weaken the case for import-substitution strategy and planning even in India, where the hold of export pessimism and suspicion of world markets had been virtually absolute.

Third, and equally important, inward-oriented economies by and large failed to produce growth miracles of the kind produced by the outward-oriented economies. Though countries such Brazil and Mexico showed rapid growth during the 1960s and 1970s, this had been achieved to a substantial degree by expanding debt. Public debt had gone up from $3.2 billion in 1970 to $37.8 billion in 1980 in Brazil, and from $3.2 billion to $33.5 billion in Mexico over the same period. Moreover, by early 1980s, growth in these countries had begun to unravel with public debt still growing apace. The GDP growth rate in Brazil fell from 8.1 percent over 1970–1980 to 1.3 percent over 1980–1985 with public debt rising to $73.9 billion in 1985. Growth rates in Mexico fell from 6.3 percent to .8 percent between the same time periods, and public debt rose to $72.5 billion in 1985. Observations like these were complemented by reports of per-

Table 8.4
Unweighted and weighted tariffs in Asia

Country and year	Primary products		Manufactured products		All products	
	Unweighted average	Weighted average	Unweighted average	Weighted average	Unweighted average	Weighted average
Hong Kong						
1985	0.0	0.00	0.00	0.00	0.00	0.00
1989	0.0	0.00	0.00	0.00	0.00	0.00
1993	0.0	0.00	0.00	0.00	0.00	0.00
Singapore						
1983	0.1	0.5	0.4	1.4	0.3	1.1
1987	0.1	0.7	0.4	1.4	0.3	1.2
1989	0.2	1.9	0.4	1.9	0.4	1.9
1993	0.3	1.9	0.4	1.9	0.4	1.9
Indonesia						
1980	23.0	13.6	31.3	28.5	29.0	23.5
1987	14.7	10.4	19.4	21.7	18.1	18.2
1990	14.8	9.1	22.5	22.6	20.3	18.0
1992	13.6	8.5	18.3	14.7	17.0	12.6
Korea						
1987	21.8	15.2	23.4	22.5	22.9	20.2
1990	14.9	10.5	12.3	11.8	12.9	11.3
1992	12.9	9.7	10.5	10.2	11.1	10.0

Malaysia						
1981	4.3	2.0	12.7	13.0	10.6	9.7
1987	8.6	6.4	15.4	17.7	13.6	14.7
1988	7.7	5.4	14.8	14.5	13.0	11.5
1992	7.3	5.3	14.7	14.1	12.8	11.2
Philippines						
1980					41.4	21.4
1985					27.6	18.3
1990					27.8	19.7
1995					19.0	14.0
Taiwan*						
1979						10.6
1985						7.7
1992						5.1
Thailand						
1981	26.3	13.7	34.6	28.7	32.3	24.8
1985	28.0	16.5	32.5	30.4	31.2	26.9
1989	33.4	31.5	43.7	40.9	40.8	38.0
1991	26.2	26.4	41.8	41.6	37.8	36.9
China						
1982	46.5	22.7	50.5	36.6	49.5	31.9
1987	33.1	20.6	41.9	33.2	39.5	29.2
1990	34.1	19.1	42.7	34.3	40.3	29.2
1993	31.7	17.8	39.7	37.1	37.5	30.6

Table 8.4 (continued)

Country and year	Primary products		Manufactured products		All products	
	Unweighted average	Weighted average	Unweighted average	Weighted average	Unweighted average	Weighted average
Bangladesh						
1983	70.7	58.8	111.2	94.7	99.9	85.4
1986	57.5	48.3	91.3	70.8	81.8	65.1
1988	72.5	44.4	114.3	92.1	102.2	76.0
1993	73.3	62.1	84.5	81.1	81.2	75.9
India						
1981	69.6	37.2	75.9	70.9	74.3	59.9
1987	90.8	69.1	101.9	99.4	98.8	90.0
1990	69.9	34.3	82.7	76.4	79.2	62.4
1992	44.9	19.9	56.1	53.9	53.0	42.6
Pakistan						
1982	65.1	36.3	82.3	68.7	77.6	57.7
1984	65.5	40.1	82.8	68.8	78.0	59.7
1988	53.7	33.1	60.9	43.9	58.8	40.1
1992	54.1	37.8	63.6	65.2	61.1	56.2
Sri Lanka						
1983	45.7	24.5	39.5	27.0	41.3	26.3
1987	28.4	32.9	27.0	19.5	27.3	23.6
1990	29.3	34.4	26.2	19.4	26.9	24.3
1993	26.7	29.1	26.0	21.2	26.1	23.7

Sources: UNCTAD (1994), except for Philippines and Taiwan. Philippines: Intal et al. (1996). Taiwan: Baldwin, Chen, and Nelson (1995).
*The tariff rate for Taiwan is "collection rate" calculated as total tariff revenue over imports times 100.

sistent shortages in the Soviet Union and Eastern and Central European countries throughout 1980s.

Fourth, research and education by economists helped change the prevailing ethos. Even at the time that import-substitution ideology was dominant, some economists had begun to advocate and document the benefits of outward-oriented policies and the costs of protection. Prominent among earlier writings in this vein were Keesing (1967), Bhagwati and Desai (1970), Little, Scitovsky, and Scott (1970), Balassa (1971), Corden (1971), Krueger (1974, 1978), and Bhagwati (1978).[12]

Subsequently, during the 1980s and 1990s, the IMF and the World Bank signaled their intention to aggressively promote trade liberalization and market-oriented policies (judged to be desirable in these studies) in developing countries. This signal, in turn, swung the economists at these institutions into action. On the one hand, they produced innumerable country reports, which formed the basis of structural adjustment loans and became powerful instruments for spreading pro-liberalization ideas. On the other hand, they produced major documents such as the World Development Report (World Bank 1987) and detailed cross-country studies such as Thomas, Nash, et al. (1991) and Papageorgiou, Choksi, and Michaely (1991), which helped advance pro-trade-liberalization ideology.

Working independently, key trade economists also helped build support for liberal trade policies by writing for the media, lecturing, and promoting pro-trade-liberalization research. Thus, Bela Balassa and Anne Krueger at the World Bank promoted research and helped shape the World Bank's policy advice during the 1980s. Max Corden, who had begun to argue in favor of a removal of quantitative restrictions and a rationalization of tariffs in Australia as early as 1958, played a key role in shaping that country's trade policies.[13] Mohamed Ariff helped advance the case for liberal trade policies in Malaysia. Ammar Siamwalla played the same role in Thailand, though with less success. In India, consistent advocacy of a liberal trade regime by Bhagwati, Desai, and Srinivasan provided the necessary intellectual support to mild liberalization during 1980s and the major opening up in the 1990s (Bhagwati and Desai 1970 and Bhagwati and Srinivasan 1975). In 1993, upon invitation from then Finance Minister Manmohan Singh, Bhagwati and Srinivasan (1993) made detailed recommendations for future reforms in India.

Finally, the role of key statesmen has been crucial in shaping trade regimes. In Singapore, the contribution of Deputy Prime Minister

Goh Keng Swee in promoting an outward-oriented regime against the prevailing ethos of import substitution was crucial. In India, without Finance Minister Manmohan Singh's determined effort, trade reform could have come to a halt soon after macroeconomic stabilization had been achieved. In Taiwan, Chiang Ching-Kuo, who became the country's premier in 1972 and its president in 1978, played a crucial role in shaping that country's policies. Chiang remained the President of Taiwan until his death in January 1988 and was succeeded by Lee Teng Hui. In Korea, Park Chung Hee, who served as the country's President from 1963 until his assassination in 1979, must be credited with the first two phases of trade liberalization in 1965–1967 and 1978–1979 as well as for Korea's reliance of an export-oriented strategy of development.

Interests

Both external and internal interests contributed to liberalization in developing countries. As a result of the phenomenal growth in Asian developing countries, developed countries came to realize by the early 1980s that the markets they had previously thought of as marginal were now significant. They saw lucrative opportunities for their exporters in these markets and began to exert pressure for increased access through unilateral threats such as those under the United States Super 301 provision of the Omnibus Trade Practices and Competitiveness Act, 1988, as well as the multilateral forum of the Uruguay Round.[14] In addition, the Reagan administration played a key role in switching the focus of the World Bank's lending from projects to structural adjustment.

Internally, at least two factors were important. In countries such as India, Indonesia, and Korea, as industries grew bigger, they began to lobby for the removal of tariff and nontariff barriers facing imported inputs. In India, firms sold the bulk of their output in the domestic market on which no duty exemption or drawback was available. In Korea, over time even export-oriented firms eventually found themselves selling in the rapidly growing domestic market for which no relief was provided from tariffs on inputs used in production. More subtly, because nontariff barriers raised the cost of imported inputs well above the world price plus tariff, even exporters became opponents of nontariff barriers on inputs.

The second factor has to do with the astronomical costs with which protection came to be associated in certain countries. The discussion of figure 8.1 revealed that policy changes typically generate redistributive effects, which are much larger than efficiency gains. Rodrik (1994) argues that since the public often accepts the status quo income distribution as fair, it is politically costly for governments to make changes that generate large redistributions. This factor perhaps delayed trade liberalization for a long time. It may be argued, however, that in some countries eventually the cost of protection had become sufficiently large that they could outweigh redistributive effects. This can be illustrated best by comparing India and China. Growing at rates ranging from 8 to 12 percent per annum by adopting export-oriented policies, in fifteen years' time China was able to bring higher living standards to even those who had benefited from protection prior to the adoption of outward-oriented policies. Recognition of this fact presumably facilitated the continuation of trade reform in India beyond what was necessary to satisfy the World Bank–IMF conditionality.

Institutions

Two institutional changes, both at the international level, are important to note. First, during the 1970s, the world abandoned the adjustable peg system and moved to a system of floating exchange rates. Though the developing countries generally did not immediately shift to the new system due to continued export pessimism, the change did pave the way for the eventual replacement of trade restrictions by exchange-rate policy to correct imbalances in payments. This institutional change was essential if the break in export pessimism was to translate into action.

Second, as already noted, the IMF and the World Bank also played some role in promoting trade liberalization through their structural adjustment programs. This factor has been less important in Asia, however, than in Africa or Latin America. Even though the World Bank gave fast-disbursing loans to countries such as India and Indonesia, these loans cannot be considered to have been the cause of the liberalization that took place. In these cases, the loans followed the policy decisions that had already been made by the governments.

The discussion in this section has been at a broad level and does not capture fully either the extent of changes that have taken place or

their political economy in individual countries. In the following section, I attempt to fill these gaps through in-depth studies of three
countries: Singapore, Taiwan, and India. These studies are complemented by shorter profiles of seven other countries: Hong Kong,
Malaysia, Thailand, and the Philippines in East Asia and Bangladesh, Pakistan, and Sri Lanka in South Asia.

8.5 Three Case Studies

We now take an in-depth look at the experience of three countries,
Singapore, Taiwan, and India. The choice of the countries has been
motivated by a desire to study a wide range of experiences. Leaving
aside a mild and short-lived episode of import substitution, Singapore has been a virtual free trader during the entire period under
review. India, on the other hand, pushed import substitution to its
limit and was perhaps surpassed in this area only by the Soviet
Union and Eastern European countries. Taiwan falls somewhere in
the middle of these two extremes; it pursued import substitution
policies during the early period, quickly became a successful exporter, but did not fully liberalize until recently. These countries
have also had different experiences with trade liberalization. When
Singapore introduced import-substitution policies in the 1960s, future liberalization was built into those policies by stipulating that
"infant" industries, which fail to grow within a short, prespecified
period, will lose protection automatically. Taiwan's liberalization
was more gradual and was greatly influenced by the U.S. intervention in later years. India was the slowest to see the benefits of liberalization. After some piecemeal liberalization during the 1980s, it
took a serious balance-of-payments crisis to launch a deeper phase of
trade reform. Though initially the World Bank–IMF conditionality
played a key role, the process subsequently became self-propelled.

Singapore: How It Escaped Protection

With the exception of Hong Kong, Singapore has been the most open
economy in the world over the last half century. Today, no more
than 10 percent of its tariff lines are subject to positive tariff rates and
they are all 5 percent or less. The import-licensing system is used for
a limited number of products as a part of the country's international
agreements or for health, safety, or security reasons. With the ex-

ception of rice, no quantitative restrictions are practiced. There are no other significant trade restrictions on merchandise trade. Nor does Singapore operate any domestic schemes to protect narrowly defined industries (GATT 1992b).

Though the ultimate credit for pro-free-trade policies must go to its far-sighted leaders, Singapore does have certain features, which made it a natural candidate for pro-free-trade policies. First, geography of the country offers large benefits of free trade. The country is an island city with strategic location and a natural port to serve as entrepôt for Southeast Asia. It is flanked by Malaysia to the north and east, Indonesia to the south and east, and the Philippines to the northeast. This location makes the country an ideal waystation for storage and final processing of goods destined to and originating from the neighboring countries. Not surprisingly, traditionally, the proportion of re-export in total trade has been extremely high. During 1960–1967 when the country's trade policies were taking shape, it was as high as 85.6 percent (Aw 1991, table 1.10).[15] Ceteris paribus, these large shares of re-exports make the cost of trade barriers high and give pro-export interests a greater political power.

Second, Singapore's history interacted with its geography to generate an outward-oriented policy regime. Sir Stamford Raffles founded the modern city of Singapore in 1819. In 1867, under the Straits Settlement, it became a Crown Colony. The British gave the Singapore port free-trade status and adopted laissez-faire policies in it. Entrepôt trade flourished and strengthened the hands of pro-free-trade interests.

Third, a small population of 1.45 million (Saw 1986, table 6.1) helped policymakers appreciate better the smallness of domestic market and, hence, resist temptation to promote industrialization through import substitution.[16] Small land area—barely 246 square miles—and a poor natural resource base meant that the country started out as a net exporter of industrial products. This, in turn, implied that if the objective was to promote industrialization, on balance, export promotion rather than import substitution was the superior approach.

Fourth, because a large proportion of the population in Singapore was engaged in trading, a sizable entrepreneurial class already existed there. For example, in 1970, only 3.78 percent of Singapore's labor force was engaged in agriculture, fishing, and quarrying. As much as 23.44 percent of the labor force was engaged in trade, and

21.98 percent in manufacturing. The remaining 50.8 percent was engaged in construction, utilities, transport and communications, financial, business, and other services.[17] This employment structure is quite different from a typical country in the early stages of development and suggests the existence of a substantial entrepreneurial class. Thus, one of the motives for protection in many developing countries—creation of an entrepreneurial class—did not exist in Singapore and Hong Kong.

Finally, due to a steady flow of foreign capital, high price elasticity of its exports (mainly manufactures), and prudent monetary and fiscal policy management, Singapore never faced a balance-of-payments crisis. On the contrary, due to surpluses in the balance of payments, from 1960 onward there was pressure on the Singapore dollar to appreciate. The Monetary Authority of Singapore had to sell Singapore dollars to counter deflationary pressures. The government budget was also persistently in surplus. These facts meant that Singapore was spared the trade barriers induced by balance-of-payments crises.[18]

All these factors contributed significantly to the fostering of a free-trade regime in Singapore. But they are insufficient to *guarantee* the adoption of free trade policies in the absence of decision makers capable of seeing and interested in internalizing the benefits of openness. This conclusion is supported by a closer examination of policies in the country. In 1959 when Singapore achieved internal self-rule, the dominant ideology was export pessimism and import substitution. The incoming government was under pressure to assume a proactive role in promoting growth and could not be immune to this ideology and ethos. And soon after coming to power, the leadership did succumb to the allure of import substitution. But, unlike many other developing countries, it did not lose sight of the fact that Singapore's future lay in conquering world markets and gave protective policies a short fuse. By 1973, the country had instituted the regime, which remains approximately intact even today. Therefore, the central question we must answer is how Singapore was able to pull out of import substitution policies adopted during the 1960s. I will argue below that this was the result of a unique interaction between historical events and a far-sighted leadership.

As noted earlier, under the 1867 Straits Settlement, Singapore had been declared a free port. Except for the brief period 1942–1945 when Japan occupied it, it remained under British control until 1959.

During this period, the colonial government followed a laissez-faire policy and developed Singapore for entrepôt trade and as a base for managing and financing their investments in rubber estates, tin mines, and related activities in Malaya and Singapore. The colonial government limited its role to the maintenance of law and order and external defense, leaving even the provision of infrastructure, including telephone services and port management, to private companies (Ow 1986, 228). Thus, a strong tradition of reliance on the private sector had developed by the time Singapore achieved full internal self-government in 1959.

In June 1959, the People's Action Party (PAP), which continues to rule today, came to power with Lee Kuan-Yew as the first prime minister and Goh Keng Swee as finance minister.[19] In its election manifesto, PAP had called for the establishment of a common market with the Federation of Malaya to obtain free access to the latter's market. Therefore, when Tunku Abdul Rahman, prime minister of the Malayan Federation, proposed the formation of a Federation of Malaysia comprising his own nation, Sarawak, British North Borneo, and Brunei, despite opposition from some party members, Lee Kuan-Yew supported it and prevailed. In September 1963, Singapore became a part of the Federation of Malaysia.

The merger proved a mistake for Singapore, however. Indonesia, its second-largest trading partner, refused to recognize the Federation of Malaysia and adopted a policy of confrontation with it. Singapore's entrepôt trade suffered a serious setback and, for the first time since World War II, the country experienced negative growth of −4.3 percent (Ow 1986).

During 1963–1965, Singapore went through internal strife as well as confrontation with Malaysian leaders, which culminated in its separation from the federation on August 9, 1965. Although the separation helped bring Indonesian confrontation to an end in June 1966, Singapore then had to face Malaysian hostility. On top of that, in 1967, the British announced their intention to withdraw all military forces by March 31, 1971, later postponed to December 31, 1971. At $550 million, the British military expenditure in Singapore was 12.7 percent of the country's GDP in 1967 (Ow 1986, 229). The prospect of withdrawal of this spending was sure to affect growth adversely.

These events had a profound impact on economic policymaking in Singapore. In its election manifesto, PAP had identified free port, lack of free access to markets in the Federation of Malaya, and orientation of entrepreneurs toward trade rather than manufacturing as three key weaknesses of the economy. The manifesto clearly signaled a switch from the British laissez-faire policy to active interventionism if PAP came to power.

Upon taking office, PAP introduced several measures to promote industrialization. I do not describe domestic policy measures toward this objective, which can be found in Tan and Ow (1982) and Aw (1991). Instead, I focus exclusively on trade policies. Until 1960, Singapore had no protective tariffs or quantitative restrictions. The only custom tariff, applying to liquor, tobacco, and petroleum, was for revenue purposes. An equivalent excise duty was levied on domestic production of the same commodities (Lloyd and Sandilands 1986).

Protective duties to promote industrialization were inaugurated, however, with tariffs on hard soap and detergents in 1960 and paints in 1962. In 1963, based on the strategy outlined in the First (and only) Development Plan (1961–1964), quantitative restrictions were also inaugurated with import quotas imposed on flashlights, radio batteries, monosodium glutamate, and wheat flour. After merger with the Federation of Malaya, additional quotas were introduced. By May 1965, the number of commodities subject to licensing had risen from their pre-Malaysian level of 8 to 230.

Although at independence on August 9, 1965, all but 88 quotas were removed, due to the introduction of high tariffs, on balance, the period 1965–1969 can be defined as the import substitution phase in Singapore. Of the 142 items freed from quota restrictions, 68 were replaced by tariffs. Several previously unprotected items were also brought under the tariff net with the result that the total number of dutiable items, defined at six-digit tariff lines, rose to 199 in 1966. This number kept climbing up steadily in subsequent years, rising to 229 in 1967, 295 in 1968, and 398 in 1969.[20]

It is useful at this point to discuss the extent of protection provided by these tariffs and quotas. Fortunately, Tan and Ow (1982) carry out detailed calculations of nominal and effective protection for the year 1967. This exercise required them to draw a correspondence between highly detailed, six-digit Singapore Trade Classification (STC) and Singapore Industrial Classification (SIC). As a result, they aggregated protected commodities into 104 products. Of these, 59 were subject to tariffs only, 25 to tariffs and quotas, and 20 to quotas only.

It is fair to say that virtually all economists who have studied Singapore are of the view that the level of protection during this period was extremely low (e.g., Lloyd and Sandilands 1986, 185–186) and Aw 1991, Table 3.1). This view is substantiated on the ground that, at its peak, the average nominal protection rate was approximately 4 percent (Aw 1991, table 3.1). In my view, this "average" rate greatly understates the extent to which tariffs and quotas distorted the "relative" price structure. Thus, consider three facts provided by Tan and Ow (1982).

First, tariff rates on many products were comparable to those in other developing countries. Of the 84 commodities subject to tariffs, 49 had tariff rates below 25 percent, 21 had rates between 25 percent and 50 percent, and the remaining 24 had rates between 50 percent and 200 percent. High-tariff items included products such as refrigerators (150%) and matches (160%).

Second, quotas were stringent. They were set at 1 percent to 120 percent of import value in a particular year between 1962 and 1966. For 28 out of 45 commodities subject to quotas, the percentage allowed was 30 percent or less than in one of the years during 1962–1966. Thus, the quota system, which concentrated on three commodity groups—bicycles and parts, tires and tubes, and miscellaneous chemical products—provided a high degree of protection to selected products.

Finally, products subject to tariffs only accounted for 11.5 percent of total manufacturing output at world prices, those having tariffs and quotas accounted for .4 percent of the output, and those having quotas for 9.7 percent. Thus, tariffs and quotas covered 21.6 percent of manufacturing output. Remembering that protected industries are likely to be the ones that have low output rather than those that are flourishing and are successful exporters, this coverage is far from insignificant.[21] In any case, when compared to Singapore's own pre-self-rule status as a free trader, this protection represents a major break from its own past.

Two factors contributed to this rise in protection. First, as already noted, the PAP government was inclined favorably to import substitution as an instrument of industrialization. Its original decision to enter the Federation of Malaysia was the result of its desire to gain free access to a protected market. Second, the separation from Malaysia led to a loss of that market and pushed Singapore further toward protecting its own market.

To their credit, policymakers in Singapore never lost sight of the basic rule of successful import substitution: Protection must be temporary and, within a reasonable time, the industry should either be able to compete without protection or allowed to liquidate. The annual report by the Singapore Department of Trade (1968), quoted in Tan and Ow (1982, 281–282), articulated the role of quotas as follows:

The need for this control on the import of each commodity was reviewed once in every six months from the date it was fist enforced and decisions made in such reviews were announced quarterly. Where the particular industry had fairly found its feet but still needed some protection, the form of protection was modified by either changing the quota or replacing it by tariffs. In other cases, where the particular industry was found not making any serious effort to succeed in its ventures, import quota protection was withdrawn. Quotas were also removed when industries were able to function without further protection from Government.

Balassa (1982), drawing on the same report, notes that tariffs too were to be gradually lowered and eventually eliminated. This is a policy stance that few trade economists will hesitate to endorse even today except on the grounds of time inconsistency or infeasibility. Once protection is granted and an inefficient industry established, it might no longer be a welfare-enhancing policy to liquidate the latter through withdrawal of protection. Alternatively, even if it is welfare enhancing to liquidate the industry, vested interests may make such liquidation impossible.

Finally, Britain's announcement that it would withdraw its forces from Singapore by 1971 also speeded up the switch to proactive, outward-oriented policies. The withdrawal was to lead to a substantial decline in local demand, making it even more urgent to look for external markets for Singaporean products. As a result, several incentives were announced for exporters in 1967 and, presumably, removal of trade barriers accelerated.

By 1974, Singapore had eliminated all import quotas and removed or lowered duties on a large number of products. As already noted, today there are no duties in excess of 5 percent, and 90 percent of tariff lines are entirely free of duty.

As is well known, Singapore has had a remarkable growth record. Thus, even during the politically turbulent years of 1960–1967, despite a negative growth of −4.3 percent in 1964, the average annual growth rate was 6.8 percent. The shift away from import substitution during 1968–1973 was accompanied by an acceleration of growth rate to an annual average of 13.2 percent. This was followed by 8.5 percent annual growth during 1974–1982 (Aw 1991, table 1.2).

Taiwan: Liberalization under External Pressure[22]

Taiwan became a province of China in 1886. In 1895, after the Sino-Japanese war, it was ceded to Japan. Substantial economic and population growth occurred in Taiwan during the following fifty years under Japanese occupation. In 1945, after the conclusion of World War II, Taiwan was receded to the Republic of China (ROC). This led to an abrupt end to the economic ties between Taiwan and Japan with China becoming Taiwan's major export market. But by 1949, the communists had taken over mainland China and the Nationalist government of the ROC was forced to relocate itself to Taiwan.

Few believed that the ROC government in Taiwan would survive the communist government. Indeed, on January 5, 1950, President Harry Truman declared that the United States had no plans to provide military assistance to the Nationalist army. But the Korean War, which broke out in June 1950, turned Taiwan into a strategic base for the United States for averting further communist aggression in the Pacific region. The Seventh Fleet was sent to patrol the Taiwan Strait and an aid program was resumed by 1951.

The resumption of aid, both military and economic, ushered in an era of deep U.S. involvement in policymaking in Taiwan. Since Taiwan was not a member of GATT, the United States was able to exert bilateral pressure freely. The fact that Taiwan also had an authoritarian government further facilitated this process. The ROC government was able to implement the policies negotiated with the United States with greater ease than would have been possible under a democratic regime.

An overview of the changes in direct controls on imports and average tariff rates in Taiwan from the early 1950s is provided in tables 8.5 and 8.6, respectively. Both tables appeared in Baldwin, Chen, and Nelson (1995). Tariffs in table 8.5 are measured in terms of collection rates and are not directly comparable to those in table 8.4. By the mid-1970s, direct controls had been substantially removed, though tariffs remained relatively high.

Table 8.5
Import controls in Taiwan

Year and month	Permitted imports		Controlled imports		Prohibited imports	
	Number of items	Percent of total	Number of items	Percent of total	Number of items	Percent of total
1953	280	55.2	185	36.5	28	5.50
1956	252	48.1	241	46.0	25	4.80
1960	506	53.7	381	40.5	33	3.50
1966	493	52.3	395	41.9	36	3.80
1968/12	5,451	57.9	3,770	40.1	191	2.30
1970/7	5,612	57.1	4,030	41.0	190	1.90
1972/7	10,860	82.1	2,365	17.9	5	0.04
1974/2	12,645	97.7	293	2.3	4	0.03
1975/1	12,688	97.5	318	2.4	4	0.03
1976/6	12,846	97.2	362	2.7	13	0.10
1978/7	15,773	97.6	375	2.3	17	0.10
1979/12	15,836	97.6	380	2.3	17	0.10
1980/12	15,818	97.4	410	2.5	21	0.10
1981/12	25,681	97.8	833	3.1	17	0.10
1982/12	25,657	96.5	904	3.4	17	0.10
1983/12	25,664	96.5	921	3.5	17	0.10
1984/6	25,847	97.2	749	2.8	14	0.10
1984/12	25,972	97.1	744	2.8	14	0.10
1985/6	26,084	97.5	662	2.5	14	0.06
1985/12	26,289	98.2	470	1.8	9	0.03
1986/6	26,286	98.2	470	1.8	9	0.03
1986/12	26,443	98.4	421	1.6	8	0.03
1987/6	26,461	98.4	411	1.5	8	0.03

Sources: Tsiang and Chen (1984) and Tu and Wang (1988), as reported in Baldwin, Chen, and Nelson (1995).

1951–1978: Import Substitution and Export Expansion

The period from 1951 to 1958 is regarded as the import-substitution phase. During this period, the ROC government relied heavily on high tariffs, strict import controls, and multiple exchange rates. The U.S. aid was used to support designated infant industries, most notably textiles. Imports of inputs for the textile industry were financed by this aid at a favorable exchange rate. Other imports, especially consumer goods, were subject to an unfavorable exchange rate. A defense surcharge on private imports other than inputs was introduced in 1953 and extended to all imports in 1954. Exports of sugar and rice, which were a state monopoly, were subject to an unfavorable rate. Other exports, by public as well as private enterprises were given a favorable rate.

Despite these controls, trade balance remained unfavorable, and by 1954 foreign exchange reserves fell to the point that foreign exporters began to reject the letters of credit issued by the Bank of Taiwan. The authorities appointed two eminent economists, S. C. Tsiang and T. C. Liu, to advise necessary reforms. Recommendations by Tsiang and Liu led to some immediate reforms and to some additional ones in 1958. By November 1958, the currency had been devalued by 50 percent and the exchange rate fully unified. Moreover, import licensing was eliminated for the "permissible" imports. The defense tax was also reduced, though tariffs remained high.

In 1959, the Commission on U.S. Aid (CUSA), consisting of officials of the ROC government and advisers from the United States Agency for International Development (USAID), produced the Nineteen-Point Financial and Economic Improvement Plan. The plan covered import liberalization and export promotion, among other areas. It was implemented under the auspices of CUSA, which also controlled aid flows. Under the plan, statutes governing foreign investment were also modified to encourage direct foreign investment, which began to surge after the mid-1960s.

These policy changes, accompanied by trade liberalization by industrial countries under the auspices of GATT led to a period of sustained export expansion in Taiwan. Exports of textiles and apparel, electronics, and consumer manufactures—including plywood, toys, furniture, footwear, sporting goods, and travel gear—surged. The electronics industry flourished largely through direct foreign investment by multinational firms based in the United States and Japan. By contrast, largely Taiwanese small and medium-sized firms produced the consumer goods exports.

Though exports surged during the 1960s, there was little import liberalization. As table 8.5 shows, until July 1970, permissible imports accounted for 57.9 percent of the total number of items with 42.1 percent items still "controlled" or prohibited." At 11–12 percent, the tariff collection rate also remained high. It was not until 1972 that rising trade surplus and consequent monetary expansion generated sufficient pressures on prices to trigger major import liberalization. Because hyperinflation on the mainland had contributed to the

Table 8.6
Tariff burden in Taiwan (million new Taiwanese dollars)

Year	Total tariff revenue (1)	Total imports (2)	Tariff burden (1)/(2) (percent)	Tariff/total government revenue (percent)
1952	520	2,533	20.53	21.98
1953	513	2,754	18.63	17.31
1954	611	3,304	18.49	15.26
1955	658	3,146	20.92	14.62
1956	807	4,800	16.81	14.73
1957	978	5,259	18.60	15.15
1958	1,312	5,605	23.41	18.02
1959	1,316	8,420	15.63	16.47
1960	1,341	10,797	12.42	14.51
1961	1,655	12,894	12.84	17.32
1962	1,743	12,174	14.32	15.77
1963	2,046	14,483	14.13	17.24
1964	2,458	17,162	14.32	17.65
1965	3,302	22,296	14.81	20.81
1966	3,445	24,957	13.80	18.72
1967	4,291	32,314	13.28	20.02
1968	5,362	36,222	14.80	19.32
1969	6,134	48,629	12.61	17.24
1970	6,800	61,110	11.13	17.45
1971	8,373	73,942	11.32	19.31
1972	12,197	100,791	12.10	22.85
1973	17,687	145,079	12.19	24.5
1974	26,659	265,395	10.05	27.57
1975	25,717	226,460	11.36	23.75
1976	30,584	289,139	10.58	23.5
1977	35,090	323,839	10.84	23.25
1978	46,225	408,378	11.32	24.18
1979	56,467	532,958	10.60	23.57
1980	57,821	711,433	8.13	20.05
1981	57,988	778,633	7.45	17.59
1982	53,519	736,084	7.27	16.18
1983	62,818	813,904	7.72	17.41
1984	69,438	870,861	7.97	17.8
1985	62,094	801,847	7.74	15.99
1986	71,409	917,033	7.79	17.18
1987	78,154	1,113,871	7.02	15.18
1988	82,023	1,423,101	5.76	13.27

Table 8.6 (continued)

Year	Total tariff revenue (1)	Total imports (2)	Tariff burden (1)/(2) (percent)	Tariff/total government revenue (percent)
1989	87,061	1,385,720	6.28	11.82
1990	79,543	1,471,803	5.40	9.47
1991	84,121	1,690,772	4.98	9.61
1992	93,057	1,816,295	5.12	9.09

Source: Baldwin, Chen, and Nelson (1995).

nationalists' defeat at the hands of the communists, the ROC government was especially sensitive to inflationary pressures.

For licensing purposes, Taiwan's imports have been traditionally divided into three categories: prohibited, controlled, and permissible. Prohibited items are not permitted under any circumstance and have traditionally accounted for a very small proportion of all items. Controlled items cannot be imported unless special permits are issued under extraordinary circumstances. Until 1970, as many as 41 percent of the items fell into this category. Finally, permissible items are allowed relatively freely though, in many cases, they too are subject to administrative regulations. Some items such as gold are allowed to be imported by producers only. Items such as oil, fertilizers, and sugar are allowed by state enterprises only. Certain imports are subject to the "source" restriction, implying that they can be imported only from certain countries. Certain imports require approval of designated government agencies. Two major rounds of liberalization in 1972 and 1974 substantially trimmed the controlled and prohibited lists. The proportion of items under the permissible list rose to 82.1 percent in 1974 and to 97.7 percent in 1974. Though this did not mean that 97.7 percent of the items were fully freed, the changes constituted a major liberalization.

The 1970s saw a revival of import substitution in Taiwan. The government decided to develop heavy industries including steel, petrochemicals, and shipbuilding. The state became directly involved in this process through investment of state funds. A licensing scheme was introduced to protect these industries against foreign imports. For example, imports of steel required permission by the state-run China Steel Company. Similarly, the state-run China Petroleum Company monopolized the imports of naphtha used in its cracking plants. Local shipping companies were encouraged to purchase their vessels from the state-owned China Shipbuilding Company.

1978–1992: Liberalization under Pressure from the United States

Starting in 1978, the United States aggressively began to seek market access in Taiwan. This development took place at a time when Taiwan was finding itself increasingly isolated politically. Recall that it had lost its seat in the United Nations to the People's Republic of China (PRC) in 1971. In 1979, the United States also de-recognized it in favor of the PRC. This isolation made Taiwan an easy target for the United States' aggressive unilateralism whose foundation had been laid down by Section 301 of the United States Trade Act of 1974. It is interesting in this context to quote Baldwin, Chen, and Nelson (1995, 93), who provide a fascinating account of sector-by-sector negotiations forced on Taiwan by the United States over the years:

U.S.–Taiwan trade negotiations, begun in early 1978 under the U.S. initiative, have been the most important force shaping Taiwan's trade policy since the late 1970s. Annual negotiations have taken place each year since 1984, with the number of meetings held each year increasing over time. Until recently, the United States always set the agenda for the negotiations. Furthermore, the bargaining process has been one-sided, with the United States proposing restrictions on Taiwan's exports or demanding market liberalization for potential American imports, and the Republic of China defending its protectionist positions. The reason the ROC has been willing to participate in these no-win negotiations year after year is obvious: the country gains politically and economically by maintaining U.S. ties. The strategy followed by ROC in the negotiations has been to make the minimum concessions needed to keep the United States reasonably satisfied and, at the same time, to prevent significant pressures within the Taiwanese economy.

The U.S.–Taiwan Trade Agreement and Tariff Concessions The United States initiated the negotiations in 1978 with a view to gaining trade concessions from Taiwan in return for extending its Tokyo Round concessions to the latter. The outcome was the U.S.–Taiwan Trade Agreement under which Taiwan pledged to observe the same obligations as those applicable to developing countries set forth in the nontariff agreements concluded in Tokyo. In the subsequent negotiations, the focus shifted to tariffs. Under pressure from the United States, Taiwan revised its tariff schedule almost every year, sometimes twice a year. By 1984, tariffs had been cut on 465 import items.

In 1985, the United States asked for concessions on 174 items, including many agricultural products, with a favorable outcome on 112 items. In 1986, the ROC gave concessions on 58 items against 71 items put on the agenda. In 1987, tariffs concessions were sought on 66 items with positive outcome on 62 items.

Concessions in Agriculture Following the U.S. failure to launch another multilateral round to liberalize trade in agriculture and services in 1982, market access in these areas became an issue in the U.S.–Taiwan negotiations as well. The United States sought concessions for American tobacco and alcohol, banking and insurance services, and agricultural products, especially fruits. In many cases, it succeeded in getting concessions on a discriminatory basis. It also successfully limited Taiwanese exports of certain products.

Since 1978, the United States has obtained access to Taiwan's market for apples, oranges, grapefruit, grapes, pears, and peaches. These products have been subject to import licensing and, in a clear violation of the 1978 U.S.–Taiwan Trade Agreement, the access to the U.S. exporters has been given on an exclusive basis. The biggest import item among fruits is apples. The United States accounted for 59.2 percent of all apples bought in 1990.

Taiwan also gave concessions on beef though, in this case, the U.S. sellers had to compete against imports from Australia and New Zealand. The ROC government has also sent "buy American missions" to purchase U.S. grains each year. Not surprisingly, the United States accounts for 90 percent of Taiwan's total imports of grains. On the export side, in 1984, the U.S. Rice Millers' Association sought restrictions against subsidized rice exports from Taiwan. The result was an agreement under which Taiwan undertook to export rice only to extremely poor countries.

An interesting conflict arose between the United States and Taiwanese domestic interests when, in the second half of 1987, imports of turkey wings increased sharply. This led to a decline in the price of chicken, which is a close substitute for turkey. Chicken farmers lobbied and were successful in getting automatic licensing revoked in January 1988. The United States trade representative (USTR) demanded immediate consultation. At the first meeting in Taipei, the United States got the ROC to agree to reinstate automatic licensing starting May 1, 1988. Chicken farmers were angry and held a demonstration in Taipei. In response, the ROC imposed a ban on imports of turkey parts. But this was insufficient to calm down the farmers who organized a demonstration in front of the Legislative Yuan on May 20, 1988. The demonstration resulted in the first ever street riot in Taipei by a farmers' group since the ROC government had relocated to Taiwan.

At the second round of negotiations in August 1988 in Hawaii, the ROC made only token concessions. This led the U.S. Trade Policy Review Group to recommend consideration of retaliation under the Super 301 section of the Trade and Competitiveness Act of 1988. Pressured on both sides, the ROC issued an Import Relief Measure for Agricultural Products in December 1988, providing relief to farmers hurt from import competition. Simultaneously, in the third round of negotiations in Washington, D.C., in January 1989, the ROC government agreed to reinstate automatic licensing for all turkey meat imports.

Tobacco and Wine Traditionally, tobacco and wine were a state monopoly in Taiwan. All production, imports, and sales were under the Taiwan Tobacco and Wine Monopoly Bureau (TTWMB). The United States had begun to seek liberalization in early 1980s. But it was not until October 1985 that, under a Section 301 threat, the ROC government and the United States signed an agreement under which the former agreed to liberalize imports of tobacco, beer, and wine. The details of how imports were to be liberalized were to be negotiated over the next year.

Due to the formidable lobbying power of the domestic industry, the United States was mainly interested in access to the Taiwanese tobacco market. But the two sides failed to come to an agreement. Taiwan initially proposed a quota while the United States wanted a tariff. Taiwan then proposed a 210 percent tariff, which the United States rejected, and sought a specific tariff that would have been equivalent to a 120 percent ad valorem tariff at the time. In addition to this disagreement, the two sides also differed on the issue of advertising. The ROC wanted to limit advertising to posters inside the stores selling American cigarettes and only reluctantly agreed to allow limited magazine advertising. The United States, by contrast, wanted access to broadcast advertising. The ROC negotiators argued that such advertising would lure youngsters into the market and was, therefore, socially hazardous.

With no agreement in sight, in October 1986 President Reagan approved the USTR's recommendation to retaliate under Section 301. This immediately returned the two sides to the negotiating table, and an agreement was reached on December 12, 1986. The tariff was set at the level sought by the United States though it was not given the permission to advertise in newspapers and broadcasting media. Soon after, many posters advertising American cigarettes appeared in the streets of Taipei and within a year American brands captured 12 percent of the market. Smoking among youngsters expanded rapidly.

Financial Services   The United States has persistently kept the issue of liberalization in the financial services area on the agenda since 1978 and won concessions on a discriminatory basis in all major areas, namely, banking, insurance, and securities.

Banking   Traditionally, state-owned banks have dominated the banking sector in Taiwan. The first foreign bank, from Japan, entered Taiwan's banking market in 1959. Following that event, for a long time Taiwan allowed one foreign bank per country. This one-bank-per-country quota was later replaced by regulations, which greatly favored the U.S. banks. Consequently, of the thirty-six foreign banks operating in Taiwan in December 1992, eleven were from the United States. Not surprisingly, the United States has never complained about these regulations. Instead, the United States has focused on national treatment for its banks. But since this issue was unresolved even in the multilateral negotiations until the signing of the financial services agreement, Taiwan was able to defend the policy of discrimination in favor of home firms with greater ease than is likely now.

The United States has also sought and received concessions in areas of new branches, debit card business, savings deposits and long-term loans, and deposit and lending limits. In August 1986, the ROC government allowed foreign banks to open more than one branch per bank. In August 1988, it allowed foreign banks to enter the debit card business. Later, it also allowed foreign banks to issue credit cards in U.S. dollars. In 1989, foreign banks were also permitted to accept savings deposits and to give loans with a maturity of more than seven years. Finally, limits on deposits and lending were also relaxed considerably over time.

Insurance   In the insurance sector, the key issue pushed by the United States was that of entry of the U.S. firms. In October 1987, the ROC government agreed to grant two licenses for property insurance and two for life insurance each year. Soon the interest in property insurance was exhausted, and the United States asked for and was granted the right to pool the licenses. The United States next demanded that U.S. insurance firms be permitted to invest in the Taiwanese real estate and securities market. The ROC refused the former demand but granted the latter one.

In May 1990, Taiwan amended the Insurance Law and further opened the door to local firms. In 1992, eight Taiwanese firms were granted licenses. This rapid expansion is likely to result in stronger demands by the United Sates for national treatment for the U.S. firms.

Securities   The securities market was also liberalized under U.S. pressure. Initially, in July 1987, four mutual fund management firms in the form of international joint ventures were approved. American banking and security firms represented the foreign side in these ventures. Because the foreign exchange flows were tightly controlled, the approval of these ventures led to the liberalization of at least an outward flow of remittance of foreign exchange. But the restrictions on inward remittances remained in place.

The boom in the Taiwanese stock market during 1986 and 1987 generated further pressure from the United States for access to the market in brokerage services. In 1988, the ROC government amended the Securities and Exchange Law to permit foreign securities firms to operate in Taiwan as minority-owned subsidiaries. The upper limit on foreign interest was set at 40 percent. In December 1990, the foreign institutional investors were permitted to invest directly in Taiwan's stock market. By 1993, the share of these investors in the transactions in the Taipei Stock Exchange at .5 percent was still small.

India: A Case of Autonomous Liberalization[23]

Though the origins of trade liberalization in India can be traced to late 1970s, a true break from protectionist policies began only in July 1991. As such, the discussion below is divided into the years 1951–91 and 1991 to date.

1951–1991: The Years of High Protection

The machinery for import controls in India had existed since May 1940 when the British government first introduced it. The objective behind the controls at that time was to alleviate shortages of foreign exchange and shipping created by World War II. After the war, import policy alternated between liberalization and tighter controls. In 1951, four years after independence, India launched the First Five Year Plan. The period covering this plan, 1951–1956, was broadly characterized by increased liberalization.

In 1956–1957, India faced a foreign exchange crisis.[24] The natural reaction of the government was to resort to import controls. Unfortunately, once introduced, the controls became a part of the overall planning framework and were extended with time. By the early 1960s, the regime of controls was firmly in place with virtually all uses of foreign exchange requiring administrative approval. Tariff rates also rose to levels that were quite high by international standards.

Self-reliance had always been a stated objective of Indian policymakers. During the 1960s and 1970s, protection against imports became a key instrument of achieving this objective. The existence of an eager and proficient civil service reinforced the prevailing view, shared by the country's policymakers and economists, according to which priority sectors had to be protected and offered adequate access to foreign exchange. It was unclear how the priority sectors were to be selected.[25] The result was the creation of a regime dominated by bureaucratic discretion. Over time, as the industrial structure grew more diverse, so did the structure of foreign trade and regulations needed to govern it.

Starting in the late 1970s, two factors helped initiate a phase of partial liberalization. First, pressures for better access to foreign inputs began to build from industries that had developed during 1960s and 1970s. Second, import compression, improved export performance during the 1970s, and a large inflow of worker remittances from the Middle East helped build a healthy foreign exchange reserve.

The process of liberalization, which began in 1977, was very slow and limited, but it continued through 1980s without major reversals. The most significant trade liberalization took place during Prime Minister Rajiv Gandhi's term, which began in January 1985. Much of the liberalization derived from the expansion of the Open General

Licensing (OGL) list and involved a relaxation of import controls on raw materials and capital goods.[26] According to Pursell (1992), imports not subject to either canalization or licensing (mainly those coming under OGL) as a proportion of total imports grew from 5 percent in 1980–1981 to 30 percent in 1987–1988.[27]

Unfortunately, steep escalation of tariff rates marred even the partial liberalization of controls during the 1980s. According to the Tax Reforms Committee (TRC 1993) report, the import-weighted average tariff rate rose from 38 percent in 1980–1981 to 87 percent in 1989–1990. The report also estimates that the duty collection rates rose from 20 percent to 44 percent over the same period. Tariff increases were particularly large after 1984–1985.

1991 to Date: The Period of Liberalization
At the beginning of 1991, all categories of import goods—consumer, intermediate, and capital—were subject to controls. Consumer goods imports were completely banned except those imported by governmental agencies or those judged essential for everyday existence, such as edible oils, drugs and medicine, kerosene, and food grains. Capital goods imports were either restricted or on OGL. Items on the OGL list could be imported without a license though not without question. For example, the importer had to be the "actual user." Similarly, productive capacity to be created by the imported machines had to have been approved by industrial licensing authorities. Imports of intermediate inputs fell into four categories. Listed according to stringency of controls, these were: banned, restricted, limited permissible, and OGL.

As noted before, in 1987–1988, items on the OGL accounted for 30 percent of the total value of imports. Even this figure overstates the extent of liberalization since it is based on ex post data. If all imports had been free, the items on the OGL list would have accounted for a much smaller proportion of total imports.

For products not on OGL, licenses were issued with relative ease when imports were required for the production of exports. In all other cases, the system was highly discretionary and decisions were made on a case-by-case basis. Each firm, whether private or public, had some arm of the government (e.g., a ministry, department, or marketing board) as its "sponsoring agency" who had to certify that the product being imported was essential. Yet another governmental agency had to certify that the product was not available domestically.

The imports of many goods were subject to canalization and could be imported only by a designated governmental agency. Canalized items included crude oil and petroleum products, iron and steel, fertilizers, edible oils, newsprint, sugar, cereals, cotton, and so forth. In 1986–1987, the only year for which information is readily available, one third of total imports were canalized.

The high level of tariffs in India defied all international standards. In 1990, the maximum tariff rate was 340 percent. Of the 5,000 positions in the Harmonized System of Tariff Codes, fewer than 4 percent had tariff rates of 60 percent or less. As many as 60 percent of the tariff lines were between 110 percent and 150 percent. Due to exemptions, particularly those given on raw materials used by exporters, the actual incidence of tariffs was lower, but it was still much higher than in other developing countries. Thus, in 1990, the duty collection rate (tariff revenue as a proportion of imports) in India was 42 percent. This dwarfed rates of 13 percent in Turkey, 8 percent in Argentina in 1989, and 7 percent in Brazil in 1990.

A balance-of-payments crisis in June 1991 triggered a process of liberalization resulting in a substantial decline in protection. With the exception of consumer goods, direct controls on virtually all items have been abolished. Some liberalization of consumer goods imports has also taken place. According to Pursell (1996), as a result of the reforms in 1991 and 1992, the share of manufacturing value added protected by NTBs fell from 90 percent to 46 percent in India. He estimates that by mid-1995, this share had gone further down to 36 percent. In a significant move, under separate agreements with the United Sates and the European Union (EU), India also undertook to liberalize its textiles and clothing, which includes consumer goods. Some of this liberalization began in 1995 with more to come in 1998, 2000, and 2002. Beyond these agreements, consumer goods imports remain subject to NTBs.

India has also gone some way toward liberalizing tariffs, though considerable liberalization remains to be done. Tables 8.7 and 8.8, taken from Pursell (1996), provide a detailed picture of the state of liberalization in industry (as of July 1996) and agriculture (as of May 1995), respectively. Table 8.7 includes the information on the changes expected under the Uruguay Round commitments and tex-

Table 8.7
Manufacturing and mining: Tariffs in March 1995 and tariff objectives

	Actual tariffs		Chelliah Committee objective for 1996/1997 (NR = no rec.)	Uruguay Round binding for 2001/2002 (NB = no binding)	U.S./E.U. Textiles Treaty target for	
	March 1995	July 1996			1998	2000
Maximum: Consumer goods	50	50	50	40		
Maximum: All goods	50	50	30	40		
Petrochemicals/plastics						
Building Blocks (ethylene, propylene, etc.)	10	10	15	25		
Intermediates (neoprene, isobutene, etc.)	10–40	10–40	20	40		
Polymers (PVC, LDPE, HDPE, etc.)	40	30	25	40		
Plastic Products/articles	50	40	30* or 50*	40		
Synthetic textiles						
Fiber intermediates (P-Xylene, MEG, PTA, Caprolactum, etc.)	35–45	35–45	20	25, 40		
Wood pulp	25	5	10	25		
Caustic soda	40	40	20	40		
Textiles fibers (polyester, etc.)	45	30	25	40	35	20
Filament yarns	45	30	30	40	35	20
Fabrics	50	50	30	NB	40	25
Apparel	50	50	30	NB	50	40

Cotton/Cotton textiles						
Cotton fiber	0	0	NR	100	35	20
Cotton yarn	25	25	NR	25	35	20
Cotton fabrics	50	50	30*	40	40	25
Cotton apparel	50	50	30*	40	50	25
Chemicals						
Basic inputs (toluene, O-Xylene, etc.)	10–20	10	20	40		
Chemicals	50	40	20	40		
Inputs for fertilizer production (ammonia, phosphoric acid)	0	0	5	25		
Fertilizers	0	0	NR	5		
Metallic minerals						
Coking coal	5	5	5	25		
Noncoking (bituminous) coal	35	20	10	25		
Iron ore	10	10	NR	25		
Copper ores	10	10	NR	40		
Uranium/thorium ores	10	10	NR	40		
Other metallic ores	19	10	NR	25		
Nonmetallic minerals (salt, sulphur, sands, gypsum, limestone, etc.)						
Rock phosphate	0	0	NR	5		
Crude sulphur	0	0	NR	10		
All other	30 or 50	30 or 50	NR	40		

Table 8.7 (continued)

	Actual tariffs		Chelliah Committee objective for 1996/1997 (NR = no rec.)	Uruguay Round binding for 2001/2002 (NB = no binding)	U.S./E.U. Textiles Treaty target for	
	March 1995	July 1996			1998	2000
Nonferrous metals						
Unwrought aluminum	10	10	15	NB		
Aluminum products	40	40	25	NB		
Unwrought nickel	20	20	15	25		
Nickel products	30	30	25	40		
Unwrought tin	30	30	15	25		
Tin products	40	40	25	40		
Unwrought copper, lead, and zinc	35	35	20	NB		
Copper, lead, and zinc products	40	40	30	NB		
Iron and Steel						
Iron ore pellets	5	5	5	25		
Sponge iron/steel scrap	5	5	10	40		
Refractories	35	35	15	25		
Pig iron	20	20	15	25		
Semis and finished steel	20–50	30	20	40		
Stainless and other alloy steels	20–50	30	20	40		
Articles of iron or steel	15–50	15–50	30	40		

Machinery and equipment

Nonelectrical	Mostly 25	Mostly 25	20	25 or 40
Electrical	Mostly 25	Mostly 25	25	25 or 40
Electronic products				
Raw materials	0–50	0–50	20	25 or 40
Parts, components, subassemblies, etc.	25–35	25–35	30	25 or 40
Instruments for industrial and commercial uses	Mostly 35	Mostly 35	30	25 or 40
Medical equipment	Mostly 15	Mostly 15	20	25 or 40
Computers	20	20	30* or 50*	40
Consumer products (TVs, etc.)	50	50	50*	40

Source: Pursell (1996).

*In this case, there is no explicit tariff recommendation in the Chelliah Committee report, but it has been assumed that their general recommendation of a tariff of 50 percent for consumer goods and 30 percent for "final" intermediate goods would apply.

Table 8.8
Major agricultural products: Import tariffs and trade policy status, May 1995

Commodity	Tariff in April 1995 (%)	Uruguay Round binding (%)	Average implicit nominal protection rate (price comparisons) (%)		Quantitative restrictions	
			Imports	Exports	Exports	Imports
1. Animals	0	100			Mostly restricted	Mostly restricted
2. Meat						
Fresh, chilled, frozen	10	150			Mostly restricted	Restricted
Processed	50	150			Mostly free	Restricted
Processed-homog. meats, hams	50	55			Mostly free	Restricted
Hides and skins incl. leather	0	25			Restricted	Free
3. Fish and crustaceans	10	150			Free	Mostly restricted
4. Dairy products						
Milk and cream	40	100			Restricted	Restricted
Yogurt	40	159			Free	Restricted
Powdered milk ($<1.5\%$)	0	0			Free	Free
Powdered milk ($>1.5\%$)	0	0			Free	Restricted
Powdered milk ($>1.5\%$) sweetened	40	40			Free	Restricted
Butter	40	40			Free	Restricted
Butter oil	40	40			Free	Free
Cheeses	40	40			Free	Restricted
5. Rice						
Common	0	0	−43	−30	Free	Canalized
Basmati	0	0			Restricted	Canalized
6. Wheat and wheat flour						
Durum (hard) wheat	0	100	−31	21	Free	Canalized
Other wheat	0	100			Restricted	Canalized

7. Coarse grains and flours						
Maize	0	0	0	33	Restricted	Canalized
Sorghum	0	0	9	40	Restricted	Canalized
Millet	0	0			Restricted	Canalized
Barley	0	100			Restricted	Canalized
Rye	0	100			Restricted	Canalized
Oats	0	100			Restricted	Canalized
Other	0	100			Restricted	Canalized
8. Processed cereals						
Baby foods					Free	Canalized
Baker's dough					Free	Canalized
Breakfast cereals					Free	Canalized
All others					Free	Canalized
9. Pulses	10	100	3		Restricted	Free
10. Vegetables	10	100		−3 to −32	Mostly free	Restricted
Dried mushrooms, Onions and potatoes	10	35			Free	Restricted
11. Fruits	50	100		−48 to 5	Mostly free	Restricted
Grapes and plums	30	30			Free	Restricted
Dried prunes	50	55			Free	Restricted
12. Preparations of fruits and veg.	50	100		−39 to 13	Free	Restricted
About 13 vegetables	50	55			Free	Restricted
Orange juice	50	85			Free	Restricted
Other fruit juices	50	85			Free	Restricted
13. Coffee (unprocessed)	10	100			Restricted	Restricted
Roasted and decaffeinated coffee in bulk	10	150			Restricted	Free
14. Tea	10	150			Mostly free	Restricted

Table 8.8 (continued)

Commodity	Tariff in April 1995 (%)	Uruguay Round binding (%)	Average implicit nominal protection rate (price comparisons) (%)		Quantitative restrictions	
			Imports	Exports	Exports	Imports
15. *Spices*	50	100/150			Mostly free	Restricted
Caraway seeds	35	35			Free	Restricted
Thyme, bay leaves	35	35			Free	Restricted
16. *Oilseeds*	40/50	100	72		Mostly restricted	Canalized
17. *Oil cakes, meals, and flours*	50	150	negative	0	Free	Restricted
18. *Edible oils*						
Soya, rapeseed, olive, & cloza oils	30	45			Mostly restricted	Free
Coconut oil	30	300			Mostly restricted	Canalized
Other edible oils	30	300			Mostly restricted	Free
19. *Raw cotton*	0	150	-17	-10	Restricted	Mostly free
20. *Greasy wool, jute, sisal, etc.*	0	40	0		Free	Free
21. *Sugar*	0	150	-11		Restricted	Mostly free
22. *Natural rubber*	25	25	24		Free	Free
23. *Raw tobacco*	50	100		Zero or negative	Mostly free	Restricted
24. *Wood and wood products*	25–50	25–40			Restricted	Mostly free

Source: Pursell (1996).

[a] The implicit nominal protection rates are averages for the years indicated. Under "Imports" column, the domestic price is compared to the import price adjusted for port, transport, marketing, and other costs. Under "Exports" column, the domestic price is compared to similarly adjusted export price. A blank space means that the relevant estimate is not available.

[b] "Mostly restricted" means that most products in the category are subject to licensing or other NTBs. "Mostly free" means the products are free of such restrictions. "Canalized" means that a designated state agency has the monopoly on exports or imports.

tiles and clothing agreements with the United States and the EU. Table 8.8 includes tariff bindings chosen by India in various agricultural products. It also shows that a considerable liberalization has taken place in agriculture. Some further idea of the changes that have taken place can be gained by looking at the changes in the highest tariff rate and tariff-collection rates. As noted above, prior to the 1991 reform, the highest tariff rate was 340 percent. Today, it stands at 40 percent.[28] The tariff-revenue-collection rate was 49 percent in 1990–1991, falling to 29 percent in 1994–1995.

The pace of liberalization has been clearly faster in the first three years than in the subsequent five years, however. The Narsimha Rao government, which had initiated the process under the able guidance of Finance Minister Manmohan Singh, had itself begun to slow down in its last two years. Subsequent coalition governments have been even less reformist and have, in some respects, reversed the liberalization undertaken under the Rao government. In the 1996–1997 budget, the first year of the United Front government, the new Finance Minister Chidambaram introduced a 2 percent across-the-board special customs duty. In addition, he maintained the peak tariff rate of 50 percent. In the 1997–1998 budget, while the peak rate applicable mainly to consumer goods did fall to 40 percent, status quo of 30 percent duty for most industrial raw material was maintained. Furthermore, through an ordinance, the special customs duty was raised from 2 to 5 percent within six months of the budget presentation.

In March 1998, the Bhartiya Janata Party (BJP)–led coalition came to power. In its export-import policy, released in April, it carried out some liberalization of consumer goods imports. The upcoming Trade Policy Review at the World Trade Organization (WTO) in the middle of April 1998 essentially forced this on the government. The government dropped 330 items from the restricted list, trimming the list of 2,700 items by one eighth.[29] A hike in the tariff rate quickly followed this liberalization, however. In the budget, presented on June 1, 1998, the new Finance Minister Yashwant Sinha introduced an across-the-board (with a handful of exceptions) 8 percent tariff.[30]

Before I turn to a brief discussion of the factors leading to the movement toward liberalization during the 1990s, it is important to note that as a part of the process, the government has used the exchange rate extremely effectively to facilitate liberalization. Prior to the beginning of the reform process, in 1991 the exchange rate was approximately Rs. 18 per dollar. By February 1993, the rupee had depreciated to Rs. 31 per dollar. By June 1998, it had gone down to Rs. 41 per dollar. This steady depreciation has kept the incentive for exports up and at the same time provided a temporary cushion to domestic industries in the wake of liberalization.

Explaining the Liberalization

Four main explanations can be given for the advent of the liberalization phase in the Indian economy during the 1990s. First, by the late 1980s, *ideas* favoring outward orientation were beginning to take hold. The traditional consensus among Indian policymakers, economists, and bureaucrats had at last broken down under the weight of mounting evidence from all quarters against protectionist and interventionist policies. A key element that helped drive the pro-liberalization lesson home to Indian policymakers and economists was the demise of the Soviet Union and the success of China. Second, the balance-of-payments crisis of June 1991 helped trigger the process of liberalization. Indian policymakers have been traditionally hesitant to take bold actions and lean heavily in favor of maintaining the status quo. A crisis was essential to get the process started while the changed consensus helped sustain liberalization beyond the initial World Bank–IMF conditionality. Third, the newly created *institution* of Trade Policy Review (TPR) at the WTO has helped preserve some of the momentum toward liberalization. The successive governments since 1991 have been reluctant to open the consumer-goods sector to imports. The TPR has provided the necessary pressure to open at least some of the consumer goods sectors and is likely to continue to do so in the future. The institutional shift to the flexible exchange rates system has helped the TPR process further by making it difficult for India to defend quantitative restrictions under the GATT balance-of-payments exception (Article XVIIIB). Finally, both domestic and foreign *interests* have played an important role in liberalization. By the early 1980s, India's licensing regime had become so oppressive that India's businessmen using imported inputs were ready to assert themselves over the producers of these inputs. This factor made a quick withdrawal of import licensing on inputs feasible. A corresponding lobby was missing for consumer goods due to the obvious fact that consumers do not have the same voice in policymaking as producers. As a result, much of the pressure to liberalize consumer goods has come from foreign producers seeking access to the Indian market. This is clearly true with respect to textiles and clothing. Liberalization in this consumer goods sector has been induced by pressure from and agreements with the United States and the European Union. Similarly, tariff bindings under the Uruguay Round were the result of pressures from trading partners.

8.6 Conclusions

In this chapter, I have offered an overview of trade liberalization in Asia in the post-1980 era and the reasons underlying this development. I have shown that in virtually all the important countries in the region, considerable liberalization occurred during the 1980s and 1990s. With some notable exceptions, import licensing was virtually abolished during this period and tariffs were dramatically scaled down. Broadly speaking, the countries in East Asia liberalized more than those in South Asia did.

The chapter has also looked closely at the experience of three countries: Singapore, Taiwan, and India. These countries provide a wide array of experience. Leaving aside a brief and mild phase of import substitution in the second half of 1960s, Singapore followed an essentially free trade policy throughout the past half century. Though Taiwan resembles Singapore in being outward oriented, it actively pursued import substitution policies first in the 1950s and then again in the 1970s. Moreover, it has never come as close as Singapore to having a free trade regime. India provides an example of the most rampant protection. It pushed import substitution to the extreme and did not seriously begin to liberalize the economy until 1991.

The free trade policy in Singapore was entirely unilateral. From a welfare standpoint, this is not surprising since Singapore is a small economy. But from a political economy standpoint, it does pose a puzzle: Why was Singapore able to virtually escape import substitution while the entire world, save Hong Kong, felt compelled to follow this route? I have argued that this was partly due to the fact that at independence, Singapore was already a free trading country with a substantial industrial and services sector and only a tiny agricultural sector. As such, the pressure for import substitution coming from the desire to industrialize was far less in Singapore than in other countries. In addition, Singapore's leadership was farsighted in that during the brief import substitution phase, it committed itself to the withdrawal of protection according to a predetermined schedule.

In contrast to Singapore, trade liberalization in Taiwan during the 1980s was driven almost entirely by pressures from the United States. Having lost its seat in the United Nations back in 1971, by 1979 Taiwan had also lost recognition as a nation by the United States. This political isolation, a lack of membership in GATT, and heavy dependence for its exports on the U.S. market gave the United States enormous leverage over Taiwan, which it exercised freely to promote the interests of its export lobbies. Virtually every reduction in trade barrier—some even in violation of the 1978 U.S.–Taiwan Agreement to adhere to the most-favored-nation (MFN) principle—resulted from demands from the United States.

Finally, India offers a mixed case. The first set of reforms in July 1991 had a clear element of reciprocity: They were undertaken in response to the IMF–World Bank conditionality. But soon after this initial action, the initiative was seized by the government of India, which chose the speed and sequencing of much of the liberalization in the subsequent years. Though the World Bank did give policy loans during these reforms, virtually all decisions were taken by India. At various stages, the bank had wanted deeper and faster reforms but the government of India chose its own path with little concern for its implications for the bank willingness to lend. The key outside pressure for liberalization in the Indian case came during the Uruguay Round negotiations when the textiles and clothing agreements were negotiated with the United States and the EU and in April 1998 when, as a part of the WTO TPR process, the country was forced to withdraw 330 consumer goods items from the restricted list of imports.

Appendix: Additional Country Profiles

In this appendix, I provide country profiles of Hong Kong, Malaysia, the Philippines, and Thailand in East Asia and Bangladesh, Pakistan, and Sri Lanka in South Asia. My main objective here is to fill some details of the liberalization story and identify its sources.

Hong Kong

According to GATT (1994), Hong Kong has been free of all export and import duties since the beginning of its occupation by the British. The country is also free of all quantitative restrictions on export and imports.[31] The policy was originally adopted by the British superintendent of trade in 1841 and was subsequently maintained by the colonial government. Hong Kong is also one of the few countries with no participation in a preferential trade arrangement whatsoever.

Free trade in goods does not translate automatically into free trade in services. This is because interventions in this area do not take the form of border restrictions. Instead, they result from a lack of "national treatment" of foreign suppliers. As noted by Fung, Wong, and Wong (1997), in areas such as telecommunications, air transport, and banking, Hong Kong does limit market access. Furthermore, according to the documentation in Altinger and Enders (1995), Hong Kong's offers for liberalization under the Uruguay Round were better than those of most developing countries but less impressive than those of the European Union, Japan, and the United States.

Malaysia

Historically, trade barriers in Malaysia have been low in relation to other countries in the region except for Hong Kong and Singapore. The average nominal tariff rate was 13 percent in 1965 (Power 1971), which rose to 18 percent in 1970 (Ariff 1975) and to 22 percent in 1978 (Lee 1986). According to Ariff (1991, 20), "there was no major overhaul of tariff rates in the 1980s." Indeed, UNCTAD (1994) reports the import-weighted average tariff rising from 9.7 percent during 1980–1983 to 14.7 percent in 1984–1987 and then declining to 11.2 percent in 1991–1993. According to GATT (1993a), the simple average nominal tariff was 14 percent.

Tariff structure in Malaysia is characterized by substantial escalation. According to GATT (1993a, 59–61), while primary products are subject to an average tariff of 5 percent, semi-processed and processed products receive an average rate of 15 percent. Tariff peaks of 50 percent are frequent in sectors such as food products, beverages, textiles and clothing, printing, chemicals, rubber products, nonelectrical machinery, and transport products. Depending on value, motor vehicles attract a duty of from 140 percent to 300 percent.

GATT (1993a) notes some liberalization in recent years. Tariffs on 1,100 items were reduced during 1988–1992. In October 1992, duty reductions on a further 600 items were announced. Information on the extent of liberalization is not provided, but from the reported tariff averages, it can be conjectured that it was minimal.

Malaysia also offers some trade preferences under the ASEAN (Association of South-East Asian Nations) Preferential Trade Area (APTA), which is to be converted into ASEAN FTA (AFTA) by 2003. The proportion of imports covered by preferences and the extent of preferences actually granted by Malaysia is not known. Under separate bilateral agreements, Malaysia also gives tariff preferences on certain items to Australia and New Zealand.

Nontariff barriers are relatively low in Malaysia. Malaysia has never taken any safeguard, antidumping, or countervailing duty actions (GATT 1993a). A number of products are subject to licensing on a negative-list basis. Though most of the products on the list are for sanitary, phytosanitary, safety, environment protection, and copyright reasons, a few of them are intended to protect domestic producers of the products. Motor vehicles are the most prominent example of the latter.

Malaysia has always been open to foreign investment (Ariff 1991, chap. 4). According to GATT (1993a, 49), since 1968 the Malaysian government has maintained a wide range of investment incentives for sectors such as manufacturing, agriculture, and tourism. These were greatly expanded in 1986 with the result that 60 percent of recent investment in manufacturing has been based on foreign capital, largely directed to export-oriented activities. The incentives are selective and focus on exports, high technology, and domestic value added.

Projects, which export 80 percent or more of their output, are allowed 100 percent foreign equity. Projects that export between 50 and 79 percent of their output are allowed 100 percent equity provided their product has 50 percent domestic value added, have RM 50 million or more in fixed assets, and do not compete in the domestic market with products already available. Projects exporting from 51 to 79 percent of their output are allowed from 51 percent to 79 percent foreign equity depending on satisfying other conditions. Projects exporting from 20 to 50 percent of output can have foreign equity from 30 percent to 51 percent depending on satisfying additional conditions. For projects exporting 20 percent or less of their output, foreign equity is permitted up to 30 percent. Projects with a high level of technology or those producing priority products are permitted foreign equity up to 51 percent even if directed to the domestic market.

Malaysian currency, ringgit, was pegged to pound sterling until 1973 and for a brief period after that to the U.S. dollar. Since 1975, the ringgit has been allowed to float and commercial banks are free to determine exchange rates and to deal forward in currencies. Malaysia accepted the obligations of the IMF Article VIII and, thus, instituted current account convertibility as early as 1968.

In sum, though Malaysia has not carried out major trade reforms in recent years, its trade regime has been characterized by low barriers by developing-country standards. As in the case of Singapore, the credit for this must go to the country's leadership, which adopted liberal trade policies unilaterally. Though I have not studied the case of Malaysia in detail, it may be conjectured that much of the analysis of Singapore in the text applies to it. The main differences are that the Malaysian internal market was much larger than Singapore's in the 1960s and that its exports had a very large proportion of primary products. Both of these factors led the country to pursue import substitution policies on a wider scale and for a longer period. Moreover, whereas the leadership in Singapore adopted a policy of time-bound liquidation of protection and did not let import-competing interests becoming entrenched, Malaysia has been more tolerant of such interests.

Thailand

Like Malaysia, Thailand has only a few nontariff barriers, applying to less than 5 percent of imports. But unlike Malaysia, it has very high tariffs, indeed the highest among the countries in East Asia included in this study. A tariff reduction program was launched in October 1982 under the Fifth Five Year Plan, but had to be abandoned due to a major revenue shortfall. In reaction, tariffs were raised in 1985 by 5 percentage points on raw materials and 10 percentage points on finished products. As a result, tariff protection to the manufacturing sector increased sharply (GATT 1991b, 6 and 73, n. 5). According to GATT (1991a), the simple and import-weighted average statutory tariff rates in 1988 were 44 percent and 35.7 percent, respectively, with the top tariff rate as high as 200 percent.

In the late 1980s, tariff revenue still accounted for a quarter of tax revenue. But the appearance of a budget surplus in 1988 allowed Thailand to launch a program of trade liberalization. If we go by the information available in UNCTAD (1994), however, the extent of liberalization until 1991–1993 was minimal. According to this source, the import-weighted average tariff, which was 38 percent during 1989–1990, fell to only 36 percent in 1991–1993.

The picture is more upbeat, however, if one relies on PECC (1995, 32). Accordingly, a Tariff Restructuring Scheme was first introduced in 1990. This scheme lowered tariff rates and simplified customs classifications. The second stage of the scheme, aimed partially to fulfill Thailand's Uruguay Round and AFTA commitments, was announced in 1994.[32] As a result of these commitments, the simple average tariff rate declined from 27.24 percent in 1994 to 17.01 percent in 1997 (PECC 1995, 32). In addition, the number of tariff rates was to be reduced from thirty-nine to six with a peak tariff of 30 percent with some exceptions such as alcohol and tobacco (60%) and autos and auto parts (over 60%). Information on the implementation of these changes was not available at the time of writing, and it is not clear how the currency crisis will impact the reforms.

In 1990, Thailand liberalized its foreign exchange regulations substantially and accepted the obligations of Article VIII of the International Monetary Fund (IMF). Thus, Thailand has full current-account convertibility now. Thai currency, baht, was devalued in November 1984 by 14.8 percent against the U.S. dollar and switched to a more flexible exchange-rate regime. The baht further depreciated against the U.S. dollar until 1988 but subsequently, until the recent crisis, remained stable.

Thailand welcomes foreign investment though there are restrictions on foreign ownership. Up to 49 percent foreign ownership is permitted in almost all sectors, but beyond that the list of industries is limited. By and large, investment incentives in Thailand do not discriminate between foreign and local sources.

The Philippines

According to Intal et al. (1996), the ADB country study of the Philippines, the initial tariff reform program during 1981–1985 brought the top tariff rate to 50 percent. Based on the Philippines Tariff

Commission calculations reported in GATT (1993b, table IV.2, 70), the simple nominal average tariff rate fell from 41.37 percent in 1980 to 27.60 percent in 1985. Over the same period, the import-weighted average tariff rate fell from 21.4 percent to 18.30 percent. According to Tan (1994), the average effective rate of protection fell from 50 percent in 1983 to 46 percent in 1985.

The period 1985–1990 saw a substantial dismantling of quantitative restrictions (see below) but few reductions in tariffs. It was in August 1991 that tariff liberalization took off again with the issuance of Executive Order No. 470. This order established four tariff rates in all to be phased in by 1995: the top rate of 30% applying to finished goods, 20 percent to intermediate and capital goods for which domestic substitutes existed, 10 percent to intermediate inputs and capital goods for which no domestic substitutes existed, and 3 percent to basic raw materials previously subject to 5 percent or lower tariff. As a result of this program, by 1995, the simple average tariff rate had come down to 19 percent. The corresponding import-weighted average tariff rate was reduced to 14 percent (Intal et al. 1996, 12).

Remarkably, the Philippines has kept the momentum of trade reform going. In 1994, a year before the program under Executive Order No. 470 was to be fully implemented, Executive Orders No. 189 and 264 were issued (PECC 1995, 31). The former aims to bring tariffs on capital equipment to 10 percent and those on spare parts to 3 percent by 2000. The latter aims to lower tariffs on all industrial products. By the year 2000, 76 percent of the country's tariff lines will come within 0 to 10 percent. By the year 2003, only two tariff rates will remain: 3 percent for raw materials and 10 percent for finished products. By 2008, a uniform tariff of 5 percent will be applied to all industrial products.

The program for rationalizing nontariff barriers began in 1981. According to GATT (1993b, 4 and 84), between 1981 and 1986, 999 commodities classified according to the Philippines Standard Classification Code (PSCC) were deregulated. In the first phase of the Import Liberalization Program (ILP), extending from April 1986 to April 1988, 1,229 commodities were liberalized. By April 1992 when the second phase of the ILP was still in progress, 533 additional items had been liberalized, leaving only 5 percent of PSCC commodities "regulated." In terms of import coverage, according to Austria and Medalla (1996) on whom Intal et al. (1996, table 1.12) draw, import-restricted items accounted for 35.2 percent of imports in 1982, 29 percent in 1984, 21 percent in 1986, and 13.6 percent in 1990.

The Philippines peso is allowed to float, though the Central Bank does intervene in the market as per instructions given by the Monetary Board. The currency is convertible on the current account. In August 1992, several restrictions were lifted even on capital account transactions (GATT 1993b, 47). For example, exporters can now retain 100 percent of their foreign exchange and invest it abroad. Under relatively liberal conditions, residents are also allowed to invest abroad.

During the 1950 and 1960s, nationalism was closely linked to opposition to foreign investment. But the investment-led boom in other southeast Asian countries and a low savings rate led to a shift in thinking and, beginning in 1968, the Philippines began to liberalize its foreign investment laws. These efforts culminated in the Omnibus Investment Code of 1987 and Foreign Investment Act of 1991. Under the provisions of the latter act, the Philippines expanded the permission for 100 percent foreign equity ownership to include to all sectors except those included in three lists. The latter, for which foreign equity was limited to 40 percent, included List A, containing sectors in which the constitution or other laws forbid 100 percent equity; List B, consisting of sectors considered to protect for national defense or moral reasons; and List C, comprising sectors served adequately by local firms. In March 1996, List C was eliminated and minimum equity requirement was lowered from $500,000 to $200,000 to allow smaller firms to operate in the country.

Trade liberalization in the Philippines has been influenced partially by the IMF and World Bank programs. But from what I can judge (and this remains to be verified), as in the case of India discussed in detail in the text, these institutions were more pivotal in *initiating* the liberalization program. The actual liberalization, especially in recent years, has gone much farther than could have been pushed by the World Bank and IMF programs and has been driven by internal initiative. Two key factors appear to be the demonstration effect flowing from other southeast Asian neighbors and commitments under AFTA.

Bangladesh

An excellent summary of trade policy changes in Bangladesh can be found in World Bank (1996). Bangladesh has employed both trade barriers and exchange controls to restrict trade. Its trade liberalization program began in the mid-1980s, though it intensified only in 1992. The first important step was taken in January 1985 when the "positive list" approach to import controls was replaced by a "negative list" approach. Accordingly, items not listed as subject to controls could be imported either freely or by fulfilling certain specified requirements.

In July 1988, Bangladesh adopted the Harmonized System (HS) of classification, which has 1,239 items at a four-digit level. In 1985–1986, imports of 41.4 percent of all four-digit HS products were restricted for trade reasons and those of 4.9% for environmental, sanitary, phytosanitary, and security reasons. The percentage of items restricted for trade reasons declined to 20.4 percent in 1989–1990, 11 percent in 1991–1992, 3.2 percent in 1993–1994, and 2 percent in June 1995. Of the twenty-six items still restricted for trade reasons in June 1995, half were in the textiles sector.

Progress in tariff reduction prior to 1992 was minimal. Some attempts at liberalization were made in early 1986, resulting in a reduction in the number of duty rates from twenty-four to eleven. But the rates remained high and dispersed, ranging from 0 to 400 percent. Moreover, discriminatory sales tax, development surcharge, and import license fees continued to be charged in addition to the custom duty.

The 1991–1992 budget took the first major step toward tariff liberalization by replacing import-discriminating multiple-rate sales tax with a 15 percent uniform value-added tax to be levied on imports and domestic supply. Regulatory duty and development surcharge on imports were also abolished. There were modest reductions in tariff rates in 1992–1993 and 1993–1994. For example, in the latter period, duties on all machinery and capital equipment for industrial use were reduced to 7.5 percent and the top statutory rate was lowered to 100 percent for almost all products. The top rate fell to 60 percent in 1994–1995 and to 50 percent in 1995–1996 with tariff bands declining to 7 percent. The overall impact of these reforms has been to bring down the average nominal tariff from 90 percent in 1989 to 25 percent in 1996. The import-weighted average tariff rate is approximately 21 percent.

There is a high degree of tariff escalation in Bangladesh. As a rule, duties on inputs and machinery are low while those on finished goods high. It must be acknowledged, however, whether the net impact of this structure is to increase or reduce anti-export bias. In

Bangladesh, inputs are mostly imported for use in exports. As such, they may very well lead to a reduction in anti-export bias.

So far, Bangladeshi currency, taka, is not convertible on the current account under Article VIII of the IMF. Traditionally, based on its projections of foreign exchange earnings from exports, remittances, aid, and various capital flows and import policies framed by the Ministry of Commerce, the Ministry of Finance prepares a foreign exchange budget. All imports except those purchased directly by the government departments are subject to the issuance of letters of credit (GATT 1992a, 65).

According to the ADB study by Reza, Rashid, and Rahman (1996), Bangladesh has a very open regime with respect to foreign investment, both direct and portfolio. Investors are allowed to invest in all but five areas, which are on a reserve list. Foreign investors are allowed to own 100 percent equity in these sectors, and repatriation is permitted with minimal restrictions. Unlike many countries in East Asia, there is no minimum investment requirement.

In relation to its import bill, Bangladesh has been the recipient of substantial assistance from the World Bank. Therefore, it would seem to be an obvious candidate for aid-induced trade reform. Yet, evidence seems to indicate only a limited influence of the World Bank and the IMF. Throughout the 1980s, despite substantial aid flows limited liberalization occurred, certainly much less than what the World Bank and the IMF would have liked to see.[33] Similarly, though the liberalization in 1990s was initiated by conditionality under Economic Structural Adjustment Facility (ESAF) of the IMF negotiated following a balance-of-payments crisis in 1991, as in the Indian case discussed in detail in the next section, initiative for subsequent phases has come from within. For example, the *structure* of tariffs bears little resemblance to what World Bank and IMF would have recommended. These institutions have consistently advocated tariff uniformity and opposed tariff escalation. Yet the structure of tariffs in Bangladesh remains highly variegated with high tariffs on finished goods and low tariffs on raw materials and intermediate inputs. Thus, my personal impression is that while the World Bank played an important role through advocacy of the benefits of liberalization in their country-specific studies and served as a catalyst to the process, conditionality itself played only a limited role in the liberalization that has taken place to date. For that the credit must go to the country that—perhaps in the light of East Asian experience, its own success in expanding exports of garments and shrimp, and massive trade liberalization by developing countries around the world—overcame export pessimism and came to appreciate the benefits of a liberal trade regime.

Pakistan

Despite being small, Pakistan started with a low trade-to-GDP ratio. Between 1960 and 1972, exports averaged 4 percent and imports 10 percent of the GDP. This was partially the result of stringent controls on imports and exports that were introduced starting in 1952 following the collapse of the export boom and ensuing balance-of-payments crisis. Following a major devaluation (131%) in 1972, these figures rose to 9 percent and 18 percent for the period 1973–1983 (Guisinger and Scully 1991, 224).

Guisinger and Scully (1991) identify two early episodes of what they call "tortoise-like" piecemeal liberalization, one during 1960–1965 under Ayub Khan and the other in 1972 under Z. A. Bhutto. The first phase of liberalization was initiated with the primary objective of export expansion and began, in January 1959, with the replacement of a positive list of exports by a negative one consisting of sixteen products. It was immediately followed by the introduction of the Export Bonus Scheme under which freely tradable bonus vouchers were issued to exporters. These vouchers allowed the holder a large number of raw materials included in a positive list. In 1964, for the first time, products also began to be freed from licensing via a positive list. Initially, the list included only four items. But by July 1965, it had expanded to a modest degree to include fifty-one items. But the breakout of war with India in November 1965 put an end to this limited phase of liberalization.

The second phase of liberalization under Bhutto went deeper. Under Ayub and Yahya regimes, import controls had created a class of privileged bureaucrats and industrialists. As such, according to Guisinger and Scully (1991), Bhutto saw and sold liberalization to the populace as an attack on corruption and economic privilege. Efficiency gains from liberalization were never even mentioned as an issue. The liberalization involved three steps taken simultaneously in May 1972, a 131 percent devaluation, rationalization, and liberalization of the licensing regime and an elimination of the export bonus scheme. The main change to the licensing regime was to reduce the number of (positive) lists from six to two. Although these lists were more liberal, many consumer products were omitted from them. Moreover, the availability of foreign exchange still remained a constraint. Goods on the free list could be imported provided foreign exchange was available.

Because of widespread belief that the 1955 devaluation had failed to produce the desired expansion of exports and fears of instability, in 1959 a devaluation had been ruled out from the outset. Bhutto, on the other hand, came to power *after* the breakup of the country had taken place. This fact undoubtedly made the massive devaluation possible.

In recent years, compared to the highly restrictive trade regime of 1960s and 1970s, substantial liberalization has taken place. Nontariff barriers include a Negative List, consisting of items that are prohibited, and a Restricted List, comprised of items that require a license. The number of items on the former was 215 in 1990 and fell to 77 in 1993–1994 and 75 in 1994–1995. Imports of a large majority of these items are prohibited for environmental, safety, and religious reasons. The number of items on the Restricted List has also declined from 105 in 1990 to 50 in 1994. Items on the two lists together account for 10 percent of all HS items at the four-digit level.

Though tariffs have also been brought down, compared with other countries they remain high. According to the ADB study by Khan (1996), the maximum tariff rate was reduced from 225 percent in 1986–1987 to 92 percent in 1993–1994 and to 65 percent (inclusive of import fee, *iqra* or education surcharge, and import license fee) in 1995–1996. The simple average tariff rate fell from 79.2 percent to 59.8 percent in 1991 and to 58.2 percent in 1994. Thus, if we go by the change in the average tariff rate in 1990s, the level of tariffs has not declined perceptibly. According to UNCTAD (1994), the import-weighted average tariff fell from 59.7 percent in 1984–1987 to 40.1 percent in 1989–1990 but rose back to 56.2 percent in 1991–1993. In 1993–1994, 76 percent of tariff lines were subject to a 50 percent or higher tariff rate (Khan 1996, 24).

As of July 1, 1994, Pakistan has adopted current account convertibility of the rupee under Article VIII of the IMF Articles of Agreement. Thus, foreign exchange availability no longer serves as an added restriction on imports. It has also liberalized many capital-account transactions. For example, residents are allowed to maintain foreign currency accounts and are free to transfer their balances abroad. Restrictions on repatriation of profits and capital associated with direct foreign investment have also been removed.

The reform of the rules on direct foreign investment was initiated in 1988. Until then, foreign investment was subject to prior approval, with restrictions on equity participation and capital and dividend remissions. Currently, none of these regulations remain. Virtually all industrial sectors are open to foreign investment and 100 percent foreign equity ownership is permitted. The issuance of shares, re-mission of dividends, and repatriation of capital by foreign investors is permitted.

Sri Lanka

Like Singapore, Sri Lanka is an island economy and had a relatively small population of 6.7 million in 1946 (Cuthbertson and Athukorala 1991, table 2.1).[34] At independence in 1948, it too had accumulated a long history of free trade policies under British rule. But beyond these similarities, vast differences exist between the two countries. Sri Lanka is a multiparty democracy with regular elections. It has a much larger land area than Singapore—25,000 square miles com-pared with latter's 246 square miles—and relies heavily on agri-culture. In 1953, 52.9 percent of Sri Lanka's labor force was in agriculture. Despite attempts at industrialization, in 1981 this per-centage remained high at 45.9 percent (Cuthbertson and Athukorala 1991, table 2.4).

Through much of its history, Sri Lanka has been ruled by either center-right governments led by the United National Party (UNP) or center-left governments led by the Sri Lankan Freedom Party (SLFP). And trade policies, as well as other economic policies, have been influenced greatly by which of these two types of governments hap-pens to be in power. The former have leaned toward liberal policies while the latter toward protectionist policies. In 1947 and 1952 elec-tions, UNP won. Under its rule from 1948 to 1956, trade regime was extremely liberal. An SLFP-led coalition won in 1956 and again in 1960 and, during 1956–1965, introduced very restrictive trade poli-cies. In 1965, UNP returned to power and attempted to undo some of the protectionist policies but was voted out again in 1970. From 1970 to 1977, an SLFP-led coalition ruled and introduced state interven-tion with a vengeance, channeling 80 percent of imports and 30 per-cent of exports in 1976 through the state. In 1977, UNP came back

with an unprecedented mandate and embarked upon a decisive program of trade liberalization. This program dealt largely with quantitative restrictions, and tariff reform was not seriously addressed
until 1991. Nevertheless, there was no major reversal of the 1977 reform through the 1980s.

A closer look at the evolution of trade policy in the democratically
run economy of Sri Lanka offers an interesting contrast with Singapore. At independence, a key feature favorable to liberal trade policies in Sri Lanka was a flourishing export sector. Plantation crops of
tea, coconut, and rubber constituted a solid export base at the time.
In 1950, exports and imports amounted to 38.3 percent and 31.8
percent of the GDP, respectively, yielding a trade-to-GDP ratio of
70.1 percent. Thus, even ex post, the economy was highly open. The
balance of payments was positive, and the country had substantial
pound sterling reserves.

The center-right Senanayake government, which was at the helm
at independence, was favorably inclined to private initiative and
liberal trade policies. Thus, there was a coincidence of pro-free-trade
circumstances and ideology, leading to a broadly liberal trade regime until 1956.[35] There were a few import and export taxes at relatively low rates to collect revenue. The main bias toward import
substitution came from domestic policies designed to expand the
production of rice and subsidiary food crops.

A rise in the world price of rice led to a fundamental shift in Sri
Lankan politics. Rice subsidies had already accounted for 30 to 40
percent of Sri Lanka's public expenditure. The price rise led to a
large balance-of-payments deficit. In response, Prime Minister Senanayake tried to raise the price of subsidized rice but was confronted
with civil disturbances culminating in his resignation. Though UNP
survived the rest of its term with a new prime minister, the episode
paved the way for its removal from power in the next election.

From 1956 to 1965, Sri Lanka was ruled by a center-left coalition,
led first by S. W. R. D. Bandaranaike and later, after his assassination
in 1959, by Mrs. S. Bandaranaike. Unlike their predecessor governments, Bandaranaike governments believed in state intervention,
planning, and import substitution industrialization. Though trade
regime remained relatively liberal until the end of 1950s, starting with the 1957–1958 fiscal year protective duties had begun to
emerge. In addition, from 1957 on the balance of payments showed a
persistent deficit. For a while, previously accumulated reserves pro-

vided the necessary cushion but, with no improvement in prospects for exports, the situation began to look grim by early 1960s. The government responded by imposing import duties and exchange controls. The 1960 budget substantially raised duties on cars, petrol, liquor, and tobacco. In 1961, an across-the-board 5 percent duty surcharge was imposed, and imports of several consumer items including cars, watches, and radios were banned entirely. By the end of 1964, all "luxury" items were banned, imports of essential foodstuffs, fuels, fertilizers, and drugs became monopolies of public corporations, and all remaining goods were subject to import licensing. The Foreign Exchange Budget Committee at the Ministry of Finance assumed control of all foreign exchange allocation based on national priorities. From a free trade economy, Sri Lanka was transformed into a completely inward-looking economy.[36]

In 1965, UNP came back to power under Dudley Senanayake, the son of the elder Senanayake. This paved the way for a modest episode of trade liberalization. A Bonus Voucher Scheme for some nontraditional exports was introduced in December 1966 followed by a 20 percent devaluation of the rupee in November 1967. A Foreign Exchange Entitlement Certificate scheme was also launched in May 1968. Some 22 percent of imports, in value terms, were freed from quantitative restrictions under this scheme.

For reasons that are difficult to explain, despite a 5 percent rate of growth, Dudley Senanayake lost the election in 1970 and the SLFP-led United Front came back to power. Mrs. Bandaranaike quickly reversed the liberalization and brought all imports back into the fold of licensing. She then introduced legislation, which gave the government the right to nationalize any business enterprise. Using the power derived from this legislation, she went on to bring foreign trade substantially under direct control of the state. According to Lakshman and Athukorala (1985), by 1976 the state accounted for 88 percent of total import trade and 30 percent of export trade. The cumulative effect of trade restrictions and perhaps reduced opportunities for Sri Lanka's exports led to a decline in trade-to-GDP ratio to 35.9 percent in 1975.

The 1977 election saw a return of the right-center UNP with a sweeping victory. Led by J. R. Jayawardene, the party had fought the election on a platform of opening the economy and revitalizing the private sector. The government quickly launched a wide-ranging reform program that included trade liberalization, exchange rate realignment, new incentives for foreign investors, overhaul of financial markets, limits on public-sector participation in the economy, and the removal of price controls and government monopolies in domestic trade.

The key element in trade reform was the freeing of imports, except 280 items accounting for 8 percent of the total value of imports in 1980, from quantitative restrictions. For most of the 280 items remaining under licensing, licenses were issued freely. Though quantitative restrictions were replaced by higher tariffs, overall protection declined and the regime became more transparent. A six-band tariff structure was introduced with the highest rate being 100 percent. The rates escalated with the stage of production so that effective protection on finished products was quite high. Finally, the exchange rate was unified and subject to a managed float. The result was a 100 percent devaluation of the rupee. The cumulative effect of these changes was a substantial depreciation of the real exchange rate.

Despite these decisive reforms, the process lost steam almost immediately and no follow-up reforms took place. In 1980, a Presidential Tariff Commission (PTC) was set up with a mandate to establish a tariff structure, which will reduce the level of protection with minimal disruption of domestic industries.[37] Though the PTC produced several studies over the years—one each in 1980, 1983, and 1987—little action was actually taken.

How do we explain this inaction? To some degree, the political tension between minority Tamil people and the Sinhalese may have diverted the attention from the reforms. But this factor did not assume urgency until 1983. An alternative explanation is that the government may have decided to wait to assess the impact of the 1977 reform before embarking on a second round of liberalization. As it turned out, massive investment projects, inflow of aid, and poor management of the nominal exchange rate led to a significant appreciation of the real exchange rate. This appreciation, in turn, sabotaged the gains from liberalization from being realized rapidly and led to a loss of support for further trade liberalization. According to Athukorala and Rajapatirana (1991), who take the view that the benefits of liberalization failed to materialize, three public investment projects, including the billion-dollar Mahaweli Development Project, accounted for 75 percent of public investment between 1978 and 1982. Similarly, after 1981, the Central Bank began intervening heavily to support the rupee.[38]

There is some truth in this explanation, but it raises another puzzling question. If the support for reforms had waned, why was there no reversal of them? One hypothesis is that a reversal would have been equivalent to the admission that the government had made a mistake. Worse still, the public could have viewed this as a renunciation of the long-standing UNP stance in favor of liberal trade policies. Therefore, a reversal could have taken place only if the government had changed. But Jayawardene remained firmly in control of power until he retired in 1988. And even then, he handpicked Prem Dasa to succeed him.

An alternative hypothesis, which remains to be verified, is that the reform had replaced state monopolies on imports, created under Mrs. Bandaranaike, with private monopolies. This led to the creation of powerful vested interests that ensured that nontariff barriers were not reimposed. This hypothesis is logically correct but remains to be verified.

It was in 1991 under President Prem Dasa that liberalization went back into a high gear. By this time, ethnic conflict had calmed down. But it is not clear what additional factors gave impetus to the process. In any case, tariff bands were reduced to four at 10 percent, 20 percent, 35 percent, and 50 percent. Thus, the maximum tariff rate (with some exceptions) fell to 50 percent. In 1994, this rate was reduced further to 45 percent. In 1995, further compression of tariffs occurred with the number of bands reduced to three, 10 percent, 20 percent, and 35 percent.

To what extent has Sri Lanka's liberalization been influenced by the World Bank–IMF conditionality? Cuthbertson and Athukorala (1991), who have analyzed the 1968 and 1977 liberalizations in detail, conclude that the outside support did not affect the first episode much. They are less sure about the second episode, however, offering no conclusion. My own judgment is that the liberalization was primarily the result of internal initiative. UNP had a history of working closely with the World Bank.[39] As such, Jayawardene had been open to aid, which was going to come in response to liberalization, and perhaps used that fact to sell the policy change to public. On the other hand, during the post-1977 period when substantial aid did come, little liberalization took place. In 1979, the World Bank even sponsored a project to estimate effective rates of protection resulting from the 1977 reform with the ultimate aim of encouraging further reform of the tariff. Though the project was completed in 1981, little action took place throughout the 1980s, the decade when the Structural Adjustment Programs proliferated elsewhere in the world.

Singapore and Sri Lanka provide sharply contrasting examples of trade policy. How do we explain the differences? Clearly, the political system and leadership made the greatest difference. In Singapore, one-party rule permitted a far-sighted leadership to concentrate on the implementation of good economic polices. Sri Lanka has been a multiparty democracy that alternated between right-center and left-center governments, which led to a cycling between liberal and closed policies. Moreover, even when reform-minded governments came to power, they found themselves preoccupied by issues that were unrelated to economic policies. In addition to this key factor, Sri Lanka's predominantly agricultural structure also made it a better candidate for protectionist policies. It gave Sri Lanka a clear basis for export pessimism and reliance on import substitution for industrialization.

Notes

I thank Jagdish Bhagwati and T. N. Srinivasan for comments on an earlier draft.

1. Within the strict partial equilibrium framework, we should think here in terms of an export tax by the rest of the world. But by the Lerner Symmetry Theorem, a uniform export tax is equivalent to a uniform tariff on imports.

2. For a small country, the optimum tariff is zero. Therefore, as we saw above, a reduction in or elimination of *any* positive tariff is beneficial to it.

3. The rule is more complicated in practice because it is difficult to determine the precise tariff reductions that will leave the terms of trade unaffected.

4. Though infant-industry argument was often invoked, the key to the advocacy of import substitution was export pessimism. Thus, apart from rare exceptions such Keesing (1967), few authors advocated the case for promoting infant industries that will sell primarily in the world market.

5. With development economists preoccupied with Latin America and South Asia, principally India, East Asia had the least involvement of economists. Moreover, countries such as the Republic of Korea also chose to ignore the advice of the World Bank during this period.

6. Corden (1995) and Little et al. (1993) have emphasized this point in the context of trade liberalization.

7. In particular, see Pritchett (1996).

8. The list of countries is comprehensive though not exhaustive. Main omissions include Brunei, Cambodia, Laos, Maldives, Myanmar, Nepal, and Vietnam. Australia, Japan, and New Zealand are not a part of "developing" Asia.

9. These tables are updated versions of those in Panagariya (1993).

10. For example, on p. 30, PECC (1995) reports that Malaysia's average (unweighted) nominal tariff rate declined from 37.9 percent in 1978 to 27.3 percent in 1987, and to 14 percent in 1992. Even the direction of movement suggested by these figures is contradicted by figure 3.6a, which shows the tariff rate starting a little above 10 percent in 1980–1983, rising to 14 percent in 1984–1987, and declining to 13 percent in 1991–1993. The average nominal tariff for 1978 also differs markedly from the rate of 22 percent reported by Lee (1986). There are other similar discrepancies.

11. Dean (1995) and Dean, Desai, and Riedel (1994) have put together data on trade liberalization during 1985–1992 for as many as thirty-two developing countries in Asia, Africa, and Latin America. In most cases, UNCTAD (1994) provides more up-to-date information than was available to these authors.

12. Quite interestingly, by the 1960s, Prebisch himself had begun to note the deleterious effects of a high degree of protection. According to an excerpt provided by Keesing (1967), in UNCTD (1964), Prebisch wrote, "(R)ecourse to very high protective tariffs ... has had unfavorable effects on the industrial structure because it has encouraged the establishment of small uneconomical plants, weakened the incentives to introduce modern techniques, and slowed down the rise in productivity ..." This stood in sharp contrast to United Nations (1950), which was also authored by Prebisch.

13. See Corden (1995) for details.

14. See Bhagwati and Patrick (1990).

15. According to Aw (1991), this share fell to 53.4 percent in 1968–1973 and to 39.4 percent in 1974–1982. But by 1973, Singapore's trade policies had taken the final form.

16. I hasten to note that like other factors described here, this one too is a facilitating factor and does not provide a compelling explanation of free trade policies adopted by Singapore and Hong Kong. Balassa (1982) rightly criticized scholars who argued that the two countries adopted free trade policies *because* they did not have domestic markets large enough to serve as the initial base for industrialization. Balassa reasoned, "With a population of 2 million in 1950 and relatively high per capita income derived from trading activities, ... Hong Kong had a larger domestic market for manufactured goods than the majority of the developing countries, many of which nevertheless embarked on industrialization behind high protective barriers. Tunisia, for example, with a home market smaller than that of Hong Kong, attempted to provide for domestic needs in small local plants that were to receive continued protection."

17. These percentages have been calculated from data available in Saw (1986, table 6.16). It must be admitted that during the late 1950s and 1960s, the share of manufactures in the labor force was low and the country did go through a brief import substitution phase. This is discussed in detail below.

18. See Aw (1991, 327–331) for details on monetary and fiscal policy.

19. Keng Swee Goh, who served as finance minister during 1959–1965 and 1967–1970 and as defense minister during 1965–1967 and 1970 until his retirement in the late 1980s, played a key role in shaping Singapore's economic policies.

20. Because starting in 1967, the government had begun to introduce several export-oriented domestic policy measures, Tan and Ow limit the period of import substitution to 1965–1967. Based on the continued rise in the number of protected items,

I have chosen the longer period of 1965–1969 as being characterized by import substitution.

21. This argument is reinforced by the fact that products subject to both tariffs and quotas, though twenty-five in number, accounted for a mere .4 percent of manufacturing output.

22. This section draws liberally on the excellent documentation and analysis in chapters 1, 2, and 5 of Baldwin, Chen, and Nelson (1995).

23. This case study draws heavily on Panagariya (1994, 1999).

24. The year 1956–1957 refers to India's financial year, which begins on April 1 and ends on March 31.

25. Discussing the allocation of Actual User licenses during the 1960s, Bhagwati and Desai write:

The problem was Orwellian: all industries had priority and how was each sponsoring authority to argue that some industries had more priority than others? . . . It is not surprising, therefore, that the agencies involved in determining industry-wise allocations fell back on vague notions of "fairness," implying *pro rata* allocations with reference to capacity installed or employment, or shares defined by past import allocations and similar other rules of thumb without any clear rationale.

26. Items on the OGL list could be imported without having to obtain a license. The OGL had been used as an instrument of liberalization soon after World War II. It was reintroduced in 1976 to free up the imports of seventy-nine items in the capital goods category.

27. Canalized imports are an exclusive monopoly of a governmental agency.

28. This figure does not include the impact of the recent 8 percent across-the-board hike in tariff rates by the BJP-led coalition.

29. Approximately eight hundred of these items are on Special Import License (SIL) list. The SIL, which are issued to big export houses and are tradable give the holder the right to import the items on the SIL list. Imports of these items are otherwise not permitted.

30. Tariff hikes by both Chidambaram and Sinha were introduced ostensibly for revenue reasons. Their impact is, nevertheless, to increase protection. They clearly reflect a lack of resolve on the part of the government to less distortionary, domestic taxes or to reduce spending.

31. The only export licenses in existence are those resulting from the Multfibre Arrangement (MFA). In addition, Hong Kong employs an import quota on rice on grounds of national security.

32. Like Indonesia, Thailand is proceeding to meet its AFTA liberalization through nondiscriminatory liberalization so far.

33. I am reminded of a conversation, during my tenure (1989–1993) at the World Bank, with a Bangladesh country economist who lamented how he had been finding it difficult to persuade Bangladesh authorities to publish a book of custom duties, which did not exist at the time. When asked why the World Bank did not have sufficient clout to accomplish this despite large amounts of aid, he candidly replied that the authorities understood the bank had its own loan targets to meet.

34. For the period up to 1983, the case study below draws heavily on the excellent study of Cuthberston and Athukorala (1991). For recent reforms, I rely on the ADB study by Rajapakse et al. (1996).

35. For a short period, the government had to adopt import and foreign exchange controls at the request of the British government, which was worried about pressures that rapid decline in Sri Lankan sterling reserves might generate. But in 1950 and 1951, in view of improved balance of payments, these restrictions were largely removed.

36. Simultaneously, public-sector participation in industrial activity expanded, especially in heavy industry, the oil industry was nationalized, and the banking sector was brought under strict control of the government. Nationalization of foreign-owned rubber and tea plantations was seriously considered but eventually abandoned.

37. In February 1978, a new constitution, modeled on that of the Fifth French Republic, was adopted and Mr. Jayawardene was installed in the strong executive presidency.

38. There are some limits to this story, however. The export-to-GDP ratio did rise from 19.1 percent in 1977 to 28.3 percent in 1980. The import-to-GDP ratio rose from 18.1 percent to 54.5 percent over the same period. The latter ratio rose primarily because of the aid-funded imports for the public projects just mentioned.

39. For example, in designing the 1954–1959 Six Year Investment Plan, the elder Senanayake government had relied on World Bank advice for some key provisions.

References

Altinger, L., and A. Enders. 1995. "The Scope and Depth of GATS Commitments." Mimeo.

Ariff, Mohamed. 1975. "Protection for Manufactures in Peninsular Malaysia." *Hitotsubashi Journal of Economics* 15, no. 2.

Ariff, Mohamed. 1991. *The Malaysian Economy: Pacific Connections.* Singapore: Oxford University Press.

Athukorala, P., and S. Rajapatirana. 1991. "The Domestic Financial Market and Trade Liberalization Outcome. The Evidence from Sri Lanka." PRE Working Paper 590, February.

Austria, M., and E. Medalla. 1996. "A Study of Trade and Investment Policies of Developing Countries: The Case of the Philippines." Discussion paper series no. 96–103, Philippine Institute of Development Studies.

Aw, Bee-Yan. 1991. "Singapore." In Papageorgiou, Demetris, Armeane Choksi and Michael Michaely, *Liberalizing Foreign Trade. Lessons of Experience in the Developing World*, vol. 2, ed. Demetris Papageorgiou, Armeane Choksi, and Michael Michaely, 309–428. Cambridge, Mass.: Basil Blackwell.

Balassa, Bela. 1971. *The Structure of Protection in Developing Countries.* Baltimore: Johns Hopkins University Press.

Balassa, Bela. 1982. "Development Strategies and Economic Performance: A Comparative Analysis of Eleven Semi-industrialized Economies." In *Development Strategies in*

Semi-industrialized Economies, ed. Bela Balassa, 38–62. Baltimore: Johns Hopkins University Press for the World Bank.

Baldwin, R., T. J. Chen, and D. Nelson. 1995. Chapters 1, 2, and 5 in *Political Economy of U.S.-Taiwan Trade.* Ann Arbor: University of Michigan Press.

Bhagwati, Jagdish. 1978. *Anatomy and Consequences of Exchange Control Regimes.* Lexington, Mass.: Ballinger Press.

Bhagwati, Jagdish. 1982. "Directly Unproductive Profit-seeking (DUP) Activities." *JPE* 90, no. 5 (October): 988–1002.

Bhagwati, Jagdish. 1988. *Protectionism.* Cambridge, Mass.: MIT Press.

Bhagwati, Jagdish. 1997. "The Choice between Reciprocity and Unilateral Freeing of Trade." Columbia University, mimeo.

Bhagwati, Jagdish, and Padma Desai. 1970. *India: Planning for Industrialization and Trade Policies since 1951.* London: Oxford University Press.

Bhagwati, Jagdish, and B. Hansen. 1973. "A Theoretical Analysis of Smuggling." *QJE* 87: 172–187.

Bhagwati, J., and H. Patrick, eds. 1990. *Aggressive Unilateralism: America's 301 Trade Policy and the World Trading System.* Ann Arbor: University of Michigan Press.

Bhagwati, Jagdish, and T. N. Srinivasan. 1975. *Foreign Trade Regimes and Economic Development: India,* New York. New York: Columbia University for the National Bureau of Economic Research.

Bhagwati, Jagdish, and T. N. Srinivasan. 1980. "Revenue Seeking: A Generalization of theory of Tariffs." *Journal of Political Economy* 88: 1069–1087.

Bhagwati, Jagdish, and T. N. Srinivasan. 1993. *India's Economic Reforms.* New Delhi: Government of India, Ministry of Finance.

Bhagwati, Jagdish, and T. N. Srinivasan. 1999. "Outward Orientation and Development: Are the Revisionists Right?" Columbia University, mimeo.

Corden, Max. 1971. *The Theory of Protection.* Oxford: Clarendon Press.

Corden, Max. 1995. "Protection and Liberalization in Australia and Abroad." Forty-Fourth Joseph Fisher Lecture in Commerce, University of Adelaide, September 26, mimeo.

Cuthbertson, A. G., and P. Athukorala. 1991. "Sri Lanka." In *Liberalizing Foreign Trade. Lessons of Experience in the Developing World,* vol. 5, ed. Demetris Papageorgiou, Armeane Choksi and Michael Michaely, 283–416. Cambridge, Mass.: Basil Blackwell.

Dean, Judith M. 1995. "The Trade Policy Revolution in Developing Countries." *World Economy* 18, no. 4: 173–189.

Dean, Judith M., Seema Desai, and James Riedel. 1994. "Trade Policy Reform in Developing Countries since 1985: A Review of the Evidence." World Bank Discussion paper no. 267.

Fung, K. C., Kar-yiu Wong, and Richard Y. C. Wong. 1997. "Unilateral Liberalization and Hong Kong: Political Economy, History and Theory," mimeo.

General Agreement on Tariffs and Trade. 1991a. *Trade Policy Review: Indonesia*, vol. 1. Geneva: GATT.

General Agreement on Tariffs and Trade. 1991b. *Trade Policy Review: Thailand*, vol. 1. Geneva: GATT.

General Agreement on Tariffs and Trade. 1992a. *Trade Policy Review: Bangladesh*, vol. 1. Geneva: GATT.

General Agreement on Tariffs and Trade. 1992b. *Trade Policy Review: Singapore*, vol. 1. Geneva: GATT.

General Agreement on Tariffs and Trade. 1993a. *Trade Policy Review: Malaysia*, vol. 1. Geneva: GATT.

General Agreement on Tariffs and Trade. 1993b. *Trade Policy Review: The Philippines*, vol. 1. Geneva: GATT.

Guisinger, S., and G. Scully. 1991. "Pakistan," in *Liberalizing Foreign Trade. Lessons of Experience in the Developing World*, vol. 5, ed. Demetris Papageorgiou, Armeane Choksi and Michael Michaely, 197–282. Cambridge, Mass.: Basil Blackwell.

Intal, P., M. Lamberte, C. David, M. Austria, C. Cororaton, E. Medalla, and V. Pineda. 1996. "The Emerging Global Trading Environment and Developing Asia: The Case of the Philippines." Asian Development Bank, revised report.

Keesing, Donald B. 1967. "Outward-Looking Policies and Economic Development." *Economic Journal* 77, no. 306 (June): 303–320.

Khan, Ashfaque H. 1996. "The Emerging Global Trading Environment and Developing Asia: Pakistan." Asian Development Bank, August.

Krueger, Anne O. 1974. "The Political Economy of Rent-Seeking Society." *AER* 64, no. 3 (June): 291–323.

Krueger, Anne O. 1978. *Foreign Trade Regimes and Economic Development: Liberalization Attempts and Consequences*. Lexington, Mass.: Ballinger Press.

Lakshman, W. D., and P. Athukorala. 1985. "Analysis of Trading Channels for Sri Lanka." In *Transnational Trading Corporations in Selected Asian and Pacific Countries*, ESCAP/UNCTC Joint Unit on Transnational Corporations. Bangkok: United Nations.

Lee, K. H. 1986. "Malaysia: The Structure and Causes of Manufacturing Sector Protection." In *The Political Economy of Manufacturing Protection: Experiences of ASEAN and Australia*, ed. C. Findlay and Ross Garnaut. Sydney: Allen and Unwin.

Little, I. M. D. 1982. *Economic Development: Theory, Policy and International relations*. New York: Basic Books, Inc.

Little, Ian, R. N. Cooper, W. M. Corden, and S. Rajapatirana. 1993. *Boom, Crisis and Adjustment: The Macroeconomic Experience of Developing Countries*. New York: Oxford University Press for the World Bank.

Little, Ian, Tibor Scitovsky, and Maurice Scott. 1970. *Industry and Trade in Some Developing Countries*. London: Oxford University Press.

Lloyd, P. J., and R. J. Sandilands. 1986. "The Trade Sector in a Very Open Re-export Economy." In *Singapore: Resources and Growth*, ed. Chong-Yah Lim and P. J. Lloyd, 183–219. Singapore: Oxford University Press.

Martin, Lawrence, and Arvind Panagariya. 1984. "Smuggling, Trade and Price Disparity." *JIE* 17: 201–217.

Nurkse, Ragnar. 1959. *Problems of Trade and Development.* Stockholm: Almquist and Wicksell.

Ow, Chin-Hock. 1986. "The Role of Government in Economic Development: The Singapore Experience." In *Singapore: Resources and Growth,* ed. Chong-Yah Lim and P. J. Lloyd, 221–267. Singapore: Oxford University Press.

Pacific Economic Cooperation Council (PECC). 1995. *Milestones in APEC Liberalization: A Map of Market Opening Measures by APEC Economies.* Singapore: APEC.

Panagariya, Arvind. 1993. "Unravelling the Mysteries of China's Foreign Trade Regime." *World Economy* 16, no. 1: 51–68.

Panagariya, Arvind. 1994. "India: A New Tiger on the Block?" *Journal of International Affairs* (Summer): 193–221.

Panagariya, Arvind. 1996. "The Free Trade Area of the Americas: Good for Latin America?" *World Economy* 19, no. 5 (September): 485–515.

Panagariya, Arvind. 1999. "Trade Policies in South Asia: Recent Liberalization and Future Agenda." *World Economy* 22: 353–378.

Panagariya, Arvind. 2000. "Preferential Trade Liberalization: The Traditional Theory and New Developments." *Journal of Economic Literature* 38: 287–331.

Papageorgiou, Demetris, Armeane Choksi, and Michael Michaely. *Liberalizing Foreign Trade. Lessons of Experience in the Developing World.* Cambridge, Mass.: Basil Blackwell.

Pitt, Mark. 1981. "Smuggling and Price Disparity." *JIE* 11: 447–458.

Power, J. H. 1971. "The Structure of Protection in West Malaysia." In *The Structure of Protection in Developing Countries,* ed. Bela Balassa, 203–222. Baltimore: Johns Hopkins University Press.

Pritchett, Lant. 1996. "Measuring Outward Orientation in LDCs: Can It Be Done?" *Journal of Development Economics* 49 (May): 307–335.

Pursell, Garry. 1992. "Trade Policies in India." In *National Trade Policies: Handbook of Comparative Economic Policies,* vol. 2, ed. Dominick Salvatore, 423–458. New York: Greenwood Press.

Pursell, Garry. 1996. "Indian Trade Policies since the 1991/92 Reform." World Bank, mimeo.

Rajapakse, R., S. Jayanetti, P. Steele, and N. Arunatilake. 1996. "The Emerging Global Trading Environment and Developing Asia: Economic Implications for Sri Lanka." Asian Development Bank, August 15.

Reza, S., M. Ali Rashid, and M. Rahman. 1996. "The Emerging Global Trading Environment and Developing Asia: Bangladesh." Asian Development Bank, May.

Rodrik, Dani. 1994. "The Rush to Free Trade in the Developing World: Why So Late? Why Now? Will It Last?" In *Voting for Reform: Democracy, Political Liberalization and Economic Adjustment,* ed. S. Haggard and S. B. Webb, 61–88. New York: Oxford University Press.

Saw, Swee-Hock. 1986. "Population and Manpower in Singapore." In *Singapore: Resources and Growth*, ed. Chong-Yah Lim and P. J. Lloyd, 142–182. Singapore: Oxford University Press.

Singapore Department of Trade. 1968. *Annual Report*. Singapore: Ministry of Finance.

Srinivasan, T. N. 1996. "Economic Liberalization and Economic Development: India." *Journal of Asian Economics* 7, no. 2: 203–216.

Tan, Augustine H. H., and Chin Hock Ow. 1982. "Singapore." In *Development Strategies in Semi-industrialized Economies*, ed. Bela Balassa, 280–309. Baltimore: Johns Hopkins University Press for the World Bank.

Tan, E. 1994. "Trade Policy Reform in the 1990s: Effects of E.O. 470 and the Import Liberalization Program." Research Paper Series No. 94–111. Manila: Philippine Institute of Development Studies.

Tax Reforms Committee. 1993. *Final Report, Part II*. New Delhi: Government of India.

Thomas, Vinod, John Nash, et al. 1991. *Best Practices in Trade Policy Reform*. Oxford: Oxford University Press for the World Bank.

Tsiang, S. C., and Wen-lang Chen. 1984. "Development Toward Trade Liberalization in Taiwan, Republic of China." In *1984 Joint Conference on the Industrial Policies of the Republic of China and the Republic of Korea*, 185–200. Taipei: Chung-Hua Institution for Economic Research.

Tu, Chaw-hsia, and Wen-thuen Wang. 1988. "Chin kuo tzu yu hua tui kung yeh fa chan chih chung chi" ("The Impact of Trade Liberalization on Industrial Development"). Taipei: Chubg-Hua Institution for Economic Research.

United Nations. 1950. *The Economic Problems of Latin America and Its Principal Problems*. New York: United Nations.

United Nations Conference on Trade and Development (UNCTAD). 1964. *Towards a New Trade Policy for Development*. Report by the Secretary-General, Geneva.

United Nations Conference on Trade and Development (UNCTAD). 1994. *Directory of Import Regimes. Part I*. New York: United Nations.

Westphal, Larry E. 1990. "Industrial Policy in an Export-Propelled Economy: Lessons from South Korea's Experience." *Journal of Economic Perspectives* (Summer): 41–59.

Westphal, Larry E., and Kwang Suk Kim. 1982. "Korea." In *Development Strategies in Semi-Industrialized Economies*, ed. Bela Balassa, 212–279. Baltimore: Johns Hopkins University Press.

World Bank. 1996. "Trade Policy Reform in Bangladesh." Private Sector Development and Finance Division, South Asia Country Department 1, April 14.

World Bank. 1987. *World Development Report*. New York: Oxford University Press.

9 Central Europe during the 1990s: From Unilateralism to Bilateralism

Patrick A. Messerlin

Within half a decade (1989–1994), the Central European Countries (CECs) have shifted from high protection and artificial openness under Soviet rule to a bold, unilateral, and nondiscriminatory trade liberalization under market rule, and then, for most of them, to bilateral trade agreements with the European Community (EC) and among themselves, combined with increased protection vis-à-vis the rest of the world.[1] Why so many changes at such a speed?

Undoubtedly, political tensions played a role unsurpassed in the rest of the world: "[Policy changes] took everybody by surprise, as the internal events moved considerably faster than anybody—abroad or at home—was able to comprehend or predict. Even domestic policy makers were often only responding to actual events" (Drabek 1997). Under the Soviet rule, each Central European economy was made as much dependent as possible from the Soviet Union and the other CECs: It was made "excessively" open, with a high ratio of trade to GDP achieved through almost systematic trade diversion, and with planned trade flows having little consideration for comparative advantages.[2] The political tensions imposed by Soviet rule have been so huge that the 1990s have been echoing them: independence from Russia, defense behind the West shield, and political links with Western Europe have been crucial factors in the Central European governments' minds when trade choices were made.

This political context has induced almost all the European policymakers to deny any noticeable role to a trade policy based on the most-favored-nation (MFN) principle. Because it bans discriminatory treatment among trading partners, the MFN provision was (still is) seen as incompatible with political factors that, by essence, give more weight to certain countries than to others. Preeminent political factors were (still are) seen as "naturally" implying discriminatory trade agreements with the politically key countries. The argument is so strong that few Europeans remember that their own history runs against it: During the fifty-four years between the 1860 Franco-British free trade treaty and World War I, the MFN rule was followed by the three world archrivals—Britain, France, and Germany—amid fierce political rivalries and despite wars (Tumlir 1984). And the argument is so strong that many European economists reverse the causality: They take as granted the existence of political benefits necessary for justifying the existence of discriminatory trade agreements that are shown to be costly from an economic point of view.

The chapter takes an opposite view, based on the increasing recognition of the net economic costs generated by discriminatory trade agreements (Bhagwati and Panagariya 1996). It shows that the CECs have obtained large economic and political benefits when, in the early 1990s, they have been following an MFN unilateral liberalization approach. It argues that, in the mid-1990s, when the CECs turned to reciprocal trade, an MFN approach would have provided yet *larger* economic and political benefits than the discriminatory agreements signed with the EC. It shows that the CECs will increasingly suffer economic and political costs from these bilateral discriminatory trade agreements. Last, it argues that the CECs would achieve their economic and political goal of accession to the EC at better terms if they would come back to an MFN-based approach.

The chapter is organized as follows. Section 9.1 examines the MFN unilateral trade liberalization followed by the CECs when they left the Soviet COMECON. Section 9.2 looks at the CECs' subsequent swing to the EC "hub and spoke" trade system—that is, a net of bilateral discriminatory trade agreements between the EC and the CECs, and to Central European increased protection with respect to the rest of the world. Section 9.3 examines the metastases of the "hub-and-spoke" trade regime in a series of free trade agreements among the CECs themselves. The conclusion suggests the economic and political benefits of a return to an MFN approach for the CECs and the whole Europe.

This presentation deserves a last remark. The chapter never uses the terms *regional trade agreement* or *regionalism* for two factual reasons. First, there are no regional trade agreements involving Central Europe: the agreements between the EC and the CECs as well as those between the CECs themselves are purely *bilateral*, and the negotiations on the CEC accessions to the EC are also bilateral. Second, the term "regionalism" does not fit well the increasing number of discriminatory trade agreements: Out of the 55 agreements notified to the GATT and its heir, the World Trade Organization (WTO), and enforced in 1995, 41 involve the EC, the EFTA countries, or the CECs—so that the "worldwide rise of regionalism" mirrors a European addiction to bilateralism.

9.1   The MFN Inilateral Trade Liberalizations of Central Europe: Economically and Politically Beneficial

This section describes the bold MFN unilateral trade liberalizations that the CECs undertook almost immediately after the fall of the Berlin Wall.[3] It argues that this policy has been very beneficial for the CECs from both an economic and political perspective. The political aspect is essential: Between 1989 and 1991, the CEC unilateral liberalization has literally "forced" an initially very reluctant EC to liberalize its own trade policy with respect to the CECs. In other words—and contrary to what is often argued—the Central European unilateral trade policies have had the capacity to improve the CECs' leverage (and terms of trade) with respect to the EC at least as well as a "reciprocity" approach would have been able to do.

Bold Unilateral and MFN-Based Trade Liberalizations

There have been three successive waves of CECs' unilateral trade liberalization. The first includes Czechoslovakia, Hungary, and Poland, immediately after the 1989 fall of the Berlin Wall. One year later, the second wave consists of Bulgaria, Romania, and one successor state of Yugoslavia (Slovenia). Two years later, the third wave includes the Baltic countries (Estonia, Latvia, and Lithuania) after they regained their political independence.

Among the first wave, Czechoslovakia offers the purest case of full-fledged MFN unilateral trade liberalization. During the second half of 1990, she unilaterally abolished all her foreign trade monopolies and nontariff barriers on exports and imports, greatly reduced foreign exchange restrictions, provided for a range of guarantees to foreign investors, abandoned payments on transactions with the other CECs and the Soviet Union, and adopted an exchange-rate policy based on a single and more accurate (though undervalued) exchange rate. By the same token, Czechoslovakia immediately became a very open economy: The country's unweighted average tariff was 5 percent (few tariffs being higher than 10%), almost all bound under GATT rules (for comparison, see below the substantially higher figures for the EC).[4]

Poland followed the same policy as Czechoslovakia, with two major differences. First, Poland had to reduce dramatically the new tariff schedule adopted only a few months before: The average tariff declined from 18.3 percent in January 1989 to 5.5 percent in July 1991. Second, Poland did not bind its tariffs at their new (low) level under GATT rules. These two features opened an era of uncertainty caused by the possibility of easy and rapid tariff reversals. By contrast, Hungary took a more cautious approach than Czechoslovakia or Poland. The country introduced tariff reductions that lowered the average tariff from 15 percent (1989) to 13 percent (1991). However, most of these reductions were conditional concessions dating from the Tokyo Round, and they were not bound under GATT. Moreover, Hungary kept its "global quota" and licensing system, though the country reduced its coverage to 10 percent of its imports.

The unilateral liberalization of the second wave (Bulgaria, Romania, and Slovenia) followed the Hungarian approach, with additional hesitations that partly mirrored the then ongoing shift of the first Central European wave toward discriminatory trade agreements with the EC. They did not dismantle all the quantitative restrictions on exports as well as on imports, and when they did, they often substituted for them price-based measures (tariffs and other domestic taxes). Their preferred liberalization instrument was exemptions from existing tariffs and other border duties under a wide range of often complicated schemes, such as temporary (often annual) tariff reductions, tariff-free imports in case of joint ventures with foreign firms, and so forth.[5] Last, these more limited efforts have been eroded by domestic political turmoil (Bulgaria), the upholding of the communists in power (Romania), or war risks (Slovenia). Despite all these imperfections, trade barriers have been significantly reduced. The Bulgarian average tariff declined from 13 percent (1989) to 11 percent (1991), Romania reduced its average tariff from 17.8 (1990) to 12.3 percent (1992), and Slovenia adopted a new tariff law only in 1995, which lowered its unweighted average tariff to 14.6 percent.

With the third wave of trade liberalization of the Baltic states, bold MFN unilateral liberalizations are back. In 1992, Estonia adopted a flat zero tariff schedule, except for two dozen products. After some hesitations, Estonia eliminated almost all its export controls—making itself an economy as open as Hong Kong. The two other Baltic countries needed more time to follow this approach. If both countries eliminated rapidly quantitative restrictions on imports and many exports, it took two years (1993–1995) for Lithuania to adopt a very open tariff structure, with an unweighted average MFN tariff of 4.5 percent (11.7 percent for food products and 2.6 percent for the other goods). Similarly, Latvia shifted slowly from an initial regime of opaque specific tariffs toward moderate ad valorem tariffs, based on a basic tariff of 15 percent with many exceptions (at 0 or 1% tariff rates) and few (but high) peaks (particularly in agriculture).

It is fair to say that all these trade liberalizations have been counterbalanced by several factors. First, some CECs (notably Lithuania, Poland, or Romania) have frequently changed their unbound tariffs. Other CECs have introduced domestic measures as protectionist as tariffs: for instance, Czechoslovakia imposed import surcharges (up to 18 percent) on 25 percent of the tariff items (12 percent of import values) in December 1990, whereas Romania maintained substantial price controls or massive subsidies in a few key sectors.[6] Second, exchange-rate policies have helped protect Central European producers from foreign competition in the CECs experiencing a sharp depreciation. Last, noticeable "private" border barriers have been substituted for official tariffs because the increasingly difficult situation of many CEC public budgets tended to increase the level of corruption at the customs level. For instance, in Romania, the average tariff estimated on the basis of the tariff revenues divided by imports was 6.7 percent: a large portion of the difference with the above-mentioned 12.4 percent average tariff was generally attributed to customs corruption.

However, the real impact of these negative factors is debatable because of low enforcement capability and smuggling. During this first period, large-scale smuggling was an option easily available because of the collapse of the CEC border polices and of their geographical proximity with open countries (Bratislava is 40 kilometers from Vienna, the Polish border and Prague are a 2-hour drive from Hamburg and Munich, respectively, etc).[7]

Fragile Forces behind Bold Policies

Similar dramatic changes in trade policies occurred in other countries—for instance, in Chile or in Mexico (chap. 10; chap. 11). However, important differences exist between the Latin American and Central European experiences—all of them suggesting that the forces behind trade liberalization were more fragile in Central Europe than in Latin America.

First, there were no significant groups of domestic policymakers with a strong economic background in the CECs—in sharp contrast to what could be observed in Chile or in Mexico where the central banks, the high administrations at the finance ministries, and a few universities or think-tanks played a key role. Moreover, the supportive role of Central European individuals who, after having fled under Soviet rule, returned to their country after the fall of the Berlin Wall has been modest, all the more because it was often blurred by the exiles' financial interests in repossessing their property and ownership of the precommunist era.

Second, the Central European policymakers did not benefit from the same intellectual support in Western Europe that Latin American countries got from the United States. Most EC policymakers did not have a higher economic knowledge in trade issues than their Central European counterparts. The wide consensus among U.S. economists about the gains from nondiscriminatory free trade and market economies had no equivalent in Western Europe (ironically, the fall of the Berlin Wall and the superiority of markets over central planning came as a surprise to many Western Europeans). After the fall of the Berlin Wall, many Western European economists have devoted their efforts to the means that could have kept the COMECON in place. Two factors reinforced this tendency. The West-European economists who were initially the most visible in Central Europe were generally Marxist: They needed some time to be converted to market economics, and they never really forgot their fondness for discrimination. The experts the EC has sent to the CECs were often chosen on the basis of implicit quotas by EC member states—limiting the availability of free trade and market-oriented European economists (who happened to be concentrated in a few member states).

Third, during these few years, the role of the Bretton Woods institutions has also been more limited in Central Europe than in Latin

America or Asia. The World Bank and the International Monetary Fund (IMF) often had a limited knowledge of the Central European economies for several reasons: The knowledge that these institutions have accumulated during the central planning period proved to be of limited help; or the CECs in question were not members (or very recent members) of the Bretton Woods institutions when they liberalized their trade, so that these institutions would have very limited valuable information on these economies. As a result, if the World Bank and the IMF were supportive of the unilateral and MFN-based trade liberalization undertaken by the CECs, the World Bank and IMF were not at its forefront—and they were even rapidly afraid when they felt that the moves were too bold (Hansson 1994). Turning to GATT, the international forum for the world trade regime, one observes that it is an institution more concerned with reciprocity and liberal trade (and disciplines such as nondiscrimination) than with free trade per se. As a result, it has intrinsic difficulties to be a good supporter of unilateral liberalization. Moreover, the few CECs that were GATT members were subject to ad hoc protocols of accession that were obsolete because they had been drafted in terms adapted to centrally planned economies, such as quantitative targets based on import penetration indicators.[8]

As a result, the main motive for the dramatic changes in trade policies was mostly a "freedom ideology" relatively unaware of hard market realities. Except for a few policymakers, Central Europeans were more driven by an instinctive reaction against the many constraints imposed by autarkic central planning and dictatorship during the previous decades than by a deep understanding of the gains from economic freedom and the limits to be imposed on state discretionary actions.

As a result, the choice of MFN unilateral trade liberalization by the CECs was very fragile. It could even be argued that this choice was made essentially because it benefited from an almost complete absence of active protectionist forces. In market economies, an economic restructuring of the scale experienced by the CECs would have triggered huge pressures from vested interests. In sharp contrast, the existing domestic lobbies in the CECs have been inert during the first years of transition (except for collective agriculture and very few manufacturing sectors in certain CECs, such as Czech steel or Polish cars and shipyards). This inertia can be explained by the sudden realization by Central Europeans of the magnitude of the economic disaster caused by central planning, leading to a massive discredit of the established domestic vested interests: State firms could not argue that high trade barriers could be beneficial for their survival; there were almost no private owners (except farmers) to ask for protection; skilled labor (managers or engineers) was lining up in order to take over the privatization process, and independent trade unions were nonexistent—except in Poland.

The Economic and Political Benefits from the CEC Unilateral Policies

In the couple of years following these bold changes in CEC trade policies, the trade pattern of all the CECs changed dramatically. Table 9.1 presents the evolution of CEC import shares (in percentage of total imports) between 1989 and 1995. It can be summarized in three points: the collapse of the intra-CEC trade, the boom in the EC-CEC trade, and the decline of the trade between the CECs and the non-EC, non-CEC countries. The first two changes reflect the economic benefits to be expected from MFN trade liberalization (including the removal of export barriers and domestic price controls)—a return to trade flows based on comparative advantages, as shown by Kaminski, Wang, and Winters (1996) and by Hoekman and Djankov (1997). The decline of the CEC trade with the non-EC countries seems inconsistent with MFN-based policies: But it could be explained by the information and transaction costs associated with the suddenness of the changes in Central Europe and the short life of the CEC MFN unilateral trade liberalizations, as shown below.

Beyond these expected economic gains, the CEC unilateral policies have provided a crucial political benefit—unanticipated at that time and still often ignored today: They have been essential to "forcing" the EC to liberalize deeper and quicker that the EC wanted initially. Until late 1990, the EC was following its traditional approach with centrally planned economies: negotiating "cooperation agreements" allowing for a slow and partial elimination of nontariff barriers over a period of four years. The bold unilateral MFN trade liberalizations of the first wave of CECs forced the EC to abandon its traditional policy. The EC did so gradually and on an annual basis—leaving the door potentially open to rapid reversal. Concerning tariffs, the EC included Hungary and Poland (already under MFN treatment) in its Generalized System of Preferences for a period of five years. In 1991, it added Czechoslovakia. Concerning nontariff barriers (NTBs), the EC eliminated all its quantitative restrictions on Hungarian and Polish exports for one year—except for a long list of "sensitive" products. In 1991, this measure was renewed for another year for these countries, and it was extended to Czechoslovakia, Bulgaria, and Romania. All these concessions excluded the "sensitive" sectors—agriculture, steel, and apparel for all the CECs—and also many other items specific to each CEC (such as glass for the Czech Republic).

The CECs greatly benefited from the EC successive shifts, as shown by the time concomitance between the EC reactions and the large increase of Central European exports to the EC. The Hungarian case is of particular interest because there is a one-year lag between the Cooperation Agreement and the EC tariff and NTB dismantlement (whereas they occurred almost simultaneously for Czechoslovakia and Poland): Hungarian exports have been inert during the first year following the Cooperation Agreement, whereas they increased dramatically within three months after the EC reactions to the CEC trade liberalization.

Why did not the EC take the initiative? First, if the fall of the Berlin Wall did trigger among Western Europeans a political movement in favor of Central Europeans, it was also the symbol of the superiority of markets—a result that many Western Europeans immersed in state-dominated economies were not prepared to hear. Second, a wealthy EC economy implied that, in sharp contrast with the CECs, European vested interests were well alive. As mirrored later by the negotiations between the EC and the CECs, there were a few, but powerful, industries concerned with competition from the CECs in "sensitive" sectors. For counterbalancing these vested interests, neither the European Commission nor the member states have been able to mobilize a coalition of exporters—maybe because prospects for growth in Central Europe were too far away and too small in the short run (in the early 1990s, the total GDP of the ten CECs was smaller than the Dutch GDP *alone*). Last, when negotiating the agreements with the CECs, more often was the European Commission on the liberal side than were member states captured by their industrialists. But the commission has not had a vision comparable to what the U.S. Secretaries Cordell Hull and General Marshall have had after World War II. Anecdotal, but convergent, information suggests that, when negotiating the discriminatory trade agreements with the CECs, EC officials did insist on the fact that the CECs

Table 9.1
The CEC trade flows under discriminatory trade agreements, 1989–1995

	1989	1990	1991	1992	1993	1994	1995	1996
A: CEC imports from the EC (% of total imports)								
CSRs	30.2	39.7	42.4	51.0	56.3	60.7	—	—
Czech Rep.	—	—	—	—	51.3	59.1	53.9	60.6
Slovakia	—	—	—	—	30.8	41.0	44.4	37.0
Hungary	39.7	42.3	56.7	60.0	54.4	61.1	63.1	60.9
Poland	37.4	42.9	59.1	62.0	64.7	65.3	64.7	63.9
Bulgaria	25.8	27.0	26.4	35.5	33.5	38.9	54.1	38.9
Romania	9.4	19.7	30.9	41.8	44.7	48.2	48.8	52.2
Estonia	—	—	—	28.3	23.3	22.6	63.7	65.0
Latvia	—	—	—	24.3	18.9	27.5	52.0	46.5
Lithuania	—	—	—	49.7	48.0	26.4	46.0	42.6
B: CEC export/import ratios: trade with the EC								
CSRs	100.3	89.1	110.9	104.8	94.5	94.9	—	
Czech Rep.	—	—	—	—	96.1	81.6	73.6	
Slovakia	—	—	—	—	72.8	84.7	81.1	
Hungary	92.8	108.5	92.3	99.8	75.4	76.6	84.9	
Poland	107.6	150.4	104.5	86.6	81.0	84.8	85.4	
Bulgaria	51.5	49.5	84.1	77.8	65.8	88.0	69.7	
Romania	527.6	132.2	92.0	62.2	67.7	86.4	94.2	
Estonia	—	—	—	72.2	68.4	66.7	59.4	
Latvia	—	—	—	109.4	136.5	80.9	62.8	
Lithuania	—	—	—	144.2	117.0	76.4	86.5	
C: CEC imports from the CECs (% of total imports)								
CSRs	15.1	12.2	7.4	5.5	5.0	5.2	—	—
Czech Rep.	—	—	—	—	17.9	21.3	13.1	14.2
Slovakia	—	—	—	—	34.5	47.7	36.7	29.4
Hungary	10.9	8.5	6.9	6.7	6.0	7.1	8.3	8.5
Poland	11.3	6.3	4.9	4.4	3.8	4.4	6.5	6.1
Bulgaria	8.3	7.2	5.7	5.3	4.3	5.4	4.9	3.8
Romania	10.3	7.8	6.9	6.9	4.9	4.8	5.6	5.1
Estonia	—	—	—	—	7.0	5.4	4.7	6.1
Latvia	—	—	—	6.0	15.3	13.1	13.7	15.9
Lithuania	—	—	—	6.6	11.1	11.8	16.2	14.6
D: CEC export/import ratios: trade with the other CECs								
CSRs	97.2	84.4	184.0	162.5	157.3	174.6	—	
Czech Rep.	—	—	—	—	119.6	124.5	116.7	
Slovakia	—	—	—	—	80.8	86.7	97.1	
Hungary	104.1	100.2	75.1	88.6	87.7	76.4	118.6	
Poland	114.9	207.7	114.7	109.8	104.1	94.0	87.6	

Table 9.1 (continued)

	1989	1990	1991	1992	1993	1994	1995	1996
Bulgaria	95.9	106.0	114.6	84.4	76.0	58.0	59.2	
Romania	90.8	48.4	62.0	62.3	79.5	105.2	66.4	
Estonia	—	—	—	—	188.9	180.6	150.3	
Latvia	—	—	—	124.5	73.5	66.3	67.2	
Lithuania	—	—	—	515.0	145.1	120.3	56.9	

Sources: UN-ECE trade statistics (1989–1994) and IMF Trade Statistics (1997). Author's computations.
Note: Dashes indicate data are not available.

should use these agreements as an opportunity to *raise* their MFN tariffs. Three major motives could explain this attitude: a lack of economic knowledge (the belief that protection does not harm the country imposing it, but its trading partners); the hope to make Central Europe an EC "hinterland" (a fashionable idea in Europe at this time, promoted by powerful magnates such as Sir James Goldsmith); and, last but not least, the understanding that high Central European MFN tariffs would greatly simplify the EC position in future negotiations at the World Trade Organization (WTO), which will inevitably follow the EC enlargement to CECs. What is crucial is that these three motives received a strong echo among Central Europe, as shown below.

9.2 The "Europe Agreements:" Their Economic and Political Costs

The first wave of unilateral trade liberalizations (Czechoslovakia, Hungary, and Poland) lasted less than two years (only one year in Poland, from August 1990 to August 1991). Despite the more limited magnitude and scope of its unilateral trade liberalization, the second wave (Bulgaria, Romania, and Slovenia) rapidly followed a similar evolution. One after the other, all these CECs turned to bilateral discriminatory trade agreements with the EC and to increased protection vis-à-vis the rest of the world. These trade agreements with the EC were included in the Europe Agreements (EAs), perceived as the necessary intermediary step toward CEC full accession to the EC.

Table 9.2 summarizes the progressive emergence of the EAs. The EAs are purely *bilateral* agreements—between each CEC and the EC.

Table 9.2
CECs' trade agreements: The "state of the unions"

with:	Agreements signed by									
	Bulgaria	Czech Republic	Estonia	Hungary	Latvia	Lithuania	Poland	Romania	Slovakia	Slovenia
Central European countries										
Bulgaria		1996							1996	
Czech Republic	1996		1996	1993	1996		1993	1995	1993	1994
Estonia		1996			1994	1994			1996	1995
Hungary		1993					1993		1993	1995
Latvia		1996	1994			1994			1996	
Lithuania			1994		1994					
Poland		1993		1993					1993	
Romania		1995							1995	
Slovakia	1996	1993	1996	1993	1996		1993	1995		1994
Slovenia		1994	1995	1995					1994	
Eastern European (CIS) countries		1996				1996				
European Community										
Cooperation agreements			1993		1993	1993				
Free trade agreements			1995		1995	1995				
Interim agreements	1994	1992		1992			1992	1993	1992	1997
Europe agreements	1995	1995		1994			1994	1995	1995	
Eur. agr. in negotiation			yes		yes	yes				

EFTA									
Free Trade Agreement	1993	1992	1991	1993	1991	1991	1993	1993	1992
Status at the World Trade Organization (WTO)									
Member		1948	1992	1973	1992		1967	1971	1948 1995
Observer					1992	1992			
Negotiation		yes			yes	yes			yes
Renegotiation					yes				yes

Sources: EBRD (1994), Phare Trade Policy Programme (1996), and Drabek (1997).

In addition to trade provisions (defining how and at which speed the EC and the CEC in question will dismantle their bilateral trade barriers), they include provisions related to "deeper integration" issues—that is, the progressive convergence of CEC laws and enforcement regime toward the EC regulatory system. Since March 1992, the EC has implemented the Interim Agreements (i.e., the EA provisions limited to trade and trade-related issues) with Hungary, Poland, and the Czech and Slovak Republics (March 1992), Romania (May 1993), Bulgaria (January 1994) and Slovenia (January 1997). As a result, there is no such a thing as a regional trade agreement at the European level—hence, the hub-and-spoke image for the EAs (and the Interim Agreements) and a key difference with NAFTA. One may argue that the bilateralism of the EAs was politically convenient: The CECs were not ready to sign the EAs at the same time and to implement them at the same speed. It remains that this strict bilateralism has allowed for the introduction of many differences among the EAs (as best illustrated by the wide differences in the number of pages for the various EAs or by the existence of an extremely complex net of rules of origin).

The EA-based discriminatory approach and the CEC increased protection with respect to non-EC countries can hardly be seen as mere coincidences. Rather many arguments suggest the following causality: The EAs have induced the CECs to become more protectionist with respect to non-EC trading partners. The previous section ends by sketching three motives linking these two evolutions from the EC point of view. These three motives could only receive strong echoes in Central Europe: Lack of economic knowledge was hiding the costs of the new trade policy; the hinterland motive was pleasing the Central European political thirst for unity with Western Europe, and it left the impression that the EC markets were large enough to solve the scale economies constraint; Central European trade officials could only be sympathetic to the problems raised by the perspective of post-enlargement negotiations within the WTO. And there was an additional reason: Higher CEC tariffs (even if only with non-EC countries) could only please the many CEC firms (privatized or not) that could not survive in a market environment.

Evidence suggesting that the causality of the EAs on CEC increased protection vis-à-vis non-EC countries after 1992 is provided in what follows. It is indirectly mirrored by the fact that the Baltics (the third wave of CEC unilateral trade liberalizations), which—so far—has been later involved in the EA hub-and-spoke regime, has been able to keep its tariffs low. As of today, Estonia has kept its zero tariff schedule—and managed to even scrap the few existing exceptions and to include agriculture (despite permanent debates). Meanwhile, Latvia and Lithuania have lowered their tariffs during the two last years (though at the cost of some dispersion of tariff rates). In other words, the CECs did not need to sign the EAs in order to maintain a free trade regime, contrary to what the so-called "credibility" argument suggests (liberalizing countries gain in credibility by anchoring their trade policy to a large trading partner) in favor of discriminatory trade agreements. Indeed, the recent adoption (September 1997) of a new customs law by Estonia (allowing the government to impose tariffs on farm products on a transitory basis, without parliamentary vote) was the first sign of increased protection accompanying the EC-Estonian EA.[9]

The section examines three points more in detail. It shows that the CECs have granted much larger preferences to the EC than did the EC to the CECs. It argues that the economic net costs of the EAs for the CECs will increase during the late 1990s, and that the political benefits from the EAs have not been significant—if they have been anything.

The Hub-and-Spoke Regime of the Europe Agreements: The CEC Preferences

The magnitude of the preferences that each CEC has granted to the EC in its EA is determined by the MFN trade policy of the CEC involved. As each CEC has accompanied its EA by a substantial increase of its MFN protection on imports from non-EC countries, it has, by the same token, increased the magnitude of its preferences to the EC—sometimes, in a huge proportion. In Poland, the unweighted average MFN tariff was increased from 5.5 (1991) to 18.4 (1992) percent. In Hungary, it was increased from 13 (1991) to 15 (1993) percent.[10] Even if the unweighted average tariff remained stable in the Czech Republic and Slovakia, it has increased by one percentage point when weighted by imports (mirroring the reshuffling of the tariff schedule).

This substantial tariff reprotection has taken various legal forms depending on the GATT status of each CEC. Because the country's tariffs were bound under GATT rules, Czechoslovakia had to request a waiver from GATT members in order to renegotiate them "in view of exceptional circumstances": In 1991, Czechoslovakia was authorized to reshuffle its tariff schedule under the condition of keeping a constant average tariff, but the country circumvented this constraint by introducing transitory import surcharges under the GATT balance-of-payments provision. For the other Central European signatories of the EAs, much larger tariff increases were made possible because existing CEC tariffs were not "bound" under GATT. As a result, these CECs were able to increase their MFN tariffs without having to pay "compensations" to their trading partners. When the three CECs that were GATT members before 1991 (Hungary, Poland, and Romania) became market economies, they were permitted by their GATT partners to negotiate a new protocol of accession with new tariff concessions. These negotiations started during the last year of the Uruguay Round negotiations—giving these CECs the possibility to renege a large portion of their previous unilateral trade liberalization. Last, Bulgaria (not a GATT member when signing its EA) could negotiate a complete protocol of accession, without feeling committed by any previous unilateral decision about trade liberalization.

I now focus on these changes for two typical CECs—the Czech Republic and Poland. It suggests three lessons. First, to the extent that the CECs have negotiated higher MFN tariffs after their EA signature, they have *unilaterally* increased the level of their preferences to the EC for roughly a decade—a huge grant to EC producers. Second, the tariff commitments taken by the CECs under the Uruguay Round have effectively postponed to the year 2001 the level of openness these countries had unilaterally reached in 1991. Last, the only CEC that has been able to keep a more or less stable protection is Czechoslovakia, which was, at this time, the only CEC with a strong GATT anchor.

The Hub-and-Spoke Regime of the Europe Agreements: The EC Preferences

Similarly, the magnitude of the preferences that the EC has granted to each CEC is determined by the MFN trade policy of the EC. This policy has generated small preferences to the CECs for two reasons: the low level of EC additional preferences granted to each CEC at the time of the EA signature, and the continuous erosion of these preferences. These points deserve more attention.

Concerning tariffs, EC duties imposed on Central European exports were already very low before the signature of the EAs because, since 1991, all the Central European signatories of the EAs were eligible to the EC GSP. Moreover, the EC tariff commitments under the Uruguay Round and under the 1996 Singapore Information Technology Agreement (which include many products that CECs could envisage producing), the EC hub-and-spoke regime with the Mediterranean countries (and maybe, the future trade agreements with South Africa, Mexico, and Mercosur) have eroded these initially low preferences.[11]

Concerning NTBs, the EC preferences granted to the CECs by the EAs have also been small for many products because in 1990–1991, as mentioned above, the EC did scrap many NTBs in reaction to the first wave of Central European MFN unilateral liberalization. But, there were two important limits to these EC initial concessions: They were granted on an annual basis, and they left untouched agriculture, clothing and steel. The EAs modified these limits, but not in a very substantial way. First, they have made *permanent* the transitory (annual) elimination of the EC NTBs. However, this benefit obtained in 1992–1994 had little value: It merely duplicated the commitments that the EC took in 1994 when signing the Uruguay Agreement on Safeguard. In this Agreement, the EC agreed to scrap all its NTBs, except the VER on Japanese exports of cars.[12] It should be stressed that the EC Uruguay commitment has more muscle than the EAs: under the purely bilateral EAs, the CECs cannot gang up against an unscrapped EC NTB, whereas they can do so under the WTO dispute settlement procedures (and can even get the support of world heavyweights, such as the United States or Japan). In agriculture, the EAs did not provide any progress. In clothing, the EAs have included large "outward processing traffic" (OPT) quotas in addition to the quotas granted under the MultiFibre Agreement. OPT quotas benefited from tariff rebates, but they exclusively concerned goods produced in the CECs from raw materials or intermediate goods imported from the EC. This condition has imposed severe constraints on the OPT regime: It has tended to give to EC firms a large discretionary power of negotiation over Central European firms during the period preparing the complete elimination of NTBs (which has occurred in January 1998). As a result, the exact value of these preferences is debatable.[13]

Last, concerning contingent protection, the CECs got less satisfactory rules under the EAs than under WTO commitments. On the one hand, the CECs did not get EC preferential antidumping rules against their exports. From 1990 to early 1998, the CECs have been accused of alleged dumping in twenty-five cases (as much as before 1989), in particular in the steel sector (making almost illusory the EC concessions in the steel sector). On the other hand, the CECs had to accept extensions of the safeguard clause: In the EAs, this clause can be invoked in circumstances that do not exist in the WTO framework, such as in case of "serious disturbance."

In sum, the preferences granted by the EC to the CECs were modest, all the more so because the EAs did not offer any new opportunities of market access to the CECs in terms of services or labor markets. It is fair to nuance this survey of the EAs by mentioning the provisions about EC support in case of CEC balance-of-payments problems. During the 1990s, the EC has granted a massive financial support to CECs in difficulties, as well as an important amount of aid. Some observers perceive these factors as EC preferences in the EA context (Drabek 1997). However, one could also argue that the EC macroeconomic support could (should) have been granted independently from trade-based EAs—as it has been the case in the early 1990s.

The previous description shows that the often celebrated "asymmetrical" nature of the EAs—the fact that the EC tariffs on Central European products were eliminated more rapidly than the Central European tariffs on EC goods—is largely a myth. This is confirmed if one examines the time pattern of the "preferential average concession" (defined as the difference between the preferential and MFN tariffs). The evolution of EC and CEC concessions during the decade 1991–2000 shows that after a peak around 1996–1997, the preferential average concession granted by the EC to the CECs *declined* over time.[14] By contrast, the preferential average concession granted by the CECs to the EC *increased* after 1996–1997 (because of the MFN reprotection) until the final year.

The Economic Net Costs of the EAs for the CECs: Increasing in the Future

In the case of discriminatory trade agreements, benefits and costs follow the mercantilist logic: Benefits come from exports, and costs from imports. As emphasized by Panagariya, in a discriminatory trade agreement:

the effect of freer trade has a strong mercantilist bias: a country benefits from receiving a discriminatory access to the partner's market and is hurt by giving the partner a similar access to its own market. When the country gives access to the partner on a preferential basis, it loses the tariff revenue collected on imports from the partner. The revenue goes to boost the terms of trade of the latter. The reverse happens when a country receives a preferential access from the partner. (Panagariya 1996, 486)

In other words, a country that wants to maximize its gains from a discriminatory trade agreement should prefer partners to which it exports a lot and from which, initially, it imports little. Table 9.1 shows that the CECs' situation does not fit with these two lessons: Even before the EA signature, CECs import from the EC a large percentage of their total imports (Box A), and they export significantly less from the EC than they import (as shown by their low export-import ratios in Box B). In other words, the CEC trade pattern does not fit the mercantilist logic of discriminatory trade agreements.

Economic benefits of the EAs for the CECs would essentially flow from the export side, that is, from additional preferential access to EC markets. Since the CECs were already enjoying a large access to the EC markets for all products (except the sensitive sectors) *before* the EAs, the EAs could not provide substantial additional gains. Moreover, scale economies is an especially weak argument in the CEC context because the relatively small size of the Central European economies implies that CEC producers could enjoy scale economies with world markets, even if they were imperfectly open. Large additional gains for the CECs necessarily involve the sensitive sectors: But these sectors are also key issues in the WTO forum (agriculture, steel, antidumping) so that any noticeable progress outside the WTO forum seems implausible.

Economic costs imposed by the EAs on the CECs come from the import side, that is, the large import flows from the EC existing before the EA implementation. Because of the EA "asymmetry" provision, the CECs have really entered the EAs only since 1996 (they began to substantially reduce their tariffs on EC goods only then). As is well known, the discriminatory EAs trigger two opposite effects when a CEC unable to produce goods in an efficient manner decides to buy them from the EC: They increase the CEC welfare ("trade creation" effect) when the EC is an efficient world producer of these goods; they reduce the CEC welfare ("trade diversion" effect) when the EC is an inefficient producer (by the world standard) of the goods demanded, and when the CECs buy these products from the EC only because the elimination of CEC tariffs on EC exports gives the EC producers a price advantage over producers from countries not pertaining to the EAs.[15] These opposite forces raise two questions.

First, are costly "trade diversion" cases more *frequent* than profitable "trade creation" cases? The usual answer to this question is that the EC is a large and open economy—hence, it "should surely" be an efficient economy.[16] This answer is much debatable. The EC is neither such a large nor such an open economy. At current exchange rates, the EC economy is only slightly larger (by 10%) than the U.S. economy alone, and it represents only 60 percent of the economies belonging to the Pacific Rim (APEC) zone (at mid-1997 exchange rates). In addition, more than a few EC industries benefit from high protection when NTBs, antidumping duties, or VERs are taken into account. Estimates of the EC unweighted MFN average tariff and border protection rate for 1990 have been provided above. In 1995, the EC unweighted average tariff is 6.4 percent (with sectoral peaks up to 17.5 percent), and the unweighted average border protection rate is still roughly 13–14 percent (with sectoral peaks up to 25–30 percent) (Messerlin 2001).

Second, *how costly* can be these trade diversion cases? As by Bhagwati and Panagariya (1996) emphasized, the larger the imports from the EC by the CEC, the higher the costs from trade diversion are likely to be. When the CECs cut their tariffs on EC imports (of goods where there are no EC-efficient producers), they will still gain from the fact that EC producers will provide goods at a lower price than those which would have been charged by Central European producers. But the CECs will lose the difference between the EC and world prices: It would have been preferable for them to buy these goods from the rest of the world, and to keep for them the difference between the EC and world prices (including under the form of tariff revenues). These losses of the CECs are gains for the EC producers. That the EC is the source of roughly 60 percent of CECs' imports (as shown in table 9.1) thus suggests large redistributive transfers from the CECs to inefficient EC producers.

The "Political" Costs of the EAs for the CECs

The Central European U-turn toward discriminatory trade agreements has often been presented as motivated by considerations not narrowly related to trade, but rather "political." These considerations can be divided into three major components singled out by the economic analysis of discriminatory trade agreements (Fernández 1997): security, credibility, and insurance. In the CEC case, these considerations refer to the desire to leave the Soviet sphere of influence and to join the Western world as quickly and as irreversibly as possible. What follows however argues that, once applied to Central Europe, these arguments are much weaker than they seem at a first glance—indeed, the EAs may well have generated political costs higher than that of benefits.

An extensive discussion of the political gains related to *security*, defined as the desire of an irreversible independence from and a strong defense against Russia, goes beyond the scope of this chapter. However, it is hard to see how the EAs could have enhanced the political "situation" of the CECs vis-à-vis the Soviet Union. In the early 1990s, many Central Europeans perceived the Soviet retreat from Central Europe as temporary and were afraid of a "coming back." Were the EAs an appropriate answer? Almost certainly, no. This is because, despite the expected minute impact of competition from Central Europe, the EC did not want to compromise on agriculture, steel, apparel, or other sensitive sectors in the EA context. This could hardly serve to reassure Central Europeans that Western Europeans were ready to fight and die for them. And it could hardly be better news for Soviet generals eager to come back to Central Europe, and for Central Europeans favoring this return.

The EAs are also presented as an instrument of *credibility* for the CEC transition and reforms. An MFN approach is often said to be not credible because it is not locked in by strong commitments with respect to a powerful partner. By contrast, a discriminatory approach is said to be credible because it is locked in by commitments involving such a powerful trading partner. The argument is much weaker than it looks at first glance because it compares unilateral liberalization and discriminatory agreement, whereas it should compare existing WTO membership and discriminatory agreements. Is a trade reform better monitored by one major partner (EC) than by two or three major trading partners (for instance, the EC, the United States, and Japan) as could be the case within the current WTO framework? The argument that "fewer cops are better than more cops" can be valid only if the unique cop has more means of action than all the cops together and if it has little to lose from enforcing rules on its fellow trading partner. Both conditions are very problematic (to say the least), all the more since 1995 because the WTO dispute settlement mechanism has been strengthened—allowing the possibility of massive and coordinated retaliation against a trading partner reneging on its commitments.

Indeed, two other reasons suggest that the EAs have not enhanced the credibility of the Central European trade policies.[17]

In a forward-looking perspective (from now to the day of CEC accessions to the EC), the EAs could have possibly generated credibility to Central European trade policies only if the CECs had negotiated those after having increased their MFN tariffs, according to the following scenario: After a few semesters of unilateral trade liberalization, the CECs gave up their efforts and increased their MFN tariffs; but they decided to stop this protectionist drift by signing the EAs with the EC. But, as described earlier, this is not the observed time sequence: The EAs were signed before the CECs adopted looser WTO commitments. Having obtained market access to the large EC market, the Central European governments maneuvered in the WTO as if they did not care about the rest of the world. In such a time sequence, the EAs have *reduced* the Central European credibility in trade policy matters rather than enhancing it.[18]

In a backward-looking perspective (from the day of accession to now), the EAs have inevitably blurred the Central European credibility because they have necessarily raised the issue of the most favorable Central European trade policies from the EC perspective in the following sense: The long-term explicit objective of the EAs is to prepare the CEC accession to the EC. This implies that the CECs and the EC will adopt a common tariff schedule. Taking into account the EC political and economic preeminence, this strongly suggests that the CECs joining the EC will adopt the EC common external tariff—raising the following problem (already evoked). If the Central European MFN tariffs are lower than the EC MFN tariffs, difficult negotiations between the enlarged EC and its trading partners from the rest of the world have to be expected under WTO rules: The EC could be asked by its trading partners to "compensate" them for the tariff increases of the CEC joining the EC. As a result, from the EC perspective, it would be much simpler to negotiate with CECs having MFN tariffs *higher* than those of the EC.

This situation is best illustrated by the ongoing saga of the WTO accession of two Baltic countries (Estonia and Lithuania). These countries have been taken as hostages by the EC and the United States with respect to their future GATS commitments in audio-visuals. For pleasing the EC (and its most protectionist member states, such as France or Belgium) and for avoiding any risk of compensations, these two Baltic countries could choose to align their commitments to the EC lowest common denominator on audiovisuals (i.e., a complete exemption of the sector). On the other hand, Estonian and Lithuanian broadcasters provide services that do not comply to EC rules (a minimum of 50% European content) to the greatest pleasure of their viewers. Based on this fact, the U.S. argues that these two Baltic countries could adopt a slightly more liberal approach, more in line with the de facto position of more liberal EC member states. Sadly, the EC and the United States are blocking the WTO accession of these two Baltic countries—mostly because of this conflict.

The fact that the EAs are presented as economically and politically costly to the CECs raises a last question: Why then have these EAs been signed by the CECs?

A first answer could come from the fact that the Central European political systems have been highly unstable since 1990: Majorities have been changed after most of the major electoral campaigns. One could interpret this phenomenon as an argument in favor of discriminatory trade agreement: the EAs would have been the means to tie up the hands of Central European governments not keen to look westward. But it could also be analyzed in a very different way: In chaotic political environments, such in the Central Europe of the 1990s, politicians are induced to pick up actions with almost immediate benefits (such as press or TV headlines related to EA negotiations) and delayed costs. As suggested above, the EAs have offered precisely this cost-benefit structure desired by myopic politicians—contrary to MFN trade agreements that tend to impose costs in the short run and to grant benefits in the long run.

A second explanation would be the desire of Central Europeans to *insure* themselves against the possible volatile trade actions of their powerful and huge neighbor—in particular against EC contingent protection such as antidumping measures. As already mentioned, the EAs have not been a success in this respect: The EC has not softened its contingent protection with respect to the CECs (it has even been argued above that it has made it more opaque and pervasive) so that "living near the Vesuvius" is as hard after the EAs as it was before. Notwithstanding these facts, the logic of the "insurance" motive for discriminatory trade agreements is particularly weak when it applies to an agreement between a large and a small country (as with the bilateral EAs). How could a bilateral and asymmetric (in terms of power) agreement provide to the less powerful signatory stronger guarantees than a multilateral agreement?

To summarize, whatever the motives for the EAs were, they announce trouble. When the costs of the EAs for the CECs fully emerge, Central European politicians looking for press coverage will throw them in the public, myopic politicians will include them in their time horizon, and the thirst for European "citizenship" may fade in Central Europe. Indeed, the nascent interest for discriminatory trade agreements between the CECs may be the harbinger of this evolution.

9.3   The CEFTA Web and Its Economic Costs

In 1991, almost one year before the implementation of the EAs, the first wave of CECs (Czechoslovakia, Hungary, and Poland) signed the Central European Free Trade Agreement (CEFTA). It went into effect in March 1993, almost one year after the EA (Interim Agreement) implementation. These two lags reveal the two different rationales of CEFTA. Its initial purpose was to limit the trade collapse between the CECs following the COMECON end. After 1992–1993, it was rather to reduce the negative consequences on the CECs of the hub-and-spoke regime generated by the EAs and to contribute to the ultimate objective of joining the EC. Slovenia (in 1996) and Romania (in 1997) have joined CEFTA. Bulgaria is expected to become a CEFTA member by late 1998, and several other countries have expressed some interest: the Baltics, Croatia, Macedonia, and Ukraine.

Besides CEFTA, there are a few other discriminatory agreements: BAFTA (the Baltic Free Trade Agreement between Estonia, Latvia and Lithuania), specific bilateral agreements between CECs and CIS countries (Ukraine and Moldova), and several regional initiatives (the "Danube Valley Cooperation," "South-East European Cooperation," etc.). One may wonder whether these initiatives have any chance to play a role. As a result, this section focuses on CEFTA.[19]

Table 9.2 shows the roughly 40 de facto bilateral free trade agreements between the CECs (if one includes those with the EC and with the EFTA countries, and one excludes dubious initiatives). Most of these agreements are unlikely to conform to WTO crucial requirements about regional trade agreements laid down in GATT Article XXIV and in the Uruguay Round understanding on its interpretation. In particular, they do not cover "substantially all the trade" between partners, if only because agriculture and sensitive industrial sectors are excluded.

CEFTA: A Web of Bilateral Transitory Agreements

Despite its name, CEFTA is not one trade agreement, but a set of trade bilateral agreements. Within a loose common framework, each CEC negotiates bilateral trade agreements with other CEFTA members for the transition period: For instance, Hungarian tariffs imposed on Polish goods may be different from Hungarian tariffs imposed on Czech goods. As a result, CEFTA is a trade regime that exacerbates discrimination during the transition period (since, for a given product, each CEC does not liberalize at the same pace with respect to all its CEFTA partners). It is probably one of the best illustrations of the "spaghetti bowl" that Bhagwati (1993) anticipated from the drift to discriminatory trade agreements.

The initial CEFTA framework has a limited coverage of concessions (under a complex set of guidances), and it anticipated a progressive move to liberalization (with a final deadline of 2001). In 1996 and 1997, it was supplemented with additional agreements enlarging the product coverage to more industrial goods and farm products, shortening the schedule of concessions by from one to three years, harmonizing rules of origin, and allowing the opening of CEFTA to other CECs.

Because CEFTA was finally conceived as alleviating the negative consequences of the hub-and-spoke regime of the EAs, it has been clearly designed as subservient to the EAs. First, CEFTA membership is subject to two conditions (imposed by the former Czech Prime Minister V. Klaus): A prospective CEFTA member must have concluded an EA with the EC, and it must be a WTO member. Second, CEFTA covers only trade—hence it has a more limited coverage than the EAs that deal with topics related to "deep integration," such as approximation (convergence) of laws and regulations. Last, CEFTA excludes sensitive industrial goods (cars and some textiles) and farm products—as the EAs do.

CEFTA is a free trade area: Signatories are left free to determine their own MFN rates with respect to the third countries (in contrast to the "customs union" formula where signatories enforce a common tariff schedule). This choice may have been motivated by political reasons beyond the scope of this chapter. But, it has certainly been a consequence of the fact that, starting with very large differences in terms of MFN protection between the CECs, agreeing on a Central European common external tariff would have been difficult (Economic Commission for Europe 1996).[20]

The Economic Costs of Central European Free Trade Agreements

The first years of implementing CEFTA have not been easy: Initial intra-CEFTA liberalizations have been followed by protectionist reactions (BAFTA's history has been smoother, with a progressive convergence to a relatively free trade stance). First, between 1995 and 1997, almost all the CEFTA countries have imposed import surcharges (from 5–10%, depending on the CEFTA member) on a noticeable range of products (alcoholic beverages, tobacco products, fuels, cars). Second, CEFTA rules allow for temporary increases of custom duties under the structural adjustment clause. CEFTA members have not hesitated to use this provision, such as Poland recently for steel, oil, and farm products. Last, contingent protection (under the form of safeguard measures) has been implemented more often and strictly on imports from CEFTA partners than on imports of similar products from the EC (and there are cases where complaining firms in the CECs against CEFTA or non-EC firms have been EC firms). In fact, many of the trade disputes between CEFTA members and the EC have reemerged in the bilateral CEFTA context. For instance, in 1995, Hungary decided to prohibit imports of used automobiles for four years—echoing the segmentation of the Central European markets under EA-related provisions on cars.[21] More recently, Hungarian and Slovak authorities have been more vocal about the loss of fiscal revenues, as a result of intra-CEC trade liberalization, than about the similar—though much larger—consequence of the EAs.

Leaving these implementation difficulties aside, a discriminatory trade agreement between small countries (as CEFTA) can generate two types of costs in addition to those (mentioned above) associated with discriminatory agreements with a large country, such as the EAs.

First, a trade agreement between two small countries that also trade with a third large country (a typical situation for two CEFTA members associated with the EC) harms the small importing country whenever imports from the large country are required to clear the market of the small importing country. In this case, the price in the small importing country remains unchanged (it is determined by the export price of the large country plus the tariff)—leaving unchanged the welfare of the domestic consumers in the small importing country. However, the government of the small importing country is losing tariff revenues, which become either additional surplus of producers from the small exporting country or deadweight losses dissipated by these producers. Globally, the small net importing country is thus loosing, as well as the free trade area as a whole (despite the fact that the small exporting country can be a net beneficiary).

Second, CEFTA is a discriminatory trade agreement among countries with large differences in MFN tariffs. This could bring net gains to the extent that the producers behind high MFN tariffs will be eliminated by the producers behind low MFN tariffs. But these gains depend on the capacity of the most efficient producers to supply the initially highly protected country—a capacity that depends on the likelihood of direct or indirect trade "deflection." Direct trade deflection (the fact that goods enter the CEC with the lowest MFN tariffs, and then sneak in the CECs with the highest MFN tariffs) is very limited for two reasons: It generates strong and permanent pressures for strict rules of origin; even if these rules of origin are not well enforced, net gains will still be limited because lax enforcement requires either lobbying or bribery costs (lax enforcement is not a free good). In sharp contrast, indirect trade deflection (the fact that goods enter the initially low tariff CEC in order to take the place of domestically produced goods that are sold in the initially high tariff CEC) is out of the reach of rules of origin. But it exists only if there is enough excess production capacity in the low-tariff country; and it does offer to the exporters (from the most open CEC to the least open CEC) opportunities for monopolistic behavior—that is, it does not necessarily offer large gains to the consumers of the highest tariff CEC. These two aspects are likely to play a strong role in the case of CECs' bilateral trade agreements: Price differences—even between members of a customs union, as shown by the EC history—can remain amazingly high, even for decades.

The Central European Free Trade Agreements: Which Political Gains?

It is often argued that the rationale of CEFTA and BAFTA flows from the fact that the CECs are neighbors—that they are "natural" trading partners (a point in line with the "gravity" regressions showing that CECs should trade between them to a much larger scale than they are doing now). However, applying this idea (and the gravity technique) to the CECs is highly debatable.

From a purely economic point of view, the notion of "natural" trading partners (and the gravity regressions) is prone to underestimate (1) the ongoing technical progress that lowers transport and transaction costs to such an extent that it makes potentially every country a "natural" trading partner of the whole world (if the involved countries benefit from modern technology), and (2) the magnification effect of ongoing liberalizations (such as deregulations in telecoms or transports) on technical progress and growth.

From a political point of view, it tends to ignore the very ambiguous (to say the least) feelings between these countries and to give too little attention to the fact that, during almost a century, the CECs have seen their history stolen by their powerful neighbors—making it difficult for them to provide their own solutions to brewing ethnic and national disputes. In Central Europe, threatening minorities and shaky borders are not limited to former Yugoslavia. By tending to equate "close" to "friendly," the natural partner notion slips easily in historical misinterpretations. These tensions between Central European countries lead to an examination of the argument that discriminatory trade agreements can be used as a common "guarantee" scheme by the members in order to reduce security threats between them (Schiff and Winters 1997). However, it is difficult to see how, in the Central European case, CEFTA as it is can play such a role— simply because CEFTA has been voluntarily conceived as down-to-earth and as limited as possible. This may reflect the distrust between Central European countries—but it may also (and perhaps above all) mirror the explicit CEFTA subservience to the EAs. The case of BAFTA might have looked better: But, the EC proposal to include Estonia in the first wave of candidates for accession seems the "kiss of death" to Baltic deep integration.

9.4 Conclusion

This review of the Central European trade liberalizations between the fall of the Berlin Wall and the late 1990s suggests two lessons: The economic costs of the large number of European trade discriminatory agreements are higher than expected—to the point where they can create serious troubles in the future; the political benefits of nondiscriminatory trade policies are higher than expected, including in terms of wide political aspects, such as negotiating leverage (reciprocity), security, credibility, and so forth.

These conclusions suggest two lessons. The first sheds light on the desirable trade policy for a particularly troubled European region: the Yugoslav successor countries (for details, see Messerlin and Maur 2000). The economic and political benefits of a nondiscriminatory and uniform trade policy are boosted by the sur-imposition of ethnic and conventional "interstate" trade in the Balkan region. Such ethnic trade could lead to de facto ethnic free trade areas, or, on the contrary, to an even greater fragmentation of the region (each ethnic region applying for its own sake the trade policy of the state to which it pertains). The best option for the Balkan countries would then be to adopt the *same*, uniform (uniform meaning that the same tariff is imposed, across the board, on all products), and moderately positive tariff *between* themselves—a tariff roughly equivalent to the external EC tariff (say, between 5% and 10%).

The advantages of such an unique intraregional tariff enforced by all the Balkan countries with respect to one another would be to eliminate the many potential distortions that can be the source of wasteful and large rents inhibiting the institutional reform process, namely: (1) those related to the import origin (including those related to ethnic-based trade management, smuggling and corruption); (2) those related to investment issues (investors will consider the region as a single market in the sense that exporting from one Balkan country to another one will not be a matter of tariff differences since all intraregional transactions will be taxed at a similar rate); and (3) last but not least, those related to the fear of different paces of development, since it maintains a reasonable level of protection while imposing the same tax on all goods. This last aspect is essential since Balkan countries will need some time to finance their reconstruction and to find their own niches of specialization (they have to recognize the products in which their neighbors have comparative advantages;

if they don't find that in their own markets, they will discover it in the EC markets where competition between the Balkan producers will be unfettered).

The second lesson to be drawn from this chapter concerns the Central European countries per se. The chapter suggests that they should come back to a less discriminatory approach: Is such a comeback possible? And is it consistent with the long-term objective of the CEC accession to the EC?

A concrete answer to these two questions would be a Central European Joint Initiative on tariff convergence: the CECs would jointly declare that they would reduce the differences between their own MFN tariffs and the corresponding EC MFN tariffs during a given period (say, 1998–2004). This initiative is a de facto joint program of additional trade liberalization limited to the MFN dimension of the CEC trade policies.[22] It should only cover the Central European MFN tariffs higher than the EC tariffs, and it should not be applied to the Central European MFN tariffs lower than the EC tariffs. It will bring *economic* gains to the CECs—and to the EC—to the extent that the CEC accession to the EC will reduce the high (relative to Central European duties) EC tariffs.

This MFN-oriented initiative will also bring three large *political* gains. First, it can shorten the very long delays expected for CEC accessions to the EC: If CECs do not take initiatives, thereby leaving less room for EC temporization, almost no CEC could realistically expect to become an EC member before the years 2010–2015. Second, the initiative can bring the EC-CEC discussions on the *acquis communautaire* into a perspective much different from the "take-it-or-leave-it" approach adopted so far: The past, the relative size, and the current and future levels of development of the Central European economies make the nonnegotiability of the entire acquis communautaire an untenable position in the long run. Last, a more open MFN trade policy is a good substitute for the CECs (which are small economies) to many policies—competition policy, disciplines on subsidies or tax arrears, incentives to get a modern and well-enforced tax system, and so forth.

A last point deserves attention. This entire chapter relies on the assumption that the CECs want to join a united and increasingly federal (at an unexpectedly rapid pace) Europe. This assumption raises the following question: Is it correct to assume that the CECs will rapidly give up a substantial amount of their fresh independence and sovereignty as eagerly as France, Germany, or even Britain did, and do? This question deserves attention because, contrary to the Western European countries, the CECs are still suffering from centuries of frustrated independence. The question is all the more important because NATO is within the reach of the CECs—and because the CECs may have wrongly perceived the existing Europe Agreements and the future accession to the EC as substitutes for NATO.

Notes

This chapter comes from a paper presented at the American Enterprise Institute & Ford Foundation Conference on "Unilateral Trade Liberalization," October 24–25, 1997, held at The American Enterprise Institute, Washington. I would like to thank Jagdish Bhagwati, Zdenek Drabek, David Henderson, Francis Ng, and Alan Winters for very helpful comments and observations on a first draft.

1. In this chapter, Central Europe covers the sixteen countries located between, on the one hand, the EC and, on the other hand, Russia, Bielorussia, and Ukraine (Eastern Europe). However, the chapter covers de facto only ten countries: Estonia, Lithuania, Latvia, Poland, the Czech Republic, Slovakia, Slovenia, Hungary, Romania, and Bulgaria. The six other CECs (Croatia, Serbia, Bosnia-Herzegovina, Macedonia, Albania, and Moldova) are so absorbed by stabilizing their external borders or their domestic institutions that they are not taken into account in the chapter.

2. Ironically, the dependency policy was such a success that the collapse of the German Democratic Republic (the largest economy in Central Europe) triggered the general collapse of the Soviet empire, including the Soviet Union itself.

3. The case of the former German Democratic Republic is left aside. Borders between Western and Eastern Germany were almost instantaneously open at an unrealistic exchange rate—giving one of the best examples in the history of a costly (because full of domestic distortions) trade liberalization (despite the preferential trade regime existing between the Federal Republic and the GDR since the 1960s).

4. When a centrally planned economy, Czechoslovakia, kept her tariffs very low as a window dressing operation. Tariff binding under GATT means that tariffs could not be increased by the country in question without granting compensations to its trading partners or running the risk of retaliatory measures in response to tariff increases. Relying on unweighted average tariffs can be misleading: Because trade is always a matter of relative prices, what counts is tariffs on a product basis (no foreign exporter faces an "average" tariff, and no domestic producer benefits from an "average" tariff). However, the small dispersion of the CEC tariffs during this first period limits the ambiguity of the average tariff notion.

5. Legally, these exemptions were often restricted to intermediate and equipment goods—hence, they tended to increase effective protection of consumer goods. But, lax enforcement has often made possible import final products under such schemes.

6. In all the CECs, the subsidy problem has been less acute in manufacturing than in service sectors (which are not examined in this chapter). Subsidies—be explicit

subsidies or implicit subsidies under the form of cumulated tax arrears—have plagued Central European service sectors, in particular banking. For a legal analysis of the subsidy issue in the Europe Agreements context, see Evans (1996).

7. From 1990 to 1994–1995, CEC borders with the EC were essentially controlled by Western European Customs, which were willing to stop immigrants and illegal imports from the CECs, but were not interested in reducing illegal exports to the CECs (except stolen cars).

8. Czechoslovakia was the only exception because she was a founding member of GATT in 1947 (before being forced to join the Soviet rule): As a result, she had a protocol of accession to the WTO similar to the protocols of market economies.

9. In this perspective, the fact that the EC has decided to include Estonia (and Estonia alone) in the first set of potential candidates to EC accession is rather intriguing—in particular, knowing the EC condition that, upon accession, the new EC members will have to terminate any preferential agreements they may have with third countries.

10. These numbers rely on unweighted average tariffs that are a less accurate source of information for the post-1991 period because the increase of the CEC MFN average tariffs has been accompanied by a broadening of the range of these tariffs.

11. For instance, all the present or *future* new EC concessions to non-CECs (such as the Mediterranean countries) reduce the *current* value of the existing EC concessions to the CECs. Similarly, a CEC granting a preferential status to another CEC erodes the economic value of its concessions under its EA. This explains that many preferential agreements have only marginal a effect on trade pattern, but generate much political frustration.

12. Indeed, one may argue that the EC was able to sign the Uruguay Agreement on safeguards because it had already scrapped its NTBs against the CECs, which were by far the most numerous. NTBs against market economies (particularly from Asian economies) were already in the process of being "translated" in antidumping cases.

13. The OPT provisions may have been useful for giving CEC producers an easy start (by quasi-integrating them in Western European firms). But they can become either a binding constraint (if CEC producers are efficient) or an empty shell (if they are not). According to Pellegrin (1997), the trade volume under the OPT clause has been significant only for Czech firms, whereas it has steadily declined for the other CECs.

14. The results are based on the following simplifying assumptions: annual constant tariff decreases and no consideration of the "sensitive" sectors and of the other discriminatory trade agreements signed by the EC and the CECs. If the CECs have on average six to seven discriminatory agreements, the EC has contractual and reciprocal agreements with 26 countries (including the CECs), contractual but nonreciprocal agreements with 70 countries (the Lomé convention), and noncontractual and nonreciprocal agreements with roughly 100 countries (the GSP). All this creates much more uncertainty about the *real* economic value of EC preferences than the preferential agreements that the CECs have been able to generate.

15. Because this chapter focuses on trade issues, it does not explicitly mention problems related to foreign direct investment (FDI). However, FDI can be "created" or "diverted" as well as trade flows. It is created when it reacts to higher rates of return existing in the free trade area members as a consequence of their trade liberalization. And it can also be diverted when free trade area tariff structures create artificially high (with respect to the rest of the world) rates of return in the free trade area members.

16. It could also be argued that economic analysis shows that a discriminatory trade agreement may be more trade creating if it includes a member with high MFN tariffs—because it is more likely to eliminate the industry of the least efficient member. To the extent that CECs are the high-tariff members after their MFN reprotection, this argument could be applied to them. But it would be somewhat awkward to do so since the CECs have increased their MFN protection on an ex post basis (*after* having signed the EAs). It seems inappropriate to laud the EAs for reducing ex post the costs of CEC tariff increases that the EAs have contributed to generate ex ante.

17. For a lively debate, see Baldwin, Francois, and Portes (1997), and the discussion accompanying their paper. See also Panagariya (1996, 499) for another illustration of the causality issue in the NAFTA case.

18. This is particularly true for Hungary and Poland. For the second wave of the CECs, the time sequence is less clear because they have signed the EAs at roughly the same time as their WTO commitments.

19. BAFTA survival is more a political than an economic issue. BAFTA is implemented since April 1994, and it intends to be a customs union. It covers almost all the manufactured goods, and it has recently been supplemented by the Trade Agreement in Agricultural Products (signed in 1996), which extends trade liberalization to farm products. However, the fate of BAFTA will essentially depend on its ability to survive to Estonian withdrawal, once Estonia has become an EC member state.

20. The exception of the Czech and Slovak customs union is more apparent than real: The frequent use of surcharges on the top of tariffs transform this customs union into a de facto free trade agreement.

21. And, indirectly, echoing the EC–Japan agreement. The EAs allow for Central European quotas on EC cars—the best example having been the Polish quota. These provisions have de facto given a privileged position to one or two EC car makers in each Central European market.

22. This "APEC-type" proposal would have the same effects as a formal customs union aimed at liberalizing the existing CEC MFN tariffs. The only cost of the proposal (compared to a customs union) is that the issues related to rules of origin are likely to stay. On the other hand, this proposal does not have to solve the issue of harmonizing the CEC low MFN tariffs, nor to face the problem of sharing tariff revenues and other political problems associated with a customs union (for details, see Messerlin 1995).

References

Baldwin, Richard, Joseph Francois, and Richard Portes. "The Costs and Benefits of Eastern Enlargement: The Impact on the EU and Central Europe." *Economic Policy* (April): 127–176.

Bhagwati, Jagdish. 1993. "Regionalism and Multilateralism: An Overview." In *New Dimensions in Regional Integration*, ed. J. de Melo and A. Panagariya. Cambridge, UK: Cambridge University Press.

Bhagwati, Jagdish, and Arvind Panagariya. 1996. "Preferential Trading Areas and Multilateralism: Strangers, Friends or Foes?" Washington, DC: American Enterprise Institute.

Drabek, Zdenek. 1997. "Regional and Sub-regional Integration in Central and Eastern Europe: An Overview." Mimeo., World Trade Organization.

Economic Commission for Europe. 1996. "The Re-emergence of Trade among the East European and Baltic Countries: Commercial and Other Policies Issues." *Economic Bulletin for Europe* 48: 75–92.

European Bank for Reconstruction and Development (EBRD). 1994. *Transition Report*. London: EBRD.

Evans, Andrew. 1996. "Contextual Problems of EU Law: State Aid Control under the Europe Agreements." *European Law Review* (August): 263–279.

Fernández, Raquel. 1997. "Returns to Regionalism: An Evaluation of the Nontraditional Gains from Regional Trade Agreements." The World Bank Policy Research Working Paper #1816, August.

Hansson, Ardo H. 1994. "The Political Economy of Macroeconomic and Foreign Trade Policy in Estonia." In *Trade in the New Independent States*, ed. C. Michalopoulos and D. G. Tarr. Studies of Economies in Transformation, Number 13, The World Bank/UNDP.

Hoekman, Bernard, and Simeon Djankov. 1997. "Determinants of the Export Structure of Countries in Central and Eastern Europe." *The World Bank Economic Review* 11: 471–487.

Kaminski, Bartlomiej, Zhen Kun Wang, and L. Alan Winters. 1996. "Export Performance in Transition Economies." *Economic Policy* (October): 423–442.

Messerlin, Patrick A. 1995. "The MFN and Preferential Trade Policies of the CECs: Singapore and Geneva Are on the Shortest Road to Brussels." Mimeo., Phare Trade Policy Program.

Messerlin, Patrick A. 2001. *Measuring the Costs of Protection in Europe: EC Commercial Policy in the 2000s*. Washington, DC: Institute for International Economics.

Messerlin, Patrick A., and Jean-Christophe Maur. 2000.

Panagariya, Arvind. 1996. "The Free Trade Area of the Americas." *The World Economy* 19, no. 5 (September): 485–516.

Pellegrin, Julie. 1997. "The Outward Processing Traffic Quotas in the EC-CEC Trade." Ph.D. diss., European Institute of Florence, Florence, Italy.

Phare Trade Policy Programme. 1996. "Reviews of Selected Central European Trade Policies." PCU. Bratislava.

Schiff, Maurice, and L. Alan Winters. 1997. "Regional Integration as Diplomacy." Mimeo., World Bank.

Tumlir, Jan. 1984. *Economic Policy as a Constitutional Problem*. London: Institute of Economic Affairs.

10 The Political Economy of Unilateral Trade Liberalization: The Case of Chile

Sebastian Edwards and
Daniel Lederman

10.1 Introduction

Chile has become a model for reforming economies throughout the world. Policymakers, academics, and consultants in Latin America, Eastern Europe, South Asia, and Africa are analyzing the Chilean experiment to get insights on how to reform their economies. Yet when Chile launched an ambitious market-oriented program under the aegis of a military dictatorship in 1974, observers throughout the world were openly critical. Chile's economic reforms have been looked at with optimistic interest only in recent years, in light of the success of the reforms: Economic growth averaged more than 7 percent per year for more than a decade (1986–1998), the annual rate of inflation has declined to around 4 percent, and unemployment declined drastically during this period—see table 10.1.[1]

The purpose of this chapter is to analyze the political and economic circumstances surrounding Chile's unilateral trade liberalization, which was implemented simultaneously with other reforms, including an effort to eliminate a stubborn inflationary process, financial reforms that ended decades of financial repression, and a massive privatization program. In less than four years, Chile dismantled quantitative restrictions and replaced a surrealistic tariff structure (with an average tariff in excess of 100%) with a uniform 10 percent tariff. Following Bhagwati (1988), we investigate the role played by ideas, interests, and institutions.[2] More specifically, we examine the role played by the "reform team," investigate some of the distributive consequences of the reforms, and analyze the mechanisms the government used to maintain a minimum level of political support for the liberalization process. A recurrent question is whether authoritarian governments—such as the Pinochet

Table 10.1
Chile: Macroeconomic indicators, 1974–1999 (period averages, percentages)

	1974–1975	1976–1979	1980–1981	1982–1983	1984–1985	1986–1989	1990–1993	1994–1996	1997–1999
1. Economic activity									
GDP growth	-6.2	7.4	6.7	-7.6	4.4	7.3	6.9	6.6	3.3
Investment/GDP*	15.4	15.6	19.5	12.9	14.8	23.5	26.5	27.2	21.1
Unemployment rate*	13.5	13.8	10.9	18.6	12.2	5.3	5.9	5.7	9.7
2. Domestic prices									
Inflation	358	69	20	22	25	18	18	8.7	4.3
Real wage variation	-4.1	14.3	8.8	-5.5	-2.1	2.6	3.9	5.1	2.2
Real exchange-rate variation	83.0	1.4	-13.2	15.7	13.3	4.5	-2.8	-3.7	0.2
Real interest rate	15.9	43.9	24.8	25.1	11.1	8.9	11.1	9.9	9.6
3. External sector									
Terms of trade variation	-33.1	2.6	-3.5	-3.6	-5.4	7.3**	-3.6	1.6	-3.0
Export volume variation	22.2	15.3	2.0	2.7	6.8	11.1	9.5	9.3	8.6
Trade balance/GDP*	-2.0	-2.8	-10.3	2.7	2.8	4.5	-2.3	8.6	2.5
Current account/GDP*	-5.2	-5.4	-14.5	-5.4	-8.3	-1.8	-4.8	0.1	-0.1
External debt/exports*	3.1	1.6	3.1	4.0	4.6	1.7	1.6	1.1	1.8
4. Macroeconomic policies									
Fiscal surplus/GDP*	2.1	5.2	3.3	-1.2	-0.2	5	0.8	2.1	-2.1
Growth of M1	260	112	31	6	23	37	28	19.7	11.2
Nominal exchange-rate variation	390	47	—	49	45	13	5	-0.8	7.3

Sources: Central Bank of Chile, National Institute of Statistics (INE, in Spanish), S. Edwards (1984), Fontaine (1996, table 1).

Note: Dash indicates data are not available.

*Refers to the value corresponding to the last year in the period.

**1987–1989.

Key:

GDP Growth — refers to the variation of annual average GDP, measured at constant prices of 1977 for the period 1976–1985, and at 1986 constant prices for the period 1986–1996.

Investment/GDP — refers to the fixed investment coefficient of GDP, where both numerator and denominator are measured at constant prices.

Terms of trade — refers to the average annual variation of the index measuring exports of goods and services in relation to the unitary value of imports of goods and services.

Unemployment rate — 1974–1981, see table 10.7; otherwise, refers to the value from Oct. to Dec. of each year, based on the National Survey conducted by INE.

Inflation — refers to the variation of the official CPI calculated from Dec. to Dec. of every year.

Real wage — variation in real wages calculated by INE, from Dec. to Dec. of each year (overlapping in 1982 and 1983 to cover methodological redefinitions.

Real exchange rate — multilateral index in relation to Chile's commercial trading partners, as calculated by the Banco Central (for 1974–1978, IMF series used for the other periods). A positive variation reflects a depreciation.

Real interest rate — refers to the average short term (30–89 days) rate of credit that banks offer, deflated by a variation of the CPI.

Export volume — defined at constant prices for non financial goods and services.

Trade balance/GDP — measures non financial goods and services, net imports of non financial goods and services as a fraction of GDP, all expressed at current prices of each year.

Current account/GDP — balance of the current account of the balance of payments, as a fraction of GDP at current prices.

External debt/exports — total external debt in relation to exports of goods and services.

Fiscal surplus/GDP — fiscal balance, excluding interest payments as a percentage of GDP.

Growth of M1 — variation from Dec. to Dec. in nominal terms of M_1A (plus liquid deposits).

Nominal exchange rate — variation from Dec. to Dec. of nominal exchange of the peso in relation to the dollar.

dictatorship that ruled Chile during 1973–1989—are sensitive to political considerations when implementing major policy changes. We also present econometric results obtained by using household-level survey data to analyze the effects of trade liberalization on Chile's unemployment.

The rest of the chapter is organized as follows: Section 10.2 presents an overview of Chile's liberalization, sketching the initial conditions, and tracing the evolution of trade policy from 1974 to the 1990s, while distinguishing among five stages of the process of trade liberalization. Section 10.3 focuses on the role of ideas, beginning with a brief discussion of analytical aspects associated with the dynamics of economic reforms in general, and with some key practical issues related to the speed and sequencing of economic reforms, and the postreform tariff structure. We then discuss the ideas of the change team, their original plan of reform, and its actual implementation, and, finally, we review the views of dissenters in the context of Chile's restricted market for ideas. After a brief review of analytical issues related to the role of interest groups in general, and after providing a taxonomy of Chilean interest groups, section 10.4 analyzes the application of compensation mechanisms that were used by the authorities to raise support for and reduce opposition to the reforms. Section 10.5 presents the econometric results regarding the employment effects of trade liberalization. Section 10.6 concludes by arguing that Chile has begun to abandon its staunchly pro-unilateralism position and is now flirting with regionalism.

10.2   Five Stages of Trade Liberalization in Chile, 1974–1990s

On September 11, 1973, after three years of a democratically elected socialist administration led by President Salvador Allende, the military staged a coup and took over Chile's government. At the time of the military coup, import tariffs averaged 105 percent and were highly dispersed, with some goods subject to nominal tariffs of more than 700 percent and others fully exempted from import duties. In addition to tariffs, a battery of quantitative restrictions were applied, including outright import prohibitions, prior import deposits of up to 10,000 percent, and a distortionary multiple exchange-rate system consisting of fifteen different rates (see table 10.2).

Despite a temporary and moderate reversal in the midst of a severe balance-of-payments crisis during 1983–1985, Chile has been

Table 10.2
The elimination of nontariff barriers (NTBs)

Instruments	The situation in 1973: Number of product categories affected (approx. 63% of total)	Dates when relaxed and eliminated
A. Import prohibitions	187	August 1976: Down to 6 products April 1978: Down to 5 products August 1981: All eliminated
B. Prior deposits*	2,872	January 1974: Waivers granted August 1976: Eliminated
C. Import licenses**	2,278	January 1974: Eliminated

Source: de la Cuadra and Hachette (1991, 218–219) and Mendez (1979, 81).
*A 90-day-non-interest-bearing prior deposit to the Central Bank, equivalent to 10,000 percent of the c.i.f. value of imports.
**Official approval required for importing.

able to sustain a continuous process of unilateral liberalization since 1974. This achievement becomes even more interesting when one considers that in the meantime Chile experienced the breakdown of its democratic system, sharp business cycles, several dramatic shifts in other aspects of economic policy, a return to democratic government, and important changes in the world trading system. From a political economy perspective, it is useful to distinguish among five stages in Chile's unilateral trade liberalization, each stage being characterized by the use of different types of "compensation schemes," as we show in section 10.4.

In terms of policies, the first phase (1974–1978) was characterized by a dramatic reduction and simplification of its trade barriers, which was part of a comprehensive program of economic stabilization and restructuring. The second stage (1978–1982) was characterized by a change in the stabilization program, and by a buildup of a significant degree of real exchange-rate overvaluation. The third stage was the temporary reversal phase (1983–1985) that occurred when Chile faced a deep economic crisis. The fourth period covers the resumption of unilateral liberalization in the context of a speedy economic recovery and the beginning of the end of the military government (1985–1990). The fifth stage began with the transition to democracy and the tariff reduction of 1991 and may be ending with Chile's turn toward preferential trading arrangements (PTAs), high capital inflows (at least through 1997), and vigorous economic growth.

Stage I: Initial Liberalization with Real Exchange-Rate Depreciation, 1974–1979

In October 1973, the minister of finance of the recently installed military regime stated that Chile's "best prospects for growth are in opening to international competition" (Méndez 1979, 63–64). Initially, however, the authorities had no precise idea about how deep and how fast the liberalization should be. In fact, only after Chile withdrew from the Andean Pact in December 1977 did the chief economic strategist, Minister Sergio de Castro, announce that the final goal was to reduce tariffs to a uniform rate of 10 percent by mid-1979. In explaining this change in tariff policy, de Castro pointed out that the prevailing differentiated tariff structure of rates between 10 percent and 35 percent generated an unjustifiable discriminatory situation.

Table 10.3 contains the itinerary of import tariff reductions for 1974–1991 and shows that the liberalization was actually somewhat abrupt during the first phase (1974–1979). By June 1976, the average tariff was 33 percent, representing a reduction of more than 60 percentage points from the average tariff of December 1973. This achievement was particularly impressive, since quantitative import restrictions had been eliminated by August 1976 (see table 10.2). By June 1979, when the first phase of the trade reform came to an end, all items, except automobiles, had a nominal import tariff of 10 percent. The impact of this liberalization phase was different across sectors. Table 10.4 shows the evolution of the rate of effective protection for eighteen industries within the manufacturing sector during 1974–1979. Clearly, both the level and dispersion of the effective rates of protection were reduced as the reforms progressed.[3] By June 1979, the average effective tariff was 13.6 percent, and the range between the highest and lowest effective tariffs was only six percentage points. Another notable consequence of the reform was that it increased the level of effective protection granted to agriculture. Historically, through the imposition of price controls on agricultural products and high import tariffs on inputs, most crops had suffered from a substantial negative rate of effective protection. In 1974, for example, the agricultural sector had a negative average rate of effective protection of 36 percent.[4]

This initial phase of trade liberalization was supplemented by an active exchange-rate policy aiming to maintain a competitive real

Table 10.3
Itinerary of import tariff reductions, 1973–1993 (percentage of c.i.f. value of imports, nominal tariffs)

Date (m/d/yr)	Maximum tariff	% of items subject to maximum tariff	Tariff mode	% of items	Avg. tariff
12/31/73	220	8.0	90	12.4	94.0
03/01/74	200	8.2	80	12.3	90.0
03/27/74	160	17.1	70	13.0	80.0
06/05/74	140	14.4	60	13.0	67.0
01/16/75	120	8.2	55	13.0	52.0
08/13/75	90	1.6	40	20.3	44.0
02/09/76	80	0.5	35	24.0	38.0
06/07/76	65	0.5	30	21.2	33.0
12/23/76	65	0.5	20	26.2	27.0
01/08/77	55	0.5	20	24.7	24.0
05/02/77	45	0.6	20	25.8	22.4
08/29/77	35	1.6	20	26.3	19.8
12/03/77	25	22.9	15	37.0	15.7
06/78[a]	20	21.6	10	51.6	13.9
06/79[a]	10	99.5	10	99.5	10.1
03/23/83	20	99.5	20	99.5	20.0
22/09/84	35	99.5	35	99.5	35.0
03/01/85	30	99.5	30	99.5	30.0
06/29/85	20	99.5	20	99.5	22.0
01/05/88	15	99.5	15	99.5	15.0
06/91	11	99.5	11	99.5	11.0
01/99	10	99.5	10	99.5	10.0
01/00	9	99.5	9	99.5	9
01/01	8	99.5	8	99.5	8
01/02	7	99.5	7	99.5	7
01/03	6	99.5	6	99.5	6

Source: Ffrench-Davis (1980 [1986]) and Saez, Salazar, and Vicuña (1995).
[a] During 1978 and the first half of 1979 the tariff schedule was linearly reduced.

Table 10.4
Effective rates of protection in manufacturing sectors (percentages)

Sector	1974	1976	1978	1979
Foodstuff	161	48	16	12
Beverages	203	47	19	13
Tobacco	114	29	11	11
Textiles	239	74	28	14
Footwear	264	71	27	14
Timber products	157	45	16	15
Furniture	95	28	11	11
Paper products	184	62	22	17
Publishing	140	40	20	12
Leather products	181	46	21	13
Rubber products	49	54	26	15
Chemicals	80	45	16	13
Petroleum and coal	265	17	12	13
Nonmetallic minerals	128	55	20	14
Basic metals	127	64	25	17
Metallic industries	147	77	27	15
Nonelectrical machinery	96	58	19	13
Electrical machinery	96	58	19	13
Average	151.4	51.0	19.7	13.6
Standard deviation	60.4	15.7	5.3	1.7

Source: Aedo and Lagos (1984).

exchange rate. In fact, the reduction of trade barriers and the deterioration of Chile's terms of trade after 1974, *required* a depreciation of the equilibrium real exchange rate. The depreciation of the real exchange rate was first achieved via the maxi-devaluation of October 1973, then was maintained by a crawling exchange rate system, which lasted until January 1978.[5] The importance assigned by the government to a "depreciated" real exchange rate was clearly articulated by General Pinochet in a 1976 speech (Méndez 1979, 195): "We shall continue to encourage nontraditional exports.... The Minister of Finance will announce the manner in which the exchange rate shall be established in order to guarantee a viable and permanent value for foreign currency."[6] At the end of 1976, the real effective exchange rate was almost 150 percent more depreciated than in the third quarter of 1973. In an attempt to break inflationary expectations, the peso was slightly revalued in June 1976, and again in March 1977. In the second half of 1977, to compensate partially for the effects of the new rounds of tariff reductions, the rate of nominal devaluation with respect to the U.S. dollar was once again increased.

Stage II: Liberalization with Real Exchange-Rate "De-Protection," 1979–1982

A change in the stabilization program took place in 1978, when the exchange rate became the main anti-inflationary anchor. The rate of devaluation was announced for a year and was preset at a rate below ongoing inflation, and in 1979, the exchange rate was fixed to the dollar. Between 1978 and 1982, and partially as a consequence of the new exchange-rate policy, a significant degree of real exchange-rate appreciation developed. This appreciation became increasingly unsustainable, and a major balance of payments crisis erupted in 1982. The country ran out of reserves, a major devaluation was implemented, and numerous firms and banks went bankrupt. As a consequence, unemployment skyrocketed, and GDP declined by over 14 percent in 1982 alone (see Edwards and Edwards 1991).

Stage III: Temporary Setback, 1983–1985

The third phase of Chile's trade reform saga encompasses the period between March 1983 and June 1985, when, in the midst of a severe balance of payment crisis, the uniform tariff was raised from 10 percent to 35 percent as part of a series of measures designed to speed up the adjustment process (see table 10.3). In addition, the government reintroduced price bands for three commodities—wheat, sugar, and edible oil—in 1983, which were meant to provide, on average, a rate of nominal protection equivalent to the uniform tariff rate.[7] Between 1982 and 1983, Chile experienced a severe economic contraction, which was accompanied by a fast adjustment of its current account (see table 10.1). Unlike previous historical experiences with increases in trade protection to correct external imbalances (such as during the 1930s), this time the tariff hikes (no quantitative restrictions were imposed) were short-lived, but the price bands have been maintained for twenty years.

Stage IV: Unilateral Liberalization Once Again, 1985–1990

The process of unilateral liberalization resumed on June 1985, when the uniform tariff was reduced to 20 percent. Later, in May 1988, the tariff was again reduced to 15 percent. This was the last trade policy reform conducted by the military government, since Pinochet lost the referendum or plebiscite vote of 1988. Democratic elections took place in 1989, and the administration of Patricio Aylwin came to power in March 1990. During this time, and especially between 1988 and 1990, a high degree of uncertainty reigned over the future economic policies of a democratically elected government. Consequently, several important economic policy measures were undertaken, including the establishment of an independent Central Bank, which aimed to reassure markets that a dramatic change in economic orientation could not take place after the political transition.[8]

Stage V: Trade Liberalization under Democratic Rule, 1991–?

A further reduction of the uniform tariff from 15 to 11 percent took place on June 1991, thus consolidating the trade liberalization that had survived the economic crash of 1982–1983 and the transition to democracy of 1988–1990. Since mid-1991, Chile began to implement a new trade strategy emphasizing PTAs. The most intense domestic debates have focused on Chile's negotiation of a free trade agreement with Mercosur (implemented in 1997), and its potential accession to the North American Free Trade Agreement (NAFTA). A number of Chilean analysts (especially economists based at the *Universidad Católica*) and even the National Society of Agricultural Producers (SNA, in Spanish) supported the idea of unilaterally reducing the uniform tariff. This renewed interest in unilateral liberalization was driven by three interrelated factors: First, there is a growing concern that the pursuit of PTAs will generate a significant degree of trade diversion. Second, the producers of traditional agricultural products are concerned about the real appreciation of the currency, and about the increased competition from Argentine and Brazilian exports of wheat and edible oil, since the associate membership agreement with Mercosur stipulates the elimination of the price bands in approximately eighteen years. Third, the PTAs imply that the "tariff structure has again become differentiated in the range of 0–11 percent, depending on the country of origin [of the imports]" (Corbo 1997, 76).

After a prolonged public debate during 1997 and 1998, the Chilean legislature approved a new schedule of further reductions in the uniform tariff on November 1998. Beginning on January 1999, the tariff was reduced to 10 percent and is scheduled to be reduced an additional one percentage point annually, until it reaches 6 percent in 2003. But this renewed interest in unilateral liberalization was then followed by a warming of relations with Mercosur in 1999, when the newly elected president, Ricardo Lagos, who is a personal friend of Brazil's President Fernando Henrique Cardoso, traveled to Brazil and announced that Chile should become a "full member" of the South American trade bloc. However, it remains unclear what "full membership" means, because Lagos received Brazil's blessing for maintaining its own external tariff. Moreover, at this time (August 2000) it is also unclear what additional concrete benefits Chile will get from its "full membership" status, beyond those already included in the preexisting agreement. Another factor that has tainted this latest rebirth of unilateral liberalization in Chile is the continued use of the agricultural price bands and the toughening of administered protection legislation concerning the use of antidumping and countervailing duties (Fischer and Meller 1999, 12). Concluding remarks at the end of this chapter return to the prospects for a continuation of unilateral liberalization in Chile.

10.3 The Role of Ideas

The political economy literature emphasizes the role of ideas in promoting changes in economic policies. However, the politics of changes in policy regimes are also affected by economic crises and by the sequencing of the implementation of various policies. Hence the following paragraphs review contributions to this literature, which help understand the Chilean experience.

Dynamics of Reform

Bates and Krueger (1993, 454) wrote that "[t]here is no recorded instance of the beginning of a reform program at a time when economic growth was satisfactory and when the price level and balance-of-payments situations were stable. Conditions of economic stagnation ... or continued deterioration are evidently prerequisites for reform efforts." Likewise, Rodrik (1994, 63) explains that "the reasons for the free trade bandwagon are more or less unique and derive from the intense, prolonged macroeconomic crisis that surrounded developing countries during the 1980s ... which overshadowed the distributional considerations."[9] According to this "crisis hypothesis," in the midst of an economic crisis, social scientists are called by politicians to find a way out of the crisis. Based on the Anglo-Saxon economic tradition and consistent with the views of the multilateral institutions, the incoming *technopols'* ideas become highly influential.[10] Proponents of the protectionist development strategy try to dismiss the new approach as foreign and/or imposed by the multilateral institutions; at the same time, the technopols try to persuade politicians and the public that their program is based on sound scientific principles, supported by international empirical evidence. During the implementation stage, the technopols usually find that the realities of politics conflict with the simple world of economics. Their ability to understand political trade-offs, and to design politically viable strategies that rely on adequate compensation mechanisms, may determine the fate of the reform effort.

As the crisis subsides, efforts by the opposition to stop the modernization process can be successful if the reforms have not generated sufficient improvement in economic growth, lower inflation, higher real wages, and lower unemployment. Pressures to reverse the reforms can emerge in democratic and authoritarian settings. In some cases the "populist temptation" is strong enough to bring the reforms to a standstill; in others, reformers are able to consolidate the reforms.[11] In order to regain public support, the authorities may reduce the pace of reforms, or may relax the public-sector budget constraint to face a political challenge, such as a midterm election or a plebescite in the case of an authoritarian ruler seeking to enhance its legitimacy.[12]

Speed, Sequencing, and Protective Structure

The role of "transition costs" has been at the center of discussions about the political economy of trade liberalization. Analysts have argued that a gradual liberalization is preferable to a Big Bang approach, because gradual reforms give firms time to restructure their operations, resulting in lower unemployment, fewer bankruptcies, and therefore, less political opposition to the liberalization program than under a fast liberalization. Other analysts have argued that slower reforms tend to lack credibility, thus inhibiting serious restructuring.[13] Whether trade reform generates an increase in aggregate unemployment is an empirical issue. A World Bank study on liberalization episodes in nineteen countries led by Michaely, Papageorgiou, and Choksi (1991) suggests that even in the short run, the employment costs of reform can be small; although losing industries will release workers, export-oriented sectors will tend to create employment opportunities.

The *sequencing* of components of reform programs was first addressed during the 1980s, in discussions dealing with the experiences of Argentina, Chile, and Uruguay. It is now generally agreed that the fiscal accounts have to be under control at the time that a major structural reform effort is launched, and that financial reform should only be implemented once a modern and efficient supervisory framework is in place. The debate over the order of liberalization of the trade and capital accounts revolves around the behavior of the real exchange rate. The liberalization of the capital account can bring an appreciation of the real exchange rate, which sends the "wrong" signal and frustrates the reallocation of resources demanded by the trade reform.[14] McKinnon (1982) and Edwards (1984) argue that the effects will be particularly serious if the transition period is characterized by "abnormally" high capital inflows that result in temporary real appreciations. According to this view, only after the new allocation of resources is consolidated should the capital account be liberalized.[15]

Some authors have argued recently that labor market reform, particularly the removal of distortions that discourage labor mobility, should precede the trade reform (as well as the relaxation of capital controls). Edwards (1988; 1995, 122) argues that trade liberalization under distorted labor markets can even generate overall welfare losses. Labor market reform can also have political ramifications, because owners of capital that would otherwise oppose a trade reform may support it if trade liberalization comes with more flexible labor market regulations, but unions in the formal sector will usually oppose labor market reforms that reduce their political and economic influence.[16]

A common feature of protected economies is that import tariffs and effective rates of protection are dispersed.[17] Harberger (1991) has argued that differentiated tariffs will always be subject to greater interest-group pressures than a uniform tariff structure. Firms, or business associations, will lobby for high tariffs on their goods and for exemptions for their imported inputs. Different arguments will be used, including the fact that a particular sector is "strategic," or that it creates employment, or that it allows the country to absorb advanced technology, or that it is important to safeguard a country's "national security." These pressures can be ameliorated by implementing a uniform import tariff, with no exemptions. Harberger (1991, 19) has argued that uniform tariffs "provide a natural guarantee against the huge efficiency costs ... in the exaggerated rates of effective protection that flow from grossly differentiated tariff structure. What is the key political economy tactic that the strategy involves? Putting each individual protectionist interest group *on* the defensive."[18]

Most of the issues identified by the political economy literature—speed, sequencing, unemployment, and real exchange-rate behavior, among others—played an important role in the unfolding of the Chilean trade liberalization that occurred from 1974 to the 1990s. In the end, both the policies as well as their effects were significantly different from what Chilean policy makers and other observers had anticipated.

Ideas and the Change Team

Bates and Krueger (1993, 456) argue that one explanation for the failure of interest groups to derail recent economic reforms is that "in the context of comprehensive economic policy reform, it is difficult for particular groups to calculate where their interests lie. Ideological struggles therefore can outweigh competition among organized interests as a determinant of policy change." Williamson (1994) similarly argues that the probability of success of the reform effort will be higher with "the existence in government of a team of economists (headed by a technopol ...) [and] with a common, coherent view of what needed to be done and commanding the instruments of concentrated executive authority" (26).

In Chile, the change team was composed mostly of economists trained at the University of Chicago during the 1960s and early 1970s.[19] These economists, many of whom had joined the faculty of Catholic University upon returning from Chicago, believed that excessive government intervention, high inflation, and rampant protectionism were at the heart of Chile's historical lackluster economic performance. Although they had produced some of the best applied research in Chile, for years their views were dismissed by the political establishment as mildly amusing, not worthy of being taken seriously.

A prominent group of "Chicago boys," including Sergio de Castro and Sergio de la Cuadra—both would later become finance ministers under Pinochet—had participated in the design of the economic program of conservative presidential candidate Jorge Alessandri in 1970.[20] Three years later, in the midst of the *Unidad Popular* economic crisis, this group began to prepare a new economic plan for an eventual postsocialist administration. Their work was funded by some private-sector foundations and carried out under strict confidentiality. By September 1973, the group had already produced a draft of a document titled "A Program for Economic Development," which proposed what at the time were considered radical economic reforms.[21] In the weeks preceding the coup d'état, a copy of the program had been made available by the group's coordinator to the Navy high command. In retrospect, it is not surprising that when Admiral Lorenzo Gottuzzo was named the Junta's first finance minister, he asked some of the Chicago boys to become his advisers. At the same time, the new minister of planning, a retired senior navy officer, also hired some of the Chicago boys as advisors. Others joined the staff of the Central Bank, which without international reserves faced the tremendous challenge of disciplining monetary policy and taming an inflationary process approaching the four-digit level.

Hence the Chicago boys' initial participation in the military government was restricted to advisory roles. The military, with a nationalistic doctrinal perspective, naturally gravitated toward more traditional views and contacted some respected "wise men" to offer them influential positions within the regime.[22] The views of these individuals were more moderate than those of the Chicago boys; they believed in gradual corrections of the distortions, in maintaining a prominent role for the state as a producer, and in maintaining moderate levels of protectionism. As Garretón (1986) and Valdés (1995) have pointed out, it was only slowly that the Chicago boys' views became dominant within the Pinochet administration. This increase in influence was the result of two factors: First, the original gradualist approach to solving the *Unidad Popular* imbalances, especially inflation, were not yielding the desired results. Second, in the middle of the crisis, the Chicago boys' "radical," but internally coherent policy proposals, became more attractive. In April 1975, a breakthrough took place. Jorge Cauas, a prestigious economist who had been director of the World Bank's Research Department, and who in many ways was an "honorary Chicago boy," was named minister of finance. At the same time, Sergio de Castro, the dean of the Chicago group, became minister of economics. Under their leadership the gradual approach to stabilization and reform came to an end, and what came to be known as "shock therapy" was applied. In a matter of two years inflation was reduced drastically, the economy opened to international competition, and a major privatization program was launched. During 1976–1979, after two years of recession, the Chilean economy grew at over 7 percent per annum, and the views of the "Chicago boys" seemed vindicated. The boom years lasted through 1980–1981, but in 1982–1983 the economy plummeted into a crisis as a result of the significant overvaluation of the real exchange rate, high real interest rates, and a hostile external environment—see table 10.1.

Although the original reform program of the Chicago boys was seen as revolutionary in 1973, from today's perspective it looks rather tame. The original document was divided into two parts: diagnosis and policy recommendations. The second part, which is of greater interest for our purposes, dealt with eight policy areas: decentralization, international trade, prices, monetary and fiscal policies, taxation, capital markets, social security, and income distribution. In addition, it provided some recommendations with respect to unemployment, education, foreign investment, agriculture, and industrial policies.[23]

Trade Reform: From Plan to Implementation

Trade liberalization played a prominent role in the Chicago boys' program of 1973. The document focused on two main aspects of Chile's trade-related policies: (1) the traditional "noncompetitive" level of the real exchange rate; and (2) the resource misallocation caused by the country's protective structure. Although both of these subjects had been extensively documented, the Program correctly pointed out that during the *Unidad Popular* the situation had worsened significantly.[24]

In order of appearance in the document, the program made the following specific proposals regarding trade policy:

• *Engineer a real exchange rate depreciation.* It was argued that a more competitive real exchange rate would encourage exports and help avoid the recurrent balance of payments crises that had plagued the country.

• *Implement a crawling peg exchange rate regime aimed at maintaining the real exchange rate at a competitive and depreciated level.* The document deliberately ruled out a flexible nominal exchange-rate regime, arguing that it would create unnecessary short-run volatility. It was argued that the level of international reserves should be used as an indicator of "fundamentals" behavior. A rapid loss of reserves would reflect that an "equilibrium" depreciation was warranted. Interestingly enough, an asymmetric approach toward exchange-rate adjustment was advocated. It was argued that "an 'excessive' accumulation of reserves would not necessarily be translated into a decline [appreciation] in the exchange rate; it would be preferable to reduce import tariffs" (75).

• *Reduce import tariffs.* A preannounced and programmed tariff reduction was proposed. The new protective structure would be characterized by a new 30 percent uniform import tariff. Four points were made regarding this aspect of the reform. First, the tariff reduction should be undertaken *at the same time* as the real exchange-rate depreciation. Second, uniformity was considered essential. This aspect of the reform was rationalized on the basis of the desirability of granting the same degree of effective protection to all activities.[25] Third, it was argued that, although politically infeasible, the ideal would be to completely eliminate tariffs. And fourth, the program pointed out that in order to avoid dumping problems, reference prices would be used to calculate the import tariff. These reference prices would, in turn, be calculated as a three-year moving average of the international price.

• *Eliminate all import licenses and prohibitions.* It was argued that these should be replaced by equivalent import tariffs.

• *Implement export promotion schemes* aimed at offsetting the discriminatory effect of the uniform import tariff.

The program then argued that these policies would, in principle, create two problems: First, the devaluation required to achieve a more depreciated real exchange rate would provoke inflation. Second, and more serious, it was argued that the tariff reduction would increase unemployment. According to the document, however, this problem could be ameliorated if labor mobility was enhanced.

The program also argued that Chile should negotiate relatively low tariffs in the Andean Pact; if this was not done, it would be impossible to reap the benefits of a more open external sector. It was also argued that, at least in the short to medium run, it would be necessary to maintain capital controls to avoid capital flight. Interestingly enough, there was no hint of the possibility that the country could suffer the opposite problem of being flooded with external funds. Finally, the document was not very explicit about the speed of reform. While at one point it said that a uniform 30 percent tariff should be implemented "as soon as possible," elsewhere it states that the tariff reduction should proceed in a "programmed and gradual" fashion.

Finance Minister Gotuzzo announced on January 7, 1974, that "the study of a complete reform of the tariff schedule requires the collaboration of various groups ... the Commission in charge of this project will contact the different organizations of the private sector ..." (Méndez 1979, 81). This commission was known (in Spanish) as the *Comisión de Asesoría de Política Arancelaria* (CAPA), and Dr. Sergio de la Cuadra became its first president. The commission established the basic principles that would guide the liberalization process:

• There was an explicit recognition that reductions in the degree of protection had to be compensated through real exchange-rate devaluations.

• International agreements—including those with the Latin American Integration Association (LAIA)—and the Andean Pact would be respected.

• The final tariff structure—called the "definitive tentative tariff"— would be comprised of three levels: 25 percent for primary products, 30 percent for intermediate goods, and 35 percent for capital goods. The CAPA established that this structure responded to political considerations and recognized that it was very difficult (if not plainly impossible) to justify it on economic grounds.

• The liberalization process would be carried out gradually, during a three-year period.

By late 1974, the country had eliminated import licenses, the maximum tariff stood at 140 percent, and the average tariff was 67 percent, down from over 100 percent in September 1973. However, and in spite of the decisions reached by the CAPA, the economic authorities were still uneasy about the final tariff structure.

At a conference that took place in December 1974, Sergio de la Cuadra, the chairman of the CAPA, disclosed a new proposal (de la

Cuadra 1976). This remarkable document recognizes the existence of major political constraints associated with trade liberalization. In the introduction, de la Cuadra stated that "trade liberalization has created a political problem, as long as there are people that gain and people that lose" (81, translated). The author goes on to argue that in this type of situation, members of the bureaucracy—and especially lower-level officials—become increasingly powerful when they have some discretion in the implementation of general policies. He argues that in designing the new tariff structure, the authorities "should accept the existence of pressure groups . . . [and should] provide mechanisms that prevent those pressures from becoming mechanisms that prevent the accomplishment of the authorities' goals" (82, translated). Hence, "in the absence of a uniform tariff, it should be recognized that tariffs will be manipulated for protectionist purposes. Thus, it is necessary to establish rules that regulate these manipulations" (88–89, translated). His specific proposal was a tariff structure with a 10 percent mode and a 30 percent maximum nominal tariff. Notice that this proposition is significantly closer to free trade than either what the Chicago boys had originally envisaged in the program, or what the CAPA had decided to do only a few months earlier. De la Cuadra then argued that this more daring tariff proposal should be compensated with a more depreciated real exchange rate. He went so far as to say that "to the extent that it is not possible to devalue the currency, the magnitude of tariff reduction would have to be smaller" (92, translated). With regard to the Andean Pact, de la Cuadra argued that a fait accompli strategy would be beneficial; if the new tariff structure were to be implemented rapidly, Chile could then negotiate with the other members of the pact from a position of strength.

In discussing the design of the Chilean tariff structure, de la Cuadra (1976) barely touches on the employment costs of the transition. This reflects a combination of beliefs and political realities. According to the program, the Chicago boys believed that in the context of a flexible labor market, the unemployment costs of a major trade reform would be rather small. One of the early policies of the military regime had been to establish a de facto flexible labor market: Union activities had been banned, minimum wages had declined steeply, and other labor legislation had been relaxed (see section 10.4 for details). However, opponents of the reforms argued throughout the process that the main effects of this "radical" program were to destroy Chile's industrial base and to generate unemployment. Naturally, the fact that the rate of unemployment had indeed increased significantly made their argument appealing.[26]

Between 1975 and mid-1977, eight rounds of tariff reductions took place, and in August of that year the average tariff stood at 19.8 percent. The maximum tariff had reached the 30 percent target, and the mode was 20 percent. During this process the authorities faced a number of unexpected developments. First, the extent of political opposition was smaller than anticipated, even when the nature of the political regime was taken into account. This was largely the result of the "compensation mechanisms" approach discussed in greater detail in what follows. Second, the reform seemed to be bearing fruit faster than anticipated. Exports were growing rapidly and, perhaps more importantly, they were becoming increasingly diversified (see figure 10.1). And third, negotiations with the Andean Pact partners were proving tougher than anticipated. This was particularly the case with respect to the pact's direct foreign investment provisions—the *Acuerdo de Cartagena* (in)famous article 24—that greatly restricted the role of foreign ownership in the member countries.

As early as June 1976, then Economics Minister Sergio de Castro expressed Chile's disagreement with the Pact's Article 24. In a speech in Cartagena, Colombia, he said: "We are absolutely sure that in order to attract the investment we require, it is necessary to modify Article 24 and to make it suitably flexible" (Méndez 1979, 206). He added that the only responses Chile had received from its partners were "expressions of goodwill which have never gone any further. Only the firm attitude of the Chilean government has finally achieved the initiation of serious discussions on the modification of Article 24" (Méndez 1979, 208). But he was wrong. Time passed and no progress was made on this issue. As a result, it became increasingly clear to the authorities that the pact was a serious obstacle for achieving the military government's goals of integrating the Chilean economy into the rest of the world. In mid-1977, the government decided that the costs of remaining in the pact greatly outweighed the benefits, and Chile announced its withdrawal. Shortly after, Minister de Castro, by then holding the finance portfolio, announced that the government's final goal was to achieve a uniform 10 percent tariff by mid-1979. He assured the population, however, that just as it had been done all along, those affected by these measures would

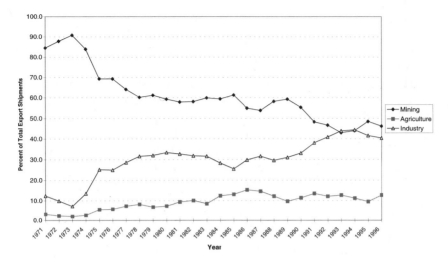

Figure 10.1
Chile's export structure, 1971–1996

be compensated by real exchange rate depreciations. Specifically, he said:

[T]he lower are tariffs the higher should exchange rates be ... [A]s a compensation for the tariff reduction corresponding to the current month, we have decided to devalue by 4.3 percent ... For the following months the exchange rate adjustment will correspond to inflation in the preceding months, plus an additional amount to compensate for the tariff reduction. (*Boletín Mensual, Banco Central de Chile*, December 1977, 1960–1961)

Dissenting Views in a Restricted Market for Ideas

Although traditional democratic channels to express dissenting views had been eliminated after the coup, those intellectually opposed to the market-oriented reforms expressed their views in a variety of ways. In particular, prominent economists associated with the opposition think tank CIEPLAN, launched a series of attacks against the program.[27] The liberalization process was criticized on three accounts: its excessive reliance on free prices and market forces; the reduced role of the government in economic matters; and the opening of international trade and financial transactions to foreign competition. These criticisms were channeled through articles in weekly magazines, and in more specialized journals. The diffusion of these ideas to a broader public was severely restricted, however. In fact, for a while the military authorities did not allow the CIEPLAN group to release its collection of articles in the form of a book amid the 1982 economic crisis.[28]

The opening of the economy—including its speed and intensity— was the subject of some of the most severe criticisms. For example, in October 1976, Ffrench-Davis argued that import tariffs of the order of 65 percent were "decisively moderate for countries of our degree of development." In July 1977, Ffrench-Davis wrote in the weekly *Hoy* that "a mistaken approach that moves the country excessively towards free trade, means closing some lines of production ..." And in February 1978, he said that "the saddest aspect of trade liberalization is that it has been carried out at great speed ...," and he argued that the government should "undo the mistakes made ... [F]irst, undo immediately part of the trade liberalization ... [and return] to the Andean Pact" (Arellano et al. 1982, 349, 354).

During the late 1970s, much of the criticism of the liberalization program was centered on the potential effect of trade reform on employment and social conditions. In July 1978, Foxley wrote in the weekly *Hoy* that "the rapid reduction of import tariffs ... [is one] of the factors that explain the high rate of unemployment" (Arellano et al. 1982, 383). In December 1976, Meller argued that a rapid liberalization of trade could be extremely costly in terms of increased unemployment. He argued that as a result of the government reforms, including the deep liberalization of foreign trade, "[the] unemployment rate could easily increase to 23% of the labor force" (Arellano et al. 1982, 387–389). The critics argued that Chile should abandon the experiment and move rapidly toward a program where the state would play a fundamental role in supporting key industries through higher tariffs and other forms of subsidies. For instance, in 1983, Foxley argued that "the State should articulate a 'vision' about the country's productive future ... The idea is to pick and develop 'winners' ... [To this effect] the State would use every instrument available..., including special credit lines, subsidies, import tariffs and tax exemptions."[29]

Starting in 1985, the Chilean economy began to recover vigorously; by 1989, it had accumulated a very strong record of growth, which surprised most analysts, including the domestic critics. As the presidential elections of 1989 approached, it had become clear that criticism of a market-based development path had subsided. In fact, the three presidential candidates presented remarkably similar economic proposals that shared many important elements. What was particularly important was that (future president) Patricio Aylwin's program—drafted mostly by the CIEPLAN group—proposed to continue with the most important market-oriented policies. The program argued for "low import tariffs," and for ensuring that the economy had "positive real interest rates that maintain some relation with productivity."[30] By the early 1990, it was clear that the incoming government was not going to fiddle with the main elements of the market reforms. If anything, the new authorities were ready to move even further in some areas, such as a further reduction of the import tariff.[31] Coming from those that had relentlessly criticized the reforms, this action represented an important victory for free trade ideas.

The Aylwin government's decision to maintain the main aspects of the market reforms was clearly stated by Minister of Finance Alejandro Foxley, who in a 1990 interview granted to *Newsweek International* pointed out that "preserving the former government achievements means maintaining an open economy fully integrated into world markets, dynamic growth in exports, with a private sector fully committed to the task of [economic] development ..."[32] Although once in power the leaders of the new democratic government supported some of the most fundamental market reforms of the 1970s and 1980s, they still had some important disagreements with the former rulers regarding the role of social and redistributive policies. In that regard Foxley was equally clear in the 1990 interview: "Remedying the former government shortcomings means recapturing the balance between economic growth and the deteriorated conditions of the middle and, above all, the lower classes." What is particularly important, however, is that in seeking funding for new social programs the new Chilean government strongly and decisively rejected traditional formulas based on inflationary finance. On the contrary, the new administration made it clear from day one that the only way to increase social spending without generating unsustainable macroeconomic pressures was to find additional government revenues. Furthermore, the new government continued the policy of targeting social programs for the poor, and avoiding blanket subsidies that historically benefited the middle and upper classes. In short, the populist policies of yesteryear had no role in the new Chilean government.

An important political decision made by the new government was to address two critical economic reforms during its first year: a tax package aimed at funding the new social programs, and a reform of the labor law that had been criticized by union leaders and political commentators. Government officials were careful to explain that these two pieces of legislation constituted the only important modifications to the economic model established by Pinochet. In this way, and especially by tackling these issues early, the government sought to minimize possible negative effects on private investment associated with policy uncertainty (Boeninger 1992).

10.4 Compensation Mechanisms and the Political Economy of Trade Reform

Distributive Conflicts and Interest Groups

Analyses of the politics of trade liberalization usually focus on conflicts among interest groups aiming to raise their shares of the national income. A common framework is based on some variant of neoclassical trade theory, including specific-factors models, and considers a finite number of interest groups; some will be hurt by the reform and will oppose it, while those that benefit will support it. Rodrik (1994, 68) considers three groups: (1) import substituting industrialists; (2) holders of import licenses; and (3) users of imports, including producers that rely on imported inputs. Depending on the underlying model of an economy, we could add any number of groups with special characteristics, including (4) agricultural producers, who often argue that food self-sufficiency is a matter of national security; (5) organized labor, especially those employed in import-competing industries; and (6) labor in the informal sector, which tends to be dispersed and disorganized. In this setup, the political support for the reform effort will be proportional to the difference between redistributed income and net efficiency gains—what Rodrik (1994, 67) calls the "political cost-benefit ratio."[33]

Since reforms are seldom restricted to one area of economic policy, a broader set of policies and interest groups should be considered.[34] Exporters are usually among the early supporters of reform-oriented governments; they benefit directly from the reduction of import tariffs affecting their inputs of production, and indirectly from the exchange-rate depreciation that often takes place during the early stages of a liberalization program. Producers of import-competing goods usually oppose trade reforms but are often at least partially compensated by the real depreciation of the currency. If the reform process is seen as a package, some import-competing sectors may support trade liberalization if they expect to benefit from labor market reforms, privatizations, or financial liberalization, for example. Unions representing the employees of state-owned enterprises are almost always among the opponents of economic reforms, but reformers often try to win them over by offering them some participation in the newly privatized firms. Moreover, political compensation schemes can also be devised to tame opposition to reforms, such as offering political appointments to influential representatives of a particular interest group. Table 10.5 provides a description of commonly used compensation schemes.

A relevant question for the Chilean case concerns the relationship between an authoritarian political regime and constraints faced by reformers. The fact that an authoritarian government does not face electoral challenges does not mean that reformers have a free hand inside a dictatorship; within a dictatorial regime are factions that represent interest groups. Reformers also have to convince military strongmen that their policies are appropriate, and the market-oriented perspective often clashes with the strongly nationalistic, state-centered views of the military.[35] Dictators also demand results —although it may give reformers more time to obtain them—and seek to maintain some degree of legitimacy, while political repression tends to be targeted to specific groups.[36] Limited freedom of expression under authoritarian regimes may also limit the scope of the market of ideas. As we argued in section 10.3, while some limitations were imposed on the exposition of antireform ideas, especially in the immediate aftermath of the breakdown of democracy in Chile, criticisms were, indeed, published by the media during the period of reform.

From a political perspective, it is important to consider the Chilean reforms as a package. Of course, this does not mean that all reforms were designed to be undertaken simultaneously, or that all were considered equally important by their supporters. What it does mean is that interest groups had to take a position with respect to the complete package, rather than with respect to some of its components. Table 10.6 provides a taxonomy of interest groups in Chile and the expected effects of the reforms on these groups. Our contention is

Table 10.5
The political economy of reform and compensation mechanisms

Mechanisms	Main features and some examples
A. Direct compensation	*Groups directly affected by the reform policy are compensated through the transfer of cash or financial securities.* In this way the authorities expect to see a reduction in the extent of opposition from that group to that particular reform. Examples of this type of compensation mechanisms include the distribution of shares of privatized firms to workers in that particular firm, and adjustment assistance programs to workers who lost their jobs as a consequence of trade liberalization. The increase in take-home pay following a social security reform is another good example of this type of direct compensation scheme.
B. Indirect compensation	This mechanism implies *compensating groups affected by a particular reform through the adjustment of a different policy that indirectly raises their revenues or reduces their costs of production.* In some cases this type of indirect compensation is "automatic" and is the result of normal economic forces at work. In others it is the result of specific policy measures. One of the most important indirect compensation mechanisms is the real exchange rate (RER). By devaluing the real exchange rate, import-substituting sectors are partially compensated, while exporters experience an additional boon. Providing tax exemptions to sectors affected by deregulation constitutes another common form of indirect compensation.
C. Cross compensation	*This mechanism entails transferring resources—either directly or indirectly—to groups not directly affected by the reform,* in order to obtain their political support. Transferring shares of privatized firms to the population at large— as in Bolivia's capitalization program—is a good illustration of this mechanism at work.
D. Exclusionary compensation (i.e., exemptions)	*Entails excluding certain powerful groups from the effects of a reform, or implementing policies that in effect exempt some sectors from the reform in order to diffuse their political opposition.* Allowing these groups to maintain certain privileges suggests that they will not become active antagonists. The special treatment given to the Chilean armed forces regarding that country's social security reform is a classic example of this type of compensation mechanism.
E. Political compensation	*This mechanism encompasses political "carrots and sticks."* For example, the appointment of influential representatives of certain groups to high-level government jobs, which often sends a (symbolic) signal to interest groups that their concerns will be addressed. On the negative side, there are politically exclusionary practices, such as political repression and persecution, which may benefit some groups at the expense of the victims.

Table 10.6
Expected winners (W) and losers (L) of economic reforms in Chile

Measure	Import-compet-ing	Ex-porters	Nontrad-ables	Grupos (con-glom-erates)	Formal-orga-nized labor	Infor-mal labor
Trade lib.	L	W	W	W	L	W
Export promotion		W		W		
Depreciation	W	W	L	W		
Bank privatization				W		
Financial dereg.	L	W	W	W		
Pension reform				W	W	L
Capital account lib.	W	W	W	W		
Privatization of real-sector firms	W	W	W	W	L	
Labor reforms	W	W	W	W	L	W

Source: Authors.

that the political economy of Chile's trade liberalization reflected the use of a variety of compensation schemes, some of which were embodied in the components of the reform package itself. Table 10.7 shows the various compensation mechanisms that were used by the Chilean authorities through the five stages of the liberalization process; and the five stages of the process can be discerned by the types of mechanisms that were used in each phase. The rest of this section analyzes the affected interest groups, and the compensation schemes that were implemented during Chile's experiment with unilateral liberalization.

A Taxonomy of Chilean Interest Groups[37]

In order to organize the political analysis of Chile's reforms, we have divided the actors into six groups—see table 10.6. The first column lists the policy measures that were part of the reforms, while the following six columns show how each type of interest group was *expected* to be affected by each policy measure. The first group is composed of owners of capital or land in import-competing industries, which include manufacturers and producers of traditional agricultural products, such as wheat, sugar, and oilseeds. The second group is composed of export-oriented producers, including mining-related enterprises and nontraditional exporters. The third group is

Table 10.7
Compensation mechanisms and the stages of liberalization in Chile, 1974–2000

Mechanism	I 1974–1978	II 1978–1982	III 1983–1985	IV 1985–1990	V 1991–?
A. Direct					
1. Employment prog.	×	×	×		
2. Duty drawbacks	×	×	×	×	×
B. Indirect					
1. RER	×		×	×	×
2. Financial reforms	?				
3. Labor reforms	×	?			
C. Cross					
1. Privatization	×	×			
2. Pension reform		×			
3. Capital account lib.		×			
D. Exclusionary					
1. Surcharges			×		×
2. Price interventions			×		×
3. Reversals			×		
E. Political					
1. Appointments	×		×		
2. Repression	×	×	×	×	
3. Democracy					×

Source: Authors. ? = ambiguous effects.

the nontradable industries, such as the construction and transport sectors. The fourth group is composed of *grupos*, or financial conglomerates, which controlled a large share of the banking sector and significant portions of export industries. The fifth and sixth groups are the formal, unionized workers and workers employed in the informal sector.

Of the import-competing groups, manufacturers have been organized under the umbrella of the *Sociedad de Fomento Fabril* (SFF) since 1883. Historically, the SFF had been at the center of the push to raise tariffs on imports of manufactures since 1897, when Law 980 was passed, raising import tariffs on textiles and other manufactures (Douglas, Butelmann, and Videla 1980, 150). In the early 1970s the SFF represented producers of chemical products, steel, textiles, and other manufacturers that had benefited from protectionist policies. While most of its members come from large and medium firms, it has also represented a number of small manufacturers. The traditional agriculturalists have been represented by the *Sociedad Nacional de Agricultura* (SNA) since 1838. However, this organization has a mixed membership that also includes the large agricultural producers of nontraditional agricultural products, such as fruits. In addition, both the SNA and the SFF belonged to a more general umbrella association of large and medium enterprises called the *Confederación de la Producción y el Comercio* (COPROCO). Finally, the *Confederación de Productores Agrícolas* (CPA) was founded in 1973, by the fusion of two associations of small and medium agricultural producers, which included producers of wheat and other traditional agricultural products.

In any case, the import-competing sectors were expected to lose from the reduction of tariffs affecting their products, but were expected to gain from the currency devaluation that would raise the prices of their tradable goods and from the labor market reforms that were expected to reduce their costs of production. In addition, owners of capital in these sectors could also benefit from the privatization of real-sector firms and from the capital account liberalization that would reduce the costs of foreign finance. In contrast, the deregulation of domestic interest rates was expected to hurt those import-competing sectors that had benefited from the subsidized credit that was available to them during the period of import substitution.

The producers of mining goods were represented by the *Sociedad Nacional de Minería*, while the exporters of nontraditional goods did not have a specific association at the outset of the reforms but were progressively included in the umbrella of the COPROCO and the general business association *Cámara Central de Comercio*, which had been founded in 1858, and traditionally represented large export firms, including some of the most important wineries. As shown in table 10.6, these export industries were expected to gain from trade liberalization, export promotion policies, exchange-rate depreciation, and even from the interest-rate deregulation since it was expected that borrowing costs (interest rates) would fall for exporters who had not benefited from the credit controls of the protectionist period.

The nontradable sectors were represented by business organizations such as the *Cámara Chilena de la Construcción*, which was founded in 1951, and several organizations affiliated with the *Consejo de la Producción, el Transporte y el Comercio*, most of which were founded between 1918 and 1973. In fact, many of its members had been key players in raising discontent with the *Unidad Popular* government during 1970–1973, for they had participated in several transport stoppages that tended to temporarily paralyze the domestic economy during this period.[38] The construction and transport sectors were expected to benefit from trade liberalization due to the lower prices of imported inputs of production, from labor market reforms, from the privatization of public firms, from the liberalization of the capital account, and perhaps from the liberalization of interest rates. However, the currency devaluation was expected to reduce the relative price of nontradable goods.

The formation of large conglomerates—the so-called grupos—was a by-product of the financial reforms initiated in 1974 and especially of the privatization of the banks in 1975. By the early 1980s, these conglomerates owned a large share of Chile's financial system, and their lending activities were often concentrated in lending to related firms. Table 10.8 shows estimates of the extent of connected lending by several financial institutions and their share of the financial system's assets. The grupos also benefited from the liberalization of the capital account, which raised the volume of funds intermediated by their banks, and from the pension reform that increased the size of the private financial market. Since the grupos owned export-oriented firms, they also benefited from the policies that strengthened the export sectors.[39]

On the eve of the military takeover in 1973, the Chilean labor movement was represented through legal and "illegal" labor unions. The legal unions were recognized by the Labor Ministry, and they encompassed industrial and agricultural unions. The former participated mostly in decentralized (firm-level) collective bargaining, while the latter were represented at the industry level. Moreover, the *Central Unica de Trabajadores* (CUT) was the national labor federation that had tight links to left-wing political parties. Nonetheless, the CUT played only a leadership role in the process of collective bargaining and was seldom directly involved in collective bargaining (Barrera and Valenzuela 1986, 233). The illegal unions were not officially recognized by the state, but their existence was tolerated by most democratically elected governments. These unions, which often called themselves "councils" or "associations," represented most public employees, including those working in public enterprises. The

Table 10.8
Economic conglomerates and the Chilean financial system in the early 1980s

Group and bank	As % of the system in Dec. 1982			Connected lending as % of institution's total lending	
	Capital and reserves	Loans	External credits	June 1982	April 1983
BHC					
BHC[a]	2.1	3.3	3.6	28.2	27.4[c]
Chile[b]	12.5	20.0	28.1	16.1	17.8
Morgan-Finansa	1.0	1.6	1.4	7.2	7.1
Cruzat-Larrain					
Santiago[b]	11.8	11.8	12.1	44.1	47.8
BHIF	1.8	3.3	1.9	17.1	19.8
Colocadora[b]	1.4	2.0	1.5	23.4	24.2
Edwards					
de A. Edwards	2.0	3.1	3.3	15.9	14.4
Errázuriz					
Nacional	1.9	1.9	1.5	29.1	27.5
Luksic					
Sudamericano	3.1	4.6	6.4	13.0	18.1
O'Higgins	2.7	2.8	3.3	8.0	12.1
Matte					
BICE	1.0	1.2	1.4	4.0	4.2
Yarur					
Crédito e inversiones	3.8	5.1	4.9	8.6	12.1
Other Banks					
Concepción[b]	3.5	4.1	4.4	17.0	12.0
Internacional	1.2	1.1	0.6	20.1	20.5
Trabajo	2.3	2.9	2.9	1.6	3.3
Osorno	2.3	2.1	1.0	3.4	9.4
BUF[a]	1.3	2.1	1.9	5.1	7.6[c]

Source: Foxley (1986, table I.21), based on data from the *Superintendencia de Bancos e Instituciones Financieras*.
[a] Closed for bankruptcy in January 1983.
[b] "Intervened" in January 1983.
[c] December 1982.

legal union membership was expected to lose from labor market reforms that reduced the political influence of the CUT, while the illegal unions were clear losers of the privatization program. In contrast, laborers employed in the informal economy were expected to gain from cheaper imports resulting from trade liberalization, but would lose from the pension reform that eliminated their public pensions.[40]

The labor market policies implemented during the period of trade liberalization will be discussed in what follows. At this point, it should be acknowledged that the weakening of the labor movement during the military regime was dramatic. For example, union membership declined drastically from about 65 percent of total wage earners in 1973 to less than 20 percent on average for the 1980s (Cortázar 1997, 240). In spite of the military regime's policy of political repression targeting left-wing labor leaders, beginning in 1974, Pinochet invited center-right labor leaders to highly publicized "informational" meetings, thus showing the general's concern about not appearing to be a labor antagonist. In July 1974, Pinochet appointed Air Force General Nicanor Diaz to the Labor Ministry; his primary mission was to create an institutional framework for labor participation in setting wage policies—namely, "tripartite committees" encompassing government, management, and labor leaders. (Coincidentally, the International Labor Organization began an inquiry into the violation of union rights precisely on July 1974.) This institutional arrangement failed to respond to labor's rank and file, who were experiencing a rapid deterioration of the purchasing power of their wages. Between December 1975 and 1978, labor discontent with the Chicago boys' program was articulated through the declarations of the so-called Group of 10 labor leaders, and several new labor organizations were formed during 1977–1979 that were not shy in expressing their opinions (see Barrera and Valenzuela 1986). Later, during the crisis of 1983–1984, labor unions took to the streets in mass protests and later played an important role in supporting the coalition that triumphed in the 1988 plebiscite. After the transition to democratic rule in 1990, the incoming administration negotiated with right-wing opposition in the Senate to enact legislation that enhanced the right to unionize for public and temporary agricultural workers, and it abolished restrictions forbidding unions from different firms to participate in firm-level collective bargaining (Cortázar 1997, 250).

In sum, the set of affected interest groups and their representative organizations is quite extensive, reflecting a long history of collective action by the various groups. In what follows, we take a closer look at the compensations mechanisms that were used to reduce the opposition and raise support for the package of reforms, which included trade liberalization.

Compensation Mechanisms during the First Stage of Reforms

As discussed earlier, the first stage of the liberalization process led to the drastic reduction of import tariffs and the elimination of nontariff barriers (recall tables 10.2 and 10.3). Several mechanisms to compensate (potential) opponents of the trade liberalization reform were used during this phase. In terms of direct compensation mechanisms, the authorities offered several export promotion policies: a rebate of the value-added tax introduced in 1975; a rebate on import duties paid on inputs to be reexported, which was limited to direct importers of inputs; and a subsidy offered to fishing and tree planting for lumber exports (de la Cuadra and Hachette 1991, 226).[41] As mentioned earlier, throughout the reform the authorities were concerned with unemployment. For this reason, in 1975, an emergency program—the Minimum Employment Program (MEP)—was launched, aiming to provide a subsistence wage to the unemployed in exchange for limited work. Table 10.9 shows the evolution of unemployment, wages, and the number of participants in the MEP.

The depreciation of the real exchange rate was perhaps the most important (indirect) compensation mechanism used throughout this period. A weak (real) value of the peso, enticed exporters—as well as those that planned to move into the export sector—to support the program and while import-substituting sectors to reduce their opposition. Figure 10.2 shows the evolution the dollar-based real exchange rate and the modal and maximum import tariff rates. The effects of the maxinominal devaluation of October 1973 began to be reversed in mid-1976, but the real exchange rate resumed its downward trend in mid-1977. This combination of trade liberalization, export subsidies, and exchange-rate depreciation encouraged a frantic growth of nontraditional exports during 1974–1979. Figure 10.1 shows the shares of total export shipments of three product categories: mining, agriculture, and industry. The latter includes nontraditional exports such as salmon, trout, wines, lumber, fishmeal, and

Table 10.9
Unemployment and wages in Chile, 1970–1983

	(1)	(2)	(3)	(4)	(5)	(6)
Year	Labor force (1000s)	U (1000s)	Open U rate (%)	MEP (1000s)	MEP (% of labor force)	Real wages (1970 = 100)
1970	2,923.2	167.1	5.7			100.0
1971	2,968.8	112.8	3.8			125.4
1972	3,000.8	93.0	3.1			125.4
1973	3,037.0	145.8	4.8			86.0
1974	3,066.8	282.1	9.2			90.2
1975	3,152.9	425.6	13.5	41.7	1.3	88.7
1976	3,216.4	511.4	15.9	168.8	5.2	86.3
1977	3,259.7	462.9	14.2	187.1	5.7	96.6
1978	3,370.1	478.6	14.2	148.0	4.4	97.5
1979	3,480.7	480.3	13.8	128.4	3.7	98.7
1980	3,539.8	417.7	11.9	187.9	5.3	108.3
1981	3,669.3	400.0	10.9	171.2	4.7	115.7
1982	3,729.7	760.9	20.4	190.2	5.1	112.2
1983	3,797.5	706.3	18.6	391.6	10.3	n.a.

Sources: The labor force and unemployment figures (columns 1, 2, and 3 refer to June of each year) were estimated by Castañeda (1983). Column 4 is based on Banco Central (1983, 212–13). Column 5 corresponds to the quotient of column 4 divided by column 1. Column 6 was constructed using National Accounts data. See A. Edwards (1984, 85) for further details.

Notes: U means unemployment. The Minimum Employment Program (MEP) was a temporary palliative system created by the government in 1975 to alleviate the unemployment problem.

frozen fruits. It is remarkable that the share of those exports rose rapidly between 1974 and 1979, but this upward trend did not resume until the 1990s.

The liberalization of the financial sector—which included the privatization of banks and a decree passed on December 1974 prohibiting state ownership of commercial banks, and which freed interest rates (Ffrench-Davis and Sáez 1995, 73)—was another important component of the reform package. It was expected that deepening the financial sector would give more firms access to credit at relatively low rates. In a way, this (potential) availability of credit at reasonable rates was seen as a key component of the compensation package. Yet, as shown in figure 10.3, real lending rates (for short-term, 30-to 89-day credit issued by banks) were excessively high,

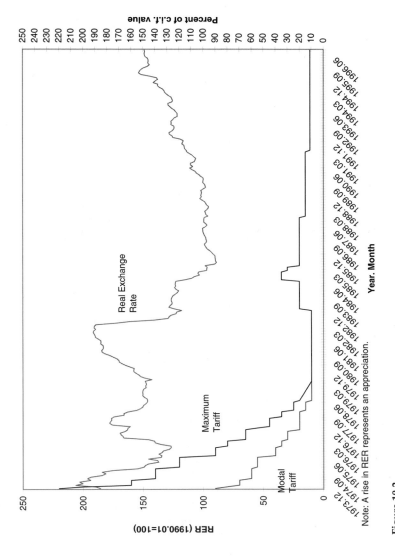

Figure 10.2
Tariff reductions and the real exchange rate, 1973–1996

ranging from 121 percent in 1975 to 35.1 percent in 1978. Hence the potential compensation to interest groups that had not benefited from subsidized credit during the protectionist period, which could have emanated from these financial reforms, was ineffective in terms of providing greater access to inexpensive credit for adjusting firms.[42]

Other forms of indirect compensations that benefited the private sector were the repression of labor unions that had aligned themselves with the Allende government, and several other measures implemented to reduce the constraints on firing and hiring workers and to promote decentralized collective bargaining. On September 18, 1973, the authorities banned the presentation of union demands (*pliegos de peticiones*) and suspended the right of union leaders to spend working time dealing with union affairs. Later that year, other decrees were issued that had the following consequences: (a) made the firing of workers easier, including the firing of workers leading "illegal" strikes; (b) suspended existing agreements regarding salaries, benefits, and other remunerations; (c) suspended automatic adjustments of pensions to compensate for inflation; and (d) suspended all organizational union activities (Barrera and Valenzuela 1986, 235–236).

A less well known fact is that the military dictatorship also offered exclusionary compensation mechanisms, even during this first stage of the liberalization process. For instance, subsidized credit to agricultural producers and a price stabilization fund for milk products, meat, wool, and even poultry, beans, onions, and potatoes were not eliminated until 1977 (de la Cuadra and Hachette 1991, 265). Moreover, in response to farm lobbies, a price band mechanism for wheat, sugarbeet, and oilseed prices was made operational in 1978, which was subsequently dismantled in mid-1979 under pressure "from the same farmer's organizations which foresaw that free trade prices would be above the ceiling price" (Quiroz and Valdés 1993, 3).[43]

Finally, it is noteworthy that also in response to the farm lobbies, the authorities offered political appointments to members of the SNA. In an interview published in July 1976, the president of the SNA, Alfonso Márquez de la Plata, said, "We are absolutely in agreement with the current economic policies and we believe that there is no alternative. But we feel that certain measures should be adopted to make this program viable ..." (qtd. in Campero 1984, 147, translated). As a result of the SNA's discontent, the cabinet was reshuffled, and a new minister and vice minister of agriculture were appointed. The vice minister position was given to a former officer (*Secretario*) of the SNA, Mr. Sergio Romero (Campero 1984, 147). Later in October 1976, the SNA's Márquez de Plata inaugurated a conference by stating, "Basic staples should be produced domestically, even at higher prices than in the international market, since they have a strategic character and they must be promoted . . ." (Campero 1984, 148, translated). The influence of the SNA would be felt during later stages of the liberalization process.

Another key political compensation mechanism was linked to the military's justification for displacing the Allende government. Namely, in spite of the initial uncertainty and an economic recession in 1974–1975, entrepreneurs that had traditionally benefited from protectionism were willing to support the economic program of the dictatorship for the sake of "saving the country" from communism. For instance, in December 1973, Mr. Orlando Sáenz, president of the SFF, wrote, "We only know the general contours of the government's economic policy . . . A model of development cannot be alienated from the idiosyncrasies of the population, nor can it go against the physical and historical continuities . . . Economic successes are merely vehicles for achieving political and social goals, but cannot become ends in themselves, this is what distinguishes a policy-maker [*Estadista*] from the technocrat: the former cannot be subjugated by the latter" (Campero 1984, 105, translated). Yet three months later, in March 1974, Sáenz said, "The process is more revolutionary than reconstructive . . . The military junta proposes to act drastically to deal with the great problems of the country . . . The reconstruction will produce a new structure of the State, a new concept of development; different productive relations that lead us to an era of prosperity" (Campero 1984, 106–107, translated). Hence it is clear that the manufacturing sector was willing to accept the challenge of economic reform because the new government had set back the socialist program of the early 1970s.

The Failure of Indirect Compensation Schemes during the Second Stage

Table 10.8 also reveals that during the second stage there was an apparent shift in the use of compensation schemes, from a reliance on indirect measures to cross-compensation schemes. In particular,

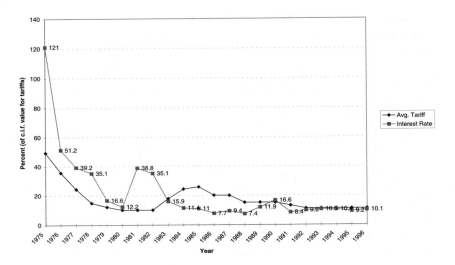

Figure 10.3
Average tariffs and real estate rates, 1975–1996

as we have already discussed, the real exchange rate began to appreciate rapidly in 1979, partly as a consequence of the change in
nominal exchange-rate policies, and partially as a result of increasingly large capital inflows. Furthermore, real interest rates began to
rise again in 1980 (see figure 10.3). Both of these developments hurt
exporters—the early supporters of the reforms. At the same time,
however, the implementation of broader aspects of the reforms,
including the labor law and massive privatization, benefited the
conglomerates, which became the more staunch supporters of the
program.

The story of labor market reforms is particularly interesting. A
new labor code was introduced in 1979, under the guidance of Labor
Minister José Piñera, a Harvard-trained economist. The code established a new collective bargaining mechanism, whereby union affiliation within a firm became voluntary, and all negotiations were to
be conducted at the firm level, thus eliminating industry-wide collective bargaining (see Edwards and Edwards 1991, 104–105, for
details). However, "in an apparent contradiction ... the authorities
made no change in the minimum wage regulation and introduced
wage indexation, both policy decisions that are only explicable in
terms of political considerations" (Riveros 1986, 24). Another observer noted, "This law, written when the Chilean economy was at

the height of its late-1970s boom, mandated essentially that every new labor contract must provide *at a minimum* a full cost-of-living adjustment from the date of the previous contract. For practical purposes, it made reduction in real wages *illegal* in any covered activity" (Harberger 1983, 6). With the nominal exchange rate pegged to the dollar at thirty-nine pesos beginning in June 1979, the wage indexation mechanism was probably another important determinant of the real exchange-rate appreciation that afflicted the Chilean economy during this phase of the liberalization process.

The process of privatization of state-owned enterprises that was initiated in 1974 proceeded throughout this period. One effect of the process was the creation and consolidation of the grupos. By 1979, the ten largest grupos controlled 135 of the 250 largest private corporations, and they controlled approximately 70 percent of all corporations traded in the stock market (Dahse 1979). During the second stage of the trade opening, the grupos benefited from several other measures. For example, the partial elimination of capital controls led to a massive inflow of foreign capital intermediated by the grupos banks and other financial intermediaries, but worsening the real appreciation of the exchange rate.[44] Another example of a cross-compensation scheme that benefited the financial conglomerates is the social security reform of 1981, which led to the establishment of privately managed pension funds, and the grupos invested heavily in these funds. Despite the fact that the grupos were "compensated" (by the partial liberalization of the capital account and the privatization of the pension system, both entailing a form of cross-compensation) as the real exchange rate continued to appreciate during this period, the profitability of industries in the tradables sector tended to deteriorate, and eventually many banks had to be bailed out on January 13, 1983.

From Backtracking to Consolidation, 1983–1991

From a political economy perspective, one of the most apparent effects of the economic recession experienced in 1983–1985 was the shift to exclusionary compensation mechanisms (see table 10.8). It has already been mentioned that the uniform tariff was raised several times during this stage, reaching 35 percent in September 1984. However, the reversal was not limited to the uniform tariff. As a matter of fact, table 10.10 lists the numerous surcharges that were

Table 10.10
Surcharges applied to imports, 1982–1986

Product	Initial surcharge (%)	Surcharge as of Sept. 1984 (%)	Surcharge as of Dec. 1986 (%)	Date of enforcement
1. Preserved fish	16	15	—	12 Nov. 82
2. Matches	12	15	5	12 Nov. 82
3. Condensed milk	18	10	—	4 Nov. 82
4. Leather footwear	18	15	—	12 Nov. 82
5. Wool fabrics	10	15	9	12 Nov. 82
6. Cement	21	15	—	12 Nov. 82
7. Fabric for bags	16	15	6	12 Nov. 82
8. Cotton yarn	15	15	—	12 Nov. 82
9. Aluminum	20	15	—	12 Nov. 82
10. Powdered milk	28	15	15	12 Nov. 82
11. Butter	16	15	15	12 Nov. 82
12. Cheese	12	15	15	12 Nov. 82
13. Water meters	22	15	—	12 Nov. 82
14. Acrylic yarn	15	15	—	12 Nov. 82
15. Cotton fabrics	20	15	6	12 Nov. 82
16. Continuous filament yarn	15	15	—	8 Jan. 83
17. Clothing	15	15	5	8 Jan. 83
18. Toys	4	15	—	15 Mar. 83
19. Cookies	10	15	—	15 Mar. 83
20. Propylene bags	23	15	—	15 Apr. 83
21. Beverage bottles	6	15	—	28 Apr. 83
22. Flat glass	7	15	10	28 Apr. 83
23. Corduroy fabrics	15	15	8	20 Jul. 83
24. Tires	15	15	8	28 Sep. 83
25. Wheat flour	15	15	—	28 Sep. 83
26. Towels	15	15	5	5 Nov. 83
27. Candies	15	15	—	9 Dec. 83
28. Rugs and carpets	15	15	5	9 Dec. 83
29. Bed sheets	15	15	7	9 Dec. 83
30. Steel cables	15	15	—	9 Dec. 83
31. Refrigerators	15	15	—	9 Apr. 84
32. Floor polishers	15	15	—	9 Apr. 84
33. Blenders	15	15	—	9 Apr. 84
34. Metal gabions	15	15	0	3 Aug. 84
35. Single-phase electric meters	—	—	6	28 Jun. 86
36. Textile appliances	—	—	5	28 Jun. 86

Source: de la Cuadra and Hachette (1991, 269), based on data from the Central Bank of Chile.
Note: Dashes indicate data are not available.

applied to imports during this period. The great diversity of products, ranging from butter to refrigerators, indicates that these surcharges were the result of industry-specific lobbying efforts—there is no apparent rationale for their imposition that would be justified by "optimal taxation" arguments. The system for setting the surcharges was launched in November 1981, at the zenith of the real exchange-rate appreciation (see figure 10.2). By December 1984, the authorities had received 123 requests for relief, alleging that imports were being subsidized by foreign governments. Yet the Chilean authorities did not follow contemporary procedures that existed under the General Agreement on Tariffs and Trade (GATT), which permitted country-specific compensatory duties, and opted for general surcharges that did not discriminate among countries.

De la Cuadra and Hachette (1991, 268) defend this position by arguing that "in the history of GATT, there has not been a single case in which a small country has been able to apply a compensatory duty on imports from a large country, because it does not have the 'power' to do so. For example, when Chile intended to levy compensatory duties on a limited number of imports from Brazil, the pressures against doing so at diplomatic levels were such that the GATT mechanism did not work." Yet the timing of the implementation of this system of surcharges indicates that the authorities became "suddenly" preoccupied by foreign subsidies. A more likely explanation is that the authorities were once again responding to political pressures, even under an authoritarian regime. In addition, "between March 1983 and January 1990, imports were subject to a 120-day minimum financing requirement ... In June 1988, the minimum financing requirement was lifted for imports below US$5,000 ... The exemption was later raised to US$20,000 in December 1988, and to US$50,000 in June 1989" (GATT 1991, 52).

Business associations were also compensated through political mechanisms. In February 1983, Manuel Martín, a leading industrialist, was appointed minister of economy. Subsequently, Modesto Collados, a construction entrepreneur, was named minister of housing, and, later minister of economy. In 1985, Manuel Délano, who had led the Chamber of Commerce, was appointed to the same office. Furthermore, in 1984, a leader of the SNA, Jorge Prado, became minister of agriculture, and in 1986, a former president of the National Society of Mining, Samuel Lira, became minister of mining (see Campero 1991, 139–140).

In the midst of the economic crisis, the COPROCO published a document titled "Economic Recovery: Analysis and Proposals" in July 1983, thus revealing that the entrepreneurs differed with the government on policy matters, including the low and uniform tariff level (Campero 1991, 139). On August 15, 1983, Finance Minister Carlos Cáceres responded to the COPROCO by stating that the government would only consider individual aspects of their proposals. According to Campero (1991, 140), "By mid-1984, the government had formulated a three-year plan ... which incorporated many of the entrepreneurs' proposals ... [including] agricultural and mining investments, a policy of job expansion, and an increase in import tariffs [from 20 to 35 percent] in order to protect national industry...." Indeed, by 1983, the government had resumed price interventions in agriculture, announcing a minimum import price for wheat that would be sustained through contingent variable import levies. In 1984, the minimum wheat price policy was incorporated into a price-band framework, and the program was extended to edible oil. Sugar was added to the system in 1985 (Quiroz and Valdés 1993). More generally, during 1983–1985 the government was forced to negotiate a recovery program with the private sector, which led to the ambiguity of its economic policies. This flirtation with an all-out reversal of the liberalization process came to an end in 1985, when Mr. Hernán Buchi became Minister of Finance and was able to reach a compromise between the orthodox views of the Chicago boys and the demands from the private sector to have a negotiated program in place (Campero 1991, 140).

As shown in figure 10.2, the real exchange rate depreciated rapidly during the crisis years, thus providing additional compensation to tradable industries. As illustrated in table 10.8, once the economic recovery got under way after 1984, and well into phases four and five of the liberalization process, few compensation mechanisms were used to make the resumption of liberalization palatable. Nonetheless, the real exchange rate (both the bilateral and the multilateral rates) became more stable, as shown in figure 10.4, thus acting as an effective indirect compensation mechanism at least by providing stability to the ratio between foreign and domestic prices.

As the economic recovery proceeded, the rate of unemployment also fell, while moderate inflation persisted in the double digits until the mid-1990s (see table 10.1). On the political side, the Constitution of 1980 had scheduled a plebescite referendum on Pinochet's regime

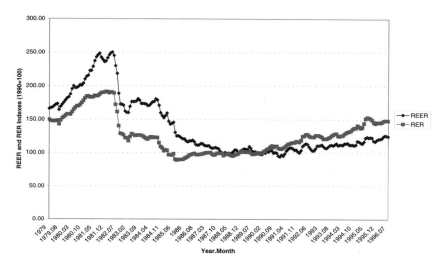

Figure 10.4
Chile: REER and RER, 1979–1996

for 1988. The democratically elected government of Patricio Aylwin lowered the uniform tariff to 11 percent in 1991. It is noteworthy that this tariff reduction was implemented in conjunction with the establishment of exchange controls. More specifically, on the same date the government instituted a reserve requirement (for a minimum of 90 days) for short-term capital inflows. This policy mix highlights the Aylwin administration's concern about real exchange-rate appreciation that Chile was experiencing as a result of a surge of capital inflows. From a political economy perspective, this combination of exchange controls and tariff reductions can be interpreted as an attempt to send a signal to the markets that the controls should not be interpreted as the beginning of a reversal of the market-oriented development model. In fact, three members of Aylwin's government who were in charge of trade policy matters have acknowledged that "even when the origin of the decision [to lower the tariff to 11 percent] had a macroeconomic motivation, the measure was consistent with the objective to consolidate the opening of the economy" (Saez, Salazar, and Vicuña 1995, 48, translated). Furthermore, a member of the Central Bank staff and a finance ministry official at the time have written that "in order to sustain the real exchange rate, in June, 1991, the government lowered tariffs ..., and imposed a series of measures on the capital market ..." (Ffrench-Davis and Labán 1996,

58).[45] Hence it cannot be overemphasized that trade liberalization in periods of uncertainty can send a strong signal that incoming, especially left-of-center, governments will continue with a market-oriented development strategy. In the words of Edgardo Boeninger, minister secretary general of the presidency during the Aylwin administration, "The [Aylwin government], whose faith in the market was initially suspect for understandable historical reasons, has invested in entrepreneurial trust, both by language and by deed, conveying signals that have contributed to creating the perception that an enabling environment for private enterprise does in fact exist" (Boeninger 1992, 286).

As mentioned earlier, Chile renewed its unilateral liberalization in 1999, and its uniform tariff is programmed to be reduced to 6 percent by January 2003. Yet it is clear that use of compensation mechanisms continues. During the late 1990s the government maintained the protectionist price bands of certain agricultural commodities and toughened the country's legislation against dumping and foreign export subsidies (Fischer and Meller 1999). These measures can be interpreted as a resurgence of the use of exclusionary compensation mechanisms, as shown in table 10.7. In this case, industries benefiting from the price-band surcharges and antidumping or countervailing duties are likely to be those that are being hurt by both the liberalization of trade with certain partners and the renewed unilateral liberalization. It is unknown at this time whether the economic benefits from further liberalization will outweigh the efficiency costs from these protectionist schemes.

10.5 Trade Liberalization and Unemployment: Preliminary Results

As we pointed out above, much of the criticism of the Chilean trade reform during the 1970s and 1980s was based on its effect on social conditions, including unemployment. Reform skeptics argued that by dismantling the protective structure—and in particular, by doing it so fast—firms were forced into bankruptcy, and unemployment soared. However, the fact that many reforms were being undertaken simultaneously made the analysis difficult. More specifically, it was difficult to disentangle the effects of trade liberalization from those of other policies, including the stabilization program aimed at taming inflation. Most analyses of labor market behavior during the Chilean reforms have been based on aggregate data (e.g., Riveros 1986). Therefore, it has been difficult to separate the effects of macroeconomic developments—including the stabilization program—from those stemming from microeconomic reforms, including the liberalization of trade.

In a recent study, Edwards and Edwards (1996) used a large unemployment survey data set to explore, at the micro level, whether the Chilean trade reform affected unemployment during the 1970s and early 1980s. They ask the following basic questions: Does the sector of origin affect the probability of being unemployed? More specifically, are workers originally employed in more "liberalized" sectors more likely to be unemployed? They used data from the University of Chile, June unemployment surveys for the Greater Santiago Area (GSA). Table 10.11 provides a summary of the data for

Table 10.11
Data set characteristics, 1976, 1979, and 1981

	Variable	Observations	Mean	Std. dev.	Min.	Max.
A. 1976	nemp	4,738	0.141	0.348	0	1
	ex	4,738	19.788	13.204	0	83
	ye	4,738	8.454	4.308	0	19
	asset	4,738	39.408	137.760	0	1,998
	dhead	4,738	0.541	0.498	0	1
	lib76	4,738	−0.10	0.196	−0.676	0.406
	sex	4,738	0.346	0.476	0	1
B. 1979	nemp	5,373	0.125	0.331	0	1
	ex	5,373	18.870	13.302	0	71
	ye	5,369	9.197	4.125	0	19
	asset	5,373	258.73	895.369	0	129,995
	dhead	5,373	0.496	0.500	0	1
	lib79	5,373	−0.015	0.034	−0.109	0.053
	sex	5,373	0.354	0.478	0	1
C. 1981	nemp	5,369	0.081	0.273	0	1
	ex	6,778	21.196	14.418	0	85
	ye	6,755	8.947	4.046	0	19
	asset	7,335	44.973	249.501	0	9,000
	dhead	7,336	0.447	0.497	0	1
	lib81	7,336	−0.004	0.015	−0.060	0.100
	sex	7,336	0.500	0.500	0	1

Source: Household surveys.

1976, 1979, and 1981. *Nemp* is a variable that takes the value of one if the individual is unemployed and zero if he or she is employed; *ex* is experience and is defined in years; *ye* is education and is also measured in years; *assets* refers to an estimate of the individual assets measured in current pesos and is used as a proxy for the individual's reservation wage; *dhead* is a binary variable that captures whether the individual is a head of household; *lib* is the degree of liberalization of each sector relative to the previous period with available data; and *sex* classifies individuals as male or female.

Edwards and Edwards (1996) analyzed whether, after controlling for other factors, the degree of liberalization affects the probability of being unemployed. In principle, this question can be addressed by estimating probit equations. A summary of their results is presented in table 10.12. As can be seen, most of the coefficients are significant at conventional levels. These results suggest that the probability of being unemployed declines with experience and schooling— although the schooling coefficient is not significant in 1979, and only slightly significant in 1981. Interestingly enough, and perhaps a bit surprising, those with lower assets appear to have a larger probability of being unemployed. Heads of households and males also ap-

Table 10.12
Estimated probability of being unemployed, 1976, 1979, and 1981 (Probit regression results, P-values in parenthesis)

Variable	1976	1979	1981
ex	−0.005*	−0.001	−0.003
	(0.019)	(0.586)	(0.210)
ye	−0.074*	−0.054*	−0.033*
	(0.000)	(0.000)	(0.000)
asset	−0.005*	−0.000*	−0.003*
	(0.000)	(0.000)	(0.000)
dhead	−0.359*	−0.255*	−0.099
	(0.000)	(0.000)	(0.176)
lib	−0.347*	−1.794*	−1.732
	(0.003)	(0.009)	(0.262)
sex	−0.391*	−0.404*	−0.254*
	(0.000)	(0.000)	(0.000)
constant	−0.049	−0.545*	−0.936*
	(0.541)	(0.000)	(0.000)
Observations	4,738	5,196	5,196

*Within 95 percent confidence interval.

pear to have a significantly lower probability of being out of work. The degree of liberalization seems to affect the probability of being unemployed positively. This supports, then, the view that in the case of Chile, trade liberalization contributed to the surge of unemployment experienced in the 1970s. As pointed out previously, however, these results should be interpreted with caution. The reason for this is that, contrary to the other variables in the analysis, *lib* is not an invariable characteristic of the individual. In fact, it is possible that the "sector" variable means different things for different people in the sample. Further analysis undertaken by Edwards and Edwards (1996) indicates that liberalization affected positively not only the probability of being unemployed but also unemployment duration. After controlling for other variables, individuals in those sectors affected more severely by the reforms experienced longer unemployment spells.

10.6   Concluding Remarks, or Flirting with Regionalism

The advent of regionalism to the Western Hemisphere has become part of Chile's economic and political realities. It is now unclear whether Chile's love affair with unilateralism has run out of passion, and it is also uncertain whether Chile's recent flirtation with regionalism will lead to the end of its remarkable experience with unilateral liberalization. Two considerations support this reasoning.

First, it is possible that the authorities may have attempted to "strengthen" their positions for the "upcoming" negotiations to enter NAFTA by maintaining the current tariff level at 11 percent.[46] Parliament was considering another reduction in the uniform tariff in 1997, but this project was temporarily shelved in the aftermath of the Asian crisis, due to a deterioration of Chile's current account.[47] In any case, most of the policy debate at that time focused on the role of tariff changes as determinants of the real exchange rate, which is a legacy of the late 1970s and mid-1980s, as well as on the fiscal consequences of the proposed tariff reduction. The lesson from past experience is that automatic adjustment mechanisms based on the downward adjustment of nontradable prices do not work, and that tariffs are an inappropriate means for raising fiscal revenues. Regarding the former, a change in the tariff by itself cannot bring about a real depreciation—it is not the proper policy lever to accomplish that. The tariff should be lowered to reap the gains from trade, not to help macroeconomic management. Since the peso had been appreciating moderately since 1995 (recall figure 10.4), many interests in tradable industries used this fact as a justification for demanding special treatment, including former allies of the military government such as the SNA.[48]

Second, some of Chile's regional partners are world-class producers of traditional agricultural products. The country has signed and implemented trade agreements with Argentina, Brazil, and Canada, and perhaps with the United States in the near future. The phasing out of the agricultural price-band mechanisms in the context of the agreement with the Mercosur countries will have obvious losers, namely the membership of the SNA. In fact, the ratification of the agreement ran into trouble in 1997, mainly as a consequence of political pressure exerted by agricultural interests on right-wing elements of Parliament. The SNA again claims that its members represent a special sector, worthy of special favors. The last two democratic governments have already used an exclusionary compensation mechanism in the form of the long phase-out period. It is reasonable to expect some "senescent industry" protection for traditional agriculture in the coming years.[49]

Eventually, in late 1998, the legislature approved Minister Eduardo Aninat's proposal to unilaterally reduce the uniform tariff to 6 percent by the year 2003. However, this renewed interest in unilateral liberalization is taking place during a time when most protectionist effects come from nontariff measures, such as the continued use of the agricultural price bands as protectionist schemes and the strengthening of administered protection. Although the latter are WTO-legal, from an economic perspective, these devices do not make much sense. Hence it is clear that while Chile continues to set the standard for developing countries in terms of unilateral liberalization, it is worrisome that it has also installed institutional mechanisms that readily heed to protectionist demands. In the end, Chile continues to move toward free trade, while compensations mechanisms continue to be used to quiet the losers. For economists, the challenge is to assess whether the potential benefits from continued liberalization are higher than the efficiency losses produced by the remaining and new nontariff barriers to trade that may be necessary to sustain the political support in favor of liberalization.

Notes

We are grateful to Arnold Harberger and Jagdish Bhagwati for helpful comments on an earlier draft of this chapter. We also benefited from suggestions provided by other participants at the AEI/Ford Foundation Conference on Unilateral Trade Liberalization of October 24–25, 1997, and participants at the 10th Inter-American Seminar on Economics held on November 21–22 in Santiago, Chile.

1. On the Chilean reforms see Harberger (1985), Edwards (1985), Edwards and Edwards (1991), and Bosworth, Dornbusch and Labán (1994).

2. Bhagwati (1988, 17) was one of the first contributions by economists that argued that protectionism was the result of a variety of forces: "Profound commitments to policies are generally due to a mix of ideological factors (in the form of ideas and example), interests (as defined by politics and economics), and institutions (as they shape constraints and opportunities)."

3. The effective rate of protection is a measure of the relative degree of inefficiency of domestic production relative to international production. A positive value means that domestic value added for that particular activity exceeds value added at international prices. The effective tariff for good $i(\gamma_i)$ is computed in the form of $\gamma_i = (t_i - \sum \alpha_{ij} t_j)/(1 - \sum \alpha_{ij})$ where t_i is the nominal tariff, a_{ij} is the input/output coefficient between input j and good i, and t_j is the nominal tariff on input j. Notice that if the good and all inputs have the same nominal tariff, then the effective and nominal rates of protection are the same ($\gamma_i = t_j$). It should be noted that from a general equilibrium perspective the usefulness of the concept of effective rates of protection is quite limited (see Bhagwati and Srinivasan 1979).

4. On the degree of effective protection in Chile's agriculture sector prior to the reform, see Varas (1975). Behrman (1976, table A.3) lists effective rates of protection for products within the agricultural sector ranging between −11 and −39 percent in 1967. Alternative measures can also be found in Balassa et al. (1971).

5. The initial maxi-devaluation responded, in part, to the need to avoid an almost imminent balance-of-payments crisis. As the tariff process proceeded, the crawling peg tried to (approximately) maintain the high level of the real exchange rate.

6. In fact, the exchange rate played a crucial role in the government's explanation of the negative effects of protectionism during the previous decades. For example, according to de Castro:

The relatively forced industrialization of the country was obtained through various mechanisms. One of these was the foreign exchange rate policy. From 1939 on, the exchange rate was maintained artificially low.... The exporting sector lost all possibility to export because ... [with a low] exchange rate ... they could not manage to cover their local production costs (Méndez 1979, 201).

7. Price bands for wheat were originally introduced in 1977, but in 1978 the president of the National Society of Agricultural Producers (SNA, in Spanish) asked the government to eliminate them, because the international price of wheat was high and the price bands did not act as an instrument of protection under those circumstances. Finally, the price bands were "legalized" on June 30, 1986, after the implementation of Law #18,525, article 12. See Chacra and Jorquera (1991, 3).

8. The Central Bank Autonomy Act was implemented in April 1990.

9. For additional arguments in favor of the crisis hypothesis, see Drazen and Grilli (1993), Williamson and Haggard (1994), Tornell (1995), and Bruno and Easterly (1996). For an skeptical view, see Rajapatirana, de la Mora, and Yatawara (1997), who show that historically many macroeconomic crises in Latin America have resulted in the "tightening" of trade policies. Support from the multilateral institutions—either in the form of technical assistance or through the provision of funds—may help the reform effort, once it has been launched. However, there is significant evidence that the multilaterals—and mostly the IMF and the World bank—have not usually played a fundamental role in the initiation of reforms (see Edwards 1997a). Moreover, Haggard and Webb (1994, 5) argue that there are no recorded reform episodes since the mid-1970s that have failed exclusively due to a lack of financial support from the multilateral financial institutions.

10. Domínguez (1997, 7) defines *technopols* as follows: "Technopols are a variant of technocrats. In addition to being technocrats ... technopols are political leaders (1) at or near the top of their country's government and political life (including opposition political parties) who (2) go beyond their specialized expertise to draw on various different streams of knowledge and who (3) vigorously participate in the nation's political life (4) for the purpose of affecting politics well beyond the economic realm and who may, at times, be associated with an effort to "remake" their country's politics, economics, and society. Technopols so defined may operate in either authoritarian or democratic regimes."

11. Boeninger (1992, 275) coined the term "populist temptation" referring to the short-term incentive faced by fiscal and monetary authorities to finance public expenditures by excessive borrowing and/or issuing currency. For detailed analysis of populist macroeconomic policies see Dornbusch and Edwards (1990).

12. In Chile, plebescite votes took place in 1980 and 1988. The former was "non-competitive" and was convened at the peak of an economic boom. Nevertheless, current expenditures grew at an average annual rate of 11 percent between 1979 and 1981 (Fontaine 1996, 14).

13. See, for example, Rodrik (1989), Calvo (1989), and Martinelli and Tommasi (1994).

14. This would be the case if the opening of the capital account is done in the context of an overall liberalization program, where the country becomes attractive for foreign investors and speculators. See McKinnon (1991).

15. Lal (1985) presents a dissenting view. Hanson (1995) has argued that under some circumstances the capital account should be liberalized early on.

16. In other words, the coupling of trade and labor reforms transforms an intersectoral distributive conflict (as would be the case in a specific-factors economy contemplating only a trade reform) into an interfactor dispute.

17. See Balassa et al. (1971) for estimates of sectoral effective rates of protection in several developing countries during the 1960s.

18. From an efficiency point of view, however, it is more difficult to defend a uniform tariff. Using an intertemporal general equilibrium approach, Edwards (1997b) shows that the optimal tariff structure would depend on a number of variables and would only by chance be characterized by a uniform nominal tariff.

19. In 1956, the University of Chicago and the Catholic University of Chile signed an agreement aimed at training Chilean economists in Chicago. See Valdés (1995).

20. Alessandri lost the elections to Marxist candidate Dr. Salvador Allende by merely 33,000 votes.

21. The document became known among the members of the group as "the brick" (*el ladrillo*, in Spanish), a reference to the size of the manuscript.

22. Several economists belonging primarily to the Christian Democratic Party (DC) were approached by Admiral Gotuzzo, who offered them jobs in his Ministry of Finance. Some of these wise men, such as Sergio Molina and Raul Saez, had served under the Frei government of 1964–1970. Carlos Massad, a more moderate Chicago graduate and former (and current, since 1997) president of the Central Bank was also approached. See Valdés (1995, 17).

23. In September 1973—a week after the coup—the Planning Ministry printed two hundred numbered copies. The document was finally published by the *Centro de Estudios Públicos* in 1992.

24. Harberger (1959), for example, provided early estimates of the effects of Chile's protective structure. See also Behrman (1976) for the Bhagwati-Krueger NBER project on trade regimes.

25. The program incorrectly argued that a uniform import tariff was second-best optimal from a welfare perspective.

26. The most important writings of the reform skeptics were collected in a volume titled *Trayectoria de una crítica* (*Trajectory of a Critique*), published in 1982 (Arellano et al. 1982).

27. During the Pinochet regime, the military did not allow open political discussions. As a result, debates on economic policy became a substitute for political discussions. The CIEPLAN economists played an important and brave role in maintaining some sense of perspective in Chile during these years.

28. Interview with Ricardo Ffrench-Davis, Santiago, Chile, August 17, 1997 (via telephone).

29. See Foxley (1983, 42–44). He goes on to suggest that under democratic rule import tariffs should be increased to an average of 30 percent, with a maximum effective rate of protection of 60 percent. He argued, however, that these policies would "not result in a return to the import substitution model, as was known in Chile and Latin America during the 1950s and 1960s" (54).

30. See Edwards and Edwards (1991, 222–226) for an early discussion of the Aylwin program.

31. Tariffs were reduced to 11 percent across the board in June 1991.

32. *Newsweek* (Latin American Edition), March 26, 1990.

33. The basic approach is based on the standard Stolper-Samuelson framework linking sectoral (factor) income shares to relative prices. It assumes that the interests of workers and capitalists are independent of the sector where they operate initially, and it ignores important macroeconomic considerations, including the potential role of the exchange rate. Extensions of the basic Stolper-Samuelson framework allow for additional actors, as well as complex relationships among them. A powerful extension, which has become popular among political scientists working on the political economy of trade, assumes that some of the factors (e.g., capital) are sector-specific. In this

case, capitalist interests differ depending on which goods they produce. In this framework, owners of capital across sectors may have conflicting interests.

34. This does not mean that the basic principles of international trade theory cease to be relevant. In fact, the extended general equilibrium framework sketched here continues to be extremely powerful.

35. For instance, a Chilean sociologist, Garretón (1986, 147), wrote that in the case of Chile, "We are ... dealing with a program to lay the groundwork for a new social order ... we must direct our attention to the capacity of diverse sectors in the dominant power bloc to achieve hegemony within it. The attempt to restructure society ... can take several directions depending on the capacity of particular sectors to generalize these interests or to impose their own ideology within the victorious coalition." In fact, the general issue of "state autonomy" from economic and social interests has had a long trajectory in the social sciences. See, for example, the first, review chapter in Hamilton (1982).

36. On the role of "legitimacy," see Linz (1978, 16–19).

37. Campero (1984, 1991) provides detailed analyses of the role of business associations in shaping the policies of the dictatorship.

38. See Campero (1984, 1991).

39. On the effect of connected lending by the grupos, see Arellano (1985) and Galvez and Tybout (1985).

40. However, the privatized, fully capitalized system that replaced the publicly managed pay-as-you-go system does offer a minimum pension.

41. The fact that from an economic viewpoint the rebate on import duties eliminates the anti-export bias of the import tariff does not mean that this compensation scheme did not have political consequences.

42. We have already mentioned that firms that benefited from directed credit prior to the reforms lost such privileges.

43. On the discretionary application of the price bands, see also Chacra and Jorquera (1991), and note 7 above.

44. According to de la Cuadra and Hachette (1991, 227), "The government gradually opened the Chilean economy to foreign capital between 1974 and 1981. Medium-term capital movements were progressively deregulated (through reductions in reserve requirements), with overall global limits on borrowing eliminated in 1979; the only limitation on total bank indebtedness [was] the maximum allowed debt-to-capital ratio (20 to 1). Restrictions on monthly inflows were eliminated in April 1980. Short-term financial credits were not allowed until 1981."

45. The controls included a reserve requirement of 20 percent of external credits that had to be deposited in a non-interest-bearing account at the Central Bank for a minimum period of ninety days. In addition, a tax of 1.2 percent on domestic credit operations was extended to cover external loans (Ffrench-Davis, Agosín, and Uthoff 1995, 121).

46. For example, Saez, Salazar, and Vicuña (1995, 46, translated) argued that when the Aylwin administration came to power in 1990, it had "to consider, to promote exports as well as better market access, the implementation of complementary policies [to

unilateralism] that would provide greater reciprocity were required ... hence the strategy began to be shaped as various opportunities changed the scenarios, thus incorporating the negotiation of free trade agreements into the trade policy agenda."

47. "Chile Backs Off from Planned Tariff Cut," *The Journal of Commerce*, March 3, 1998, p. 1A.

48. Again, trade policymakers of the Aylwin Administration wrote, "During [the early 1990s] the authorities had to face sectorial pressures to raise the level of protection ... In practice, it is possible to conclude that these pressures were not fruitful and the sectors were left to operate under a uniform protection environment" (Saez, Salazar, and Vicuña 1995, 49, translated).

49. On senescent industry protection, see Hillman (1982) and Cassing and Hillman (1986).

References

Aedo, Cristián, and Luis F. Lagos. 1984. "Protección efectiva en el sector manufacturero." Working Paper, Universidad Católica de Chile, Department of Economics, Santiago, Chile.

Arellano, José Pablo. 1985. "De la liberalización a la intervención: El mercado de capitales en Chile 1974–1983." *El Trimestre Económico* 52: 721–772.

Arellano, José Pablo, et al. 1982. *Modelo económico chileno: Trayectoria de una crítica.* Santiago, Chile: Editorial Aconcagua.

Balassa, Bela, et al. 1971. *The Structure of Protection in Developing Countries.* Baltimore and London: The Johns Hopkins University Press for the World Bank.

Barrera, Manuel, and J. Samuel Valenzuela. 1986. "The Development of Labor Movement Opposition to the Military Regime." Chap. 7 in *Military Rule in Chile: Dictatorship and Oppositions*, ed. J. S. Valenzuela and A. Valenzuela, 230–269. Baltimore and London: The Johns Hopkins University Press.

Bates, Robert H., and Anne O. Krueger. 1993. "Generalizations Arising from the Country Studies." Chap. 10 in *Political and Economic Interactions in Economic Policy Reform*, ed. R. H. Bates and A. O. Krueger, 1–20. Oxford, UK, and Cambridge: Basil Blackwell.

Behrman, Jere R. 1976. *Foreign Trade Regimes and Economic Development: Chile.* New York and London: Columbia University Press for the NBER.

Bhagwati, Jagdish. 1988. *Protectionism.* Cambridge, MA: The MIT Press.

Bhagwati, Jagdish, and T. N. Srinivasan. 1979. "On Inferring Resource-Allocational Implications from DRC Calculations in Trade-Distorted Small Open Economies." *Indian Economic Review* 14: 1–16.

Boeninger, Edgardo. 1992. "Governance and Development: Issues and Constraints." In *Proceedings of the World Bank Annual Conference on Development Economics 1991.* Washington, DC: The World Bank.

Bosworth, Barry P., Rudiger Dornbusch, and Raúl Labán, eds. 1994. *The Chilean Economy: Policy Lessons and Challenges.* Washington, DC: The Brookings Institution.

Bruno, Michael, and William Easterly. 1996. "Inflation's Children: Tales of Crises That Beget Reforms." *AEA Papers and Proceedings* 86, no. 2: 213–217.

Calvo, Guillermo. 1989. "Incredible Reforms." In *Debt, Stabilization, and Development: Essays in Memory of Carlos Diaz-Alejandro*, ed. G. Calvo et al., 30–55. Cambridge, MA: Basil Blackwell.

Campero, Guillermo. 1984. *Los gremios empresariales en el periodo 1970–1983: Comportamiento sociopolítico y orientaciones ideológicas.* Santiago, Chile: Instituto Latinoamericano de Estudios Transnacionales.

Campero, Guillermo. 1991. "Entrepreneurs under the Military Regime." In *The Struggle for Democracy in Chile, 1982–1990*, ed. P. W. Drake and I. Jaksic, 128–160. Lincoln: University of Nebraska Press.

Cassing, James, and Arye Hillman. 1986. "Shifting Comparative Advantage and Senescent Industry Collapse." *American Economic Review* 76: 516–523.

Castañeda, Tarsicio. 1983. "Evolución del empleo y el desempleo y el impacto de cambios demográficos sobre la tasa de desempleo en Chile, 1960–1983." Documento Serie Investigación no. 54, Department of Economics, University of Chile, Santiago.

Chacra, Verónica, and Guillermo Jorquera. 1991. "Bandas de precios de productos agrícolas básicos: la experiencia de Chile durante el período 1983–1991." Serie de Estudios Económicos No. 36, Banco Central de Chile, Santiago.

Corbo, Vittorio. 1997. "Trade Reform and Uniform Import Tariffs: The Chilean Experience." *AEA Papers and Proceedings* 87, no. 2: 73–77.

Cortázar, René. 1997. "Chile: The Evolution and Reform of the Labor Market." In *Labor Markets in Latin America: Combining Social Protection with Market Flexibility*, ed. S. Edwards and N. Lustig, 115–163. Washington, DC: Brookings Institution Press.

Dahse, Fernando. 1979. *Mapa de la extrema riqueza.* Santiago, Chile: Editorial Aconcagua.

de la Cuadra, Sergio. 1976. "Estrategia para la liberalización del comercio exterior chileno." In *Estudios Monetarios IV.* Santiago, Chile: Banco Central de Chile.

de la Cuadra, Sergio, and Dominique Hachette. 1991. "Chile." Chap. 2, in *Liberalizing Foreign Trade*, vol. 1, ed. D. Papageorgiou, M. Michaely, and A. M. Choksi. Cambridge, MA: Basil Blackwell.

Domínguez, Jorge I. 1997. "Technopols: Ideas and Leaders in Freeing Politics and Markets in Latin America in the 1990s." Chap. 1 in *Technopols: Freeing Politics and Markets in Latin America in the 1990s*, ed. J. Domínguez. University Park: The Pennsylvania State University Press.

Dornbusch, Rudiger, and Sebastian Edwards. 1990. "Macroeconomic Populism." *Journal of Development Economics* 32, no. 2: 247–277.

Douglas, Hernán Cortés, Andrea Butelmann, and Pedro Videla. 1980. "El proteccionismo en Chile: Una visión retrospectiva." *Cuadernos de Economía* 54–55: 141–167.

Drazen, Allen, and Vittorio Grilli. 1993. "The Benefit of Crises for Economic Reforms." *American Economic Review* 83: 598–607.

Edwards, Alejandra. 1984. "Three Essays on Labor Markets in Developing Countries." Ph.D. diss., University of Chicago, Department of Economics.

Edwards, Sebastian. 1984. *The Order of Liberalization of the External Sector in Developing Countries*. Princeton Essays in International Finance 156, Princeton University, Princeton, NJ.

Edwards, Sebastian. 1985. "Stabilization with Liberalization: An Evaluation of Ten Years of Chile's Experiment with Free Market Oriented Policies." *Economic Development and Cultural Change* 33 (January): 223–254.

Edwards, Sebastian. 1988. *Exchange Rate Misalignment in Developing Countries*. Baltimore, MD: Johns Hopkins University Press.

Edwards, Sebastian. 1995. *Crisis and Reform in Latin America: From Despair to Hope*. New York: Oxford University Press for the World Bank.

Edwards, Sebastian. 1997a. "Trade Liberalization Reforms and the World Bank." *AEA Papers and Proceedings* 87, no. 2: 43–48.

Edwards, Sebastian. 1997b. "Trade Reform, Uniform Tariffs and the Budget." In *Macroeconomic Dimensions of Public Finance: Essays in Honor of Vito Tanzi*, ed. M. Blejer and T. Ter-Minassian. New York: Routledge.

Edwards, Sebastian, and Alejandra Cox Edwards. 1991. *Monetarism and Liberalization: The Chilean Experiment*. Chicago: The University of Chicago Press.

Edwards, Sebastian, and Alejandra Cox Edwards. 1996. "Trade Liberalization and Unemployment: Policy Issues and Evidence from Chile." Mimeo., Anderson School of Management, University of California at Los Angeles.

Ffrench-Davis, Ricardo. 1980. "Liberalización de las importaciones: La experiencia chilena en 1973–1979." *Colección Estudios CIEPLAN* 4: 39–78. Also published, with minor revisions, as "Import Liberalization: The Chilean Experience, 1973–1982." Chap. 2 in *Military Rule in Chile: Dictatorship and Oppositions*, ed. J. S. Valenzuela and A. Valenzuela, 51–84. Baltimore: The Johns Hopkins University Press, 1986.

Ffrench-Davis, Ricardo, Manuel Agosín, and Andras Uthoff. 1995. "Capital Movements, Export Strategy, and Macroeconomic Stability in Chile." Chap. 4 in *Coping with Capital Surges: The Return of Finance to Latin America*, ed. R. Ffrench-Davis and S. Griffith-Jones, 99–144. Boulder, CO: Lynne Rienner Publishers.

Ffrench-Davis, Ricardo, and Raul Labán. 1996. "Macroeconomic Performance and Achievements in Chile." In *Social and Economic Policies in Chile's Transition to Democracy*, ed. C. Pizarro, D. Raczynski, and J. Vial, 43–68. Santiago, Chile: CIEPLAN and UNICEF.

Ffrench-Davis, Ricardo, and Raul E. Sáez. 1995. "Comercio y desarrollo industrial en Chile." *Colección de Estudios CIEPLAN* 41: 67–96.

Fischer, Ronald, and Patricio Meller. 1999. "Latin American Trade Regime Reforms and Perceptions." Working Paper 65, University of Chile, Department of Industrial Engineering and Center of Applied Economics.

Fontaine, Juan Andrés. 1996. *La construcción de un mercado de capitales: El caso de Chile*. Washington, DC: The World Bank.

Foxley, Alejandro. 1983. *Latin American Experiments in Neoconservative Economics.* Berkeley: University of California Press.

Foxley, Alejandro. 1986. "The Neoconservative Economic Experiment in Chile." Chap. 1 in *Military Rule in Chile: Dictatorship and Oppositions,* ed. J. S. Valenzuela and A. Valenzuela. Baltimore: The Johns Hopkins University Press.

Galvez, Julio, and James Tybout. 1985. "Microeconomic Adjustments in Chile during 1977–1981: The Importance of Being a *Grupo.*" *World Development* 13, no. 8: 969–994.

Garretón, Manuel Antonio. 1986. "Political Processes in an Authoritarian Regime: The Dynamics of Institutionalization and Opposition in Chile, 1973–1980." Chap. 5 in *Military Rule in Chile: Dictatorship and Oppositions,* ed. J. S. Valenzuela and A. Valenzuela. Baltimore, MD: The Johns Hopkins University Press.

GATT [General Agreement on Tariffs and Trade, Secretariat]. 1991. *Trade Policy Review: Chile, Volume I.* Geneva: GATT, October.

Hamilton, Nora. 1982. *The Limits of State Autonomy: Post-Revolutionary Mexico.* Princeton, NJ: Princeton University Press.

Haggard, Stephan, and Steven B. Webb, eds. 1994. *Voting for Reform: Democracy, Political Liberalization, and Economic Adjustment.* Washington, DC: Oxford University Press for the World Bank.

Hanson, James A. 1995. "Opening the Capital Account: Costs, Benefits, and Sequencing." Chapa. 14 in *Capital Controls, Exchange Rates, and Monetary Policy in the World Economy,* ed. S. Edwards, 383–430. New York: Cambridge University Press.

Harberger, Arnold. 1959. "Using the Resources at Hand More Efficiently." *American Economic Review* 49: 134–146.

Harberger, Arnold. 1985. "Observations on the Chilean Economy, 1973–1983." *Economic Development and Cultural Change* 33 (April): 451–462.

Harberger, Arnold. 1991. "Towards a Uniform Tariff Structure." University of Chicago, Department of Economics, Chicago.

Hillman, Arye. 1982. "Declining Industries and Political-Support Protectionist Motives." *American Economic Review* 72, no. 5: 1180–1187.

Lal, Deepak. 1985. "The Real Aspects of Stabilization and Structural Adjustment Policies: An Extension of the Australian Adjustment Model." World Bank Staff Working Paper 636, Washington, DC.

Linz, Juan J. 1978. *The Breakdown of Democratic Regimes: Crisis, Breakdown, and Reequilibration.* Baltimore, MD: Johns Hopkins University Press.

Martinelli, Cesar, and Mariano Tommasi. 1994. "Sequencing of Economic Reforms in the Presence of Political Constraints." Mimeo., Department of Economics, Universidad Carlos III, Madrid, Spain, and Department of Economics, University of California, Los Angeles.

McKinnon, Ronald. 1982. "The Order of Economic Liberalization: Lessons from Chile and Argentina." In *Economic Policy in a World of Change,* ed. K. Brunner and A. H. Meltzer, 26–41. Amsterdam: North-Holland.

McKinnon, Ronald. 1991. *The Order of Economic Liberalization: Financial Control in the Transition to a Market Economy*. Baltimore: Johns Hopkins University Press.

Méndez, Juan Carlos, ed. 1979. *Chilean Economic Policy*. Santiago, Chile: Budget Directorate.

Michaely, Michael, Demetris Papageorgiou, and Armeane M. Choksi. 1991. *Liberalizing Foreign Trade: Lessons of Experience in the Developing World*. Vol. 7, ed. M. Michaely, D. Papageorgiou, and A. M. Choksi. Cambridge, MA: Basil Blackwell.

Quiroz, Jorge A., and Alberto Valdés. 1993. "Price Bands for Agricultural Price Stabilization: The Chilean Exprience." Mimeo., ILADES/Georgetown University, Santiago, Chile, and The World Bank, Washington, DC.

Rajapatirana, Sarath, Luz Maria de la Mora, and Ravindra A. Yatawara. 1997. "Political Economy of Trade Reforms, 1965–1994: Latin American Style." *The World Economy* 20, no. 3: 307–338.

Riveros, Luis. 1986. "The Chilean Labor Market: From Structural Reforms of the 1970s to the Crisis of the 1980s." Mimeo. Development Research Department, Labor Markets Division, The World Bank, Washington, DC, April.

Rodrik, Dani. 1989. "Promises, Promises: Credible Policy Reform via Signaling." *The Economic Journal* 99: 756–772.

Rodrik, Dani. 1994. "The Rush to Free Trade in the Developing World: Why So Late? Why Now? Will It Last?" Chap. 3 in *Voting for Reform: Democracy, Political Liberalization, and Economic Adjustment*, ed. S. Haggard and S. B. Webb, 43–70. New York: Oxford University Press for the World Bank.

Saez, Sebastian, Juan Salazar, and Ricardo Vicuña. 1995. "Antecedentes y resultados de la estrategia comercial del Gobierno Aylwin." *Colección de Estudios CIEPLAN* 40: 41–66.

Tornell, Aaron. 1995. "Are Economic Crises Necessary for Trade Liberalization and Fiscal Reform? The Mexican Experience." Chap. 2 in *Reform, Recovery, and Growth: Latin America and the Middle East*, ed. R. Dornbusch and S. Edwards, 53–78. Chicago and London: The University of Chicago Press.

Valdés, Juan Gabriel. 1995. *Pinochet's Economists: The Chicago School in Chile*. Cambridge, UK: Cambridge University Press.

Williamson, John, ed. 1994. *The Political Economy of Policy Reform*. Washington, DC: The Institute for International Economics.

Williamson, John, and Stephan Haggard. 1994. "The Political Conditions for Economic Reform." Chap. 12 in *The Political Economy of Policy Reform*, ed. J. Williamson. Washington, DC: The Institute for International Economics.

11 Unilateral and Reciprocal Trade Reform in Latin America

Rachel McCulloch

The economic landscape of Latin America in 1980 had been shaped by decades of protectionism and import-substituting industrialization. Although Chile initiated wide-ranging trade reforms in 1974, the early results had done little to encourage emulation by other nations in the region, as Chile endured years of double-digit unemployment. Argentina had also reduced trade barriers beginning in 1976. However, effective protection rates remained high, and persistent macroeconomic instability undercut any efficiency gains that trade reforms might otherwise have generated. Mexico and Uruguay had likewise started to liberalize trade in the late 1970s. But each of these countries again tightened import restrictions in the early 1980s. Only in Chile did trade remain significantly less distorted than prior to the initiation of reforms, and even there, visible gains still fell short of signaling the clear superiority of the new market-oriented policies. Meanwhile, other countries in the region responded to the debt crisis of 1982 with further increases in trade barriers. By the middle of the decade, Latin America's external sector was the most distorted in the world (Edwards 1995).

Yet despite the decidedly mixed experience of the avant-garde, and notwithstanding significant increases in protection throughout the region in the wake of the debt crisis, the policy tide was beginning to turn. Only a few years later, greater openness had become the norm in Latin America rather than the exception. Still more recently, even Brazil—the region's most notable laggard with respect to trade reform as well as macroeconomic stabilization—succeeded in dismantling some of the inward-looking policies that insulated its economy from foreign competitors for more than a generation. By the mid-1990s, the region's move toward greater openness was no longer in doubt; the key question for Latin American policymakers was less *whether* to pursue an outward-oriented policy than *how* to achieve and sustain the required policy environment.

What accounted for the wave of trade liberalization that swept over Latin America in the 1980s and 1990s? One important force underlying the trend was a shifting consensus among mainstream economists regarding the appropriate role of trade policy in promoting development. Professional opinion in the 1950s and 1960s largely favored import substitution, and this approach was implemented throughout Latin America with the enthusiastic support of bilateral and multilateral aid agencies. But subsequent empirical research, including the landmark OECD and NBER projects on foreign trade and economic development, called the old conventional wisdom into question (Little, Scitovsky, and Scott 1970; Bhagwati 1978; Krueger 1978). The studies' conclusion, that a liberalized export-promoting trade regime is more effective than import substitution in accelerating economic development, gained further credence from the conspicuous success of export-led growth in several East Asian economies (Krueger 1997). Closer to home, the collapse across Latin America of development strategies based on import substitution and massive state intervention, together with Chile's takeoff into sustained export-led growth, pushed political leaders to embrace the opening of international trade and other market-oriented reforms (Edwards 1995).

Notwithstanding this broadly shared epiphany, the precise stimulus for and political-economic context of trade reforms in Latin America was as varied as the character, timing, and extent of the reforms themselves. A few countries unilaterally (autonomously) eliminated trade distortions as one element in a broad program of reforms (Chile, Bolivia). In other cases, liberalization was undertaken in conjunction with a regional initiative (Central American Common Market, Andean Trade Initiative, NAFTA, Mercosur). Reformers were also encouraged by strong external incentives from the U.S. government (Caribbean Basin Initiative, Section 301) or from the World Bank and International Monetary Fund (Brazil, Costa Rica, Colombia). Thus, even actions that on the surface appear to be unilateral may have entailed some form of cross-reciprocity.[1]

Some countries also initiated reforms in order to qualify for membership in a trading group with established norms, as occurred in Mexico's preparation to join the General Agreement on Tariffs and Trade (GATT).[2] New members liberalized partly to benefit from the lower most-favored-nation (MFN) tariffs negotiated in past rounds of multilateral negotiations. Similarly, late reformers may have been motivated partly by their improved access to export markets in countries that had already liberalized unilaterally. These situations might be characterized as intertemporal reciprocity in the sense that one country's willingness to liberalize has been increased by the earlier liberalization of partner countries. However, the rapid spread of liberalization across Latin America has alternative explanations that involve no implicit reciprocity. One is the demonstration effect of successful early liberalizers, most notably Chile. Some countries may also have engaged in a process of competitive liberalization, reducing trade barriers and implementing other market-oriented reforms in an effort to attract or retain footloose manufacturing investment (Bergsten 1996). A final explanation views the debt crisis of the early 1980s as a common stimulus affecting a number of countries in a similar way: conditions of "deep economic crisis ... relegated distributional issues to second place" (Rodrik 1994).

The evidence suggests that policy debate in Latin America in the 1990s no longer centered on the relative merits of import-substituting industrialization versus export-led growth. That traditional battle was over. Every Latin American country was looking for ways to expand exports, each instituted trade reforms, and some committed to further market-opening measures in the years ahead. But even before the mid-1980s, there was no scarcity of trade reform in Latin America. On the contrary, some countries in the region had already embarked on multiple prior episodes of liberalization. In almost every case, however, implementation delays and outright policy reversals halted the reform process in its tracks before the anticipated gains in productivity and growth could be realized. What made the period after 1985 different was not only that more countries liberalized, but also that fewer of the reforms were reversed subsequently.

Implementation of outward-looking policies sometimes helps establish a "virtuous circle" of liberalization through resulting economic and political changes (Krueger 1993). For example, growth of the export sector at the expense of import-competing production raises the political strength of exporters and is thus likely to increase domestic support for liberalizing imports of capital equipment and other required inputs. In other cases, however, resulting economic and political changes undermine the viability of the reforms rather than reinforcing them. In fact, a pattern of liberalization followed by tightening was typical of Latin America during the 1970s and early 1980s. A prolonged period of high unemployment, a noticeable increase in income inequality, or deterioration of the current account are among factors that raise domestic pressure for reversal of liberalization.[3]

Why were the post-1985 trade reforms less susceptible to reversal? Several important developments may help explain the increased viability of Latin American trade reforms. The first is the increasing weight of evidence in support of outward-oriented reforms as an effective means of promoting growth. An important second factor is improved macroeconomic management, and especially the dramatic reduction of inflation rates throughout the region.[4] Excluding Brazil, the average rate of inflation in Latin America fell from about 300 percent in 1980–1990 to 31 percent in 1991–1996 (Burki and Perry 1997). Brazil's successful stabilization program reduced inflation from about 2,700 percent in 1994 to 18 percent in 1996 and less than 10 percent in 1997. Earlier heterodox approaches had achieved only limited success in battling chronic inflation, and their reliance on administered prices and interest rates was fundamentally incompatible with market-oriented reforms (Thomas, Nash, et al. 1991). Moreover, World Bank and IMF resources were increasingly deployed in support of outward-oriented reforms. These external resources allowed reform-minded governments to soften unfavorable initial effects of the new policies and thus to defuse potential pressure for policy reversal. A World Bank study (Burnside and Dollar 1997) confirms that providing multilateral aid to developing countries with "sound policies" increases the probability that reforms will persist.

A final explanation links sustained trade reforms to the proliferation of regional trade agreements (RTAs) that accompanied MFN liberalization beginning in the mid-1980s. Because unilateral liberalization and formation of regional trade areas are associated with significantly different adjustment paths, they differ also in their ability to withstand the inevitable domestic pressure for reversal. Membership in an RTA may therefore allow some countries to go forward with market opening even when unilateral liberalization faces insurmountable political obstacles. To be sure, the potential for this kind of complementarity depends crucially on the underlying objectives of regional cooperation. The inward-oriented Latin American RTAs of the 1960s and 1970s were explicitly intended to foster import substitution at the regional level and were thus antithetical to unilateral liberalization by member nations. In contrast, regional agreements of the 1980s and 1990s sought to enhance the international competitiveness of their members, with the ultimate goal of achieving full integration into global markets.

The purpose of this chapter is to document Latin America's reopening to international markets, to assess the role of unilateral trade liberalization in the region's move toward openness, and to shed light particularly on the zeal with which Latin American countries pursued regional trade initiatives. The chapter identifies a number of obstacles to sustaining trade liberalization and ways in which successful liberalizers in Latin America were able to overcome them. The focus is trade reform as an ongoing process, including the packaging of reform measures, their timing and sequencing, and the political-economy issues central to the viability of reforms in progress.

11.1 Documenting Trade Reform in Latin America

To evaluate Latin America's progress toward openness, an important first step is to consider the large menu of policy changes potentially included under the general heading of trade liberalization. Everyone can agree that Chile's dramatic across-the-board tariff cuts in the 1970s and 1980s were indeed liberalization. But outward-oriented reforms in a number of Latin American countries focused on creating new incentives for *exporting* (much as was done in countries as diverse as South Korea, Mauritius, and Morocco on other continents) and especially for nontraditional export products and markets, as in Costa Rica and Brazil. Moreover, it was not unusual for a country to maintain import substitution policies in some industries while offering export incentives in others, or even to tax traditional exports while promoting nontraditional exports, as Brazil and Argentina did. Finally, most countries in Latin America reduced MFN barriers to imports while at the same time making still larger cuts within regional arrangements.

Because many policy variables potentially affect a country's trade, even the direction of the net change in openness or outward orientation can be less than obvious. The NBER study of trade reform in developing countries classifies as liberalization any policy change that reduces the traditional anti-export bias of a country's trade regime (Bhagwati 1978; Krueger 1978). Revisionist interpretations of the paradigmatic East Asian experience (e.g., Rodrik 1995) suggest that an active government role rather than merely "getting prices right" was central to the export-led growth strategies of South Korea and Taiwan; by the Bhagwati-Krueger criterion even explicitly targeted export incentives qualify as liberalization.

Baldwin (1989) distinguishes between *incidence-based* measures of policies affecting trade, such as average tariff rates, and *outcome-based* measures, usually the relative size of trade flows. Because many factors apart from policies toward trade affect openness as measured by the relative importance of trade, outcome-based measures are useful in evaluating change in the openness of a single country rather than in making comparisons across countries. Moreover, a country may reduce its tariffs, thus appearing to liberalize according to one standard incidence-based measure, yet maintain import-licensing arrangements or exchange controls that in effect nullify the reduced import barriers. In this case, an outcome measure such as the ratio of trade to gross domestic product (GDP) will show little progress.

Pritchett (1996) proposes three concepts of trade liberalization or outward orientation. *Neutrality* refers to a reduced bias toward production of import substitutes, *liberality* to a lower degree of market intervention, and *openness* to an increase in trade intensity.[5] Comparing alternative summary measures of outward orientation from the empirical literature on growth and openness, Pritchett shows the indicators to be almost completely unrelated in cross-country data for less-developed countries. This finding suggests that openness has several dimensions; countries making the best progress according to one measure will not necessarily look as good in terms of another.

Whereas Chile's broad reductions in tariffs and nontariff barriers qualify under all three of Pritchett's concepts, some export promotion efforts in East Asia improved neutrality and openness while increasing rather than reducing the extent of market intervention. As elsewhere, the move toward outward orientation in Latin America was far from synonymous with laissez-faire. Although most Latin American countries liberalized trade while at the same time pursuing other market-oriented reforms such as privatization and deregulation, only in Chile was trade reform imbedded in an all-encompassing movement toward free-market policies. However, tables 11.1–11.4 suggest substantial progress according to all three types of indicators.

Table 11.1
Latin American import barriers by country, 1984–1993

Country and years	Mean tariff rates, weighted (percent of import value)			Mean total charges, weighted (percent of import value)			NTM incidence, weighted (percent of trade)		
	84–87	88–90	91–93	84–87	88–90	91–93	84–87	88–90	91–93
Argentina (1987, 1990, 1993)	24.8	20.3	9.7	38.6	26.8	16.6	21.2	29.6	3.1
Bolivia (1986, 1988, 1993)	19.5	16.5	9.8	19.5	16.5		32.1	3.5	
Brazil (1986, 1990, 1993)	50.2	28.4	14.7	75.2	28.4	16.9	44.1	22.2	14.3
Chile (1987, 1988, 1992)	19.0	14.3	10.7	20.2	18.3	21.2	16.1	20.7	0.4
Colombia (1986, 1988, 1992)	28.7	25.9	11.7	73.7	43.5	11.7	76.9	80.4	2.3
Costa Rica (1985, 1992)	53.0		15.0						0
Ecuador (1986, 1989, 1993)	29.4	26.7	8.2	39.1	37.4	10.2	51.0	52.2	
Mexico (1987, 1990, 1992)	9.1	8.9	12.3	13.4	9.5	15.8	24.1	22.2	19.0
Paraguay (1984, 1992)	9.2		12.9	63.6		12.9	22.5		4.6
Peru (1984, 1988–1989, 1992)	57.0	66.0	17.0					100.0	0
Venezuela (1987, 1989, 1992)	31.4	26.2	14.6	31.4	31.4	16.2	46.1	11.7	2.8

Sources: UNCTAD (1994), except Costa Rica and Peru from Dean, Desai, and Riedel (1994).
Notes: UNCTAD data weighted by product shares in world trade flows. Tariff data for Costa Rica and Peru weighted by domestic production; NTMs are percent of tariff lines covered by licensing requirements or quantitative restraints.

Table 11.2
Average minimum and maximum tariff rates by selected country, 1984–1993

Country and years	Average minimum tariff rates, weighted (percent of import value)			Average maximum tariff rates, weighted (percent of import value)		
	1984–1987	1988–1990	1991–1993	1984–1987	1988–1990	1991–1993
Argentina (1987, 1990, 1993)	14.5	17.7	8.2	34.0	21.7	10.3
Bolivia (1986, 1988, 1993)	19.5	16.3	9.5	19.5	16.7	9.9
Brazil (1986, 1990, 1993)	39.3	19.7	9.7	59.1	34.2	18.3
Chile (1987, 1988, 1992)	18.6	14.2	10.5	19.5	14.4	10.9
Colombia (1986, 1988, 1992)	23.1	19.9	9.0	32.6	30.2	14.0
Ecuador (1986, 1989, 1993)	18.6	16.5	6.0	42.0	39.6	10.3
Mexico (1987, 1990, 1992)	4.5	3.9	9.3	12.7	12.9	14.9
Paraguay (1984, 1992)	7.8		10.0	10.6		15.7
Venezuela (1987, 1989, 1992)	17.6	16.5	10.8	46.4	35.1	18.0

Source: UNCTAD (1994).
Note: Sectoral tariff rates weighted by shares in world trade flows.

Table 11.3
Exchange rates by selected country, pre-reform and 1995

Country and date of reform	Black-market premium		Real effective exchange rate 1995 (1990 = 100)
	Pre-reform	1995	
Argentina (1989)	40	0	
Bolivia		0	90
Brazil (1987/88)	41	0	
Chile (1985)	16	11	120
Colombia (1985)	9	0	134
Costa Rica (1986)	214	0	101
Ecuador		0	129
Mexico (1985)	15	0	
Paraguay		11	114
Peru (1989)	82	0	
Uruguay		0	157
Venezuela (1989)	103	25	140

Sources: Reform dates and pre-reform black-market premiums, Dean, Desai, and Riedel (1994); official and black-market exchange rates for 1995, *World Currency Yearbook, 27th edition* (1995); real effective exchange rates for 1995, *International Financial Statistics Yearbook* (1997).

Tables 11.1 and 11.2 display several indicators of import policy reform in eleven Latin American countries for which detailed information is available on a comparable basis.[6] Table 11.1 shows both weighted[7] mean tariff rates and weighted mean total import charges, the latter including a range of "paratariffs" that further raise the cost of imports. Between the mid-1980s and the early 1990s, mean tariff rates fell in nine countries. The exceptions are Mexico and Paraguay, which had the lowest mean rates in the initial period. Mean total charges also fell, sometimes dramatically, in nine countries. Here the exceptions are Chile and Mexico, both early reformers that had already reduced import barriers before the start of the period. However, given Chile's reputation as the region's liberalization superstar, it is interesting that its mean total import charges are the highest of the group and nearly double its mean tariff rate alone. The table likewise shows dramatic declines in the incidence of nontariff measures (NTMs), including quantitative restrictions. The modest increase in Paraguay's weighted mean tariffs may reflect tariffication of remaining NTMs in compliance with Mercosur and WTO commitments, rather than an increase in overall protection. The large

Table 11.4
Income, exports, and growth in Latin America, 1980–1995

Country	1995 GDP (billion $US)	1995 Exports (billion $US)	1995 GNP per capita		Exports as a share of GDP (%)		Export growth (% per year)		GDP growth (% per year)	
			$US	PPP est.	1980	1995	1980–1990	1990–1995	1980–1990	1990–1995
Argentina	281.1	21.0	8,030	8,310	5	9	3.7	6.9	−0.3	5.7
Bolivia	6.1	1.1	800	2,540	21	20	3.5	6.7	0.0	3.8
Brazil	688.1	46.5	3,640	5,400	9	7	7.5	7.4	2.7	2.7
Chile	67.3	16.0	4,160	9,520	23	29	7.0	9.2	4.1	7.3
Colombia	76.1	9.8	1,910	6,130	16	15	7.5	7.2	2.7	4.6
Costa Rica	9.2	2.6	2,310	5,850	26	41	6.1	9.5	3.0	5.1
Ecuador	17.9	4.3	1,390	4,220	25	29	5.4	7.4	2.0	3.4
Mexico	250.0	79.5	3,320	6,400	11	25	6.6	6.8	1.0	1.1
Paraguay	7.7	0.8	1,690	3,650	15	36	11.5	13.8	2.5	3.1
Peru	57.4	5.8	2,310	3,770	22	12	−1.7	8.3	−0.2	5.3
Uruguay	17.8	2.1	5,170	6,630	15	19	4.3	4.4	0.4	4.0
Venezuela	75.0	18.5	3,020	7,900	29	27	2.8	4.9	1.1	2.4

Source: World Bank (1997a).

Notes: GDP and GNP per capita are converted to U.S. dollars using a three-year average of exchange rates. PPP estimates of GNP per capita are calculated using purchasing power parities rather than exchange rates as conversion factors. Export and GDP growth rates are calculated using constant-price data. Thus, for a country with deteriorating terms of trade the share of exports in GDP can decline even if export growth exceeds GDP growth over the period.

decrease in Paraguay's mean total import charges supports the conclusion that its overall protection was declining.[8]

Table 11.2 shows that average minimum and average maximum tariff rates fell in nine countries. Mexico and Paraguay are again the exceptions, although with final rates in the same range as other countries in the group. Because the inefficiency associated with protection comes in part from "chaotic" incentives (Bhagwati 1978), tariff reform is most beneficial when it is associated with a reduction in the dispersion of rates as well as in their height. Chile's flat tariff schedule gives most domestic production a uniform advantage over competing imports; a flat schedule implies that effective protection rates are the same as nominal rates. Dean, Desai, and Riedel (1994) report sizable reductions in tariff dispersion (standard deviation) associated with trade reforms in Argentina, Brazil, and Costa Rica, along with a small increase in dispersion for Peru. A cruder measure of dispersion is the ratio of the average maximum tariff rate to the average minimum rate. The higher the ratio, the greater is the possibility that effective protection rates have been maintained or even increased despite reductions in both averages. Table 11.2 shows that the ratio fell in only four of nine countries, although these falls occurred in the countries with the highest initial ratio. The final ratios of average maximum to average minimum tariff rates range from close to 1 in Bolivia and Chile to 1.9 in Brazil.[9]

In addition to direct restrictions on trade flows, an important dimension of outward orientation broadly conceived is the foreign-exchange regime. Devaluation of an overvalued currency fits the Bhagwati-Krueger definition of trade liberalization since it reduces the bias against exports. Similarly, the composite binary measure of openness adopted by Sachs and Warner (1995a) classifies a country as closed if it meets even one of several criteria of significant insulation from global market forces, including a large differential between the official and black-market exchange rates as well as the extent of policies directly limiting trade. In the Sachs-Warner scheme, removal of trade barriers alone is insufficient to qualify as opening if the official exchange rate is kept so overvalued as to prevent development of export activities along lines of comparative advantage. Other analysts focus on changes in trade policies only and treat exchange-rate policy separately if at all.[10]

All eight Latin American countries studied by Dean, Desai, and Riedel (1994) reduced the extent of intervention in foreign-exchange

markets after 1985, eliminating multiple exchange rates and abolish-
ing most exchange controls. Moreover, the countries with the highest
black-market premiums prior to reform achieved the largest reductions in their premiums. For the region as a whole, the average
black-market premium fell from 72 percent in 1989 to 2 percent in
the mid-1990s (Inter-American Development Bank 1996). Table 11.3
shows that the black-market premium fell, often dramatically, for all
countries for which 1995 data were available.

Exchange controls are almost always associated with maintenance
of an overvalued exchange rate, although the black-market premium
is likely to overstate the extent of overvaluation. Liberalization of the
exchange regime is therefore typically accompanied by a nominal
devaluation of the currency.[11] Adoption of a more liberal exchange
regime also tends to increase allocative efficiency in international
transactions and to reduce efficiency losses due to rent seeking.
Michaely, Papageorgiou, and Choksi (1991) note that devaluation
has been a universal element in stabilization packages and a "common—sometimes crucial—instrument of trade liberalizations," even
those not associated with stabilization programs.

Most Latin American countries implemented large real devaluations in the wake of the debt crisis (Edwards 1995), thereby shifting
domestic production in favor of tradable goods and promoting export growth. But as these countries succeeded in implementing and
sustaining market-oriented policy reforms, inflows of private capital
from abroad often contributed to real appreciation and slower export
growth. Table 11.3 shows that real effective exchange rates appreciated
between 1990 and 1995 for seven of the eight countries in the group for
which the International Monetary Fund (IMF) publishes such a rate,
the exception being Bolivia. In the cases of Colombia and Chile, capital
controls were applied to limit certain types of inflows and thus the
associated real appreciation. A persistent tendency to real overvaluation was likewise a problem in Argentina, Brazil, and Mexico, each of
which used a nominal-anchor strategy to combat domestic inflation.

Table 11.4 compares several outcome indicators of openness for
twelve Latin American economies. Of the twelve countries, ten experienced faster growth of export volume from 1990 to 1995 than in
the preceding decade. Export growth slowed slightly in Colombia
and Brazil, although in both cases exports grew at a faster rate than
GDP over the entire period. However, the share of exports in GDP
rose in only seven of the twelve countries, declining modestly for

four and dramatically for Peru. The seeming paradox of a fall in export share over a period in which the average growth of exports is greater than that of GDP reflects differences in the two types of measures. The export share in GDP is calculated using current price data, while growth rates are calculated using constant prices and thus measure changes in volume rather than value. Relative prices of most agricultural and mineral raw materials declined sharply between 1980 and the mid-1990s. With primary commodities accounting for more than four-fifths of its exports, Peru experienced a large deterioration in its terms of trade over the period.

Because the ultimate goal of policy reform is to accelerate economic growth, the most important outcome measure is the rate of growth. Of course, many types of policy change contributed to Latin America's improved overall economic performance. Perhaps most important was macroeconomic stabilization. Even within the category of efficiency-enhancing structural reforms, trade liberalization is only one of a broad spectrum of market-oriented policies implemented since the mid-1980s. Still, the data confirm that Latin America's far-reaching trade reforms were at least consistent with higher overall growth rates. Eleven of the twelve countries experienced higher average annual GDP growth in the period after 1990. The average growth rate was the same in both periods for Brazil. For the region as a whole, the weighted average of the annual growth rates was 3.2 percent from 1990 to 1995, compared to 1.7 percent over the previous decade (World Bank 1997a,b). Moreover, the aggregate figures include the slow growth in Mexico and Argentina in the wake of Mexico's December 1994 peso crisis. With a strong recovery in those economies, the regional average reached 3.5 percent for 1996. But higher economic growth in the 1990s did not necessarily translate into reduced unemployment (Burki and Perry 1997). The region's average unemployment rate in the mid-1990s was in fact higher than in the 1980s, reflecting sharply higher unemployment in Argentina and smaller increases in Mexico and Venezuela.

Table 11.5 dates the initiation of trade reforms in the major South American countries plus Mexico and Costa Rica as determined in several studies using alternative criteria. The table also classifies the *initiation* of reforms as representing unilateral liberalization or influenced by some combination of (trade) reciprocity, cross-reciprocity, and/or intertemporal reciprocity. Reciprocity is based on a trading-bloc affiliation at the time reforms were initiated, although this does

Table 11.5
Initiation of trade liberalization in Latin America (liberalizations still in place by 1997)

Country	Sachs and Warner (1995a)	Edwards (1995)	IDB (1996)	Dean, Desai, and Riedel (1994)	Type of opening
Chile	1976	Early	1975, 1985s	1985	Unilateral (1970s), cross-reciprocal
Bolivia	1984 (1956–1978)	Early	1986s	Not covered	Unilateral
Mexico	1986	Early	1985s	1985	Cross-, intertemporal reciprocal
Costa Rica	1986 (1952–1961)	Second phase	1986g	1986	Reciprocal, cross-reciprocal
Paraguay	1989	Third phase	1989g	Not covered	Intertemporal reciprocal
Uruguay	1990	Second phase	1978, 1991s	Not covered	Reciprocal, cross-reciprocal
Argentina	1991	Third phase	1978, 1985, 1989s	1989	Cross-reciprocal (1985), reciprocal
Brazil	1991	Third phase	1990g	1987	Reciprocal, cross-reciprocal
Colombia	1991	Third phase	1991s	1985	Cross-reciprocal
Ecuador	1991 (1950–1983)	Nonreformer	1990g	Not covered	Reciprocal; cross-, intertemporal reciprocal
Peru	1991 (1948–1967)	Third phase	1990s	1989	Reciprocal, cross-reciprocal
Venezuela	(1950–1959), (1989–1992)	Third phase	1989s	1989	Cross-reciprocal

Notes: Sachs and Warner (1995a) clasify a country as open if nontariff barriers cover less than 40 percent of trade, the average tariff rate is less than 40 percent, the black-market exchange rate of the domestic currency is less than 20 percent below the official rate, and there is no government monopoly on major exports. Dates in parentheses indicate liberalizations satisfying these criteria that were later reversed. Other dates are based on trade policies only. Timing in Edwards (1995) is based on changes in average tariff and nontariff protection, coverage of nontariff barriers, and range of tariff rates. Dean, Desai, and Riedel (1994) and IDB (1996) date liberalizations since 1985. IDB (1996) also distinguishes shock (s) and gradual (g) trade reform. A shock reform cuts average tariffs by at least 50 percent and removes most NTBs in a two-year period.

not establish a causal link. A motivating role of cross-reciprocity is cited by Michaely, Papageorgiou, and Choksi (1991) for Argentina (1967) and Peru (1979). Thomas, Nash, et al. (1991) cite external financing between 1979 and 1987 from the World Bank and the IMF as "intended to facilitate the policy change" in Argentina, Brazil, Chile, Colombia, Costa Rica, Mexico, and Uruguay. Edwards (1995) estimates that nearly four-fifths of World Bank programs from 1983 to 1989 included conditions relating to trade liberalization goals. He emphasizes, however, that the role of the international organizations and the U.S. Treasury in "forging the new consensus" on the need for openness may have been as important as conditioning release of funds on specific reforms. Because of the evolving views of Latin American leaders, reforms implemented sometimes went far beyond those specified in loan conditions (e.g., Mexico, Colombia). Table 11.5 attributes possible motivating factors only to the *initiation* of reform. From the late 1980s onward, all the reformers benefited from after-the-fact external technical and financial support from the World Bank and IMF. By early 1996, all twelve countries (along with all remaining Latin American countries) had joined the WTO (nine were already GATT members in 1994). By the mid-1990s, each of the twelve had also entered into at least one regional trade arrangement.

11.2   Liberalization As a Sequential Process[12]

Why were most nations in Latin America able to achieve and sustain an open economy while other developing countries—often guided by the same received wisdom and even the same advice from the same foreign experts—failed to do so? The answer lies in the complex interplay of economics and politics that is central to the process of liberalization. Trade policy is inherently endogenous, shaped by underlying political forces. The economic results of implementing each new policy alter the political balance within a country, thus strengthening or weakening the position of reformers.

To consider the underpinnings of successful and sustained trade reform, it is helpful to divide the process of liberalization into four sequential components: (1) the design of a policy package; (2) its acceptance and endorsement by top policymakers; (3) its implementation in specific policy measures and their administration; and (4) the economy's response to changed incentives. The last component in turn influences the degree of support from the policy community and the public, completing the political-economic cycle. Correspondingly, a reform package may fail for several reasons. First, the policies themselves may be poorly conceived or inappropriate to the country's economic or political circumstances. Second, the package, though well designed and appropriate, may nonetheless fail to gain the support of a country's political leadership. Third, even a package supported by top policy officials may be aborted if the relevant legislative and administrative bodies are unwilling to implement it. Finally, elements in the policy environment may prevent markets from responding appropriately to the changed incentives.

The record of Latin America shows a general progression over these stages. In the early 1970s, doubt still remained concerning the best policies to follow; industrialization via import substitution continued to enjoy wide support among Latin American economists and policymakers. To some, the domestic dislocations from the first oil shock vividly demonstrated the potential danger of greater integration into international markets. By the late 1970s, the intellectual case for open markets was ascendant, but many Latin American policymakers remained unconvinced. In the early 1980s, governments rolled back earlier trade reforms in response to debt problems. But by the late 1980s, trade reforms once initiated began to stay in place, at least in countries that had managed to achieve macroeconomic stability.[13] The most important "late" trade reformers—countries that continued to reverse earlier liberalization—were Argentina and Brazil, both of which experienced repeated failures of macroeconomic stabilization efforts. It is noteworthy that the regional macroeconomic dislocations associated with the December 1994 devaluation of the Mexican peso did not lead to a major rollback of Latin American trade reforms. The only country to retreat temporarily in 1994 and 1995 from earlier reforms was Venezuela (Inter-American Development Bank 1996).

Getting Started

In Latin America, the fundamental ideas for reform were typically imported. These ideas were assembled and put forward by foreign experts and a new generation of domestic policymakers trained in the United States.[14] But to have a reasonable chance of being implemented, a reform initiative requires support from *some* of a country's top policymakers. Drawing on four decades of experience in advising Latin American governments, Harberger (1993) concludes that the right advice is not enough. Successful economic policies "would in all likelihood have failed (or never got started) but for the efforts of a key group of individuals, and within that group, one or two outstanding leaders" (343). In a number of cases, this core group consisted of young U.S.–trained economists. Williamson and Haggard (1994), summarizing views of several development experts, likewise cite the need for visionary leadership and a "sense of history." In their own opinion, however, great vision is not always required. Given a crisis situation, any sensible leader will see the immediate political benefit of a major change in policy direction.[15]

Empirically, crisis conditions do sometimes provide the spur needed for major reforms (Chile in 1974, Argentina in 1989, Peru in 1990). Rodrik (1994) argues that crisis conditions push distributional issues into the background and thus allow trade reforms to go forward. But action taken in response to a crisis is not necessarily a move toward greater openness. On the contrary, many Latin American countries rolled back earlier trade reforms in response to the oil shocks of the early 1970s and again during the debt crisis of the early 1980s. Likewise, macroeconomic crisis appears to be the most common reason for the reversal of liberalization by individual Latin American countries (Rajapatirana, de la Mora, and Yatawara 1997). In other cases, liberalizers initiated reforms without waiting for a full-blown crisis to materialize under old policies (Costa Rica in 1986, Colombia in 1984).

Successful reform also requires support from legislators and administrators to ensure its effective implementation. To create the desired changes in economic behavior, the vision of a leader must first be translated into practical policies. However, some governments lack the necessary technical expertise to implement new policies. While help is often available from aid agencies in the OECD countries and from multilateral organizations such as the World Bank and International Monetary Fund, excessive reliance on outside assistance may exact a high price. A key role for foreign experts may alienate local officials and erode their sense of ownership of the new policies. Moreover, critics of reform often take advantage of any prominent foreign role to marshal domestic support for their opposition. The persistent appeal of populist and heterodox economic programs in Latin America (e.g., Peru in 1985, Brazil in 1986) stems partly from their rejection of neoclassical policy advice from foreign, and especially U.S., experts. In 1984, even Chile replaced its band of "Chicago boys" with mainstream advisors who raised tariffs, though a new group of Chicago-trained economists was installed the next year.

A different type of "problem" related to policy implementation is that the administrative burden of a laissez-faire approach is much lighter than that of a dirigiste economic regime. Substantial resistance to market-oriented reforms may therefore come from government officials whose jobs, salaries, prestige, and often opportunities for graft are endangered, as well as from their opposite numbers in the private sector who have learned how to operate profitably under existing policies. Thus, opposition to reform is likely to extend far beyond the firms and workers in protected import-competing sectors.

Maintaining Broad Popular Support

Support at the top is necessary but not always sufficient for political sustainability. However, the importance of broad political support depends, especially in the short term, on the form of government. An authoritarian regime may be able to force the population to accept austere policies or to shape public opinion through control over the media. Some development specialists have even raised the controversial notion that early introduction of democratic institutions may doom the prospects for needed economic reforms.[16] Indeed, authoritarian governments launched many of the successful reform efforts in both Latin America and East Asia. In most cases these reforms were not reversed by subsequent democratic regimes.[17] But any new government, whether authoritarian or democratic, may enjoy a kind of honeymoon period during which leaders benefit from greater freedom of maneuver as well as the luxury of blaming unsatisfactory economic conditions on the previous regime (Chile in 1974, Argentina and Paraguay in 1989, Peru in 1990). Of course, the new leader is often merely carrying out earlier promises regarding direction of policy change.

The need for broad political support is one explanation for the popularity of reciprocal liberalization in general and of RTAs in particular. The public and even many policymakers take a largely mercantilist view of trade reforms, finding it easy to grasp the benefits from increased exports (typically seen as expanded sales and employment) and accordingly difficult to see the benefits from increased imports. In a reciprocal agreement, the increased imports can be justified as the price of increased exports. But, given this prevalent misunderstanding of the fundamental nature of gains from trade, belief in the benefits of unilateral liberalization requires a major leap of faith.

11.3   Overcoming Obstacles to Successful Liberalization

Trade liberalization is an intensely political subject for two related but distinct reasons. The first is that costs associated with new policies become apparent almost immediately while the gains lie farther in the future. Adjustment costs along the way can mean a period of lower average living standard, even though there are always some who gain immediately from any change in policy. This is one reason why visionary leadership can be key to successful reform. A separate problem is that there are always permanent losers from any liberalization. Moreover, *trade* reform entails an especially high ratio of redistribution to total gains (Rodrik 1994). While there is no way to avoid transition costs or an uneven distribution of long-term costs and benefits, appropriate policies may reduce their extent and thus preserve the political viability of reform.

Commitment to an outward-oriented trade strategy requires complementary supporting policies and conditions. These include transportation and communications infrastructure; access to financial capital and to imported capital goods, raw materials, and intermediate inputs; a well-functioning labor market; and, above all, an appropriate real exchange rate. To the extent that potential exporters respond to profit opportunities offered by the new policy environment, their political influence increases while that of import-competing producers wanes. The result is then to strengthen political support for liberalization, allowing the reform process to go forward (Krueger 1993). But *will* potential exporters respond? The key to the virtuous cycle lies in the credibility of the new policies, and this in turn rests on the economy's ability to withstand the dislocations of the adjustment period.

Adjusting to New Policies

Liberalizing countries necessarily experience dislocation costs during the period of adjustment to new policies. These dislocation costs are of two main forms: those associated with necessary changes in the composition of durable capital, and those associated with unemployment of labor or other resources. As long as change in policy has not been fully anticipated, the economy will begin from a given stock of durable sector-specific human and physical capital that is no longer optimal. In the new situation, some types of capital will be worth more than their replacement cost, others will be worth less. Trade liberalization will typically reduce the value of capital in import-competing industries and raise the value of capital in current or potential export sectors. If real factor rewards are flexible, these resources can continue to be fully employed as the stock adjusts over time to suit new relative prices. Required changes in the returns to industry-specific factors are largest soon after the new policy comes into force; in the post-liberalization equilibrium following complete adjustment in the stock of sector-specific capital, the market value of any factor must again equal its replacement cost.

In the absence of factor-market distortions, the laissez-faire adjustment process will be socially optimal. In particular, there will be no efficiency gain from speeding up or slowing down the process through government policy, although there may be political reasons to do so. But factor prices are rarely very flexible in the short run, and other factor-market distortions are likely to be present as well. Some resources will therefore become unemployed during the transition period, necessarily raising the social cost of adjustment and thus undermining political support for the liberalization program. These temporary dislocations would seem to bolster the case for some kind of government adjustment assistance program to speed the movement of resources into expanding sectors.

In practice, however, the economic benefits from adjustment assistance appear to be slim. Where adjustment assistance is offered to workers displaced by trade liberalization, it usually takes the form of a social safety net that is more generous than the one covering workers displaced for reasons other than increased foreign competition. Providing such special benefits may be good politics—allowing liberalization to go forward in the face of strong opposition from workers. A less-benign type of adjustment assistance takes the form of subsidized loans and technical assistance to trade-impacted firms. These measures retain resources in declining sectors and thus tend to delay rather than facilitate adjustment. In either case, the primary motive for such policies is to defuse political opposition to socially desirable liberalization.[18]

Development economists formerly counseled gradual change in policy as a means of reducing costs of adjustment (e.g., Little, Scitovsky, and Scott 1970). This is another area where conventional wisdom has changed in the light of experience. In practice, gradual policy changes allow more time for opponents of liberalization to marshal their forces. Liberalization delayed can therefore mean liberalization canceled. Chile's long-lived reforms began as shock therapy, not gradualism. In contrast, when Argentina in the 1970s announced a schedule of gradual reforms, firms expecting to be negatively affected lobbied successfully to cancel the planned tariff reductions (Edwards 1995). Such observations may help explain why late reformers in Latin America moved much faster than nations that opened up earlier. Edwards (1995) points to "a clear change in what is perceived to be abrupt and rapid ... what fifteen years ago [in Chile] were seen as brutally fast reforms are now considered to be mild and gradual liberalizations." Colombia cut average import tariffs by 65 percent in one year, going from an average of 34 percent in 1990 to 12 percent in 1991. Peru eliminated quantitative restrictions in "one bold move" and cut tariffs from an average of 110 percent in 1990 to 15 percent in 1992. Table 11.6 shows that the most recent liberalizations in eight of twelve countries are classified as shock trade reforms. Of these, all but one (Venezuela) had been sustained as of 1997.

Table 11.6
Trade taxes as a share of total central government revenue: By country, 1981–1990 and 1991–1995 (percent)

Country	1981–1990	1991–1995
Argentina	13.8	7.9
Bolivia	12.5	6.6
Brazil	2.7	1.9
Chile	8.7	9.6
Colombia	17.0	9.7
Costa Rica	25.5	16.1
Ecuador	20.2	11.6
Mexico	10.1	7.1
Paraguay	14.6	14.8
Peru	20.8	9.8
Uruguay	11.4	5.6
Venezuela	12.6	9.1

Source: World Bank (1997a, table A.1).

In other parts of the world, rapid radical reform has also had a better overall record than gradualism. Based on evidence from trade reform by developing countries in the 1980s, often with support from the IMF and World Bank, Thomas, Nash, et al. (1991) conclude that "comprehensive, intense, and rapid" reform is usually preferable because its benefits are both larger and sooner than under a more gradual approach. To the extent that gradualism gives rise to uncertainty about full implementation, gradual policies may lack credibility. With domestic and foreign investors in doubt as to whether an announced program will ever be fully implemented, the new price signals may elicit little response.

Also undercutting the case for gradualism is recent evidence that the aggregate effect of successful trade liberalization on employment can be relatively small even in the short run. Although workers will be displaced from firms in contracting sectors, much of the resulting job loss can be offset by employment expansion in export industries (Edwards 1995). However, the popular mercantilist accounting of jobs created and jobs lost gives little indication of actual adjustment costs borne by displaced workers, which depend on gross rather than net changes and on worker characteristics. It also takes no account of the real gains from expanded trade—increased efficiency from replacing low-productivity import-competing output with regionally or globally efficient export production.

Real Exchange Rates

For an economy adopting an outward-oriented strategy, the most important price to "get right" is the real exchange rate. Appreciation of the real exchange rate undercuts the competitiveness of potential exports across the board and makes imports look cheap relative to their domestic counterparts; increased unemployment and deterioration of the current account result. If the nominal exchange rate is fixed, the usual policy response is a return to protectionist measures; the reversal is often billed as temporary, justified by the need to protect jobs and dwindling international reserves. Recent Latin American trade reforms have almost always begun with a large nominal devaluation (Edwards 1995), yet the single economic factor most likely to sabotage a liberalization attempt once in progress is (a return to) overvaluation of the real exchange rate. Real appreciation often occurs when the exchange rate is used as a nominal anchor in battling domestic inflation. The potential incompatibility of the nominal-anchor strategy with maintaining a viable real exchange rate gives rise to the judgment that macroeconomic stabilization must be achieved before trade liberalization has a good chance at success. The repeated reversals of trade reform in Argentina and Brazil were linked to failed stabilization programs.

Another threat to an appropriate real exchange rate comes from the capital account. Initiation of a credible reform package may attract new capital inflows. Indeed, the desire to increase inward direct investment is often an important motive for reform. A flexible nominal rate will rise (at least temporarily) as a consequence of capital inflows attracted by the new policy initiative. Under a fixed rate, increased capital inflows will swell reserves, thereby putting upward pressure on the domestic money supply and the price level. In either case, real appreciation is the likely result. This is one reason for the conventional advice that trade reforms should precede capital-account liberalization. However, rather than limiting all capital inflows, developing countries often try to discourage only inflows of short-term liquid capital, thus offering exporters some protection from volatility of the real exchange rate without losing the potential benefits from longer-term investments. Techniques used to limit short-term inflows include minimum maturity conditions, taxes, and reserve requirements on foreign borrowing, as implemented by Colombia and Chile (Burki and Perry 1997).

Macroeconomic Discipline

By the 1990s, most nations in Latin America had finally managed to achieve the degree of macroeconomic stability essential for good economic performance. Until then, structural adjustment policies including trade reform were held hostage by the need to reduce budget deficits and curb inflation. As noted earlier, battling inflation may produce an overly strong real exchange rate that taxes would-be exporters. Trade reform may also pose a fiscal problem for developing countries, which typically rely on trade taxes for a substantial share of revenue. However, table 11.4 indicates that all twelve countries covered in this chapter reduced their relative dependence on trade taxes as a source of revenue for the central government between the early 1980s and the mid-1990s.

In Latin America, taxes on major commodity exports have traditionally generated a substantial fraction of government revenue.
When Argentina eliminated export taxes at the start of the 1990s,
improved compliance with income taxes helped fill the resulting gap
(World Bank 1996). In other cases, trade reform was carried out
in tandem with the privatization of government-owned companies
(e.g., Peru after 1990). Privatization typically produces double fiscal
benefits: first from the asset sale, then from avoidance of the budget-
breaking operating subsidies often required to keep government
enterprises in operation. Import tariffs have also been a significant
source of government revenue for most Latin American countries. In
principle, a move to a simple trade regime with low uniform trade
taxes could raise rather than lower trade's contribution to government revenue, depending on the price elasticity of trade flows and
the prior extent of smuggling to avoid high tariffs and burdensome
nontariff barriers. Another potential offset is tariffication of quantitative restrictions, a policy change considered to be a move toward
trade liberalization because it reduces the role of administrative discretion. Although it boosts tariff revenues, tariffication has the political disadvantage of creating losers (former license holders) without
immediately obvious winners. In practice, such offsets have not been
sufficient to prevent total tariff collections from falling as trade is
liberalized. Some policy analysts therefore argue that the fiscal deficit should be reduced before trade is liberalized (Thomas, Nash, et al.
1991).

Increased Inequality

Regardless of the political regime, the sustainability of any policy
package eventually rests on its ability to raise, or at least not to reduce, the resources available to meet the needs of the population. A
package that delivers a rising average living standard is obviously
easier to sell than a package that requires sacrifice. The yardstick
most often used to compare economic success across countries is
growth in per capita income (PCI).[19] But the viability of reforms
depends not only on aggregate or average gains but also on their
distribution. The debt crisis of the early 1980s was associated with a
pronounced tendency toward increased inequality in Latin America,
but subsequent recovery and reforms reversed this effect, at least for
the region as a whole. The income share of the lowest quintile of the

population rose from 3.4 percent in the 1960s to 4.5 percent in the 1990s, while the income share of the highest quintile dropped from 61.6 percent to 52.9 percent over the same period (World Bank 1997b). Although income inequality remains an important policy concern in Latin America, there is little evidence that market-oriented reforms in the 1980s and 1990s exacerbated the problem.[20]

A previous generation of development economists saw in Simon Kuznetz's inverted U of temporarily increased income inequality the necessary price of future growth; concentration of income and wealth were assumed to promote essential capital formation by raising the aggregate saving rate. Today this rationalization seems less persuasive. The high saving rates that fueled growth in East Asia were achieved without increases in inequality. Moreover, in a world of internationally mobile capital, domestic saving and domestic capital formation are no longer required to move in lockstep. In Latin America, internationally mobile capital provides a barometer of investor sentiment regarding the credibility of reforms. Countries that achieve stable, market-oriented institutions have been able to supplement domestic saving with private capital inflows from abroad. Although governments rarely appreciate the daily "policy report card" provided by active financial markets, concern about losing foreign investment may well restrain officials' impulse to adopt policies with short-term payoffs but longer-term costs (McCulloch and Petri 1998). Conversely, while international investors are indeed likely to shun countries without strong market institutions, wealthy Latin American savers are highly resourceful in finding means to move their own financial assets to safe havens abroad. Anecdotal evidence strongly suggests that concentration of income and thus of savings facilitates capital flight. In this case, increased income inequality—whatever its effect on the aggregate saving rate—is likely to reduce the amount of domestic savings available to finance domestic capital formation.

Skilled versus Unskilled Labor

In earlier decades, discussion of the potential for temporary or permanent increases in income inequality resulting from liberalized trade centered on changes in labor earnings versus return to capital, especially foreign-owned capital. In the 1990s, attention began to focus more on the observed increase in the gap between earnings of Latin America's skilled and unskilled workers, which some tie to increased openness (e.g., Wood 1997). For a world of two factors, the Stolper-Samuelson theorem predicts exactly this outcome in skilled-labor-abundant countries like the United States. However, the same model also predicts a shift to a lower ratio of unskilled to skilled labor in production, the opposite of what has been observed in most industrial nations. For this reason, Lawrence and Slaughter (1993) argue that skill-biased technical change rather than trade lies at the heart of the controversial trend. Moreover, the Stolper-Samuelson model predicts a fall in the same differential for unskilled-labor-abundant countries, that is, less-developed countries, while in fact the skill premium has risen in many such nations.

One explanation for a rising skill premium in developing countries is that the technology transfer associated with growth of nontraditional exports causes a temporary increase in demand for skilled labor. Even though the exports themselves may be unskilled-labor-intensive in production, skilled labor is needed initially to adapt and implement the imported technologies (Pissarides 1997). Also, the Stolper-Samuelson and factor-price-equalization theorems predict changes in *equilibrium* factor rewards with both factors fully mobile between sectors, and then only under other special conditions. Given the pace of policy change in Latin America since the mid-1980s, the situation can hardly be viewed as such an equilibrium.

Related concerns are the perceived increase in the volatility of earnings and the increased uncertainty of job tenure associated with participation in international markets (Rodrik 1997). These concerns can to some extent be addressed through a social safety net, and indeed Rodrik demonstrates a high correlation between measures of countries' openness and social spending. Rodrik notes that international mobility of capital prevents countries from financing such a safety net primarily through taxes on income from capital. However, as long as openness produces *aggregate* gains to a nation's labor force, social insurance for workers can be financed without increased taxes on capital income.

Sustained high unemployment rates in some Latin American countries reflect slow adjustment to trade and macroeconomic reforms in the presence of labor-market distortions (Burki and Perry 1997). But whatever their cause, increased income inequality and/or volatility can undermine the perceived "fairness" of outward-oriented policies even if accompanied by enhanced growth of per capita income. While countries differ widely in the approaches used to make these changes acceptable to their citizens, the issue must be addressed if integration with international markets is to remain politically viable. During the difficult adjustments of the early 1980s, free-market-oriented Chile protected its poorest citizens with targeted employment and nutrition policies (Graham 1996). In Mexico, social and education programs were used to enhance the welfare of the poor and defuse political opposition to economic reforms in the early 1990s (Cordoba 1994). Even so, unpopular reforms, especially devaluation of the Mexican peso, are credited with helping to end the decades-long political monopoly of the Institutional Revolutionary Party (PRI). Nonetheless, most PRI-initiated trade reforms remained in place.

Sequencing of Reforms

In the developing world (as well as in centrally planned economies), an import-substitution trade regime has typically been one element in a broad complex of dirigiste policies affecting all domestic economic activity—extensive public ownership, selective subsidies, and government restrictions affecting operation of domestic capital and labor markets as well as the foreign exchange market.[21] Furthermore, many developing countries experienced double- or triple-digit inflation rates during the 1960s and 1970s, thanks to overreliance on money creation to finance government spending. Experience suggests that attention to appropriate sequencing of economic reforms could reduce the period of economic distress following liberalization. A large literature has addressed the issue of sequencing, but without achieving consensus on an optimal sequence that is independent of the special circumstances of a given country.[22] Moreover, the sequencing literature typically treats trade liberalization as a single element in a broader reform program. Questions less often addressed concern the sequencing of the individual policy changes required to complete a country's successful transformation from import substitution to outward-oriented growth, changes sometimes carried out over a period of years or even decades.

Notwithstanding theorists' concentration on the costliness of restrictions on imports, successful liberalizers most often begin the process of integrating into global markets by restoring incentives for exporters. The initial impetus for import liberalization frequently comes from the needs of current or potential exporters who must look to world markets for capital goods, raw materials, or intermediate inputs. Such measures to facilitate export growth, often enacted in advance of comprehensive reforms, may include rebates of import duties on capital equipment and/or intermediate inputs used to produce exports; establishment of export-processing zones; favorable access to licensed foreign exchange and restricted imports; and other incentives intended to raise the profitability of all or selected export-oriented activities. Subsequent reforms may include broader measures such as elimination of import licensing, tariffication of quantitative import restrictions, rationalization of the tariff structure, and elimination of multiple exchange rates used to discourage "nonessential" imports.

The first step in comprehensive reforms is usually a real devaluation, sometimes along with unification of any multiple exchange rates (Thomas, Nash, et al. 1991). In Chile, Mexico, and Bolivia, an early real devaluation tended to make quantitative import restrictions redundant, thereby facilitating their speedy removal. Although Edwards (1995) notes the increased speed and intensity of trade reform programs in the 1990s, broad tariff reductions were typically implemented in stages over several years according to a schedule announced at the start. In the first stage, the goal is less to spur exports than to move domestic relative prices closer to international prices and to eliminate large discrepancies in domestic effective protection rates.

The Lerner symmetry theorem implies that removing barriers to exports is equivalent to removing barriers to imports. Nonetheless, there may be dynamic advantages in pursuing export promotion prior to general liberalization on the import side. The most controversial aspect of trade liberalization is not the configuration of production and trade in the new equilibrium versus the old one, but the path by which the economy moves from one to the other. In the new outward-oriented equilibrium, both imports and exports will be much larger. However, the extent of overall economic losses and income redistribution, and hence the difficulty of maintaining adequate political support for needed reforms, all depend critically on whether imports grow sooner or later than exports, that is, whether the current account improves or deteriorates during the period of adjustment. Marked deterioration of the current account signals a likely return to protection (Michaely, Papageorgiou, and Choksi 1991), thus undermining credibility of the reforms. Proceeding first with export promotion (including real devaluation) also creates a set of early supporters of further trade reforms, including both local firms with export potential and foreign direct investors establishing export-oriented subsidiaries.

The External Environment

The case for import-substituting industrialization, as developed by Prebisch, Singer, and other writers, rests in part on export pessimism: the assumption that global markets offer less-developed countries little opportunity for gains through increased exports. Development along lines of international comparative advantage was interpreted narrowly to mean additional export of raw materials and commodities, since these made up about four-fifths of the value of existing exports from less-developed countries as a group. Advocates of import substitution assumed that the international prices obtained for commodity exports would decline over time, exacerbating the gap between rich and poor nations (Edwards 1995). Moreover, their narrow view of outward-oriented growth seemed to offer no role for development of a modern manufacturing sector (Krueger 1997).

Notwithstanding the past successes of export-led industrialization in Latin America and elsewhere, the question of global market receptivity to nontraditional exports continued to lurk in the background during the 1990s, and often with good reason. The World Bank study of trade policy reform in the 1980s identified growing protectionism in international markets as one of several factors constraining exporters' response (Thomas, Nash, et al. 1991). Apparel exports, the first step on the export-led-industrialization ladder for a host of countries, was also the most protected manufacturing industry in most industrial nations, including the United States.[23] Likewise, agricultural exports from Latin America were limited by quotas, tariffs, antidumping suits, and other restrictions.[24] It is of course true that export-oriented development would work better if rich countries were more willing to adjust out of sectors that have lost their comparative advantage. But, as Sachs and Warner (1995b, 15) conclude, export-oriented development has still worked, even under less-than-ideal external conditions: "With the ... exception of Haiti, there is not a single developing country that had substantially open trade and yet failed to grow by at least 2 percent per year" between 1970 and 1989.

Studies focusing instead on less-developed countries that remained insulated from global markets tell a similar story. From their
research into the causes of sub-Saharan Africa's declining share in
world exports, Yeats et al. (1996) conclude that OECD trade barriers
in potential export markets were not to blame: "Rather, the sub-
Saharan African countries' own trade and transport policies incorporate a substantial anti-export bias, which lessens their ability to be
competitive in international markets." If anything, exports from sub-
Saharan Africa should have gained an advantage in the markets of
industrial nations from trade preferences under the European Union's
Lome Convention as well as the Generalized System of Preferences,
but these preferential arrangements were apparently insufficient to
offset the anti-export bias of the nations' own policies.

11.4   Unilateral versus Reciprocal Liberalization

Along with the rest of the world, Latin America experienced a resurgence of regional trade initiatives in the 1990s (see table 11.7).
These included new regional customs unions with negotiated common external tariffs: the revamped Andean Group (1988) and Mercosur (1991). However, most of the new arrangements were free
trade areas, including NAFTA (1994) as well as a host of bilateral
agreements (Edwards 1995; Organization of American States 1997).
Unlike the inward-looking regional agreements of the 1960s, these
new agreements were formed as trade of the members was being
liberalized on an MFN basis also. Even the language of the agreements was typically outward-oriented, emphasizing enhancement
of international competitiveness, export growth, and receptivity toward foreign direct investment. Some observers were unenthusiastic
about the regional initiatives, fearing losses from trade diversion, a
return to nontransparent protection, rising external trade barriers,
and reduced interest in future rounds of multilateral trade negotiations (e.g., Bhagwati and Panagariya 1996). Other researchers,
however, argued that regional agreements could help maintain the
region's movement toward openness by enhancing credibility of reforms (e.g., Fernandez 1997).

    Given the range of potential benefits from and obstacles to suc-
cessful liberalization discussed previously, together with the intellectual climate of general support for market opening in general,

what can be said about the choice between unilateral and reciprocal liberalization? Relative advantages may reflect differences in anticipated size of eventual benefits, costs of adjustment, and political feasibility of reform. But in light of the patterns of policy change in the 1980s and 1990s, it is misleading to cast unilateral and reciprocal liberalization as mutually exclusive alternatives. Rather, they may offer complementary strategies for implementing market-oriented structural reform (McCulloch and Petri 1997), an idea that has been termed "open regionalism" in the Asia-Pacific context.

Size of Benefits

An RTA is likely to cause trade diversion—substitution of imports from higher-cost partners for goods previously obtained from non-partners.[25] The cost associated with trade diversion thus reduces potential gains from liberalization with preferential elements; in a free-trade agreement, these costs may be increased by application of restrictive rules of origin. Nonetheless, unilateral liberalization may produce an inferior final outcome for an individual country that is large enough to influence the terms of trade. If its initial tariffs are below the theoretical "optimum," a large country's unilateral liberalization raises world welfare, but the gain comes partly at its own expense. If large countries instead liberalize bilaterally or multilaterally, associated terms-of-trade effects tend to balance out, reducing the possibility that any one country can actually be worse off even after full adjustment. The members of Mercosur and NAFTA include large countries for which negative terms-of-trade effects from liberalization are a significant concern. Grouping with major trading partners neutralizes much of the potential impact.

Moreover, by promoting action on the part of countries that might otherwise choose to free-ride, reciprocal liberalization may result in *more* liberalization and thus greater global as well as national gains. This is, of course, the logic underlying the multilateral trade negotiations that have helped reduce many types of barriers to trade in the advanced countries. Essentially the same benefits might be obtained from what could be called "strategic unilateralism," a scenario in which one country's unilateral liberalization induces trading partners to follow its example (Coates and Ludema 1996). This kind of leader-follower behavior may be plausible in a repeated-game

Table 11.7
Regional trade arrangements in Latin America (arrangements still in effect in 1997)

Arrangement, date, membership	Type of arrangement	Objectives, status in 1997	Comments
Common Market of the Southern Cone (Mercosur), 1991 Argentina, Brazil, Paraguay, Uruguay	Customs union	Establish common market, eventually implement macroeconomic coordination and monetary union. Most internal tariffs eliminated by 1995, remainder to be phased out by 2000. Common external tariffs of 0 to 20 percent implemented in 1995, exceptions lists to be phased out over 5 years for Argentina, Brazil, and Uruguay, 10 years for Paraguay.	No provisions to facilitate internal labor mobility. Under 1996 agreements to phase out tariffs on trade with Mercosur, Chile and Bolivia became associate members (4 + 1 formula).
Andean Group, 1969 Bolivia, Colombia, Chile (until 1976), Ecuador, Peru, Venezuela (from 1973)	Customs union	All trade restrictions eliminated on trade between Bolivia, Colombia, Ecuador, and Venezuela; common external tariffs of 5 to 20 percent (40 percent for autos) implemented in 1995. Peru's participation lagged, but most trade between Peru and other members liberalized through bilateral agreements.	Early program largely abandoned, group revived beginning in 1989.
Central American Common Market, 1961 Costa Rica, El Salvador, Guatemala, Honduras, Nicaragua	Customs union	Establish economic union, eventually implement macroeconomic coordination and unrestricted movement of capital and labor. Many barriers to internal trade reduced or eliminated; some progress toward establishment of common external tariffs of 5 to 20 percent, but with many exceptions and reversals.	Group disintegrated during the 1980s, revived in early 1990s. CACM members and Panama established a new organization (Sistema de Integracion Centro-americana) in 1993.

	Type	Description	
Caribbean Community and Common Market (Caricom), 1973 Antigua and Barbuda, Bahamas (only Community), Barbados, Belize, Dominica, Grenada, Guyana, Jamaica, Montserrat, St. Kitts and Nevis, St. Lucia, St. Vincent and the Grenadines, Suriname (from 1995), Trinidad and Tobago	Customs union	Economic and political integration. Most members participate in a limited free trade area. Common external tariff established but not uniformly applied by members.	Bilateral agreements with Venezuela (1992) and Colombia (1994) provide for limited period of nonreciprocal preferential access and negotiations on eventual bilateral free trade.
North American Free Trade Agreement (NAFTA), 1992 Canada, United States, Mexico	Free trade agreement	Regional free trade, with eventual extension to a Free Trade Area of the Americas (FTAA). Eliminates most tariffs and nontariff barriers over a 10-year period and liberalizes some service sectors. Includes provisions on intellectual property, government procurement, investment. "Side agreements" on labor, environment, safeguards.	Expansion of Canada-U.S. free trade area created in 1988.
Group of Three, 1994 Colombia, Mexico, Venezuela	Free trade agreement	Total elimination of tariffs over a 10-year period, with some sectoral exceptions; also deals with intellectual property, services, government procurement, investment.	Colombia-Venezuela trade remains subject to Andean Group terms.

Table 11.7 (continued)

Arrangement, date, membership	Type of arrangement	Objectives, status in 1997	Comments
Bilateral agreements Chile with Mexico, 1992; Venezuela, 1993; Colombia, 1994; Ecuador, 1995 Mexico with Chile, 1992; Bolivia, 1995; Costa Rica, 1995	Free trade agreements	Regional free trade. Agreements include mechanisms for dispute resolution and clear timetables for elimination of almost all trade barriers.	Mexico's agreements similar in structure to NAFTA.
Association for Latin American Integration (ALADI), 1980 Argentina, Bolivia, Brazil, Chile, Colombia, Ecuador, Mexico, Paraguay, Peru, Uruguay, Venezuela	Regional scope agreement	Increase bilateral trade among member countries and between members and third countries through bilateral and multilateral agreements, with long-term goal of regional free trade; 32 sectoral agreements in place, mostly bilateral.	Successor to Latin American Free Trade Association (LAFTA).

Sources: Edwards (1995) and Organization of American States (1997).

context. However, the reverse is also possible: Some countries may delay trade reform hoping to get "credit" for their action in a subsequent regional or multilateral negotiation.[26]

Finally, negotiation of regional agreements may be a way to prod other trading partners into mutually beneficial multilateral or regional negotiations. Under United States Trade Representative William Brock, the Reagan administration announced its willingness to negotiate a free trade agreement with any interested country; Brock's stated goal was to increase support abroad for initiation of a new GATT round. Chile, supposedly next in line to join an expanded NAFTA, negotiated a free trade agreement with Mercosur in 1996, perhaps to remind a foot-dragging United States of its earlier declarations of interest (Chile's 1991 free trade agreement with Mexico predated NAFTA).

Cost of Adjustment

Any type of trade liberalization entails adjustment costs that must be measured against the eventual gains from superior efficiency. In the typical case, distorted domestic factor markets exacerbate these costs. The simultaneous opening of several national markets reduces the extent of dislocation and required adjustment for any one of them. An important aspect of this advantage is the reduced need for adjustment of the real exchange rate, important for countries still fighting domestic inflation. Lower cost of adjustment constitutes an economic benefit in itself, but it also reduces the political difficulties of implementing and maintaining the liberalized trade regime. Moreover, in both NAFTA and Mercosur, much of the new regional trade was intra-industry trade (in both cases, autos and parts account for a substantial share of increased trade), presumed by some analysts to be associated with lower adjustment costs than inter-industry trade.

Political Feasibility

An element of reciprocity usually reduces the political obstacles to trade reform. Indeed, greater political feasibility appears to be the most important reason why countries engage in various types of reciprocal rather than unilateral liberalization. In particular, discriminatory liberalization, although almost always suboptimal in at least its initial outcome, offers clear benefits to readily identified domestic sectors in the form of trade diversion, thus ensuring the support of export interests that are known to be regionally but perhaps not globally competitive. In contrast, unilateral liberalization holds out immediate benefits only to the much smaller number of export firms and sectors that appear ex ante to be globally competitive (ex post, the general-equilibrium consequences of a successful liberalization bring to light export potential not apparent in advance). A reciprocal process, whether regional or multilateral, also enhances public acceptance of liberalization. Reciprocity undercuts the public perception that the country's policymakers are giving away something of value (market access) with no quid pro quo.

On the other hand, the negotiations required to achieve reciprocal liberalization may in practice mean a lengthy delay of needed reforms. The decision to liberalize unilaterally seems to occur in conjunction with comprehensive across-the-board reforms. In such instances, liberalization on the part of trading partners would be welcome for the reasons noted earlier, but the cost of delay is considered too high to make this a condition for the country's own action. In particular, a crisis calls for prompt action, and so may be associated with unilateral trade reform, as in the case of Chile (1974), Bolivia (1985), and Peru (1990), though cross-reciprocity eased the way for Peru.

Complementarity

Unilateral, multilateral, and regional initiatives are often discussed as if they were mutually exclusive alternatives. The conventional wisdom is that RTAs induce costly trade diversion and increase political opposition to future reductions in external trade barriers (e.g., Bhagwati and Krueger 1995). Yet Latin American experience in the 1980s and 1990s suggests that these three liberalization strategies may represent complementary ways for a country to move toward greater integration into global markets. During the period, most of the countries in the region reduced their own MFN trade barriers, joined RTAs, *and* participated in GATT-WTO negotiations. Argentina and Brazil were among the last countries to join the region's wave of trade reform, in both cases after previous failed attempts. It is plausible that the Mercosur agreement helped to minimize backsliding despite significant external shocks including the Mexican peso crisis in 1994 and the Asian crisis in 1997. In the first test of the common external tariffs that went into effect in 1995, immediate protests from Mercosur partners forced Brazil to roll back new tariffs and quotas that had been announced unilaterally in response to balance-of-payments problems. While the announced compromise still included new protection directed toward nonmembers, the episode suggests that speedy pressure from significant partners can help to sustain openness at least within the region if not globally.

The apparent complementarity of unilateral and reciprocal liberalization may reflect scale effects from formation of a larger integrated market as well as changed political and economic circumstances and incentives resulting from the RTA. In a world of constant costs and perfect competition, trade diversion is necessarily welfare reducing for the importer. But if non-Vinerian benefits such as increased competition and larger market size are sufficiently important, trade diversion may transform the favored partner into a low-cost producer that is competitive globally as well as regionally. And when non-Vinerian benefits are minor, trade diversion associated with formation of a free trade area gives each member the incentive to reduce its own external tariffs on product categories where trade diversion is most damaging (Richardson 1993).[27] Moreover, nonmembers who have lost export markets because of trade diversion may be motivated to join later, as occurred in the European Union and ASEAN.

The trade diversion associated with RTAs also provides a way to raise political support for a more-open trade regime. In addition, by promoting a shift in each member's production structure toward sectors that are at least regionally competitive, an RTA can serve as a stepping-stone to future nondiscriminatory trade reforms. Of course sectors benefiting from trade diversion will lobby to retain their favored positions. However, these sectors would have opposed multilateral liberalization in any case, while the initially weakest and thus most protection-oriented sectors in each member country have been vanquished through the milder discipline of the RTA and are thus no longer present to oppose further liberalization (McCulloch and Petri 1997). Formation of Mercosur, with its member economies all shaped by decades of import substitution, may help eliminate the many domestic firms and sectors that cannot prove themselves to be even regionally competitive, thus setting the groundwork for further liberalization in the future.[28]

Finally, participation in international agreements to open markets can raise the viability of reforms by increasing the domestic and international political cost of reversing them. Like GATT-WTO membership, RTAs therefore lend greater credibility to reforms, especially in countries whose recent history has included numerous liberalization reversals. For Mexico, NAFTA membership was billed explicitly as a way to lock in market-oriented reforms and thus increase their credibility (Tornell and Esquivel 1997). Likewise, establishment of Mercosur helped bolster the credibility of the latest trade liberalizations in countries with prior records of many policy reversals.

11.5   Promoting Favorable Dynamics with RTAs

The proliferation of RTAs in Latin America, together with the evident enthusiasm on the part of the United States for these arrangements, has raised concerns about their compatibility with further progress toward multilateral liberalization. The key issue is the way RTAs evolve over time and the associated effects on the political viability of future regional or multilateral liberalization. Theory has demonstrated that formation of RTAs can have either positive or negative effects on the success of subsequent multilateral liberalization (Haveman 1996; Levy 1997; Richardson 1993). But compared to their theoretical counterparts, real-world RTAs seem decidedly benign in their effects. As indicated earlier, the evidence for Latin America suggests considerable complementarity between regional and multilateral liberalization. In fact, not only do regional blocs appear to facilitate their members' shift from inward-oriented to open trade regimes, but their formation is sometimes explicitly motivated by this goal.

Critics of RTAs worry that these arrangements will be dominated in their effects by costly trade diversion[29] and will cause their members to lose enthusiasm for further multilateral negotiations. Yet much of the evidence from actual RTA behavior suggests that policymakers do not typically choose this strategy over participation in multilateral liberalization but, rather, see the two types of liberalization as complementary ways of pursuing gains from integration into international markets. Often the anticipated gains from an RTA are exactly the efficiency-boosting effects of a larger market that theorists find most difficult to capture in a model: scale and scope economies, increased competition, technology transfer.

Nor do members of actual RTAs show signs of systematically exploiting their collective market power by raising their protection toward nonmembers. Nations interact over many issues other than trade, rendering adherence to a blatantly exploitive external trade policy short-sighted. In any case, GATT/WTO rules place limits on the impulse toward higher external barriers. Rather, the increased protection associated with RTAs has typically taken the form of restrictive rules of origin for free trade areas and discriminatory application of safeguards. These developments are significant worries because they represent a return to the inefficiencies associated with nontransparent barriers, not because the RTA members are optimally exploiting their joint market power in trade with nonmembers.

Theory suggests that an RTA may help overcome political obstacles to future multilateral liberalization to the extent that trade creation shrinks the size and political power of the region's least competitive firms (McCulloch and Petri 1997). Conversely, trade diversion under an RTA might be expected to strengthen resistance to any future enlargement or multilateral liberalization. In practice, however, it appears that RTAs dominated by trade diversion are ones that never get off the ground because potential members are reluctant to accept the associated losses (e.g., the Andean Pact of the 1960s). The observed tendency for established RTAs to grow in size and diversity over time suggests that membership in an RTA gradually changes the balance of producer interests in ways that promote eventual inclusion of new members who were previously "too competitive" to be allowed to join.

The renewed prominence of RTAs in the 1990s has raised interest in a revision of GATT/WTO rules to increase the likelihood that such arrangements will make positive contributions to multilateral liberalization. One possible approach is suggested by Kemp and Wan's (1976) theoretical demonstration that the external barriers of a bloc can always be adjusted to leave trade with third countries unchanged—that is, to rule out trade diversion—while allowing net gains for members. Variants of a no-trade-diversion rule have been proposed as alternatives or supplements to Article XXIV of the GATT, which currently restricts RTAs principally through the requirement that countries must fully eliminate internal barriers (Bhagwati 1992;

McMillan 1993). However, minimizing diversion does not necessarily produce the most favorable dynamics. Trade diversion may be critical to the political viability of a particular RTA, and if the RTA represents an essential step in the transformation of a country's industrial structure, then a no-trade-diversion constraint may actually retard subsequent multilateral liberalization.

11.6 Conclusions

Beginning in the mid-1980s, greater openness became the norm rather than the exception in Latin America. This increase in openness was confirmed by changes in policies and by changes in trade intensity. Moreover, the increased trade intensity was associated with an increased average rate of growth in the region and in almost all individual countries. In a region where past trade reforms were usually reversed, the key question for policymakers in the 1990s was less *whether* to follow an outward-oriented strategy than *how* to achieve and sustain the required policy environment. The chapter identifies political and economic obstacles to trade liberalization in Latin America and looks at ways successful liberalizers were able to overcome them. A central element in sustained progress toward openness is achievement of macroeconomic stabilization; failed stabilization is usually accompanied by new trade restrictions.

The focus of the chapter is on trade reform as an ongoing process, in which implementation of outward-looking policies helps establish a virtuous cycle of liberalization. In the 1990s, the process of unilateral and reciprocal MFN trade reform proceeded in conjunction with negotiation of new regional and bilateral trade agreements. Although they usually imply a sacrifice of efficiency relative to global free trade, such agreements have the potential to overcome domestic political resistance to liberalization and to reduce the costs of adjustment. They may also help avoid backsliding toward protection by raising the cost of future policy reversals, thus enhancing the credibility of reforms.

Rather than representing a rejection of multilateral liberalization, an RTA may help reshape member economies so as to allow further multilateral liberalization that was not politically feasible previously. Because trade creation under an RTA promotes shrinkage of each member's least competitive sectors, adjustment to the RTA leaves each country with a larger proportion of firms that are globally as well as regionally competitive and thus raises political support for further liberalization at the multilateral level. At the same time, the renewed popularity and changed emphasis of RTAs suggests that GATT/WTO rules governing regional agreements are due for reassessment. Although losses from trade diversion remain a valid concern, the larger problem to be addressed is the association of RTAs with reversal of progress toward greater transparency of the trade regime.

Notes

An earlier version of the chapter was presented at the AEI/Ford Foundation project conference on unilateral trade liberalization, Washington, DC, October 24–25, 1997. I am indebted to Jagdish Bhagwati and the conference participants for comments and suggestions.

1. Rather than coordinated reduction of trade barriers in two or more countries, cross-reciprocity links trade reform in one country to other types of anticipated benefits. Most common is some form of financial assistance—for example, structural-adjustment lending—that helps to offset the immediate political and economic costs of liberalization.

2. By the mid-1990s, all Latin American countries had joined the GATT or its successor, the World Trade Organization (WTO), and many had reduced or eliminated some trade barriers (especially nontariff measures) in the process. However, although eight Latin American countries participated in the Uruguay Round of multilateral trade negotiations, Finger, Reincke, and Castro (chapter 5) conclude that none offered significant tariff cuts as part of the round's "reciprocal" tariff concessions.

3. Rodrik (1994) highlights distributional conflict as a limit to sustaining openness. However, a World Bank study concludes that a balance-of-payments deficit was the primary factor in eight of fourteen countries whose liberalizations were subsequently reversed; of five countries in which no reversals occurred, only one had experienced balance-of-payments difficulties (Michaely, Papageorgiou, and Choksi 1991).

4. Rodrik (1994) also suggests that trade reforms included in broader policy packages benefited from a kind of halo effect. Once inflation was firmly under control, some of the success was attributed—rightly or wrongly—to open trade policies. Conversely, failed stabilization is often associated with reversal of trade reform (Rajapatirana, de la Mora, and Yatawara 1997), although this may be in direct response to an associated balance-of-payments problem.

5. Broad reductions in import barriers—for example, across-the-board tariff cuts—generally improve both neutrality and liberality. However, application of additional interventions may, for second-best reasons, improve neutrality while reducing liberality. Improvements in either neutrality or liberality may in turn raise openness as measured by trade flows. But openness measures such as the value of exports as a share of GDP are also affected by exogenous changes in world prices.

6. Inter-American Development Bank (1996) provides qualitative indicators of increased openness for twenty-five countries in Latin American and the Caribbean. The

report concludes that virtually all countries in the region participated in the trend: "The region's trade and foreign exchange systems are currently [in 1996] freer than they have been since the period before the Great Depression."

7. In UNCTAD data, sectoral rates are weighted by product shares in *world* trade. Compared to the usual practice of weighting by shares in the country's own imports, this procedure avoids a downward bias in the weight given to sectors with unusually high protection—ones more protected in a given country than the global average for the industry. However, there is still a downward bias for sectors highly protected on average worldwide, such as steel and autos.

8. Although cuts in tariffs are often regarded as an essential element in trade liberalization, less than half of the liberalization episodes in a major World Bank study included tariff reduction; in contrast, reduction in the severity of quantitative restrictions was almost always included (Michaely, Papageorgiou, and Choksi 1991).

9. In principle, unification of tariff schedules could be accomplished by raising some especially low tariffs. However, actual tariff unifications in Latin America and elsewhere have been achieved almost exclusively through tariff reductions (Michaely, Papageorgiou, and Choksi 1991).

10. As in the NBER project, the binary Sachs-Warner openness measure relies on subjective evaluation of information from diverse sources. Other researchers attempting to establish statistical links between trade and growth have used a variety of statistical measures of openness. See Harrison (1996) for a survey. Openness measures based on export or import volume or on divergence between domestic and foreign prices implicitly consider effects of both trade and exchange-rate policies.

11. But liberalization cannot ensure that an exchange rate consistent with purchasing power parity will be maintained over time. As discussed later, successful reforms may promote capital inflows and an associated real appreciation.

12. This section is adapted from McCulloch (1999).

13. In a chapter titled "The Emergence of a New Latin American Consensus," Edwards (1995) thus sums up the sea change in economic thinking during the 1980s and early 1990s: "The once-dominant view based on heavy state interventionism, inward orientation, and disregard for macroeconomic balance slowly gave way to a new paradigm based on competition, market orientation, and openness. In 1992 the United Nations Economic Commission for Latin America and the Caribbean (CEPAL), a historical supporter of inward-looking and government-led development, recognized that the most appropriate course was now to emphasize openness." Bruton (1998) provides a detailed intellectual history of "the new orthodoxy" of outward orientation but expresses his doubts regarding its adequacy as a full solution to the problems of underdevelopment.

14. Not necessarily or even mainly at the University of Chicago, as José Piñera, a Chilean free-marketeer educated at Harvard, emphasizes (Piñera 1994).

15. Conversely, Bresser Pereira (1994) attributes the failure of his 1988 inflation-fighting initiative in Brazil to President Sarney's unwillingness to support the unpopular plan in the absence of an outright emergency.

16. Concerning the slow pace of reform in Ecuador, *Trends in Developing Economies 1996* notes the nation's "long democratic traditions" but also that "considerable polit-

ical fragmentation and divisiveness makes the pursuit of long-term policies difficult" (World Bank 1996).

17. If individual voters are unsure whether they will be winners or losers from liberalization, majority voting may reject even a trade reform that benefits the median voter (Rodrik 1996). Myopia and risk aversion exacerbate the problem of getting voters to support efficiency-raising reforms.

18. In the United States, the first trade adjustment assistance program was created by the 1962 Trade Expansion Act, which authorized U.S. participation in the Kennedy Round of multilateral trade negotiations. For a number of useful contributions on the theory and empirical record of trade adjustment, see Bhagwati (1982).

19. This standard is highly but not perfectly correlated with others that give a better picture of changes in the living conditions of a "typical" member of the population, such as infant mortality, longevity, access to clean water, and literacy. Another recent concern not captured by conventionally measured growth in PCI is degradation of the environment, including inefficiently rapid depletion of natural resources. This concern is addressed in the emphasis on *sustainable development*—development that doesn't mortgage the welfare of future generations.

20. For a sample of less-developed countries worldwide, Dollar and Kraay (2000) find that openness to foreign trade benefits the poor to the same extent on average that it improves overall economic performance. Improvements in rule of law and fiscal discipline are likewise found to benefit the poor to the same extent as the economy as a whole.

21. Krueger (1993) points out that the perceived need for these policies may arise from the negative consequences of import substitution—a vicious policy cycle.

22. Edwards (1995) summarizes the main findings of the sequencing debate but comments that sequencing of reforms has come to be viewed as largely a political issue.

23. The Uruguay Round of multilateral trade negotiations produced an agreement to phase out the Multifibre Agreement (MFA), the global network of quantitative restrictions on trade in textiles and apparel, over a ten-year period. However, many trade policy experts remained pessimistic about a return to open markets for these important developing-country exports. They interpreted the long phase-out period as indicating a lack of real commitment to liberalization on the part of OECD nations. Some analysts believed the extent of OECD protection of these import-competing industries would actually increase, at least temporarily, during the phase-out process.

24. As discussed below, concern about finding export markets underlies much of the interest in RTAs. Yet even NAFTA failed to prevent Mexican tomato growers from hitting the closed door of restrictive U.S. agricultural policies.

25. In a world of many overlapping preferential arrangements, apparent trade diversion may in fact represent redirection of trade flows along lines of comparative advantage, that is, correction of previous trade diversion. The NAFTA-induced shift of U.S. import orders to Mexico from the Caribbean is an example.

26. Uruguay Round negotiators agreed informally to give developing countries credit for earlier unilateral tariff reductions that were subsequently bound under the GATT/ WTO. Finger, Reincke, and Castro (chapter 5) find evidence from the pattern of total and bound concessions that developing-country binding of earlier unilateral reductions was "treated at the round as an action of substantial value."

27. Trade diversion due to bilateral trade agreements with Mexico (1991), Venezuela (1993), Colombia (1993), Ecuador (1994), and Mercosur (1996) prompted Chile to announce further cuts in its already low unified import tariff.

28. A controversial study by Yeats (1998) compares Mercosur's internal trade pattern with what would be predicted given only the members' MFN liberalization since 1988 and shows that much of the new intra-Mercosur trade is in industries in which members are not globally competitive. However, this methodology does not distinguish between the traditional categories of trade diversion and trade creation. Moreover, the study compares an actual situation with one that may not have been a feasible option, that is, sustained unilateral liberalization in countries with a prior record of multiple reversals. As Yeats notes, the study takes no account of credibility of reform strategies or dynamic effects. Also, by comparing Mercosur's intrabloc trade with members' exports to other markets, the study ignores the potentially important role of protection elsewhere; this may be significant given that transport equipment and machinery products account for much of the increased intratrade.

29. The traditional literature, following Viner's lead in focusing on the case of constant opportunity cost in production, has probably overemphasized the costliness of trade diversion. As noted earlier, benefits associated with creation of a larger integrated market can transform a high-cost trading partner into a globally competitive one (Wonnacott 1996; McCulloch and Petri 1997). Moreover, apparent diversion can include welfare-increasing reversal of previous diversion, as in the expansion of U.S. imports from Mexico at the expense of higher-cost goods already afforded preferential access under the Caribbean Basin Initiative.

References

Baldwin, Robert W. 1989. "Measuring Nontariff Trade Policies." NBER Working Paper 2978, May.

Bergsten, C. Fred. 1996. "Competitive Liberalization and Global Free Trade: A Vision for the Early 21st Century." Asia Pacific Economic Cooperation Working Paper 96–15. Washington: Institute for International Economics.

Bhagwati, Jagdish N. 1978. *Foreign Trade Regimes and Economic Development: Anatomy and Consequences of Exchange Control Regimes.* Cambridge, MA: NBER.

Bhagwati, Jagdish N. 1992. "Regionalism versus Multilateralism." *The World Economy* 15 (September): 535–55.

Bhagwati, Jagdish N., ed. 1982. *Import Competition and Response.* Chicago: University of Chicago Press.

Bhagwati, Jagdish, and Anne O. Krueger. 1995. *The Dangerous Drift to Preferential Trade Agreements.* Washington: American Enterprise Institute.

Bhagwati, Jagdish, and Arvind Panagariya. 1996. "Preferential Trading Areas and Multilateralism—Strangers, Friends, or Foes?" In *The Economics of Preferential Trade Agreements,* ed. Jagdish Bhagwati and Arvind Panagariya, 1–78. Washington: American Enterprise Institute.

Bresser Pereira, Luis Carlos. 1994. "Brazil." In *The Political Economy of Policy Reform,* ed. John Williamson, 333–354. Washington: Institute for International Economics, January.

Bruton, Henry J. 1998. "A Reconsideration of Import Substitution." *Journal of Economic Literature* 36 (June): 903–936.

Burki, Shahid Javed, and Guillermo E. Perry. 1997. *The Long March: A Reform Agenda for Latin America and the Caribbean in the Next Decade.* Washington: World Bank, August.

Burnside, Craig, and David Dollar. 1997. "Aid Spurs Growth—in a Sound Policy Environment." *Finance and Development* 34: 4–7.

Coates, Daniel E., and Rodney D. Ludema. 1996. "Unilateral Tariff Reduction as Leadership in Trade Negotiations." Working paper. Washington, DC: Georgetown University and U.S. General Accounting Office.

Cordoba, Jose. 1994. "Mexico." In *The Political Economy of Policy Reform*, ed. John Williamson, 232–284. Washington, DC: Institute for International Economics, January.

Dean, Judith M., Seema Desai, and James Riedel. 1994. "Trade Policy Reform in Developing Countries Since 1985: A Review of the Evidence." World Bank Discussion Paper.

Dollar, David, and Aart Kraay. 2000. "Growth *Is* Good for the Poor." Working paper. Washington, DC: World Bank Development Research Group, March.

Edwards, Sebastian. 1995. *Crisis and Reform in Latin America: From Despair to Hope.* Washington, DC: World Bank.

Fernandez, Raquel. 1997. "Returns to Regionalism: An Evaluation of Nontraditional Gains from Regional Trade Agreements." Research Policy Working Paper 1816. Washington, DC: World Bank, International Trade Division, August.

Graham, Carol. 1996. "From Safety Nets to Social Sector Reform: Lessons from the Developing Countries for the Transition Economies." Washington, DC: Brookings Institution, September.

Harberger, Arnold C. 1993. "Secrets of Success: A Handful of Heroes." *American Economic Review (Papers and Proceedings)* 83 (May): 941–958.

Harrison, Ann. 1996. "Openness and Growth: A Time-Series, Cross-Country Analysis for Developing Countries." *Journal of Development Economics* 48 (April): 419–447.

Haveman, Jon D. 1996. "Some Welfare Effects of Sequential Customs Union Formation." *Canadian Journal of Economics* 24 (November): 941–958.

Inter-American Development Bank (IDB). 1996. *Economic and Social Progress in Latin America: 1996 Report.* Baltimore, MD: Johns Hopkins University Press.

International Financial Statistics Yearbook. 1997. Washington, D.C.: International Monetary Fund.

Kemp, M. C., and Henry Wan, Jr. 1976. "An Elementary Proposition Concerning the Formation of Customs Unions." *Journal of International Economics* 6 (February): 95–98.

Krueger, Anne O. 1978. *Foreign Trade Regimes and Economic Development: Liberalization Attempts and Consequences.* Cambridge, MA: NBER.

Krueger, Anne O. 1993. "Virtuous and Vicious Circles in Economic Development." *American Economic Review (Papers and Proceedings)* 83 (May): 351–355.

Krueger, Anne O. 1997. "Trade Policy and Economic Development: How We Learn." *American Economic Review* 87 (March): 1–22.

Lawrence, Robert Z., and Matthew Slaughter. 1993. "International Trade and American Wages in the 1980s: Giant Sucking Sound or Small Hiccup?" *Brookings Papers on Economic Activity* 2: 161–225.

Levy, Philip I. 1997. "A Political-Economic Analysis of Free Trade Agreements." *American Economic Review* 87 (September): 506–519.

Little, Ian, Tibor Scitovsky, and Maurice Scott. 1970. *Industry and Trade in Some Developing Countries*. London: Oxford University Press.

McCulloch, Rachel. 1999. "On the Dynamics of Trade Policy Reform." In *Asia-Pacific Economic Linkages*, ed. Mordechai E. Kreinin, Michael G. Plummer, and Shigeyuki Abe, 129–147. Oxford: Pergamon/Elsvier Science.

McCulloch, Rachel, and Peter A. Petri. 1997. "Alternative Paths Toward Open Global Markets." In *Quiet Pioneering: Robert M. Stern and His International Economic Legacy*, ed. Keith Maskus et al., 149–169. Ann Arbor: University of Michigan Press.

McCulloch, Rachel, and Peter A. Petri. 1998. "Equity Financing of East Asian Development." In *Capital Flows and Financial Crises*, ed. Miles Kahler, 158–185. Cornell: Cornell University Press.

McMillan, John. 1992. "Does Regional Integration Foster Open Trade? Economic Theory and GATT's Article XXIV." In *Regional Integration and the Global Trading System*, ed. Kym Anderson and Richard Blackhurst, 292–310. New York: St. Martin's Press.

Michaely, Michael, Demetris Papageorgiou, and Armeane M. Choksi, eds. 1991. *Liberalizing Foreign Trade (Volume 7): Lessons of Experience in the Developing World*. Cambridge, MA: Basil Blackwell.

Organization of American States (OAS). 1997. *Trade and Integration Arrangements in the Americas*. Washington, DC: Trade Unit, Organization of American States.

Piñera, Jose. 1994. "Chile." In *The Political Economy of Policy Reform*, ed. John Williamson, 225–231. Washington, DC: Institute for International Economics, January.

Pissarides, Christopher A. 1997. "Learning by Trading and the Returns to Human Capital in Developing Countries." *World Bank Economic Review* 11 (January): 17–32.

Pritchett, Lant. 1996. "Measuring Outward Orientation in LDCs: Can It Be Done?" *Journal of Development Economics* 49 (June): 307–335.

Rajapatirana, Sarath, Luz Maria de la Mora, and Ravindra A. Yatawara. 1997. "Political Economy of Trade Reforms, 1965–1994: Latin American Style." *The World Economy* 20 (May): 307–338.

Richardson, Martin. 1993. "Endogenous Protection and Trade Diversion." *Journal of International Economics* 34 (May): 309–324.

Rodrik, Dani. 1994. "The Rush to Free Trade in the Developing World: Why So Late? Why Now? Will It Last?" In *Voting For Reform: Democracy, Political Liberalization, and Economic Adjustment*, ed. Stephan Haggard and Steven B. Webb. New York: Oxford University Press.

Rodrik, Dani. 1995. "Getting Interventions Right: How South Korea and Taiwan Grew Rich." *Economic Policy* 20 (April): 55–107.

Rodrik, Dani. 1996. "Understanding Economic Policy Reform." *Journal of Economic Literature* 34 (March): 9–41.

Rodrik, Dani. 1997. *Has Globalization Gone Too Far?* Washington, DC: Institute for International Economics, March.

Sachs, Jeffrey, and Andrew Warner. 1995a. "Economic Reform and the Process of Global Integration." *Brookings Papers on Economic Activity* 1: 1–95.

Sachs, Jeffrey, and Andrew Warner. 1995b. "Economic Convergence and Economic Policies." NBER Working Paper No. 5039.

Thomas, Vinod, John Nash, et al. 1991. *Best Practices in Trade Policy Reform.* Oxford: Oxford University Press.

Tornell, Aaron, and Gerardo Esquivel. 1997. "The Political Economy of Mexico's Entry into NAFTA." In *Regionalism versus Multilateral Trade Arrangement*, ed. Takatoshi Ito and Anne O. Krueger, 25–56. Chicago: University of Chicago Press.

UNCTAD. 1994. *Directory of Import Regimes.* New York: United Nations.

Williamson, John, and Stephan Haggard. 1994. "The Political Conditions for Economic Reform." In *The Political Economy of Policy Reform*, ed. John Williamson, 525–596. Washington, DC: Institute for International Economics, January.

Wonnacott, Ronald J. 1996. "Free-Trade Agreements: For Better or Worse?" *American Economic Review (Papers and Proceedings)* 86 (May): 62–66.

Wood, Adrian. 1997. "Openness and Wage Inequality in Developing Countries: The Latin American Challenge to East Asian Conventional Wisdom." *World Bank Economic Review* 11 (January): 33–58.

World Bank. 1996. *Trends in Developing Economies 1996.* Washington: World Bank.

World Bank. 1997a. *World Development Report 1997.* Washington: World Bank.

World Bank. 1997b. *World Development Indicators 1997.* Washington: World Bank.

World Currency Yearbook, 27th edition. 1995. Brooklyn, N.Y.: International Currency Analysis, Inc.

Yeats, Alexander. 1998. "Does Mercosur's Trade Performance Raise Concerns about the Effects of Regional Trade Arrangements?" *World Bank Economic Review* 12 (January): 1–28.

Yeats, Alexander, Azita Amjadi, Ulrich Reincke, and Francis Ng. 1996. "What Caused Sub-Saharan Africa's Marginalization in World Trade?" *Finance and Development* 33 (December): 38–44.

III

Sectoral Experience

12

Unilateral International Openness: The Experience of the U.S. Financial Services Sector

Lawrence J. White

12.1 Introduction

The 1990s were a decade in which international trade in services, and especially financial services, was an area of special policy concern. In the wake of the United States' ratification of the North American Free Trade Area (NAFTA) agreement in 1993 and the GATT's Uruguay Round of trade liberalization in 1994 (and the creation of the World Trade Organization), trade in financial services received heightened attention. After one attempt at an international agreement on liberalization stalled in 1995 (because of the U.S.'s refusal to be a signatory), two years of further negotiation finally yielded an agreement in late 1997, with twenty-nine countries becoming signatories.[1]

This agreement was reached in the shadow of, and possibly as a consequence of, the Asian debt crisis of 1997, which exposed the widespread weaknesses and inefficiencies of the financial sectors of Thailand, Korea, and Indonesia. Banks and other lending institutions in those countries were revealed to have exercised poor judgment (often in response to their governments' formal or informal pressures) in their lending/investment decisions and in their decisions with respect to foreign currency risk exposure. The financial failures that followed were seen as indicative of the more general shortcomings of these countries' governmental policies of heavily regulating and influencing their financial sectors and resisting the disciplines that a more open market-oriented approach would have encouraged.

Finally, 1997 was also a year in which the financial difficulties of Japan's commercial banks were increasingly recognized and were seen as indicative consequences of the widespread restrictive/

protective policies that the government of Japan had pursued for decades with respect to its financial sector.

In contrast, by the late 1990s the United States' financial services sector was seen as a beacon of health and efficiency (though the same description could not have been offered a decade earlier). And, as opposed to the closed and restrictive financial-sector policies of these Asian countries (and of many other developed and developing countries), the U.S. financial services sector could be fairly described as quite open internationally: Non-U.S. firms that wish to offer financial services in the U.S. markets are generally offered "national treatment;" namely, they are generally treated in a manner similar to U.S. firms and do not face adverse discrimination because of their non-U.S. nationality.

A striking feature of this U.S. openness is that historically it was achieved almost entirely through unilateral actions by the United States; negotiated reciprocity with other countries has not been essential to this openness. Despite the threats of negotiated reciprocity that became a feature of U.S. negotiation strategy with respect to financial services in the 1990s, unilateral openness has remained the de facto stance of the United States.

This openness stands in stark contrast not only with the policies of many other countries, which place substantial restrictions or outright prohibitions on the provision of banking, insurance, securities, and other financial services by nonnationals,[2] but also with the experiences of most U.S. industrial sectors, where openness is only partial and/or has been achieved only through negotiated and reciprocal reductions in protectionist barriers.

At one level, this unilateral openness of the U.S. financial services sector, which accounts for about 7 percent of U.S. GDP, is remarkable. Despite the long-standing theoretical case for the unilateral maintenance of free trade as a welfare-maximizing policy for a country, the practice of nearly all countries is otherwise. Mercantilism, nationalism, allegations (and the occasional reality) of market failures, distributional concerns, rent-seeking behaviors, interest-group politics, and a host of other real-world intrusions have created extensive systems of trade barriers and foreign investment barriers that have been eroding only slowly—mostly on a reciprocal basis—in the five decades since the end of World War II. Financial services in other countries are often as prone, if not more so, to these forms of protectionism.

At another level, this openness in the United States is somewhat less remarkable. Like many other services, the provision of financial services has tended to require a local presence by the seller; indeed, because financial services are prone to problems of asymmetric information, this need for a local presence has probably been stronger than for many other services. Accordingly, on-site facilities by the seller—in essence, inbound foreign direct investment (FDI) by a nonnational—have been essential for the effective sale of the services. As compared to its history of protectionism with respect to trade, however, the United States has been more open with respect to inbound FDI generally,[3] including the local provision of financial services by nonnationals. Also, as a net capital exporter for the first three-quarters of the twentieth century, the United States experienced relatively small amounts of inbound FDI generally. With small amounts of inbound FDI, there were only modest demands for the local provision of financial services by the overseas-based financial services firms that might be best suited for the task (but that also might trigger protectionist sentiments). As late as 1975, for example, the percentage of U.S. banking assets accounted for by foreign banks was only 5 percent. In contrast, two decades later (1996), the comparable percentage was over 20 percent.

In an era of widened focus on the role of services and especially financial services in economic growth[4] and on trade issues related to services, the experience of the unilateral openness of the U.S. financial services sector may prove instructive. This chapter addresses the questions of the openness of the U.S. financial services sector, why it has arisen, and whether it has served the United States well. A major theme of the chapter is that the phenomena of asymmetric information, which are endemic to finance, have had an important influence on the specific types and levels of foreign involvement that are found in the U.S. financial services sector. Though differing levels of foreign involvement in the various parts of the financial services landscape can be observed, this pattern is not an indication of U.S. discrimination or differential treatment but instead is largely consistent with openness *and* the asymmetric information phenomena.

I proceed as follows: Section 12.2 lays out some categorizations that are particularly useful for understanding financial services. Section 12.3 discusses the general nature of financial services and why they are special. Section 12.4 discusses the regulatory regimes that apply to financial services in the United States, since the openness of the financial services sector has not been synonymous with an absence of regulation. Section 12.5 describes the generally open nature (internationally) of the U.S. financial services sector. Section 12.6 explores the origins of this openness and whether it has served the United States well; this section also addresses in detail the application of the asymmetric information paradigm to the pattern of foreign involvement in the U.S. financial services sector. And section 12.7 provides a brief conclusion.

12.2   Some Useful Categorizations

The financial services sector encompasses a broad collection of types of firms and specific services. It will be useful for the discussion in the following sections to delineate and explain a number of useful categories among the firms in this sector.

Broad Industry Categories

The financial services sector has traditionally been analyzed (and regulated) in terms of broad industry groupings. Though recent technological and regulatory changes have tended to blur some of the distinctions, these groupings are still useful.

1. *Banking.* This encompasses banks and other depositories (e.g., savings institutions) that primarily make loans and fund those loans by accepting deposits from the public.

2. *Finance Companies.* These are firms that make loans and fund those loans through debt instruments (e.g., commercial paper) that are not deposits. Finance companies in the United States tend to be of three types: (a) free-standing firms; (b) subsidiaries of banks; (c) subsidiaries of commercial enterprises, primarily providing credit to the customers of the parent company (in essence, financing the customers' purchases—e.g., auto loans) but sometimes also operating as a general-purpose finance company.

3. *Securities (including options and futures and similar derivatives).* This encompasses firms that are involved in the originating and trading of tradable, liquid financial claims.

4. *Mutual Funds.* These firms are usually considered to be part of the securities industry. They invest in securities and fund themselves by selling shares to the public.

5. *Insurance.* This encompasses firms that promise to pay contingent claims (e.g., life insurance, health insurance, property/casualty insurance) and use the premium income collected to fund their holdings of securities, loans, real estate, and other assets (that are the wherewithal for the payment of those claims).

6. *Pension Funds.* These financial arrangements promise to pay sums upon the retirement of an employee, while accumulating (and investing) sufficient funds in the interim so as to assure that the payout commitment can be met. Pension funds can be owned by an employer, by a union, or by an employee. Some of the financial services firms that advise and/or manage these funds are specialists in the field; others are subsidiaries of banks, insurance companies, securities firms, or mutual funds.

Financial Intermediaries and Financial Facilitators

A second broad distinction can be made between financial intermediaries and financial facilitators. Again, the distinctions are not airtight, but they are useful.

1. *Financial Intermediaries.* These include banks (and other depositories), finance companies, insurance companies, pension funds, mutual funds, venture capital firms, and leasing companies. These are enterprises that invest largely in financial assets (e.g., loans, mortgages, securities, etc.) and fund those investments by issuing liabilities on themselves (e.g., deposits, debt obligations, insurance policies, pension claims, mutual fund shares, etc.).[5] As an example, table 12.1 provides a stylized balance sheet for a typical bank. Its loans are its assets, its deposits are its liabilities, and the difference between its loan assets and its deposit liabilities is its net worth or "capital." An insurance company would have a similar-looking balance sheet, except that the potential claims of its insureds would constitute its liabilities.[6]

Table 12.1
A stylized bank balance sheet

Assets	Liabilities
$100 (loans)	$92 (deposits)
	- - - - - - - - - - - -
	$8 (net worth)

2. *Financial Facilitators.* These include stockbrokers, underwriters, dealers, market makers, investment bankers, mortgage bankers, advisers, and accountants. These enterprises facilitate the transactions between borrowers and lenders and between equity issuers and investors, but are generally not the direct investors themselves.

Primary and Secondary Markets

A third useful distinction can be made between primary and secondary markets.

1. *Primary Markets.* The origination of a loan or mortgage and the underwriting of an equity issue are primary market activities. The user of the funds is being provided directly with finance.

2. *Secondary Markets.* The trading of stocks, bonds, and other financial instruments on exchanges (or among dealers or other market makers) is a secondary market activity. Direct finance to users is not being provided, but the liquidity provided by secondary markets widens investment opportunities and improves the efficiency of finance.[7]

12.3   The Nature of Financial Services

Finance is special. First, it is ubiquitous. All enterprises need finance of some form (even if it is just the owner's personal savings and investment) to begin operations, to maintain themselves, and to expand. Governments need finance to cover revenue shortfalls over short and long periods. Individuals need finance to convert savings into liquid instruments and to obtain resources to bridge income shortfalls (e.g., home mortgage loans, car loans, credit card loans, etc.).

Second, finance inherently has a time dimension: A loan or investment is made at an "early" time, and repayment and returns occur at a "later" time. But repayment and returns are usually far from certain and are subject to potential problems of asymmetric information: moral hazard and adverse selection. (Insurance similarly has a time dimension and is prone to similar asymmetric information problems.) These asymmetric information problems are pervasive and shape the pricing, structure, and availability of financial services, as well as the types of firms that offer them and the types of behaviors displayed by these firms. For example, extensive information gathering about loan applicants and extensive monitoring of loans after they have been granted are common features of banks and other loan originators.

One important consequence of the asymmetric information problems of finance and of the extensive monitoring efforts that attempt to mitigate those problems is the tendency for finance to be locally oriented. Because the costs of monitoring often rise with distance, a lender/investor often wants to be geographically close to the borrower. Similarly, because of transactions costs, a depositor usually wants to be close to his or her bank.

Proximity is not an absolute, however. Larger, better established and better known borrowers—for example, the United States government, the General Motors Corporation—have always been able to access lenders from farther afield than can less well known borrowers, because of the greater informational transparency of the former. And the rapid improvements in the technologies of data processing/computerization and telecommunications over the past three decades have made proximity progressively less important. Computerized credit-scoring techniques have made it possible for lenders to assess potential borrowers, at least for relatively modest size loans (e.g., credit card loans), from afar, and automated teller machines (ATMs) have made it easier for depositors to access their banks from afar. The increasing globalization of financial markets, resting on those rapid technological improvements, is a real phenomenon.[8]

Nevertheless, geographical proximity has historically been extremely important and remains important for many types of financial transactions. An immediate implication of this proximity principle is that non-U.S. firms that wish to offer their financial services to U.S. customers would likely have to establish local facilities in the United States, so as to know their potential customers better and also to be better known by them.[9]

A second implication of the general asymmetric information paradigm is that, other things being equal, a lender will prefer to lend to borrowers with which it is familiar and will tend to shun those with which it is unfamiliar. A non-U.S. company that was establishing branch facilities in the United States would tend to be unfamiliar to domestic U.S. lenders but would likely be more familiar to lenders from its home country. To the extent that the company wanted credit and other financial services for its U.S. operations, home country banks and other lenders would have an incentive to establish facilities in the United States. Further, to the extent that the non-U.S. entity wants investment and other financial advice for operating in the U.S. financial markets, it will favor financial services firms with which it is familiar—very likely, financial services firms from its home country. Again, these firms will have an incentive to establish facilities in the United States.

In sum, the asymmetric information paradigm is a powerful one for financial services, and it has a number of important implications—proximity and familiarity—for foreign provision of these services in U.S. markets.

12.4   Understanding Financial Regulation

Extensive regulation is the hallmark of virtually all countries' treatment of their financial sectors. In many countries this regulation includes severe or absolute restrictions on entry by nonnationals (as well as restrictions on entry by nationals).

But the converse has not been true for the United States. The international openness of the U.S. financial services sector has not been synonymous with an absence of regulation. Indeed, despite substantial deregulation activity over the past two decades, the financial services sector remains extensively regulated.[10] For some financial services (e.g., pension funds), the federal government is the primary regulator; for others (e.g., insurance), the states are the sole regulators; for yet others (e.g., banking, securities), regulatory responsibility is shared between the federal government and the states, but with the federal government's role becoming increasingly dominant.

International openness has largely meant national regulatory treatment of foreign-based financial services providers.[11] But, since U.S. financial regulation is so extensive and is often different in substance and in detail from what foreign-based financial services providers face in their home countries, it can present a barrier even when it adheres to national treatment standards; and some aspects of regulation must inherently make a distinction between national and foreign-based providers, to the potential disadvantage of the latter. Some discussion of the form and substance of U.S. financial regulation is therefore warranted as part of any discussion of the openness of the U.S. financial services sector.

A threefold classification of regulation in general and its manifestation in the financial services sector will be useful.

Economic Regulation

This form of regulation involves government control over prices, profits, entry, and/or exit (including must-serve requirements). Familiar examples of this type of regulation include taxicab regulation in many cities; the states' regulation of electricity, natural gas, and local telephone prices; and the former Civil Aeronautics Board's regulation of airline fares, routes, and entry/exit. Barriers to international trade and to FDI would be in this category as well.

In the U.S. financial services sector, this is the category of regulation that has been the primary focus of the deregulation efforts of the past two decades. Nevertheless, substantial remnants of economic regulation are present (as of 1997) throughout the financial services sector. For example, banks cannot pay interest on checking accounts provided to commercial customers.[12] They are limited by some states in the interest rates that they can charge on loans (usury ceilings), as are other lenders; they are limited by some states as to the fees and charges that they can attach to credit card transactions. Some states limit banks' ability to establish branch locations within the state or across state boundaries.[13] Federal law prevents banks from directly engaging in corporate securities activities and restricts their ability to underwrite or sell insurance; banks and their holding companies are largely restricted to activities that are associated with traditional banking and are barred from owning commercial or industrial enterprises.[14] And federal and state laws require banks to "serve the needs of their communities." Many states regulate the premiums charged on politically sensitive types of insurance, such as automobile insurance and health insurance, and impose must-serve requirements with respect to insurance companies' provision of health, automobile, homeowner, and flood/disaster insurance.

Health-Safety-Environment (HSE) Regulation

This form of regulation involves government control over production processes and/or types or qualities of goods or services produced. Familiar examples include the Food and Drug Administration's (FDA's) regulation of pharmaceuticals, the Federal

Aviation Administration's (FAA's) regulation of airlines, the Environmental Protection Agency's (EPA's) regulation of air and water quality standards, and the Occupational Safety and Health Administration's (OSHA's) regulation of workplace safety.

Safety regulation is pervasive among some types of financial intermediaries—notably banks and other depositories, insurance companies, and pension funds.[15] Federal regulation imposes minimum capital (net worth) requirements on banks and other depositories, restricts their activities (so as to reduce their riskiness), and imposes suitability and competence requirements on officers and directors; an extensive labor force of examiners and supervisors enforces this regulation in the field.[16] State safety regulation of insurance companies mimics federal bank regulation in most ways. Federal regulation of pension funds includes fiduciary obligations, prudent-person investing rules, and (for defined-benefit pension plans) requirements for employer prefunding of promised retirement benefits.[17] Federal regulation of the securities industry includes capital requirements for broker-dealers, licensing of stockbrokers ("registered representatives"), and restrictions on the riskiness of the short-term debt instruments that can be held by money market mutual funds. Securities sales personnel are expected to be familiar with their customers' financial status and have a fiduciary obligation to serve their customers' best interests.

Information Regulation

This form of regulation involves attaching specified (and often standardized) pieces of information to products or services. Familiar examples include the FDA's requirement that detailed descriptions and instructions accompany pharmaceutical packages, the Department of Agriculture's labeling requirements for processed foods, and the Department of Transportation's fine-print requirements for airline advertising.

The federal and state governments regulate the securities industry extensively in terms of information requirements. Companies (and the financial firms that serve them) are required to make extensive disclosures at the time that they issue securities and then to report their relevant financial information according to a standardized accounting framework ("generally accepted accounting principles," or

GAAP) on a quarterly basis,[18] as well as reporting any significant events as they occur.[19] Corporate insiders must publicly disclose "inside" information before trading on it. Mutual funds are required to mark their portfolios to market on a daily basis and to reveal the net share value, to reveal their portfolio holdings periodically, and to report recent performance results on a standardized basis. Banks must disclose interest rates on loans and on deposits, on a standardized basis, and must provide a copy of their balance sheets to anyone who asks. Insurance companies must provide extensive information to their insured on a standardized basis.

A Summing Up

This brief description of financial regulation does not do full justice to the many linear feet of printed state and federal laws and regulations that envelop the financial services sector. But as even this brief summary illustrates, the regulatory thicket is a nontrivial barrier that any entrant must penetrate, and nonnational potential entrants might well find the thicket yet more daunting.

12.5   The Openness of the U.S. Financial Services Sector

There is no good summary measure of the openness of the U.S. financial services sector. Instead, one has to look to the policies that have been pursued by federal and state regulators of the various categories of financial services to determine whether national origin has been a determinant of how the regulators have assessed the worthiness of potential entrants or how the regulators have treated incumbents.

Despite some exceptions, national treatment is a reasonably good approximation of the regime that applies to nonnational firms that wish to supply financial services in the United States.[20] If nonnational firms otherwise meet the qualifications for entry, their nationality generally is not an issue;[21] and once established as incumbents, their nationality does not influence their regulatory treatment (with the exception of some difficult aspects of safety regulation that pertain to foreign-based banks and insurance companies).[22] This openness is in sharp contrast to the practices of many other countries, which refuse entry to nonnational providers of financial services and/or differentially limit what nonnational providers can do.

This openness has had different consequences and manifestations among the major categories of financial services in the United States. In the remainder of this section I provide some of the data that pertain to foreign firms' provision of financial services in the United States.[23] In section 12.6 I discuss the reasons—especially the proximity/familiarity arguments developed in section 12.3—that can explain much of the pattern that these data reveal.

Banking

Table 12.2 provides data on the percentages of all commercial bank assets in the United States that have been accounted for by foreign banks located in the United States, from 1973 through 1996. Though there are two alternative sources of data—the Federal Reserve Bank of New York and the *American Banker*—their estimates are only slightly different in levels[24] and are quite consistent in trends. As can be seen, the foreign bank percentage grew steadily in the 1970s and the 1980s, but peaked in the early 1990s at about 23 percent and then leveled or declined slightly.[25]

Table 12.3 shows the ten leading countries of origin for foreign banks in the United States. Japan is by far the leader; France is a distant second.

It is worth noting that only a handful of foreign banks have succeeded in establishing significant branch networks (and in at least one case the foreign bank simply bought an existing New York bank with an extensive New York branch network).

No readily available data exist on foreign ownership of savings institutions (savings and loan associations and savings banks); but until the late 1980s, there were no foreign-owned savings institutions, and since then only a handful have been acquired by foreign owners. It is likely that the percentage of assets accounted for by foreign-owned institutions is less than 1 percent of the total.[26]

Credit unions are mutual organizations with no explicit owners except their members/depositors, so foreign ownership is not a relevant concept for these institutions.

Insurance

Table 12.4 provides information on foreign firms' involvement in U.S. insurance markets for 1992–1995. (Unfortunately, consistent

Table 12.2
Foreign banks in the United States: Their U.S. assets as a percentage of all bank assets in the United States, 1973–1996

Year	Federal Reserve Bank of New York data	*American Banker* data
1973	3.8%	n.a.
1974	4.9	n.a.
1975	5.3	n.a.
1976	5.8	n.a.
1977	6.4	n.a.
1978	8.0	n.a.
1979	9.9	n.a.
1980	11.9	n.a.
1981	13.5	n.a.
1982	14.4	n.a.
1983	14.6	16.3%
1984	15.9	17.7
1985	16.1	18.6
1986	17.3	18.4
1987	19.0	20.9
1988	19.6	20.2
1989	20.6	21.2
1990	21.4	21.7
1991	22.6	22.5
1992	22.2	23.3
1993	21.1	22.0
1994	21.3	22.0
1995	21.7	22.6
1996	n.a.	22.1

Sources: U.S. Treasury (1994); U.S. Department of Commerce, *Statistical Abstract of the United States,* various issues; *American Banker,* February 20, 1997, 16.
Note: n.a. indicates data not available.

Table 12.3
Foreign banks in the United States: Top ten countries, 1996

Country	U.S. bank assets ($ billions)
Japan	$355.6
France	121.4
Canada	70.3
United Kingdom	64.1
Germany	58.7
Switzerland	54.3
Netherlands	53.3
Italy	28.2
Korea	17.1
Australia	16.6

Source: American Banker, February 20, 1997, 19–23.

Table 12.4
Foreign insurers in the United States: Their U.S. assets as a percentage of all insurers' assets in the United States, 1992–1995

	Life insurance	Property/Casualty/Health Insurance	All insurance
1992	10.7%	11.2%	10.9%
1993	11.6	11.7	11.6
1994	10.8	10.6	10.8
1995	10.8	10.4	10.7

Source: OECD (1997).

data for a longer time series or for countries of origin are not readily available.) These limited data show that foreign involvement in U.S. insurance in the mid-1990s was at about half the relative level as was true for banking.[27]

Investment Banking–Securities

No readily available summary measures of foreign firms as providers of services in the U.S. securities markets (that would be comparable to the summary measures that are available for banking and insurance) exist. Though the "household names" in U.S. securities markets and investment banking—for example, Merrill Lynch; Gold-

Table 12.5
Leading underwriters of all U.S. securities, 1996

Rank	Underwriter	Market share
1	Merrill Lynch	16.3%
2	Lehman Brothers	10.6
3	Goldman, Sachs	10.3
4	Salomon Brothers	10.1
5	Morgan Stanley	8.8
6	J. P. Morgan	7.2
7	**Credit Suisse First Boston**	6.3
8	Bear, Stearns	4.4
9	Donaldson, Lufkin, & Jenrette	3.6
10	Smith Barney	3.1
11	Nationsbank	2.0
12	Chase Manhattan	1.8
13	PaineWebber	1.7
14	Prudential Securities	1.5
15	**UBS**	1.1
Total for top 15:		88.8%

Source: Investment Dealers' Digest, January 13, 1997, 32.
Note: Foreign-headquartered firms are in bold.

man, Sachs; Salomon Brothers; Morgan Stanley Dean Witter; Paine-Webber; Smith Barney; Lehman Brothers; Bear, Stearns; Donaldson, Lufkin & Jenrette—are headquartered in the United States, there are a number of foreign-owned (wholly or substantially) investment banking–securities firms that are active in the U.S. markets: for example, Nomura; Credit Suisse First Boston; ABN AMRO; SBC Warburg (including Dillon, Read); Lazard Freres; UBS; Deutsche Morgan Grenfell. Though a few of these latter firms sometimes appear on annual "league tables" (the leading X firms in a category) of securities and investment banking activities (e.g., securities underwriting, merger-advising activity), it is the former group that is far more prominent. Table 12.5 provides a list of the leading securities underwriters in the United States in 1996. As can be seen, two foreign firms ranked seventh and fifteenth, respectively, among U.S. underwriters, together accounting for 7.4 percent of underwritings. Since this list of the top 15 accounted for almost 90 percent of all underwritings, it is reasonably inclusive. The smaller firms that would fill out the remainder of the list tend to be domestic underwriters.[28]

Table 12.6
Leading underwriters of all U.S. securities, 1975

Rank	Underwriter	Market share
1	Merrill Lynch	12.3%
2	First Boston	10.7
3	Salomon Brothers	10.4
4	Morgan Stanley	9.8
5	Goldman, Sachs	7.4
6	Blyth Eastman	6.2
7	Lehman Brothers	5.6
8	Halsey, Stuart	5.4
9	Kidder Peabody	5.1
10	Smith Barney	3.8
11	Dean Witter	3.8
12	Paine Webber	3.2
13	Kuhn, Loeb	3.2
14	White, Weld	3.2
15	E. F. Hutton	2.3
Total for top 15 (out of total for top 20)		92.4%

Source: Hayes, Spence, and Marks (1983), 118–119.

The overall foreign share is likely to be only slightly larger than 7.4 percent.[29]

Even modest appearances by these non-U.S. firms in the 1990s lists exceeded their frequency of appearance on similar lists in the 1970s and earlier, when (with one exception[30]) the only firms that appeared on the lists were U.S. securities firms. Table 12.6 provides an example of a 1975 list, when no foreign firms reached the top 15.[31] Further, no foreign-headquartered securities firms have established (or even bought) extensive retail distribution systems comparable to the "wirehouses" of Merrill Lynch, PaineWebber, Dean Witter, and so forth.

By contrast, in the government securities market, of the thirty-nine primary dealers (as of 1994) with which the Federal Reserve Bank of New York trades securities (in the implementation of the Federal Reserve's open-market monetary policy), nineteen were foreign-headquartered firms, representing seven countries.

In the area of options and futures, non-U.S. firms appear to have a modest presence. About 5 percent of the firms that participate in the options and futures markets are foreign based.[32]

As a first approximation, it appears that foreign firms' provision of financial services in the securities area in the United States, as a fraction of all securities services provided by U.S. and foreign firms in the United States, is substantially smaller than the comparable fractions for banking and insurance—except in the government securities area.

A second potential dimension to the concept of international access to U.S. securities markets exists: foreigners as *users* of the financial services (e.g., as borrowers or investors).[33] The globalization of financial markets has clearly had its manifestations in foreigners' access to the U.S. securities markets. For example, the number of non-U.S. companies that were listed for trading on the New York Stock Exchange (NYSE) rose from 59 in 1986 to 290 by the end of 1996; the volume of trading in non-U.S. stocks on the NYSE rose from 4 percent of total NYSE trading in 1988 to 9 percent in 1996.[34] Since the focus in this chapter is on the openness of the financial services sector with respect to the *providers* of the services, we will not pursue this second aspect further.[35] But a potential link between nonnational users and nonnational providers is clear: To the extent that non-U.S. users find the U.S. securities markets increasingly attractive and their volume of usage increases, the opportunities for non-U.S. providers of services (as the financial firms that are the most familiar to and familiar with the non-U.S. users, but who can also guide the non-U.S. users through the maze of the U.S. securities markets) will concomitantly increase.

Mutual Funds

Those involved in managing and selling mutual funds are largely U.S. companies. Though a few non-U.S. securities firms offer a few mutual funds, the overwhelming presence in the field is by U.S. companies (some of them specialists in the mutual fund area; others offering mutual funds as part of their larger securities business), and most of the familiar names in the area—e.g., Fidelity, Dreyfus, Vanguard, Franklin, Merrill Lynch, Prudential, etc.—are U.S. companies. In the late 1990s two significant purchases of U.S. mutual fund groups by an overseas buyer occurred: Zurich Insurance's purchase of Kemper and Scudder, and Invesco's purchase of AIM. In both instances the asset share positions amounted to 2 percent or less of the U.S. mutual fund industry's aggregate assets.

Finance Companies

Among the leading one hundred finance companies in 1995, there were no free-standing foreign-owned companies and only nine subsidiaries of foreign-owned banks or commercial enterprises (of which 8 were subsidiaries of banks and the ninth was Toyota Motor Credit Corp). Those nine accounted for 7.8 percent of the total assets of the one hundred.[36] It appears that foreign relative participation in this area is substantially smaller than is true for foreign participation in U.S. banking and U.S. insurance.

Pension Funds

Securities firms, banks, mutual funds, and insurance firms are frequent pension fund advisors and/or managers; there are also specialized pension fund managers and advisers. One standard reference source[37] lists 1,590 firms as serving as advisors and/or managers, as of early 1997; 109 of them were foreign-based firms. The list of the top 15 firms (see table 12.7) shows only one foreign firm (albeit in first place); all 109 firms account for about 17 percent of all pen-

Table 12.7
Leading pension fund managers/advisors, 1997

Rank	Firm	Market share
1	**Barclays Global Investors**	6.9%
2	State Street Global	6.4
3	Fidelity	5.3
4	TIAA-CREF	4.0
5	Bankers Trust	3.9
6	J. P. Morgan	3.1
7	Alliance Capital	2.0
8	Northern Trust	1.7
9	Pacific Investment Management	1.7
10	Vanguard	1.7
11	Capital Research & Management	1.5
12	Prudential	1.4
13	Brinson Partners	1.3
14	MetLife	1.3
15	Capital Guardian Trust	1.2

Source: Standard & Poor's (1997).
Note: Foreign-headquartered firms are in bold.

sion funds under management. A list of the top 15 firms in a specialized area, 401(k) plans (see table 12.8), shows only one foreign firm (in fifth place).

A Summing Up

Foreign firms clearly do participate in the financial services sector of the United States. But the extent of their participation varies extensively across the different subsectors. In the next section, I argue that this differential pattern of participation is not indicative of any (perhaps hidden) discriminatory policies by the U.S. government but instead is quite consistent with a financial sector that is internationally open *and* that is subject to the asymmetric information phenomena endemic to finance.

12.6 The Causes, Manifestations, and Ramifications of Unilateral Openness

This section addresses three questions: Why has unilateral openness arisen in the U.S. financial sector? Why has this openness man-

Table 12.8
Leading 401(k) plan managers/advisors, 1996

Rank	Firm	Market share
1	Fidelity	15.0%
2	Vanguard	8.5
3	State Street Global	7.3
4	Merrill Lynch	4.4
5	Bankers Trust	4.1
6	**Barclays Global Investors**	4.1
7	Prudential	3.4
8	UAM	3.1
9	Principal Financial Group	3.1
10	T. Rowe Price	2.8
11	CIGNA	2.8
12	Putnam	2.6
13	Aetna	2.5
14	MetLife	2.5
15	INVESCO	2.2

Source: Cerulli Associates.
Note: Foreign-headquartered firms are in bold.

ifested itself in the pattern described in section 12.5? And has this openness benefited the U.S. economy?

Why Has Unilateral Openness Arisen?

As was argued in section 12.3, the asymmetric information problems that are inherent in finance have made information gathering and monitoring crucial to the successful provision of financial services. And, traditionally, the costs of information gathering and monitoring have caused geographic distances to be a barrier; equivalently, proximity between lender and borrower (or between insurer and insured, etc.) has been important.

An important implication of proximity has been the relative absence of pure "trade" in financial services, in the sense of a firm located in one country selling its services across the border to purchasers in another country. Instead, for the most part, the provision of finance has required a local presence; in essence, the provider of financial services has had to make a local investment in facilities and personnel (and information) and then sell the services from the local location. Another way of stating this proposition is that the provision of financial services by a foreigner has required substantial inbound FDI into the United States.

Generally, the United States has not had a tradition of hostility to inbound FDI. There are important exceptions to this last statement: The United States has restricted foreign ownership of airlines serving domestic routes, of shipping companies serving the coastal trade routes (cabotage), of companies using the electromagnetic spectrum for telecommunications (broadcasting or telephone), and of companies serving national defense needs. Also, prior to the mid-1970s a patchwork of restrictions on foreigners applied in commercial banking.[38] And, in the 1980s and early 1990s, as the United States became a net capital importer, media and political attention focused on foreigners' purchases of high-profile assets (e.g., movie studios, New York City's Rockefeller Center).[39] Still, compared to its history of protectionism in manufacturing and compared to many other countries' restrictions on FDI, the United States' stance on inbound FDI has been relatively open and encouraging.

Since foreigners' provision of financial services required inbound FDI, and since the United States was relatively encouraging toward inbound FDI, a general attitude of openness—unilateral openness, without any need for reciprocity—toward foreigners' provision of financial services was a natural stance.

Further, as a net capital exporter for the first three-quarters of the twentieth century, the United States experienced relatively small amounts of inbound FDI generally. Without a great deal of inbound FDI, there was little demand for the special expertise—the knowledge of the creditworthiness of the enterprises of their fellow nationals, as well as the ability to help their fellow nationals navigate the U.S. financial markets—that foreign providers of financial services could otherwise bring to the United States. Consequently, there was less opportunity for foreign providers to establish themselves,[40] but also less opportunity for domestic (U.S.) resentments against foreigners to build into protectionist sentiments. In effect, the international (unilateral) openness of the U.S. financial services sector had few consequences (and few potential political costs) for much of the twentieth century.

The history of commercial banking until the 1970s is somewhat of an exception to this openness, but the story is a complicated one.[41] At the federal level, though otherwise suitable foreigners could obtain a national bank charter from the Comptroller of the Currency, all of the directors of the bank would have to be U.S. citizens. Some states explicitly prohibited the presence of foreign banks or treated them as the equivalent of a branch of an out-of-state bank (which was generally prohibited); others limited their operations severely. A few states, such as California, Illinois, and New York, were favorably disposed; but even as late as 1960 New York did not permit foreign banks to establish full-fledged branches that could conduct a general banking business. On the other hand, foreign banks that had facilities in the United States were free of many federal regulations that applied to domestically owned banks: for example, limitations on interstate branching, interest rate ceilings on deposits, and reserve requirements.

This harsher treatment of foreign banks than of most other inbound FDI or of other foreign providers of financial services was consistent with the harsh attitudes that the states generally had toward out-of-state banks (i.e., banks with out-of-state headquarters) and that the federal government tolerated and reinforced until 1994. In many respects, the "foreignness" of foreign banks was less important than the fact that they were simply another out-of-state bank.

In any event, federal legislation in 1978 (the International Banking Act) brought foreign banks into greater parity with domestic banks at the federal level (and allowed a minority of the directors of national banks to be non-U.S. citizens). Simultaneously, most states began to see the wisdom and benefits of encouraging the establishment of foreign banking facilities within their boundaries, and banking moved toward the openness enjoyed by the other parts of the U.S. financial services sector.[42]

Why This Pattern of Foreign Involvement?

The pattern of differing levels of foreign involvement in the U.S. financial services sector described in section 12.5 could possibly be indicative of differing levels of U.S. governmental discrimination against foreign firms. But my earlier discussion of U.S. policies argues otherwise. Further, a closer examination of this pattern of differential involvement reveals that it is quite consistent with an open financial services sector and the application of the asymmetric information paradigm of finance and the consequent needs for proximity and familiarity between lender and borrower, as discussed in section 12.3. Equivalently, these proximity/familiarity propositions lead us to expect differing levels of involvement by foreigners across subsectors, and those expectations are consistent with the actual pattern found among the subsectors of the U.S. financial services markets.

For the most part, foreign providers of financial services in the United States have not had special technological expertise, special brand names, special products, or special efficiencies that would give them comparative advantages or niches in U.S. financial markets. They are probably at an informational disadvantage with respect to dealing with most domestic borrowers in the United States, and their brand names are generally unfamiliar.[43]

However, foreign providers often do have special knowledge about the creditworthiness of the enterprises of their fellow nationals, as well as a familiar brand name to their fellow nationals.[44] Accordingly, it is the wave of inbound FDI that the United States has experienced since the mid-1970s that has created the greatest opportunities for foreign providers.[45] The time-series data for foreign banks and inbound FDI, cross-section data by country for inbound FDI and foreign bank assets in the United States, and the relative presence of foreign providers across the subsectors of financial services are all consistent with these proximity-familiarity propositions. I address each in turn.

1. *Time-Series Data on Foreign Banks and Inbound FDI.* Table 12.9 provides the time-series data on total foreign bank assets in the United States.[46] and the levels (i.e, the stock) of total inbound FDI for the years 1973–1996. As can be seen, the foreign bank assets series and the inbound FDI series generally increase similarly from the mid-1970s through the early 1990s (but diverge in the mid-1990s, with foreign bank assets falling[47] and the stock of inbound FDI continuing to rise). Of course, this similarity in movement does not necessarily imply causality.[48] Further, it could be the case that the growth in foreign bank assets in the United States was just one aspect of the rising tide of inbound FDI in the United States since the late 1970s; that is, U.S. banking operations were just another activity that overseas investors saw as profitable investments. Still, the time-series pattern is consistent with the proximity-familiarity propositions.

2. *Cross-Section Analysis of Foreign Banks and Inbound FDI.* For 1996, data have been assembled, by country, on the levels of foreign bank assets in the United States and levels (stock) of inbound FDI in the United States. As can be seen in table 12.10, a simple linear regression between the two cross-section data series shows a significant positive relationship; an extra dollar in the level of inbound FDI for a country is associated with an extra $1.36 of foreign bank assets in the United States. About half of the variance in foreign bank assets can be explained. When the regression is repeated in logs, a significant relationship continues to hold; a 10 percent increase in inbound FDI is associated with a 5.7 percent increase in foreign bank assets. About half of the variance can again be explained.

As was true for the time-series data, it might be the case that this positive association is just an aspect of the general process of inbound FDI, even on a cross-section basis (i.e., those countries that invested more extensively in the United States also tended to invest more heavily in banks). Still, the pattern is again consistent with the proximity-familiarity propositions.

Further, the relative absence of extensive branch networks among foreign banks is another piece of support. Foreign banks' comparative advantage is at the "wholesale" level, dealing with fellow-national enterprises, with few branches needed, rather than at the

Table 12.9
Foreign bank assets in the United States and the stock of inbound FDI, 1973–1996 (in billions of dollars)

Year	Foreign bank assets (Federal Reserve Bank of New York data)	Foreign bank assets (*American Banker* data)	Inbound FDI
1973	$32.3	n.a.	$20.6
1974	46.1	n.a.	25.1
1975	52.4	n.a.	27.7
1976	61.3	n.a.	30.8
1977	76.8	n.a.	34.6
1978	109.1	n.a.	42.5
1979	149.6	n.a.	54.5
1980	200.6	n.a.	83.0
1981	250.6	n.a.	108.7
1982	299.8	n.a.	124.7
1983	328.8	$321.6	137.1
1984	394.4	380.9	164.6
1985	440.8	423.8	184.6
1986	524.3	461.0	220.4
1987	592.6	571.9	263.4
1988	650.6	638.3	314.8
1989	735.7	706.0	368.9
1990	791.1	768.3	394.9
1991	860.7	832.0	419.1
1992	869.0	887.0	423.1
1993	855.6	872.7	467.4
1994	943.7	893.7	496.5
1995	982.9	989.1	560.8
1996	n.a.	948.7	630.0

Sources: U.S. Treasury (1994, 77); U.S. Department of Commerce, *Statistical Abstract of the United States*, various issues; *American Banker*, various issues; Bargas (1997a, b).
Note: n.a. indicates data not available.

Table 12.10
OLS cross-section regressions: Foreign bank assets in the United States and levels of inbound FDI, by country of origin, 1996

42 countries

Mean of foreign bank assets in the U.S. (FBKASS): $22.5 billion
Mean of level (stock) of inbound FDI (IFDI): $14.4 billion

Linear regression:
FBKASS = 2.91 + 1.36 IFDI
$\quad\quad\quad$ (0.44) (7.08)
$\quad$ R-sq. = 0.564

Linear regression in logs:
Ln(FBKASS) = 1.12 + 0.57 Ln(IFDI)
$\quad\quad\quad\quad\quad$ (4.96) (6.59)
$\quad\quad$ R-sq. = 0.52

Note: t-statistics in parentheses.

"retail" level, dealing with consumers and local (domestic) small businesses, where branches are important.[49]

3. *Savings Institutions.* The absence of foreign interest in the ownership of savings institutions when they were primarily consumer oriented (for which foreigners would have no comparative advantage), and the growing foreign interest in owning them when legal changes allowed thrifts to act more like commercial lenders, is consistent with the proposition that foreigners would be more interested in owning institutions that could be used in ways that were closer to the foreigners' comparative advantage.

4. *Insurance Companies.* The lower penetration of foreign insurance companies in the United States, as compared with banks, is consistent with the proximity-familiarity propositions. U.S. insurance companies in the property-casualty area would likely be willing to offer insurance to U.S. operations of foreign enterprises in circumstances where U.S. banks would be unwilling to lend, because domestic insurance companies can more readily familiarize themselves with the local facilities and risks of a foreign enterprise than can a domestic bank familiarize itself with the more general risks of lending to that same (foreign) enterprise. In addition, foreign insurers would have less of an advantage (vis-à-vis domestic insurers) in retail lines, such as life insurance, motor vehicle insurance, and homeowners' insurance.

5. *Securities-Investment Banking Firms.* We would expect foreign enterprises in the United States, when seeking credit, initially and primarily to be interested in bank finance. Banks are information and monitoring specialists and are accustomed to dealing with smaller scale requests.[50] Only when an enterprise graduates in size and reputation do the possibilities of raising funds through the securities markets arise.[51] Accordingly, the proximity-familiarity propositions would predict that the foreign presence in investment banking would be less than in commercial banking, and this is the pattern that is indeed found. Though the increased globalization of securities markets may increase the demand for foreigners' investment banking services in the United States even in the absence of inbound FDI, that increased demand has not yet proved sufficiently important.

The exception is in the government securities market, where foreigners have a substantial presence; but this is an exception that, in an important sense, proves the rule. As part of the U.S. economy's becoming a net foreign debtor, the U.S. government has sold a significant amount of its debt to foreigners. As of year end 1996, a third (over $1.1 trillion) of the privately held debt of the U.S. government was held by foreigners. It is not surprising that foreign securities firms, in the service of their overseas customers, would want a substantial presence in the U.S. government securities area.

As was true for banking, the relative absence of extensive retail branch networks among foreign-headquartered securities firms is further support for the proximity-familiarity propositions, since foreign firms would be unlikely to have a comparative advantage in dealing with the retail public in the United States.

6. *Options-Futures.* Prior to the 1970s, the U.S. futures exchanges focused exclusively on agricultural and mineral commodities. Though some commodities were of interest internationally, many were domestically oriented. From the early 1970s onward, financial futures and options became increasingly important. The initial focus was on instruments that were related to U.S. securities, though trading in foreign exchange contracts and then contracts on foreign securities were added over time. It is not surprising (and it is consistent with the proximity-familiarity propositions) that foreign-based financial services providers would not generally have a special advantage in these markets and hence would not be especially prominent.

7. *Mutual Funds.* Mutual funds are generally retail oriented. It is quite consistent with the proximity-familiarity propositions that foreigners would have only a modest presence in this area.

8. *Finance Companies.* Finance companies tend to be lending specialists and do not offer the wider range of services that commercial banks or investment banks offer. Furthermore, finance companies that lend to commercial enterprises (as opposed to consumers) tend to focus their efforts on smaller enterprises. It is consistent with the proximity/familiarity propositions that foreigners have only a modest presence in this area and that there are no free-standing foreign-controlled finance companies—that is, they are all subsidiaries of foreign-owned commercial enterprises (e.g., Toyota) or of foreign-owned banks.

9. *Pension Funds.* At first glance, the significant presence of a number of foreign firms in the U.S. pension fund area seems inconsistent with the proximity-familiarity propositions. Pension funds encompass hundreds of thousands of enterprises and millions of workers—not the area where foreign-based financial services firms should have their comparative advantage. But pension funds, as comparatively sophisticated investors, are increasingly concerned about the international diversification of their investments. Foreign-based financial services firms may well have a comparative advantage in advising and guiding pension funds in their international investments.

However, though a foreign firm (Barclays Global Investors) is the leading provider of services in the overall pension area, it is merely the fifth-ranked firm in the 401(k) area (and there are no other foreign firms in the top 20), and it is the sixth-ranked firm in all defined contribution plans.[52] Since 401(k) and defined contribution plans generally are subject to much greater control by individual workers, who would tend to be less familiar with foreign firms or even with the importance of diversifying internationally, this lesser role in the defined contribution area (and the implied greater role in the defined benefit area, where knowledgeable enterprises would be more important) is consistent with the proximity-familiarity propositions.

10. *A Summing Up.* The mosaic of relative presences and penetrations by foreign providers in the financial services markets of the United States—cross-sectionally, over time, and across subsectors—is largely consistent with the proximity-familiarity propositions, and

thus with the asymmetric information paradigm of finance, which were developed in section 12.3. This pattern also gives support to the notion that the U.S. financial services sector is basically open to international providers, since the pattern is consistent with what would arise from an open sector that was subject to the asymmetric information problems that are well known for financial services.

Has the United States Benefited from Its Openness Policies?

As a general matter, the U.S. economy generally must have benefited from its openness policies. Foreign providers have delivered a set of services that domestic providers would have delivered with more difficulty and less efficiency; foreign providers meshed nicely with the larger wave of inbound FDI from the late 1970s onward, and with the increasing globalization of markets generally and of financial markets more specifically.

On the other hand, it is not the competition from foreigners in U.S. financial markets that has spurred the efficiency and innovation of U.S. financial services providers. Foreign providers have not generally been at the forefront of innovation in the financial services sector.[53] New products and services—financial options and futures, asset securitization, financial engineering, etc.—have come primarily from domestic financial services providers. The vigor of American financial services providers and their international expansiveness and competitiveness rests with the firms that are headquartered in the United States. In turn, this vigor, competitiveness, and innovativeness is due largely to the large internal market for financial services in the United States and the multiple arenas (including regulatory arenas) in which competition and innovation can and have occurred: the 50 states and their 150 separate regulatory regimes for banking, insurance, and securities; three federal bank regulators; a federal savings institution regulator; a federal credit union regulator; a federal securities regulator; a federal commodities-futures regulator; and two federal pension fund regulators. At one level, this structure can appear chaotic and inefficient;[54] but it can also create beneficial competition and innovation: among firms; among markets; and even among regulators.[55]

Has the U.S. economy been harmed by the policy of openness? It is tempting to suggest that the United States might have been more successful in prying open other countries' financial services sectors (and thus would have benefited America's efficient and dynamic financial services providers) if the United States had been less open and had pursued a policy of reciprocity, offering selective openness only to those countries that offered equivalent openness to American providers. Perhaps this strategy would have worked vis-à-vis Japan and a handful of other industrial countries. But it probably would have been useless vis-à-vis most developing countries, which have cared a great deal about keeping U.S. providers out and have cared little about access for their providers to the U.S. financial services markets. And it would have created the risks of failure with respect to the opening of even other industrial countries' financial services sectors and of fanning the flames of protectionism within the United States. The game could well have not been worth the candle.

12.7 Conclusion

Unilateral international openness has been a real and important feature of the U.S. financial services sector. This unilateral openness has stood as a "beacon" among countries in today's increasingly globalized markets. It is a standard to which most other countries and most other sectors of the U.S. economy should aspire. The United States' financial openness has been a significant example for the advocates of openness in other countries, and this openness has probably helped nudge other countries (e.g., those in East, Southeast, and South Asia) in the direction of more openness,[56] although the Asian debt crisis of 1997 showed that there was considerably more work that could be done. Indeed, an important lesson that emerged from that crisis was that the protected/restricted financial sectors of most Asian countries were ill-adapted to the growing globalization of financial markets; arguably, had these countries earlier adopted openness policies that were closer to those of the United States, their financial institutions would have been exposed earlier and more gradually to greater competition and to greater pressures to be efficient in their lending/investing/intermediation practices and would have been less prone to the failures that actually occurred.[57]

In the 1990s the United States shifted its nominal international negotiating stance to one of an insistence on reciprocity. It was this stance that caused the United States to refuse to sign the 1995 international agreement on liberalizing trade in financial services. As was

argued in section 12.6, the risks of a move to reciprocity are substantial, although its seductive lure is understandable; it may well be
that the United States' tougher bargaining position was the reason
for the improved outcome of the December 1997 agreement.

Fortunately, despite this tougher stance and threats that it might
prospectively insist on reciprocity in its decisions, the U.S. government has not (yet) imposed any real restrictions that would undo its
basic openness posture. With luck, the threats alone will be sufficient
and will not require restrictive enforcement, and the de facto openness of the U.S. financial services sector will continue.

Notes

This chapter was written for and presented at the Ford/AEI Conference on Unilateral
Trade liberalization, October 24–25, 1997. The author would like to thank Jagdish
Bhagwati, Jose Campa, Andrew Dick, Sydney Key, Xavier Martin, John Rea, Richard
Sylla, Lawrence Uhlick, Paul Wachtel, and Mira Wilkins for helpful comments on an
earlier draft and to thank Liu Linan for her research assistance.

1. For a discussion of the negotiations leading up to the 1997 agreement, see Key
(1997).

2. The United Kingdom is one of the few other countries that has practiced extensive
openness with respect to their financial services sector.

3. As will be discussed in section 12.6, this openness to inbound FDI has had some
major exceptions.

4. See, for example, King and Levine (1993a, 1993b) and Levine (1996).

5. The claims of the liability holders are on the institution and are not claims on any
specific assets in which the institution has invested.

6. Similarly, mutual funds would have various financial instruments as their assets
and the shares of their shareholders as their liabilities, and pension funds would have
as their liabilities the claims of present and future retirees.

7. Analogies for primary and secondary markets can be found in insurance: The writing of an insurance contract is a primary activity; reinsurance is a secondary activity.
Similarly, for options and futures, the initial writing of a contract is a primary activity,
and its subsequent trading is a secondary activity.

8. It has been noted that the globalization of finance has proceeded the farthest in the
area of foreign-exchange trading, next for government debt, next for corporate debt,
and least for corporate equity. See Bodner (1990). And garden-variety bank commercial loans, with few exceptions, are not traded at all, even on a national basis.
This ordering is consistent with the relative transparency and simplicity of the various types of instruments and the relative informational disadvantages that nonnational (from afar) transactors and traders would experience compared to national
transactors.

9. Again, there are exceptions. The reputation of Swiss banks for maintaining depositors' anonymity has been so great that some U.S. depositors have been willing to buy deposit services from Swiss banks, even in (or possibly because of) the absence of a local presence by these banks.

10. A more complete overview can be found in White (1994).

11. In the case of banking, surprisingly, through quirks in U.S. banking laws prior to 1978, foreign-based banks were less tightly regulated in some respects than were U.S.-based banks.

12. This is the surviving remnant of the Federal Reserve's "Regulation Q", which formerly (from 1933 until the early 1980s) specified the interest rates on all types of deposits in banks.

13. The restrictions by states used to be much more extensive and comprehensive. Along with the elimination of most of the reach of Regulation Q, this rolling back of state (and federal) restrictions on branching has been one of the major accomplishments of the economic deregulation of banking of the past two decades.

14. Securities firms, insurance companies, and commercial-industrial companies are symmetrically barred from owning a bank. These ownership limitations arise from the Glass-Steagall Act of 1933 and the Bank Holding Company Acts of 1956 and 1970. These limitations apply to banks' U.S. operations. When operating abroad, U.S. banks are largely exempt from these limitations, so long as the activities are conducted outside the U.S. bank (e.g., in the bank's holding company or in a separate subsidiary of the holding company).

15. Common elements among all three broad categories of intermediaries that might justify safety regulation are the arguments that their liability holders—depositors, insurance policyholders, and pension fund claimants—are generally ill-equipped to monitor their institutions on their own and that the financial consequences to them of their institution's failure could be substantial. Also, for banks, concerns about systemic contagion—depositor runs and/or successive failures (toppling dominoes)—are also an important motivation for safety-and-soundness regulation. See White (1991, chap. 10; 1996).

16. Also, since 1993 the premiums on federal deposit insurance have been risk based.

17. Pension plans can be classified into defined-benefit and defined-contribution plans. In the former category, employers promise to pay specified sums upon a worker's retirement, often linked to the preretirement wages of the retiree, and are required to set aside sufficient sums in advance so as to meet the expected commitment. In the latter category, retirees receive whatever has accumulated as a consequence of their own and their employer's earlier contributions and the returns and appreciation on those investments. It is the defined-benefit plans for which the possibility of an employer's bankruptcy raises the threat of the employer's inability to meet its pension commitment and hence the argument for a funding-in-advance requirement.

18. Extensive disclosure regulation has been accompanied by extensive corporate governance regulation. This latter body of regulation might be considered a weak form of safety regulation; arguably, "appropriate" corporate governance rules make investments "safer" for investors.

19. As a first approximation, the guiding regulatory philosophy in the securities area is that of information disclosure, whereas the guiding philosophy in banking (and insurance and pensions) is that of safety; but as my description indicates, all three forms of regulation apply to all sectors.

20. See U.S. Treasury (1994). The history of national treatment and openness differs by subsector. For example, for commercial banks, national treatment fundamentally began in 1978, with the passage of the International Banking Act; see Key and Brundy (1979) and Segala (1979). Ironically, before then, though foreign banks were discouraged or prohibited by some states and even at the federal level, those foreign banks that were established faced less federal regulation in some dimensions—e.g., no restrictions on interstate branching, no ceilings on deposit interest rates, no reserve requirements—than did domestic banks; see Benston (1990). At the other extreme, American acceptance of the investment banking services of foreign-headquartered institutions extends back to the first half of the nineteenth century. See Wilkins (1989; 1991).

21. A few states still prohibit the entry of foreign banks and place extra burdens on foreign insurance companies. See U.S. Treasury (1994).

22. If the foreign bank's operations are through a branch rather than a separately capitalized entity, then there are difficult questions of how U.S. regulators can assure themselves that the bank is solvent and that it will be able to satisfy the claims of its U.S. depositors; see Key (1990), Key and Scott (1991, 1992), and Misback (1993). Similar questions pertain to foreign insurance companies and the claims of their U.S. insureds.

23. As will be clear, we will focus on the financial services that are provided "on the ground" in the U.S. by foreign providers and not those that may be provided from afar (e.g., the loan to a U.S. borrower that might be provided from the overseas office of a foreign bank or the Swiss bank deposit that is owned by a U.S. resident).

24. Part of the differences is surely due to the fact that the Federal Reserve Bank of New York data are measured as of year end, while the *American Banker* data are measured as of June 30 of each year.

25. This change in pattern appears to be due largely to the financial difficulties experienced by the Japanese banking system in the mid-1990s, with ramifications for their operations in the United States. Between 1995 and 1996, for example, the assets of Japanese banks operating in the United States declined by $95 billion, or over 20 percent from their 1995 levels. In a widely reported example, in early 1998 Sumitomo Bank decided to sell its California subsidiary (with about $5 billion in assets) to Zions Bancorp. of Utah; see Domis (1998).

26. Also, a significant number of savings institutions (albeit, the smaller ones) have remained as mutual institutions, with no explicit owners except (arguably) their depositors, so foreign ownership would not be relevant for these institutions.

27. Mutual ownership is still a significant element in insurance, which would tend to reduce the share held by foreign firms.

28. In 1993 foreign firms, not including CS First Boston, were lead underwriters for 3.5 percent of all new debt and equity issues. See U.S. Treasury (1994, 82).

29. This list includes only the lead underwriter ("manager") for each issue. As the "tombstone" advertisements for underwritings indicate, there are often multiple underwriters for an issue, and foreign firms do participate in many underwritings; but

so do smaller domestic firms. A listing that allocated shares among all underwriters would likely yield similar results.

30. That exception is Lazard Freres, which is a joint U.S.-French partnership.

31. Lazard Freres was eighteenth that year.

32. See U.S. Treasury (1994, 85).

33. See, for example, Grundfest (1990), Miller (1990), Baumol and Malkiel (1992), Edwards (1992), Smith (1992), and Cochrane, Shapiro, and Tobin (1996).

34. See Smith and Sofianos (1997); see also Cochrane, Shapiro, and Tobin (1996).

35. A major issue in this second arena is the extent to which the SEC should try to protect U.S. investors vis-à-vis foreign securities issuers by requiring the latter to conform to U.S. GAAP in their information-accounting disclosures. See, for example, Baumol and Malkiel (1992) and Cochrane, Shapiro, and Tobin (1996).

36. These data are from *The American Banker*, June 21, 1997, 7–8. Since the one-hundredth largest finance company had less than $50 million in assets, the total assets for the 100—$732 billion—is probably not too far from the industry total, so the foreign share is unlikely to be much different from the 7.8% cited in the text.

37. See Standard & Poor's (1997).

38. See Summers (1976), Lees (1976), Kim and Miller (1983), and Jones (1993).

39. But rarely did this attention actually lead to successful efforts to block the foreigners' purchases.

40. Investment bankers from foreign-headquartered institutions were active in the United States in the nineteenth century; but this was a period when the United States was a net capital importer. See Wilkins (1989; 1991).

41. See Summers (1976), Lees (1976), and Kim and Miller (1983).

42. See Key (1985), Key and Welsh (1988), and Benston (1990).

43. For a discussion and description of the difficulties that British banks—for whom the problems of language and culture should have been substantially less than they would be for banks headquartered in non-English-speaking countries—have had in maintaining a profitable presence in the U.S. banking markets, see Jones (1993).

44. In the discussion that surrounded the sale of Sumitomo Bank's California operations (to Zions Bancorp. of Utah), it was noted that 45 percent of Sumitomo Bank of California's customers were Japanese-Americans. See Domis (1998).

45. The connection between FDI and international banking—domestic banks following their fellow nationals' business operations and establishing overseas locations so as to provide financial services to those business operations—is a widely discussed phenomenon. For discussions and efforts to explain the pattern of U.S. banking abroad, see Kindleberger (1983), Nigh, Cho, and Krishman (1986), and Sagari (1992). Once established locally in the United States and serving their home country enterprises, foreign providers of financial services might try also to provide services to domestic U.S. customers. And, in some instances, as part of the general pattern of capital inflow into the U.S., foreigners might simply buy a U.S. financial institution and hope that its local expertise and brand-name reputation would remain intact.

46. By this we mean the assets of U.S. branches or other facilities of foreign banks.

47. Again, the fall in foreign bank assets in the mid-1990s is largely due to the financial difficulties experienced by the Japanese banking system generally.

48. One formal effort to test causality between foreign bank assets and inbound FDI yielded inconclusive results; see DeLong (1993). For other efforts to explain the pattern of foreign banks' presence in the United States, see Ball and Tschoegel (1982), Hultman and McGee (1989), and Heinkel and Levi (1992).

49. Many of the British banks that attempted to establish branch networks subsequently abandoned them, and the ones that remained were considered to be performing poorly; see Jones (1993).

50. See Bhattacharya and Thakor (1993).

51. See Berger and Udell (1993).

52. See *Institutional Investor*, April 1997, 62.

53. An exception may be in the development of smart card technology, where an international consortium (Mondex) is one of the industry leaders.

54. See Coffee (1995).

55. See Bloch (1985) and White (1996).

56. See White (1995).

57. Of course, as the U.S. savings-and-loan debacle of the 1980s and the equally serious wave of failures of over 1,000 commercial banks in the 1980s and early 1990s showed, openness alone is no guarantee that substantial numbers of financial institutions will avoid self-destructive lending policies; see White (1991) and FDIC (1997). But these problems did not create large-scale problems for the U.S. economy, unlike the consequences of the Asian debt crisis of 1997 for Thailand, Korea, and Indonesia.

References

Ball, Clifford A., and Adrian E. Tschoegel. 1982. "The Decision to Establish a Foreign Bank Branch or Subsidiary: An Application of Binary Classification Procedures." *Journal of Financial and Quantitative Analysis* 17 (September): 411–424.

Bargas, Sylvia E. 1997a. "Direct Investment Positions for 1996: Country and Industry Detail." *Survey of Current Business* 77 (July): 34–41.

Bargas, Sylvia E. 1997b. "Foreign Direct Investment in the United States: Detail for Historical-Cost Position and Related Capital and Income Flows, 1996." *Survey of Current Business* 77 (September): 75–118.

Baumol, William J., and Burton G. Malkiel, "Redundant Regulation of Foreign Security Trading and U.S. Competitiveness." 1992. In *Modernizing U.S. Securities Regulation: Economic and Legal Perspectives*, ed. Kenneth Lehn and Robert W. Kamphius Jr., 39–55. Homewood, Ill.: Business One Irwin.

Benston, George J. 1990. "U.S. Banking in an Increasingly Integrated and Competitive World Economy." *Journal of Financial Services Research* 4 (December): 311–339.

Berger, Allen N., and Gregory F. Udell. 1993. "Securitization, Risk, and the Liquidity Problem in Business." In *Structural Change in Banking*, ed. Michael Klausner and Lawrence J. White, 227–291. Homewood, Ill: Irwin.

Bhattacharya, Sudipto, and Anjan V. Thakor. 1993. "Contemporary Banking Theory," *Journal of Financial Intermediation* 3 (October): 2–50.

Bloch, Ernest. 1985. "Multiple Regulators: Their Constituencies and Policies." In *Market Making and the Changing Structure of the Securities Industry*, ed. Yakov Amihud, Thomas S. Y. Ho, and Robert A. Schwartz, 155–182. Lexington, Mass.: Heath.

Bodner, David E. 1990. "The Global Markets: Where Do We Stand?" In International Finance and Financial Policy, ed. Hans R. Stoll, 201–206. New York: Quorum.

Cochrane, James L., James E. Shapiro, and Jean E. Tobin, "Foreign Equities and U.S. Investors: Breaking Down the Barriers Separating Supply and Demand." *Stanford Journal of Law, Business & Finance* 2, no. 2 (1996): 241–263.

Coffee, John C. Jr. 1995. "Competition versus Consolidation: The Significance of Organizational Structure in Financial and Securities Regulation." *Business Lawyer* 50 (February): 447–484.

DeLong, Gayle L. 1993. "The Influence of Foreign Banking on Foreign Direct Investment: Association and Causality." Mimeo., New York University.

Domis, Olaf de Senerpont. 1998. "Utah's Zions to Buy Sumitomo of Calif. for 1.3 Times Book." *American Banker* (March 27): 1.

Edwards, Franklin R. 1992. "SEC Requirements for Trading Foreign Securities on U.S. Exchanges." In *Modernizing U.S. Securities Regulation: Economic and Legal Perspectives*, ed. Kenneth Lehn and Robert W. Kamphius, 57–76. Bur Ridge, Ill.: Irwin.

Federal Deposit Insurance Corporation (FDIC). 1997. *History of the Eighties; Lessons for the Future*. Washington, DC.

Grundfest, Joseph A. 1990. "Internationalization of the World's Securities Markets: Economic Causes and Regulatory Consequences." *Journal of Financial Services Research* 4 (December): 349–378.

Hayes, Samuel L. III, A. Michael Spence, and David Van Praag Marks. 1983. *Competition in the Investment Banking Industry*. Cambridge, MA: Harvard University Press.

Heinkel, Robert L., and Maurice D. Levi. 1992. "The Structure of International Banking." *Journal of International Money and Finance* 11 (June): 251–272.

Hultman, Charles W., and L. R. McGee. 1989. "Factors Affecting the Foreign Banking Presence in the U.S." *Journal of Banking and Finance* 13 (June): 383–396.

Jones, Geoffrey. 1993. *British Multinational Banking*. Oxford: Oxford University Press.

Key, Sydney J. 1985. "The Internationalization of U.S. Banking." In *Handbook for Banking Strategy*, ed. Richard C. Aspinwall and Robert A. Eisenbeis, 267–292. New York: Wiley.

Key, Sydney J. 1990. "Is National Treatment Still Viable? U.S. Policy in Theory and Practice." *Journal of International Business Law* 9 (1990): 365–381.

Key, Sydney J. 1997. *Financial Services in the Uruguay Round and the WTO*. Occasional Paper #54, Group of Thirty, Washington, DC.

Key, Sydney J., and James M. Brundy. 1979. "Implementation of the International Banking Act." *Federal Reserve Bulletin* 65 (October): 785–796.

Key, Sydney J., and Hal S. Scott. 1991. *International Trade in Banking Services: A Conceptual Framework*, Occasional Paper #35, Group of Thirty, Washington, DC.

Key, Sydney J., and Hal S. Scott. 1992. "International Trade in Banking Services: A Conceptual Framework." In *The Internationalization of Capital Markets and the Regulatory Response*, ed. John Fingleton, 35–68. London: Graham & Trotman.

Key, Sydney J., and Gary M. Welsh. 1988. "Foreign Banks in the United States." In *The Bankers' Handbook*, ed. William H. Baughn, Thomas I. Storrs, and Charls E. Walker, 58–71. Homewood, Ill.: Dow Jones-Irwin.

Kim, Seung H., and Stephen W. Miller. 1983. *Competitive Structure of the International Banking Industry*. Lexington, MA: Heath.

Kindleberger, Charles P. 1983. "International Banks as Leaders or Followers of International Business." *Journal of Banking and Finance* 7: 583–595.

King Robert G., and Ross Levine, 1993a. "Finance and Growth: Schumpeter Might Be Right." *Quarterly Journal of Economics* 108 (August): 717–737.

King, Robert G., and Ross Levine. 1993b. "Finance, Entrepreneurship, and Growth: Theory and Evidence." *Journal of Monetary Economics* 32 (December): 513–542.

Lees, Francis A. 1976. *Foreign Banking and Investment in the United States: Issues and Alternatives*. New York: Wiley.

Levine, Ross. 1996. "Foreign Banks, Financial Development, and Economic Growth." In *International Financial Markets: Harmonization versus Competition*, ed. Claude Barfield, 224–254. Washington, DC: American Enterprise Institute.

Miller, Merton H. 1990. "International Competitiveness of U.S. Futures Exchanges," *Journal of Financial Services Research* 4 (December): 387–408.

Misback, Ann E. 1993. "The Foreign Bank Supervision Enhancement Act of 1991." *Federal Reserve Bulletin* 79 (January): 1–10.

Nigh, Douglas, Kang Rae Cho, and Suresh Krishnan. 1986. "The Role of Location-Related Factors in U.S. Banking Involvement Abroad: An Empirical Examination." *Journal of International Business* 17 (Fall): 59–72.

OECD (Organization for Economic Cooperation and Development). *Insurance Statistics Yearbook, 1988–1995*. Paris: OECD, 1997.

Sagari, Silvia B. 1992. "United States Foreign Direct Investment in the Banking Industry." *Transnational Corporations* 1 (December): 93–123.

Segala, John P. 1979. "A Summary of the International Banking Act of 1978." *Economic Review* (Federal Reserve Bank of Richmond) 65 (January/February): 16–21.

Smith, Clifford W. Jr. 1992. "On Trading Foreign Securities in U.S. Markets." In *Modernizing U.S. Securities Regulation: Economic and Legal Perspectives*, ed. Kenneth Lehn and Robert W. Kamphius, 77–82. Bur Ridge, Ill.: Irwin.

Smith, Katherine and George Sofianos. 1997. "The Impact of an NYSE Listing on the Global Trading of Non-U.S. Stocks." NYSE Working Paper 97–02, June.

Standard & Poor's. 1997. *The Money Market Directory of Pension Funds and Their Investment Managers*. New York: Standard & Poor's.

Summers, Bruce J. 1976. "Foreign Banking in the U.S.: Movement toward Federal Regulation." *Economic Review* (Federal Reserve Bank of Richmond) 62 (January/February): 3–7.

U.S. Treasury. 1994. *National Treatment Study 1994*. Washington, DC: Government Printing Office.

White, Lawrence J. 1991. *The S&L Debacle: Public Policy Lessons for Bank and Thrift Regulation*. New York: Oxford University Press.

White, Lawrence J. 1994. "U.S. Banking Regulation." In *International Financial Market Regulation*, ed. Benn Steil, 15–35. London: Wiley.

White, Lawrence J. 1995. "An Analytical Framework; Structure of Finance in Selected Asian Economies; Financial Infrastructure and Policy Reform in Developing Asia." In *Financial Sector Development in Asia*, ed. Shahid Zahid, 3–165. Hong Kong: Oxford University Press.

White, Lawrence J. 1996. "Competition versus Harmonization: An Overview of International Regulation of Financial Services." In *International Financial Markets: Harmonization versus Competition*, ed. Claude Barfield, 5–48. Washington: American Enterprise Institute.

Wilkins, Mira. 1989. *The History of Foreign Investment in the United States to 1914*. Cambridge, MA: Harvard University Press.

Wilkins, Mira. 1991. "Foreign Banks and Foreign Investment in the United States." In *International Banking 1870–1914*, ed. Rondo Cameron and V. I. Bovykin, 233–252. New York: Oxford University Press.

13   The Japanese Big Bang as a Unilateral Action

Koichi Hamada

13.1   Introduction

For more than a quarter of a century, Japan has been the greatest capital exporter in the world thanks to the country's large surplus in savings. In quantity, Japan has been a great financial nation. In quality, however, its financial market has been far from efficient.

In spite of the enormous scale of financial sectors, the efficiency in financial intermediation in Japan was dwarfed by government regulations that protected the interests of financial industries at the expense of individual users.[1] These weaknesses of Japan's financial sectors were brought to the world's attention by the recent financial turmoil that involved banking, insurance, and securities sectors.

Japan, of course, has tried to rebound from this crisis by taking a unilateral action. The country considered the revitalization of the British financial market to be a compelling example. On November 11, 1996, (then) Prime Minister Ryutaro Hashimoto of Japan announced an ambitious plan for a "Big Bang" in Japan's financial market (Imai 1997; Nihon Keizi Shinbun 1997).[2]

Since the plan involves not only the liberalization of the security industry but also the banking and the insurance industries, Japan's Big Bang is expected to be, if it is realized as was conceived, even more spectacular than the original Big Bang in the United Kingdom in 1986 (Imai 1997). In England, the main emphasis in deregulation was in the security market. In Japan, the plan is expected to cover all the financial sectors, including banking, insurance and securities.

Japan's Big Bang is the reaction of Japan's government to the declining position of Tokyo's financial market in the world (Imai 1997). There is consensus that, due to the suppression of an effective incentive mechanism by the monetary authorities, Japan's financial market lost its relative importance in the world. The Big Bang plan is a "last resort" rescue plan for Japan's financial market.

Japan's Big Bang attempts to deregulate Japan's financial market by opening the borders of its financial market. "Free," "fair," and "global" are the key words. Politicians choose these generic words not because they are well defined, but because they appeal to the emotions of the people. But the underlying logic seems to be that the "globalization" of the market, when implemented, will create a "free" and "fair" market in Japan. An internationally open market obliges policymakers to terminate domestic regulation because an open market with domestic regulation will either export financial activities abroad or give foreign financial institutions the lion's share of the domestic market. In other words, if regulation in the domestic market is tight, funds will flow abroad. If foreign firms can operate in the domestic market, they can exploit arbitrage opportunities due to the existence of regulation. While the openness necessitates deregulation, deregulation generally promotes openness but does not absolutely require the openness of an economy as a prerequisite. Thus, the best way to deregulate is to open the market to the world.

The scheduled actions by Japan are unilateral. Nothing is stated about reciprocity with respect to other countries' policies. Hardly any new conditions are imposed as prerequisites on foreign firms as requirements for participating in Japan's financial market. In this sense Japan's Big Bang is a typical example of unilateral liberalization. An analysis of the economic reasons that led to Japan's failure, as well as of the endogenous political factors that initiated the move toward liberalization, is the central task of the chapter.

13.2 Japan's Traditional Financial System

In order to understand the nature of Japan's financial system, a historical account is useful. In fact, the history of Japan's banking is the history of strengthening control by the MOF.[3]

The history of Japan abounds with examples of borrowed foreign institutions and technologies. At first, "foreign" implied China, from which Japan imported language, religion, and legal as well as bureaucratic systems as early as the seventh century. "Japanese spirit and Chinese talent" was the motto. After the Meiji Restoration, Western industrialized countries replaced China as the foreign source. The Japanese government sent delegates to find the best institutions existed for their purpose. Thus the army is from the French system, the Navy is from the British Royal Navy, and so forth (Morishima 1984). Western talent, technologies, and institutions were supposed to be tamed for domestic use by the Japanese spirit.

The monetary system was no exception. The Central Bank, the Bank of Japan (BOJ), modeled after the Belgian Central Bank, was chartered in 1882. The Bank of England was considered at that time to be the most prestigious in the world, but the Belgian Central Bank became the example emulated because it allowed more influence by the government. The National Banking System was introduced, but in this case the introduction caused the emergence of too many "national banks," the excessive creation of money and inflation.

World War I (1914–1918) brought Japan a period of prosperity through the export demand that was followed by a stock market boom. The boom was interrupted by a stock market crash in March 1920. On March 15, the Tokyo Stock Exchange prices lost their values as if "autumn leaves were driven by wind" (Tokyo Stock Exchange 1928). The Tokyo Stock Exchange closed its operation for the following two days. On April 7, Masuda Broker Bank—a bank that financed stock brokers—suspended its payments and, consequently, the Tokyo as well as the Osaka Exchange had to cancel trading. Seven commercial banks (including Konoike and Sumitomo) agreed to finance rescue lending to the Masuda Broker Bank. Each stock market, when reopened on April 13, continued to decline and triggered a decline in commodity markets, notably those of cotton and silk. Many small banks were under attack by withdrawals of savings and suspended business. In May a substantial bank, Shichiju-yon (Seventy-Fourth) Ginko, went bankrupt. The stock price index was not yet calculated when this occurred, but the stock in the Tokyo Stock Exchange is estimated to have declined almost 50 percent between the beginning of March and the middle of April. From April to July, 169 bank offices were under bank runs, and 21 banks had to suspend business. Two hundred and thirty-three firms went bankrupt during the period from May to the middle of July.

To cope with the financial crisis and the collapse of the credit system, the BOJ extended loans amounting to 240 million yen (the exchange rate at that time was about Y2 = $1) in order to provide reserves and sufficient liquidity for troubled banks, as well as for brokers and dealers in the stock and commodity markets. Most of them were paid back to the BOJ in two years. These loans signaled to the public the role of the Central Bank as the lender of last resort, and they were in fact repeated in the subsequent financial squeeze on a smaller scale in 1922.

On September 1, 1923, the eastern part of Japan was hit by a devastating earthquake that registered about 7.9–8.2 on the Richter scale. Seventy-five percent of the residents in Tokyo and 95 percent of those in Yokohama suffered from the earthquake and resulting fires. More than 140,000 people died. The total physical damage caused by the earthquake was estimated to be 5.5 billion yen (equivalent to 2.2 billion dollars), which was 42 percent of the GNP of the year.[4] Banks and financial institutions were seriously affected.

The government tried to provide necessities to the devastated area. It issued the Ordinance of Moratorium that allowed a thirty-day postponement of debt payments, except for wage payments, salaries, and deposits under a certain amount. It was also stipulated that the BOJ would rediscount "earthquake bills" until the end of March 1924. Earthquake bills were defined as commercial bills that were either bank bills due for payments in the affected areas or bills issued by firms operating in the affected areas. The moratorium was discontinued after thirty days, but the large accumulation of these earthquake bills set the stage for the financial crisis of 1927.

In 1926, the ailing Taisho emperor met his demise. The new name chosen for the era was Showa"—from the Chinese classic *The Documents of Yao*—meaning that the emperor as well as the people cooperate for world peace (Goto 1990). On the contrary, the first half of the Showa era turned out to be a history of economic depression and Japan's militaristic aggression in Asia.

The main drama of the 1927 financial crisis (the second year of Showa) started on March 14 when, in the Diet that was discussing the process of redeeming the earthquake bills, Finance Minister Naoharu Kataoka said, "Today at noon, Watanabe Bank in Tokyo finally failed to meet the demand for withdrawals" (Bank of Japan 1982). The fact was, it is now told, that Watanabe Bank went into financial difficulties in the morning, but through concerted efforts it managed to deal with customers in the afternoon. However, these words by the finance minister in the Diet created a reaction of distrust and fright among depositors. Many banks that were rumored to be unsound faced bank runs due to withdrawal by depositors.

At that time, Taiwan Bank was considered most insecure in terms of delinquent debts in its operation with Suzuki & Company. Suzuki

& Company operated aggressively in Asian trade and had a monopoly on camphor trade with Taiwan. The company also held a number of earthquake bills amounting to 430 million yen, 26 percent of which were financed by loans from Taiwan Bank. Taiwan Bank, as well as Ohmi Bank, which was important in the Western cloth trade, suspended their business. The chain reaction of rumors created a panic situation in Japan, and on April 23 and 24 all the banks were closed in an allegedly voluntary, coordinated action. To order a moratorium, a special imperial ordinance was needed. This would have caused traumatic panic, which is why voluntary actions were first requested from the banks. After the two-day closing, a moratorium of three weeks was announced, and the BOJ started supplying money by lending to the banks that were dealing with unprecedented bank runs. Thirty-two banks suspended operation in April and May, and forty-five banks followed suit during 1927. The BOJ acted as the lender of last resort. The BOJ had to print bank notes so rapidly that they issued two hundred yen bills with white backs— that is, without any printing on the other side. Incidentally, the degree of the stock market crash during that year was about 20 percent and milder than that in 1920.

In the meantime, Japan was contemplating its return to the gold standard that it had left after the outbreak of World War I. The new finance minister, Junnosuke Inoue, strongly believed that returning to the gold standard was a necessary step in making Japan a respectable member of the club of industrialized nations. In 1929, he staged the return to the gold standard with a yen value substantially appreciated by about 18 percent. The Japanese economy therefore went into a severe depression. Prices went down precipitously. Output declined only around 10 percent, but the consumer price and the investment goods price declined 27 percent and 33 percent respectively during 1926 to 1931. The rural sector was severely depressed by the decline of the relative price of agricultural to industrialized products. It was certainly one of the factors that promoted the fascist movements that led Japan into the reckless World War II.

The rescue lendings by the BOJ amounted to 679 million yen. This is almost 5 percent of the national income of 1927. It was not until 1952—twenty-five years later—that banks could repay their liability to the BOJ from this emergency measure. This alone demonstrates the magnitude and the gravity of the Showa financial crisis.

Even before the outbreak of the financial crises of 1927, the MOF had been planning to legislate a bank regulation law. Coincidentally, it was exactly in the middle of the financial crisis, March 30, 1927, that the Diet passed the Banking Act. The MOF regulations started to reorganize the banks by merger. They proposed the principle of one bank for each prefecture (at that time Japan had 47 prefectures). In fact, the number of banks was reduced from 1,283 to 61 in 1945.

The MOF increased its control with the enactment of the Banking Act in 1927. The MOF now controlled entry, jurisdiction of business, deposit interest rates, and the opening of new branch offices. Through the assistance of the BOJ as well as the MOF, even loan interest rates and various fees were fixed by the associations of banks and other financial institutions. In return, the MOF promised the protection of financial institutions, the policy called "Banking Administration by Convoys." Thus, it became reasonable for bankers and financial businessmen to watch for signals from the MOF and not market signals.

In the meantime, the Industrial Bank of Japan (IBJ) developed entrepreneurial capacities to screen the borrowers. Ueda (1994) considers this to be the beginning of the main banking system, a kind of co-insurance system in which banks delegate monitoring to a designated bank (the main bank of the borrowing firm).

The Japanese economy grew with alternating recessions and booms generated mainly by the stop-and-go policy of the Japanese government that was constrained by the balance of payments under the fixed exchange rate. In the late 1950s, the economy grew faster and the stock market advanced. In the late 1950s, the motto of the security companies was "Goodbye banks and welcome security companies." The government encouraged newly introduced mutual funds and, in particular, public-bonds mutual funds that would facilitate the issue of bonds of public electric companies. Many customers also thronged around stock brokers in order to buy the newly introduced mutual funds.

Starting in 1961, however, the stock market began to decline. The stock market index declined about 40 percent from its peak in July 1961 to its trough in July 1965. Difficulties developed in the security companies. Many clients demanded liquidation of mutual funds, and they began to withdraw securities from the "broker managed" accounts—namely, those accounts that were managed by security companies like deposits in the form of securities. In many cases, security companies had already sold the securities that were supposed to be in the account. In particular, the Yamaichi Security Company and the Oi Security Company were in deep trouble.

As difficulties developed, commercial banks started helping security companies by building the Nihon Kyodo Shoken (Japan Cooperative Securities), a holding company of stocks. Two hundred billion yen (at that time the exchange rate was Y360 = $1) were provided as relief funds for the stock market. Security companies, which were afraid of the increased control by banks in the future, built another institution called Nihon Shoken Hoyu Kumiai (Japan Securities Holding Union) which engaged in price-supporting operations in the stock market. Banks like Fuji, Mitsubishi, and the IBJ were trying hard to rescue Yamaichi and Oi.

The MOF had asked major newspaper and news agencies in Tokyo to refrain from leaking the news that there might be securities and financial difficulties. That the MOF exercised such influence may come as no surprise to a critic of Japan, such as van Wolferen (1989). However, Nishi Nippon (The Western Japan Press), which was not a member of the major press club, leaked the news that Yamaichi Securities had serious financial difficulties. Customers who held management accounts in Yamaichi and other security companies started runs as they withdraw from their accounts. The BOj was reluctant to engage in an extensive relief operation.

On May 28, 1965, Finance Minister Kakuei Tanaka, a very interesting but down-to-earth politician,[5] met with the responsible central banker and commercial bankers. The meeting was with the presidents of the IBJ, Fuji, and Mitsubishi, and the vice governor of the BOJ. One commercial bank president said that they should proceed in a gradual, conservative way. Another suggested the closing of the securities market for a few days in order to calm public anxieties. According to the political scientist Kusano (1986; see also Goto 1990), Tanaka, who favored forceful action, instead shouted, "Shut up! How can you be a responsible president of a large bank?" Kusano interprets this as a ritual to save the face of the BOJ vice governor. It was not any of the commercial banks, but rather the BOJ that had been reluctant. However, if the finance minister had scolded the BOJ vice governor, then it would have been a disgrace and an embarrassment to the Central Bank. Therefore, a commercial bank president took the blame in place of the vice governor of the Central Bank. Consequently, the BOJ agreed to lend indirectly about 5.3

billion yen to the Oi Security Company and about 28.2 billion yen to the Yamaichi Security Company. Fortunately, the Japanese economy returned to a rapid growth path soon, and the loan was repaid in just four years.

This episode led to the MOF obtaining yet more power through the enactment of a licensing system. The approval of a license became mandatory for establishing a security company:[6] Licensing was intended as a safety measure aimed at preventing financial troubles like Yamichi's. Indeed, the licensing system passed the Diet on the same day that the bailout of Yamichi was decided politically.

13.3 Bubbles and Crashes

At the start of the 1990s, in January of the second year of the new emperor's era (the "Heisei era," marked by peace and success), the Tokyo stock market, which had enjoyed a glorious record during the 1980s, started a precipitous decline. This decline was reminiscent of the financial crisis of the first episode that began in the second year of the Showa. The Nikkei Index lost about 63 percent of its value in two and a half years. At the same time, soaring land prices ceased to appreciate and even started to decline substantially, almost for the first time in the postwar history.

Security brokerage firms struggled to recover from the loss of their public image that was caused by troubles with loss-offset practices; banks tried to reorganize their operations in the face of increased incidence of unsound loans. Commercial banks and other major financial institutions were subject to a more strict capital-asset requirement that was proposed by the Bank for International Settlements (BIS). For some of these institutions, the requirement became a substantial constraint for business. Mists of uncertainty prevailed for the future of the Japanese financial and securities market. Some people even suspected that the declining stock market and failures of some financial institutions triggered chain reactions that undermined the systemic stability of Japan's financial market.

There was a long period of excess liquidity and of land and stock price booms during the late 1980s. From 1987 to 1989, the BOJ kept its discount rate to a then historical low of 2.5 percent over a period of two years. Because of the appreciation of the yen, the price of the consumer price index and the wholesale price index remained relatively stable. However, there were tremendous land price booms or bubbles; the total value of the land in Japan was estimated to be four times as much as the land value in the spacious United States. The rapid growth of the stock market continued until the end of 1989. After Yasushi Mieno became governor of the BOJ at the end of 1989, he tightened monetary policy abruptly by raising the discount rate several times in order to recover the role of an independent and traditional Central Bank.

In the meantime, stock market "scandals" concerning illegal loss-offset deals to favorite customers by brokers emerged, and many cases of bad debts extended from banks, even from respectable banks, erupted. Land prices showed substantial decline, which was unprecedented in the land-scarce Japanese economy that had enjoyed a constant increase in land prices in modern history. The Nikkei Index that had almost been approaching 39,000 yen in 1989 plunged to 15,000 yen. The BOJ and the government watched the situation, hoping in vain that the decline would be short-lived and that the decline of asset prices would be good medicine to cure the "bubble" psychology on land and stock prices.

Indeed, the impact of disturbances on the financial sector was great, or too great, one should say. The number of bankruptcies exceeded six thousand in the first half of 1992. The magnitude of liabilities of bankrupt firms during Fiscal Year 1991 (91/4–92/3) was 8,137 billion yen. It was estimated, in one of the most pessimistic scenarios (Kenji Uchida, *Toyo Keizai*, July 25, 1992), that the credit of about 68,000 billion yen held by banks may be unsound. The Japanese deposit insurance system charged only about 0.012 percent of the value of deposits, and its standby credit line from the BOJ was only 0.5 billion yen. Thus, unless the BOJ would act as the determined lender of last resort, the Japanese financial system was threatened by an uncertain future.

In August 1992, the government finally turned to an expansionary macroeconomic policy as an emergency relief measure. This time the government would rely on a fiscal expansion package. Amazingly, there was still some room for government expenditures in Japan because the Flow of Funds account showed a recent surplus in the I-S balance of the government sector that includes social security. The stock market temporarily rebounded with this fiscal package, considering it an encouraging signal for future economic activities, but the rebound was short-lived. The stock market still lingered within a low range owing to the uncertainty that was reinforced by the loss of leadership of the Liberal Democratic Party (LDP).[7]

A basic dilemma exists if one tries to prevent systemic instability of a financial system without impairing efficient intermediation of funds. In order to be capable of screening safe borrowers, monitoring them from unsound economic activities, and verifying correctly the financial situation of a firm that declares insolvency, financial institutions should have positive and negative rewards corresponding to its economic success or failure. For that purpose, some intermediaries should be left to go into bankruptcy. However, once a systemic failure of a national financial system develops, the government is often obliged to prevent bankruptcy of financial firms in order to stop the propagation of disaster to the total payment system.

Conceptually, the dilemma for the BOJ can be seen as an example of a two-stage game. The first stage is the period before the disaster takes place, and the second stage is after the disaster takes place. Here one can easily detect the logic of time inconsistency. At the first stage of the game when financial activities are undertaken, participants are better motivated by the expectations of a cold-turkey Central Bank that does not rescue financial institutions. But, financial institutions know that, at the second stage when a crisis occurs, the Central Bank will be forced to rescue some individual institutions in order to save the system. This is the dilemma between the ex post rescues and ex ante efficient incentive mechanism. This time inconsistency of the policy process makes it difficult to construct an "incentive compatible" financial system. The carrot and the stick should be used very skillfully. One needs here a "trembling hand equilibrium," as defined by the Nobel Laureate economist Selten. The BOJ should play the game as if it may be a cruel Central Bank instead of a benevolent one. It should suggest to the public that in some cases the BOJ may not come to the rescue when a bank is bankrupt.

The Diet passed a series of laws on the rescue of financial institutions. It extended the bankruptcy clauses (the U.S. Chapters 7 and 13 equivalent) in the Bankruptcy Law to unincorporated financial institutions that had not previously been covered by the Bankruptcy Law. The National Deposit Insurance System was strengthened and the premium increased. Notably, the government promised to compensate any loss in the principal of loans from the past *for five years.*

This shows that Japan chose the way to emphasize the carrot rather than the stick. This policy choice certainly helps avoid the systemic disorder from the present financial crisis, but it may pave the way for the next financial crisis by giving agents some assurance that government help will be in order in case of financial crises.

The Tokyo financial market has hardly shown any signs of recovery. Quite recently, the Yamaichi Securities Company and Hokkaido Takushoku Bank were declared bankrupt. The glorious record of Japan's growth in the last half of this century was thus tainted by financial turmoil.

Incidentally, the current financial crisis exposed the Achilles' heel of the main bank system. According to the scheme, "the main bank" plays the principal role in screening a borrower, monitoring its managerial activities and rescuing the borrower in the event he or she is in financial trouble. By playing this role collectively, banks can not only economize screening and monitoring costs without duplicating these activities but also engage in a kind of co-insurance. The bank designated to be the main one performs the rescue operation because banks engage in a repeated game. If a bank defects from this role, sanctions will be applied later.

Even before this financial instability, defections occurred. In such cases, the main bank role was usually shifted from the defecting bank to another bank. In today's financial turmoil, many small financial institutions like "Jusen" (Special Residential Finance Company) could not stand independently. Nor could the main lenders endure the burden of debt. Finally, the government had to come to the rescue. Here the game was no longer the repeated game. This endgame situation created difficulty for maintaining efficient allocation by the logic of the Folk Theorem. The co-insurance scheme could no longer function.

Even though Japanese financial institutions are under rather extensive administrative control, their openness to the public with respect to information was insufficient. Here again the practice tended to neglect the interest of depositors. As Fuchita (1997) emphasizes, while fewer regulations are necessary in most financial behavior, additional regulations are necessary to make financial information more transparent. Otherwise, those who possess insider information will benefit substantially from using it. It is the task of Japan's leaders of the Big Bang to install necessary regulations to make information transparent to the public. Some information should be disseminated, but some should be blocked in order for the market mechanism to work with less regulated financial behavior.

13.4 The Incentive Problems with Administrative Control

It is interesting to note the difference in actions taken in the two crises that hit Yamaichi approximately thirty years apart. In the first crisis leak[8] in 1965, the Bank of Japan engaged in a rescue operation by the emergency lending of 28.2 billion yen (78 million dollars). In the recent crisis in 1997, the government decided to let the company go bankrupt after the hidden loss of 260 billion yen (2 billion dollars) was revealed.

In 1965, Japan was in a short recession in the middle of rapid economic growth. Private bankers were willingly persuaded by the government to contribute to the rescue fund. The Japanese financial market was not under fierce international competition. The government had the leadership and accountability to rescue Yamaichi. In fact, the Ministry of Finance gained more power by establishing the system that requires *approval* rather than *registration* for opening a security company.

In 1997, in contrast, Japan was in a long recession that had lasted seven years already. The Fuji Bank, the main bank of Yamaichi, is reported to have refused to help Yamaichi because of its own difficulties. The Japanese capital market is liberalized so much that the Japanese monetary policy alone cannot influence financial variables. The MOF has lost power as well as its credibility for reorganizing Japan's financial system in the failure.

The traditional system of government control of financial institutions was often called the "convoy" system. To protect the least efficient financial institutions, the MOF guided the financial industries to adjust the pace of their development so that the least efficient would survive. At the core of the convoy system, regulations prevalent in Japan could be classified into four categories (Suzuki 1997). The first category consisted of the control on interest rates, fees, and prices from financial services. The second was the restriction on jurisdiction and entry. The third was the restriction on commodity design. The fourth was to close the Japanese market from abroad. Particularly, the commodity design restriction was striking as well as stringent to the financial sectors where innovation was possible only by designing new commodities of financial institutions. A new design of financial commodities was not permitted unless a financial institution managed to obtain the approval of the MOF. Even the Ministry of International Trade and Industry (MITI) at its zenith of power did not regulate the design of automobiles.

A group of scholars maintain that the main characteristics of Japan's economic system in the postwar period was developed during the preparation and the execution processes of World War II (Okazaki and Okuno 1993). According to them, the economic system of Japan before the war was more or less like the Anglo-Saxon type of market system. The enforcement of the Foreign Exchange Control Law in 1933 was the first important step toward the controlled financial market. Moreover, it was a prototype of regulatory legislation that followed (Ueda 1994).

Recall how the MOF increased its control by enacting the Banking Act in 1927, by which it regulated entry, jurisdiction of business, deposit interest rates, and the opening of new branch offices. Perhaps with the assistance of the BOJ, as well as the MOF, loan rates and various fees were fixed by the association of banks and other financial institutions.

Now, let us compare theoretically the incentive structures under the market principle with the incentive structure under government control. Under the market principle, banks are mainly concerned with market variables such as interest rates, exchange rates, amount of deposits, and profit rates. It is most important to predict the factors that affect those market variables. Financial innovations are contrived to beat the market. Under government control and administrative guidance, on the other hand, banks have to predict what government officials will do concerning the new financial instruments, how they will fix the deposit interest rate, and how the government will guide the exchange rate. Much unnecessary effort is spent watching the government rather than watching the market. The existence of "the MOF liaison person" and "the Bank of Japan liaison person" in banks demonstrates this unsound mechanism. The incentive structure is prone to lead to corruption, to inefficiency, and to a lack of innovative activities.[9]

The incentive mechanism in Japan has worked only insufficiently through price or interest-rate signals. Under the existence of fixed interest-rate differentials between deposit rates and loan rates, which were guaranteed by the convention supported by the MOF, profitability of banks depended primarily upon the quantity of deposits they could collect. The profit of a securities broker company depended on the amount of trade in which it could engage. The profit of an insurance company reflected merely the number of contracts its marketing people, who were mainly part-time housewives, could collect. The profit of financial institutions was not much affected by the quality of services or prices such as interest rates, portfolio investment skills, or the content of insurance contracts. To collect more deposits, trade more, and write more insurance contracts, financial employees worked overtime.

Under the system of administrative guidance, it was crucially important for banks to coordinate with the BOJ, the MOF that put regulations on interest rates, brokerage transaction fees, dividend ratios, and the branch offices of these banks, securities companies, and insurance companies (financial institutions hereafter). Moreover, the MOF controlled the kinds of financial instruments that these banks, securities companies, and insurance companies could create or trade. Bankers, securities brokers, and insurance employees were at first obliged to engage in guessing games to guess what the MOF intended to do with respect to these regulations before listening to the market signals. Since most of the regulatory measures took the form of "administrative guidance," and administrative guidance is almost by definition without legal ground, these measures have the nature of discrete decision rather than of rules.

Because of this highly regulated structure, Japan's financial institutions were deprived of freedom in business behavior. For example, if a credit union issued a savings deposit with a lottery attached, it met with strong resistance from the controlling agency as well as from other financial institutions. Because of the protective nature of these regulations, not only the regulating MOF but also the regulated financial institutions seemed to have enjoyed the regulation. It was always better for banks to have lower interest rates on deposits than on market demands, to have restricted entry of newcomers, and to have fixed fees for currency exchanges. It was always profitable for securities companies to be assured of fixed brokerage fees. Therefore, the regulation regime was an outcome of collusion between those who controlled and those who were controlled.

Learning about the intention of bureaucrats is more important than learning about future prices or economic variables. This violates the principle of efficiency because learning from bureaucratic signals seldom functions to improve either national efficiency or the bank's knowledge of how prices work on economic agents. This also violates the principle of equity because only insiders to the government circle can learn information for their future advantage.[10]

Against this profitable coalition, new entrants, in particular foreign entrants, had a strong disadvantage. Foreign financial firms certainly complained. The most important victims, however, were Japan's customers of financial sectors. For a long time Japan's consumers suffered from the fixed, extremely low-interest-rate policy and sacrificed themselves for the high growth path of the economy that the low-interest rate had supported. Their only rewards were the stability of the financial system and the fruits from a high rate of growth. The latter reward ceased after the end of the high growth period (1950–1973), and the first reward was threatened after the outbreak of financial instability that began in 1990.

More precisely, the question of consumers' benefits should be considered in a dynamic context. By lowly fixed interest rates on deposits, and by the limitation of alternative savings assets by policy as well as the lack of information on comparative interest rates,[11] the Japanese consumers were deprived of the rate of return that would have obtained by the market-determined deposit rate. Thus they were exploited in the short run. In the long run, however, they used to be rewarded for their sacrifice at least partly by the fruits of a remarkable economic growth that might have facilitated the low-interest policy. These benefits, though, no longer exist now.

For example, Dixit and Stiglitz (1983) have a model of monopolistic competition with increasing returns, which is used extensively in trade theory. The welfare implication of the model is that a country can improve its welfare by imposing a lump-sum tax on consumers and giving a subsidy for firms that enjoy increasing returns. I do not know for sure that the low interest policy was a proxy of a lump-sum taxation. But, given the lack of alternative saving instruments that did not allow alternative choices of saving instruments, I may argue that the low-interest policy played the role of lump-sum taxation. Thus, consumers must have retrieved a part of the results from their thrift in the long run.

Incidentally, Sakakibara, Feldman, and Harada and other government officials once defended the system as follows (Sakakibara, Feldman, and Harada 1982):

Japan's financial markets remain quite distinct from those in Anglo-Saxon countries. Structural characteristics such as retail competition, effective syndication, long-term credit banks, and government financial institutions give the Japanese system some notable strengths that Anglo-Saxon counterparts lack. There is no reason whatsoever to change the basic institutions of Japanese financial markets. In a time of international tension and the increasing uncertainty, such institutions provide advantages to both Japanese corporations and consumers. It is an ingenious mechanism of pooling and diversifying risks at a national level.

It was an interesting coincidence that one of the authors, Eisuke Sakakibara, played a substantial role in proposing the Big Bang. Even after the need for central coordination no longer existed, bureaucrats attempted and succeeded, at least partly, to keep their control intact. Incumbent financial institutions in the regime wanted its continuation. And bureaucrats continued to govern by the logic of legal legitimacy, not the nature of economic causality.

During the fast-growth period, all seemed to have worked well. Japan was the largest source of savings supply in the world economy. It suffices for Japan to continue its quantitative expansion. Now the quality of financial service is at stake. This creates the urgency that Japan undertake the measures for deregulation.

A group of scholars maintains that the main characteristics of Japan's economic system in the postwar period were developed during the preparation for and the execution of World War II (Okazaki and Okuno 1993; Noguchi 1995). Price freezes and government-guided mobilization of goods for war purposes remained as the basis of a controlled system by the MITI after the war. The seniority wage system that was considered to be one of the three sacred treasures in the labor market was formed by the national wartime wage control. According to them, the economic system of Japan before the war was more or less like the Anglo-Saxon type of market system. The enforcement of the Foreign Exchange Control Law in 1933 was the first important step toward regulation in the financial market. Also it was a prototype of the regulatory legislation that followed (Ueda 1994).

The wartime objectives before and during World War II were better served by government control than by market signals. This proposition is known as "the 1940" theory and is worth additional scrutiny. Coordination at the time of war certainly needed coordination through the center rather than through price signals. The most puzzling question, however, is why these practices remained dominant so long—roughly more than a half century—after the war period.

13.5   The Process of the Big Bang

In 1998, the amended Foreign Exchange Law, precisely named "The Foreign Exchange and Trade Control Law," was in effect and the regime of essentially free capital transactions was in principle introduced. The word *Control* as a part of the name of even the current legislation is nothing but an anachronism. It is surprising that a country with a developed international capital market and such a large current account surplus as Japan's finally joined the free international capital market only just before the turn of the century. In any event, the process finally took the form of an international opening of the market and inevitable domestic deregulation.

The process of breaking the wall of the Glass-Steagall type of regulation, built between different kinds of financial industries, has been progressing. Banks are allowed to have subsidiaries that can engage in securities business, and so forth. However, in the future, the process of mutual entry across the field will be accelerated by the allowance of holding companies in financial industries. Holding industries were severely restricted by the postwar American Occupation that regarded the "Zaibatsu" as the obstacle to a democratic market economy. Zaibatsu used to reign over the industry through holding companies.

Let us sketch the actual process of the Big Bang. Already in April 1993, the Reform Act of the Financial System (Kinyu Kaikaku Ho) had become effective. The Glass-Steagall type of restriction of mutual entries among sectors, notably between banking and securities, was relaxed, and several mutual entries became possible from banks to security businesses and vice versa. More precisely, a subsidiary of a bank is allowed to start a security business and a subsidiary of a security firm is allowed to start a banking business. Though several restraints remain, this new law breaks down one of the barriers to entry among sectors. In the spring of 1997, the Foreign Exchange Act was amended, and in April 1998 it became effective. Therefore, international barriers were taken away and free movement of capital between Japan and abroad was in principle established.

A similar process took place in the insurance industry as well. The new Insurance Industry Act (Shin Hoken-gyo Ho) became effective in April 1996. This new law now allows mutual entry from the life insurance sector to the casualty insurance sector, and vice versa. As in the case of the Reform Act of the Financial System, a subsidiary of a life insurance company can open a casualty insurance company and vice versa. The pace of deregulation has been slow in this area, and the deregulation will have been almost completed by 2001.

There were many restrictions on entry and on the financial or instrument designs. Regulation of the design of financial instruments worked severely against efficiency in the financial market. In the securities business, the fee restrictions were being relaxed but only gradually. For example, with respect to regulated fees, in 1998 the fees for securities' deals were deregulated only for more than $400 million worth of transactions. But, for smaller transactions, fees continued to be regulated.

In short, Japan had indeed been planning to relax domestic regulations, but quite gradually. On the other hand, the pace of the opening of the market by the Foreign Exchange Control Law amendment was quite fast. Thus, the following dilemmas occurred (Suzuki 1997). If the high speed of opening is combined with the fast pace of activities of domestic regulation, then shocks to Japanese financial sectors would be large. However, if the government and BOJ were reluctant to advance domestic deregulation because of possible negative shocks to the industry, then a large part of the cream of financial business would be absorbed by foreign bankers and financiers, and a large amount of capital outflow would take place. The Tokyo market would be "hollowed out" even more. As Suzuki argues, there is a tradeoff between efficiency and protection of incumbent Japanese financial business. If you were to protect the domestic financial sector, then most of the financial transactions would leave for foreign markets. That would be an expensive efficiency loss. On the other hand, if the government wishes to keep the efficiency and deregulate fast, then it would endanger the survival of certain financial institutions.

By 2002, the attempt to deregulate financial sectors has proceeded almost as planned. Even the sectors like life and casualty insurance industries are deregulated to a considerable degree. The effect of this Big Bang is rather moderate. First, the Japanese economy went into deep recession and deflation with a large overhang of delinquent debts. Financial sectors benefited from opening of the market to the world as well as from deregulation. Japan has enjoyed the show-window effect to observe closely the entrepreneurship of foreign bankers. For example, Citibank and investment companies introduced financial innovations. In particular, problematic practices of Japanese banking were relieved by the financial skills of foreign financial firms. Also it was difficult to change the traditional Japanese pattern in financial intermediation through lending by the banking sector rather than through the stock market. Thus, in retrospect, the effect of the Big Bang has been limited. In order to rejuvenate Japan's financial activities, it will need a combination of trials by foreign financial skills and learning by Japanese bankers.

13.6 Economics of the Unilateral Action

First, let us consider the economics of unilateral actions in general. The process of unilateral action in a trade model consisting of commodity trade or with trade of services in absence of any direct investments are as follows: Suppose there are three sectors in the economy—two regulated sectors where a unilateral action takes place, and the third sector is the export sector of the country where free trade prevails. Figure 13.1 illustrates a simple case of unilateral action. The aggregate production of financial services is depicted on the horizontal axis, and the aggregate production of other goods is depicted on the vertical axis. A unilateral action has a domestic as well as an international effect. The domestic effect comes from the increased mobility of resources between sectors and usually expands the production possibility locus. Figure 13.1 illustrates a special case of a rectangular production opportunity. There the supply of the financial sector's output increases from P to Q. The international effect is the worsening of the terms of trade. Only if this effect is stronger than the domestic gain, as in the case of immiserizing growth (Bhagwati 1958), then the national welfare will deteriorate.

If a country is small, it will not change the terms of trade. A unilateral action in a small country will thus certainly improve the national welfare, as indicated by C_0 (we assume trade restriction at the beginning) to C_1 in figure 13.1 where by the "small country" assumption the terms of trade remain the same as the dotted line. In a unilateral action in a large country, where it can create the terms-of-trade advantage by trade restriction as with tariffs and quotas, the unilateral action may work against national welfare because of the loss due to the worsened terms of trade. If the terms of trade worsen

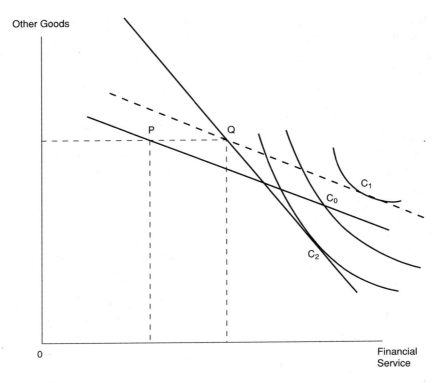

Figure 13.1

as depicted by the solid line in figure 13.1, the equilibrium shifts from C_0 to C_2. The tariff rate, or effective tariff rate corresponding to the quota, is lower than the optimal tariff rate for a country. Then reduction of an outside tariff will worsen welfare.

A unilateral action is often discussed in a group of countries. Suppose there are three countries. Two of them are closer, and they reduce the tariff rates on their traded goods for each other. The trade creation effect helps the participants. If there is a third country, the unilateral action will imply the reduction of the tariff of the third country as well. To repeat, one effect is the effect of liberalizing tariffs within the zone, and the other effect is opening a zone to a third party.

So far, we have abstracted from foreign direct investment (FDI). Unilateral liberalization of the service industry by industrializing the FDI can be analyzed in the same way. FDI shifts up the production frontier, and as long as the required rate of return to foreign investor does not increase substantially, the unilateral action is always profitable. As long as the domestic economy is sufficiently open, there is no room for the effect to work (Brecher and Diaz-Alejandro 1977; Uzawa 1969). Accordingly, FDIs will benefit the national economy in general.

There is an analogy to unilateral action like the Big Bang in Japan described previously. If you liberalize among three major financial sectors, banking, securities, and insurance, and between subsectors like casualty and life insurance, then the unilateral action will increase the supply of services produced by domestic industry. This is a definite gain. The terms of trade of the services, however, may worsen and offset the effect of integration by lifting regulations on domestic sectors and resulting in more competition in domestic sectors. The unilateral action will benefit the Japanese economy, unless the liberalization of the financial market to foreign entrants increases the price of financial services and leads to an increase in foreign financial firms' profits to such an extent that the effect of the upward-sloping supply curve of the financial service offsets the domestic gain in financial service production. Foreign investors cannot benefit from the protected price of services because the unilateral action implies that the domestic market is deregulated. Unless the loss from terms of trade is large enough to immiserize the country, the Japanese economy as a whole will gain. If the political process, due to sectoral interests, does not prevent the Big Bang, there is a national incentive to create it.

In spite of the positive economic benefits for the nation, in the past neither the MOF, nor the BOJ, nor bankers were willing to open the Japanese economy. The reason is, of course, that we have neglected the political process aspect of financial deregulation. It is not a nation as a whole, but each interest group that has a reservation welfare (utility) level in order to be induced to participate in a reform. Crisis deteriorates the welfare at status quo, the reservation utility level. Now the Japanese economy is in trouble and financial sectors are in serious trouble. Japan can afford to adopt drastic measures to get out of this impasse. For example, there are signs of the decline of Japan's role in the world market. During 1989–1995, New York's market increased its share from 43 percent to 52 percent in foreign-exchange transactions. London's share went from 30 percent to 29 percent. In the meantime, Tokyo lost its weight going from 27 percent to 19 percent. In the volume of transactions, during the ten-year period 1985–1995, New York kept its share from 64 percent to 60 percent and London increased its share from 6 percent to 23 percent; Tokyo went from 30 percent to 17 percent.

This loss of transaction volume was triggered by the action of the Japanese government. In response to scandals related to derivatives, the MOF raised for a while the margin requirement and other fees in the Osaka exchange. The policy backfired and the MOF had to reverse it. Anyway, now Japan is in such deep financial trouble that any lifeboat is welcome in this situation—as a Japanese proverb says, "A drowning man will grab at even a straw." Many vested interests in financial sectors or bureaucracies are no longer strong obstacles. Participants now understand the need for reform of the Japanese financial system.

13.7 The Political Economy of the Big Bang

The first question that comes to mind concerning the political economy of Japan's Big Bang is, Is it real? Japanese financial sectors and the Japanese government had a long history of resistance to pressures from abroad to open the Japanese market. During the early 1980s, the U.S. Congress and the U.S. administration tried to open the Japanese market in order to arrest the excessive overvaluation of the yen before the Plaza Accord. There was a joint group called the Yen-Dollar Ad-Hoc Committee. However, as Frances Rosenbluth (1990) vividly describes in her report to the Joint Economic Committee of the U.S. Congress, Japan's Minister of Finance did not wish to open the domestic market and to lose the authority to regulate it, and the Bank of Japan hesitated to open the Japanese market fearing loss of control of the money supply. Those efforts on the part of the United States had limited success.

Therefore, an interesting question is, Why now? Japan is taking the initiative in this unilateral action. One skeptical view is that Japan is neither serious about opening the domestic financial market nor prepared to deregulate the financial market substantially. In this view, Japan is using the Big Bang as an excuse for the slow process of deregulation or as a means of drawing attention away from the difficulties of the financial market and the failure of monetary policies. I do not, at least for the moment, adopt this skeptical view and proceed to the question: What can we normally expect if the government's intention is to trigger a serious Big Bang?

Probably until the recent period, Japan's government or the MOF had an interest in protecting the ancient regime against foreign pressure. Now after the great financial collapse of the system, the government might have changed its assessment of protection of Japan's financial industries. With the older system, sufficient incentives can no longer be secured. With the Big Bang, the government can expect the emergence of a sound market mechanism in the financial market. Also, the Big Bang can divert the people's attention from the waste and corruption of the older system to the forward-looking vision of a financial market open to the world.

Then, how can this deregulation due to the Big Bang revitalize the Japanese financial market and succeed in fostering financial entrepreneurship in Tokyo? I am rather optimistic because human capital able to effect sophisticated financial activities abounds in Japan. The elimination of incentive restraints that originated in the 1940 system will help the revitalization of Japan's financial market, which has enormous strength in terms of the amount of savings it generates.

Institutional reform does not materialize if participants agree to adopt a new rule or, at least, are reluctantly persuaded or forced to follow a new rule. In this weak sense, the "individual rationality" requirement is necessary. In theoretical writing, individual rationality implies that the new plan encourages individuals to keep their reservation utility level. In international negotiations, nations are motivated to agree with a new plan if it improves or at least sustains the welfare level of interest groups. Thus, "group rationality" is desired. In other words, every group has to be convinced and the welfare of the group will not deteriorate. It is, of course, difficult to satisfy completely this condition for groups with different interests. Thus, domestic impasses create obstacles for international negotiations. In practice, it is difficult to satisfy all the interest groups. The idea of "win-set" in a two-level game (Putnam 1988) implies that the negotiation is conducted on the set in the bargaining box where the outcome will not jeopardize the reelection of the incumbent party. By the Ulysses and Sirens effect, the government bound by domestic restrictions may find more bargaining power in international negotiations (Putnam 1988). In some cases, however, strongly bound governments may not be able to reach an agreement.

Consumers have been neglected for a long time in the Japanese financial intermediation process. Interest rates on deposits were often below the rate of inflation in CPI. The control of the MOF on the financial industries—that is, banking, securities, and the insurance industry—was very tight. However, since those financial industries benefited from many patterns of control, such as restriction of entry and the fixing of interest rates and fees to levels that are favorable to them, financial institutions also enjoyed this lucrative state. Politicians obtained contributions from interest groups like financial institutions, and they influenced the bureaucracy. Rosenbluth (1989) is right in recognizing the power of politicians in determining the balance of interests among the financial institutions, that is, bankers, stockbrokers, and insurance professionals. However, it seems spurious to ask who controls whom, or who influences whom. Economic agents in the financial industries, bureaucrats, and politicians seem to have been enjoying a salonlike coalition. Only the consumers are out of this coalition.

As already discussed, the economic process can be regarded as a two-stage game, which consists of first agreeing on a set of rules and then engaging in economic behavior given the chosen set of rules.[12] It is not easy, however, for participants, to agree on a set of rules. Evolutionary game theory emphasizes natural selection. A viable or efficient rule will be chosen by a repeated process of survival of adaptable participants. This seems to be too long-run a view to be applied to economic organization.

Once a big dislocation of the environment takes place, then more likely the present status quo turns unsatisfactory. For the Japanese financial industries, the present rule is no longer something to defend. The current crisis will make it easier for groups to agree on a new rule. As Samuelson (1967, 699) puts it, "One does not have to be cynical, but merely realistic to guess that if fundamental changes are to come, they will come in the wake of some international crises rather than as a result of predetermined planning and agreement."

At an impasse, political leadership plays a role. Many groups may be reluctant to join the reform. But, provided that a new rule is potentially beneficial, side payments can be made by those who gain from the new rule to those who lose. And, the side payments can be facilitated by the leadership of politicians. As Frohlich, Oppenheimer, and Young (1971) convincingly argue, politicians put inputs in terms of effort, persuasion, and funds to realize political benefits that these authors called "leadership surplus," like the "producers' surplus." Moreover, an attempt to change the perception or the images of people of the new rule is crucially important (Haas 1992).

Thus, political entrepreneurship will understand the payoff structure for the participants, change the perception of the payoff structure to other participants, spend his or her resources to collect leadership surpluses later, make necessary side payments to make the new system satisfy the reservation utility constraint, and use his (or her, which is unlikely in Japan) power as a threat to nonconformism. Thus, political leadership can work as a catalyst to shorten the time by which evolutionary solutions are chosen by natural selection. The fact that finally this liberalization and deregulation are likely to be realized depends on the strong leadership of Ryutaro Hashimoto.

Looking at the situation a little more carefully, one finds that the first stage of the choice of regimes resembles a one-shot game or a once-and-for-all game. Countries decide whether or not to join a regime. If countries of sufficient numbers and countries that have sufficient relative mass in the world agree, then a new regime is adopted. Once a certain rule is adopted, countries develop expectations about others' behavior, and the repeated play continues. When a strong shock hits the system, the ongoing rule may turn out to be nonviable, and again a new rule may be adopted.

Incidentally, the role of the Postal Saving System (PSS) needs some explanation. This time, the Japanese government imitated the British Postal Saving System, and, surpassing its originator, has created a gigantic financial intermediary, probably the largest financial intermediary in the world. Banks are criticizing this large rival institution. They say that the Ministry of Post and Telecommunication (PSS) is highly subsidized by the consolidated account with the post and telecommunication activities of the system, that the system does not follow the market principle, and that this nonprivate institution will be an obstacle to the Big Bang. The PSS argues, on the other hand, that banks are colluding by giving the depositors low rates of interest through the protection of the MOF.

Basically, this is a tug of war, or a zero sum game, between banks and the PSS. The following remarks are in order:

1. Because of the economies of scope that deposits are collected by the post offices that engage in mailing activities, and because of the low labor and building cost of the PSS, the cost of fund collection is

often less expensive in the PSS. This advantage of fund absorption of the PSS should be utilized.

2. On the other hand, the PSS does not have sufficient skills in entrepreneurship or in managing this huge pool of funds. In fact, the use of the fund was managed by the "Fund Managing Account" of the MOF. This fund supply was a major source of the Fiscal Investment Loan Program (FILP) and an effective measure of conducting the industrial policy. Now the need for the industry-specific supporting policy became less important.

13.8   Concluding Remarks

The huge surplus of savings by Japan was good for the world and used to be a major source of strength in Japan's financial business. By the mere amount of its savings, Japan can assume a monopolistic position in international finance. Any reference by a minister to the possibility, if not the serious intention, of Japan withdrawing money from the initial bid for the newly issued U.S. treasury bills could cause turbulence in the U.S. bond market as well as the currency exchange market.

Recent incidents that cast doubt on the health of Japan's sector suggest that this quantitative dominance was not necessarily accompanied by the quality of financial services nor by the efficient financial market and organizations. Moreover, the huge financial flows from Japan were facilitated by consumers and depositors that endured substantially lower interest rates and lower quality of financial services for a long time. From the standpoint of consumers, who provided savings, they were hardly rewarded. Now Japan has to earn income by its human skills and not merely by its massive savings.

We have argued that Big Bang can be regarded as a unilateral action, and that economic rationales exist for Japan to proceed to this unilateral action. Also the present turmoil in Japan's financial market may mitigate the political-economic resistance to a reform of the system.

The Big Bang proposal was considered as a measure to draw public attention to a somewhat rosy picture in the future and to create a new image of a deregulated world. These intentions were welcomed but so far have had limited effects. The open financial system that the Big Bang intended to realize is, however, crucially instrumental in creating the hope that the Japanese banking system will really learn the benefit of market mechanism through show-window effects and practices by international entrepreneurship.

The Big Bang is an attempt to revive Japan's financial world. It is also a typical example of a unilateral action for liberalization. If it succeeds, then it will help Japan's economy become one that effectively uses its large savings.

As we have seen, the Japanese Big Bang, as a unilateral action, has been processed more or less as announced. Many legal barriers have been lifted on cross-business activities among domestic financial subsectors as well as against foreign entry into Japan. The Ministry of Finance will be partitioned into a few divisions and will lose its past glorious authority. In spite of the legal and procedural progress, the Big Bang does not seem to work as a panacea. The realization of its benefit remains to be seen. However, some signs of progress are visible. Many mergers and takeovers are occurring in Japan, including the takeover of bankrupt large investment banks like the successors of the Japan Long-term Credit Bank and the Nippon Credit Bank. Mergers and takeovers in the market are the signs of prospective better management and performance. Competitive mechanisms released by the Big Bang process have the potential to turn the Tokyo market into an advanced capital market.

Notes

I owe much to the insightful comments by Jagdish Bhagwati, David Weinstein and Lawrence White. I also thank Fumiko Takeda and Shiro Yabushita for their helpful discussions and Carolyn M. Beaudin for her editorial contributions.

1. According to the 61st Report of the Bank for International Settlements (BIS), Japanese banks accounted for about 35 percent of the total assets owned by the BIS member banks and about 34 percent of their total liabilities at the end of 1990. Tokyo, along with its offshore banking facilities, has become one of the three largest stock and currency markets.

2. He directly addressed his plan to the finance minister and the justice minister of his cabinet. This is interpreted as an indication that the prime minister has seriously considered the legislative implementation of the plan (Imai 1997).

3. The following few paragraphs are excerpts from Hamada (1995).

4. We rely on the GNP estimates by Ohkawa, Takamatsu, and Tamamoto (1974) and by Yamada (1951).

5. Although only an elementary school graduate, Tanaka became the prime minister who would later see his career end with the bribery charge that related to the Lockheed-All Nippon Airline (ANA) airbus procurement scandal.

6. This system may be working as a good device for monitoring and controlling security companies; but it has recently been criticized by foreigners as yet another form of nontariff barrier.

7. One structural policy in the fiscal package was even amusing. The MOF asked for commercial banks to refrain from selling stocks. This request could not be really effective because it simply implied the postponement of supply and those unsold stocks could be factors in being an excess supply for the future. This was typically Japanese, though, because this kind of moral suasion has been popular and was used by the MITI as an emergency measure for declining industries like aluminum (see Dore 1986).

8. The MOF was almost controlling the news media as well, but it was not perfect.

9. Of course, there are activities that are facilitated by watching what government will do. Using a market process to decide on which side of the road to drive, for example, will take a long time and yield a lot of chaos. (One cannot wait until the evolutionary stable Nash outcome emerges.) Careful studies are still needed to see exactly at what point market signaling starts dominating government signaling.

10. This reminds me of the recent story on financial firms that looked more to the group of Sokai-ya, literally gang members, often referred to as Yakuza (the Japanese Mafia), who ask companies for money in exchange for securing the order of shareholders' meetings. Neither is this an incentive-compatible scheme.

11. For a long period, the advertisement involving the comparison of interest rates among financial institutions was "refrained" by the agreement by the Bankers' Association. The MOF at least allowed that practice, if not enforced it.

12. Take, for a moment, the example of international finance: the choice of the international monetary regime. Monetary policies interact when a monetary regime is chosen to be a fixed exchange-rate system or a flexible exchange-rate system. The first stage was governed by the expectation of what happens if a certain regime is chosen. The subgame of perfectness is usually required.

Nakasone's leadership, with economist Kato's help, enabled the most successful privatization, that is, the dissolution of the National Railway (NR) to Japan Railways (JRs).

References

Bank of Japan. 1982. *Nihon Ginko Hyakunen-shi*, Vol. 3 (The one-hundred-year history of the Bank of Japan). Tokyo: Bank of Japan.

Bhagwati, J. 1958. "Immiserizing Growth: A Geometrical Note." *Review of Economic Studies* 25 (June): 201–205.

Brecher, R. A., and C. F. Diaz Alejandro. 1977. "Tariffs, Foreign Capital and Immerising Growth." *Journal of International Economics* 7, no. 4 (November): 317–322.

Dixit, A., and J. Stiglitz. 1983. "Monopolistic Competition and Optimal Product Variety." *American Economic Review* 67, no. 3: 297–308.

Dore, R. 1986. "Government and Business Enterprise." In *Flexible Rigidities*, R. Dore, 128–149. Stanford: Stanford University Press.

Frohlich, N., J. A. Oppenheimer, and O. R. Young. 1971. *Political Leadership and Collective Goods*. Princeton: Princeton University Press.

Fuchita, Y. 1997. *Shoken Biggu Ban* (The Big Bang in the Security Market). Tokyo: Nihon Keizai.

Goto, S. 1990. *Showa Kinyu-shi* (Financial History of Showa). Tokyo: Jijitsushin-sha.

Haas, P. 1992. "Introduction: Epistemic Communities and International Policy Coordination." *International Organization* 46, no. 1 (Winter): 1–35.

Hamada, K. 1995. "Bubbles, Bursts and Bail-outs: Comparison of Three Episodes of Financial Crises in Japan." In *The Structure of the Japanese Economy: Changes on the Domestic and International Fronts*, ed. M. Okabe, 263–286. New York: St. Martin's Press.

Imai, K. 1997. *Nihon ban Biggu Ban* (The Big Bang in the Japanese Style). Tokyo: Toyo Keizai.

Kusano, A. 1986. *Showa 40-nen 5-gatsu 28-nichi Yamaichi Jiken to Nichigin Tokuyu* (The Yamaichi Incident and the Bank of Japan Relief Loans). Tokyo: Nihon Keizai Shinbun.

Morishima, M. 1984. *Why Has Japan Succeeded?* Tokyo: TBS Brittanica.

Nihon Keizai Shinbun, ed. 1997. *Do naru Kinyu Biggu Ban* (What Happens in the Financial Big Bang?). Tokyo: Nihon Keizai.

Noguchi, Y. 1995. *1940-nen taisei: saraba "senji keizai"* (The 1940 Regime: Good-Bye to the "War-Time Economy"). Tokyo: Tokyo Keizai Shinposha.

Ohkawa, K., N. Takamatsu, and Y. Tamamoto. 1974. *Kokumin Shotoku*. Tokyo: Toyo Keizai Shinposha.

Okazaki, I., and M. Okuno, eds. 1993. *Gendai Nihon Keizai Sisutemu no Genryu* (The Origin of the Modern Japanese Economic System). Tokyo: Nihon Keizai Shinbun.

Putnam, R. D. 1988. "Diplomacy and Domestic Politics: The Logic of Two-Level Games." *International Organization* 42 (Summer): 427–460.

Rosenbluth, F. 1989. *Financial Politics in Contemporary Japan*. New York: Cornell University Press.

Rosenbluth, F. 1990. *Foreign Pressures and Liberalization of Japan's Financial Market: Japan's Economic Challenge*. Report to the Joint Economic Committee, October.

Sakakibara, E., R. Feldman, R. and Y. Harada. 1982. "The Japanese Financial System in Comparative Perspective," *Report to the Joint Economic Committee*, U.S. Congress.

Samuelson, P. 1967. *Economics*, 7th ed. New York: McGraw-Hill.

Suzuki, Y. 1997. *Biggu Ban No Jiremma* (The Dilemma of Big Bang). Tokyo: Toyo Keizai.

Tokyo Stock Exchange. 1928. *The Fifty Years History of Tokyo Stock Exchange*. Tokyo: Tokyo Stock Exchange.

Ueda, K. 1994. "Institutional and Regulatory Frameworks for the Main Bank System." In *The Japanese Main Bank System: Its Relevance for Developing and Transforming Economies*, ed. M. Aoki and H. Patrick, 89–108. Oxford: Oxford University Press.

Uzawa, H. 1969. "Shihon Jiyuka to Kokumin Keizai" (Liberalization of Foreign Investments and the National Economy). *Ekonomisuto* 23 (December): 105–122.

van Wolferen, K. 1989. *The Enigma of Japanese Power*. New York: Knopf.

Yamada, Y. 1951. *Nihon Kokumin Shotoku Suikei Shiryo*. Tokyo: Toyo Keizai Shinposha.

14

Internet-Induced Liberalization and Reciprocity: The Case of Telecommunications

Cynthia Beltz Soltys

14.1 Introduction

Telecommunications provides the backbone for the modern trade arena. It actually has two trade roles: first, as a medium for trade; and, second, as a traded service itself. Telecommunications, as a result, has been on the front lines of two fundamental revolutions. The advance of digital technologies is transforming the industry from the bottom up, while the creation of a multilateral trade regime and procompetitive trade rules is transforming the industry from the top down. The impact of the digital revolution on telecommunications was marked in February 1997 by the launch of the first toll-quality Internet voice service, which made it possible to use ordinary phones for international phone calls at sharply reduced rates. Meanwhile in Geneva, with considerably more fanfare and media attention, more than 60 nations in February 1997 concluded a landmark agreement under the auspices of the World Trade Organization (WTO) to bind open the global telecommunications market to competition and foreign investors.

The century-old tradition of monopolies and closed markets has now been replaced, declared U.S. Trade Representative Charlene Barshevsky, "by market opening, deregulation, and competition." The agreement broke new ground by establishing the first multilateral framework of binding rules and procompetitive regulatory principles in basic telecommunications services. It was the first of the negotiations left over from the Uruguay Round to reach a successful conclusion under the WTO, successor to the General Agreement on Tariffs and Trade (GATT). The agreement thus also provides an important bridge from the traditional trade issues of the past fifty years that focused on border barriers to the trade issues in services that often focus on market-access barriers in the internal market.

The WTO telecommunications negotiations also marked the continued rise in specific reciprocity demands in the post–Cold War period. Calls for unilateral liberalization in telecommunications and the elimination of U.S. foreign ownership restrictions in the mid-1990s, for example, were dismissed as detrimental to U.S. welfare and politically naive on the grounds that they would sacrifice the leverage needed to pry open foreign markets to competition. During the multilateral telecommunications negotiations, U.S. trade officials further argued that "without reciprocity we will not get freer trade."[1]

But, the case of telecommunications demonstrated just the opposite. First, the WTO telecomm negotiations demonstrated that the increased complexity and the sector-specific nature of the WTO trade negotiations in services limited the role of reciprocity in accelerating the actual pace of liberalization beyond that determined by other factors. Second, thanks to these other factors, even without strong reciprocal WTO commitments that matched the U.S. telecommunications commitments, trade is opening up and expanding. Indeed, it can be argued that were it not for the factors transforming telecommunications from the bottom up, there would not have been a 1997 WTO telecommunications agreement. The 1997 WTO telecommunications agreement further suggests that U.S. demands for reciprocal matching commitments, particularly in foreign investment, helped to weaken, rather than strengthen, the final set of commitments.

This is significant because the WTO itself is in danger of being overtaken by the speed at which new technologies, infrastructure demands, and globalization pressures are rewriting the rule-book and transforming the trade arena. The ten years spent discussing and negotiating the WTO telecommunications agreement contrasts with the breathtaking speed with which the Internet and the digital revolution are transforming the communications business. When the multilateral talks on telecommunications first started in the late 1980s under the Uruguay Round, the World Wide Web didn't even exist. When the next round of talks started in 1994, the Internet was just beginning its metamorphosis into a global communications and computing medium. Yet by 1997, the Internet had redefined the communications landscape.

In this chaotic environment of converging markets and complex competition, the Internet has also been breaking down barriers between industries and nations far faster than formal rule-making institutions have been able to react. The new services are undermining the old monopoly regime, once seen as unassailable. The Internet has further demonstrated the benefits of unilateral liberalization and getting ahead of the curve while increasing the political-economic cost of protective telecommunications regulations and internal demands in laggard nations for their elimination.

Even as U.S. officials struggled to devise reciprocity-based instruments that would increase their leverage at the WTO negotiating table, the Internet quietly undercut the incentive and ability of foreign officials to maintain restrictive regimes. Without competition in basic telecommunication services, prices remain high and the information gap between countries widens. With competition, countries are finding they can deliver more services for less. The competition to increase Internet access, as a result, has helped create a far more potent force for "freer trade" than any reciprocity instrument that could be devised by trade officials.

14.2   Shifting Paradigms in Telecommunications

The Old Order: International Exchange without Competition

In the beginning, telecommunications was government-owned and treated as a natural monopoly, with the rules set from the top down to limit entry and the number of carriers that could carry phone traffic. The system of national monopolies was in turn held together by a cooperative international system designed to fortify and protect the power of those monopolies.

Before the late 1980s, for example, there was little support for including telecommunications in the multilateral trade regime because telecommunications services were still supplied by monopoly providers in most countries. International telecom agreements were instead limited to technical concerns about cross-border connectivity and the ability of different systems to exchange messages. Market entry was strictly controlled, international prices were administered, international competition was discouraged, and international calls were treated as a jointly provided service between national monopolies.

Under this system, instead of competing to provide services, national operators arranged with each other for the exchange of each other's calls through a set of rules known as the accounting rate system. The system is based on an imaginary line drawn halfway between two countries marking the point where an outgoing call is passed off from one carrier to the recipient carrier's network. It operates on the basis of a dual-price arrangement: the collection charge (retail price) that end users pay to the originating carrier, and an accounting rate (wholesale price) that determines the termination fee (settlement rate, usually half the accounting rate) paid by the originating carrier to the other carrier for completing the call in its market.

Each carrier charges its domestic customers for the outbound call (collection charge), but reimburses the other company for terminating the call based on the accounting rate that is negotiated bilaterally. The accounting rate in the past could be reduced only if both carriers agreed. In trade terms, an outgoing call is an import of a foreign carrier's call termination service. And, an incoming call is an export of a domestic carrier's termination services to the foreign carrier. Periodically, the accounts are settled between correspondent carriers with net payments made to the carrier receiving more incoming calls.[2] At the time the accounting rate system was created, the international facility itself was the dominant cost involved with connecting two domestic networks. But this is no longer the case. International facilities now account for a trivial portion of the cost.

But accounting rates did not adjust to fully reflect the changes in the cost of providing an international call. When competition has been limited on international routes, accounting rates and user retail rates have diverged sharply from the collapsing cost of delivering an international phone call. Before alternative calling methods started to proliferate in the 1990s, for example, the rates for international phone calls were set to extract as much as possible from consumers of international services. In addition to this tax on international communications, the bilateral nature and secrecy of the accounting rate negotiations have also promoted discrimination between countries.[3] A price charged for terminating traffic from one country, for example, could be ten times greater than the price charged to a carrier in another country even if the cost of terminating the call from both countries is similar.

The New Order: Rules for Competition

Pressure to dismantle the national monopolies and the supporting regulatory policies increased as technological advances changed the

Table 14.1
Changing paradigm for international telephony

Old telecom regime	Emerging trade regime (Early 1990)
International telephony a jointly provided service	International telephony a traded service
	Basic telephony as a key intermediate service for other traded services
	Enhanced services as a traded service (delivered direct to end-user)
Monopoly service provision	Competitive Service Providers
Traffic travels mainly over Public Switched Telephone Network (PSTN)	Traffic over PSTN, leased lines, private nets, CSP networks, satellites, Internet, etc.
Voice traffic dominant	Multimedia traffic

underlying economics of long-distance communications and the importance of telecommunications as a trade medium increased. (See table 14.1.)

Telecom Trade Issues

The market access barriers include overt, discriminatory restrictions on a foreign firm such as limits on foreign ownership. They also include barriers that are not inherently discriminatory such as restrictions on the number of carrier licenses issued or the lack of transparency in regulatory procedures. Some of the major barriers to trade in basic telecommunication services can be classified by the major modes of supply. (See table 14.2.) In terms of cross-border trade, for example, the barriers include quantitative limitations on the number of permitted service suppliers, total value of transactions, and total number of operations. Restrictions on commercial presence include limits on foreign equity participation, limits or requirements on the type of legal entity permitted to supply a service, and quantitative limits on number of available frequencies for foreign service providers. Government administrative measures (not addressed in GATS country schedules) can also affect trade and market access.

By the 1990s, the limits on foreign market access in telecommunications had become a major international trade issue. Regulatory reforms in the early mover countries had opened up segments such as computer-based (enhanced) communication services to increased

Table 14.2
Trade barriers in basic telecommunications services

Sector or subsector	Limitations on market access	National treatment limitations
Telecommunication services (a) through (g) and (o)	(1) Quantitative limitations/needs test applied to the number of service suppliers (including monopolies, duopolies, etc.), total value of transactions, total number of operations, or quantity of output.	(1) Preferences given to domestic suppliers or restrictions imposed on foreign suppliers in the allotment of frequencies
Local/long-distance/international service: wire-based radio-based on a resale basis for public use for nonpublic use	(3) Quantitative limitation on the number of available frequencies to be allowed to foreign service suppliers. Restrictions or requirements regarding the type of legal entity permitted to supply the services (also, a requirement of certain forms of commercial presence could rule out cross-border supply). Limits on foreign equity participation. (4) Limitations/needs test applied to the total number of natural persons that may be employed.	(3) Preferences given to domestic suppliers or restrictions imposed on foreign suppliers in the allotment of frequencies. Limitations on the nationality or residency of directors or board members. Restrictions on foreign ownership of facilities.

Source: World Trade Organization.
Note: Based on scheduling methodology used by the World Trade Organization. Numbers in parentheses indicate the mode of delivery: (1) cross-border supply; (2) consumption absorbed; (3) commercial presence; and (4) presence of natural persons.

competition, which in turn required a framework of accepted rules to limit the growing range of conflicts over foreign market access. (See table 14.3.) Advances in communications technologies, by accelerating the speed and efficiency of transmitting information worldwide, had also significantly changed the nature of all international transactions in information-based services by increasing their transportability. Large user groups such as financial service firms played a key role in making telecommunications an international trade issue. In addition, with the service component of manufacturing industries rising, the ability of goods-producing industries to remain internationally competitive had become closely linked to the availability of competitively priced intermediate telecommunication service inputs.[4] A particular concern in this context was the monopoly provision of telecommunications services and restrictive domestic regulations that presented a major barrier to the expansion of trade in services.

There was the additional concern that without an accepted framework of rules for progressive liberalization countries could take a step away from the old monopoly model, but increased foreign market access or effective competition would still be blocked. Countries could, for example, remove some overt discriminatory trade barriers such as a restriction on foreign ownership, but market access (for domestic and foreign-owned providers) could still be limited by regulatory measures that influenced market structure, licensing requirements, pricing policies, or interconnection arrangements. Restrictive regulations that prohibit the use of leased lines or that make it costly to interconnect to the local PSTN, for example, inhibit not only the cross-border supply of telecommunication services but also the development of private networks used by multinationals and all service industries that depend on telecommunications. Another concern was the lack of transparency in regulatory procedures. For example, even if a country did not put restrictions on the number of licenses that would be issued, entry by a foreign firm could still be precluded by the lack of information on the regulatory procedures.

Making the Impossible Deal Possible
Thus, unlike past trade issues, which focused on tariff rates imposed at the border, the issues in telecommunications services intrude much further into the domain of domestic politics. Many thought that it would be impossible to conclude a procompetitive

Table 14.3
Major trade barriers in enhanced and value-added services (U.S. industry view, 1988)

Generic trade barriers

Denial of national treatment

Denial of right of establishment (including denial of commercial presence)

Denial of cross-border access

Denial of access to and use of domestic distribution systems

Lack of transparency, notification, or due process

Government subsidy

Barrier to movement of personnel

Exchange controls

Discriminatory government procurement practice

Barriers related to use of telecommunications services

Restriction on access and use of public telecommunications services

Restriction on movement of information among countries (including intracorporate data flows)

Restrictions on attachment of customer equipment (adherence to more than a "no harm to the network" standard)

Imposition of non-cost-based and discriminatory pricing (including volume-sensitive pricing of leased circuits and pricing mechanisms that force selection of a less desirable service)

Barriers related to provision of enhanced and value-added services

Restriction of access to and use of public telecommunications services

Restriction on movement of information among countries (including imposition of taxes or customs tariffs on information)

Restrictions on attachment of CPE (adherence to more than a "no harm to the network" standard)

Restrictions on ability to provide value-added/enhanced, computer, and information services

Imposition of non-cost-based and discriminatory pricing (including volume-sensitive pricing of leased circuits and pricing mechanisms that force selection of a less desirable service)

Prohibition on resale and shared use of telecommunications services

Forced use of international protocols beyond the necessary compatibility of physical characteristics to interconnect

Source: Based on U.S. Council for International Business, "Value-Added and Information Services in the Services Trade Negotiations," April 1988.

agreement on telecommunications because of the political sensitivity of the sector. Liberalization, for example, touched on sensitive areas such as the nation's control of its infrastructure and employment policies (the national telephone system has often been the largest single entity and employer). Liberalization was further complicated by telecommunication's role (international services in particular) in many countries as a fiscal tool for generating revenue to fund a wide range of social objectives.

Two key factors helped make the impossible deal possible. The first key factor was the regulatory distinction between basic and enhanced services. Basic telecommunications services in the 1980s were largely the domain of monopoly providers while enhanced services (alternatively referred to as value-added and nonbasic) included the new computer-based services that were supplied by a variety of firms.[5] Enhanced services were also the segment of the market most open to foreign competition. (See table 14.4.) The regulatory distinction let trade negotiators build the telecom framework by focusing first on trade in enhanced services while the more controversial issue of trade in basic voice services was largely left to the 1994 to 1997 trade negotiations.[6] The agreement on enhanced services in 1994 also ended up having a far greater liberalization impact than negotiators had expected because of the unexpected Internet advances in the late 1990s that expanded the range and influence of computer-enhanced services.

A second key factor that made the 1997 WTO telecom agreement on basic voice services possible, particularly in terms of developing country participation, was the unprecedented liberalization movement already taking place in the WTO member countries. Led and fed by the competitive pressures emanating from more open markets and pushed by huge infrastructure demands that far exceeded domestic resources, countries started dismantling their state-owned monopolies at an unprecedented rate in the mid-1990s. The changes were particularly prominent in the Asia-Pacific region, where more than eighty new operators were created between 1990 and 1996.[7] "The progress made towards competition and open, private markets," remarked the former head of the FCC International Bureau in early 1997, has been "nothing less than astonishing."[8] Competition is now being promoted in some shape on every continent, in every region, and in countries from Guatemala to Germany to Korea.

Table 14.4
Market structure and level of foreign participation allowed in selected countries in 1993

Type of service		Basic voice local	Long-distance and international	Mobile/cellular	Enhanced services
Europe	United Kingdom[1]	Open and Competitive	Open and Competitive[2]	Multiple Licenses: Open to foreign firms	Open and Competitive
	Germany	Monopoly	Monopoly	Duopoly: Foreign consortia in both carriers	Open and Competitive
	France	Monopoly	Monopoly	Duopoly: Foreign consortia in one carrier	Open and Competitive
	Sweden	Monopoly	Open and Competitive	Analog monopoly, digital competition	Open and Competitive
	Italy	Monopoly	Monopoly	Duopoly: Closed to foreign firms	Open and Competitive
United States	U.S.	Regional Monopoly	Open and Competitive	Regional Duopoly: Open to foreign firms	Open and Competitive
Asia	Australia	Duopoly: Closed to foreign firms	Duopoly: Closed to foreign firms	Three firms licensed: One foreign firm	Open and Competitive
	New Zealand	Open and Competitive	Open and Competitive[3]	Open and Competitive	Open and Competitive
	South Korea	Monopoly	Monopoly	Regulated Duopoly: Limited foreign participation	Open and Competitive

Japan	Managed Competition: Closed to foreign firms	Managed Competition: Closed to foreign firms	Regionalized Competition: Foreign firm participation minimized	Open and Competitive
Singapore	Monopoly	Monopoly	Monopoly	Competitive but Closed to foreign firms
Malaysia	Monopoly	Managed Competition: Closed to foreign firms	Regulated Duopoly: Closed to foreign firms	Competitive but Closed to foreign firms
China	Monopoly	Monopoly	Monopoly	Closed to foreign firms

Sources: Local and long-distance data for Europe from Office of Technology Assessment, *U.S. Telecommunications Services in European Markets*, Washington, DC: GPO, August 1993. Mobile/cellular data for Europe from U.S. International Trade Commission, *Global Competitiveness of U.S. Advanced-Technology Industries: Cellular Communications*. (Washington, DC: Government Printing Office, 1993.) Data for Asia from "The State of Telecommunications Infrastructure and Regulatory Environment of APEC Economies," *Asia-Pacific Economic Cooperation*, Volumes 1 & 2, November 1993 and June 1994; Erik Olbeter and Lawrence Chimerine, *Crossed Wires* (Washington, DC: Economic Strategy Institute, 1994).

[1] The United Kingdom and Finland were the only two countries without foreign ownership restrictions.

[2] Only resale is permitted in international basic services.

[3] While New Zealand regulations restrict the number of international carriers, the two existing providers are both partly owned by foreign firms.

In many countries, the market liberalization push in telecommunications was also part of a broader shift in policy. The push to facilitate foreign investment was reflected in the increasing popularity of bilateral investment treaties, which surged from less than 400 at the beginning of the 1990s to more than 1,300 in 1996 with 180 concluded in 1996 alone. Also in 1996, more than 65 countries moved in the direction of liberalizing foreign investment. Between 1991 and 1996, 95 percent of the more than 600 changes in rules governing foreign direct investment were in the direction of liberalization. And, by 1996, more than 120 privatization laws were passed that opened the sale of state-owned enterprises in infrastructure industries to foreign investors.[9] The sale of telecommunications firms led the privatization push in infrastructure projects, accounting for 20 percent of total privatization revenue.

The WTO Telecom Framework

These trends created the opportunity for the WTO telecommunications framework, which was instituted through two separate agreements.

The first major piece of the framework was put in place in 1994 as part of the General Agreement on Trade in Services (GATS), which included a Telecommunications Annex and specific commitments in the country schedules for providers of enhanced services.[10] (See table 14.5.) The annex represented a key innovation for trade policy because it established the right of users (downstream industries) to use a foreign country's phone network to supply covered services in that market, even if a country had reserved its right under the WTO to maintain a telecom monopoly.[11] In general, the obligations of the telecom annex apply to any WTO government even if it has not scheduled commitments on telecommunications. In the process, the annex created a multilateral framework of restraints on the abuse of monopoly position without challenging the rights of countries to maintain those monopolies in basic telecommunications services. In operational terms, the annex created the "right to plug in" to national telecom networks, defined as an ability to lease telecommunications circuits to transport information within a country and across borders, with freedom from restrictions on equipment and interconnection standards.[12]

The issue of provider rights in voice services was addressed by the second major piece of the framework that was put in place with the

Table 14.5
Uruguay Round GATS telecommunication commitments

Service activity	DC	LDC	Transition	Total
Basic services				
a. Voice telephone services	0	10	0	10
b. Packet-switched data transmission services	2	9	0	11
c. Circuit-switched data transmission services	2	10	0	12
d. Telex services	1	6	0	7
e. Telegraph services	0	6	0	6
f. Facsimile services	1	8	2	11
g. Private leased circuits	1	7	0	8
Enhanced services				
h. Electronic mail	25	19	4	48
i. Voice mail	25	17	4	46
j. Online information and data base retrieval	25	21	4	50
k. Electronic data interchance (EDI)	25	17	4	43
l. Enhanced/value-added facsimile services, including store and forward, store and retrieve	9	16	4	29
m. Code and protocol conversion	25	12	4	41
n. Online information and/or data processing (including transaction processing)	9	16	4	29
o. Other	4	15	2	21

Source: Laura Altinger and Alice Enders, "The Scope and Depth of GATS Commitments," *World Economy* 19, no. 3 (May 1996): 329.
Note: DC = Developed Countries; LDC = Less Developed Countries.

1997 conclusion of the WTO negotiations on basic telecommunication services and voice services, traditionally the largest segment of the business.[13] A major innovation in this negotiation was the inclusion of a reference paper on "procompetitive" regulatory principles for the first time in the country schedules of specific commitments.

Taken together, the GATS general obligations, the Telecommunications Annex, and the individual country schedules in enhanced and basic services form a multilateral framework of rules for progressive liberalization in telecommunications. Thus, much like the GATT did for trade in goods fifty years ago, there now exists under the GATS a framework for defining an "open" market in telecom-munications as well as several mechanisms for promoting procom-petitive transition paths.[14]

Limits of the WTO Telecommunications Agreement
The ten years needed to put the WTO telecom framework in place reflects the inordinate difficulty of getting countries with a diverse range of political and regulatory regimes to agree on a common set of rules and principles. The conclusion of the basic telecom agree-ment is, therefore, itself a major achievement. But, despite the many significant achievements of those negotiations, gaps remain. The pact needs to be extended, for example, to include many of the emerging and developing countries that represent 45 percent of the world's population. China and Russia, for example, were not part of the deal.

For the countries that did sign the agreement, the scope of the commitments differs significantly by country and region. Of the schedules that committed to liberalize voice services, 55˙ will be phased in over a ten-year period. On international services and facilities, of the 59 countries that guaranteed market access, only 26 did so without reservations, 6 opened for selected market segments, and 23 committed to implement their obligations at later dates (from 1999 to 2013). On satellite services, of the 49 countries that made commitments, 23 will implement them at various times over the 1999–2004 time period.[15]

A great deal of work will also need to be done to improve the weak commitments of the Asian countries, which offer some of the greatest growth opportunities for telecommunications. The OECD, most of which was already liberalizing at the time of the WTO ne-gotiations, account for more than 75 percent of the world telecom-munications market. But, with future growth centered elsewhere, a major benefit of a multilateral agreement would be to bring the other areas into the framework of accepted trading rules.

Trade and telecom officials will also be tied up for years inter-preting and implementing the new rules. Existing commitments may not be fully phased in until after 2010. Getting countries to live up to their commitments is always difficult. But in telecommuni-cations, the transition path will be particularly difficult because of the novel nature of the regulatory policy issues (regulating to pro-mote rather than impede competition) and the many key details yet to be resolved. If implementation of the United States' own rule-making revolution (the 1996 Telecommunications Act) is any model of what we can expect in this situation, the process will be contentious and lengthy. Incumbents have taken every opportunity to delay the introduction of competition, and implementation has gotten bogged down by lobbyists and lawyers using the courts to refight battles they had previously lost.[16]

In addition, whereas the United States had already been debating the transition to competition for more than ten years, many of the other WTO members are just getting started. Many will need to change their legal systems and a Kafkaesque maze of protective regulations to implement their WTO commitments and embrace such concepts as "transparency and independent regulation." Unlike the United States, many of the other countries are also starting from a position where they do not enjoy universal telephone access. More than half of the signatories are less-developed nations, which will have significant technical and political obstacles to overcome in just the training of regulators to enforce the WTO commitments.

Even after domestic rules have been changed to conform with the WTO-scheduled commitments, foreign firms will still face incumbent carriers and regulatory agencies who can be expected to be particularly creative in their tactics to delay or impede interconnection. Loopholes or "regulator rights" have been built into the WTO's telecommunications provisions, which permit access conditions to be imposed to safeguard public service responsibilities, such as universal service, or to protect the "technical integrity" of the public telecommunications system.[17] When and how such restrictions can be attacked as an illegitimate nontariff trade barrier will have to be resolved through the WTO dispute settlement process.

This process itself will be time-consuming. Because of the government-to-government nature of the WTO process, companies must first convince their own governments to champion their case. Once a case is accepted, the government still needs to prove that a foreign government has behaved in a way that is inconsistent with the law and spirit of the WTO agreement.

14.3 Driving from the Bottom Up

Given the inherent limits of the WTO and the limits of the existing commitments on telecommunications, too much should not be expected too soon from the rule-making revolution embodied in the

1997 WTO agreement. But, thankfully for telecommunications, freer trade and the savings from increased innovation and lower prices do not depend on the new WTO rules, reciprocity, or even strong-arm U.S. negotiating tactics. The most powerful forces pushing for market liberalization did not even have seats at the negotiating table.

Excessive regulation and artificially high rates have instead created an engine of their own destruction. Technological innovations have made it easier for end-users to bypass overpriced networks, while inflated profit margins have attracted entrepreneurial firms from within and outside the traditional telecommunications industry. End-user pressure for lower prices and new services in international markets, intertwined with changes in technology and national liberalization trends, are in particular forcing carriers to become more consumer sensitive in their product and pricing strategies. Thus far the impact has been the strongest in the long distance and international service markets where the trends have worked together to destabilize protectionist regimes and accelerate the elimination of century-old market barriers once seen as unassailable.[18]

Technology
The cracks in the old telecommunications order and its underlying regulatory structure first started to appear in the late 1950s with the development of microwave communications, which opened the door to the possibility of competition in long-distance service. Since then, advances in technology have multiplied the channels for transmitting telecommunication signals (copper cable, fiber-optic cable, satellite), slashed the cost of long-distance communications, increased the tradability of services, and created new platforms for delivering communications services that are further restructuring the cost structure of the industry.

The integration of computers into telecommunications in particular put in motion a fundamental transformation of the telecommunications industry.[19] The advances increased the range of services and opened the door to a new set of actors. Some of today's most dynamic communications technologies, for example, have their origin not in the core of the telecommunications industry, but rather in areas that used to be considered peripheral to the business such as the routing of data traffic over leased lines and the Internet. Two key factors driving the ongoing transformation are the microelectronics revolution and advances in transmission technologies, particularly in the area of fiber optics and satellites. For three decades each new generation of computer chips has contained roughly twice the capacity as its predecessor with the performance per unit cost doubling every eighteen to twenty-four months (Moore's law, named after Intel's co-founder). Computer-processing power in the late 1990s costs one-hundredth of 1 percent of what it did in the early 1970s.

In terms of transmission, advances in fiber-optic cables, satellites, and compression techniques have also made it possible to provide far greater capacities at much lower costs. When the first Trans-Atlantic One (TAT-1) cable was completed in 1956, it had a capacity of 89 simultaneous telephone calls (voice paths) with the cost of each around $600,000. The TAT-12/13 cable launched in 1996 made 600,000 voice paths possible at less than $1,000 each. Capacity increased so dramatically in the first part of the 1990s that supply outstripped demand, leaving a substantial share of transoceanic capacity idle.[20] The cost of adding capacity is also falling while new technologies are making it possible to carry more calls on existing fibers. Advances in the form of wave division multiplexing (WDM), for example, are increasing the capacity of each fiber by allowing multiple wavelengths to be transmitted.

Recent policy decisions have further boosted the trend in collapsing costs by increasing the supply of available capacity and diversifying its ownership. In 1996, for example, the United States and the European Union relaxed restrictions that had previously limited the ability of utilities and others from leasing their excess capacity.[21] Firms can now buy capacity from new service providers that are building their own fiber networks and applying Internet technology to create high-capacity networks. In addition, the nature of the market for wholesale capacity is changing as a result of global fiber-optic projects financed by those that have been traditionally outside the industry, rather than incumbent international carriers.

Taken together, these trends changed the de facto rules and transformed the economics of the international telecommunications industry by slashing the price of international calls and opening the field to new forms of competition. Distance, for example, is no longer a meaningful determinant of an international phone call's underlying cost. In the late 1990s, it cost far less to call across the world than to call a regional partner or neighboring country. It was more expensive, for example, to call across the English Channel from the United Kingdom to France than to Los Angeles, 6,000 miles away.

It was also cheaper in 1996 to call from Geneva to Honolulu than it was to call from Geneva to Barcelona. Instead of distance, the unusual geography of telecommunications in the 1990s reflected the distorted prices and inefficiencies created by outdated (protective) regulations and asymmetrical rates of liberalization.

Inflated Profit Margins

The price distortions in turn helped create bypass opportunities. Incumbent phone operators providing long distance services were particularly vulnerable because traditionally they passed to consumers only a small part of the cost savings made possible by technological advances. The deviation of retail price from cost was especially large on international routes.[22]

There were also significant differences in per minute rates and price-cost margins across countries that could not be justified by the different degrees of digitalization across countries. Part of this was due to the discriminatory nature of the closed bilateral negotiations on accounting rates. Part was also due to the impact of competition in some of the early mover markets. In the United Kingdom, for example, competition has brought retail rates toward cost on routes between the United Kingdom and other markets open to international competition. Lower accounting rates and collection charges for calls from continental Europe to the United States through the United Kingdom have in turn helped make it a key hub for international traffic and international finance.

Consumer Pull and Globalization

Driven by the rising pressures of international competition and the shift toward an information-based economy, corporate customers started looking beyond incumbent national carriers to satisfy their communication needs. In particular, they become much more aggressive and sophisticated in their use of new technologies to devise routes around inefficient pricing systems.

At the same time, inflated profit margins had attracted new competitors to the business to exploit the opportunities created by unmet consumer demand and lower-cost networking technologies.[23] By 1997, instead of a few hundred telephone companies setting rates for international calls, there were more than a thousand.[24] New competitors came into the industry from other countries, from other industries, and from technological advances that enabled alternative delivery mechanisms. Competition had also started to emerge between rival groups that were themselves a shifting mix of national affiliations. The ability to tax international calls, as a result, declined with the growth in options for bypassing carriers and countries charging excessive rates.

Early movers on the market liberalization path like the United States played a key role in opening the door to international competition. Relatively permissive lease line policies in the United States, for example, made it possible for a new generation of operators to enter the international marketplace without owning their own facilities, undersea cables, or satellites. By purchasing the excess capacity of the phone companies (an estimated 43 percent on transoceanic routes in 1995) and then reselling it at a discount, new carriers were able to enter the market. All the resellers and some of the callback operators in the United States, for example, used leased lines to provide their services.

The Bypass Revolution

These trends together encouraged the development of complex, circuitous, distance-insensitive routing systems that used software advances and leased lines to pass traffic over less expensive routes.[25]

In 1997, the range of alternative calling procedures for increasing competition included refile, callback, international simple resale, international virtual private networks, and voice over data networks.[26] Some of the services such as callback and refiling use the public switch network (PSTN) as well as software advances and innovative strategies to bypass high-cost routes and minimize accounting rate liability. Others such as international simple resale and voice over the Net or Internet telephony bypassed the accounting rate system altogether.[27]

Callback provided a prime example of how computer advances were exploited in the 1990s by a new generation of carriers to increase the contestability of markets even when direct forms of competition were prohibited.[28] To do this, callback operators purchased bulk capacity on international routes and applied least-cost routing software to find the cheapest commercial routes. The service let consumers establish a virtual presence in lower-cost telecommunications markets by exporting a high-tech version of the old college trick: Call home, let the phone ring twice, hang up, and wait for your parents to call you back. In the case of a callback service, a computer (automatic dialer) reads the encoded message in the signal and calls back giving consumers a low-cost dial tone that can be used to call almost anywhere in the world.

By switching the origin of the call, callback transfers some of the cost-saving benefits of competition to markets dominated by state-owned monopolies or inefficient suppliers. Depending on the destination of the call, customers could save from 20 to 70 percent on their international calls. Consumers in countries like Argentina were able to save on domestic calls that took an 11,000-mile detour through an U.S. callback operator. In Hong Kong, the national monopoly on international voice calls initially was not scheduled to expire until 2006, and it was treated as a reserved service in the country's WTO commitments. But this reservation did not protect it from competition. Competitors instead made inroads through callback services that cut into the monopoly's market share by as much as 20 percent over the 1996–1997 period.[29] In Brazil, as a result of callback innovations, Embratel made only 22 percent of what it once did on an international direct-dial call. The callback operator received 5 percent, a local representative received 3 percent, and the customer pocketed a 70 percent saving.[30]

More than twenty-five countries (including China, India, Indonesia, Philippines, Thailand, Vietnam, and South Africa) tried to fight back by making bypass services such as callback illegal. But the laws were openly circumvented. Technical devices were also tried to block callback by modifying switches and other aspects of the phone system. But callback services proved to be annoyingly durable. Unlike imports that can be seized at the border, dial tones are difficult to track and block. Technically, it was difficult to distinguish callback traffic from other traffic, which made it difficult for governments to block callback without also disconnecting a user's phone service.

New methods for providing callback services were also being devised faster than legislation and restrictive rules could be written. When Uganda tried to block all calls to the Seattle area code where a callback company was based, the company redirected the calls through a different area code. When others banned callback services using uncompleted call signaling, firms used different technologies to exploit loopholes in the rules and regulations. The rise of callback services over the Internet further aggravated the control problem. Even when countries were able to limit callback, they found it impossible to erase its impact. Once consumers realized that cheaper rates and greater choice were possible, they became increasingly unwilling to accept the higher rates of incumbent providers.

The callback market, as a result, exploded. By 1997, there were more than three hundred firms (including more than 100 American firms) that were offering callback services around the globe, and the market was growing at an annual rate of 20 to 25 percent.[31] In one of the more ironic twists of the callback story, callback even became popular with government ministries in countries that were actively trying to limits its growth.[32]

Callback's popularity will diminish over time as increased competition reduces the margins and discounts that have fueled its growth. But its popularity and durability signal the bypass opportunities that exist as long as significant price distortions persist and national liberalization trends continue to enable resale and the entrance of entrepreneurial firms. The evolution of the callback market also highlights the potential for lower long-distance prices to benefit both consumers and incumbent carriers by releasing the market potential hidden by inflated rates. After the United Kingdom and Australia deregulated their long-distance markets, for example, British Telecom and Telstra watched their market shares and gross revenues per minute of long distance steadily decline. But traffic volumes surged. Each company, as a result, has posted record profits. Likewise, in the international market, in which demand is relatively price elastic, significant increases in volume may more than offset reductions in price.[33]

Callback also signaled how incumbent operators were being forced to compete ahead of schedule because of unexpected market developments. For example, apparently persuaded by the principle that if "someone is going to eat your lunch it may as well be you," traditional phone companies around the world started to get into the bypass business as well by offering call-reorigination and other services that cannibalized international message telephone service. Carriers were forced to put aside their fears of cannibalizing existing activities in order to focus on the larger goals of holding onto their customers and generating new revenue streams. In early 1997, for example, Hong Kong Telecom hit back at twenty plus callback operators by offering its own cut-price international direct dial-tone services. AT&T, which had previously protested callback at the FCC, also started actively marketing third country calling through the United States and using callback techniques as a vehicle to undercut rival operators and break into the voice market of foreign countries. Through these and other moves, incumbent carriers helped make both the regulations and national boundaries that traditionally protected their profit margins more porous.

Converging technologies further spurred on the bypass revolution by blurring the boundaries between regulated and unregulated industries and enabling competition between the phone companies and firms that previously did not compete. For example, there used to be different technologies for different networks with different rules for different types of traffic (voice, data, and video) that targeted different customers. But, by the late 1990s, the lines were no longer distinct. The move from analog to digital signal transmission enabled the emergence of integrated service networks that include basic voice as only one component in a bundle of applications and services. Desktop computers became "communication cockpits" that could handle e-mail, take phone calls, and share applications with other users around the world.

The Internet: A Virtual "Trade Partner"

With the emergence of this chaotic marketplace, telecommunications changed from a business about phone companies to one in which voice services could no longer be relied on as a mainstay of the business. In the process, multimedia advances and the Internet unraveled the definition of a phone call and launched a new age in service trade.

The Internet embodies the multimedia and borderless marketplace made possible by advances in transmission and computing technologies. Its growth has been driven by the powerful intersection of Moore's law (progressively greater computer power for a given cost) and network economics (exponential increases in the value of the network with each additional user).[34] The power of this intersection took everybody by surprise in the mid- to late-1990s when interest in the Internet exploded after the introduction of user-friendly navigational tools for the World Wide Web.[35] From 1993 to 1997, for example, the Internet grew from 1.8 million hosts (the computers that are directly connected to the Internet) to 19.5 million.[36]

By relaxing the grip of geography on business, the Internet has also created a new generation of international actors, accelerated investment in the development of a global information infrastructure, and created an infinitely flexible trade medium. It also did not require legislation, fast-track authorization from the U.S. Congress, or a multilateral agreement to become the closest example yet of a global free trade area. Instead, while government officials and business leaders have labored over the negotiating table, the Internet has slashed communications costs and increased the speed with which a widening array of services can cross national borders.

U.S. negotiators couldn't have asked for a better "trade partner" to promote freer trade in communication services. In a far more convincing fashion than anything U.S. negotiators could say or do, the Internet has highlighted the benefits of competition and the costs of protection in infrastructure services. The speed with which the Internet emerged as a major communication medium also disarmed many that might have otherwise opposed or tried to managed its entry. Telecommunications providers, as a result, were left scrambling to get on the Internet bandwagon. Regulators worldwide were left trying to figure out what just passed them, and governments were racing to get their countries connected.[37]

Herein lies perhaps the greatest strength of the Internet in the context of the trade liberalization process. By opening the global marketplace to firms of all sizes, the Internet has captured the interest of governments worldwide and forced them to confront the inefficiencies of their telecommunications systems. By entering into the communications arena under the "enhanced service" or "value-added network" label, the Internet has the added advantage in many countries of being outside the entrenched system of rules designed to protect incumbent carriers in basic voice services. This means advances in areas such as Voice over the Internet have helped enlarge the areas bound open to competition under the WTO by adding functionality and voice services to unregulated or lightly regulated delivery mechanisms. Such advances are also just the tip of the e-commerce revolution that is transforming both telecommunications and the larger trade arena.

Creating Borderless Trade in Services
Any service that can be easily digitized and transmitted electronically can potentially be delivered to most cities in the world in just a few seconds or minutes. Services from architectural design to telecommunications providers all have the potential to go global over the Internet.[38]

In telecommunications, by the late 1990s, millions were already using the Internet like a phone to set up appointments, hold conferences, and exchange messages around the world. The biggest impact initially was on international and business markets, where 40 percent of international corporate traffic was traditionally for fax messages. But until prices come into line with cost, other forms of long distance and international communications will continue to gravitate toward the Internet or something like it. This will be true not only for types of traffic like the fax, but also for those that may not initially be suited for Internet delivery such as real-time voice services.

Even as the WTO telecommunications talks were collapsing in Geneva in April 1996, the first annual Voice over the Net conference, Dialing the Net, was taking place in London. It was not attended by trade officials, did not attract much media attention, and did not try to forge a consensus on what national governments should do to increase competition and build global networks. Instead, the meeting showcased the shifts already taking place in the marketplace toward cheap, global, communications services. Companies such as the Israeli firm VocalTec demonstrated in particular how Voice over the Net had made it possible for phone calls to be made around the world for the price of a local call.

The savings come from the bulk purchase of leased lines, speech compression, and the bandwidth efficiency savings provided by the use of packet switching instead of the circuit-switched technology used for conventional phone calls. Ordinarily when you pick up the phone to call someone, it requires a dedicated two-way circuit for the duration of the call. For Internet calls, voices are cut up into digital packets of information, which travel separately through a web of routes across the network before they are reassembled and turned into sound at the other end. Conventional calls work like a highway with a lane reserved for each conversation. Even if neither party is talking, with no cars using the road, the lane remains reserved. On the Internet, however, cars can use any lane that has space. Voice signals from one conversation can slip in between silences of another conversation. The net result is that much more traffic can be squeezed into the same amount of bandwidth.[39] The savings made possible by voice compression over the Internet could reduce the one-minute cost for a trans-Atlantic call to less than 10 cents compared to the $1 a minute average charge under the accounting rate system for a conventional call.

Despite the potential savings, voice over the Net at first was not taken seriously because the quality was far inferior to conventional phone service and it was a hassle to use. But, voice over the Net has been developing at a mind-spinning rate. The first wave of software in 1995 demonstrated the technical feasibility of voice over the Net as well as its potential savings. User friendliness significantly improved in 1996 with software advances that opened the door to a new generation of users that will not need a computer to capture the cost-saving advantages of voice over the Net. Then in 1997, voice over the Net came of age as a serious business application that made it possible for corporations to shift their intracorporate traffic onto the Internet, generating huge savings particularly in the area of international phone service.

Changing the Game: Creating A New Center of Gravity

If and when voice over the Net will become a mainstream consumer service is impossible to predict. But, until a more rational pricing structure emerges, voice services will be a weak link in the evolution of the communications chain and crossover technologies like Internet telephony will continue to emerge. "Technology," notes Andrew Grove, chief executive officer of Intel, is "like a natural force that is impossible to hold back. It finds its way no matter what obstacles people put in its path."[40] The obstacles and bottlenecks in key segments of the telecommunications market, created by the lack of competition and excessive regulation, have become in effect a lightning rod for industry attention because of the businesses that can be created by circumventing or eliminating them altogether. The infrastructure role that telecommunications plays in expanding service trade and the global trading community has also intensified the focus on those obstacles. Voice over the Net represents just the edge of the shock wave recreating the global communications industry.

Over time the price advantage of voice over the Net, like callback, will diminish as increased competition and national policy reforms force international rates toward cost on conventional phone service while the shift to more efficient Internet pricing models and improvements in the quality of service increases the cost of Internet-based services. But the enduring value of voice over the Net is the role it has already played in changing the very nature of the telecommunications market. In particular, it has accelerated the shift from simple voice communication to those services, which can be integrated with computer applications.

By providing a single ubiquitous protocol for voice and data, voice over the Net also provides a vast platform for innovation. When the Internet reached a critical mass, it attracted an unprecedented flood of resources aimed at fixing every known deficiency. It became in effect a global communications laboratory that attracted the best and brightest from the converging fields of telecommunications, computers, and entertainment. Every problem area from bandwidth capacity constraints, to local access bottlenecks, to standards, to the security of transactions, to the user-friendliness of consumer access devices became the subject of intensive research and new service offerings.[41]

In the process, the Internet shifted the time frame and the terms of the transition to freer trade and a more competitive communications marketplace. Instead of the carefully planned transition paths (envisioned in the 1997 WTO telecom commitments), carriers have been forced out of their protective monopoly enclaves ahead of schedule to compete in a much more chaotic marketplace than the one they had anticipated just a few years ago.[42]

The Internet, as a result, has done what trade negotiators and government officials could not—that is, turn the industry upside down and accelerate the shift to data services (the most open segment of the market), making it the industry hot spot. (See table 14.6.) On some international routes, the crossover point between data and voice had already been reached by the late 1990s. Between the United

Table 14.6
Worldwide explosion of new services

Category	Installed base, 1991 (million)	Installed base, 1996 (million)	Forecast installed base, 2001 (million)	CAGR, 1991–1996	CAGR, 1996–2001
Telephone main lines	545.0	741.1	1,000	6.3%	6.2%
Cellular subscribers	16.3	135.0	400	52.76%	24.3%
Personal computers	123.0	245.0	450	14.8%	12.9%
Internet host computers	0.7	16.1	110	85.8%	46.8%
Estimated Internet users	4.5	60	300	67.9%	38.0%

Source: International Telecommunication Union, *Challenges to the Network: Telecommunications and the Internet*, 1997.

States and Japan in 1996, for example, the volume of Internet traffic was greater than traditional voice and fax traffic.[43] It changes, in the words of former U.S. FCC chairman Reed Hundt, "everything about the way we communicate and all our government communication policies."[44] Some of the most basic definitions have been called into question such as when is a phone call not a phone call? Or, who is a phone company?[45]

By reducing the underlying cost of delivering service, increasing the range of service options, increasing the tradability of communications services, and enlarging the area of competition covered by liberalized trading rules, Internet advances opened the door to a more fundamental form of competition (domestic and international) than the competition that regulators and legislators have tied themselves in knots trying to foster (or limit).[46] It is more in the line of the Schumpterian form of competition that comes from new technology, new sources of supply, and new type of organization—"competition which commands a decisive cost or quality advantage that strikes not at the margins of the profits and the outputs of existing firms but at their foundation."[47]

Bypassing and Unraveling Restrictive Rules

The Internet furthermore confounds those that would like to draw lines around it and limit its growth. The first problem that regulators confront is that it has traditionally been treated as an enhanced service, the area already bound open to competition by multilateral trade agreements. Voice over the Net (even in the case of phone-to-phone services) has been treated as a value-added rather than a basic service.[48]

The Internet further highlights the growing importance of marketplace developments in setting the de facto rules of the game for the emerging trade environment. New technologies and actors are arising from areas that used to be considered peripheral to telecom (and often regulated with a lighter touch than voice services) to redefine both telecom and the broader trading arena before regulators have been able to react.[49] Major communications innovations used to emerge gradually, giving governments decades to develop the rules for incorporating them into the international system. But the information revolution and the arrival of the Internet have been equated with "going from horse and carriages to jet planes in less than a year." The formal rule-making revolution taking place in telecommunications via the WTO, by contrast, has taken more than ten years.[50]

The Internet's strength as a new communications medium also comes from its decentralized and packet-switched architecture, which make it much more difficult to monitor or block particular services. Instead of the hierarchical model of the traditional telecommunications industry, the Internet is based on a network of links between networks established on the basis of open standards and thousands of autonomous agents. This far more decentralized architecture makes it difficult, if not impossible, to contain its influence by national boundaries. The technical means for tracking and monitoring forms of Internet traffic will no doubt continue to improve, but the administrative cost will also increase, potentially making it more costly to trace and bill according to the path taken by a data packet than the total cost involved with sending the call.

Increasing Protection's Punishment

Technological advances are not only outstripping legislative mechanisms and making protection less effective, they are also changing the interests of government in maintaining that protection. For example, to get connected and capture some of the benefits made possible by the Internet, countries around the world are learning they must first break down the barriers to competition in both infrastructure and Internet access services.

Since much of the Internet runs over leased lines and the conventional phone network, if a country has high line rates and poor telecommunications facilities, it is also likely to have low rates of Internet use.[51] Many of the developing countries in particular have had to contend with telephone systems that are dominated by state-owned monopolies, dilapidated, and outrageously expensive. In the late 1990s, relatively few citizens had phones and even fewer had access to the Internet. In 1997 the continent of Africa, excluding South Africa, had fewer Internet hosts than Estonia. Although Asia experienced some of fastest Internet growth rates over the 1993–1996 period, it was still far behind the United States and much of Europe in penetration rates. Iceland, with its population of 250,000, in 1996 had more than four times as many Internet hosts per inhabitant than India with its population of 930 million. Indonesia was ranked only one step above India in multimedia access.

Such gaps increasingly matter to governments because the cost-saving potential of the Internet is exploding across a wide range of service and manufacturing industries. To those that are connected, the Internet offers unparalleled opportunities to cut cost, expand domestic service, and increase participation in the global market-place. Countries around the globe, as a result, are desperately trying to catch up.

14.4   Ahead of the Curve

Benefits of Going It Alone

Those who moved unilaterally to open their telecommunications markets to competition are ahead of the curve in the Internet revolution, reflecting a strong link between market liberalization, pricing reform, and Internet growth. In the OECD countries, for example, leased line rates in the monopoly markets fell between 1992 and 1994, but they were still 30 percent (56/64 kbits/s) or 46 percent (1.5/2 Mbits) more expensive than those in countries that permit competition in fixed network facilities.[52]

Higher leased line prices are important because they raise both the direct cost of connections to the Internet as well as the total cost of the underlying infrastructure. When Internet access providers are forced to pay steep charges to the public telecommunications operator (PTO), they pass those charges onto business and residential users. In 1995, dial-up Internet access was three times more expensive in monopoly markets. In those OECD countries that permit competition in infrastructure services, the penetration of Internet hosts is five times greater than in those countries with a monopoly provider. (See figure 14.1.) When the rate of growth is compared, weighted by the time since Internet service started, Internet access in OECD countries with infrastructure competition has also grown six times faster than monopoly markets.[53]

The Internet's development thus highlights some of the gains from moving on your own to promote competition rather than waiting for others to do the same. Beyond the Internet, the dynamic gains include the introduction of new services, increased productivity, and accelerated infrastructure development.[54] For all the OECD economies, most of the performance indicators (the pricing of services, network development, and industry efficiency) suggest that increased

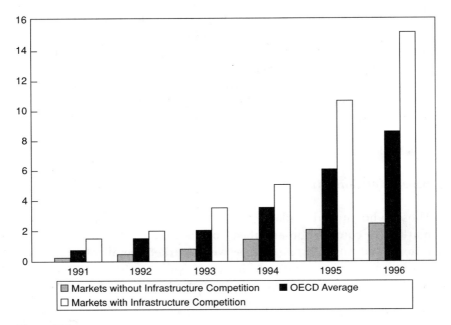

Figure 14.1
Impact of competition: Internet hosts per 1,000 inhabitants
Source: OECD, "Information Infrastructure Convergence and Pricing: The Internet" (Mar. 1996).

market entry generated significant benefits. Competition increased the depth and size of the telecommunications market while offsetting declines in the market share of incumbent firms. Productivity increased in terms of lines per staff as well as revenue per staff.

In terms of individual countries, the U.S. experience demonstrates both the benefits of competition and the dynamic impact that market liberalization has in generating pressure for reform elsewhere in the system.[55] U.S. long-distance telecommunications firms, for example, were forced to become more efficient and quicker to market with innovative products and services. They in turn became some of the most sought after partners for international business alliances in large part because of their experience with competition.

By becoming an early mover in its permissive use of leased lines and private networks, the United States also became a center of innovative activity and a test bed for advanced communications services. American telecommunications firms pioneered many of the popular alternative calling procedures and have been at the center of the Internet revolution. They have provided much of the infrastructure (in 1997 almost every byte of Internet traffic between continents passed through the United States), made cyberspace more user-friendly, and pushed (along with Israeli firms) the envelope with service innovations such as Voice over the Net.

The benefits of competition are further reflected in the experience of the Scandinavian carriers, which have thrived in a tough market-oriented environment. Sweden was the first European country outside the United Kingdom to open its telecommunications industry. It opened cellular services in 1981 and then started opening fixed-line telephony at the end of the 1980s. Since deregulation in 1993, the Swedish telecommunications market has grown at a 10 percent annual rate—three times faster than the pre-deregulation rate.[56]

Among the Nordic countries, the experience of Finland provides a particularly strong demonstration of the dynamic benefits (innovation and new services) of competition, particularly in local services. The benefits include high ownership of mobile phones (4 for every 10 inhabitants), the world's highest rate of Internet penetration, more public phones per capita than the rest of Europe, the second lowest business call charges in the OECD after Iceland, and the fifth lowest residential charges after the other four Nordic countries (Iceland, Norway, Sweden, and Denmark). Telecom Finland has also demonstrated that it is possible to survive and thrive in an open market. In 1994, when the long-distance market was opened, Telecom Finland lost half its market share in its core long-distance phone business. But since then the carrier has registered higher profits as it has been forced to develop a new range of services, in particular cutting-edge Internet and wireless services.[57]

In Latin America, Chile was the first to start the market liberalization process. The legal framework for the reforms was put into place in 1987 when the state-owned monopoly operator responsible for long-distance and international service (Entel) was privatized, which included substantial foreign investor participation.[58] Although the reforms did not result in a full liberalization of the sector, they still played a key role in revitalizing it. In the first three years after the reforms, the annual growth of new lines increased from 5 percent to 20 percent, access to phone service doubled, and the waiting list fell from ten years to one. Labor productivity improved to 7 staff per 1,000 lines (comparable to industrialized countries) from 13 per 1,000 lines. Consumers, according to World Bank studies, captured the largest increases in domestic welfare, resulting primarily from accelerated investment in infrastructure, increased teledensity, and the introduction of new services.[59] After the long-distance market was opened to competition in 1994, prices plummeted and consumer welfare increased by $120 million in 1995 alone.[60] Chile also had the highest rate of Internet use in the region with penetration rates twice that of Brazil and three times higher than Argentina.[61]

In terms of market segments, those most open to competition have been growing the fastest. In international services, the countries that permitted direct competition have achieved higher rates of growth than countries that retained monopolies in the 1990s. (See figure 14.2.) Developed countries that permitted competition experienced annual growth rates of 9.3 percent in traffic per subscriber compared to the 5.6 percent experienced in other countries. In emerging economies, those with competition achieved growth rates of 11.7 percent compared to the 5.2 percent of those providing services under monopoly conditions.[62]

The mobile telephone market, which is far more open than fixed line services, has become one of the industry's fastest growing segments. Within region and income groups, the growth in mobile telecommunications subscribers has also not been uniform across countries. The available evidence suggests that on average business and residential customers pay lower rates in open markets in the OECD, which are growing three times as fast as monopoly markets. The developing countries with the largest number of new operators have also been the ones with the highest rates of diffusion and cellular substitution.[63]

It should also be noted that when the United States promoted competition at home, it helped open foreign markets as well. This was not the result of U.S. reciprocity demands but rather market forces operating in downstream industries and international markets. Even groups that criticized unilateral liberalization as unilateral disarmament and an irrational sacrifice of bargaining chips have been forced to concede the power of market forces. "The sole impetus for telecommunications liberalization in most countries," one report notes, "originates from foreign business fearing that their firms will be less competitive relative to U.S. firms as a result of a less liberalized domestic telecommunications market."[64]

Downstream American users in the corporate community benefited in particular from prices for long-distance and private com-

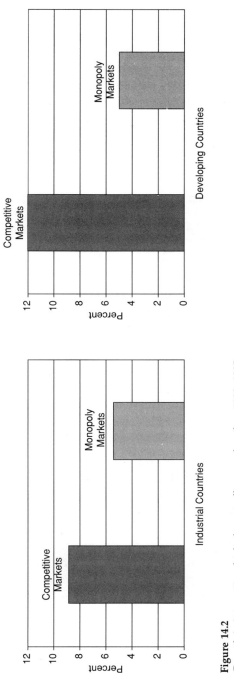

Figure 14.2
Growth in international telephone traffic per subscriber, 1990–1995
Source: World Bank, *Global Economic Prospects and Developing Countries* (1997).

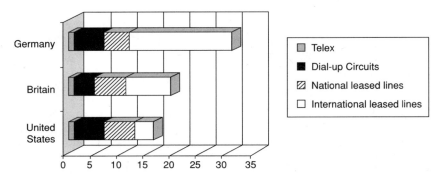

Figure 14.3
Competition pays: Telecommunications costs (as percentage of business turnover) of a sample financial services company
Source: PA Consulting.

munications data services that were significantly lower than those facing their rivals laboring under more restrictive regimes. In Latin America, users have been forced to pay up to five times as much to call the United States as compared to calls that originate in the United States. In Germany prior to liberalization, the cost of key telecommunications services such as high-speed leased lines was five times as high as in the United States and twice as high as in Britain. (See figure 14.3.)

Catching Up

To catch up to the early reformers and improve their competitive position, almost every industrialized nation by the early 1990s had begun a comprehensive review of its telecommunications policies to make their markets more attractive to international network users. And in a radical shift from the state-owned monopoly world of the 1980s, when privatization was viewed as a strange British experiment, the European Union (EU) targeted national monopolies for elimination.[65] The EU, driven by a desire to boost the efficiency of Europe's infrastructure and its competitive position relative to the United States and the Far East, passed in particular a series of directives requiring member countries to open.

In developing countries, the factors driving liberalization in the industrialized countries have been amplified by two factors: the low teledensity rates and infrastructure demands. In the late 1990s, more than 50 percent of the world's population had never made a phone call. The access when available was often of low quality. Upgrading and expanding the telecommunications networks accordingly presented a vast financial challenge for developing countries. More than $60 billion a year, according to the World Bank, was needed just to implement basic service plans.

The needs far exceeded the capabilities of national governments, domestic firms, and capital pools.[66] In India, the situation is particularly challenging: Infrastructure needs in the power, transportation, and communications sectors may exceed capabilities by up to 50 percent what the country alone can realistically afford.[67] India is also not an isolated case. To cope with the sheer volume of infrastructure investment required for upgrading their networks, nations have been turning in increasing numbers to foreign investors for help. Foreign investment, as a result, became the single most important source of external financing for developing countries in the late 1990s.

In telecommunications, between 1984 and 1996, forty-four public telecommunications operators (PTOs) were privatized and from one-third to two-thirds of the investment came from outside the home country of the privatized operator. In 1996, foreign investment accounted for roughly 45 percent of the $22 billion raised in PTO privatizations.[68] Foreign investors have also been courted for their particular expertise in new communications technologies that will let developing countries leapfrog past traditional development cycles. Cellular communications in Latin America, for example, has been aggressively promoted to improve the region's low teledensity rates and cut the cost of development.

Barriers to trade in communications services and monopolies (private as well as public) clearly still exist and will continue to do so for some time. But, the price of sustaining them and the pressure to eliminate them is rapidly rising. Countries like Argentina have paid a high price for dragging their feet. Argentina replaced its public monopoly with the private monopolies of Telefonica, Telecom (local and long distance), and Telintar (international long distance), which were protected from competition by regulation. But, the monopolies kept rates high, curtailed Internet access, dragged down economic growth, and cost the Argentine economy the full benefits of a sophisticated, efficient telecommunications system.[69]

In India, frustrations over the information-technology gap led to a rising chorus of demands from the business community for a

more competitive telecommunications infrastructure and relaxing
of market access conditions. Thanks to its restrictive regulations, for
example, India has had some of the highest leased line and Internet
access rates in the world. Then in September 1997, after a barrage of
criticism from users, the government eliminated the state-controlled
operator's (VSNL) monopoly on Internet access, waived license fees
for new ISPs for five years, promised to provide new ISP "bandwidth without delay," and directed VSNL to upgrade its data communications facilities. ISPs have also been given permission to use
the surplus communications capacity owned by the country's railways network and to "have access to multiple gateways for international connections, if necessary." The government also said it would
allow foreign firms to take stakes of up to 49 percent in private
ISPs.[70] The primary force behind the shift toward liberalization was
fear that the competitive position and aspirations of major Indian
industries would be severely curtailed unless the underlying communications infrastructure was rapidly and radically improved.[71]

The decisions represent just the tip of what needs to be done to
open telecommunications markets to trade and competition. But, they
reflect the growing strength of internal forces that favor increased
competition and more open markets. By making the cost of protective
regulations more tangible (in terms of foregone benefits) and increasing the range of domestic interest groups with a stake in eliminating
unnecessarily burdensome restrictions, the Internet has created a formidable force for liberalization that few could have imagined just a
few years ago.

14.5   Slowing the Top Down

On the flip side, just as the Internet has accelerated the push for reform from the bottom up, the limits of reciprocity-induced and top-
down liberalization have become more apparent.

The Short Arm of Slow-Moving Regulators

Part of the problem in telecommunications is that reciprocity-
induced liberalization depends on government levers and regulation
to speed competition and secure "effective," "timely," "cost-oriented"
market access. The incremental and progressive nature of the WTO
liberalization process and the excruciatingly slow pace of deregulation highlight, however, the limits of topdown directed change in

fast-moving industries. At the national level, regulatory reforms have often been spread out over many years for hearings and reconsideration, thereby providing ample grounds for practically indefinite delays if any of the parties find them to be in their interest. Even before the dynamics and distractions of the trade arena were added, regulatory processes have been slow to change (akin to turning a tanker around).

"Telecommunications is the fastest moving industry," lamented the outgoing head of Hong Kong's regulatory authority, "with the slowest moving regulators."[72] Refining the official rule-making process can take ten years or more, even for those countries considered to be far advanced in the liberalization process (1996 U.S. Telecommunications Act). That experience contrasts sharply with the 6- to 18-month technology cycles and the rapid development of the Internet. An industry rule of thumb is that one human year is equal to about five Internet years. Bureaucratic inertia and regulatory overload pose particular problems for Asian telecommunications authorities, who have become entangled by the design and implementation of "master plans" for restructuring telecommunications markets. New market developments keep pushing the plans back while the political challenge of the enabling legislation and recent financial crisis has further impeded progress.

For its part, the United States has convincingly demonstrated how a nation's legal culture and institutions can further impair reform efforts even after sweeping legislation has been passed. The outgoing FCC chairman Reed Hundt bemoaned in August 1997, for example, "the harsh desert" of America's legal culture—"with its thousand devices of tortuous delay and questioning of every phrase, word, and punctuation mark of the 1996 Telecommunications Act"—that encourages "unceasing argument and ineffective delay-ridden decision making."[73]

Given the nature of these institutional and cultural hurdles already complicating the transition to freer markets, it hardly seems reasonable to expect reciprocity demands in a sector-specific trade negotiation to speed the transition to freer trade and competition in other countries through the process of regulatory reform.

Reciprocity and Services

A second problem for reciprocity-induced liberalization in the new trade arena is that defining and achieving reciprocity is much more difficult in services than in the case of traded goods under the GATT. The intangible nature of trade in services, which often takes place electronically, makes it more difficult to monitor or measure trade as easily measured as trade in goods. In contrast to tariffs at the borders for goods, many of the barriers to trade in telecommunications (and other services) are also embedded in diverse, domestic regulatory institutions and business practices that are inherently more difficult to quantify.

A related problem is that the regulations that impact trade are also often tied to legitimate social objectives. The appropriate course of action for removing the trade barrier, as a result, is not as clear as the removal of a tariff or quota. It may not simply be the removal of the regulation. A third major problem is that the regulatory and technical complexity of the trade issues have led to sector-specific negotiations, which has in turn limited the cross-issue linkages and trade-offs that could help increase political support, particularly in developing countries, for binding liberalization moves under the WTO. Together these changes in the trade-negotiating environment have made it much more difficult to both define reciprocity and achieve it in practice in multilateral trade negotiations.

U.S.-specific reciprocity demands, particularly in the WTO telecommunications negotiations, furthermore compounded the problem by first slowing the liberalization process in the United States and then detracting from the willingness of other countries to anchor their liberalization measures in their WTO commitments. Instead of strengthening WTO commitments, U.S. reciprocity demands (particularly in the area of foreign investment) helped weaken them as other countries moved to preserve bargaining chips for future trade negotiations.

U.S. Reciprocity-Induced Delays: Setting a Bad Example

In February 1996, the United States passed the landmark Telecommunications Act, which promised to sweep away six decades of communications law and promote vigorous competition in all areas of telecommunications. But, despite this 300-page "revolution" in rule making, the remaining restrictions on foreign ownership in telecommunications were left largely untouched.[74] Congress opted instead for minor changes, repealing only a provision that had restricted the ability of foreigners to serve as officers or directors in U.S. firms with a radio license. Those in favor of the other restrictions argued that dropping them would be a foolish act of unilateral disarmament, which would sacrifice key bargaining chips needed to pry open foreign markets.[75]

This demand for reciprocity was also reflected in the November 1995 decision of the U.S. Federal Communications Commission to adopt a specific reciprocity approach to the regulation of foreign carrier entry. The FCC adopted in particular a market access test that made its waiver of restrictions on foreign carrier participation conditional on the availability of "effective competitive opportunities" (ECO) for U.S. carriers in that carrier's home market.

The ECO test took a national security provision (Section 310(b)(4)) and turned it into a trade statute in an effort "to encourage foreign governments to open their telecommunications markets" to U.S. participation and investment. Under the ECO test, absent other public interest factors, the FCC conditioned its waiver of the 25 percent indirect foreign ownership restriction on a demonstration that the home market (principle place of business) provided "effective competitive opportunities" (ECO) to U.S. telecommunications firms.[76] The ECO test also promoted the specific reciprocity principle that a foreign ownership interest in a U.S. market should be limited to the extent that American firms can take an equity stake in the same market segment in the home country of the parent firm.

The moves of the FCC into the trade arena over the 1995–1997 period contrasts with its prior reluctance to use its regulatory authority as a trade tool. In 1980, for example, the FCC rejected foreign ownership restrictions on cable operators as a means of prying open foreign markets to U.S. investment, concluding that it lacked the "responsibility for investment policy with respect to communications in foreign countries." The FCC continued, "We do not believe a desire for reciprocity in international investment policies by itself provides an adequate basis for action on our part. Nor are we, in any case, in a position to know if such a policy on our part would have the result intended or if, to the contrary, it would lead to increasing trade barriers in other areas."[77] Yet, by November 1995, the FCC had been pulled so far into the trade debate that it suggested the United States "hold foreign carriers accountable for the policies of their home governments" in an effort "to ensure that U.S. investors have similar opportunities to compete in foreign markets."[78]

The shift at the FCC reflected the larger shift in U.S. trade policy toward the use of sector-specific reciprocity measures that linked the relaxation of market access restrictions to foreign liberalization. The argument was that unilateral liberalization eliminates the incentive of foreign governments to open their markets. But such logic, particularly in telecommunications, underestimates the power of the other technology, market, and institutional forces at work while overestimating the trade leverage of the United States and the ability of trade policy to speed the pace of reform in other countries. Meanwhile at home, the ECO test delayed the market-opening process by making trade considerations a legitimate "public interest" concern that could outweigh any procompetitive benefits associated with entry and operation of a foreign carrier in the United States.[79]

By holding onto foreign investment restrictions and the ECO test over the 1995–1997 period, the United States in particular demonstrated its willingness to do good for U.S. consumers only if other countries did the same for their consumers. By not moving unilaterally to complete the liberalization process and relax its foreign ownership restrictions, the United States demonstrated that it would sacrifice significant public-interest benefits, delay the domestic transition to more competitive markets (especially in outbound international services), curtail investment in U.S. infrastructure, and limit the flow of much-needed capital to new entrants.[80] U.S. reciprocity tests, as a result, helped shelter U.S. carriers from effective competition and curtail the ability of U.S. firms to enter new markets. The Section 310(b) foreign investment restrictions in particular disadvantaged those U.S. firms that were more dependent on foreign equity links for their development strategies or did not have the legal resources and expertise to navigate the FCC's review process.

Problems at the Bargaining Table

Given the high profile of U.S.-specific reciprocity demands (such as the ECO test) during the WTO negotiations, some may be tempted to conclude that those demands accelerated the liberalization pace and strengthened the WTO commitments. But, just the opposite occurred. The unprecedented liberalization wave discussed earlier testifies to the power of the other forces driving the communications revolution from the bottom up. In addition, the response of countries to these pressures has tended to be shaped more by local political-economic concerns than U.S. reciprocity demands. The countries that have significantly liberalized their markets have done so unilaterally.

Hoarding Bargaining Chips

On the flip side, despite U.S. demands for reciprocal market-opening measures, most of the Asian countries held out and scheduled weak commitments on basic telecommunications services. (See table 14.6.) In addition, despite intense U.S. demands that its major trading partners match its offer to permit 100 percent indirect foreign investment with commitments to permit majority control, both Canada and Japan refused to budge during the negotiations. Canada reserved its right to maintain its 46.7 percent limit on foreign ownership, and Japan did the same with its 20 percent limit on foreign investment in NTT and KDD.[81]

U.S. reciprocity demands thus had the perverse effect of limiting, rather than expanding, WTO liberalization commitments by convincing other countries that they should follow the U.S. example and hoard bargaining chips. India, in particular, seemed to define success at the WTO by how much it held its ground against U.S. demands. India was more open in practice than its 1997 WTO commitments suggested. It committed only to permitting foreign investment up to 25 percent although national policy since 1994 permits foreign equity up to 74 percent in telecommunications ventures.[82] The commitments of Chile, France, Korea, and Japan also reflect the decision of government officials to withhold liberalization commitments in order to preserve bargaining chips for future negotiations. Chile, for example, even though competition was increasing in local service, did not bind open local services. Chile thus was more open in practice than on paper—in terms of their WTO commitments. As a result, Chile has a bargaining chip for future negotiations. There was also some evidence that U.S. reciprocity demands in the WTO financial service negotiations sparked significant resentment that spilled over to the telecommunications negotiations, where countries took advantage of the opportunity to frustrate the United States by limiting their scheduled commitments to less than the status quo. Reciprocity demands in this case thus detracted from liberalization by weakening the set of WTO commitments.

Strengthening Resistance to Liberalization

History further suggests that, in an atmosphere of distrust, countries may refuse to "be encouraged" on the liberalization path and may decide to drag their feet instead. Free traders in Britain in the late 1800s, for example, came to the conclusion that insisting on reciprocal market-opening moves only made their task of opening markets more difficult. They found that so much suspicion existed regarding their motives that their free trade demands were being used by foreign protectionist interests to incite popular unrest with claims that the English sought to prostitute the domestic industries. To take away this pretense, the Anti-Corn Law League emphasized the British gain from a free trade policy but did not insist that foreign governments come to the same conclusion.[83]

In more recent times, Malaysia has been one of the countries most resistant and suspicious of U.S. efforts to open up telecommunications and information technology markets to competition. Yet, particularly in the case of tariff reductions on information goods under the WTO's Information Technology Agreement (ITA), Malaysia is one of the Asian countries that has the most to gain from liberalization. It is one of the world's largest exporters of computer chips and disk drives. But, with Prime Minister's Mahathir Mohamad's innate distrust of anything proposed by the West, Malaysia initially dug in whenever the United States tried to apply market-opening pressure.

India's experience further highlights the limits of reciprocity-induced liberalization. In 1991 Prime Minister P. V. Narasimha officially opened India's door wider to trade and private foreign capital. But the decision to start the privatization of the state-owned international telecommunications operator, VSNL, was repeatedly delayed until April 1997 due to shifting political winds, which exploited a tendency to distrust markets and foreign firms. In particular, as the fall 1996 elections approached, the left-wing opposition parties attacked Prime Minister Narasimha Rao's government for letting MNCs and foreign investors compromise India's self-reliance. At the other extreme, the Hindu nationalist party advanced a commitment to homegrown industries (or *swadeshi*). When the Congress party government of Prime Minister Rao was defeated in the 1996 election, disagreements about the appropriate treatment of foreign investment broke out in the thirteen-party coalition that formed the next two governments. The instability of the coalition has created opportunities for other parties to gain political points by appealing to nationalistic sentiments again.[84]

Given the context of India's institutional arrangements and the political dynamics of the reform process, there was little that U.S. reciprocity demands, particularly in sector-specific negotiations, could do to speed up the transition. Instead, U.S. reciprocity demands compounded the problem by engendering more ill will than they were worth (uniting the opposition, for example, against the foreigners).

During the WTO negotiations on basic telecommunications services, many of the Asian countries were concerned that liberalization would mean Americanization. Telecommunications liberalization commitments at the WTO were viewed as a one-way street that would primarily benefit giant U.S. companies since most of the Asian companies were not big enough to compete in the United States or Europe. Many could, however, still gain from increased access to smaller markets in their region or Africa. But, the sector-specific nature of the negotiations combined with the United States as the primary demandeur aggravated negotiator concerns about domestic perceptions of lopsided concessions that favored the United States.

Many of the Asian countries questioned in particular what they would be able to show for their market-opening concessions because they did not have carriers actively seeking to participate in the U.S. market. In addition, while demanding significant reductions from other countries and portraying itself as the gold standard of a high-quality offer, the United States retained a 20 percent limit on direct foreign investment and significant regulatory discretion to condition foreign carrier access. These factors together bred significant resistance and resentment of U.S. demands that will come back to haunt the United States in future negotiations, much like the financial services did in telecommunications.

Section 310(b): A Cracked Crowbar

Aside from these limits, the specifics of the ECO tests and Section 310(b) created additional problems for U.S. negotiators looking for more leverage at the negotiating table. A study commissioned by AT&T during the WTO negotiations concluded that "without a credible threat, the U.S. would have no bargaining leverage."[85] But, for the threat to be credible, it must be relevant and the foreign government must believe that the United States has the will and the capability to follow through: Foreign governments must expect that their firms will be denied entry or restricted from expanding their U.S. telecommunications operations *unless* they fulfill the market-opening conditions demanded by the United States. To the extent that these conditions are negotiable, the threat is less credible.

Yet, this was precisely the problem with Section 310(b) and its assigned trade role during the WTO telecommunications negotiations. The FCC made it quite clear in November 1995 that the ECO guidelines would be applied on a case-by-case basis with no general commitment to the reciprocity test as the determining factor in the analysis. Instead, the ECO test was listed as only one of many factors that would be considered as part of the FCC's public-interest review. Even if the ECO conditions were not met, an investment could still be permitted. Or, on the flip side, if the ECO test was satisfied, a foreign investment could still be denied. Given the FCC's discretion to accept or reject a petition for a 310(b) waiver irrespective of the results of the ECO test, it hardly seems rational to attribute any major change in government policy or the WTO negotiations to the U.S. reciprocity test.

Section 310(b)'s credibility problem as a trade tool was further accentuated by the nature of the instrument. On the one hand, some telecommunications experts have argued that foreign governments have exaggerated the importance of Section 310(b) restrictions as an investment barrier because it really is only "a mole hill" that can easily be circumvented.[86] But, how can a mole hill be a credible threat that gives U.S. negotiators significant new leverage at the bargaining table? If the Section 310(b) restriction did not significantly impair the access of foreign telecommunications firms to the United States, how could it also be a significant bargaining chip? U.S. leverage at the negotiating table was also limited because it was not offering its trading partners a clean slate, that is, 100 percent direct foreign ownership. Instead, under Section 310(b) and the FCC authority to waive the 25 percent limit, the United States offered only 100 percent indirect foreign ownership. France and Korea, as a result, kept their 20 percent limits on direct foreign ownership.

An even more important problem for Section 310(b) in its role as a trade tool was that it was not commercially relevant to countries that the United States was trying to pry open in telecommunications. Countries such as India or Malaysia, for example, did not have firms operating in the United States.

Threats of Emulation

Section 310(b) restriction on foreign ownership, as a result, did not add much to the United States' negotiating hand. But the decision to use it as a trade tool and delay liberalization at home may come back to haunt the United States in future negotiations.

Some, for example, may follow the U.S. lead and keep in place foreign investment restrictions until they are compelled by their WTO commitments to remove them. Or they may be unwilling to schedule commitments under the WTO until they receive market access concessions. Developing countries are, for example, demanding with increasing force and frequency concessions that share the political burden for binding their market-opening moves in a multilateral trade agreement.

In implementing existing WTO commitments, some may also follow the U.S. lead and preserve considerable regulatory discretion over foreign entry as the FCC did it its November 1997 *Foreign Carrier Order*. The European Union has already criticized the United States for reserving the authority to restrict foreign operations in order to protect the "public interest," which leaves ample room for protectionist mischief. Other countries, for example, may imitate the United States, as in the case of the antidumping laws, and adopt their own broadly defined "public-interest" tests that permit the licensing of a foreign service provider to be determined on the basis of undefined "other trade factors."[87] By 1997 telecommunications already showed some signs that public-interest tests and safeguards were poised to become a significant trade barrier and source of trade tension in the years ahead.[88] This problem was swept under the rug during the WTO negotiations because there was not time to address it. It was also not the best forum. Over the next few years, WTO members will need to discuss at a technical level, in a less politically charged environment, the factors for determining when a public-interest test is more burdensome than necessary and an unwarranted distortion of trade.

If public-interest tests proliferate that are not administered as judiciously as the FCC intended in telecommunications, the United States may not be the one gaining leverage at the negotiating table over the longer term. With over 40 percent of the world's multinational corporations headquartered in the United States, which is the leading supplier of foreign direct investment, the United States is particularly vulnerable to the harassment tactics of foreign governments.[89] Any regulatory cross fire of thinly disguised discriminatory investment measures would tend to cut against the interests of multinational firms in reducing the fragmentation of the global information infrastructure.

Another threat is that U.S. trading partners may emulate U.S. trade negotiating tactics in future service negotiations and "hold foreign investors accountable for the policies of their home governments" that they deem to be unfair. Another challenge may arise from a different direction if other countries find it useful to emulate the United States and twist national security provisions to restrict market access and foreign investment for commercial reasons. The use of Section 310(b) foreign investment restrictions as a trade tool put the United States on the slippery slope of advocating "Do as I say, not as I do."

14.6 Hayek's Triumph

Taken together, the various barriers and limits of reciprocity-induced liberalization suggest trade officials will be forced to rely more on the private sector and unregulated forces for the transition to freer trade and competition. With digital advances rapidly altering the boundary lines between industries and nations, "no country in the world," acknowledges Indonesia's telecommunications minister Joop Ave, "has the capability and regulatory skills to keep up with technological change."

Given the vast political-economic and regulatory complexities involved with designing and implementing government plans and trade treaties for removing the barriers to competition in communications services, there seems little cause to believe that they will open telecommunications markets to competition faster than the forces embodied in the Internet revolution. Indeed, the radically different speeds at which the top-down and bottom-up revolutions are unfolding in telecommunications have raised anew the age-old question about the ability of government (particularly multilateral) institutions to keep pace with the problems demanding a solution.

Nobel Laureate Herbert Simon captured the essence of the restraint facing governments and regulators worldwide. "The capacity of the human mind for formulating and solving complex problems," such as the appropriate transition path from monopoly to competition, Simon notes, "is very small compared with the size of the problems whose solution is required."[90] Add the legal and economic issues (such as setting cost-oriented prices) that are far from straightforward, the dynamics of multilateral trade negotiations, and the political-economic challenges involved with using regulation to open centuries-old monopolies, and the complexity of the decision problem increases exponentially.

The missed deadlines and the incremental nature of the telecommunications liberalization process under the WTO reflect, for example, the limits of the process. They reflect the inherent complexity and difficulty of using the collective bargaining process to secure a multilateral agreement on internal issues such as foreign investment and national regulatory principles that have long been the responsibility of sovereign states. On the flip side, the rapid rise of the Internet as a communications medium and platform for trade signals the rising importance of forces outside the regulatory process in driving and shaping the evolution of the communications revolution. The Internet, in the words of Hayek, seems to be "far outstripping the plans men consciously contrive" to increase competition and free trade.

14.7   Net Implications for the WTO

Although the WTO is not an organization for the impatient, it still has an important role in promoting and securing some of the liberalization advances fueled by the other (technological, economic, and political) revolutions taking place. But, it cannot move beyond what individual countries are willing to accept. In telecomm, reciprocity demands (especially those perceived to be unfair) detracted from what individual countries were willing to accept and bind in their scheduled commitments. The sector-specific nature of the negotiations aggravated the problem because it limited the cross-issue linkages that may otherwise have helped a country generate the internal political support for making stronger liberalization commitments under the WTO.

Many have pointed to the successful conclusion of the WTO telecommunications negotiations as evidence that concerns about sector-specific negotiations are misplaced. But telecommunications is a special case. The infrastructure role of telecommunications in trade and the information economy, the underlying revolution in communication technologies, and the shift in attitudes that favored liberalization all helped overcome the limits of sector-specific negotiations. In other service negotiations, where the impact of the bottom-up revolution is weaker, developing countries may be less forthcoming if the negotiating context is sector-specific or the agenda is too narrowly focused to permit a greater trading of commitments across sectors.

This is important because the WTO plays a unique role in promoting infrastructure investment and liberalization over the long term. For example, to attract the long-term investments needed to upgrade the telecommunications infrastructure, developing countries need a predictable and reliable set of rules. If there is not a credible commitment that the capital assets or generated returns will not be expropriated once the infrastructure is deployed, for example, the investment (domestic or foreign) in non-redeployable assets may not take place. Vague and shifting regulations governing taxation and commerce can, as a result, be a significant deterrent to infrastructure investment.

Countries with unstable or weak political institutions have had a hard time breaking this cycle. In this case, governments acting alone often face significant pressure to overturn prior commitments to investment projects because of short-term budget difficulties or the complaints of disadvantaged groups on which officials rely for support. There has also been a tendency to direct investment not to infrastructure but rather to the hiring of additional workers who can then be used as a base for lobbying within the government for additional fiscal support for the communications ministry.

As a result, many developing countries on their own confront the dilemma of needing both more investment (domestic and foreign) and strong, credible political commitments to secure it. The WTO can help countries out of this dilemma by increasing the cost of overturning a prior liberalization decision. The threat of trade sanctions under the WTO in many cases may carry more weight than a complaint filed with a ministry that has ties to the local monopoly carrier.

The WTO thus offers developing countries, independent of any market access concessions from the other side of the bargaining table, a significant opportunity to increase the credibility of their liberalization programs and thereby gain more from the communications revolution taking place. Reciprocity demands, especially in sector-specific negotiations, only confuse the issue.

In telecomm in particular, the argument for specific reciprocity clouded the debate by implying that those who do not open their markets gain at the expense of those who do. This is clearly not true from the perspective of telecommunications users, which includes businesses whose ability to compete is impaired by poor service and inflated costs. Such zero-sum logic (let them in only to the extent they let you in) furthermore conflicts with the U.S. experience in telecommunications and the Internet. As for the impact on foreign governments, the bottom-up forces at work such as the Internet have proven to be a far more potent force in persuading countries to open their markets. With the emergence of a global information economy, there is also no such thing as a free ride anymore. Those countries that choose to hold onto their restrictions in telecom risk falling further behind the curve with the burden of underdeveloped infrastructures.

Notes

This chapter was completed in February 1998. Its focus is mainly, though not exclusively, on the thesis that rapid technological change led to liberalization in the telecommunications sector, not reciprocity.

1. Paul Lewis, "Is the U.S. Souring on Free Trade?" *New York Times,* June 25, 1996, D1.

2. Charges are based on the balance of minutes on a route, as opposed to all the minutes delivered. There is rising pressure, however, to abandon the accounting rate system in favor of a system based on call termination charges that would be set separately (rather than jointly) by operators based on all the minutes delivered. Among others, see Tim Kelly, "Is There Life for the Accounting Rate System," *Telegeography 1997/98: Global Telecommunications Traffic Statistics and Commentary,* October 1997, 33–38.

3. For a useful analysis of the accounting rate system and its inconsistencies with a multilateral trading system, see Leonard Waverman, "The Options for Reforming International Tariffs and Settlement Procedures: The Need for Multilateralism," paper presented at *Financial Times* World Telecommunications conference, London, December 5, 1991; see also Henry Ergas, "International Trade in Telecommunication Services: An Economic Perspective," in *Unfinished Business: Telecommunications After the Uruguay Round* (Washington, DC: The Institute for International Economics, January 1998), 89–106; L. Johnson, "Dealing With Monopoly in International Telephone Service: A U.S. Perspective," *Information Economics and Policy* 4 (1989): 225–247.

4. GATT secretariat note, MTN.GNS/W/52, May 19, 1989. See also Geza Feketekuty, "Why Telecommunications Has Become a Trade Issue," paper presented at *Financial Times* World Telecommunications Conference, London, December 1, 1986; R. Brian Woodrow, *Global Services and Trade Liberalization: Implications for International Business and Major Service Sectors,* The First Geneva International Forum on Global Services and Trade Liberalization, Applied Service Economic Center (ASEC), Geneva, May 16, 1990; R. Bruce, "International Trade in Telecommunications Services," paper presented at Emerging International Telecommunication Regimes, McGill University/University of Vermont, Montreal, October 15–17, 1989; and R. Brian Woodrow, "Telecom and Trade in Services—Never the Twain Shall Meet," *Transnational Data and Communications Report* (April 1990): 17–24.

5. The FCC through a series of computer inquiry decisions, for example, made a distinction between basic and enhanced (any offering over telecommunications network that is more than a basic transmission service). The FCC then exempted from regulation all enhanced services offered over common carrier transmission facilities used in interstate communications that employ computer-processing applications that act on format, content, code, protocol, or similar aspects of the subscriber's transmitted information; provide additional different or restructured information; or involve subscriber interaction with stored information.

6. On the importance of the enhanced and basic service regulatory distinction in building the WTO framework, see Robert R. Bruce, Jeffrey Cunnard, and Mark Director, *From Telecommunications to Electronic Services: A Global Spectrum of Definitions, Boundary Lines, and Structures,* International Institute for Communications (London: Butterworth, 1986); Geza Feketekuty, U.S. Counselor to the U.S. Trade Representative, "The New World Information Economy and the New Trade Dimension in Telecommunications Policy," 1989; G. Russel Pipes, "Telecommunications," in *The Uruguay Round: Services Papers on Selected Issues* (New York: UNCTAD/ITP/10, 1989), 105–113, and as G. Russel Pipe, "Telecommunication Services: Considerations for Developing Countries in Uruguay Round Negotiations," *Trade in Services: Sectoral Issues, UNCTC,* (New York: United Nations, 1989), 49–112.

7. Pekka Tarjanne, secretary general of the International Telecommunications Union (ITU), as reported by James Kynge, "Telecom Groups Look to Wider Ventures," *Financial Times,* June 10, 1997.

8. Scott Blake Harris, "Smile—The Revolution's Gathering Pace," *Communications Week International,* February 3, 1997.

9. Privatization refers only to a change in the ownership of a telecommunications entity and therefore does not necessarily imply deregulation (increase domestic competition) or liberalization. But, with the range of forces at work and other changes accompanying the wave of privatizations in the mid-1990s, there appears to be a growing consensus that they reflect a shift toward deregulation and liberalization. United Nations, *World Investment Report 1997: Transnational Corporations, Market Structure, and Competition Policy,* (New York: United Nations, 1997), 18–20; United Nations, *World Investment Report 1996: Investment, Trade, and International Policy Arrangements* (New York: United Nations, 1996), 25.

10. Under the U.N. Central Product Classification (CPC) codes, enhanced telecommunications services have been included in 7,523 (electronic mail, voice mail, online information, and database retrieval, electronic data interchange (EDI), enhanced/value added facsimile services (including store and forward, store and retrieve)) and 843 (online information and/or data processing (including transaction processing)). Under the GATS, enhanced services have also included code and protocol conversion, for which there is no CPC code. For more on enhanced services and international commitments, see International Trade Commission, *General Agreement on Trade in Services: Examination of the Schedules of Commitments Submitted by Asia/Pacific Trading Partners,* publication 3053, August 1997, 5–3.

11. Covered services are those in which a nation has scheduled liberalization commitments such as financial services. For background on the Telecommunications Annex that was modeled in part on the annex in the U.S.-Canada Free Trade Agreement, see Daniel Rosen, *Towards a New International Framework For Telecommunications and Information Services: Issues and Prospects,* Institute for Research on Public Policy, April 1988. For an analysis of the GATS Telecommunications Annex, see Lee Tuthill, "Users' Rights," *Telecommunications Policy* 20, no. 2 (1996): 89–99; and Tuthill, "The GATS and New Rules For Regulators," *Telecommunications Policy* 21, no. 9/10 (1997): 783–798.

12. "New Policy Directions, Analysis of the Relevance of the Trade Committee's Conceptual Framework for Trade in Services to Trade in NonBasic Telecommunication Network-based Services," Submission of the United States to the OECD/ICCP, October 27, 1988, 11.

13. Sixty-nine individual governments made offers. But, with the addition of the European Commission, there are seventy signatures to the protocol.

14. For a detailed description of the individual documents that make up the WTO framework on telecommunications, see also International Trade Commission, *International Trends in U.S. Services Trade: 1998 Annual Report,* publication 3105, May 1998, 4-1–4-19. For general background on the negotiations, see Peter Cowhey and Jonathan Aronson, *When Countries Talk* (Cambridge: Ballinger Publishing Company, 1988); Anthony Rutkowski, "Multilateral Cooperation in Telecommunications: Implications of the Great Transformation," in *The New Information Infrastructure,* ed. William Drake (New York: The Twentieth Century Fund Press, 1995), 223–250; and the *Financial Times* series by Hugo Dixon that included "A Clearer Line to Markets Abroad," *Financial Times,* March 6, 1990.

15. Summary of Country Commitments in WTO Telecommunications Talks as of February 24, 1997, prepared by the Office of the U.S. Trade Representative; and World Trade Organization, Annex 1, "Overview of Results of WTO Basic Telecommunications Negotiations.

16. See Catherine Young, "Telecom: Congress Should Reform Its Reform," *BusinessWeek,* January 12, 1998.

17. Lee Tuthill, "Users' Rights," *Telecommunications Policy* 20, no. 2 (1996): 89–99.

18. For a more detailed analysis of the technology and market forces driving both the breakdown of the economic arguments for a regulated monopoly and the liberalization process, see *Changing Rules: Technological Change, International Competition, and Regulation in Communications,* ed. Robert Crandall and Kenneth Flam, 221–253. (Washington, DC: The Brookings Institution, 1989); and Peter Cowhey and Jonathan David Aronson, *When Countries Talk: International Trade in Telecommunications Services* (Cambridge: American Enterprise Institute/Ballinger Publishing Company, 1988); and Edward E. Zajac, "Technological Winds of Creation and Destruction in Telecommunications: A Case Study," in *Evolving Technology and Market Structure: Studies in Schumpeterian Economics,* ed. Arnold Heertje and Mark Perlman (Ann Arbor: University of Michigan Press, 1990), 247–262.

19. Digitalization in particular increased the speed and reliability of telecommunications and led to service convergence, whereby different services could be provided through the same storage/transmission medium. The advances also enabled connectivity and interoperability such that many users (persons or devices) could share resources across network boundaries. See G. Russel Pipes, "Telecommunications"; Peter K. Pitsch, *The Innovation Age: A New Perspective on the Telecom Revolution* (Indianapolis: Hudson Institute and the Progress and Freedom Foundation, 1996); OECD, Committee for Information, Computer, and Communications Policy, *The Telecommunications Industry: The Challenges of Structural Change* (Paris: OECD, 1988).

20. Telegeography, *Telegeography 1996–1997* (Washington, DC: Telegeography, 1990), xv.

21. See also Frost & Sullivan, *Strategic Assessment of U.S. Utility Companies Opportunities in the Telecommunications Industry,* Report #5647–60, 1998.

22. For analysis of the inflated rates on international routes, see Leonard Waverman, "Options for Reforming International Tariffs and Settlement Procedures"; OECD, *New Technologies and Their Impact on the Accounting Rate System,* February 1997; and Rob Frieden, *International Telecommunications Handbook* (Boston: Artech House Inc., 1996).

564 Cynthia Beltz Soltys

23. New entrants made use of new transmission technologies to operate long-distance services at lower cost than incumbents operating with older plant and equipment. In local services, by contrast, the traditional scale advantages enjoyed by incumbent carriers have not been undermined as quickly by the development of alternative transmission technologies. Andrew Davies, *Telecommunications and Politics: The Decentralized Alternative* (New York: Pinter Publisher, 1994); OECD, Directorate for Science, Technology, and Industry, *Local Telecommunication Competition: Developments and Policy Issues*, 1996.

24. ITU, *Asia Pacific Telecommunications Indicators 1997: New Telecommunication Operators*, June 1997.

25. See, for example, Hugo Dixon, "Reconnecting Charges With Costs," *Financial Times*, April 3, 1990. For early discussion of discontinuities in rates and competition for transit traffic in the 1980s, see Leland L. Johnson, *Competition, Pricing, and Regulatory Policy in the International Phone Industry* (Santa Monica, CA: Rand, 1989); in the 1990s, see OECD, *New Technologies and the Accounting Rate System*, 1997; for a more recent analysis of accounting rate avoidance strategies and the creation of new networking options see Rob Frieden, "The Impact of Call-back and Arbitrage on the Accounting Rate Regime," *Telecommunications Policy* 21, no. 9/10 (1997): 819–827.

26. For a useful discussion of alternative calling procedures and their implications for international telecommunications, see OECD, Committee for Information, Computer, and Communications Policy, *Refile and Alternative Calling Procedures: Their Impact on Accounting Rates and Collection Charges*, (Paris: OECD, 1995); OECD, *New Technologies and Their Impact on the Accounting Rate System*, February 1997.

27. Networks and services have been designed to avoid or minimize settlement charges rather than to minimize cost and improve service quality. The bypasses helped increase in the short term the contestability of markets that domestic regulatory reform efforts and multilateral institutions such as the WTO have been unable to accomplish. They have also helped reduce resistance and increase momentum for reform. But, over the longer term, distortions in the accounting rate and international payment system will still need to be eliminated to promote infrastructure development and price signals that accurately reflect underlying costs and market opportunities.

28. The relevant margin in the case of callback is the gap between wholesale prices in a country such as the United States and a foreign country's retail rate or collection charge.

29. In January 1998, Hong Kong Telecom, in exchange for a compensation package from the government, gave up its monopoly on international direct-dialed services as of the year 2000. John Ridding and Alan Cane, "Hong Kong Telecom: Company Gives Up Monopoly," *Financial Times*, January 21, 1998; and Sean Kennery, "Hong Kong Telecommunications Losing Market Share," *Reuters News Service*, May 4, 1997.

30. Reuters Newswire, "Callback Systems Eat into Brazil Phone Revenues," October 1, 1996; and USA Global Link, available at ⟨http://www.usagl.com⟩.

31. Stephen Young and Paul Lee, *Resale and Call-back: Opportunities and Threats* (London: Ovum Limited, 1996). On role of callback in increasing competition and consumer benefit, see Punn-Lee Lam, "Erosion of Monopoly Power: Lessons From Hong Kong," *Telecommunications Policy* 21, no. 8 (1997): 693–695.

32. Glenn Manoff, "Callback Sparks Diplomatic Incident," *Communications Week International*, July 14, 1997.

33. In Australia, where collection rates are relatively low, the price elasticity of demand for switched outbound minutes is significantly greater than −1.0. For outgoing calls on which accounting rates and collection rates are highest, the price elasticity of demand approximates −1.5 such that a 10 percent decrease in collection rates would lead to a 15 percent increase in the volume of international calls. See Ergas, "International Trade in Telecommunications Services: An Economic Perspective," 101. In the United States, price elasticity of demand for international service is greater than −1.0, see FCC, *Trends in the U.S. International Telecommunications Industry*, Industry Analysis Division, June 1997; and FCC International Settlements Rates, Report and Order (Released August 18, 1997), at paragraph 10.

34. The digitalization and the price/performance curves described by Moore's Law impact both the computers through which users access the Internet and the routers that direct traffic through the Internet.

35. The World Wide Web is the multimedia portion of the Internet that also permits the interlinking of documents and data. For the Internet's evolution, see Katie Hafner and Matthew Lyon, *When Wizards Stay Up Late* (New York: Simon and Schuester, 1996); Jeffrey K. MacKie-Mason and Hal Varian, "Economic FAQs About the Internet," *Journal of Economic Perspectives* 8, no. 3 (Summer 1994): 75–96; and OECD, Committee for Information, Computer, and Communications Policy, *Information Infrastructure Convergence and Pricing: The Internet* (Paris: OECD, 1996).

36. Network Wizard, *Internet Domain Survey, July 1997*, available at ⟨http://www.nw.com⟩; and OECD Information Technology Outlook 1997, 143–144, available at ⟨http://www.oecd.org/dsti/sti/ib/prod/itour-97.pdf⟩. These numbers represent only a minimum size of the Internet because they do not include the much larger intracorporate Internet traffic (Intranets), which may be four times the size of the public Internet. The host counts also do not include the potentially unlimited number of mult-iuser computers. America Online, for example, in 1996 had only a handful of host computers for its millions of users that access the Internet through its proprietary network.

37. See Cynthia Beltz, "Global Telecommunications Rules: The Race with Technology," *Issues in Science and Technology* (Spring 1997): 63–70.

38. OECD, "Commerce Goes Electronic," *OECD Observer*, no. 208, October/November, 1997.

39. Richard Jay Solomon, "Anything You Can Do, I Can Do Better," working paper MIT Research Program on Communications Policy, 1996; Steve G. Steinberg, "Making the Connection Between Voice Calls and Computers," *Los Angeles Times*, July 21, 1997, 9.

40. Andrew Grove, "What Can Be Done, Will Be Done," Forbes *ASAP*, December 2, 1996, 193.

41. Slow local access conditions have, for example, played a key role in limiting the growth of the Internet. But, firms are actively seeking solutions (ISDN, xDSL, cable modems, wireless, and satellites) to get around the bottleneck. See Kevin Werbach, "Digital Tornado: The Internet and Telecommunications," Federal Communications Commission, Office of Plans and Policy Working Paper, March 1997, 74–75. See also Rich Karlgard, "Digital Warriors Want Baby Bells Blood," *Wall Street Journal*, December 8, 1997, A24.

42. The Internet's commercial growth was initially encouraged by the phone companies as a means of soaking up some of the excess capacity created by technological advances and investment in fiber-optic cables, on long-distance and international routes (i.e., new demand for old networks). But, no one ever expected the Internet to challenge their core business. Like the Kudzu vine planted for soil stabilization that has grown out of control and become the bane of the South, the Internet has become a thorn in the side of telecommunications providers worldwide.

43. David Molony, "IP Traffic Drives Capacity Buildout," *Communications Week International*, July 14, 1997; Carl Malamud, *A World's Fair for the Global Village* (Cambridge: MIT Press, 1997); and Vint Cerf, "A Vision of Convergence," *Telegeography 1997/98*, October 1997, 50.

44. Chairman Reed Hundt, Federal Communications Commission, address to the *Wall Street Journal* Business and Technology conference, September 18, 1996, Washington, DC.

45. Cynthia Beltz and Claude Barfield, "The Borderless Economy: Global Trade Rules and the Internet," paper presented at Coalition of Service Industries Conference at Electronic Commerce, Santiago, Chile, September 28, 1998; and Cynthia Beltz, "Talk Is Cheap," *Reason* (August/September 1996): 45–49.

46. See Werbach, "Digital Tornado"; Lee McKnight and Joseph P. Bailey, eds., *Internet Economics* (Cambridge: MIT Press, 1997); and International Telecommunications Union, *Challenges to the Network: Telecoms and the Internet*, September 1997.

47. Joseph A. Schumpeter, *Capitalism, Socialism and Democracy* (New York: Harper & Row, [1942] 1975), 84; R. Fels, *Business Cycles: A Theoretical, Historical and Statistical Analysis of the Capitalist Process*, R. Fels, (Philadelphia: Porcupine Press, [1939] 1964), 315.

48. In the case of the European Union, the regulatory distinction between value-added and basic means that all countries need to permit voice over the Net. Even in the case of the five countries (Greece, Spain, Luxembourg, Portugal, and Ireland) that have not liberalized basic telecommunications services will need to permit Voice over the Net to be offered without requiring a license as a telecommunications operator.

49. See Beltz, "Global Telecommunications," 64, 66–68; and Patrick Low et al., *Electronic Commerce and the Role of the WTO*, Special Studies 2, The World Trade Organization, 1998.

50. See OECD, "Gateways to the Global Market: Consumers and Electronic Commerce," background paper, 1997, available at ⟨http://www.oecd.org/daf/ccp/cons/bpaper.htm⟩; Department of Commerce, *Emerging Digital Economy*, 1998; and, Cynthia Beltz, "The Internet Economy," *The World and I Magazine*, Washington Times, January 1998.

51. The other major barriers include high license fees for Internet service providers, high Internet access charges for consumers, and low personal computer penetration rates. See OECD, Committee for Information, Computer, and Communications Policy, *Information Infrastructure Convergence and Pricing: The Internet*, March 1996; and OECD, Internet Access Pricing, paper presented at OECD and European Commission workshop, Dublin, June 20–21, 1996.

52. These rates do not include bulk discounts, which tend to be more widely available in competitive markets. They thus tend to understate the gap between competitive and monopoly rate positions. OECD, *Communications Outlook, 1997* (Paris: OECD,

1997), 124–129; Sam Paltridge, "How Competition Helps the Internet," *The OECD Observer* (September 1996): 25–27; OECD, Committee for Information, Computer, and Communication Policy, *Information Infrastructure Convergence and Pricing: The Internet* (OECD: Paris, March 1996). In 1995, the OECD countries with infrastructure competition included the United States, the United Kingdom, Finland, Canada, New Zealand, Sweden, Australia, and Japan.

53. OECD, *Information Infrastructure Convergence and Pricing*, 13.

54. After reform, the average price for telephone services fell by 63 percent in the United Kingdom and 41 percent in Japan. In Finland the price for long-distance calls fell by 66 percent. It is important to note, however, that reductions in price may also in part be attributed to other factors. OECD, *Report on Regulatory Reform: Sectoral Studies* 1 (1997): 43–44.

55. For a detailed analysis of impact of telecommunications competition by sector, see U.S. Department of Commerce, National Telecommunications and Information Administration, *NTIA Competition Benefits Report*, Staff Papers regarding the Benefits of Competition and Deregulation in Selected Lines of Communications Commerce (Washington, DC: NTIA, November 8, 1985). For a useful overview discussion, see Robert R. Bruce, "Restructuring the Telecommunications Sector: Experience in Some Industrial Countries and the Implications for Policymakers," in *Implementing Reforms in the Telecommunications Sector: Lessons from Experience*, ed. Bjorn Wellenius and Peter A. Stern (Washington, DC: World Bank, 1994).

56. Sweden's telecommunications reform in 1993 forced state carrier Telia AB into competition in the international, long-distance, and business sectors five years before most of the other European countries.

57. Andreas Evagora, "The Nordic Track," *Tele.com*, January 1998, available at ⟨http://www.teledotcom.com⟩.

58. With the exception of Chile, the results of recent moves to privatization and liberalization are not adequately developed or obvious. International rates have declined but this may in part be attributed to the growth of bypass services such as callback rather than a change in policy. In general assessing the impact of increased competition due to trade liberalization (rather than deregulation) in telecommunications in developing countries is difficult because the two may occur simultaneously or privatization and deregulation may be a step toward trade liberalization. Many of the studies that have examined the impact of the market liberalization process in developing countries have, as a result, focused on the impact of privatization. But although privatization can be an important first step, increased competition may not be the result due to the creation of a duopoly or administrative barriers to competition. Thus a simple correlation between privatization and reduced prices and increased teledensity alone does not signify that the benefits have been generated by increased competition, let alone trade liberalization. For useful early studies in the field see Robert Saunders, Jeremy J. Warford, and Bjorn Wellenius, *Telecommunications and Economic Development*, 2d ed. (Baltimore: Johns Hopkins University Press, 1994), 313–329; Pablo T. Spiller and Carlo G. Cardilli, "The Frontier of Telecommunications Deregulation: Small Countries Leading the Pack," *Journal of Economic Perspectives* 11, no. 4: 127–138. For discussions on the observed correlations between privatization and improved teledensity trends, see ITU, *World Telecommunications Development Report, 1996/97*; and Michael Beardsley, "Getting Telecommunication Privatization Right," *McKinsey Quarterly*, January 1, 1995, 32. See ITU, *Asia Pacific Telecommunication Indicators 1997*, June 1997, for contrasting examples of the Philippines and Pakistan privatization experiences.

59. Bjorn Wellenius, "Telecommunications Restructuring in Latin America: An Overview," in *Implementing Reforms in the Telecommunications Sector: Lessons from Experience,* ed. Bjorn Wellenius and Peter A. Stern (Washington, DC: World Bank, 1994).

60. Information refers to Chile. See Spiller and Cardilli, "The Frontier of Telecommunications Deregulation"; Crandall and Waverman, *Talk Is Cheap: The Promise of Regulatory Reform in North American Telecommunications* (Washington, DC: Brookings Institution, 1995).

61. Increasing capacity, as for many countries, is a major challenge for Chile. In 1997, Chile connected to the outside world at roughly 9 Mb/sec, the same size pipe that a small U.S. service provider uses to connect to the Net. See Declan McCullogh, "The Globalization of Chile," The Netly News Network, October 10, 1997, available at 〈http://netlynews.com〉.

62. The first steps toward market liberalization in some of the developing countries focused on the privatization of state-owned monopolies with some international participation and some competition in nonbasic services. The early reformers included Chile (1987), Argentina (1990), Mexico (1990), and Venezuela (1991). For an early study of the differences and lessons from the reforms see Bjorn Wellenius and Peter Stern, eds., *Implementing Reforms in the Telecommunications Sector: Lessons from Experience,* (Washington, DC: World Bank, 1994).

63. OECD, *Report on Regulatory Reform,* 43–44; ITU, *Asia-Pacific Telecommunication Indicators 1997: New Telecommunication Operators,* June 1997; Frances Carincross, "Airborne," *The Economist* Survey of Telecommunications, September 13, 1997, 16.

64. Erik Olbeter and Lawrence Chimerine, *Crossed Wires,* (Washington, DC: The Economic Strategy Institute, 1995), ix; see also Linda Spencer, *Foreign Investment in the United States: Unencumbered Access* (Washington, DC: The Economic Strategy Institute, 1991).

65. End-user complaints, which played a key role in fueling the liberalization drive, included excessive rates and poor service with call failures averaging one in four. G. Russel Pipes, "Euro-Telecom Liberalization Advances," *Transnational Data and Communication Report* (January 1990): 5–7.

66. On the role of capital needs and efficiency gains from competition in driving privatization and deregulation push in Asia, see Charles P. Oman, Douglas H. Brooks, and Colm Foy, eds., *Investing in Asia* (OECD, Paris, 1997).

67. National Council of Applied Research, The India Infrastructure Report, New Delhi, 1997, as reported by Mark Nicolson, "Indian Report Paves Way for Infrastructure Spending Boost," *Financial Times,* January 17, 1996, 8.

68. ITU, World Telecommunications Development Report, 1996/97, summary figure 2; see also United Nations, *World Investment Report 1996: Investment, Trade, and International Policy Arrangements* (New York: United Nations, 1996), table 1.10, 25.

69. Juan Manuel Valcarcel, "Dial M for Monopoly," *Wall Street Journal,* August 16, 1996.

70. Statement of India's Telecommunications Commission Chairman A. V. Gokak at a New Delhi news conference on the Department of Telecommunications Internet guidelines, October 20, 1997.

71. Amy Louise Kazmin, "Long Way to Go on a Bumpy Road," *Financial Times,* special issue on India's software industry, December 3, 1997.

72. See, for example, comments of the outgoing Hong Kong regulator, Alex Arena, as reported in "Hong Kong Regulator Tells Asia, 'Keep Authorities Slim,'" *Reuters News Service,* June 12, 1997.

73. Reed Hundt, "The Light at the End of the Tunnel vs. the FOG: Deregulation vs. the Legal Culture," speech given at the American Enterprise Institute, August 14, 1997.

74. U.S. foreign ownership restrictions include a 20 percent limit on direct foreign ownership of a common carrier radio license and a 25 percent on indirect investment. An amendment proposed by Congressman Michael G. Oxley (R-Ohio) would have eliminated the indirect limit in Section 310(b) of the 1934 Communications Act, but it was rejected early on in the legislative process. For history of Section 310(b) and analysis of the telecommunications bills in the 104th Congress, see Gregory Sidak, *Foreign Investment in Telecommunications* (Chicago: University of Chicago Press, 1997), 239–247.

75. Letter from Senators Trent Lott and Ernest Hollings, respectively the Senate whip and ranking minority member of the commerce committee; and, Nancy Dunne, "Congress Warns Clinton Over Telecoms," *Financial Times,* April 29, 1996, 4.

76. FCC, Foreign Carrier Market Entry Rule, Dkt 95–22 (Rel. November 30, 1995), at 6, 203, 213–219.

77. FCC, Second Cable Order, 77 FCC 2d at 79.

78. FCC Foreign Carrier Order (November 1995), para. 187.

79. See Cynthia Beltz, "Foreign Investment and Telecommunications," in *Beyond Us and Them,* ed. Douglas Woodward (Westport, CT: Greenwood Publishing, 1998); and Lawrence Spiwak, "Anti-Trust, the 'Public Interest,' and Competition Policy," in *Anti-Trust Report* (December 1997): 18–19.

80. Foreign Carrier Order (November 26, 1997), at 35. Thomas J. Duesterberg and Kenneth Gordon, *Competition and Deregulation in Telecommunications: The Case for a New Paradigm* (Indianapolis: The Hudson Institute, 1997); Thomas Duesterberg, "Telecoms Market in Need of a Freer Line," *Financial Times,* May 5, 1997, 16.

81. Some trade officials involved with the negotiations argue that without the ECO test the Europeans would not have been as forthcoming in their offer on regulatory principles and international services. But the delay in the European offer was also related to internal difficulties involved with getting a consensus and giving DGI adequate time to understand the implications of the commitment on regulatory principles. The EU for much of the WTO negotiation was also still working through its directive on interconnection and licensing. Until the language for this directive was worked out internally, the EU was unable to commit on the WTO reference paper. In addition, the trend for increasing liberalization in practice was already set by EU directives such that after January 1, 1998, opening the telecommunications sectors to full competition, any established EU firm in any segment would be protected from discriminatory access conditions. See also Peter Holmes, Jeremy Kempton and Francis McGowan, "International Competition Policy and Telecommunications," *Telecommunications Policy* 20, no. 10 (1996): 764–765.

82. India permits up to 49 percent direct ownership and up to 49 percent indirect ownership of the remaining 51 percent.

83. Jagdish Bhagwati and Douglas A. Irwin, "The Return of the Reciprocitarians—U.S. Trade Policy Today," *The World Economy* 10, no. 2: 109–130. 114–120.

84. On the determining role of political factors in shaping the nature of India's reform process (liberalization without privatization), see Ben A. Petrazzini, "Telecommunications Policy In India: The Political Underpinnings of Reform," *Telecommunications Policy* 20, no. 1 (1996): 39–51; Nikhil Sinha, "The Political Economy of India's Telecommunication Reforms," *Telecommunications Policy* 20, no. 1, (1996): 23–38.

85. Strategic Policy Research, "The U.S. Stake in Competitive Global Telecommunication Services: The Economic Case for Tough Bargaining," 1993, 32.

86. Eli Noam, Testimony on foreign ownership reform, before the U.S. Senate Committee on Commerce, Science, and Transportation on SR-253, March 21, 1995; Erik Olbeter, "Opening the Global Market for Telecommunications," *Issues in Science and Technology*, (Winter 1994–1995): 63–64.

87. Initially promoted in the United States as a "trade remedy" for leveling the playing field, antidumping laws have spread around the world to the detriment of U.S.-owned multinationals. More than forty nations—half of them developing countries—have adopted antidumping laws. There has also been a sharp increase in cases since 1990 with U.S. exporters the target more often than any other country. Other examples of countries following the unfortunate lead of the United States include the introduction of quantitative restrictions (textiles in the 1970s: China, Mexico, Turkey; cars in the 1980s: Japan, Malaysia, Indonesia, Germany) and Europe's New Commercial Instrument, which is modeled on U.S. Section 301 of the trade laws. Stephen Woolcock, "European and North American Approaches to Regulation: Continued Divergence?", working paper, 1995.

88. For the misuse of public interests tests, see Sidak (1997). On the international side, the United States in particular will be watching the Philippines and their use of the public convenience test. During the negotiations, the Philippines were forced to drop their economic means test, which is treated as a market access barrier, in favor of a broader public interest test.

89. United Nations, *World Investment Report 1994* (Geneva: United Nations, 1994), 4, 17.

90. Herbert Simon, *Models of Man: Social and Rational* (New York: Wiley, 1970); Herbert Simon, "Theories of Decision Making in Economics and Behavioral Sciences," *American Economic Review* 69, no. 2 (June 1959): 273.

Recommended Reading

Aronson, Jonathan, and Peter F. Cowhey. 1988. *When Countries Talk: International Trade in Telecommunication Services*. Washington, DC: Ballinger / AEI Press.

Beltz, Cynthia. 1997. "Global Telecommunication Rules: The Race with Technology," *Issues in Science and Technology* (Spring): 63–70.

Beltz, Cynthia. 1998. "The Internet Economy," *The World and I Magazine*, Washington Times (January).

Frieden, Robert. 1996. *International Telecommunications Handbook*. New York: Artech House, Inc.

Low, Patrick, et al. 1998. *Electronic Commerce and the Role of the WTO*, Special Studies 2. Geneva: The World Trade Organization.

Organization for Economic Cooperation and Development. 1996. *Information Infrastructure Convergence and Pricing: The Internet*. Paris.

Paltridge, Sam. 1996. "How Competition Helps the Internet," *The OECD Observer*, (August/September).

Rutkowski, Anthony. 1995. "Multilateral Cooperation in Telecommunication: Implications of the Great Transformation." In *The New Information Infrastructure*, ed. William Drake. New York: Twentieth Century Fund.

Index